MATTHEAN BEATITUDES IN SOCIO-HISTORICAL CONTEXT

Christian Heritage Rediscovered

The Series, as the name suggests, is meant to focus on Christian Faith & Living vis-à-vis topics like Literature & Poetry, Indigenous Philosophizing, Ethical response towards Agriculture, Health & Healing, Science & Technology, Eco-feminist Theology, Sociological approach towards Human Rights, Law & Politics, Arts, History of Ideas, Ancient Civilizations, Cultural Contiguity, Religious Cosmologies & Mysticism, Footsteps of famous Theologians, World Peace & Harmony, Global Capitalism, Network Marketing, Cybertheology, Population & Demographics, Epigraphic Studies, Contextualized Education, and many others. We welcome a Mss. on any topic/s mentioned, whether they are original works, scholarly monographs, collections of conference papers, revised dissertations, or translations of historical documents. Through the Series we, the Publishers, are striving to put forward published works that may help Institutions, Academic Bodies, Researchers, Scholars and the World at large in furthering their respective knowledge and understanding on the concerned subject. We welcome your comments on our efforts and further suggestions on how we can foster the upcoming thought provoking theologically grounded books.

Christian Heritage Rediscovered - 36

MATTHEAN BEATITUDES IN SOCIO-HISTORICAL CONTEXT

Their Implications for Contemporary Christian Discipleship

Vanlalchhawna Khiangte

CWI

Christian World Imprints™

First Published in 2016 by

Christian World Imprints™
Christian Publishing & Books from India
H-12 Bali Nagar, **New Delhi-110015**
info@christianworldimprints.com
www.ChristianWorldImprints.com
Phone: +91 11 25465925

ISBN: 978-93-5148-119-5 (HB) ISBN: 978-93-5148-128-7 (PB)

Cataloging in Publication Data--DK
Courtesy: D.K. Agencies (P) Ltd. <docinfo@dkagencies.com>

Khiangte, Vanlalchhawna, author.
Matthean Beatitudes in socio-historical context : their implications for contemporary Christian discipleship / Vanlalchhawna Khiangte.
pages cm. -- (Christian heritage rediscovered ; 36)
ISBN 9789351481195 (HB)
ISBN 9789351481287 (PB)

1. Beatitudes.--Socio-rhetorical criticism. 2. Bible. N. T. Matthew.--Socio-rhetorical criticism. 3. Christian life. I. Title. II. Series: Christian heritage rediscovered ; 36.

BT382.K45 2016 DDC 226.93 23

Printed at D. K. Fine Art Press Pvt. Ltd.

This Humble but Sincere Work

is

dedicated to

My Beloved Mother

Lt. Ranghnuni

(1919-2009)

Whose love I cannot fathom

Being her youngest son, my mom always longed to see me. However, after I had grown up, I had to live most of my time in places faraway from her because of my undeserved service for the good Lord. And she left us for our heavenly home on March 27, 2009 while I was in Tübingen, Germany for the purpose of my doctoral research. I am looking forward to meet her again in the eternal Kingdom of Heaven where our loving God will give us complete comfort from all our mourning here on earth.

This book, in its original form, is the thesis submitted to the Senate of Serampore College, towards the Doctor of Theology degree, accepted by the Senate in 2011. It is published with written permission. The original title of the thesis is "**A Study of the Matthean Beatitudes and Its Implications for Contemporary Christian Discipleship**." The candidate is responsible for the title, contents and opinions expressed in this book. Although few changes have been made from the original thesis the idea expressed remains the same.

The Book

This book presents a study of the Matthean Beatitudes (Matt 5:3-12) from social-historical perspective and their implications for contemporary Christian discipleship.

The author meticulously investigated the socio-historical background of the Matthean community at first instance, and then has done an exegetical study on the Matthean Beatitudes (Matt 5:3-12) using the historical critical method as the main tool. Also, he has employed insights on the socio-historical experience of the Matthean community for drawing exegetical conclusions. The author concludes that the Matthean Beatitudes can be subsumed under the category of apocalyptic beatitudes. While the first, the second, the fourth, the eighth and the ninth beatitudes (Matt 5:3, 4, 6, 10, 11-12) mainly pronounce consolation to the suffering people of God (the Matthean community); the third, the fifth, the sixth and seventh beatitudes (Matt 5:5, 7, 8, 9) carry ethical exhortation too.

This scholarly work not only fills an important gap in Matthean studies by refocusing on the importance of these prefatory beatitudes in St. Matthew's gospel, but it does so from the vantage point of the wider hermeneutical perspective provided by contemporary New Testament investigations.

The author affirms that these beatitudes have important implications for Christians in India today, both as a consolation to the downtrodden, impoverished and persecuted Christians; and as an exhortation to the Christians in general to pursue ethical conduct as required in their specific contexts befitting the followers of Jesus Christ. This well-researched work is a treat for all the theological students across the globe due to its clarity, use of scholarly materials and systematic exploration of relevant materials.

The Author

Rev. Dr. Vanlalchhawna Khiangte is an ordained minister of the Baptist Church of Mizoram (BCM). After working as a missionary for seven years (1985-1992) he studied B.D. at Union Biblical Seminary, Pune (1992-1996). He worked as a pastor for four years (1996-2000) under the BCM. After he finished M.Th. (New Testament) from United Theological College, Bangalore (2000-2002), BCM deputed him to teach at the Academy of Integrated Christian Studies (AICS) in 2002, which is continuing.

He completed his doctoral study under the SATHRI of the Senate of Serampore College/University in October, 2011. He was the Vice Principal, and now is the Academic Dean and Dean of Ministerial Training at the AICS, Aizawl, Mizoram.

Foreword-I

The significance of the Beatitudes in St. Matthew (Mt 5:1-12) have received mainly tangential attention in scholarly studies. Their importance for the gospel is underscored by its placement as the preface to the Sermon on the Mount, the emphasis by the iterative use of the key Matthean terms such as "righteousness" and "the Kingdom of Heaven". The studies generally consign it to a treatment of the Sermon on the Mount (and correctly so) or to an analysis within a study of a theme or a commentary. So, it is pertinent to point out that no major study of the Matthean Beatitudes itself has appeared since the pioneering investigation by Dupont, which appeared in French.

It is here that the publication of the revised version of Khiangte's doctoral thesis on the Matthean Beatitudes must be commended for several reasons. It is a necessary fillip to the important research produced by New Testament students in India. There is a tendency to neglect much of the investigations in New Testament in India due to the difficulties involved in their publication. So, there is a benign neglect of such material while pursuing New Testament research in India, easily demonstrated by the scanty references to such resources in recent studies or to the preponderance of published works originating in Western countries. True, much of the valuable work is available mainly in these studies. Nonetheless, there are many important insights afforded by New Testament students in India that are worth pursuing. And it is by their being published, and thus receiving scholarly attention in ongoing discussions that they gain a wider currency.

New Testament studies in India have exploited the deeper hermeneutical insights produced by recent scholarly investigations. It has strongly advocated a contextual application that has not been present in a purely historical-critical analyses of the NT texts. And in this it has attempted to bridge the chasm that has appeared in the West between the text, the Church and a relevant ministry. It is in responding to the deep pain and plight of the existential situation of the people that the New Testament texts will once again resound with the inspiring relevance that they once possessed. Moreover, these studies are situated against the broader canvas of the Roman Empire, and to its sociological implications so as to elicit a more pertinent examination of the texts. Such a perspective affords the text the ability to appeal to a multiplicity of concerns without imposing on it a singular interpretation.

It is evident now why this publication is significant. Not only does it fill an important gap in Matthean studies by refocusing on the importance of these prefatory Beatitudes in St. Matthew's gospel, but it does so from the vantage point of the wider hermeneutical perspective provided by contemporary New Testament investigations. Khiangte has not only been thorough in pursuing the studies on the Matthean Beatitudes available in recent scholarly publications but has also brought out their implications by investigating them from the contours of the Roman Empire and not merely from the perspective of Judaism. And just as importantly, he has attempted to flesh out their existential implications so that they are not merely academic, but resound with the demands of the new righteousness that Jesus demanded of His followers as they heard Him, even if it is through the mouthpiece of His evangelist St. Matthew. There is no doubt that the relevance of what the gospel lies in, how it addresses the welter of issues that confront the Christian community in India. No singular perspective can provide the meaning of what it communicates, as each community looks to it for responses to the problems they confront. And in exploring what the Matthean Beatitudes mean, Khiangte has presented the many implications they contain for Christianity in India. As St. Matthew himself as observed, Khiangte has endeavoured to become a good scribe who brings rich treasures out of the old (Mt 13:52).

Publications of scholarly research from India suffers from benign neglect from others. It would be a tragic loss to New Testament studies, if engagement with this valuable publication were to be confined to India. There would be much to gain from Khiangte's scholarly investigations if scholars were to interact with it and further the boundaries that the author has explored. It will be furthering these dimensions through a careful study of the Matthean Beatitudes that this work holds promise. It is a fervent hope that this publication will open rich vistas of engagement with New Testament scholarship from India in general and with this work in particular.

Dr. Youhanon Mar Demetrios
Metropolitan
Diocese of Delhi

Foreword-II

Dr. Vanlalchhawna Khiangte has made a significant contribution to the field of New Testament by writing a book *Matthean Beatitudes in Socio-Historical Context: Their Implications for Contemporary Christian Discipleship* which is a revised version of his D.Th thesis. He has been a systematic researcher, pastor and theological educator over the past two decades and his contributions are widely appreciated by his students as well as his church. As there is a significant growth in the field of theological colleges and theological students, it is high time to think of Indian scholars writing and publishing quality materials. In this context, Dr. Khiangte's book is an important attempt portraying the ethical, theological and exegetical insights of the Beatitudes in Matthew 5:1-12. Many scholars over the past decades have interpreted the beatitudes by applying tools from historical-critical method, since historical-critical method is a result of systematic study of scripture from the point of view of socio-cultural context of Palestine.

Dr. Khiangte's work is significant as he could connect the insights from the beatitudes with the contemporary ecclesial situation and socio-political challenges. Though, he could bring the ethical codes to the forefront of discussion in a very critical manner, he could keep a balance between ethical teachings and theological framework. As a theological educator and researcher in the field of New Testament, I believe that this work will easily be accepted by the theological students across the globe due to its clarity, use of scholarly materials and systematic exploration of relevant materials.

Today, Matthean scholarship has taken a new shift. With the contributions of Warren Carter and others in the field, many have asked the question about the role of the Roman Empire in forcing Jesus Movement to accept the beatitudes as their paranetical and foundational manifesto for a better Christian living.

Dr. Khiangte has not only connected this study with the foundations of Christian discipleship, but also related with the values of the Kingdom of God. In that sense, this monograph will address many issues in the field of New Testament, and offer clear guidelines for New Testament researchers to understand the meaning of the Matthean beatitudes. I wish and pray that may the Lord help Dr. Khiangte to contribute more books and through his works many more students find guidance for their research.

Revd. Dr. C. I. David Joy
Professor of New Testament
UTC, Bangalore

Acknowledgment

This book is the outcome of my doctoral study, and therefore I would like to acknowledge here with profound gratefulness the invaluable help I received from various people in different ways for the completion of my doctoral thesis, and for its publication in book form.

To my family, relatives, friends and well-wishers who have been faithfully upholding me with prayer and were always ready to do whatever they could in order to help me whenever I need their help during my doctoral study.

To the Baptist Church of Mizoram, for giving me a valuable opportunity to take up a doctoral research, and for taking care of all my financial needs. To the principals of Academy of Integrated Christian Studies (AICS) Rev. Dr. K. Thanzauva and his successor Prof. Dr. R.L. Hnuni (now Rev. Dr. R. L. Hnuni) for helping me in every possible way.

To Dr. Youhanon Mar Demetrios (then Fr. Dr. John Mathews), who was the convener for my assessment papers during the assessment period, and who afterwards became my thesis supervisor, for his scholarly, open-minded, diligent, fatherly and friendly guidance; to say in the shortest way, who proved to be an ideal thesis guide to me.

To Rev. Dr. M.V. Abraham, a member of the committee for my assessment papers, and Rev. Dr. M. J. Joseph, another member, who gave me encouraging feedbacks on my assessment papers. To the Registrars of FFRRC in succession during my study - Rev. Dr. John Panicker, Fr. Dr. John Mathews (now Dr. Youhanon Mar Demetrios) and Rev. Dr. K.G. Pothen. To the Deans of Doctoral Studies of FFRRC in succession during my study – Fr. Dr. John Mathews (now Dr. Youhanon Mar Demetrios), Rev. Dr. Varghese Mathai, Rev. Dr. GeeVarghese Mathew, and Fr. Dr. Reji Mathew. To Mrs. Darly George, who single-handedly handles all the office work of the FFRRC. To the faculty and students of FFRRC with whom I had a good time of interaction during my stay in Kottayam.

To the Principal, Librarians and staff of Orthodox Theological Seminary and Mar-Thoma Theological Seminary. Especially to Fr. Dr. K. M. George, Principal, and Fr. Dr. Matthew Baby (now Dr. Mathews Mar Thimotheos), supervisor of Family Quarters - of Orthodox Theological Seminary, Kottayam, for providing me with a comfortable family quarters for the period of April 2006 to October 2007 (until I left it for my exposure programme to Tuebingen, Germany).

To Rev. Dr. F. Hrangkhuma, the then Principal and Mr. Yesan S, the Librarian, of SAIACS, who provided me with several important periodical articles from the facility of their library when I visited the Institute on October 2006.

To the authorities of the United Theological College, Bangalore, for giving me and my wife an accommodation inside the campus during June 2008 to May 2009, and, to Mrs. Rita Wesley, the Librarian of the United Theological College and her library staff for their invaluable help whenever I visited the library on various occasions.

To Rev. Dr. Gudrun Holtz and her husband Rev. Dr. Rolf Noorman, who have been sources of help and inspiration to me from the time of my Master Degree programme in 2000 till I completed my doctoral study, and of course even until now, and who helped me to get scholarship for study exposures to Tübingen University, Germany.

To the Diakonisches Werk der EKD, Stuttgart, and especially to the scholarship team - Dr. Schneider and his successor Rev. Christian Rave, Mrs. Sylvia Karlev, and Mrs. Katharina O'Shea, for giving me scholarship for my study exposure during October 2007 to March 2008 and for the month of March 2009. To Prof. Dr. Hermann Lichtenberger of Tübingen University, who offered me his valuable time for an interview on 27 March, 2008 to discuss about my ongoing research, and who also helped me in my second visit in March, 2009. To those participants in the English-German Colloquium in New Testament, Tübingen University, who shared insightful feedback on my paper, and especially to Dr. Scott Caulley, the organizer of the Colloquium, for giving me an opportunity to present a paper from my ongoing research and for helping me in preparing the paper.

To my wife Lalzuatpuii who has faithfully been the backbone from the beginning of my research till the end, and my cousin Lalliankimi who sacrificed her valuable times to stay with us at Kottayam for almost two years to help us in our difficult times.

To those who work in the office of Zozam Weekly magazine, Aizawl, and especially to Ms. Sangluri among them, for their warm-hearted help at the time I visited their office to sift through the old issues of the Zozam magazine.

To miss Joana Heath who kindly read through my thesis and made comments for correction of English.

To the Christian World Imprints, New Delhi, for kindly taking care of its publication in book form.

And to all others who have made an invaluable contribution toward the completion of my doctoral research and for its publication in book form in one way or another but whose names I could not mention here.

Finally, all the glory be to the loving God Almighty, whose unconditional love and unchanging care sustained me in all areas of my life during my doctoral research and enabled me to complete my thesis, and then finally to publish it in book form.

Abbreviations

General Abbreviations

A.D.	-	Anno Domini/ *in the year of the Lord Jesus*
Adj.	-	Adjective
B.C.	-	Before Christ
B.C.E.	-	Before Common Era
C.E.	-	Common Era
c./ca. (*circa*)	-	about (approximate date)
Cf./cf.(*confer*)	-	compare or see
Chap., chaps.	-	chapter, chapters
Comp., comps.	-	compiler, compilers
e.g.	-	(*exempli gratia*) for example
ed./eds.	-	editor, editors, edition, editions
esp.	-	especially
et al.(*et alii*)	-	and others
etc. (*et cetera*)	-	and others of the same class; and so forth.
f., ff.	-	and the following page (s)
i.e. (*id est*)	-	That is to say
LXX	-	The Septuagint
MLA	-	Member of Legislative Assembly
MS, MSS	-	Manuscript, Manuscripts
n.	-	footnote number
NT	-	New Testament
OT	-	Old Testament
Pl	-	plural
p., pp.	-	page, pages
par.	-	parallel
Q^{lk}	-	the Q version used by Luke
Q^{mt}	-	the Q version used by Matthew
R.C.	-	Roman Catholic
T.A./TA	-	Travelling Allowance

Trans.	-	Translator, translated by
UBS	-	United Bible Society
v., vv.	-	verse, verses
Vol., vols.	-	volume, volumes

Reference and Serials

ABD	-	*The Anchor Bible Dictionary*
ANRW	-	*Aufstieg und Niedergang der Römischen Welt*
DJG	-	*Dictionary of Jesus and the Gospels*
DLNTID	-	*Dictionary of Later New Testament and Its Development*
DNTB	-	*Dictionary of New Testament Background*
ICC	-	International Critical Commentary
IDB	-	*Interpreter's Dictionary of the Bible*
Str-B	-	Strack, Hermann L., and Paul Billerbeck. Kommentar zum Neuen Testament aus Talmud und Midrash. Muenchen: C.H.Bech'sche Verlagsbuchhandlung, MCMLXIX.
TDNT	-	*Theological Dictionary of the New Testament*
TDOT	-	*Theological Dictionary of the Old Testament*
WBC	-	Word Biblical Commentary

English Translation of the Bible

JB	-	Jerusalem Bible
KJV	-	King James Version
LB	-	The Living Bible
NAB	-	New American Bible
NKJV	-	New King James Version
NRSV	-	New Revised Standard Version
RSV	-	Revised Standard Version
TEV	-	Today's English Version

Books of the Bible

Old Testament

Cant	-	Canticles
Chron	-	Chronicles
Dan	-	Daniel
Deut	-	Deuteronomy
Eccl	-	Ecclesiastes
Exod	-	Exodus
Ezek	-	Ezekiel
Gen	-	Genesis
Hag	-	Haggai

Hos	-	Hosea
Isa	-	Isaiah
Jer	-	Jeremiah
Jon	-	Jonah
Josh	-	Joshua
Judg	-	Judges
Lev	-	Leviticus
Mal	-	Malachi
Mic	-	Micah
Neh	-	Nehemiah
Num	-	Numbers
Prov	-	Proverbs
Ps	-	Psalms
Sam	-	Samuel
Zech	-	Zechariah
Zeph	-	Zephaniah

New Testament

1Jn	-	1 John
Cor	-	Corinthians
Eph	-	Ephesians
Gal	-	Galatians
Heb	-	Hebrews
Jas	-	James
Jn	-	John
Matt	-	Matthew
Pet	-	Peter
Phil	-	Philippians
Rev	-	Revelation
Rom	-	Romans
Thess	-	Thessalonians
Tim	-	Timothy
Tit	-	Titus

Apocrypha, Pseudepigrapha and Early Patristic Books

Asc. Isa	-	Ascension of Isaiah
Bar	-	Baruch
Did	-	Didache
Ecclus	-	Ecclesiasticus
En	-	Enoch
Eth. En	-	*Ethiopic Enoch*

Chrysostom Hom. on Mt. - John Chrysostom, *Homilies on the Gospel according to St. Matthew* (trans. of Commentarius in sanctum Matthaeum Evangelistam, in PG 57 and 58), in NPNF 10

Ign.	*Eph*	-	Ignatius, *Letter to the Ephesians*
	Mag	-	Ignatius, *Letter to the Magnesians*
	Philad	-	Ignatius, *Letter to the Philadelphians*
	Pol	-	Ignatius, *Letter to Polycarp*
	Smyrn	-	Ignatius, *Letter to the Smyrnaeans*
	Trall	-	Ignatius, *Letter to the Trallians*
Jub		-	*Jubilees*
Macc		-	Maccabbees
Ps. Sol		-	Psalms of Solomon
Sib. Or		-	Sibylline Oracles
Sir		-	Sirach
Slav. En.		-	*Slavonic Enoch*
T.Judah		-	Testament of Judah
Tob		-	Tobit
Wis/Wisd		-	Wisdom

Qumran Scrolls

1QM	-	*Milhāmāh* or *War Scroll* from Qumran cave 1
1QS	-	*Serek hayyahad* (*Rule of the Community, Manual of Discipline*)
4QpHos[a]	-	Fragment of a commentary on Hosea from Qumran's Fourth Cave
4QpPs 37	-	Commentary on Psalm 37

Rabbinic Writings and Tractates in Mishnaic Literature

m. 'Abot	-	*'Abot* of Midrash
m. Pe'a	-	*Pe'a* of Midrash
m. Kelim	-	*Kelim* of Midrash
Mek. on Exod	-	*Mekilta* on Exodus

Targum

Tg. on Isa	-	Targum on Isaiah

Josephus

Ant/Antig.	-	*Antiquities of the Jews*

Periodicals

ActaPatByz	-	*Acta Patristica et Byzantina*
ActaTheol	-	*Acta Theologica*
AnglTheolRev	-	*Anglican Theological Review*
BibToday	-	*Bible Today*
BibTrans	-	*The Bible Translator*
CathBibQuart	-	*Catholic Biblical Quarterly*
CriswellTheolRev	-	*Crisswell Theological Review*
CurTheolMiss	-	*Currents in Theology and Mission*
EphTheolLov	-	*Ephemerides Theologicae Lovanienses*
ExpTimes	-	*Expository Times*
HarvTheolRev	-	*Harvard Theological Review*
HervTeolStud	-	*Hervormde Teologiese Studies*
HervTeolStudSupp	-	*Hervormde Teologiese Studies Supplement*
JournEvangTheolSoc	-	*Journal of the Evangelical Theological Society*
JournTheolSAfric	-	*Journal of Theology for Southern Africa*
JournBibLit	-	*Journal of Biblical Literature*
JournJewStud	-	*Journal of Jewish Studies*
JournStudNT	-	*Journal for the Study of the New Testament*
LuthTheolJourn	-	*Lutheran Theological Journal*
NovTest	-	*Novum Testamentum*
NTStud	-	*New Testament Studies*
RelStudRev	-	*Religious Studies Review*
RestorQuart	-	*Restoration Quarterly*
RevExp	-	*Review and Expositor*
StudRel/SciRel	-	*Studies in Religion/Sciences Religieuses*
StudBibFranlibAnn	-	*Studium Biblicum Franciscanum Liber Annus*
TriJourn	-	*Trinity Journal*

Introduction

The gospel of Matthew emphasizes the teaching of Jesus more than the other two synoptic gospels,[1] and the teaching materials in Matthew's gospel center on the nature of discipleship.[2] Obviously, the author structured this gospel in accordance with his emphasis on the teaching of Jesus on discipleship[3] and therefore he, in a stylistic manner, presents the teachings of Jesus in five blocks of discourses.[4] It is also evident that in order to accentuate his emphasis on the teaching of Jesus on discipleship all the more Matthew deliberately places the Sermon on the Mount (Matt chaps. 5-7), which contains most of Jesus' core teachings on discipleship,

1 The teaching materials occupy about 75 per cent of Matthew's gospel while they occupy about 50 percent of Mark's gospel and about 60 percent of Luke's gospel. See Barclay M. Newman, Jr., "Some Translational Notes on the Beatitudes," *BibTrans* 26/1 (Jan 1975), 108. See also Stanley D. Toussaint, *Behold the King. A Study of Matthew* (Portland: Multnomah Press, 1980), 22. [Note: The titles of the periodicals are cited here and afterwards either in full or abbreviated forms as far as possible as they are cited in the NT Abstracts. Those that are not found in the NT abstracts are given either in full form (especially the shorter titles) or in the format used in the NT Abstracts (especially the longer titles). And the reference works and serials are entered in abbreviated forms].

2 Wilkins notes that each of the major discourses in Matthew's gospel is primarily directed to the disciples (5:1; 10:1; 13:10, 36; 18:1; 23:1; 24:1–3), and Matthew often transforms the teaching segments into explicit discipleship-teaching pericopae by including the term "disciple" (8:21, 23; 9:27; 10:42; 12:49; 13:10; 15:23; 16:5; 17:6; 17:10; 18:1; 19:10; 21:20; 24:3; 26:8, 40, 45). See M.J. Wilkins, "Discipleship," *DJG*, edited by Joel B. Green, Scott McKnight and I. Howard Marshall (Downers Grove, Illinois: InterVarsity Press, 1992), 182.

3 Warren Carter notes that in the view of most of the modern scholars "Matthew creatively shapes and interprets material passed on to him by early communities" in writing the Sermon on the Mount as well as the rest of the gospel. See Warren Carter, *What are They Saying about Matthew's Sermon on the Mount?* (New York: Paulist Press, 1994), 9.

4 Though scholars give different explanations to the structure of Matthew's gospel, the five blocks of discourses is undeniably discernible, such as chaps. 5:1-7:29; 9:36-11:1; 13:1-53; 18:1-19:1 and 23:1-26:2. See S. McKnight, "Matthew, Gospel of," *DJG*, edited by Joel B. Green, Scott McKnight and I. Howard Marshall (Downers Grove, Illinois: InterVarsity Press, 1992), 526-541.

toward the beginning of this gospel as the first of Jesus' teachings.[5] The above observation is corroborated further by the perceptible fact that this sermon was gleaned and systematically arranged by Matthew to suit his special purpose (that is drawing attention to the nature of discipleship) from the teachings of Jesus at different times under different circumstances during his earthly ministry.[6] Thus, at least two central features of Matthew's gospel become explicit. First, the main emphasis (or special purpose) of the first evangelist[7] in writing this gospel is to lead his readers to the understanding of Jesus' teachings on the nature of discipleship. Second, the mode of its formulation as well as its contents and its position in the framework of the first gospel[8] show that the Sermon on the Mount is Matthew's special instrument in clinching his emphasis of Jesus' teachings on discipleship. In addition to these two vital aspects, Matthew has situated his own understanding of the beatitudes[9] at the beginning of this sermon encapsulating what constituted the new righteousness professed in this extended discourse.[10] Its content and its position in the Sermon on the Mount suggest that for Matthew the Beatitudes sums up the essence of the fundamental characters required in the Kingdom of Heaven/God.[11] To put in other words, the Beatitudes constitutes the core of Jesus'

---

5 See the following - Eduard Schweizer, *The Good News According to Matthew*, translated by David E. Green (Atlanta: John Knox Press, 1975), 78; Newman, Jr., "Some Translational Notes on the Beatitudes", 107-109; and Donald Hagner, *Matthew 1-13*, WBC, Vol. 33A (Dallas, Texas: Word Books Publisher, 1993), 82-83.

6 Newman, Jr., "Some Translational Notes on the Beatitudes", 109.

7 The term "the first evangelist" is used here and in some other places of this thesis to refer to the writer of the gospel traditionally assigned to Matthew, which is placed first among the four gospels in the New Testament and for which it is often termed as "the first gospel."

8 The gospel traditionally assigned to Matthew is often termed as "the first gospel." Therefore, the same term is used here and in some other places of this thesis in the same sense. The use of the term in this thesis only means that Matthew appears first among the four gospels in the New Testament, and it does not mean that it was written first among them.

9 Please note that when the word "Beatitudes" begins with capital letter, it is used as a single unit, and when it begins with a small letter, ("beatitudes") it is used to refer to individual beatitudes.

10 See Matt 5: 20. Luz observes that "righteousness" and "kingdom of heaven" are the two catchwords in the beatitudes forming "the righteousness of the kingdom of heaven," which permeate the whole Sermon on the Mount, befitting to be called its theme. See Ulrich Luz, *Matthew 1-7: A Continental Commentary*, translated by Wilhelm C. Linss (Minneapolis: Augsburg Fortress, 1989 [1985]), 214.

11 Betz argues that "the rest of the Sermon is nothing else than the concretization and elucidation of the first macarism." See Hans Dieter Betz, *Essays on The Sermon on the Mount* (Philadelphia: Fortress, 1985), 17-36. Even before Betz, Austin Farrer has already proposed, in *St. Matthew and St. Mark* (Westminster: Dacre, 1954), 176, that the Sermon on the Mount was composed by Matthew on the basis of the beatitudes. Also Michael Goulder has suggested in *Midrash and Lection in Matthew* (London: SPCK, 1974), 251-254, that the first eight beatitudes are Matthew's creation in rabbinic style to form the summary of, or heading for, the Sermon on the Mount.

teaching on the nature of discipleship.[12] An unavoidable conclusion, therefore, is that an in-depth investigation of the Matthean Beatitudes is inevitable for a proper understanding of Jesus' teaching on the nature of discipleship. The fact that Matthew's gospel reveals Jesus' teaching on discipleship more than the other two synoptic gospels do, also underlines this conclusion.

Meanwhile, the application of sociological principles, especially a socio-historical approach in the study of Matthew's gospel, has given an impression that it is one of the most relevant methods for understanding and interpreting the message of the first gospel.[13] This also implies that an application of the same approach is vital for understanding the meaning of the Matthean beatitudes, as well as their implications for the present situation.

However, while the Matthean Beatitudes apparently holds the primary key to the understanding of Jesus' teaching on the nature of discipleship, and while an application of a socio-historical approach to it is crucial for understanding its meaning and implication, no major study has been done on this important text in recent years, especially using a socio-historical approach. Of course, there are so many writings on the Matthean Beatitudes and it could be said that it is one of the most frequently treated texts of the New Testament. However, most of them are reflections on the text without proper investigation into the background, and they are somewhat spiritual interpretations. Such interpretations take the beatitudes at face value without taking into consideration the socio-historical context behind the first gospel that influenced its writing and shaped its contents, including the beatitudes. They take all the beatitudes as spoken by Jesus, and interpret them as timeless truth, equally applicable to everyone in every age.[14] Therefore, they

The logic now is that if the "Beatitudes" comprises the core of the Sermon on the Mount, which has "righteousness of the Kingdom of Heaven" as its theme, then, the "Beatitudes" sums up the essence of the requirements needed in the Kingdom of Heaven/God.

12 Green correctly maintains that the beatitudes encapsulate "both the kind of person the disciple will be seen to be if he or she faithfully follows the requirements of the Sermon on the Mount, and, conversely, the kind of person the disciple will need to be if he or she is to rise to its demands and to persevere in the right (and narrow) path (7:13-14)." H. Benedict Green, *Matthew, Poet of the Beatitudes* (Journal for the Study of the New Testament Series 203. Sheffield: Sheffield Academic Press, 2001), 288.

13 For further discussion on this, see the introduction portion of the next chapter (2).

14 For examples of such reflections, see the following: Billy Graham, *The Secret of Happiness* (Garden City, New York: Doubleday & Company, Inc., 1955); Casimir A. Delimat, *Ascent: Spiritual Progress according to the Beatitudes* (New York: St. Paul Publication, 1960); William Fitch, *The Beatitudes of Jesus* (Bombay: Gospel Literature Service, 1961); J. Maurus, *Live a Happier Life: 8 Steps to Success and Happiness* (Allahabad: Better Yourself Books, 1970); Marylin Norquist, *Jesus' Pattern for a Happy Life: The Beatitudes* (Liquori, Missouri: Loquori Publications, 1981); F. Ripoll, *The Beatitudes: The Blueprint for Happiness*, 4th Edition (Bombay: St. Paul's, 1994[1981]); Helen Cecilia Swift, *The Beatitudes: Pattern for Christian Living* (New York: Alba House, 1990); Simon Tugwell, *Reflections on the Beatitudes. Soundings in Christian Tradition* (London: Darton, Longman and Todd, 1980). Limitation of space does not permit

lack necessary moorings to Christian discipleship. Of course, there have been few attempts, which try to see the social implications of the "Beatitudes." However, these attempts also usually lack an investigation into their socio-historical settings, which are crucial for their proper understanding.[15] Consequently, they are inadequate to offer a meaningful interpretation in the contemporary situations. Even the study of Dupont[16] and some other smaller studies which focused on historical critical methods lack an investigation into the socio-historical context behind Matthew's gospel in general and the Matthean beatitudes in particular, and therefore they are inadequate to provide contextual application.[17] Most of the previous studies, thus, fail to look into the influence of the socio-historical situations behind this text as well as the meaning of the text in such situations.

At the same time, however, there are important exceptions, on the study of the subject *per se*, apart from Dupont's major study.[18] Some of the prominent ones of such studies are: Michael Crosby's, *The Spirituality of the Beatitudes: Matthew's Challenge for First World Christians*,[19] Dennis Hamm's, *The*

---

us to highlight the content of all these books. But mention may be made here that all these works lack a proper investigation into the socio-historical context of the Beatitudes which is indispensable for its proper interpretation and for understanding the implication of all the individual beatitudes. They simply treat all the beatitudes as spoken by Jesus and interpret them as a spiritual teaching equally applicable to everyone in every age.

15 For examples of the attempts that try to see the social implications of the Beatitudes, but without an investigation into their socio-historical settings, see the following: Dietrich Bonhoeffer, *The Cost of Discipleship*, Complete edition (London: SCM Press Ltd., 1978 [1937, 1959]); Gerald Vann, *The Divine Pity: A Study in the Social Implications of the Beatitudes* (London and Glasgow: Fontana Books, 1956 [1945]); Bernard Häring, *The Beatitudes: Their Personal and Social Implications* (Middlegreen, Slough: St. Paul Publication, 1981[1976]); and John S. Pobee, *Who are the Poor? The Beatitudes as a Call to Community* (Geneva: World Council of Churches, 1987). These works are mentioned here only to show that although they try to present the social implications of the Beatitudes, they are inadequate because they lack an investigation into the socio-historical setting of the Beatitudes which is crucial for a proper interpretation of all the individual beatitudes and for a proper understanding of their implications.

16 J. Dupont, *Les Béatitudes*, 3 Vols. (Paris: J. Gabalda, 1958-73). Kindly refer to the next footnote for further reference in connection with the work of Dupont.

17 For an example of such studies, apart from the work of Dupont, see William Barclay, *The Plain Man Looks at the Beatitudes* (London: Fontana Books, 1963). Dupont's book is written in French and it is not available in English language. However it's being written on the basis of historical critical method could be understood from Raymond F. Collins, "Beatitudes," *ABD*, Vol. 1 (New York: Doubleday, 1997 [1992], 629-631, who based his study on Dupont's book along with others' writings. The point is that while these authors apply historical critical method in their study of the Beatitudes they lack an investigation into the socio-historical context behind Matthew's gospel in general and the Matthean beatitudes in particular.

18 J. Dupont, *Les Béatitudes*.

19 (Maryknoll: Orbis, 1981).

Beatitudes in Context,[20] H. Benedict Green's, *Matthew, Poet of the Beatitudes*,[21] and Charles R. Day's "An Investigation of the Beatitudes of Matthew: Between the Oral Tradition and the Greek Text."[22] Crosby tries to see the background of the beatitudes in the experience of the Matthean community and rightly maintains that Matthew's gospel was addressed to a specific community. However, this study lacks substantial insights into the social situations behind this gospel as envisaged in the recent studies on Matthew's gospel. Besides, there is also a shortage of background and linguistic studies of the beatitudes. They are mainly interpreted by the author on the basis of Matthew's gospel itself and emphasis is given on the perspective of liberation theology. Dennis Hamm, in *The Beatitudes in Context*, deals with both the Lukan and the Matthean beatitudes. His primary focus is to interpret the beatitudes of Luke and Matthew from their literary context and from their Old Testament backgrounds. He gives a brief introduction to the meaning and function of the beatitudes. Then, he separately deals with the Lukan beatitudes and the Matthean beatitudes, dealing first with the Lukan beatitudes. In both cases, he discusses the literary contexts first, and then interprets them in the light of their OT backgrounds. Of course, this is an appropriate approach to begin with. However, the socio-historical context of the primary audience is not taken into consideration, which is understood in this book as of paramount importance. In *Matthew, Poet of the Beatitudes*, Benedict Green denies the existence of Q as Matthew's source, and according to him, Matthew's gospel is fundamentally an expansion and redaction of Mark by the first evangelist.[23] According to Green, Matthew versified many of his direct quotations from the Old Testament into a poetic form, and he composed many other texts in poetic form under the influence of Old Testament texts.[24] Accordingly, Green asserts that the Matthean beatitudes are composed in a poetic form by Matthew, largely under the influence of the Old Testament, particularly the LXX; and Psalm 119 (118, LXX) offers a formal model for the composition of the Beatitudes.[25] Green explains the meanings of the beatitudes primarily based on the Old Testament passages, which presumably are influential in their composition.[26] At the same time, he also draws evidence from other places in Matthew's gospel itself to support his interpretation. He also assumes a Matthean community but he neither

20 (Wilmington, Delaware: Michael Glazier, 1990).

21 Journal for the Study of the New Testament Series 203 (Sheffield: Sheffield Academic Press, 2001).

22 (D. Lit. Thesis, University of Pretoria, 2004).

23 Green, *Matthew, Poet of the Beatitudes*, 18, 31-32, 35.

24 See the sections "Matthew as Versifier" (1) and (2) in Green, *Matthew, Poet of the Beatitudes*, 48 -150.

25 Green, *Matthew, Poet of the Beatitudes*, 23, 41, 47, 251. See especially 266-267 where Green lists the OT (LXX) passages which are, according to him, the roots of the beatitudes.

26 Green prefers to speak of "influences" rather than "sources." Green, *Matthew, Poet of the Beatitudes*, 264.

investigates the background nor highlights the nature of this community.[27] Of course, Green offers an important and unique contribution to the study of the Matthean Beatitudes. His interpretation of the individual beatitudes based on their Old Testament background or influence is also a very important approach. However, his rejection of two document-hypothesis (or the existence of Q), is difficult to swallow at this stage, and his lack of an investigation into the nature of the community behind the first gospel makes his study inadequate. Charles R. Day mainly investigates the different stages of tradition of the Matthean beatitudes before they were written down in the Greek language. His aim is to ascertain the oral tradition that gave rise to the Greek text, and to suggest a theoretical rendering of the original words of Jesus. This research suggests that the original beatitudes were composed in Aramaic and they were subsequently translated into Hebrew, and it is this Hebrew version which is the antecedent for the Greek text (which, according to Day, underwent successive modifications) known today.[28] This is indeed a valuable contribution to the study of the Matthean Beatitudes. At the same time, however, a profound investigation into the community behind this gospel and their influence upon it are lacking, which on the other hand, are vital for understanding their implications.

Meanwhile, the application of sociological principles in recent years, particularly in terms of an in-depth investigation into the socio-historical settings behind the New Testament texts, has produced the necessary corrective to such approaches of investigating the text. These studies, by locating New Testament texts especially within the dynamics of human community and issues, produced insights, which have substantial bearings on the outcome of New Testament exegesis.[29] Just to give an example, Theissen and Meeks, in their study on the

27 Green, *Matthew, Poet of the Beatitudes*, 22-23.

28 Charles R. Day, "An Investigation of the Beatitudes of Matthew: Between the Oral Tradition and the Greek Text" (D. Lit. Thesis, University of Pretoria, 2004), 238-244.

29 The application of sociological principles in New Testament studies is based mainly on an argument that every literary work reflects and responds to the social world in which it was produced. See the following for example- Salvador Giner, *Sociology* (London: Martin Robertson, 1972), 199; Bengt Holmberg, *Sociology and the New Testament: An Appraisal* (Minneapolis: Fortress Press, 1990), 1; and Thomas B. Slater, "Social Methodology and the New Testament," *Bible Bhashyam* 19 (1993), 238.
This application began as early as 1960s. One of the earliest attempts was E.A. Judge, *The Social Pattern of Christian Groups in the First Century* (London: Tyndale, 1960). But it became popular from 1970s. One of the leading works is J. G. Gager, *Kingdom and Community: The Social World of Early Christianity* (Eaglewood Cliffs, N. J.: Prentice Hall, 1975). Among other important contributions are - Gerd Theissen, *Sociology of Early Palestinian Christianity*, translated by John Bowden {Philadelphia: Fortress Press, 1978); by the same author, *The Social Setting of Pauline Christianity: Essays on Corinth* (Edinburgh: T&T Clark, 1982); Abraham J. Malherbe, *Social Aspects of Early Christianity* (Philadelphia: Fortress, 1977); Wayne A. Meeks, *The First Urban Christians: The Social World of the Apostle Paul* (New Haven: Yale University Press, 1983); H.C. Kee, *Miracle in the Early Christian World: A Study in Socio-Historical Method*

social setting of Pauline Christianity, conclude that the main problem underlying the disputes in the Corinthian church concerning eating meat (I Cor 8) and over the celebration of the Lord's Supper (I Cor 11) was the difference in socio-economic status among the members. More precisely the problem was caused by the complacency of the rich members in eating meat, as well as the special treatment given to the rich members and the neglect of the poor members at the same time by the host at the Lord's Supper.[30] These insights are crucial for understanding and interpreting this letter. In the case of Matthew's gospel, the sociological studies have attempted to reconstruct the experiences of the Matthean community as the necessary crucibles in which theology was fashioned.[31] These studies have shown that Matthew's gospel could best be understood by viewing it from the background of the Matthean community in the post 70 C.E. context. In the renewal movement within Judaism, which took place in the aftermath of the destruction of the Jerusalem temple, the overcoming of the previous separation of Judaism into groups was emphasized above all.[32] This integrating process under the leadership of the scribes and Pharisees strongly followed the Pharisaic tradition. It consequently resulted in the exclusion of Jewish groups, which were not representing the majority consensus, including the followers of Jesus Christ,

---

(New Haven: Yale University, 1983); J. Stambaugh and D. Balch, *The New Testament in Its Social Environment* (Philadelphia: Westminster, 1988); B. Malina, *The New Testament World: Insights from Cultural Anthropology* (Atlanta: John Knox, 1981); by the same author *Christian Origins and Cultural Anthropology* (Atlanta: John Knox, 1986); and J.H. Elliot, "Social Scientific Criticism of the New Testament: More on Methods and Models," *Semeia* 35 (1986), 1-33.

30 See, Theissen, *The Social Setting of Pauline Christianity*, and Meeks, *The First Urban Christians.*

31 Notable among the major contributions in this area are: Amy-Jill Levine, *The Social and Ethnic Dimensions of Matthean Salvation History. "Go nowhere among the Gentiles…" (Matt. 10:5b)* (Studies in the Bible and Early Christianity 14; Lewiston: the Edwin Mellon Press, 1988); J. Andrew Overman, *Matthew's Gospel and Formative Judaism: The Social World of the Matthean Community* (Minneapolis: Fortress Press, 1990); Graham N. Stanton, *A Gospel for a New People: Studies in Matthew* (Louisville: Westminster Press, 1993 [1992]); Anthony J. Saldarini, *Matthew's Christian-Jewish Community* (Chicago: University of Chicago, 1994); David C. Sim, *The Gospel of Matthew and Christian Judaism. The History and Social Setting of the Matthean Community* (Edinburgh: T&T Clark, 1998).

32 The Post-exilic Israel, particularly Hellenistic-Roman period was characterized by group formations such as Sadducees, Pharisees, Essenes, etc. This was followed in the Roman-Herodian Period by emergence of a number of prominent prophetic-charismatic movements, religio-political and socio-revolutionary movements. It seems that the post-70 C.E. renewal movement was trying to overcome such separation of Jewish community into groups. For more detail see Ekkehard W. Stegemann and Wolfgang Stegemann, *The Jesus Movement: A Social History of Its first Century*, translated by O. C. Dean, Jr. (Minneapolis: Fortress Press, 1999 [1995]), 138-222.

labeling them as deviants.[33] It is therefore believed that Matthew's gospel largely reflects and responds to the experience of the Matthean community in that situation. Moreover, it is also believed in this study that the first gospel reflects even the experience of the Matthean community, which it shared along with the other Jewish community in the aftermath of the first Jewish war against Rome (66-73 C.E.), socio-politically and economically. In addition to these factors, it also seems that the author of the first gospel took into consideration the experience of his community from the Gentiles, its experience (along with their neighbors) of frequent death and illness due to the unhygienic living condition and frequent natural disasters, as well as the internal experience of the community resulting from the mixed membership of both Jewish and Gentile converts.[34] Consequently it is held in this book that all these experiences of the Matthean community need to be taken seriously in the interpretation of this gospel. However, as far as the knowledge of this researcher is concerned, those important insights envisaged in recent Matthean studies on the socio-historical situation of the Matthean community, have not been employed so far in the study and interpretation of the Matthean Beatitudes. Hence, this study is undertaken.

This research work, therefore, aims to explicate the meaning of the Matthean beatitudes by interpreting them with the help of insights offered by recent scholarship on the socio-historical setting of Matthew's gospel. Such an interpretation will bring out the significance of the ways of life of Jesus' disciples spelled out in this text, such as poverty in spirit, mourning, meekness, hunger and thirst for righteousness, showing mercy, purity in heart, peacemaking, persecution for righteousness' sake, and sufferings for Jesus' sake, in their specific contexts. Hence, this research will help the contemporary Christians to relate in

33 This is indicated in the new formulation of the so-called *Birkat ha-minim* "heretic benediction." Stegemann and Stegemann, *The Jesus Movement*, 222.
Recent studies on the Matthean community usually use the sociological model of either sectarian or deviant to describe this community's struggle against formative Judaism. For example, Overman and Stanton use the term 'sectarian' while Stegemann and Stegemann, and Saldarini employ deviance theory. On the basis of the detailed explanations of sectarian model and deviance theory this researcher sees the deviance theory as the more appropriate designation of the Matthean community. For a detailed explanations of the term "sect" see the following - Max Weber, *The Sociology of Religion* (Boston: Beacon Press, 1963), 65, 92-93; Ernst Troeltsch, *The Social Teaching of the Christian Churches*, translated by Olive Wyon (London: George Allen & Unwin LTD; New York: The Macmillan Company, 1956 [1931/1922]), 331ff.; Bryan Wilson, *Religion in Sociological Perspective* (Oxford: Oxford University Press, 1982), 90-92; and B. Johnson, "On Church and Sect," *American Sociological Review* 28 (1963): 539-549. And for a detailed explanation of deviance theory see the following - H.S. Becker, *Outsiders: Studies in the Sociology of Deviance* (New York: Free Press, 1963), 8-9; K.T. Erikson, *Wayward Puritans: A Study in the Sociology of Deviance* (New York: John Wiley and Sons, 1966), 13; and Ben-Yehuda, *Deviance and Moral Boundaries: Witchcraft, the Occult, Deviant Sciences and Scientists* (Chicago: University of Chicago Press, 1985), 19-20.

34 All these factors will be discussed in the next chapter.

their respective situations the implication for Christian discipleship encapsulated in these beatitudes. The outcome of this research is expected to be especially meaningful for many poor and downtrodden Christians in India who, at the same time, often suffer persecutions. And it will also be consequential for the Mizo Christians[35] in North East India, who are being intruded deeper and deeper by moral corruption, particularly financial corruption, in which even many church leaders are not spared.[36] Moreover, it will also have an important bearing upon

35 The author of this book belongs to Mizo Christian community of the North East India, and he focuses more on the Mizo Christians and other communities of North East India because he is one of them and he has a concern for them.

36 This researcher belongs to this Mizo community and has a first hand knowledge of the problems facing this community. According to 2001 census report about 85 per cent of the population of Mizoram state is Christians. The remaining population, approximately 15 percent is made up basically of non-Mizo communities living in this state. Within the Mizo community, more than 99 per cent confessed to be Christian. The remaining less than one per cent is made up of those who lately claim themselves to be members of Israelites. In this state as well as in this community corruption is very much rampant, especially among government officers and legislatures. This is clearly revealed in the constant outcry of the general public through news papers and news magazines, who feel deprived of their shares in the government's development plan. Especially in the year (2006) the regular chorus of News papers and news magazines from the beginning of the year till the end is the problem of corruption. Just to give an example, it has been revealed by one vernacular magazine on 22, August, 2006 that 15 out of 38 members of Mizoram state legislators availed Leave Traveling Concession, amounting to lakhs of rupees per person without going on actual travels. "The magazine only highlighted these 15 legislators coming from all parties because they were the ones who could be proved that they were in Mizoram while the claim in their TA bills said they were traveling." See Bureau Report, "Legislators Fake TA Bills Revealed," *News Link* (22.08.2006), 1 of 1, available from www.zoram.com (accessed 11.12.2006). This matter has been mentioned again and again in the news papers. See for example, Revd. Chuauthuama, "MLA Free Travel Hman Dik Loh Chungchang (Matter Relating to the Misuse of Free Travel by MLA)," *Vanglaini*, 06 September 2006, 3. It would not be an exaggeration to say that in the opinion of the general public most of the government officers and legislators are suspected to be involved in financial corruption. As such, the Bureau Report quoted above began the report with the statement "In what could be a shocking revelation in other places other than Mizoram but not in Mizoram." A significant thing in relation to corruption in Mizoram is that many of those government officers and legislators, who are suspected to be involved in corruption, are church elders and active participants in church's activities. See for example K. L. Rochama, "Zin Loh Hlawh (Salary/Payment for not Traveling)," *Vanglaini*, 21 September 2006, 3. Here, Rochama mentions a government officer who is also a church elder, as stating that even all the government officers, including many church elders among them, are drawing advance bill for traveling concession, but either without really going for the trips or spending only a portion of the bill for traveling. The enormity of this corruption problem can be seen from the fact that even the Mizoram Upa Pawl (Association of Elderly People in Mizoram) declared this year (2006) "a year of fighting against corruption." See for example, "MUP-in MLA hlawh nawr hniam tum" (posted on 20 February 2009), 2 of 2, http://emizoram.com/news/?p=4387&cpage=1 (accessed 23.04. 2009). Even Former Legislators' Association of Mizoram is taking similar steps. Not only that, but also Mizoram People's Forum has been formed this year under the patronage of the Presbyterian church of Mizoram to fight against

many Christians in India, particularly in the North East, who have often been engaged in the killing of other people, even other Christians, due to ethnic and ideological conflict. The insights gained from this study also will have an important bearing upon Christians within the larger context of India in general, reminding them of their true identities and responsibilities as disciples of Jesus Christ in different contexts, which confront them, such as where the gap between the rich and the poor becomes wider and wider, where there is an unending division on the basis of caste and class with its resultant exploitation, where religious intolerance increases particularly against Christians from the dominant religious community, where corruption enters deeper and deeper even into the life of many Christians, and where ethnic enmity prevails over Christian brotherhood among certain Christian communities.[37]

---

corruption and other related problems. See for example, "Kohhran leh Politics [Church and Politics]," *Zozam* (July 4-10, 2006), 18.

37 The situation in India is understood in general. However, at least two particularly challenging situations may be mentioned. As it is generally understood the Indian economy is growing at a fast pace in recent years. Basically because of technological development and globalization the rich becomes richer. However, at the same time the poor becomes poorer. This is clearly indicated by the fact that during the same period many farmers have committed suicide because of debt burdens, and the trend of farmers' suicide continues. It is claimed that during 1997 to July 2005 more than 25000 (twenty five thousand) farmers committed suicide, and in 2006 alone more than 1000 (thousand) farmers have committed suicide in Maharastra state alone. See Chad Heeter, *Rough Cut. Seeds of Suicide. India's Desperate Farmers* (26.07.2005), 1-2 of 6. http://www.pbs.org/ frontlineworld/rough (accessed 12.12.2006). See also Gadkari, "Over 1000 farmers committed suicide in 2006," *Maharastra News* (29.11.2006), 1 of 1, available from www.newsKerala.com (accessed 11.12.2006). The ethnic rivalry in Manipur state which resulted in the death of hundreds of people and burning of several houses and villages during the last decade and even at the beginning of this decade is not yet properly healed. A very sad thing is that the communities involved in this rivalry are Christians. For an overview of the problem during 1990s, See Shin-wha Lee and Deepa Khosla, *Nagas in India* (updated 09/04/99), 1-19 of 19. http://www.bsos.umd.edu/cidcm/mar/indnaa.htm (accessed 12.12.2006).

All these situations call for a thoroughgoing reflection on the nature of Christian discipleship, based on scriptural text, reinforced with proper research. This research is aiming at providing a useful tool for a meaningful reflection.

Contents

Chapter 1

The Socio-Historical Setting of Matthew's Gospel

1.1. Preface

First, we will try to explain in brief why a study of the Matthean socio-historical setting is important and which specific areas of this setting are focussed on in this book.

The interrelationship between literature and the social life-settings behind it has been noted and given importance in recent years more than ever before in the study of Biblical literature, particularly of the New Testament.[1] This emphasis is basically an outcome of the sociology of literature which posits that specific types of social life-settings (*Sitze im Leben*) influence and shape types or genres (*Gattungen*) of literature.[2] Accordingly, sociologists approach literature as a document through which the inner structures of a society can be investigated. It is claimed, "no matter how fanciful or farfetched the literary act of creation may be," literature "is still a document which, if properly decoded, is bound to reveal the latent relationships, values and beliefs of the writer's world."[3] In line with

---

1 See for example, David Rhoads, "Social Criticism: Crossing Boundaries," in *Mark and Method: New Approaches in Biblical Studies*, edited by Janice Capel Anderson and Stephen D. Moore (Minneapolis: Fortress, 1992), 384. Here Rhoads notes:

> The New Testament is a profoundly social document. Each writing in the New Testament emerged from a community. Each writing addressed specific people with a unique message for a given time, place, and circumstance. Each writing was deeply embedded in a particular culture and history. Each writer shared a common social system with readers that enabled communication to take place. The writings of the New Testament were social acts.

2 Holmberg, *Sociology and the New Testament: An Appraisal*, 383-384. See also Slater, "Social Methodology and the New Testament," 237-248, 244.

3 Giner, *Sociology*, 199, and 201, n. 7.

the emphasis given in the sociology of literature, even literary critics of the New Testament recognize that an understanding of social and cultural realities behind the stories of the New Testament texts is essential in order to decode the meaning inherent in those stories.[4] Because of all these emphases, an understanding of the social world behind New Testament literature has been regarded in current New Testament scholarship as highly important in order to understand their meaning and interpret them meaningfully. As a result, several writings on the varied subjects of the New Testament from a sociological perspective have come out,[5] and are continuing to come out. In the case of the gospels in particular, their connection to their socio-historical context is clearly noted in Brown's statement, where he says that experiences stemming from the decades that separated Jesus from the writers of the canonical gospels coloured the presentation of these gospels, and "relevance to Christian problems determined the selection of what was preserved from the Jesus tradition."[6]

Hence, it is believed in this research that an investigation into the social world behind Matthew's gospel is of paramount importance in order to enhance the proper understanding of this gospel and its meaningful interpretation in the present context.[7]

---

4 Mark Allan Powell, *What is Narrative Criticism?* (London: SPCK, 1993), 97.

5 Some of the leading works in the area may be mentioned as examples, such as - Malherbe, *Social Aspects of Early Christianity*; Theissen, *Sociology of Early Palestinian Christianity*; Kee, *Miracle in the Early Christian World*; Theissen, *The Social Setting of Pauline Christianity*; Meeks, *The First Urban Christians*; Stambaugh and Balch, *The New Testament in Its Social Environment.*

6 Raymond E. Brown, *An Introduction to the New Testament* (Bangalore: Theological Publications in India, 2000 [1996]), 7. Following Brown, Ewherido further says, "Recognizing this interconnection between the text and its social history is a necessity for anyone who seeks to understand the text," because "the gospels were first lived by the early Christian communities, in which the contents of the good news were deeply embedded before they were written down." Anthony O. Ewherido, *Matthew's Gospel and Judaism in the Late First Century C.E. The Evidence from Matthew's Chapter on Parables (Matthew 13:1-52* (New York, et al.: Peter Lang, 2006), 230, n. 7.

7 Sixty years ago G. D. Kilpatrick had already indicated this in *The Origins of the Gospel according to St. Matthew* (Oxford: Clarendon Press, 1966 [1946]). The view of Kilpatrick is summarized by Stendahl, in *The School of St. Matthew and Its Use of the Old Testament* (Ramsey, New Jersey: Sigler Press, 1991 [Philadelphia: Fortress, 1968 [1954]]), 20, as follows:

> At the time when Matthew was compiled, Mark had been used for liturgical purposes for some years, as had Q and M (the discourse material peculiar to Matthew), while the narrative material peculiar to Matthew was put into writing by the evangelist himself. The liturgical use of the scriptures was the focus of the church's use of the gospel material. In expounding the text read in the services the needs of the church were connected with the words and works recorded in the gospel. The exposition was repeated time and again and developed into a more or less fixed tradition, which in its turn was admitted to liturgical use. At this state, traditions of the Matthean church were combined into a revised edition of the gospel.

Therefore, the purpose and intent of this chapter is to highlight the social world of Matthew's gospel with the conviction that it holds the primary key to the interpretation of this gospel in general and the Matthean "Beatitudes" (Matt 5:3-15) in particular. It is expected here that an insight into the social world of Matthew's gospel would help to unearth the implications of the Matthean beatitudes for Christian discipleship, especially in the present context, which is the focus of this research.

However, it is important to clarify here that while the term "social world" covers the whole range of social and cultural reality, the focus in this study is the "social-historical reality" behind Matthew's gospel. This does not mean that the two terms, namely "social world" and "social history" are understood as identical or synonymous in this study. It is acknowledged here that the term "social world" encompasses the whole area within the purviews of the basic approaches of sociological principles such as social description, social history, sociology of knowledge and cultural anthropology.[8] While all these approaches are inter-related and cannot be totally separated in the study of the New Testament, each of them, however, has a specific emphasis. Accordingly, the degree of their applicability to each book of the New Testament is also different. That means that while one approach is more appropriate or useful for the study of a specific book or text of the New Testament, other approaches may be more functional for studying other books or texts of the New Testament. At this juncture, the application of sociological principles in the study of Matthew's gospel so far has shown that a socio-historical approach is one of the most appropriate methods for the study of this gospel.[9] In fact, it has been revealed by sociological studies of Matthew's gospel that the most important factor affecting and influencing its writing and its theological formulation was the socio-historical reality experienced by the community behind this gospel.[10]

Therefore, an attempt is made in this chapter to explore the socio-historical experience of the community behind Matthew's gospel, which apparently had

---

Recently Ewherido rightly notes that "both text and social history are indispensable and interdependent in the articulation of Matthew's self-understanding and social context. Ewherido, *Matthew's Gospel and Judaism in the Late First Century C.E.*, 198.

8 For a brief explanation of these approaches, see Rhoads, "Social Criticism: Crossing Boundaries," 136-143.

9 A brief explanation of social history may be drawn from the words of Gager, "a social history need not concern itself with anything more than a *description* of the relevant social data." See J. G. Gager, "Social Description and Sociological Explanation," *RelStudRev* 5 (1979b), 174-180, 175.

10 For example, see the following works which are based on this conviction: Overman, *Matthew's Gospel and Formative Judaism*; Stanton, *A Gospel for a New People*; Saldarini, *Matthew's Christian-Jewish Community*; Sim, *The Gospel of Matthew and Christian Judaism*; Magnus Zetterholm, *The Formation of Christianity in Antioch. A Social-scientific Approach to the Separation between Judaism and Christianity* (London and New York: Routledge, 2003).

affected the writing of this gospel and influenced its contents. In the process, however, the so-called "traditional questions" such as authorship, intended audience, date, and geographical location of Matthew's gospel are taken up first as preliminary considerations. This is followed by an analysis of a significant historical event behind the Matthean setting, namely the first Jewish war against Rome (66-73 C.E.), especially its aftermath upon the Jews. This is important because, this war resulted in the emergence of the so-called "formative Judaism" which was a reorganization movement of the Jewish society shattered by the war. The leaders of this movement eventually came into conflict with the Matthean community, and this conflict became the major influencing factor for the writing of Matthew's gospel and for the shaping of its contents. Therefore, under the subtitle, "the Socio-Historical Setting of the Matthean Community," the following factors which are identified in this research work as significant in shaping the content of Matthew's gospel in general, and especially the Beatitudes in particular, are studied, such as: the relationship between formative Judaism and the Matthean community; the relationship between Matthew's community and the Gentiles; the ethnic composition of the Matthean community; and the socio-economic status of the Matthean community. Then the commonly proposed terms such as the theories of sectarianism and deviance are briefly analysed to suggest the most appropriate sociological term for designating Matthew's community. A summary of all these investigations furnishes a theoretical framework for the interpretation of Matthew's gospel in general and for the interpretation of the Matthean Beatitudes (Matt 5:3-12), in particular.

1.2. Preliminary Considerations

In an attempt to delineate the socio-historical setting of Matthew's gospel, an investigation of the so-called traditional questions is indispensable. This is because specific suggestions on the authorship and the intended audience of the gospel, as well as the time and place in which it was written, are important for identifying its socio-historical setting. This section is, therefore, dedicated to this purpose. The questions of authorship and intended audience are briefly considered first here, which are followed by a more detailed study on the suggestions of the date and place in which this gospel was written.

1.2.1. The Authorship of Matthew's Gospel

Based on its overwhelming Jewish nature,[11] supported by some external

11 Among various indicators of the Jewish nature of this gospel, the following may be mentioned as examples: the gospel's emphasis on the fulfillment of the OT and especially the distinctive formula quotations which point to Jesus as the Messiah and Jesus' ministry as the dawning of the messianic age (found throughout the gospel, but more concentrated in the first four chapters); the importance of Jesus' faithfulness to the law and his demand for righteousness (particularly as in 5:17-20); the omission by Matthew of Mark's explanation of Jewish customs

evidences,[12] Matthew's gospel is usually regarded as written by a Jewish author. This can be regarded as the majority consensus to date.[13] There is, however, a difference of opinion among the proponents of the Jewish authorship of Matthew's gospel on the actual identity of the author.[14] There has been an argument in favour of Matthew, one of the disciples of Jesus Christ, as its author. This argument goes back to the church fathers whose statements testify that Matthew wrote the gospel in Hebrew.[15] The possibility of this could not be totally ruled out because of the

---

(cf. Matt 15:2 with Mark 7:3-4); Matthew's formulation of several discussions in typical rabbinic patterns (e.g., a matter of divorce in 19:3-9); the apologetic motifs of the infancy narrative (against early Jewish claims of the illegitimacy of Jesus' birth), and the resurrection narrative (against the Jewish claim that the body was stolen; 28:12-15). See Hagner, *Matthew 1-13*, lxiv.

12 Such as the witness of the church fathers like Papias, Pantaenus, Irenaeus, Origen, Eusebius, and Jerome. See Hagner, *Matthew 1-13*, lxxvi.

13 Of course, there are some scholars who opt for a Gentile authorship of Matthew's gospel. Often quoted, as the proponents of Gentile authorship are - K.W. Clark, "The Gentile Bias in Matthew," *JournBibLit* 66 (1947), 165-172; P. Nepper-Christensen, *Das Matthausevangelium: Ein Judenchristliches Evangelium?* (Aarhus: Universitaetsforlaget: 1958); G. Strecker, *Der Weg der Gerechtigkeit*, 3rd ed. (Goettingen: Vandenhoeck & Ruprecht, 1971); John P. Meier, *The Vision of Matthew: Christ, Church, and Morality in the First Gospel* (New York: Paulist Press, 1978), 17-25. For an example of where these names are mentioned as supporters of Gentile authorship of Matthew, see Brown, *An Introduction to the New Testament*, 211, n. 87. However, Brown here notes that the proponents of Gentile authorship comprise only about one to four against those who favor a Jewish Christian authorship. For a detailed discussion on authorship of Matthew's gospel, as well as for support of its Jewish authorship, see W. D. Davies and Dale C. Allison, Jr., *A Critical and Exegetical Commentary on the Gospel According to St. Matthew*, Vol.1, ICC (Edinburgh: T&T Clark, 1988), 7-58. See also D. A. Carson, Douglas J. Moo and Leon Morris, *An Introduction to the New Testament* (Grand Rapids, Michigan: Zondervan, 1992), 66-74.

14 It would be good to clarify here that we are dealing with the actual author of Matthew's gospel here and not the implied author or the narrator. Literary/Narrative critics are interested in distinguishing and analyzing the real author, the implied author, and the narrator. The "real author" is the historical person who created the narrative. The "implied author" is the literary version or the second self of the real author, created by the real author himself in the process of creating the narrative. The implied author becomes known to the reader through the process of reading the story of the narrative. The "narrator" is the invisible speaker, the one who tells the story to the reader, whom the reader hears as he or she reads through the story. See, Jack Dean Kingsbury, *Matthew as Story* (Philadelphia: Fortress, 1986), 31. We are dealing here with the actual author because neither the idea of the implied author nor the narrator is relevant for the socio-historical approach, which is employed for our present research.

15 According to Patristic evidence preserved in Eusebius (*H. E.*), Matthew's gospel was originally composed in Hebrew language by Matthew, one of the disciples of Jesus. Papias wrote, "Matthew composed his history in the Hebrew dialect, and every one translated it as he was able." Irenaeus also wrote, "Matthew produced his gospel written among the Hebrews in their own dialect, whilst Peter and Paul proclaimed the gospel and founded the church at Rome...." Origen also stated that among the four undisputed gospels "the first is written according to Matthew, the same that was once a publican but afterwards an apostle of Jesus Christ, who

heavy dependence of these materials on apostolic Christianity, thus, a very early date, and especially because there was no challenge to Papias' statement in his own time.[16] The vast majority of scholars, however, contend that the gospel of Matthew as we have it now, was written in Greek and was not a translation from a Hebrew/Aramaic original.[17] Yet, there are strong arguments for the possibility of it being a translation from the Semitic original. For example, apart from other arguments, it seems that the great figures of the early church fathers such as Eusebius, Origen, Clement of Alexandria and Irenaeus, who were Greeks and who presumably knew the Greek language better than most (or all) of modern scholars, apparently took canonical Matthew to be the translation of a Semitic original.[18] Yet, another problem with the suggestion of Matthew's authorship in relation to our present canonical text is that the patristic witness to the authorship of Matthew suggests the date of this gospel as earlier than that of Mark which is generally dated in the late 60s or just after 70 C.E., that is shortly after the fall of Jerusalem.[19] However, most (or all) of the recent studies on the socio-

---

having published it for the Jewish converts, wrote it in Hebrew." Also Pantaenus (according to Eusebius) found that the gospel according to Matthew, written in Hebrew, preceded him to India when he (Pantaenus) visited the place. It was left by Bartholomew, one of the disciples and was preserved there in the Hebrew language at that time. See Eusebius, *H. E.,* 3. 39; 5. 8; 6. 25; and 5. 10, in Eusebius, *Ecclesiastical History to the Twentieth Year of the Reign of Constantine, Being the 324th of the Christian Era,* translated by C. F. Cruse, 4th, Revised ed. (London: Samuel Bagster and Sons, 1847), 144, 202-203, 258-259, 205. According to Viviano, Jerome also mentions that the Hebrew text of Matthew was still preserved in his own time in the Caesarean library. See B.T. Viviano, "Where Was the Gospel according to St. Matthew Written?" *CathBibQuart* 41 (1979), 542. It is generally observed that later patristic statements depend upon Papias' witness. See Davies and Allison, Jr., *Matthew,* Vol. I, 8-9. In any case, however, it sounds too daring to cast off all these witnesses, especially when there were no better alternatives having been put forth in their own time.

16 Craig S. Keener, *A Commentary on the Gospel of Matthew* (Grand Rapids, Michigan/Cambridge, U.K.: William B. Eerdmans Publishing Company, 1999), 38-41. See also David A. DeSilva, *An Introduction to the New Testament. Contexts, Methods and Ministry Formation* (Downers Grove, Illinois: InterVarsity Press / Leicester, England: Apollos, 2004), 235.

17 Brown, *An Introduction to the New Testament,* 210. See also John Nolland, *The Gospel of Matthew. A Commentary on the Greek Text* (Grand Rapids, Michigan/Cambridge, U.K.: William B. Eerdmans Publishing Company, 2005), 3.

18 For this and for other arguments, see Davies and Allison, Jr., *Matthew,* Vol. I, 12-17. Davies and Allison Jr. do not mention the specific writings of the church fathers in which they based this argument. Therefore, the author depends upon them, because it is too vast to sift through the writings of the early church fathers.

19 See the following - Brown, *An Introduction to the New Testament,* 163-164. Donald Guthrie, *New Testament Introduction,* Revised Edition (Downers Grove, Illinois: Intervarsity Press, 1990), 84-89. See also W.G. Kummel, *Introduction to the New Testament* (Bloomsbury Street, London: SCM Press LTD, 1977 [1973]), 97-98. Cf., however, for an earlier date for both Mark and Matthew, particularly before the destruction of Jerusalem Temple, Carson, Moo and Morris, *An Introduction to the New Testament,* 76-79. See also Nolland, *The Gospel of Matthew,* 14-17.

historical context of Matthew's gospel suggest that this gospel was written in the aftermath of the destruction of Jerusalem and the Temple in which formative Judaism began to take shape.[20] Therefore, a more probable argument, based on all the available evidence at present, is that the primary source of the materials in the gospel could be Matthew, who wrote in Hebrew/Aramaic. Then, it was translated and redacted by a Hellenistic Jew, who had extensively made use of Mark's gospel, which already existed at the time of the translation and final redaction.[21] David A. DeSilva posits in a simple way as follows:

> Matthew did compile an Aramaic sayings source, recording what Jesus taught in the course of his own apostolic ministry. This became the possession of the communities that Matthew founded and nurtured. A disciple of Matthew took his teacher's materials, other Jesus sayings familiar to the community and Mark's gospel, and fashioned a presentation of Jesus' life and instruction more complete than any of the sources on their own. Because, Matthew stood behind one of these sources, indeed the source that made the gospel distinctive, it would be quite natural for his name to continue to stand behind the finished product as author and, more importantly for the early church, authenticator of that tradition.[22]

Or, it is also quite possible, that the final editor made use of the collection of Jesus' sayings by Matthew, which was already translated into Greek, which perhaps then took the form of Q[23]. If this is the case, then there is a possibility that the Q underwent further development, before the first evangelist made use of it, resulting in the existence of Q^{mt} and Q^{lk}. This is suggested by the fact that the differences of Q materials in Matthew and Luke are sometimes difficult to explain as redactions of either of the two evangelists, although, it is uncertain how far such

---

20 See the following for example - Overman, *Matthew's Gospel and Formative Judaism*, 2, etc.; Saldarini, *Matthew's Christian-Jewish Community*, 4; Sim, *The Gospel of Matthew and Christian Judaism*, 113-115.

21 Davies and Allison, Jr., *Matthew*, Vol. I, 12-13.

22 DeSilva, *An Introduction to the New Testament*, 235-236.

23 John Nolland's observation seems worth mentioning here. According to him, if Papias' statement ('Matthew, then, compiled the oracles in the Hebrew/Aramaic language, and each interpreted/translated as they were able') is from a reliable tradition, we can presume that 'the oracles of Jesus here refer to the teaching of Jesus, and, the word of Papias 'h`rmh,neusen' here suggests 'translation' rather than 'interpreted.' "The nearest things that we have to such an ancient collection of 'oracles' are the Gospel of Thomas and the document Q." Then, "it is easier to suggests that Matthew's activity ... provided the initial stimulus for the creation of such documents than that Matthew's collection of 'oracles' directly underlies them, but the latter is certainly quite possible." In his conclusion, Nolland maintains that it is very unlikely that the apostle Matthew composed the canonical Gospel although it has never been questioned in the early centuries. "A collection of the sayings of Jesus made by the apostle Matthew may have left its mark on canonical Matthew, but we cannot be certain even of this." Nolland, *The Gospel of Matthew*, 2-4.

appeal can be made.[24] In any case, this redactor adapted his material to the needs of the Christian community of his time and place.[25] Therefore, it is assumed in this research, that Matthew's gospel was written in Greek by a Hellenistic Jewish author, making extensive use of Mark's gospel and the sayings source Q, which was probably collected by the apostle Matthew and written in Aramaic. He could have used the sayings source in its original Aramaic form, but more probably after it was translated into Greek. Further, by the time the first gospel was written the original Q probably had been redacted and it had taken two forms. Then, the author of the first gospel made use of the one, which is now, called Q^{mt}, while the other one was used by Luke and is now called Q^{lk}. Besides Mark and Q^{mt}, he also used written and oral sources, which were available to him.[26] Stendahl proposes that Matthew's gospel was a product of the school of St. Matthew as a handbook for teachers and church leaders for the purpose of teaching, preaching, and church government of the Matthean community. According to him, the school is the natural *Sitz im Leben* of the gospel.[27] It is believed in this study, however, that the *Sitz im Leben* of Matthew's gospel is the antagonism between the Matthean community and formative Judaism, as well as some possible tensions within the community.[28] Moreover, the hand of a single author seems quite discernible in the literary characteristics of Matthew's gospel.[29] The purpose, which Stendahl proposes, nonetheless, seems quite fitting into this context of the Matthean community. Therefore, it is quite possible, as Dobschütz suggests, that the author of the first evangelist was a (Hellenistic) Jewish rabbi, who became a Christian, and who made use of his Jewish rabbinic training in presenting the Christian

---

24 C. M. Tuckett, "Q (Gospel Source)," *ABD*, Vol. 5 (New York: Doubleday, 1992), 568.

25 See for instance, Saldarini, *Matthew's Christian-Jewish Community*, 7. For this and for a detailed discussion on the authorship of Matthew's gospel, see also the following - Davies and Allison, Jr., *Matthew*, Vol. I, 7-58; Hagner, *Matthew 1-13*, lxxv-lxxvii.

26 Luz assumes that Q was a written document which underwent a process of expansion from a smaller collection and circulated in different recensions. He opines that Q^{mt} is enlarged minimally and is closer to the "common" form than Q^{lk}, which was most likely enlarged substantially. According to Luz, Paleographically one might assume the collection of Q material as a rather large notebook, bound together with stings on the margin, permitting an insertion of new leaves at any time. With regard to the special Matthean materials, Luz is of the view that almost all the individual stories which Matthew inserted as additions to the Markan text (e.g., Matt 17:24-27; 27:3-10) and the infancy narratives (Matt 1:18-2:23) were taken by Matthew from oral traditions and formulated by Matthew himself in writing for the first time. Luz does not presume a written source even for fulfillment quotations. He thinks that a written source is used by Matthew for some of his larger unique parables, for the primary antithesis of the Sermon on the Mount, and for the text on almsgiving, prayer, and fasting (Matt 5:21-24, 27f., 33-37; 6:1-6, 16-18). Luz, *Matthew 1-7*, 48-49.

27 See Stendahl, *The School of St. Matthew*, 24, 29, 35, 205-206.

28 This will become clear at the end of this chapter as it is the main focus of this chapter.

29 See "the Structure of Matthew's Gospel" and "Other Important Literary Characteristics of Matthew's Gospel" in the following chapter.

gospel, particularly aiming to provide to his community with his gospel the order of the church and Christian catechism[30] in the context of their antagonism with formative Judaism and the possible tensions within the community. It is also highly probable at the same time that the elders or leaders of the Matthean community, which may be understood as representing what Stendahl calls "the school of St. Matthew," contributed the materials used by the author. In all the subsequent discussions in this study, for the sake of convenience, the name of the author will always be mentioned as Matthew, as traditionally assigned, but without necessarily meaning that the final form of the first gospel was written by the apostle Matthew. And, the text in view will be of the final redaction that is assumed to have been written in Greek by a Hellenistic Jewish author.

It is thus, believed in this research that the author of the first gospel was a Hellenistic Jew, probably a former Jewish rabbi who became a Christian, and who was one of the leaders of the Matthean community, and who wrote this gospel in Greek, using Mark and the saying source Q, as well as other traditions which were available to him both written and oral, and adapting them to the needs of his community. Probably he also was helped by other leaders of his community in collecting the materials and also by giving suggestions as to how to adapt them to the requirements of his intended audience, the Matthean community. This will take us to the consideration of the intended audience of this gospel.

1.2.2. The Intended Audience of Matthew's Gospel

There are two main lines of thought with regard to the intended audience of Matthew's gospel. Based on the overwhelming Jewish nature of the gospel,[31] and at the same time, the prominence of Gentile interest from beginning to end,[32]

30 Ernst von Dobschütz, "Matthew as Rabbi and Catechist," in *The Interpretation of Matthew*, edited by Graham Stanton (Philadelphia: Fortress Press; SPCK: London, 1983), 19-29. Dobschütz, here, maintains that the author of the first gospel was a Jewish rabbi. The term "Hellenistic" in the bracket is added by this researcher because he believes that the first evangelist was a Hellenistic Jew, which is suggested, especially by the fact that the Greek language used in the first gospel is not a translation from Hebrew/Aramaic, as pointed out by various scholars. See for example, Brown, *An Introduction to the New Testament*, 210; and Nolland, *The Gospel of Matthew*, 3.

31 For the Jewish nature of the gospel, see "the Authorship of Matthew' gospel" above.

32 The Gentile interest of the first gospel can be seen in many places of the first gospel. The following may be mentioned as some explicit examples: the inclusion of four women in the genealogy, who are usually regarded as gentiles, namely – Tamar, Rahab, Ruth and the wife of Uriah (Matt 1:1-17); the coming of the wise men from the east to worship infant Jesus (2:1-12); the flight of the infant Jesus to Gentile Egypt (2:13-15; Jesus' making of his home in Galilee of the Gentiles (4:13-15); the story of the centurion whose child was healed (8:5-13); the story of a Canaanite woman whose daughter was healed (15:21-28); Pilate's wife (27:19); the centurion at the crucifixion (27:54); and in the great commission (28:16-20). See, Ulrich Luz, *Studies in Matthew,* translated by Rosemary Selle (Grand Rapids, Michigan / Cambridge, U.K.: William B. Eerdmans Publishing Company, 2005), 12. Luz here mentions that these are

some scholars suggest that the intended audience of this gospel consisted of Jewish Christians as the majority members with some Gentile members among them, who were not proselytized to Judaism.[33] However, some other scholars maintain that the intended audience of the gospel were only Jewish Christians. These scholars hold that if Gentiles were included at all, they were fully proselytized into Judaism leaving aside their Gentile identity. Therefore, they were not Gentile Christians any more, but were Jewish Christians. A good number of recent studies on the Matthean community have come to this conclusion while some commentators also share the same view.[34] This question will be discussed later when we come to the sub-section "the ethnic composition of Matthew's community." At this level we will maintain that the overwhelming Jewish nature of the gospel on one hand, and the prominence of Gentile interest from beginning to end on the other, suggest that Matthew's community was composed of Jewish Christians as the majority members with some Gentile Christians as minority members among them. And, obviously because of the influence of the Jewish Christians Matthew's church was basically a Jewish-oriented church, as indicated in the first gospel.[35] This would imply that even the Gentile members of the community were Jewish-oriented.

1.2.3. The Date on which Matthew's Gospel was Written

Scholars' suggestions on the date of Matthew's gospel range from 40 C.E. to 105 C.E.[36] However, it seems that at present, while some scholars still argue for a pre-

---

indicators of Matthew's interest in the mission to the Gentiles. Especially, for the prominence of Gentile interest in the beginning chapters of Matthew's gospel, see also F. P. Viljoen, "The Matthean Community according to the Beginning of His Gospel," *ActaTheol* 26/2 (2006): 242-262. With regard to the four women in Matt 1:1-17, Talbert notes that "they could be regarded either as sinners or foreigners [cf. Gal 2:15 –'Gentile sinners'], people who though irregular were the means of God's providence. Jesus, the son of Abraham and David, came from a lineage that was inclusive." C. H. Talbert, *Reading the Sermon on the Mount. Character Formation and Decision Making in Matthew 5-7* (Colombia: South Carolina Press, 2004), 10.

33 See the following for example, Brown, *An Introduction to the New Testament*, 213; Stanton, A *Gospel for a New People*, 123-134; and Raymond E. Brown and John P. Meier, *Antioch and Rome. New Testament Cradles of Catholic Christianity* (New York/Ramsey: Paulist Press, 1983), 46-47; Douglas R. A. Hare, "How Jewish is the Gospel of Matthew?" *CathBibQuart* 62/2 (April 2000), 264-277, available from http://search.atlaonline.com. Accessed 30 October 2006.

34 See the following for example - Overman, *Matthew's Gospel and Formative Judaism*, 4-5; Saldarini, *Matthew's Christian-Jewish Community*, 1, 74, 82; Sim, *The Gospel of Matthew and Christian Judaism*, 256, 299; Hagner, *Matthew 1-13*, lxix-lxx; Keener, *A Commentary on the Gospel of Matthew*, 49-50; Aaron M. Gale, *Redefining Ancient Borders. The Jewish Scribal Framework of Matthew's Gospel* (New York /London: T&T Clark, 2005), 2, 39, 162-163.

35 Cf. DeSilva, *An Introduction to the New Testament*, 236-238.

36 For the various dates proposed and the scholars who proposed them, see Davies and Allison, Jr., *Matthew*, Vol. I, 127-128. It seems that even today no further proposal goes beyond these dates.

70 C.E.[37] the majority of scholars view the date within the period 70-100 C.E. Within this period, some scholars further suggest 80 C.E. - 90/95 C.E. as the most plausible date for this gospel.[38] Scholars have put forth several arguments in favour of the date after 70 C.E., and before 100 C.E. Though, not all of them are equally forceful, there are a good number of reasonable arguments, which may be briefly highlighted as follows.

The overwhelming probability that Ignatius, bishop of Antioch in Syria, who died *c.* 107 C.E.,[39] knew the gospel in written form, suggests the upper limit of the composition of this gospel at 100 C.E. Ignatius wrote seven letters during his fateful journey to Rome at the beginning of the second century to face his martyrdom,[40] and these epistles contain a number of citations or allusions to Matthew's gospel.[41] If Ignatius could have used Matthew's gospel in his letters,

---

37 See for instance, Carson, Moo and Morris, *An Introduction to the New Testament*, 76-79; and Nolland, *The Gospel of Matthew*, 14-17.

38 Brown, *An Introduction to the New Testament*, 216. See also Davies and Allison, Jr., *Matthew*, Vol. I, 138. For arguments against the suggestion of the date after the First Jewish War against Rome, see Nolland, *The Gospel of Matthew*, 14-17.

39 On the dating of Ignatius' death, see C. Trevett, *A Study of Ignatius of Antioch in Syria and Asia*, SBEC, Vol. 29 (Lewiston: Edwin Mellen, 1992), 3-9.

40 Ignatius' seven letters were addressed to six churches such as – Ephesus, Magnesia, Tralles, Philadelphia, Smyrna, Rome, and to Polycarp, bishop of the church in Smyrna. See M.W. Holmes, "Ignatius of Antioch," *DLNTID*, edited by Ralph P. Martin and Peter H. Davids, A Compendium of Contemporary Biblical Scholarship (Downers Grove, Illinois / Leicester, England: InterVarsity Press, 1997), 530-531. See also William R. Schoedel, "Ignatius, Epistles of," *ABD*, Vol. 3 (New York: Doubleday, 1992), 384-387.

41 Sim, *The Gospel of Matthew and Christian Judaism*, 31. E. Massaux argued that Ignatius' letters contain no less than nine certain and five probable allusions to Matthew's gospel. As certain allusions, Massaux lists *Eph.* 5:2/Matt. 18:19-20; *Eph.* 14:2/Matt 12:33; *Mag.* 8:2/Matt 5:11-12; *Trall.* 11:1/Matt 15:13; *Philad.* 2:2/Matt 7:15; *Philad.* 3:1/Matt 15:13; *Smyrn.* 1:1/Matt 3:15; *Pol.* 1:2-3/Matt 8:17; *Pol* 2:2/Matt 10:16, while the probable references are *Eph.* 17:1/ Matt 26:7; *Mag.* 9:2/Matt 27:52; *Rom.* 9:3/Matt. 10:40-41; *Philad.* 6:1/Matt 23:27; *Smyrn.* 6:1/Matt 19:12. See E. Massaux, *The Influence of the Gospel of Saint Matthew on Christian Literature before Saint Irenaeus*, edited by A. J. Bellinzoni, 3 Vols., New Gospel Studies 5, Vol. 1 (Macon, GA: Mercer University Press, 1990), 85-95. But, some scholars criticized Massaux's argument and claimed that Ignatius did not use Matthew but both of them used the same source, as evidenced in the fact that all the parallel accounts are found in Matthew's special source M. See the following for example, W. R. Schoedel, "Ignatius and the Reception of the Gospel of Matthew in Antioch," in *Social History of the Matthean Community: Cross-Disciplinary Approaches*, edited by David L. Balch (Minneapolis: Fortress Press, 1991), 129-177 [176]; J. Smith Sibinga, "Ignatius and Matthew," *NovTest* 8 (1966), 263-283. Trevett, *A Study of Ignatius of Antioch in Syria and Asia*, 22-23. C. Trevett, "Approaching Matthew from the Second Century: The Under-Used Ignatian Correspondence," *JournStudNT* 20 (1984), 59-67. However, David C. Sim argues that in spite of these refutations at least some of Ignatius' writings betray a reproduction from Matthew. A good example is found in *Smyrn.* 1:1 which says, "for it is fitting for us to fulfill all righteousness." This is a clear allusion to Mat 3:15. See Sim, *The Gospel of Matthew and Christian Judaism*, 31-32. It would be logical to think on the

one could posit with confidence that the gospel of Matthew was written not later than 100 C.E. Another important factor relates to the suggestion (see below) that Matthew's gospel was written in Antioch of Syria. Kilpatrick maintains that the gospel bears no sign of influence from Pauline epistles, and (if it were written in Antioch) it is very difficult to imagine such a state of affairs in a city church of any importance outside Palestine after 100 C.E.[42]

There are strong points of argument to fix the lower limit of the date of the gospel at 70 C.E. Based on Markan priority it is accepted by the majority of the New Testament scholars that the author of Matthew's gospel (as well as Luke) knew and used Mark's gospel. Moreover, it is generally agreed that Mark wrote in the late 60s or just after 70 C.E. that is shortly after the fall of Jerusalem.[43] It is quite possible that Mark wrote a few years before the fall of Jerusalem. This suggestion is based on Mark 13:14, as well as Mark's lack of an explicit reference to the fall of Jerusalem.[44] If this is the case, the date of Matthew's gospel, which uses Mark as its main source, cannot be earlier than 70 C.E. This suggestion is strongly supported by the allusion to the destruction of Jerusalem in Matt 22:7, which says, "the king was enraged. He sent his troops, destroyed those murderers, and burned their city" (NRSV). According to most critical scholars, this verse is *ex eventu*, referring to the destruction of Jerusalem in 70 C.E.[45] Therefore, this suggests that Matthew's gospel was written after the destruction of Jerusalem.

Another important argument in favour of the date after 70 C.E. is the triadic formula in Matt 28:19. Though, there are admittedly other Trinitarian-type formulae in other places of the New Testament (e.g., 1 Cor 12:4-6; 2 Cor 13:14; Tit 3:4-6; 1 Pet 1:2; Jude 20-21), the loaded phrase "in the name of the Father and of the Son and of the Holy Spirit" has no parallel in the New Testament, as well as in first century Christian literature (excepting Didache 7, which most

---

basis of this evidence that if Ignatius took this one from Matthew, he could have taken even other parallels from Matthew, and not from the source M.

42 Kilpatrick, *The Origins of the Gospel according to St. Matthew*, 130.

43 For a detailed discussion on Markan priority and the dating of Mark's gospel, see the following - Guthrie, *New Testament Introduction,* 84-89, 136-208. Brown, *An Introduction to the New Testament*, 111-116, 163-164. Kummel, *Introduction to the New Testament*, 97-98. See also Burton H. Streeter, *The Four Gospels* (New York: Macmillan, 1925), 150-360. For an alternative view, that is for Matthean priority, see William R. Farmer, *The Synoptic Problem* (New York: Macmillan, 1976 [1964]). John Nolland also briefly notes, "Increasing scholarship seems to be freshly open to the possibility of a pre- A.D. 70 date for Mark." Nolland, *The Gospel of Matthew*, 14.

44 Guthrie, *New Testament Introduction,* 54.

45 Davies and Allison, Jr., *Matthew*, Vol. I, 131. See also DeSilva, *An Introduction to the New Testament*, 238.

probably depends upon Matthew), and is the most advanced step towards a later Trinitarian thought.[46]

The higher level of controversy with the Pharisees in Matthew's gospel more than in Mark and Luke, and the condemnation of the free use of the title 'Rabbi' (Matt 23:8) also fit well into the early rabbinic period after 70 C.E.[47] In fact, most of the recent studies on the community behind Matthew's gospel suggest that the gospel was written for the Jewish Christians who were in severe antagonism with the leaders of formative Judaism, which was a movement for the reconstruction of Judaism after the catastrophe of the first Jewish war against the Romans (66-73 C.E.), particularly after the destruction of the Jerusalem Temple in 70 C.E.[48]

All these arguments strongly suggest that Matthew's gospel was written after 70 C.E., but before 100 C.E. Within this range, there are slight differences in narrowing down the date.[49] In the light of scholars' arguments, this researcher is of the view that the most probable date for Matthew's gospel is between 75-93 C.E. There are two basic reasons behind this suggestion, apart from other evidences. First, formative Judaism, a reorganization movement within Judaism after the destruction of Jerusalem and the Temple, and with which Matthew's community were in serious antagonism, as the gospel indicates,[50] would have needed some time to develop and become dominant, especially outside Palestine, as it appears in Matthew's gospel.[51] It is quite possible that it must have been in conflict with Matthew's community for some time before Matthew's gospel was written, and the writing of the gospel must have taken place when the conflict reached its peak. Therefore, it is unlikely that the gospel was written before 75 C.E. Second, Matthew's gospel, on the other hand, does not seem to reflect the persecution

---

46 Davies and Allison, Jr., *Matthew*, Vol. I, 133. See also Brown, *An Introduction to the New Testament*, 217.

47 Brown, *An Introduction to the New Testament*, 217. For a more detailed discussion, see Davies and Allison, Jr., *Matthew*, Vol. I, 133-138. Here, Davies and Allison, Jr. note that the term "rabbi" was a mark of courtesy up to 70 C.E., but at Jamnia it became a title for ordained scholars authorized to teach. See also the following - Davies, *The Setting of the Sermon on the Mount*, 271; Keener, *A Commentary on the Gospel of Matthew*, 42.

48 See the following for example: Overman, *Matthew's Gospel and Formative Judaism*; Saldarini, *Matthew's Christian-Jewish Community*; Sim, *The Gospel of Matthew and Christian Judaism*.

49 Davies and Allison Jr. suggest the year between 80-95 C.E. See Davies and Allison, Jr., *Matthew*, Vol. I, 138. Meier opts for the years between 80 and 90 C.E., while Harrington prefers the period between 85 and 90 C.E. See Brown and Meier, *Antioch and Rome*, 17; and Daniel J. Harrington, *The Gospel of Matthew*, Sagra Pagina (Collegeville, Minnesota: The Liturgical Press, 1991), 8. According to David C. Sim, on the other hand, a date between 85-95 C.E. seems best suited to the internal evidence of the gospel and the relevant external evidences. See Sim, *The Gospel of Matthew and Christian Judaism*, 40.

50 See the following for example - Overman, *Matthew's Gospel and Formative Judaism*, 1-5. Sim, *The Gospel of Matthew and Christian Judaism*, 2, 27-28.

51 This research adopts the view that Matthew's gospel was written outside Palestine in Syrian Antioch. This will be dealt with in the next section.

under Domitian which happened between 93-96 C.E.[52] It is therefore, likely that Matthew's gospel was written before 93 C.E.

Thus, it is maintained in the above discussions that Matthew's gospel was written between 70-100 C.E., most probably between 75-93 C.E. It was written by a Hellenistic Jewish author for an audience of a community comprised of Jewish Christians as the majority members, with Gentile Christians as minority members, some of whom were fully proselytized and some others were partially proselytized to Judaism.[53] With these assumptions in mind, we will now proceed to another crucial issue that is the geographical location where Matthew's gospel was written.

1.2.4. The Geographical Location of Matthew's Gospel

Several places have been suggested by scholars as the place where Matthew's gospel originated,[54] such as Alexandria,[55] Jerusalem or Palestine,[56] Galilee,[57] Tiberias or

52 For Domitian's persecution, see the following - Bo Reicke, *The New Testament Era. The World of the Bible from 500 B.C. to A.D. 100*, translated by David E. Green (Philadelphia: Fortress Press, 1979 [1964]), 292-293. Sim, *The Gospel of Matthew and Christian Judaism*, 231-236. Here, Sim explains that the Gentile persecutions in Matthew's gospel point basically to those persecution suffered by Matthew's community in the hands of their Gentile neighbors during the Jewish revolt of 66-74 C.E.

53 Here, "fully proselytized" refers to those Gentile Christians who followed all the Jewish laws including circumcision, while "partially proselytized" refers to those who followed four Jewish laws, but not circumcision. These were accepted as partakers into the eschatological blessings along with the Jewish Christians, but could not have full table-fellowship with the Jewish Christians. This will be discussed later in the section, "The Ethnic Composition of Matthew's Community."

54 Brown correctly asks whether we are dealing with the place where the gospel was written from or written to or both as if the author lived among the addressees. See Brown, *An Introduction to the New Testament*, 161. It is assumed in this study, however, that both the writer of Matthew's gospel and his intended audience lived in the same location.

55 The suggestion of Alexandria is mainly associated with Brandon. Brandon's suggestion is based mainly upon his rejection of Antioch and his contention that the best alternative is Alexandria. According to him the narrowly Jewish and at the same time anti-Gentile sentiments of Matthew's gospel are incompatible with the liberal Christianity of Antioch. He also holds that since Luke is closely associated with Antioch, Matthew must be situated elsewhere. On the other hand, the flight to Egypt in the Matthean infancy narrative would have appealed to the Alexandrian Christians who fled to the Egyptian capital during the Jewish war. See S. G. F. Brandon, *The Fall of Jerusalem and the Christian Church* (London: SPCK, 1981 [1951]), 226-227 [217-243].

56 According to Brown, this suggestion began with the church fathers in the 2nd century C.E., and it has substantial supporters even today. This proposition is based, it seems, mainly on the earlier tradition that Matthew wrote in Hebrew or Aramaic, and on the striking Jewish features of the gospel, particularly the internal evidence of controversies with Jews. See Brown, *An Introduction to the New Testament*, 212.

57 M. Gnanavaran suggests the rural area of Galilee without giving a specific location. He argues that Matthew's gospel indicates a rural setting more than an urban setting, and Matthew

Sepphoris,[58] Caesarea Maritima,[59] Phoenicia,[60]

---

has a particular concern for Galilee. He further argues that the suggestion of Galilee is also compatible with the Jewish characteristic of the gospel, as well as Matthew's interest in the Gentiles. See M. Gnanavaram, *Treasure in Heaven and Treasure in Earth. Attitude Towards Poverty and Wealth in the New Testament Communities and in the Early Church* (Delhi: ISPCK, 2012 [2008]), 77-84.

58 The suggestion of Tiberias or Sepphoris is given by Andrew J. Overman. Overman maintains that if one takes the struggle of the Matthean community with formative Judaism seriously, then Palestinian provenance is virtually assured, because both formative Judaism and its successor rabbinic Judaism were Palestinian in origin. He furthers posits that Matthew's concentration of Jesus' activities, as well as the activities of the Pharisees, who are portrayed regularly in this gospel as Jesus' opponents, in Galilee points to the region of Galilee as the origin of this gospel. Furthermore, he holds that as the language and some of the imagery of Matthew suggest a city, the most plausible location must be either Tiberias or Sepphoris, which were the only seat of Sanhedrin or court of the region at different times in the first century. See Overman, *Matthew's Gospel and Formative Judaism*, 158-159. Overman is recently supported by Aaron M. Gale. See Gale, *Redefining Ancient Borders*, 3, 46-63, 164-165.

59 Caesarea Maritima has been strongly suggested by B. T. Viviano. According to Viviano, Caesarea was a centre of Christian life as far back as can be traced and it was also from earliest times a centre of Christian learning, dominated by a school and a library and bishops with a taste for learning. And, the ones who began this learned dialogical tradition could have been the author or authors of the gospel called "according to Matthew." See Viviano, "Where was the Gospel according to St. Matthew Written?" 542-543. To support this view, Viviano further argues, quoting Jerome, that the gospel according to Matthew was written in Hebrew by the apostle Matthew, also called Levi, and a copy of that Hebrew text was preserved in the Caesarean library during the time of Jerome. Viviano, "Where was the Gospel according to St. Matthew Written?" 542, quoting Jerome, *De viris inlustribus* 3 (ed. Richarson; TU 15.1). See also by the same author, *Matthew and His World: The Gospel of the Open Jewish Christians Studies in Biblical Theology* (Fribourg: Academic Press; Goettingen: Vandenhoeck & Ruprecht, 2007), 9-23.

60 The Phoenician origin of Matthew's gospel is suggested by G. D. Kilpatrick. Like Brandon, Kilpatrick rejects Antiochene hypothesis on two major grounds. First, he holds that while Antioch was an important Pauline centre Matthew seems uninfluenced by Pauline thought. Second, he maintains that Ignatius of Antioch had no connection with the very Jewish gospel of Matthew, and therefore it is unlikely that Matthew wrote his gospel in Antioch. Then, Kilpatrick suggests Phoenicia mainly on the grounds of terminology used by Matthew, for example, τα ὑδατα for the sea of Galilee while Mark uses ἡ θαλασσα for the same which Matthew reserves for the much greater Mediterranean Sea. Kilpatrick argues that this distinction suggests a location for Matthew in a port city. See Kilpatrick, *The Origins of the Gospel According to St. Matthew*, 130-134. See also Sim, *The Gospel of Matthew and Christian Judaism*, 48-49.

Transjordan (Pella),[61] Syria (in general),[62] Edessa (in Syria),[63] and Antioch of Syria (on the R. Orontes).[64] All these suggestions have been analysed by John P. Meier, Davies and Allison, Jr., and David C. Sim, and therefore, it is not necessary to repeat here what they have done.[65] However, important factors that need to be considered in determining the geographical location of Matthew's gospel will be highlighted here and the different suggestions will be viewed through the lens of these factors.

1.2.4.1. *Important Factors for Determining the Geographical Location of Matthew's Gospel*

It would not be possible to give an exhaustive list of the important factors for determining the place where Matthew's gospel originated, because different scholars can give importance to different factors. Therefore, the following factors are given importance in this research:

1) Three important conclusions have been drawn in the discussions above, such as - (a) Matthew's gospel (the final redaction) was written in Greek. (b) It was

61 This suggestion has come from Slingerland, who suggests that, the phrase 'beyond the Jordan' in two texts of Matthew 4:25 and 19:1 point to the eastern side of Jordan as the place where Matthew lived. He suggested Pella, the Decapolitan city where, According to later Christian tradition, many members of the Jerusalem church fled, prior to the outbreak of the Jewish war, as the likeliest place of composition of this gospel. See H. D. Slingerland, "the Transjordan Origin of Matthew's Gospel," *JournStudNT* 3 (1979), 18-28.

62 For examples of the suggestion of Syria in general, see the following - Goulder, *Midrash and Lection in Matthew*, 149-152; F. V. Filson, *The Gospel according to Saint Matthew*, BNTC (London: A & C Black, 1977), 14-15. Harrington, *The Gospel of Matthew*, 73. The main reason for suggesting Syria is mainly the difficulties involved with locating Matthew's gospel inside Palestine, and a minor point in favour of Syria is Matt 4:24 where the writer of this gospel expands his Marcan source and then writes that Jesus' fame spread throughout Syria. See Sim, *The Gospel of Matthew and Christian Judaism*, 51.

63 The suggestion of Edessa as the place of Matthew's origin first came from B.W. Bacon. His main argument is that Matthew shows ability for 'targuming', by which is meant translation by preachers of Jesus' words with an accompanying explanation. According to him, this practice was particularly well known in the Christian communities of North Eastern Syria. At the same time, Bacon holds that the gospel was brought to Antioch, the Syrian capital early on, and then it was disseminated from there. See B. W. Bacon, *Studies in Matthew* (London: Constable, 1930), 15-23. Bacon was followed by J. Kennard and R. E. Osbourne. See the following - J. Kennard, "The Place of Origin of Matthew's Gospel," *AnglTheolRev* 31 (1949), 243-246. R. E. Osborne, "The Provenance of Matthew's Gospel," *StudRel/SciRel* 3 (1973), 220-235.

64 The first major proponent of this suggestion was B. H. Streeter, who put forth several arguments in favour of his suggestion. See Streeter, *The Four Gospels*, 500-523. It seems that this suggestion is supported by majority of the Matthean scholars. See Keener, *A Commentary on the Gospel of Matthew*, 41. We will soon see the arguments for Antioch of Syria in detail.

65 For a detailed analysis of these suggestions see the following - Brown and Meier, *Antioch and Rome*, 18-27; Davies and Allison, Jr., *Matthew*, Vol. I, 138-148; and Sim, *The Gospel of Matthew and Christian Judaism*, 40-62.

written between 70 and 100 [75-93] C.E. (c) it was written by a Hellenistic Jewish author for the community where Jewish Christians formed the majority members, mixed with Gentiles Christians among them as minority members. In addition, it is held in most of the recent studies on the social location of Matthew's gospel that it was written in the context where Matthew's community was in a serious conflict with formative Judaism[66] led by the scribes and Pharisees.[67] All this suggests that Matthew's gospel was written in a place where there was a substantial Jewish population who spoke Greek as the common language of their communication at the time of 70-100 C.E., with sizeable Gentile neighbours.

2) On the basis of the language and some of the imagery used in Matthew's gospel, scholars observe that it must have been written in an urban location. This conclusion has been drawn mainly on the basis of a comparison between Matthew and Mark, which shows that – Matthew uses the word *polis* ("city") more frequently than Mark;[68] Matthew mentions more of commerce than Mark;[69] Matthew has greater differentiation of the retainer group;[70] Matthew has increased references to slaves.[71] All these factors suggest that Matthew's gospel was written in an urban milieu.[72]

3) The overwhelming prominence of Peter in Matthew's gospel suggests that it came from the place where Peter had greater influence than any other apostle or early church leaders.[73]

4) Matthew's gospel shows substantial interest in the Gentiles, especially, when compared with Mark. The interest of Matthew in the Gentiles has two aspects, presenting both a negative and positive view.[74] Such a considerable interest in the Gentiles would suggest that the gospel originated from the place,

---

66 For the term "formative Judaism," see "the Emergence of Formative Judaism" below.

67 See the following for example - Overman, *Matthew's Gospel and Formative Judaism*; Saldarini, *Matthew's Christian-Jewish Community*; Sim, *The Gospel of Matthew and Christian Judaism*. See also Davies, *The Setting of the Sermon on the Mount*, 256-315.

68 The word occurs 27 times in Matthew while it occurs only 8 times in Mark.

69 Such as for example, children playing in the market place (Matt 11:16), and the vineyard owner hiring day labourers in the market place (Matt 20:3ff.). Especially the second one is not found in Mark. Also the wedding banquet in Matt 22:1-14, especially Matt 22:5 where one goes away to his farm and another to his business, is not found in Mark.

70 Such as tax collectors, judges, Roman officers (*centurion*) and high priest guard. Mark lacks 'judge/s'.

71 The word occurs 17 times in Matthew while it occurs only five times in Mark.

72 For these comparisons between Matthew and Mark, see Stegemann and Stegemann, *The Jesus Movement*, 227-228.

73 The prominence of Peter in Matthew than in any other gospel is seen in Matt 14:28-31; 16: 17-19; 17: 24-27. Also, in the list of the Twelve taken from Mark, Matthew (10: 2) adds "first" before Peter's name. See Brown, *An Introduction to the New Testament*, 214.

74 For a discussion on Matthew's positive attitude on the Gentiles, see Donald Senior, "Between Two Worlds: Gentiles and Jewish Christians in Matthew's Gospel," *CathBibQuart* 61 (Ja 1999), 1-23. For a discussion on Matthew's negative attitude on the Gentiles, see David C.

whose immediate neighbours were Gentiles.[75] Particularly the indications in the gospel that the community had suffered persecutions in the hands of the Gentiles suggest that the community underlying Matthew's gospel lived in close proximity to the Gentiles.[76]

5) It seems that the ascription of Matthew as the author of the first gospel took place only in the beginning of the first century, and it was anonymous before this time.[77] Therefore, the success of the gospel, in spite of its being anonymous, is ascribed to the support given by an influential church. In other words, Matthew's gospel became accepted as having apostolic authority by the church in general because it originated in the context of a prominent church.[78]

6) The Jewish war against Rome (66-73 C.E.) also needs to be taken into account because this war resulted in the destruction of Jerusalem and the Temple, and in the devastation of most of the Jewish habitations in Palestine.[79] While, the gospel was written after the Jewish war (66-73 C.E.), it is not so emphatic in its description of the war. This suggests that the gospel originated in a place and a community, which was not directly involved in the war.[80]

Sim, "The Gospel of Matthew and the Gentiles," *JournStudNT* 57 (Mr 1995): 19-48; and by the same author, *The Gospel of Matthew and Christian Judaism*, 215-256.

75 The texts of Matthew's gospel often cited as indications of Matthew's positive attitude to the Gentiles are - the description of Jesus as the son of Abraham, the father of all nations (1:1); the inclusion of four Gentile women in the genealogy such as Tamar, Rahab, Ruth and Bathsheba/ the wife of Uriah (1:3, 5, 6); the story of the Magi worshipping infant Jesus (2:1-12); Two of the formula quotations (4:15-16; 12:18-21); the healing of the centurion's son (8:5-13); Jesus' visit to and work of miracles in the Gentile regions of Gadara (8:28-34), Tyre and Sidon (15: 21-39); the healing of the daughter of a Canaanite woman (15:22-28); Parables of the kingdom (21: 28- 22:14); the Gentile centurions confession (27:54); and Jesus' command to evangelize all nations (28: 19). See Sim, *The Gospel of Matthew and Christian Judaism*, 217.
At the same time, Matthew's negative portrayal of the Gentiles is also undoubtedly seen in Matt 5: 46-47; 6:7-8; 6:31-32; 18:15-17. Sim, *The Gospel of Matthew and Christian Judaism*, 225-229.

76 The persecution of Matthew's community by the Gentiles can be inferred at least from Matt 10:17-22; 22:4-14. See discussion on this in Sim, *The Gospel of Matthew and Christian Judaism*, 231-236.
Kingsbury seems right in observing that the intended readers of Matthew's gospel (Matthew's community) lived in close proximity to hostile pagans and a vigorous Jewish community. See, Kingsbury, *Matthew as Story*, 153-157.

77 Davies and Allison, Jr., *Matthew*, Vol. I, 8. For the possibility of early attribution of the authorship of the first gospel to Matthew, see Carson, Moo and Morris, *An Introduction to the New Testament*, 66-67.

78 Davies and Allison, Jr., *Matthew*, Vol. I, 144.

79 For the historical account of this war, see Josephus, *The War of the Jews*, in *Josephus. Complete Works*, trans. William Whiston (Grand Rapids, Michigan: Kregel Publications, 1983 [1960]), 490-605.

80 Though Matthew seems to refer to the destruction of Jerusalem in 22:7, there is no description or emphasis on the event to give the impression that Matthew's community had the first hand

The criteria listed above would not be exhaustive. However, these factors would be sufficient for determining the most plausible place from among the various suggestions for the geographical location of Matthew's gospel. Therefore, remembering these criteria, we will now examine the various suggestions mentioned above.

1.2.4.2. *Analysis of Various Suggestions for the Geographical Location of Matthew's Gospel*

First, most of the places in Palestine, including Galilee, can be excluded because of language and the Jewish war. Although many Palestinians undeniably spoke Greek in the first century, the dominant language in the region, most probably, remained Aramaic. Therefore, if the gospel (the final redaction) was written in any place within Palestine it is very likely that it would have been written in Aramaic and not in Greek.[81] Moreover, in the Jewish war (66-73 C.E.) Jerusalem was almost completely destroyed,[82] and the war caused major disruptions in both Jewish and Jewish-Christian communities throughout Palestine.[83] It is therefore, difficult to see the possibility for the production of a document such as Matthew's gospel in the midst of such physical, economic and social turmoil.[84] Besides, it seems that Mathew's community did not have first hand experience of the war.[85] Furthermore, there is no knowledge that Peter had any prominence in the cities of Palestine after he lost his prominence in Jerusalem church prior to Jerusalem council.[86] Because, of all this problems, it is difficult to uphold the suggestions of Palestine and any specific place within it such as Jerusalem, Galilee, Trans-Jordan and Caesarea Maritima.[87]

Among the suggested places within Palestine, the only place, which deserves further consideration, seems to be Sepphoris. As already mentioned above[88] it is

---

experience of the catastrophe. It seems therefore that they observed it from a far. Davies and Allison, Jr., *Matthew*, Vol. I, 140.

81 Sim, *The Gospel of Matthew and Christian Judaism*, 41. See also Davies and Allison, Jr., *Matthew*, Vol. I, 141-141.

82 Josephus, Wars of the Jews VI. V. 1, 2 and VII. I. 1 in *Josephus. Complete Works*, 581-582, 589. See also Sim, *The Gospel of Matthew and Christian Judaism*, 40-41.

83 Martin Goodman, *The Ruling Class of Judea: The Origins of the Jewish Revolt against Rome, A.D. 66-70* (Cambridge: Cambridge University Press, 1987), 250.

84 Sim, *The Gospel of Matthew and Christian Judaism*, 41.

85 Davies and Allison, Jr., *Matthew*, Vol. I, 140.

86 Sim, *The Gospel of Matthew and Christian Judaism*, 45, 55, 58-59.

87 There are additional problems with Caesarea Maritima. There was a massacre of Jews in Caesarea in 66 C.E. and there is no evidence of the Jewish resettlement in the following decades. Besides, Eusebius who lived in Caesarea did not mention any connection of this place with Matthew or Matthew's school. See Davies and Allison, Jr., *Matthew*, Vol. I, 141. See also Josephus, *War of the Jews* II. XVIII. 1 in *Josephus. Complete Works*, 492.

88 See p. 5.

Overman who strongly suggests either Tiberias or Sepphoris. Overman maintains that formative Judaism and its successor rabbinic Judaism were Palestinian in origin and therefore, if one takes the struggle of the Matthean community with formative Judaism seriously, then Palestinian provenance is virtually assured. He further notes that Matthew concentrates Jesus' activities, as well as the activities of the Pharisees, who are portrayed regularly in this gospel as Jesus' opponents, in Galilee, and this suggests the region of Galilee (within Palestine) as the place of origin of this gospel. Furthermore, Overman asserts that as the language and some of the imagery of Matthew suggest a city, the most plausible location within Galilee must be either Tiberias or Sepphoris, because, these were the only seats of the Sanhedrin or court of the region at different times in the first century.[89] The suggestion of Overman, particularly that of Sepphoris, deserves a serious consideration because of various reasons. Apart from what has been mentioned above, Sepphoris was the largest city of Galilee and it was spared a serious calamity during the first Jewish war against Rome (66-73 C.E.) because, the people there received the Romans without resistance, but with acclamations and joy. The city also withstood Josephus' attempt to capture it during the same war.[90] Besides, from the time of its appearance in history, that is 103 B.C.E., until it was destroyed by Varus in 4 B.C.E, it was a Greek city. After it was rebuilt by Herod Antipas as a Hellenistic city and a centre of Hellenistic culture,[91] soon after he inherited Galilee from his father Herod the Great in 4 B.C.E.,[92] it became a loyalist Roman city with Jewish and Gentile population.[93] There was also evidence of a strong pagan presence besides the Jews and Christians in the first century.[94] Therefore, Sepphoris suits well, to some extent, as the suggested location for the antagonism between Matthew's community and formative Judaism, and it explains well the prominence of Gentiles in Matthew's gospel. However, the main problem with the suggestion of Sepphoris is that there is no information on the connection of this city with Peter, who is prominent in Matthew's gospel more than in any other gospel.[95] Moreover, while it could be assumed that Greek was quite well-known

89 Overman, *Matthew's Gospel and Formative Judaism*, 158-159.

90 See Josephus, *War of the Jews* II. XVIII. 11, and III. II. 4, and III. 4. 1 in *Josephus. Complete Works*, 495, 503-504.

91 Richard A. Horsley and John S. Hanson, *Bandits, Prophets, and Messiahs: Popular Movements in the Time of Jesus* (Harrisburg, Pensylvania: Trinity, 1999 [1985]), 34.

92 David C. Braund, "Herod Antipas (Person)," *ABD*, Vol. 3 (New York: Doubleday, 1992), 160.

93 James F. Strange, "Sepphoris," *ABD*, Vol. 5 (New York: Doubleday, 1992), 1091.

94 See Eric M. Meyers, "Early Judaism and Christianity in the Light of Archaeology," *Biblical Archaeologist* 51/2 (1988), 76, available from http://search.atla-online.com. Accessed 30 October 2006.

95 Cf., however, while there is no specific information on the Jewish Christian community specifically in Sepphoris in the first century, there was information on such groups in Palestine in the second century. They were mentioned as Ebionites, Nazarenes or Elkasites. However,

among the inhabitants because it was a Greek city till 4 B.C.E., and because it was rebuilt after that as a Hellenistic city and a centre of Hellenistic culture, archaeological excavation, on the other hand, suggests that Hebrew and Aramaic were preferred to Greek in the region of Galilee in the first century.[96] Because, of all these difficulties involved, the suggestion of Sepphoris is also not strong enough. Therefore, it seems finally, that the gospel was written outside Palestine where there was a considerable size of Jewish population.

However, there are different problems even with most of the suggested places outside Palestine.

With regard to the suggestion of Alexandria, there are certain major problems in spite of the fact that S.G.F. Brandon has made strong points of argument for it. Brandon rightly points out that Alexandria was the second largest city of the Roman Empire, after Rome, and it had a huge Jewish population.[97] However, the Jews of Alexandria had been severely destroyed during the Jewish war against Rome (66-73 C.E.). According to Josephus, fifty thousand Jews were killed in Alexandria, and though, there were some survivors, this was a complete destruction as their houses were plundered and burnt.[98] Therefore, a big question is, would the city have accommodated again a big Jewish community by the time Matthew's gospel was written to facilitate the composition of such a document? Even if a substantial number of Jews were still left there, another major problem is that there is almost a total lack of knowledge about the origin of the Christian community in this city.[99] Although, Brandon has strongly argued for the presence of the law-observant church in Alexandria,[100] and for the possible involvement of Peter there,[101] his points are based highly on speculation without concrete evidence.[102]

The suggestion of Phoenicia is also problematic because, apart from other difficulties, very little is known about this place in the final quarter of the first century. It is therefore, difficult to assign Matthew to such a very little known place

these groups affirmed the primacy of James, the brother of Jesus, over Peter in the Church's leadership. See Meyers, "Early Judaism and Christianity in the Light of Archaeology," 71-73.

96 Meyers, "Early Judaism and Christianity in the Light of Archaeology," 74.

97 Brandon, *The Fall of Jerusalem and the Christian Church*, 221.

98 See Josephus, *War of the Jews* II. XVIII. 8, VII. X. 1 in *Josephus. Complete Works*, 494, 604. According to Victor A. Tcherikover and Alexander Fuks, Josephus' number is probably an exaggeration. But they affirm that the Alexandrian Jews were terribly stricken in 66 C.E., far more terribly than the pogrom of 38 C.E., See Victor A. Tcherikover and Alexander Fuks, eds., *Corpus Papyrorum Judaicarum*, Vol. I (Cambridge / Massachusetts: Harvard University Press, 1957), 79.

99 Davies and Allison, Jr., *Matthew*, Vol. I, 139.

100 Brandon, *The Fall of Jerusalem and the Christian Church*, 6, 17-18, 24-26, 224-225, etc.

101 Brandon, *Ibid.*, 211-212, 225, 232, 242.

102 Davies and Allison, Jr., *Matthew*, Vol. I, 139. See also Davies, *The Setting of the Sermon on the Mount*, 317-324.

and which cannot be the centre of Christian learning at the time Matthew's gospel was composed.[103] The place is also incompatible especially with the suggestion of Matthew's setting in an urban milieu.

The suggestion of Syria without pinpointing any specific place is too vast and vague to analyse. It is impossible to have a close investigation into the social historical situation that underlies Matthew's gospel in such an area. Moreover, the main reasons for suggesting Syria in general are only because of the difficulties involved with locating Matthew's gospel inside Palestine, and because Matthew, in 4:24, expands his Marcan source and then writes that Jesus' fame spread throughout Syria.[104] Therefore, this will be left aside, especially because it is highly possible to suggest a specific place inside Syria, which will become clear as we go on.

Besides other problems, the suggestion of Edessa in Syria has a major obstacle in the language with which Matthew's gospel was written, that is Greek. If the gospel had originated in Edessa it must have been written in Syriac because almost all the inscriptions and literary texts recovered in Edessa were written in Syriac.[105]

The most favoured suggestion, which satisfies most of the above criteria, is the Syrian capital Antioch on the river Orontes. Therefore, the present research subscribes to the suggestion of Antioch in Syria as the most probable place where Matthew's gospel was written. We will now see how Antioch fits well with most of the important factors suggested above.

1.2.4.3. *Antioch of Syria - the Most Plausible Location of Matthew's Gospel*

One of the strongest arguments in favour of Antioch is the prominence of Peter in Matthew's gospel above all the other disciples and the other leaders of early Christian movement.[106] Based on Galatians (2:11-14), Peter appears as an influential figure in Antioch. Later patristic tradition also confirms his long-standing association with the church there.[107] Besides, apart from the fact that he was influential in the Jerusalem church prior to the apostolic council, there is no substantial evidence to tell that Peter assumed an important position in any Christian church in the eastern region of the Roman Empire other than in Antioch.[108] Therefore, the prominence of Peter in Matthew's gospel goes very well

103 Davies and Allison, Jr., *Matthew*, Vol. I, 142.

104 Sim, *The Gospel of Matthew and Christian Judaism*, 51.

105 Davies and Allison, Jr., *Matthew*, Vol. I, 142-143. See also Sim, *The Gospel of Matthew and Christian Judaism*, 52.

106 Sim, *The Gospel of Matthew and Christian Judaism*, 59.

107 For these patristic traditions, see G. Downey, *A History of Antioch in Syria from Seleucus to the Arab Conquest* (Princeton: Princeton University Press, 1961), 583-586.

108 Sim, *The Gospel of Matthew and Christian Judaism*, 55, 58-59.

with his prominence in the church at Antioch, and hence the suggestion that this gospel originated in this place.

The suggestion that a major and an influential church must have supported the gospel in order to survive also reinforces the Antiochene hypothesis. If such major churches in Jerusalem and in Caesarea could be omitted (as argued above) and if the Patristic tradition indirectly proves that Matthew was not written in the west, that is, Rome or Asia Minor,[109] then Antioch is the strongest contender for this.[110]

The suggestion of Antioch also satisfies a number of other important criteria mentioned above. Antioch was the third largest city of the Roman Empire after Rome and Alexandria,[111] and undoubtedly, the main language of the city was Greek. In the first century, the largest Jewish population within the cities of the Syrian province (outside Palestine) was found in Antioch.[112] Meeks and Wilken assume that the Jewish population of Antioch in the first century was about 22,000.[113] What percentage would the Jewish population have had in the Antioch city is not known. It may be safe to follow Zetterholm in his estimate of about 5 to 10 per cent.[114] Even in the context of the first Jewish war (66-73 C.E.) where the Jews suffered severely at the hands of the Romans, Antiochean Jews escaped a major catastrophe.[115] The existence of a Gentile neighborhood indicated in the gospel by both the negative and positive views of the Gentiles in the gospel, as

109 Streeter argues that while the witnesses of Papias and Irenaeus which place Matthew to Palestine can be discarded they have significance from negative respect in that by not locating the gospel in either Rome or Asia Minor, they indicate that it was written somewhere in the eastern region of the Roman empire. See Streeter, *The Four Gospels*, 500.

110 Sim, *The Gospel of Matthew and Christian Judaism*, 55, 59.

111 See Josephus, *Wars of the Jews*, III. II. 4, in *Josephus. Complete Works*, 503.

112 See Josephus, *Wars of the Jews*, vii. iii. 3, in *Josephus. Complete Works*, 591.

113 W. A. Meeks and R. L. Wilken, *Jews and Christians in Antioch in the First Four Centuries of the Common Era* (Atlanta: Scholars Press, 1978), 8. For other suggestion on the Jewish population of Antioch in the first century, see also C. H. Kraeling, "The Jewish Community at Antioch," *JournBibLit* 51 (1932): 136, who suggests 45,000. Binder and Levinskaya, however, believe that the lower figure of Meeks and Wilken is more reliable. See, D. D. Binder, *Into the Temple Courts: the Place of the Synagogue in the Second Temple Period* (Atlanta: Society of Biblical Literature, 1999), 264; and I. Levinskaya, *The Book of Acts in its First Century Setting, Volume 5: The Book of Acts in its Diaspora Setting* (Grand Rapids, MI: Eerdmans, 1996), 134.

114 According to Magnus Zetterholm the population of Antioch at this time was possibly over 300,000 and the Jewish population comprised about 5 to 10 percent of it. See Zetterholm, *The Formation of Christianity in Antioch*, 28, 42. But according to Warren Carter, it was estimated at about 150,000 to 200,000. See, Warren Carter, *Matthew and the Margins. A Socio-political and Religious Reading* (Journal for the Study of the New Testament Supplement Series 204. Sheffield: Sheffield Academic Press Ltd., 2000), 17. For various early references to the population of Antioch, see Downey, *A History of Antioch*, 582-583.

115 See, Josephus, *Wars of the Jews* II. XVIII. 5, VII. V. 2 in *Josephus. Complete Works*, 493, 593.

well as by the Gentile persecution of the Matthean community, also fits well with the Antiochene hypothesis.[116]

One of the strongest arguments against the Antiochene hypothesis is the strong suggestion of a Palestinian provenance by the antagonism between the Matthean community and formative Judaism.[117]

However, there are strong arguments for the validity of the Antiochene hypothesis to answer the struggle between the Matthean community and formative Judaism. Paul's story and his letters show that Pharisees were well known outside Palestine both among the Jewish circles and among Gentile circles. In the pre-war period Paul, a Diaspora Jew was a self-proclaimed Pharisee (Phil 3:5). If he received his training in Tarsus, it would mean that the Pharisaic movement had reached beyond the borders of Palestine. If he was trained in Jerusalem (cf. Acts 22:3) his choice of the very vocation would demonstrate that the tenets of Pharisaism were known in the Diaspora. Besides, the Jewish pilgrims from the Diaspora who constantly travelled to Palestine to attend the major festivals could certainly have been expected to be in contact with the leaders of formative Judaism. Paul's letter to the Philippians (3:5), where he mentions the Pharisees' attitude to the law without further explanation, shows that the knowledge of the Pharisees was widespread outside Palestine. It can also be assumed that, like Paul, many other Diaspora Jews who completed their studies in Jerusalem went back to their respective places. Since Antioch had a large Jewish population and because of its proximity to Palestine, it would be safe to assume that many of the Antiochene Jews studied in Jerusalem and went back to Antioch, and then introduced some Pharisaic influence to the Jewish community.[118]

Further, it is also highly possible that in the post-war period, many Jews left their homeland in search of a better life, and many of them went to Antioch and Alexandria because these were the two great cities of Diaspora Jewry.[119] We could also assume that the Jewish refugees would have chosen Antioch more than Alexandria because Alexandrian Jews were severely wiped out during the war while Antioch escaped such calamity, and Antioch was in close proximity to Palestine. It is indeed asserted that because of the economic problem in Palestine there was an increasing tendency among the Jews to emigrate from Palestine to the neighboring countries, especially to Syria.[120] Moreover, one could assume with confidence that Scribes and Pharisees were among these refugees. Then it would

---

116 This aspect will be discussed later in the sub-section "Matthew's Community and the Gentiles."

117 Overman maintains that any suggestion outside Palestine is incompatible with the antagonism between the Matthean community and formative Judaism. Overman, *Matthew's Gospel and Formative Judaism*, 158-159.

118 Sim, *The Gospel of Matthew and Christian Judaism*, 60-61.

119 Sim, *The Gospel of Matthew and Christian Judaism*, 61.

120 See Davies, *The Setting of the Sermon on the Mount*, 295.

be natural for these Pharisees to have had a keen interest in the developments that were taking place in Galilee, and accordingly, to have maintained a close contact with their fellow Pharisees who were actively participating in the development in Galilee. The excellent road systems that linked the two regions also guaranteed such a contact.[121] In support of this argument, it is maintained that there is good evidence, which shows that the Pharisees in Galilee travelled to the Diaspora to appeal for financial and moral support.[122] A particular case in this connection is the introduction of a rabbinic school tax of two drachmas. The Pharisaic scribes in Jamnia who were the leaders of formative Judaism and who had authoritative influence over all the Jews in the Roman Empire introduced this tax and it became gradually effective throughout the Roman Empire. The agents of the synagogues called "apostles" collected these contributions until the third and fourth centuries and sent them to the president or chief rabbi of the Palestinian school, who bore the honorific title of "prince," "ethnarch," or "patriarch."[123] It would be natural to assume that Antioch, which had a large Jewish population and which was in close proximity to Galilee, would have been a primary target for such activity.[124]

Moreover, it has been maintained that there was a close relationship between Galilee and Syria in the history of the earliest Jewish Christianity. The Jewish Christians' heartland, settled by Jewish Christian refugees from Jerusalem, includes Galilee, Pella, and then it arched into Syria through Antioch and Edessa. This is indicated in the development and communications in the church. At the same time, the Jewish sources also point to the same geographical unity, that due to this geographical contiguity the Jews in Galilee and Syria were in relatively good communication.[125]

Even among those four places mentioned above, it seems that Antioch was the only place where Greek was the common language. As we have already indicated in the analysis above, Galilee and Pella were inside Palestine, and Aramaic seems to be the common language there at the time Matthew's gospel was written.

---

121 Sim, *The Gospel of Matthew and Christian Judaism*, 61.

122 See the following: Davies, *The Setting of the Sermon on the Mount*, 295; T. Rajak, "The Jewish Community and Its Boundaries," in *The Jews among Pagans and Christians*, edited by J. Lieu, North and Rajak, 9-28 (London: Routledge, 1992), 14-15. Meeks and Wilken also maintain that on the basis of the stories in the Rabbinic literature, it is clear that "the rabbis came regularly to the area to collect funds." See Meeks and Wilken, *Jews and Christians in Antioch*, 9, and 41 n. 46.

123 Reicke, *The New Testament Era*, 288-289. See also Emil Schürer, *The History of the Jewish People in the Age of Jesus Christ (175 B.C.–A.D. 135)*, Revised, Enlarged, and Edited by G. Vermes, F. Millar and M. Black (Edinburgh: T&T Clark, 1979 [1901/1909]), 288.

124 Sim, *The Gospel of Matthew and Christian Judaism*, 61.

125 Alan F. Segal, "Matthew's Jewish Voice," in *Social History of the Matthean Community*, edited by David L. Balch, 3-37 (Minneapolis: Fortress Press, 1991), 26. See also Hans Joachim Schoeps, *Jewish Christianity: Factional Disputes in the Early Church* (Philadelphia: Fortress, 1964), 19-27.

In Edessa, it seems that the common language was Syriac as the discoveries of inscriptions and literary texts suggest.[126] Therefore, even among these four places Antioch is the most probable place for the writing of Matthew's gospel.

Based on the above discussion it can be concluded here that different qualifications, which are obviously required for the hypothesis of Matthew's geographical location, are best satisfied by Antioch in Syria. Therefore, this research will follow the assumption that Matthew's gospel was written in the context of the church in Antioch of Syria.

1.2.5. Preliminary Conclusion

Our discussion so far has led us to conclude that Matthew's gospel was written after the destruction of Jerusalem and the Temple in 70 C.E., most probably between 75-93 C.E. It was written by a Hellenistic Jewish author for an intended audience, which comprised Christ-believing Jews as dominant members, with some Gentile Christians among them as minority members. Antioch of Syria is the most probable place where this gospel was written.

Keeping these assumptions in mind, we will now look into the various aspects of Matthew's socio-historical situation, which must have necessitated the writing of this gospel and influenced its contents. The earlier studies on the social background of Matthew's gospel mainly focussed on the question of whether the author and the intended audience were Jews or Gentiles. The consensus now on this is that the first gospel was written by a (Hellenistic) Jewish author for a Jewish-Christian (including Jewish-oriented Gentile Christian) audience,[127] which was undergoing a bitter relationship with the larger Jewish society.[128]

Then more recently, studies on Matthew's social history mainly focus on the question of whether the dispute between Matthew's community and the larger Jewish society was *intra muros* or *extra muros*, that is, whether Matthew's community was still part of the synagogue or it had already broken relation with it when Matthew's gospel was written. Although this question has been asked since the introduction of redaction criticism, Matthean scholarship is more concentrated on this question especially from the 1980s with the social sciences gaining popularity in the study of the New Testament. This is an ongoing debate and there is no general consensus as yet to date.[129] However, it is generally agreed that Matthew's community was in serious dispute with the contemporary Jewish

126 See the "*Analysis of Various Suggestions for the Geographical Location of Matthew's Gospel*" above.

127 Cf. the preliminary conclusion above.

128 For a general survey on this, see Boris Repschinski, *The Controversy Stories in the Gospel of Matthew. Their Redaction, Form and Relevance for the Relationship Between the Matthean Community and Formative Judaism* (Forschungen zur Religion und Literatur des Alten und Neuen Testaments 189. Göttingen: Vandenhoeck & Rupprecht, 2000), 13-28.

129 For a general survey on this, see Paul Foster, *Community, Law and Mission in Matthew's Gospel* (Tuebingen: Mohr Siebeck, 2004), 24-79.

reorganization movement, the so-called "formative Judaism." It is understood even in this study that the major concern of the gospel is the relation of the Matthean community with formative Judaism. Therefore, we will first study here the question of how formative Judaism came into conflict with Matthew's community. Following this other important aspects of Matthew's socio-historical background will be considered, such as the relationship between Matthew's community and the Gentiles, the ethnic composition and the socio-economic status of the Matthean community and the possible problems related to these factors.

To begin with, the first Jewish War against Rome (66-73 C.E.), which is a significant historical event in the Matthean setting, and particularly its impact upon the Jews, will be highlighted. This is important especially because it was in the aftermath of this war that the so-called formative Judaism emerged and eventually came into severe conflict with the Matthean community, then necessitating the writing of Matthew's gospel and largely influencing its content.

1.3. A Significant Historical Event in the Matthean Setting: The Jewish War Against Rome (66-73 C.E.) and Its Aftermath Upon the Jews

A significant event in the history of the Jews, which had a far-reaching consequence upon both the Jews and the Jewish Christians prior to the writing of Matthew's gospel, was the first Jewish war against Rome (66-73 C.E.), and particularly the destruction of Jerusalem and the Temple in 70 C.E. by the Romans; and its aftermath, especially the rebuilding of Judaism from the chaos created by this event.[130] Although Antioch of Syria, the most plausible place for the location of Matthew's gospel was outside of Palestine, socio-historical study of Matthew's gospel has affirmed that the same event greatly affected the writing of the first gospel and influenced its contents.[131]

Palestine came under the Roman rule in 63 B.C.E.[132] After a lapse of one hundred years, that is in 66 C.E., the Jews rose in revolt against Rome. A detailed investigation into the reasons behind this revolt is beyond the purview of this study. To mention briefly, however, different factors have been proposed as the cause of this revolt, such as – (1) the failure of the Jewish aristocracy through whom the Romans ruled Judea, (2) the increasing debt burden of the poor Jews including the urban plebs, and (3) the exploitation of the peasants by the landowners and the government, and the harsh treatment of the Jews by the Romans, from the beginning of the Roman conquest of Palestine (63 B.C.E.) till the war broke out

---

130 Davies and Allison, Jr., *Matthew*, Vol. III, 692-704.

131 This will become clear as we go on from here up to the end of the sub-section 1.4.3.2.

132 See Schürer, *The History of the Jewish People*, 100. See also Reicke, *The New Testament Era*, 83.

in 66 C.E.[133] In the course of the war the Jerusalem Temple was destroyed by the Roman soldiers under the command of Titus, in 70 C.E. Not only the Temple, but the city of Jerusalem itself was severely destroyed in the war to the extent that it was difficult for those who visited it to believe that it had ever been inhabited.[134] The destruction of Jerusalem and the temple marked the victory of the Romans over the Jews. However, the war did not come to an end automatically with it. It could be said that the actual end of the war inside Palestine came with the fall of Masada, a Jewish fortress, which was situated on a high mountain on the shore of the Dead Sea, in 73 C.E.[135]

---

133 Martin Goodman, "The First Jewish Revolt: Social Conflict and the Problem of Debt," *JournJewStud* 33 /1-2 (1982), 417-427; Goodman, *The Ruling Class of Judea*; Eduard Lohse, *The New Testament Environment* (Abingdon, Nashville: Parthenon Press, 1976), 47-48. Richard A. Horsley, "Ancient Jewish Banditry and the Revolt against Rome," *CathBibQuart* 43 (1981), 412. Especially for the sufferings of the Jews under the Romans and their ally the Jewish rulers from 63 B.C.E onwards till the war erupted in 66. C.E., see Horsley and Hanson, *Bandits, Prophets, and Messiahs*, 30-43. Here (in p. 30), Horsley briefly puts a kind of summary like this, "after the highly oppressive rule of the Roman client kings (Herod and his sons), there followed direct rule by governors of the alien empire, something the Jews had not experienced since the initial Babylonian and Persian conquests. After the mid-first century C.E., moreover, the behaviour of the Jewish priestly aristocracy, the Herodian and Roman domination meant unusually heavy taxation, indeed a serious threat to their very existence, as many were cut off from their land."

134 See Josephus, *Wars of the Jews* VI. V. 1, 2 and VII. I. 1 in *Josephus. Complete Works*, 581-582, 589.

135 Lohse, *The New Testament Environment*, 47, 50-51. See also Stambaugh and Balch, *The Social World of the First Christians*, 28-29, and Horsley and Hanson, *Bandits, Prophets, and Messiahs*, 44. While scholars are more or less unanimous on the date of 66 C.E. as the beginning of the revolt, it is uncertain whether its end, that is the fall of Masada, was at 72 or 73 C.E. On the basis of Reicke's argument it could possibly be 72 C.E. See, Reicke, *The New Testament Era*, 289, n. 24. However, to be on the safe side, and following majority of the writers, 73 C.E. will be referred to in this research as the year in which the war came to an end. Even after all the Jewish resistance inside Palestine was destroyed, the Sicarii who fled the war in Judea went up to Alexandria and Cyrene. They created a problem in Alexandria in 72 C.E., and in Cyrene around 74 C.E. See Reicke, *The New Testament Era,* 289-290. However, before they caused much damage they were subjugated, and thus came the total repression of the Jewish rebellion of this time, until another rebellion came under Bar Kochba in 132-135 C.E., which, according to some scholars, may not necessarily had connections with the first rebellion. See Josephus, *Wars of the Jews*, VII. X – IX in *Josephus. Complete Works*, 603-605; Lohse, *The New Testament Environment*, 52; and Benjamin Isaac and Aharon Oppenheimer, "Bar Kokhba Revolt," *ABD*, Vol. 1 (New York: Doubleday, 1992), 599. Here Isaac and Oppenheimer mentions that most scholars ascribed the cause of the Jewish revolt under Bar Kochba in 132-135 C.E. to Emperor Hadrian's decision to turn Jerusalem into a Pagan city and his ban on circumcision. According to Applebaum, however, the severe poverty suffered by the Jews in the aftermath of the first Jewish war resulted in the recurrent emergence of outlaws and bandits, and it finally led to the revolt in 132 C.E. See S. Applebaum, "The Economic Life in Palestine," in S. Safrai and M. Stern, eds. *The Jewish People in the First Century,* Vol. 2 (Philadelphia: Fortress Press, 1976), 699.

We will now highlight the aftermath of this war upon the Jews socio-politically, economically and religiously. Our particular interest in this analysis will be the emergence of formative Judaism in the aftermath of this war, and the conflict of Matthew's community in Antioch with the leaders of the Jews in this formative period.

The first Jewish war against Rome (66-73 C.E.) had far reaching consequences upon the Jews in Palestine in particular and upon all the Jews in general. The impact of the war upon the Jews can be broadly discussed from the perspectives of the socio-political, economic, and religious praxis. We will first look into the socio-political impact of the war upon the Jews. In all the discussions in this section, the focus will be mainly on the situations during the time in which Vespasian, Titus, and Domitian (i.e., the Flavians) were emperors of Rome successively.[136] The focus will be on the situations in Palestine, because the prime effect of the war fell on Palestine. However, its universal impact upon the Jews throughout Roman Empire will also be briefly considered, because what happened in Palestine affected the Jewish world in one way or the other, and there were direct actions from Rome that affected all the Jews in the Roman Empire. Then, the link between the impacts of this war and the writing of Matthew's gospel will be brought out.

136 While the war against the Jews was going on, the Roman Emperor Nero died in 68 C.E. and there was civil war in Rome with a competition to become emperor. Within a short period, there were three emperors, namely Galba, Otho, and Vittellius. According to Josephus, Galba reigned only a little more than seven months, and was killed by treachery in the middle of the market place at Rome. Then Otho was made the emperor (Josephus, *War*, 4.2.491). However, after three months and two days he committed suicide in fear of the advance of Vitellius, commander of the German legion (Josephus, *War*, 4.9.548). Thus, Vitellius became emperor (Josephus, *War*, 4.2.588). In such a situation Vespasian was declared emperor in 1st July, 1969 by the Alexandrian legions and was quickly followed by the Judean legions. Vespasian marched toward Rome and before he reached there Vitellius was assassinated by the supporters of Vespasian. Vitellius was emperor for eight months and five days (Josephus, *War*, 4.4.652). Paul L. Maier, however, comments that the duration assigned by Josephus to those three emperors' respective reigns do not agree with any Roman historians, who also disagree among themselves. Probably the aggregate of all of their reign may be a little more than one year. See William Whiston (trans.), *The New Complete Works of Josephus*, revised and expanded edition. Commentary by Paul L. Maier (Grand Rapids, MI: Kregel Publications, 1999), 840-841. Therefore, it seems that Vespasian became emperor of Rome in 69 C.E. When he died in 79 C.E., his son Titus became emperor. Titus ruled only for 26 months and died in 13th, September, 81 C.E. Then, his younger brother Domitian became emperor until he was murdered in 18th. Sept, 96 C.E. See the following - T. S. Johnson, "Roman Emperors," *DNTB*, edited by Craig A. Evans and Stanley E. Porter (Downers Grove, Illinois / Leicester, England: InterVarsity Press, 2000), 970-971. Brian W. Jones, "Titus (Emperor)," *ABD*, Vol. 6 (New York: Doubleday, 1992), 580-581.

1.3.1. The Socio-Political Impact of the War Upon the Jews

In the first Jewish war against Rome (66-73 C.E.) a large number of Jews (not less than 500,000) perished.[137] According to Josephus, the country of Judea became desolate, and it was not peopled by Titus, and it was lying ready for the future restoration of the Jews.[138] At any rate, the Jews were still the main inhabitants of the land. However, there was a significant change in the system of administration and the status of the Jews.

As a result of the war Judea was separated from Syria and it became an imperial province.[139] The term "Judea" here seems to be used in a wider sense covering Palestine as a whole.[140] Vespasian retained the country of Judea as a private possession.[141] Titus left the Tenth Legion as a garrison in Jerusalem to

---

137 According to Josephus 1,100,000 people perished during the whole siege of Jerusalem, 97,000 were taken captive during the whole war and during the selection of those to be sent to different places after Jerusalem was taken, 11,000 perished for want of food. Out of those who perished in the siege of Jerusalem the greater part of them did not belong to Jerusalem, but they were the Jews who had come up to Jerusalem from all over the country for the Feast of Unleavened Bread. The whole number of the Jews who perished during the entire seven years war amounted to 1,337,490, and the total approximate number of those who took part in the feast was 2,700,200, excluding those who had leprosy or gonorrhoea, women who had their monthly courses, other polluted people, and any foreigners. See Josephus, *Wars of the Jews* VI. IX. 2,3,4, in *Josephus. Complete Works*, 587-588. However, Josephus' figure of the Jews who perished in the siege of Jerusalem is taken as exaggeration by some scholars and they suggest the figure of about half a million. See Applebaum, "The Economic Life in Palestine," 692.

138 Josephus, *Wars of the Jews*, VII. 6.6, in *Josephus. Complete Works*, 597. According to Reicke, while the population of Palestine was reduced after the destruction of Jerusalem Temple in 70 C.E., it was by no means dejudaized. See Reicke, *The New Testament Era*, 266.

139 Lohse, *The New Testament Environment*, 51. It seems that the separation of Judea from Syria was resolved when Vespasian was sent (in 67 C.E) there. See Schürer, *The History of the Jewish People*, 253, 276. See also Reicke, *The New Testament Era*, 257.

140 See Schürer, *The History of the Jewish People*, 392-393. The understanding of the Judean province as covering the whole of Palestine is also supported by the fact that all the sub divisions within Palestine, such as Galilee, Judea, Idumea and Perea, except only Samaria, were involved in the revolt against Rome. Vespasian waged war against all these and subdued them all. See, Reicke, *The New Testament Era*, 256-257. For a detailed description of the war, see Josephus, *Wars of the Jews* in *Josephus. Complete Works*, 427-605. It is very unlikely that Samaria, which is in the heart of Palestine, would be included in the neighbouring province of Syria. Therefore, it is reasonably safe to assume that the Judean province covers Palestine, and hence the two terms, Judea and Palestine, would be used interchangeably in this study. When the term Judea is used in a more restricted sense, it will be so indicated.

141 See Josephus, *Wars of the Jews*, vii. 6. 6, in *Josephus. Complete Works*, 597. It is not so clear whether Josephus used the term "Judea" here to mean the whole of Judean province which covers Palestine as a whole, or in a more restricted sense to mean the former administrative district of Judea excluding Idumea, Samaria, Galilee and Perea. It seems that Schürer opts for the second sense. See Schürer, *The History of the Jewish People*, 280. However, it could also be understood as meaning the whole of Palestine due to certain reasons. For example, Josephus also does not simply say "Judea" here, but he emphatically says "all Judea." This

preserve order, with certain troops of equestrians and companies of footmen.[142] According to Reicke, apart from the environs of Jerusalem, other important sites, such as Caesarea, the newly-founded Flavia Neapolis near Shechem and Emmaus, were also claimed as Roman colonies for soldiers and veterans. Some of the soldiers were also quartered at Qumran.[143] According to Josephus, however, Caesar gave orders for the sale of all Judea except Emmaus (which is different from the Emmaus mentioned by St. Luke) which he assigned for eight hundred men, whom he dismissed from his army, for their habitation.[144] The post of governor was upgraded to the rank of imperial legate of praetorian rank, and a well qualified person with experience in provincial administration was required to fill the post.[145] Thus, the governor was no longer a procurator but the general of the Tenth Legion itself (called "*Fretensis*"). Since Jerusalem had been completely destroyed in the war Caesarea remained the official residence of the governor as it previously was the residence of the procurator. The Romans took tough measures to ensure that Judea was tranquilized from any further possible uprising. They were careful to intercept any potential Messiahs before they gained a following, and they subjected the house of David to special scrutiny and persecution.[146]

So, Palestine lost its relative independence and autarchy after the war. It no longer remained the land of the Jews politically, but only ethnically. The Judean ruling class, along with the High Council, was done away with and they were never given a chance to regain their power. The other function of the old ruling class, namely the collection of taxes, was also presumably taken over by the local Gentiles who had so long been rivals of the Jews in Palestine.[147]

Since Palestine became an imperial province, it ceased to be a procuratorship. Although the Jews, in principle, could still live in Palestine or visit it, and they still looked upon it as their holy land, they no longer had citizenship of their own which they were supposed to have had during the procuratorship because of the authority of the High Council. Furthermore, all the Jews became stateless *peregrini* in the Roman Empire, except those families that had acquired Roman citizenship on the basis of special accomplishments.[148]

---

seems to indicate the Imperial province of Judea. Applebaum also states that the Jewish purple-fishers of the Galilean coast and the workers of Opobalsam plantations at Ein Geddi and Beth ha-Ramtah in Peraea seem to have become tenants of the imperial treasury since then. See Applebaum, "The Economic Life in Palestine," 696.

142 Josephus, *Wars of the Jews*, VII.1.2 in *Josephus. Complete Works*, 589.

143 Reicke, *The New Testament Era*, 266.

144 See Josephus, *Wars of the Jews* VII. VI. 6, in *Josephus. Complete Works*, 597.

145 Schürer, *The History of the Jewish People*, 276.

146 See the following- Stambaugh and Balch, *The Social World of the First Christians*, 29; Goodman, *The Ruling Class of Judea*, 247; Reicke, *The New Testament Era*, 266; Schürer, *The History of the Jewish People*, 276, 290.

147 Goodman, *The Ruling Class of Judea*, 233-235, 247.

148 Reicke, *The New Testament Era*, 283-284.

According to Reicke, "Vespasian, Titus, and Domitian treated Judaism, politically no longer bound to Zion but to Rome, with confidence, or at least with equanimity."[149] There was no general persecution of the Jews during their time, except Domitian's persecution of those Roman magnates and aristocrats, whom he thought were exhibiting too little interest in the official cult, as well as in their obligations to the state, and too much interest in biblical monotheism. However, even under Domitian Judaism remained an ethnically and legally distinct entity, which was officially inviolate.[150] In addition, after the defeat of the Jews in Palestine, the rights of the Diaspora Jews were not restricted because Vespasian and Titus confined their war to the Jews of Palestine and particularly to the Zealot leaders.[151]

1.3.2. The Economic Impact of the War upon the Jews

The economic impact of the war may be broadly considered under different sub-sections such as impact of the war upon ownership of land, impact of the destruction of Jerusalem and the temple, impact of the tenth legion stationed at Jerusalem, and the economic burden of the Jews in general.

1.3.2.1. *Impact of the War upon the Ownership of Land*

According to Josephus, after the fall of Jerusalem Vespasian "gave order that all Judea should be exposed to sale; for he did not found any city there, but reserved the country for himself."[152] According to Martin Goodman, Vespasian sold out the lands on lease to the highest bidder. With regard to the previous owners, many of them were imprisoned, enslaved or executed. Even those who escaped without physical punishment lost their land.[153] It seems, however, that there were certain areas which would have been excluded from Vespasian's policy, such as the area around Jerusalem which was allotted to the tenth legion, and various tracts allotted to Roman veterans and individual aristocratic Roman beneficiaries who received personal grants of property from the emperor in reward for their support during the civil war of 69 C.E. Applebaum highlights how such grants of land are witnessed in Rabbinic literatures particularly by reflecting two new phenomena in the land holding systems. The first incident is the appearance of a new type of

149 Reicke, *The New Testament Era*, 285.

150 *Ibid.*, 286.

151 Reicke, *Ibid.*, 284-285. Even when the unrest was reported to Vespasian in Cyrene in 74 C.E., and Jonathan, one of the Sicarii, who led the rebellion, accused the richest men among the Jews as the ones who were responsible for the rebellion, Titus persuaded him not to believe that accusation. Instead, he made an inquiry into the allegation and found out that it was false. Then he punished Jonathan and burnt him alive. Vespasian did not attack the Jews any more, but showed tolerance toward them. See Reicke, *The New Testament Era*, 291-292. See also Josephus, *Wars of the Jews*, VII. XI. 1-3, in *Josephus. Complete Works*, 604-605.

152 Josephus, *Wars of the Jews*, VII. 6.6, in *Josephus. Complete Works*, 597.

153 Goodman, *The Ruling Class of Judea*, 231.

landlord called *matzik.* The second event is the new halakic rulings which were called forth to counter the dangers that threatened the Jewish population and its hold on the land.[154]

The *matzik* was a new type of landlord, or his agent, supported by the Roman government. The *matzik* expelled the Jewish peasant or converted him forcibly into a tenant, afflicting him with constant and exorbitant exactions. In several cases, the *matzik* abandoned his new holdings after some time. It must be assumed, based on this that the *matzik* received the land in full legal proprietorship and he could again dispose it of legally. The *matzikim* were to be found over the entire country, and they were chiefly Romans, while some Jews were certainly included. The Roman *matzikim* were consuls and senators, women of the aristocracy, high-ranking officers and other military settlers. It appears that in the course of their tenures, the *matzikim* carried out military intelligence work, and they behaved with extreme oppressiveness.[155]

In order to deal with this new agrarian situation the new halakic rulings of this time (basically the period between 70 and the later second century C.E.) "were framed by restricting the conditions on which Jews might acquire the land of Jewish holders surviving or deceased, from whom it had been confiscated under the Roman *Lex Cornelia de sicariis et veneticis*."[156] The law concerned here, that is *sikarikon regulations*, stipulated that rebels against Roman rule were liable to the death penalty and to confiscation of their property. In Judea, the *sikarikon* did not apply to those who were killed in the first war, but it applied to those killed in the war from the second war onwards, and it has always applied in Galilee. A highly probable implication of this is that after the first war a large area of confiscated land was sold only in Galilee, while in Judea the authorities or new Gentile settlers held most land and therefore options were left open only for any tract that came on the market. The situation, however, changed in the second war of 132-135 C.E., and the number of casualties made an application of *sikarikon* imperative in both Judea and Galilee.[157]

What has become obvious now is that after the first war (66-73 C.E.) a large number of Jewish peasants were forced off their lands or compelled to become tenants, and other tracts continued to be held as imperial domain (*Praedium Caesaris*). Lands were confiscated most probably from those sectors, which had been directly involved in the rebellion, while those Jews who had favoured Rome from the beginning or come over to the Romans at the critical juncture were allowed to retain their land or were given new estates. Those who received new

154 Applebaum, "The Economic Life in Palestine," 694.

155 *Ibid.*," 694- 695.

156 *Ibid.*," 695. Applebaum here holds that "such at any rate is the most reasonable interpretation of the so-called *sikarikon* regulations discussed in rabbinic literature relating to conditions between 70 and the later second century."

157 Applebaum, "The Economic Life in Palestine," 695.

estates were mainly well to do but among them were also simpler peasants who were resettled by the Roman authorities.[158] Those, Jewish landholders would have formed part of the *matzikim* in the new agrarian situation.

1.3.2.2. *Impact of the Destruction of Jerusalem and the Temple*

The destruction of Jerusalem and its main centre the Temple, dealt a shattering blow to the economy of the Jews in Palestine. It was an elimination of the principal centre of Jewish commerce and crafts, as well as the destruction of the largest source of internal and external income for the Jewish community there. The enormity of this impact may be briefly highlighted.

a. Economic Impact of the Destruction of Jerusalem: Although Jerusalem was unsuitable for trade because of lack of raw-materials and water,[159] it was the centre of trade for the Jews with imported raw-materials. Because of its religious and political significance, a large amount of revenue flowed into the city. The main sources of revenue were – (1) the enormous revenue of the Temple that came from all over the world in terms of bequests, fixed tax, the *didrachma*, the sacrifices, the redemption of vows, the wood offerings, and the produce of the land owned by the Temple; (2) Revenue that flowed into the city from foreign traffic, especially at the time of the great pilgrim festivals during which the revenue was increased enormously. One of the most notable sources during this time was the so-called "second tithe," a tenth of the produce of his land which a good Jew was committed to spend in Jerusalem; (3) An important amount that must have been spent for the needs of the court and for buildings in Jerusalem from the general taxes collected by independent rulers who resided in Jerusalem (such as -Herod 37 B.C. to 4 B.C.; Archelaus 4 B.C. to A.D. 6; Agrippa I A.D. 41-44); (4) The riches brought into the city by some owners of capital, such as wholesalers, tax collectors, and Jews who had grown rich in the Diaspora; and also a few people who would settle in Jerusalem for religious purposes; (5) The articles for daily use, and luxury products such as ointments manufactured in Jerusalem;[160] (6) Moreover, it is also suggested that there was a banking operation in the Jerusalem Temple where the belongings of the widows, the orphans, as well as the rich were deposited. Evidence to suggest such banking business in the Temple is

158 Applebaum, "The Economic Life in Palestine," 695.

159 Joachim Jeremias mentions that Jerusalem lies in a part of the country very much unfavourable for trade. Most of the raw materials for trade were lacking in the area. While metals and rich ore were entirely absent, the clay, which the neighbourhood produced, was of inferior quality. Stone was the only raw material that the area yielded in large quantities. The mountainous Judaea, otherwise, provided only the products and by-products of cattle and sheep rearing such as wool and hides, and those of the olive trees such as wood and olives. At the top, and as the most serious of all, was lack of water. See Joachim Jeremias, *Jerusalem in the Time of Jesus: An Investigation into Economic and Social Conditions during the New Testament Period*, study edition, translated by F.H. Cane and C. H. Cane (London: SCM, 1969 [1962]), 27.

160 Jeremias, *Jerusalem in the Time of Jesus*, 28.

found in II Macc. 3:6, 10-11; and in various places of the Old Testament such as for example, I Kings 7:51; II Kings 18:15; 16:8; I Chron 9:26; 28:11, 12; II Chron 36:18; Neh 12, 13; Eccl 42:7; Tob 1:14; 9:5.[161] Such enormous revenue promoted trade in the city. Besides, the court and the rich residents in Jerusalem led a life that generated a variety of needs, which in turn favored the growth of the luxury trade.[162] The major trades in Jerusalem were woolen manufacture (whose workers included weavers, fullers, tailors); leather industry; smithy; food trades (which include trades in oil, bakery, selling of meat [butchery]); selling of water; manufacture of luxury goods (which include manufacture of ointments and resins, arts and crafts, jewellery, and also the profession of scrivener); and building trade. There were also doctors, barbers, and money changers. The building trade held an especially important position under the rule of the Herodian princes which expanded from 37 B.C.E. to the outbreak of the war in 66 C.E., and sometime afterwards. Although the renovation of the Temple, one of the most significant building works in first century Palestine, was completed in 62-64 C.E., and many people were without employment,[163] some more building activity was projected before the outbreak of the war in 66 C.E., probably as a means of relief for the unemployed Temple workers.[164] The destruction of Jerusalem, therefore, was indeed the destruction of the Jewish trade. Even those who were involved in the trades in one way or the other and who survived the catastrophe, had to find some other ways of survival because there was no way of reviving their trade at least for some time in Jerusalem which was completely destroyed.[165]

b. Economic Impact of the Destruction of the Temple: The Temple was, in fact, the main centre of revenue for Jerusalem. The Temple had indeed vast wealth in terms of cash, precious furnishings, and estates,[166] and the loss of wealth and

---

161 For this and for further discussion on the economic role of the Jerusalem Temple, see Sam P. Mathew, *Temple Criticism in Mark's Gospel: The Economic Role of Jerusalem Temple During the First Century CE* (Delhi: ISPCK, 1999), 55-59. Here, Mathew also suggests that although there is no direct evidence to support that the Temple gave loans, based on the very fact that the people can deposit their wealth in the Temple, it could be reasonably assumed that they can also obtain loans from it.

162 Jeremias, *Jerusalem in the Time of Jesus*, 27-29.

163 It has been said that more than 18,000 workers were rendered without work by the completion of the rebuilding of the Temple in 62-64 C.E. See Jeremias, *Jerusalem in the Time of Jesus*, 22. See also E. P. Sanders, *Judaism: Practice and Belief, 63 BCE – 66 CE* (London: SCM Press/ Philadelphia: Trinity Press International, 1992), 85.

164 For these and for further detailed discussion on trades in Jerusalem, see Jeremias, *Jerusalem in the Time of Jesus*, 4-18, 22. See also Sanders, *Judaism: Practice and Belief, 63 BCE – 66 CE*, 85.

165 See Josephus, *Wars of the Jews* VI. V. 1, 2 and VII. I. 1 in *Josephus. Complete Works*, 581-582, 589.

166 Sanders, *Judaism: Practice and Belief, 63 BCE – 66 CE*, 83. The account of Josephus offers an idea about the scale of the Temple's wealth. According to *Antig* 14. 72, 105, a Roman general Crassus, who intended to invade the Parthians raided the Temple in Jerusalem on his way

revenue because of the destruction of the Temple was enormous. A large amount of income, which used to flow into the city from the vast public, which visited the capital every year, especially during the festivals,[167] was lost. Along with this, the regular contributions, which the Diaspora Jews used to furnish to the temple, also disappeared.[168] With the destruction of the Temple, the economic basis and source of livelihood of a large number of people also had vanished. Such people who depended upon the temple treasury for their livelihood may be briefly mentioned as follows: (1) there were at least three hierarchies of priests with their families, who depended directly on the temple tax/tithes for their livelihood such as the High Priest, the chief priests, and ordinary priests.[169] (2) There were good numbers of tradesmen who earned their means of living by supplying the products required for sacrifices and the numerous temple requisites. For example, tradesmen were needed to supply large quantities of incense burned in the morning and in the evening, and a good deal of clothes, vessels, and basins.[170] Moreover, it seems that traders were engaged to supply animals required for the sacrifices, which were examined by the priests before they were sold to the people. It seems that they did this to avoid a possible pollution of the temple by the animals brought by the people.[171] (3) There were also permanent staff employed for the cultus, such as to look after the vessels and basins, which needed periodic attention.[172] (4)

---

and took cash reserves of 2000 talents, which Pompey did not touch because of his regard of religion. According to Sanders, the money was presumably kept in terms of gold or silver, and calculating a talent as equivalent to about 40 kg, what Crassus lifted amounted to about 80,000 kg of coins. Sanders observes that even if Josephus' account is taken as exaggeration, it nevertheless shows that the temple had great wealth. Sanders, *Judaism: Practice and Belief, 63 BCE – 66 CE*, 83-84.

167 There were three festivals for the Jews in a year commanded by the Torah, in which it enjoined all the Jews to go to the Temple in Jerusalem to offer sacrifices. Those festivals were Pesah (Passover) in the spring, Shavuot (Pentecost, Feast of Weeks) on the fiftieth day of the Passover, and Sukkot (Tabernacles, Feast of Booths) in the fall. In the First century before the destruction of the Temple, many Jews in Judea went up for every festival, while many went at least on Pesah. The Galilean and Syrian Jews went as often as they could. Those Jews from distant lands tried to visit the Temple at least once in their lifetime, usually for Passover. The craftspeople and shopkeepers of Jerusalem depended on the trade of pilgrims for their livelihood and they kept the city prosperous. See Stephen M. Wylen, *The Jews in the Time of Jesus: An Introduction* (New York / Mahwah, N. J.: Paulist Press, 1996), 97.

168 Applebaum, "The Economic Life in Palestine," 698.

169 Mathew, *Temple Criticism in Mark's Gospel*, 35-42. Mathew also mentions here that apart from these three hierarchies, even Levites had the right to tithes before the Herodian and Roman periods. However, in this period their right was appropriated by the priests, and there was no more mention of tithes for Levites.

170 Applebaum, "The Economic Life in Palestine," 698. See also Sanders, *Judaism: Practice and Belief, 63 BCE – 66 CE*, 85.

171 Sanders, *Judaism: Practice and Belief, 63 BCE – 66 CE*, 85-87.

172 See the following: Jeremias, *Jerusalem in the Time of Jesus*, 16, 26, 29-30; Sanders, *Judaism: Practice and Belief, 63 BCE – 66 CE*, 85.

Moreover, many workers in the city were paid from the Temple treasury. Apart from the priestly hierarchies, those who got their wages directly from the Temple treasury included maintenance workers of the city, such as those who worked for the maintenance of the buildings, the water channel, walls, towers, wells and cisterns, and those who worked in the cleaning and supervision of the streets, etc. Unemployed workers after the completion of the Temple were also given assistance from the Temple treasury, engaging them in the paving of the streets of Jerusalem and in the additional work undertaken in the Temple.[173] We could safely assume that many of those who got their livelihood from the revenue of the Temple died in the course of the war. However, for those who survived among them, their source of livelihood had gone. It was not only that those sources of income were lost, but they were diverted to Rome, "and the burden, vastly increased, fell on Judaea and Diaspora Jewry equally."[174]

1.3.2.3. *Impact of the Tenth Legion Stationed at Jerusalem*

As mentioned earlier the tenth legion had been stationed in Jerusalem. There is no explicit record about the economic effects of this military garrison upon the people and the place. At any rate, there is no attestation of any Jew possessing a large estate near the city after 70 C.E.,[175] thereby suggesting that the surrounding areas of Jerusalem became a commissariat of this military garrison and the remaining population became tenants of the army. According to Applebaum, the army officers administered them and supplies were consistently levied upon this people by the army.[176]

1.3.2.4. *The Economic Burden of the Jews in General after the War*

During the war, most of the villages and towns of the Jews in Palestine, except those, which surrendered to the Romans, had been ravaged.[177] According to Josephus, some of the villages had been ravaged by the Jews themselves.[178] All the Jews, other than those who had favoured Rome from the beginning or had come over to the Romans at the critical juncture, lost their land. Because of all this, the Jewish population of Palestine was afflicted with poverty after the war. Moreover, their existential poverty was exacerbated by a series of drought years and increased

173 Jeremias, *Jerusalem in the Time of Jesus*, 26.

174 Applebaum, "The Economic Life in Palestine," 698.

175 Goodman, *The Ruling Class of Judea*, 233.

176 Applebaum, "The Economic Life in Palestine," 693-694. Here, Applebaum also observes that the results of the administration of the district by the army were no doubt hard for the inhabitants, but it was not entirely negative because the commanders of the legion would certainly have had an interest to revive and maintain the productivity of the district.

177 Implied in Applebaum, "The Economic Life in Palestine," 698.

178 See Josephus, *Wars of the Jews*, iv. VII. 2, in Josephus, *Complete Works*, 537.

taxation.[179] It seems that the Jews paid a higher Roman tax (*tributum capitis*) than the surrounding region, and it was increased by Vespasian.[180] Johanan ben Zakkai mentions that the Jews were paying a head-tax of fifteen *sheqels* to Roman government, as a punishment for the neglect of the Temple dues before 70 C.E.[181] This amount is supposed to be the approximate average total sum the contemporary Jew of Palestine paid yearly. This is about four times the tax paid by Egyptian peasant in the late first century C.E.[182] Moreover, all the Jews throughout the Roman Empire were required to pay two drachmas every year, which they used to pay as temple tax before, to *Jupiter Capitolinus*, the Roman rival god of the Jewish God, whose temple had been burnt down in 69 C.E.[183] Although it was not a big amount, it was definitely an additional burden for many impoverished Jews. Moreover, while the tax was promulgated in the third year of Vespasian's reign, the tax itself was in force from the destruction of the Temple, and therefore, the Jews had to pay arrears for one year. Initially, it was collected from all the Jews, both male and female alike, including their slaves and freedmen, between the age of 3 to 60 or 62.[184] A Jewish master was responsible to pay the tax for all his slaves, both Jews and non-Jews, in addition to his responsibility to pay for his wife, his unmarried daughters, and his minor sons.[185] Therefore, if the family was a big one, the burden could have been very heavy in the midst of war-torn poverty. Moreover, during the reign of Domitian it was extended to all the Jews regardless of their age (from 3 years old without upper limit), and it was rigorously exacted.[186] Such abuses of exaction were abolished by Emperor Nerva,

---

179 Applebaum, "The Economic Life in Palestine," 698.

180 *Ibid.*," 698, quoting and interpreting Appian, *Syriaca* 50.

181 See Jacob Neusner, *Judaism in the Beginning of Christianity* (Whitstable, Kent: Whitstable Litho Ltd, 1984), 94. See also Applebaum, "The Economic Life in Palestine," 698.

182 Applebaum, "The Economic Life in Palestine," 698.

183 See Josephus, *Wars of the Jews*, VII. VI. 6, in *Josephus. Complete Works*, 597. See also Tcherikover and Fuks, eds., *Corpus Papyrorum Judaicarum*, Vol. I, 80. Most of the writers refer to this tax as *Fiscus Judaicus.* However, Sara Mandell argues that it is *Didrachmon* tax, a war indemnity, and not to be confused with *Fiscus Judaicus.* Mandell further argues that this tax was not paid by all the Jews, but only by the Pharisaic Jews, who were circumcised Jews who followed the paternal custom and lived a Jewish life. See S. Mandel, "Who paid the Temple Tax when the Jews were under Roman Rule?" *HarvTheolRev* 77/2 (1984), 228, 232 [223-232]. The situation might be like this - that its official name probably was *denarii duo Judaeorum* "two denarii of the Jews," and it was used up to some years of Domitian's reign. But between the 8th and 12th years of Domitian's reign the official name was replaced by a less complicated "Jewish tax" probably in connection with some reform in the central administration of the *fiscus Judaicus.* See Tcherikover and Fuks, eds., *Corpus Papyrorum Judaicarum*, Vol. I, 81.

184 Tcherikover and Fuks, eds., *Corpus Papyrorum Judaicarum*, Vol. I, 80-81.

185 *Ibid.*, Vol. II, 114.

186 Zetterholm, *The Formation of Christianity in Antioch*, 186, 188-189, quoting Suetonius, *Domitian* 12.2.

the successor of Domitian.[187] However, the tax itself continued at least untill the middle of the second century.[188] Even the voluntary payment of the priestly dues was continued.[189] The poverty, which the Jews had been undergoing in the aftermath of the war, was so severe[190] that it resulted in the recurrent emergence of groups of outlaws and bandits, which, according to some scholars, eventually became the leading factor in the outbreak of the revolt in 132 C.E. in the reign of Hadrian.[191]

1.3.3. The Religious Impact of the War Upon the Jews

The religious impact of the war upon the Jews could be seen largely in three ways, such as its direct impact upon the temple cultus, its direct impact upon the destiny of the priests, and its indirect impact for the emergence of Pharisaic Judaism.

1.3.3.1. *Direct Impact of the War Upon the Temple Cultus*

The Jerusalem Temple, which was the religious centre of the Jews,[192] was destroyed in 70 C.E., and the High Council (Sanhedrin), along with the Judean ruling class, mostly made up of the Sadducean nobility, was also done away with. Along with the disappearance of the Sanhedrin, the Sadducees also disappeared from history.[193] There are differences of opinion on the reasons the Sadducees' disappearance from history. A highly probable reason was that the Sadducees were taking leadership in the revolt against Rome. And, probably the Sadducees concentrated around Jerusalem, and being implicated in the war, they heavily suffered with the fall of the city.[194] Then, as they were diminished, the preponderance of the Pharisees

---

187 Tcherikover and Fuks, eds., *Corpus Papyrorum Judaicarum*, Vol. I, 80. See also Zetterholm, *The Formation of Christianity in Antioch*, 189.

188 Tcherikover and Fuks, eds., *Corpus Papyrorum Judaicarum*, Vol. II, 116.

189 Applebaum, "The Economic Life in Palestine," 699.

190 A story that tells the severity of the poverty in the aftermath of the war was documented thus – A contemporary sage who was riding on a donkey with provisions, was accosted by a Jew begging him for food. When he dismounted to unload his beast, the man had died before he could do so. Applebaum, "The Economic Life in Palestine," 699.

191 Applebaum, "The Economic Life in Palestine," 699. For the view that the second Jewish war might have not been necessarily connected to the first war and its aftermath, see Oppenheimer, "Bar Kokhba Revolt," *ABD*, Vol. 1 (New York: Doubleday, 1992), 599. See also Horsley and Hanson, *Bandits, Prophets, and Messiahs…*, 127-131.

192 For a discussion on the Religious role of the Temple, see Mathew, *Temple Criticism in Mark's Gospel*, 52-53.

193 Schürer, *The History of the Jewish People*, 283-284. See also W. O. E. Oesterley, *A History of Israel*, Vol. II (Oxford: Clarendon Press, 1934 [1932]), 452, 455. For more about the Sadducean nobility, see Sanders, *Judaism: Practice and Belief*, 317-340.

194 According to Horsley and Hanson, some of them were eliminated by the (Jewish) rebel groups, and others by the reconquering Roman army. Horsley and Hanson, *Bandits, Prophets, and Messiahs*, 44.

overweighed their influence in the post-war period.[195] The worship of God in the Temple came to an end with the destruction of the Temple. In addition, the sacrifices mandated in the books of the Torah could no longer be performed and they could only be maintained in the memory of the Jewish people. Although, some writings have assumed that the sacrifices were continued for some time even after the Temple was destroyed, this did not in fact take place. The sacrifices were abolished on 17th July, 70 C.E. and there is no reference to its restoration anywhere.[196] Therefore, Schürer maintains that the speaking of the sacrifices in present tense after the destruction of the Temple by Josephus and some Christian writers was only the description of "what is still allowable, but a right that was no longer actually exercised."[197] Even the priests, who surrendered to Titus after the destruction of the Temple, were put to death because Titus said that since the Temple where those priests belonged had been destroyed, it was befitting for the priests to perish along with it.[198] As also indicated earlier, the Jews were required to pay a poll-tax of two drachmas known as *fiscus Judaicus* annually to Capitoline

195 See A. C. Sundberg, "Sadducees," *IDB*, Vol. 4 (New York/Nashville: Abingdon Press, 1962), 161.
Some of the other prominent arguments are the following: According to Sandmel, "after A.D. 70, after the Temple was destroyed and the priestly cultus came to an end, … the Sadducees had no reason to persist, and they disappeared." See Samuel Sandmel, *The First Christian Century in Judaism and Christianity: Certainties and Uncertainties* (New York: Oxford University Press, 1969), 58. Porton, however, argues that Sandmel's view is based upon the assumed relationship between the Sadducees and the priesthood, and this assumption is far from grounded in the sources. All that we know about Sadducees, according to Porton, is that Josephus mentions them in the Maccabean period along with the Pharisees and the Essenes, and the Sadducees play a small role in the Jewish documents which come down to us from the period after 70 C.E. in which the Pharisees/rabbis rose to power. See Gary Porton, "Sadducees" *ABD*, Vol. 5 (New York: Doubleday, 1992), 894. According to W. D. Davies, the Sadducees were disqualified by many things for leadership after 70 C.E., such as their denial of resurrection hope, their emphasis on the temple and its services, their rigid adherence to the letter of the law, and alienation from the masses because of their former identification with the wealthy and powerful priestly and political forces. Finally, the leaders at Jamnia made a "dogma" of the resurrection from the dead in order to discredit the Sadducees, and because of this, they automatically became heretics. See Davies, *The Setting of the Sermon on the Mount*, 259.

196 Schürer, *The History of the Jewish People*, 281-283. Here, Schürer mentions that the continuance of the sacrifice after the destruction of the Temple has been maintained or indicated in the following - the Epistle to the Hebrews, the Epistle to Diognetus, Josephus (*Antiquities*, iii. 9-10); some rabbinical literature (e.g., *Pesachim*, vii. 2); and Justin, *Dialogus Cum Trypho*, c. 40, 46. However, according to Schürer, its abolition is clearly mentioned or indicated in *Taanith*, vi. 6; Josephus *Wars of the Jews*, vi.ii. 1; Mishna, such as *Pesachim*, x. 3, *Rosh hashana*, i. 4; Babylonian Talmud, such as *Rosh hashana* 31b, *Pesachim* 72b, *Sebachim* 60b. See also Goodman, *The Ruling Class of Judea*, 232, 249-250.

197 Schürer, *The History of the Jewish People*, 283.

198 See Josephus, *Wars of the Jews* VI. VI. 1, in *Josephus. Complete Works*, 583. See also Goodman, *The Ruling Class of Judea*, 231; and, Stambaugh and Balch, *The Social World of the First Christians*, 29.

Jupiter, just as they had formerly contributed to the Temple in Jerusalem.[199] This means that the Temple tax was replaced by a humiliating tax to the cult of Jupiter, who, according to the Romans, had defeated Yahweh and his people.[200] Initially Vespasian claimed this tax for rebuilding the Temple of Jupiter on the Capitol, which had been burned in 69 C.E. But, it seems that Domitian put an end to the exclusive connection between this tax and the treasury of the Jupiter Capitolinus, and redirected the sum collected from the Jews in the name of this tax to another use. Seemingly, because of the same purpose, he changed the name of the tax to *fiscus Judaicus* and he levied it not only from all the Jews by race, but also from all proselytes to Judaism.[201] Some scholars assume that it was not abolished until 361 C.E. under Julian.[202] It is quite uncertain whether this is true or not. It seems that there is evidence of its existence at least up to the middle of the second century.[203]

According to Goodman, this *fiscus Judaicus* symbolized a deliberate destruction of both the free Jewish state, with the religion and society of Judea before 66 C.E. Since Vespasian decided that the Temple cult was pernicious and was determined to do without it altogether, it is unlikely that any thought of repairing the Temple would be entertained, and though it was not impossible, it is highly unlikely that any sort of sacrificial cult was revived on the ruined site.[204] No new High Priest was appointed because of this new attitude of Rome and that of King Agrippa, who seems to have avoided all contact with the province after 70 C.E.[205]

---

199 See Josephus, *Wars of the Jews*, VII. VI. 6, in *Josephus. Complete Works*, 597.

200 Stambaugh and Balch, *The Social World of the First Christians*, 29.

201 See the following: Oesterley, *A History of Israel*, 454-455; and Tcherikover and Fuks, eds., *Corpus Papyrorum Judaicarum*, Vol. II, 113.

202 See for example, Oesterley, *A History of Israel*, 454-455.

203 Tcherikover and Fuks, eds., *Corpus Papyrorum Judaicarum*, Vol. II, 116. Reicke quotes Tertullian as maintaining that while this contribution toward rebuilding the Capitol was indeed a source of religious vexation to the Jews in general, it was not an excessive financial burden to all of them. It seems that many of them appreciated it rather as the possibility of purchasing religious liberty for roughly a dollar a year. Reicke, *The New Testament Era*, 285, quoting Tertullian, *Apology* xviii. 9. It would be legitimate to observe, however, that every single addition to the existing tax(es) would have definitely been an additional burden for many Jews who had been severely impoverished by the war.

204 Goodman, *The Ruling Class of Judea*, 232. According to Reicke, Josephus and Mishna did speak as though the cult still existed only because the Jews counted on a restoration of the Old Testament sacrificial cult and made certain attempts along these lines (Bar 1:10). See Reicke, *The New Testament Era*, 266.

205 Goodman, *The Ruling Class of Judea*, 232. When the uprising of the Jews against Rome began in 66 C.E., Agrippa went to Jerusalem to quell it. But he failed and he himself became the target of the Zealots. It seems that after this he avoided visiting Jerusalem altogether. See David C. Braund, "Agrippa (Person)," *ABD*, Vol. 1 (New York: Doubleday, 1992), 100.

Although, there was no racial hostility against the Jews themselves[206] Judaism itself was looked upon as a pernicious religion by Vespasian, Titus, and perhaps all their fellow Romans. Therefore, "it was to be tolerated in the private lives of diaspora Jews" only, and that was also "only because its suppression throughout the Mediterranean would be too vast an undertaking."[207] Public sacrifices to the Jewish God and the conversion of non-Jews to Jewish practices were strictly prohibited.[208] During the reign of Domitian the rooting out of proselytes and sympathizers with Judaism who had adopted Jewish customs reached something of a climax, and it has been said that even an old man of ninety have been hauled in front of a large bench of assessors to see whether he had undergone the operation of circumcision.[209]

1.3.3.2. *Direct Impact of the War Upon the Destiny of the Priests*

The suppression of sacrificial worship, affected by the overthrow of the city and the destruction of the Temple, also led to the gradual recession of the priesthood from public life. It seems that there was a high expectation for the priests to be able to resume their services in the near future. Accordingly, all dues were exacted even after the catastrophe as before. Only the taxes, which had been directly contributed for the maintenance of the Temple and of the public sacrifices, were declared to be suspended by the Rabbis. Even the contribution meant for the personal support of the priests, continued after the catastrophe, as a duty according to the law, and where there were priests they were directly given to them.[210] In spite of all these, the priesthood, which could no longer perform its service, lost its importance. It increasingly became only a memorial of a past age and as time went on it sank more into obscurity and decay.[211]

1.3.3.3. *Indirect Impact of the War: The Emergence of Pharisaic Judaism*

While the Sadducees disappeared from history and the priests lost their significance, the Pharisees and the Rabbis entered into the heritage of the Sadducees and priests. In the words of Schürer, "the overthrow of Jerusalem means nothing more or less than the passing over of the people to Pharisaism and the Rabbis."[212] Although, Pharisees and Rabbis are mentioned here as separate entities, in reality

206 Goodman, *The Ruling Class of Judea*, 239.

207 *Ibid*, 238-239.

208 *Ibid*, 239.

209 *Ibid*, 238-239, quoting Suetonius, *Domitian* 12.

210 Schürer, *The History of the Jewish People*, 284.

211 *Ibid.* According to W. D. Davies, Priests were still influential after 70 C.E., and posted danger to Pharisaic leadership in Jamnia and to the reconstruction movement led by these Pharisees. They were, therefore restrained by the Pharisees through enforcement of their policy. See Davies, *The Setting of the Sermon on the Mount*, 260-261.

212 Schürer, *The History of the Jewish People*, 284.

both of them were members of the same Pharisaic movement at this time. The term "rabbi" was given as an honorific title to the Pharisee sage, especially after 70 C.E. The leading figures of the reorganization movement of Judaism after 70 C.E., who were working for the renewal of Judaism along the line of the Pharisaic teachings, were usually referred to as "rabbis," for example, R. Johannan ben Zakkai, R. Gamaliel II and R. Ismael.[213] On the other hand, the great Pharisaic teachers before them like Shammai (of the first century B.C.E.) and Hillel (of the beginning of the first century C.E.)[214] were not given the title.[215]

Therefore, what happened was that after the destruction of Jerusalem Temple the Pharisees, under the leadership of their sages who were called rabbis, took control of Judaism.[216] During the past two centuries before the war, they had been making steady progress toward dominant power.[217] Now, the two main factors, which stood in their opposition, had sunk into utter insignificance, and they consequently entered into absolute sovereignty over the Jews for a time.[218] This will be further discussed later in the sub-section "the emergence of formative Judaism."

1.3.4. Preliminary Conclusion

A summary of our discussion in this sub-section may be briefly given as follows: The first Jewish war against Rome (66-73 C.E.) had far-reaching consequences upon the Jews. The impact of this war upon the Jews could be broadly seen in three aspects, namely socio-political, economic and religious. While the socio-political and economic impact was felt mainly in Palestine, the religious impact was felt by all the Jews both inside and outside Palestine.

---

213 See for example, Schürer, *The History of the Jewish People*, Vol. I, 522-528.

214 See C. A. Evans, "Shammai, House of," *DNTB*, edited by Craig. A. Evans and Stanley E. Porter (Downers Grove, Illinois/Leicester, England: InterVarsity Press, 2000), 1106-1107. For a reference to the connection of Shammai and Hillel with the Pharisees, see the following - S. Mason, "Pharisees," *DNTB*, edited by Craig. A. Evans and Stanley E. Porter (Downers Grove, Illinois / Leicester, England: InterVarsity Press, 2000), 782-787. B. D. Chilton, "Rabbis," *DNTB*, edited by Craig A. Evans and Stanley E. Porter (Downers Grove, Illinois/Leicester, England: InterVarsity Press, 2000), 914-917.

215 Hayim Lapin, "Rabbi," *ABD*, Vol. 5 (New York: Doubleday, 1992), 600-602. Here, Lapin also mentions, "the earliest evidence for 'rabbi' as a title attached to a proper name (e.g., Rab Hana) occurs on Jerusalem ossuaries which apparently date from before 100 C.E."

216 S. Mason also notes that because rabbinic literature mentions men like Hillel and Shammai, as well as the family of Gamaliel, who are elsewhere connected with the Pharisees, among its founding figures, scholars traditionally more or less identify the Pharisees with the rabbis. See Mason, "Pharisees," 785.

217 For a detailed discussion on the history and practice of Pharisees, see Sanders, *Judaism: Practice and Belief*, 380-451. See also Mason, "Pharisees," 782-787. For a discussion on "Rabbi" see Lapin, "Rabbi," 600-602.

218 Schürer, *The History of the Jewish People*, 284.

Socio-politically, the war resulted in the separation of Judea (i.e., Palestine) from Syria and it became an imperial province, having its own governor. The Judean ruling class, along with the High Council, that is the Sanhedrin, was done away with. So, Palestine lost its relative independence and autarchy after the war, and therefore, it no longer remained the land of the Jews politically, but only ethnically. As a result, the Jews no longer had citizenship of their own which they were supposed to have under the authority of the High Council. Hence, they became stateless *peregrini* except those families, which had acquired Roman citizenship because of special accomplishments.

The economic impact of the war was also very severe. Most of the Jews in Palestine lost the ownership of their land. A large number of Jewish peasants were forced off their lands by way of imprisonment or execution and many of them were compelled to become tenants. Only those Jews who had favoured Rome from the beginning or come over to the Romans at the critical juncture were allowed to retain their land or were given new estates. Most of the lands of the Jews were sold by Vespasian to the highest bidders, and thus became *latifundia*, where the forced tenants were afflicted with exorbitant exactions. Apart from the loss of landownership, the destruction of Jerusalem and the Temple was a severe blow to the economy of the Jews in Palestine. Many people who depended upon the temple treasury for their livelihood lost their source of living. Included among them were the priestly hierarchies who were responsible for the temple services, some craftsmen who tended the vessels and utensils, traders who supplied the products required for sacrifices and the numerous temple requisites, and many people who were engaged in the maintenance work of the city. In addition, a large amount of income, which used to flow into the city from the vast public that visited the capital every year, especially during the festivals, was also lost. The regular contributions, which the Diaspora Jews used to give to the Temple, also had disappeared. Not only were those sources of income lost, but they were also diverted to Rome, by way of heavily increased tax, which fell equally on Judaea and Diaspora Jewry. As a result of all this, and compounded by a series of drought years, the Jews in Palestine were severely impoverished.

While the war had such a serious impact upon the socio-political and economic spheres of the Jews, its impact upon the religious praxis of the Jews was no less serious. It could be viewed as far more consequential. With the destruction of the Temple, the worship of God in it came to an end. The sacrifices mandated in the books of the Torah also could no longer be performed. The Temple tax was replaced by a humiliating tax to the cult of Jupiter. The high council (Sanhedrin) and the Sadducees disappeared from history, and no new High Priest was appointed. Judaism became a pernicious religion to the Romans. In the Diaspora, it was tolerated in the private lives of the Jews, but public sacrifices to the Jewish God and the conversion of non-Jews to Jewish practices were strictly prohibited. Many priests were executed when Jerusalem fell, and the priesthood, which could no longer perform its service, lost its importance. It eventually sank more into obscurity and decay. As the Sadducees disappeared from history and the priests lost their significance, the Pharisees, under the leadership of their sages called rabbis, entered into the heritage of the Sadducees and priests, and they consequently entered into absolute control over the Jews.

The entry of the Pharisees and Rabbis into the limelight in the aftermath of the first Jewish War is significant in the renewal of the Jewish society and religion shattered by this war. The renewal movement under their leadership consequently had an important bearing on the emergence of Matthew's gospel. To this we now turn.

1.4. The Social Setting of Matthew's Gospel

The discussion above has brought to light that the Jewish war against Rome (66-73 C.E.) had serious impacts upon the socio-political, economic, and religious life of the Jews. In particular, the religious impact of the war upon the Jews had a direct bearing on the change in the religious leadership of the Jews from Sadducees and Priests to Pharisees and Rabbis. This change in Jewish religious leadership with its concomitant renewal movement of the Jewish religion is understood in recent Matthean scholarship as a primary factor affecting and influencing the writing of Matthew's gospel. Therefore, we will focus our attention in this sub-section on this new development within Judaism, which is termed as "formative Judaism," and how this development is related to the writing of Matthew's gospel. However, there are also other factors, which are understood as consequential in the formation of Matthew's gospel, especially influencing the composition of its content. Therefore, those factors also will be considered after studying formative Judaism and its influence upon the writing of Matthew's gospel.

1.4.1. The Emergence of Formative Judaism

The most devastating experience of the Jews in the war was the destruction of Jerusalem and the Temple. This amounted not only to a political setback for the people of Israel, but it also meant the destruction of their social, cultural and religious centre because the Temple was not only the central symbol of Judaism, but it constituted both the social and cosmic structure of Israelite society.[219]

219 Overman, *Matthew's Gospel and Formative Judaism*, 35. See also Jacob Nuesner, "The Formation of Rabbinic Judaism: Yavneh (Jamnia) from A.D. 70 to 100," in *ANRW* II (Berlin /New York: Walter de Gruyter, 1979), 21; Jacob Neusner, *From Politics to Piety: The Emergence of Pharisaic Judaism* (Englewood Cliffs, New Jersey: Prentice Hall, 1979 [1973]), 2-3.
The significance of the Temple for the Jews may be briefly explained as follows: In ancient Israel the temples were built only where the ancient Israelites understood to be a place where Yahweh, the God of Israel, or one of his messengers, had revealed himself. As such, the temple in Jerusalem was built on the place where Abraham almost sacrificed his son Isaac, and where God spoke to Abraham as is related in Genesis 22. The Jerusalem Temple achieved supremacy over all other Israelite temples, and acquired many legends which emphasize its particularly

sacred quality, such as the narratives in 2Sam 24; and Gen 14 and 22. See Benedikt Otzen, *Judaism in Antiquity. Political Development and Religious Currents from Alexander to Hadrian*, translated by Frederick H. Cryer (Sheffield: JSOT Press, 1990), 99-101. The significance of the Temple for Israelite society is mentioned in several passages of the Old Testament. It was regarded as a national centre from the beginning. As it was the abode of the ark, it was considered to be the place where divine presence is revealed, and therefore it was a preferred place of prayer, to which an individual Israelite should direct his prayer even from the remotest places. See Yehoshua M. Grintz, "The Significance of the [First] Temple," *Encyclopaedia Judaica*, Second Edition, Vol. 19 (Detroit, et al.: Thomson Gale, 2007), 608. See also the following OT texts quoted by Grintz - IKings 8:22-53, cf. Josh 7:6-9; ISam 1:10-16; IISam 7:18-29; IKings 8:44-48; cf. Dan 6:11; Joel 2:15-16. Especially, in several places of the prophetic writings, the significance of the Temple mount and the Temple itself is emphatically stated. See for example – Mt. Zion, the temple mount is the mountain of the Lord and the holy mountain (Isa 11:9; 56:7; 65:11, 25; Joel 2:1; 4:17; Zeph 3:11, et al), and it is the place where the Lord dwells (Ps 74:2). The temple is the house of God of Jacob and the Lord's house (Isa 2:2-3; Jer 23:11; Ezek 8:14, 16; Joel 1:13-16; Mic 4:1-2; Haggai 1:14, et al.). For this references and for more references, see Grintz, "The Significance of the [First] Temple," 608. In fact, in the words of Otzen, "the Jews could maintain that Yahweh dwelt simultaneously in heaven and in the temple on Zion," and "it was here that heaven and earth were thought to meet; indeed, in reality, the temple *was* heaven on earth." See Otzen, *Judaism in Antiquity*, 100-101. Otzen further notes (in p. 101) that the temple was the locus in which the Israelites made the closest contact with the forces, which determined their life and being. Their own existence, their nation's and, indeed, even that of the whole world, were dependent on the divine forces which entered the earthly sphere at precisely this spot. It was therefore of corresponding importance to ensure that the sacral rites, of inestimable origin and significance, be carried out with the greatest precision. Because of its immense significance for the Israelites, even when it was destroyed by the king of Babylon (2Kings 25:9), there was much prophecy around the visions of its reconstruction and the purification of its worship. E.g., Ezek chaps. 40-48; Hag chaps. 1-2; Zech 1:16; 2:15; 6:12; 8:3; 22:23; Mal chaps. 1-3. See Grintz, "The Significance of the [First] Temple," 608. When the Temple was rebuilt, some religious elements and values were added in it. The Holy Scriptures and other national historical literature were kept in it, and the Temple acted not only as a storehouse, but it also acted as an agency for their careful preservation and dissemination. These ancient texts kept in the Temple functioned as authority for determining the correct reading of the text of the Holy Scriptures whenever a doubt arose about it. Shmuel Safrai, "The Significance of the [Second] Temple for the People," *Encyclopaedia Judaica*, second edition, Vol. 19 (Detroit, et al.: Thomson Gale, 2007), 625. The chamber of Hewn Stone and the outer courts were the place of sitting for the Sanhedrin and the various law courts connected with it. The Sanhedrin attained its full privilege only when it sat in the Temple precincts and while the sacrificial system was in operation. In spite of all these additions, the second Temple continued basically "to be looked upon as the 'dwelling place' of the Divine presence, and as the only fitting place to bring sacrifices in His name, both communal and individual." Moreover, "the Temple and its appurtenances were pictured as symbolizing the entire universe, including the stars of the firmament, and the Temple service was considered to be a source of blessings to all the nations of the world and even to the heavens and the earth and all it contains." Shmuel Safrai, "The Significance of the [Second] Temple for the People," 625. In addition to its social, cultural and religious significance, especially under the Roman rule, many elements of autonomous self-government and political life left in the Jews' hands by the Romans were based in the Temple. Nuesner, "The Formation of Rabbinic Judaism…," 21.

Because the Temple had such a great significance in the life of the Jews, one could imagine how much consequence its destruction would have had upon the Jews. Indeed, because of its destruction, together with the devastation of their holy city Jerusalem, the Jews were in a chaotic and fluid state after the war. For the survival of Judaism, a new religio-cultural synthesis was required. "This synthesis and the process of its construction and emergence in the post-70 period are referred to as *formative Judaism*," a termed coined by Jacob Neusner.[220] During this period of the so-called formative Judaism, which lasted about 50 years between *c.* 70 C.E., and *c.* 120 C.E., a number of religious-cultural structures of the period before 70 were put together in a new synthesis, which later came to be called rabbinic Judaism.[221] Although it seems that Neusner's emphasis with the term "formative Judaism" was on the formative nature of Judaism during the period he studied, rather than on a kind of Judaism (as Ewherido has pointed out[222]), the term also can be understood as a movement for the reconstruction of Judaism, having leaders, and gradually winning people to join it (as Overman uses it[223]). In this study, the term will be basically used in this second sense, but without negating the first sense.

The important challenge to reclaim the faith of the Jews from the disaster of the war and the loss of the Temple was taken up by a coalition of forces. The most dominant element in this coalition was the Pharisees under the leadership

220 Overman, *Matthew's Gospel and Formative Judaism*, 35 and n.1. It is usually regarded now that Neusner is the one who coined the term "formative Judaism" and who popularized it. See also the works of Neusner quoted by Overman, such as "The Formation of Rabbinic Judaism...," 3-42; of the same author, "Judaism after Moore: A Programmtic Statement,"*JournJewStud* 31 (1980), 141-156. See also Ewherido, *Matthew's Gospel and Judaism*, 198-199; and the work of Neusner quoted by Ewherido, in addition to those mentioned by Overman, that is *From Politics to Piety*, 3-43. According to Ewherido's analysis (p.199), Neusner used the term "formative Judaism" as a synonym of Rabbinic Judaism, to designate a formative era in the evolution of Judaism, which according to Neusner, spanned between 200 B.C.E. and 700 C.E., and Neusner's emphasis with the term is on the "formative" nature of Judaism during the period he studied rather than on a kind of Judaism. Ewherido also here notes that Neusner popularizes the term "formative Judaism" by dedicating a series under this title [see, Jacob Neusner *Formative Judaism: Current Issues and Argument* (2 Vols.; South Florida Studies in the History of Judaism, 133, 145; Atlanta, GA: Scholars Press 1996/1997)], to study the development of different aspects of Judaism, particularly the compilation of Jewish canon and the evolution of the Talmud during this period. It seems, therefore, that the term "Formative Judaism" coined by Neusner, has been used by other scholars like Overman to refer to the re-organization movement of the Jews shattered by the destruction of Jerusalem and the Temple in 70 C.E. It is used in the same sense in this study. Cf., Stegemann and Stegemann, *The Jesus Movement*, 222, who maintain that the term "formative Judaism" was first coined by G. F Moore, in *Judaism in the First Centuries of the Christian Era*, 7th ed. (Cambridge: Harvard University Press, 1954).

221 Nuesner, "The Formation of Rabbinic Judaism...," 22.

222 Ewherido, *Matthew's Gospel and Judaism*, 199.

223 Overman, *Matthew's Gospel and Formative Judaism*.

of the rabbis. The scribal profession also seems to be an important contributor. Besides these two groups, it is likely that even representatives of the priesthood and the nobility also played their part in this coalition. Whatever may have been the actual composition, it seems clear that the scribes and the Pharisees were the real players of power and influence.[224] Hence, the two primary components of the synthesis were those emphasized by Pharisaism before 70 C.E., namely the universal keeping of the law by every Jew, not only by the priests, and the values of the scribal profession before the same period, that is the study of the Torah and the centrality of the learned man in the religious system.[225] Here, we could posit that even among the scribes the leading participants in this movement were the Pharisaic scribes.[226] Indeed, according to Twelftree, the great Pharisaic sages like Shammai and Hillel were the famous scribes before 70 C.E., and Rabban Johannan ben Zakkai was the most distinguished scribe after the fall of Jerusalem. Gamaliel I who, according to Acts 5:34–39 and 22:3, taught Paul, was another celebrated scribe.[227] Based on this observation it is quite possible that those who are referred to as the scribes and as the rabbis by different writers, as the leading figures in formative Judaism were more or less the same people who were leaders among the Pharisees.[228] This has been indicated by Joachim Jeremias in his discussion of the scribes.

According to Jeremias, **the scribes** grew up in the last century B.C.E., and a large number of them came from both the priestly aristocracy and the ordinary priests in Jerusalem, before 70 C.E. There were also scribes from the lower orders of clergy and from the patrician families who developed the Sadducean tradition. Scribes came not only from the priests, but also from every other class of the

---

224 This is indicated by an open hostility of Matthew's gospel to these two groups. See Sim, *The Gospel of Matthew and Christian Judaism*, 113.

225 Nuesner, "The Formation of Rabbinic Judaism…," 22.

226 According to G. H. Twelftree, scribes came from various sections of the Jewish society. While some scribes came from the priestly aristocracy, others came from among the ordinary priests or members of the lower orders of clergy, and the vast majority of them came from every other section of society. They were probably associated with various sects and associations including the Pharisees, (as indicated by the phrase "scribes of the Pharisees" in Mark 2:16; and Acts 23:9). See G. H. Twelftree, "Scribes," *DJG*, edited by Joel B. Green, Scot McKnight, and I. Howard Marshall (Downers Grove, Illinois/Leicester, England: Inter Varsity Press, 1998 [1992]), 733.

227 Twelftree, "Scribes," 732.

228 Cf., according to Anthony J. Saldarini, on the basis of the contents and development of the Mishna, compiled at the end of the second century, soon after 70 C.E., the rabbis were a small group formed by a coalition of scribes, Pharisees, priests, and landowners, who were interested in preserving and interpreting the practice of Judaism without the Temple, and who were seeking to define Judaism in new circumstances. But, they were not leaders in control of the community. A. J. Saldarini, "Delegitimation of Leaders in Matthew 23," *CathBibQuart* 54 (1992), 663.

people, far outnumbering the rest. Only knowledge, not their origin gave power to the scribes.[229]

Jeremias also says that a scribe had the right to be called **Rabbi**, as it is clearly indicated in Matt 23:7-8 that this title was already used for scribes at the time of Jesus.[230] And, "apart from the chief priests and members of patrician families the scribe was the only person who could enter the Supreme Court, the Sanhedrin." And, "**the Pharisaic party in the Sanhedrin was composed entirely of scribes**."[231]

Further, Jeremias says that while "the scribes were venerated, like the prophets of old, with unbounded respect and reverential awe, as bearers and teachers of sacred esoteric knowledge; ... the Pharisaic communities especially gave their scribes unconditional obedience, and **Pharisaic scribes were by far the most numerous**."[232]

Therefore, this reorganization movement in the aftermath of the war could be seen as basically a Pharisaic movement under the leadership of the scribes and rabbis who were most probably distinguished members / sages among the Pharisees. This understanding does not rule out, however, the possibility for the scribes from other sections of the society (other than the Pharisees) also to have taken active part in the movement. Therefore, following the available sources for this study, in the further discussions relating to this subject, we will continue to use the terms Pharisees, scribes, and rabbis. However, it would be right to understand the two terms, scribes and rabbis, as more or less interchangeable in this specific context, representing the Pharisaic leaders of this reorganization movement; and also to see the movement as basically a Pharisaic movement.[233]

As mentioned earlier, most of the high priestly class of Sadducees perished along with the destruction of Jerusalem and the temple, and the priests lost their influence. Even the Essenes were never heard of any more.[234] Among the major Jewish sects mentioned by Josephus before the catastrophe,[235] only the Pharisees

---

229 Jeremias, *Jerusalem in the Time of Jesus*, 233-236. Bolds are mine.

230 *Ibid.*, 236. Bold is mine.

231 *Ibid.* Bolds are mine.

232 *Ibid.*, 243. Bolds are mine.

233 Indeed, W. D. Davies and Dale C. Allison, Jr., maintain that "it was the Pharisees, first under Johannan ben Zakkai and later under Gamaliel II, who undertook to preserve and reform the Judaism that survived the war with Rome." Davies and Allison, Jr., *Matthew*, Vol. III, 693.

234 According to W. D. Davies, the Essenes were decimated although Essenism did not die in 70 C.E., and its movement was not subsequently aggressive enough to constitute a menace. See Davies, *The Setting of the Sermon on the Mount*, 259.

235 Josephus mentions that there were three philosophical sects in Judaism such as Pharisees, Sadducees and Essenes. See, Josephus, *Wars of the Jews*, ii. viii. 2 in *Josephus: Complete Works*, 476. For a detailed discussion on the Essenes, see Sanders, *Judaism: Practice and Belief*, 341-379.

survived the disaster and thus became the major player in the reorganization of the Jews who were disorganized by the war.[236]

For the instruction of their own members in their daily life and relations, the Pharisees had developed a system well before 70 C.E., which centred on the application of the laws of purity around the home and table. Though they used temple imagery in their program, a temple was not required for the execution of that program. Such a program placed them in a good position to gain influence in the post-70 C.E. period. In fact, the post-70 C.E. coalition adopted the Pharisaic laws of purity, and endeavoured to apply in a much broader manner to all the Jews.[237] In addition to the laws of purity, another attraction of the Pharisees could be their teaching on Messianic hope, with their teaching on the supremacy of Israel and the belief in the resurrection of the dead, which were implied in the Messianic hope. These ideals, which had been cherished by apocalyptists, added appeal to Pharisaic teachings because, although such an expectation was there even before, the people now, in their distressed situation after the war, became occupied with more zeal to fulfil the commandment of God to be worthy of the future glory which they confidently believed would be theirs.[238] However, the Pharisees maintained in their teaching that God would bring all such things to pass in His own good time, and the most important thing at present for God's people was to fulfil His will, which was set forth in the Law. This combination of the importance of purity laws for the present reinforced by future hope taught by the Pharisees made it easier for the people, who were in a situation of disillusionment, to accept them.[239]

Based on scholars' reconstructions from later traditions, the centre of this coalition movement was said to be the imperial city of Jamnia, although there is no documentary proof from its own time.[240] It has been said that the Jerusalem Sanhedrin was restored there, but only as a faculty of law, by the Pharisaic

236 Davies and Allison, Jr., *Matthew*, Vol. III, 692-693.

237 Overman, *Matthew's Gospel and Formative Judaism*, 35-37.

238 Schürer, *The History of the Jewish People*, 288-289.

239 Oesterley, *A History of Israel*, 456.

240 Jack P. Lewis mentions that there is no contemporary documents on the Yavneh (Jamnia) period, and "an account of actions of Yavneh must be drawn from sources redacted at a later period without any objective way to know how much the information has been distorted in the process of transmission." Lewis further says, "the extant materials do not permit writing biographies of any of the participants of the gatherings. The sources are at variance on details with each other." Therefore, "the nature of the sources makes it impossible to be specific about the nature of the Yavneh gatherings as well as specific about their enactments, especially in the ... canon, text, and the exclusion of Christians." See Jack. P. Lewis, "Jamnia (Jabneh), Council of," *ABD*, Vol. 3 (New York: Doubleday, 1992), 635. This shows that scholars depend mainly on the later traditions for their reconstruction of the Jamnia period. Although, it may be difficult to accept the detail stories about the activities of the rabbis at Jamnia due to lack of documentary proof of its own time, it seems that one cannot deny the fact that it was the centre of the Jewish renewal movement, after the catastrophe of the war, under the leadership

Rabbis.[241] Rabban Johanan ben Zakkai became the first president of this school of law during the first decade after the destruction of the Jerusalem Temple.[242] The Jamnia period came to an end with the second Jewish Revolt against Rome under Bar Kokhba in 135 C.E.[243]

At this time, many Jews wondered why they suffered such a catastrophe and what would be their future. Most of the Jews accepted that God punished them because of their sin, and the Jewish Christian community held that Jews were punished because they rejected Jesus Christ. The Jewish apocalyptists, who blamed Israel's sin for the disaster, comforted the people by promising them immediate redemption.[244] Differing from the rest of his generation, Rabban Johanan ben Zakkai focused on the prevailing needs of the surviving remnant of Israel. Instead of promising them an immediate redemption, he called them to achieve a better fortune by their own efforts. He conceived that the fulfilment of the Jewish law, as interpreted by the Pharisees, would offer a good life in this world, and it would assure a good portion in the next life. He emphasized God's *hesed,* that is, the act of loving-kindness, as the key to atonement for the Jews. Taking Hosea 6:6 as his base, he stressed the ethical element of his trilogy, such as the study of the Torah, doing the commandments and acts of loving-kindness.[245]

As already indicated above, Rabban Johannan ben Zakkai had the base of his academy at Yavneh/Jabneh/Jamnia.[246] Under him, the academy was just beginning on a small scale, but it assumed larger dimensions under Rabban

---

of the rabbis. With the acceptance of this fact, this study subscribes to scholars' reconstruction of the rabbis' activities at Jamnia, especially because there seems to be no better alternatives.

241 W. D. Davies, however, observes that while it is misleading to think of the Sanhedrin at Jamnia as the one before 70 C.E., which had political connotations, at the same time, it is not to be thought of as only a kind of an academic school. In spite of their pre-occupation with the study of the Torah, the Sages "could have never been tempted to forget that the Torah was given that men might *live* thereby," and therefore, "although they never called themselves as Sanhedrin, they exercised as many of the functions of that now extinct body as they could." See Davies, *The Setting of the Sermon on the Mount*, 294.

242 See the following - Reicke, *The New Testament Era*, 266-267, 287; Schürer, *The History of the Jewish* People, 284; Oesterley, *A History of Israel*, 456-457; Neusner, *Judaism in the Beginning of Christianity*, 89. With slight differentiation in the titles such as Rab, Rabbi, and Rabban, Moore says that Rabbi is greater than Rab (which is the Babylonian distinction from Palestinian Rabbi), and Rabban is greater than Rabbi. It means 'our master' or 'great master.' Still greater than Rabban is the man's bare name, such as for example, Hillel. See Moore, *Judaism in the First Century of the Christian Era*, Vol. III, 16.

243 Lewis, "Jamnia (Jabneh), Council of," 635.

244 Neusner, *Judaism in the Beginning of Christianity*, 89-91; see also Neusner, *From Politics to Piety*, 2-3.

245 Neusner, *Judaism in the Beginning of Christianity*, 90, 93-98. See also Davies, *The Setting of the Sermon on the Mount*, 256ff.

246 These three names are used interchangeably. See Lewis, "Jamnia (Jabneh), Council of," 634.

Gamaliel II, who succeeded him[247] and who worked until the beginning of the second century C.E. It is said that a band of scholars were working with him. Gamaliel II had highly celebrated contemporaries such as R. Joshua ben Chananja and R. Elieser ben Hyrcanus. These men had younger contemporaries and pupils such as R. Ishmael, R. Akiba and R. Tarphon.[248] These men, with their numerous colleagues and scholars, carried on the interpretation of the law with greater zeal than ever.[249] In fact, the Pharisaic tradition of legal interpretation, as advanced by this rabbinic school at Jamnia, eventually won dominance over rival methods of expounding the law.[250] After the political overthrow, the care of the law seemed to have taken the centre stage where the whole strength of the nation had concentrated as its own highest and proper task. Thus, these scholars dealt with painful particularity on everything pertaining to the law, such as the civil and criminal law, as well as the manifold religious statutes and ordinances, and the teachers drilled them into the memories of their scholar pupils. Without taking into account whether the circumstances of the time permitted these ordinances to be put into practice or not, they discussed diligently and earnestly all the minutiae of the temple service, the entire ritual of the sacrificial worship, as well as the laws of purifying, the Sabbath commandment, and other religious duties, which were still possible to be observed.[251] The task of fixing the calendar, probably the only

247 Gedalyahu Alon, *Jews, Judaism and the Classical World. Studies in Jewish History in the Times of the Second Temple and Talmud*, translated from Hebrew by Israel Abrahams (Jerusalem: the Magnes Press, the Hebrew University, 1977), 295. Here (see, pp. 269-313; 314-343), Alon discusses in detail why Rabban Johannan ben Zakkai had his base at Jabneh. He contends that Johannan and other Jewish settlers were the ones who surrendered to the Romans, whom the later sent there not because they desired, but against their will (see p. 294). He further maintains (in pp. 314-317) that Rabban Johannan ben Zakkai officiated there as Patriarch, for two facts indicate this: First, the title "Rabban" accorded to him by tradition everywhere is restricted to the Patriarchs only. Second, tradition attributes nine enactments to Johannan ben Zakkai, and such ordinances could have been instituted only by a Patriarch in the second Temple period.

248 Schürer, *The History of the Jewish People*, 285. See also Reicke, *The New Testament Era*, 288.

249 Schürer, *The History of the Jewish People,* 285.

250 Goodman, *The Ruling Class of Judea*, 234. Here, Goodman opines that it probably took many years before this dominance was achieved. However, W. D. Davies and Dale C. Allison, Jr., seem to be true in noting, giving certain analogies, that a cataclysmic events such as the revolt against Rome in 66 C.E. and the collapse of the Jewish state in 70 C.E. could have produced much more rapid changes "than scholars accustomed to the leisurely contemplation of historical events recognize." Therefore, it might have not taken such a long time for the Pharisees to establish their dominance among the Jews after the war, especially where there was a large vacuum in the Jewish society with the disappearance of the zealots, the Essenes, the Sadducees and the priests. See Davies and Allison, Jr., *Matthew*, Vol. III, 700-701.

251 Schürer, *The History of the Jewish People,* 285.
According to W. D. Davies and Dale C. Allison, Jr., there were four prominent questions with which the Pharisees had to deal with. 1) What is the identity of the people of God without state or temple? The answer of the Pharisees emphasized obedience to Torah. 2) The

remaining function of the High Priest after the destruction of the temple, was also taken up by the rabbinic leaders. It was very important for all pious Jews to know that they had celebrated the important festivals, for example, the Day of Atonement on the right day, because it would be a heinous sin to err. It may well be that the rabbinic leaders' definitive guidance about the calendar was one of the important instruments toward their eventual winning of authority over the Jewish population.[252]

The Jews now piously regarded the duties prescribed by the rabbis as obligatory without question, especially since the priests, who were previously responsible for such prescriptions, had been relegated to a condition of inactivity. The rabbis were now recognized not only as lawgivers in spiritual and temporal things, but they were also appealed to as judges in all matters of dispute.[253]

Toward the end of the first century and in the beginning of the second century C.E., the court of law at Jamnia enjoyed its highest reputation. Even though they could scarcely have had any formal recognition from the Roman authorities, a college of learned men actually stepped into the old Sanhedrin of Jerusalem, as the supreme court of law for Israel. Indeed, they seemed to have copied the Sanhedrin of Jerusalem even in the number of members. It has been mentioned in some place that R. Eleasar ben Asariah was appointed as president by the seventy-two elders.[254] The decisions on points of law, including ceremonial, civil and criminal law, issuing from this faculty of law were treated as constituting the authoritative standard.[255]

The influence of the Pharisaic rabbis in Jamnia was not confined within Palestine. All the Jews in the Roman Empire were dependent upon them and the scribes followed a policy of establishing uniformity along Pharisaic lines for all the Jews. Accordingly, Gamaliel II (the second president of the scribal school at Jamnia after Johanan ben Zakkai) is said to have laid down basic norms for defining the canon of Scripture, obviously for all the Jews, for recognizing the Halakha of Hillel, and for the compulsory recitation of the Eighteen Benedictions

---

second question is, What is Torah? The response of the Pharisees insisted upon the centrality of the oral Torah according to the House of Hillel. 3) The third question pertains to the relation between Jews and Gentiles. The Pharisees responded with requiring isolation from and continued rejection of Gentile ways. 4) The fourth question is what should one think of the Messiah and eschatology? The Pharisaic answer is symbolized by the *Birkat-ha-minim*: the Messiah had not come. Davies and Allison also maintain that the four questions are equally pertinent to the Jewish believers in Jesus, and Matthew's gospel, if carefully read, reveals that the author was acutely aware of these issues. Indeed, "the First Gospel is partly Matthew's response to them." Davies and Allison, Jr., *Matthew*, Vol. III, 701.

252 Davies, *The Setting of the Sermon on the Mount*, 261ff. See also Goodman, *The Ruling Class of Judea*, 235.

253 Schürer, *The History of the Jewish People*, 286.

254 *Ibid.*, 286-287, quoting *Sebachim*, i. 3; *Jadajim*, iii. 5, iv. 2.

255 Schürer, *The History of the Jewish People*, 287.

in the synagogue.[256] It is also said that the last two lines of the Benediction were added by Samuel the Small under Gamaliel II. The scribes also introduced a rabbinic school tax of two drachmas, as a replacement of the priestly temple tax and it competed with the Emperor's tax. This rabbinic double drachma was said to be a free will contribution and it was only gradually introduced throughout the Roman Empire. The responsibility of collecting and forwarding this fund was laid upon the agents of the synagogues, called "apostles." These agents sent the annual contributions of the Jewish communities until the third and fourth centuries to the president or chief rabbi of the Palestinian school, who bore the honorific title of "prince," "ethnarch," or "patriarch." In this matter, the place of the priests was taken by the rabbis. All this policy of the scribes contributed to the Pharisaic intensification of Judaism, and it distinguished practicing Jews from the outside world.[257]

A very important development strongly implied in this coalition movement was an integrative process in which the overcoming of the previous separation of Judaism into groups was emphasized above all.[258] This integrating process resulted in the exclusion of Jewish groups, which were not representing the majority consensus, including the followers of Jesus Christ.[259] It was in this context that

---

256 Cf., however, the assertion that the canon of the Hebrew Scripture was closed at Jamnia, has been questioned. See James A. Sanders, "Canon [Hebrew Bible]," *ABD*, Vol. 1 (New York: Doubleday, 1992), 841. See also Lewis, "Jamnia (Jabneh), Council of," 636. Therefore, we do not necessarily support the assertion of the closure of the Hebrew Scripture's canon at Jamnia, here. We are only mentioning what is said in some place in connection with the influence of the rabbis in Jamnia.

257 See the following - Reicke, *The New Testament Era*, 288-289; Schürer, *The History of the Jewish People*, 288; Davies, *The Setting of the Sermon on the Mount*, 273ff.

258 The Post-exilic Israel, particularly Hellenistic-Roman period was characterized by group formations such as Sadducees, Pharisees, Essenes, etc. This was followed in the Roman-Herodian Period by emergence of a number of prominent prophetic-charismatic movements, religio-political and socio-revolutionary movements. For a more detailed discussion, see Stegemann and Stegemann, *The Jesus Movement,* 138-222.
W. D. Davies and Dale C. Allison, Jr., note that a major concern of the Pharisees at this juncture was to deal with the disunity among the Jews, and therefore in their effort to reconstruct the Jewish faith "they sought to end sectarianism and so hold together and reconcile the various factions and divisions within the ranks of Jews as a people." Then Davies and Allison mention four steps taken by the Pharisees among several tasks, which are pertinent for interpreting Matthew. To mention them briefly – 1) they sought to undo domestic divisions among themselves, particularly between Hillelites and Shammaites; 2) the heirs of the Pharisees began the process of collecting their oral laws; 3) they recognized certain religious necessities. Particularly they sought to establish a standard calendar for the Jewish religious year, and they tried to transfer to the synagogues rites previously performed in the Temple; and 4) the rabbis most probably formulated or expanded the *Birkat-ha-minim*, to make heretics feel unwelcome, and also probably in part to bar Jewish Christians from officiating at synagogue services. Davies and Allison, Jr., *Matthew*, Vol. III, 693-694.

259 This is indicated in the new formulation of the so-called *Birkat ha-minim* "heretic benediction." See, Overman, *Matthew's Gospel and Formative Judaism*, 51 [48-56]. See also the following -

the antagonism between the leaders of formative Judaism and the Matthean community arose. This will be discussed further. Before that, however, we will try to see how this movement entered Antioch in Syria, which is the suggested location of Matthew's community in this study.

1.4.2. Influence of Formative Judaism upon the Jews in Antioch

If Antioch is the most plausible location for the origin of Matthew's gospel as is argued above, and if the gospel was written in the social milieu of the emerging formative Judaism as is contended in this study, then it is necessary to see how formative Judaism operated in Antioch or how it influenced the Jews in Antioch. It seems that there is no direct information on this question. Therefore, the connection between formative Judaism and the Jews in Antioch has to be reconstructed from other known facts as well as from the speculations of some scholars.

It has been mentioned above that the leaders of formative Judaism did not confine their influence within Palestine, but they exerted their influence throughout the Roman Empire, and accordingly all the Jews were dependent upon them. It has also been pointed out that the rabbinic school tax of two drachmas, introduced by the scribes, was also eventually imposed throughout the Roman Empire, and the agents of the synagogues called "apostles" were given responsibility to collect and send it to the president or chief rabbi of the rabbinic school in Palestine. In this connection, we can safely assume that Antioch of Syria would have been the main attraction to the Pharisees and scribes to exert their authority outside Palestine because of the huge Jewish population in this city, and because of its proximity to Palestine. We could now recollect what has been mentioned in this regard, that Antioch was the third largest city in the first century Roman Empire, after Rome and Alexandria.[260] Because of its proximity to Palestine and because of its size it had a huge Jewish population, and in fact, during the first century, the largest Jewish population in the Syrian province was found in Antioch.[261] It is safe to assume, following David C. Sim, that in the midst of such a large Jewish population scribes and Pharisees were almost certainly present in Antioch even before the Jewish war, and more scribes and Pharisees would have come as refugees after the war and quickly consolidated their position and come into conflict with Matthew's community.[262] There could have been a problem between the two parties even before the war. More probable, however, is that the problem

---

Reuven Kimelman, "Birkat haminim and the Lack of Evidence for an Anti-Christian Jewish Prayer in Late Antiquity," in *Jewish and Christian Self-Definition*, edited by E. P. Sanders, et al., Vol. 2 (Philadelphia: Fortress Press, 1981), 226-244; Davies, *The Setting of the Sermon on the Mount*, 274-277.

260 See Josephus, *Wars of the Jews*, III. II. 4, in *Josephus. Complete Works*, 503.

261 See Josephus, *Wars of the Jews*, VII. IV. 3, VII. V. 2, in *Josephus. Complete Works*, 591.

262 Sim, *The Gospel of Matthew and Christian Judaism*, 115, 151.

began when those refugees after the war came to Antioch and claimed leadership over the Jewish community, including the Matthean community there, which, although it had some Gentiles among its members, was basically a community of Jewish and Jewish-oriented Gentile Christians.[263] The antagonism between these two parties will be looked at more closely now.

1.4.3. The Antagonism between Matthew's Community and Formative Judaism

Based on most of the recent major studies on the social context of Matthew's gospel, it is maintained in this study that Matthew's community was composed of Jewish Christians and Jewish-oriented Gentile Christians.[264] Therefore, the conflict between formative Judaism and Matthew's community also was mainly a conflict within Judaism.[265] The central issues over which the conflict ensued seem to be the messianic status of Jesus and the proper interpretation of the Law.[266] Since the Gentile members of the community were simply following the Jewish Christians' interpretation of the Law and the messianic status of Jesus Christ, we could fairly assume that the Jewish leaders were mainly in opposition to the Jewish Christians because of their differing interpretation of the Law and their bestowal of messianic status to Jesus. Apart from this basic factor, however, there were also other issues, which added to the hostility of the Jewish leaders against the Jewish members of the Matthean community. First, the presence of the Gentiles in the Matthean community raised doubts among the Jews (the synagogue) about the faithfulness of the Jewish Christian members of the Matthean community to Israel's belief in one God.[267] Second, it has been said that Christians were scattered from Jerusalem when the Jewish War against Rome (66-73 C.E.) began, thus not standing with the other Jews in the Revolt. This seems to have increased the antipathy of the Jews in Jerusalem and in Antioch.[268] Therefore, we would assume with confidence that because of all these factors, leaders of formative Judaism (i.e., the Jewish leaders) were hostile to the Matthean community. Matthew's

263 Sim, *The Gospel of Matthew and Christian Judaism*, 151. Here, Sim's view is that the community was composed of basically Jews with few Gentile proselytes. However, this study assumes that there were also other Gentile adherents who were not proselytized to Judaism, but were Jewish-oriented by following some of the Jewish practices. This picture will become clearer when we come to the sub-section "the Ethnic Composition of Matthew's Community."

264 See the section of "the Ethnic Composition of Matthew's Community" below.

265 Sim, *The Gospel of Matthew and Christian Judaism*, 163.

266 Jack Dean Kingsbury, "Conclusion: Analysis of Conversion," in *The Social History of the Matthean Community. Cross-Disciplinary Approaches*, edited by David L. Balch (Minneapolis: Fortress Press, 1991), 265. See also Sim, *The Gospel of Matthew and Christian Judaism*, 139, 151.

267 Brown, *An Introduction to the New Testament*, 214, n. 93. See also DeSilva, *An Introduction to the New Testament*, 238.

268 Brown, *An Introduction to the New Testament*, 214.

gospel indicates that there was a serious antagonism between these two groups, and formative Judaism got the upper hand in this conflict. As a result, Matthew's community suffered various kinds of persecutions in the hands of the Jewish leaders and their supporters.[269] We will now briefly look at the indications of the conflict between Matthew's community and formative Judaism, and the afflictions faced by the former in the hands of the latter.

1.4.3.1. *Indications of Conflict between Matthew's Community and Formative Judaism*

The most explicit indication of the conflict between Matthew's community and formative Judaism can be seen in the negative reaction of the scribes and the Pharisees, who were the leaders of formative Judaism, to the mission of Jesus; as well as in Jesus' response to those events by denouncing the scribes and Pharisees in the harshest of tones, in Matthew's gospel.

The negative reaction of the scribes and the Pharisees to Jesus and his mission in Matthew's gospel can be seen as follows.[270] They charge Jesus with blasphemy (9:3).[271] They think evil of Jesus (9:4).[272] They attack Jesus for eating with sinners (9:11).[273] They charge Jesus with demon possession (9:34; 12:24).[274] They attack Jesus for breaking the law (12:2; 15:1-2).[275] They plot to kill Jesus (12:14).[276] They are offended by Jesus' teachings (15:12).[277] They test Jesus (19:3; 22:15-16; 22:34-35).[278]

---

269 This is acknowledged in most of the recent studies on the social setting of Matthew's community. See for example, Sim, *The Gospel of Matthew and Christian Judaism*, 109; Stegemann and Stegemann, *The Jesus Movement*, 236-237.

270 Cf., Sim, *The Gospel of Matthew and Christian Judaism*, 119.

271 Matt 9:3 - "*Then some of the scribes said to themselves, 'This man is blaspheming.'*"

272 Matt 9:4- "*But Jesus, perceiving their thoughts, said, 'Why do you think evil in your hearts?'*"

273 Matt 9:11- "*When the Pharisees saw this, they said to his disciples, 'Why does your teacher eat with tax collectors and sinners?'*"

274 Matt 9:34; 12:24- "*But the Pharisees said, "By the ruler of the demons he casts out the demons.'*"; 12:24 – "*But when the Pharisees heard it, they said, 'It is only by Beelzebul, the ruler of the demons, that this fellow casts out the demons.'*"

275 Matt 12:2; 15:1-2 -"*When the Pharisees saw it, they said to him, 'Look, your disciples are doing what is not lawful to do on the Sabbath*"; cf. 15:1-2 – "*Then Pharisees and scribes came to Jesus from Jerusalem and said, 2 'Why do your disciples break the tradition of the elders? For they do not wash their hands before they eat.'*"

276 Matt 12:14- *But the Pharisees went out and conspired against him, how to destroy him.*"

277 Matt 15:12-"*Then the disciples approached and said to him, 'Do you know that the Pharisees took offence when they heard what you said?'*"

278 Matt 19:3; 22:15-16, 34-35- "*Some Pharisees came to him, and to test him they asked, 'Is it lawful for a man to divorce his wife for any cause?*"; 22:15-16 – "*Then the Pharisees went and plotted to entrap him in what he said. 16 So they sent their disciples to him, along with the Herodians, saying, 'Teacher, we know that you are sincere, and teach the way of God in accordance with truth, and show deference to no one; for you do not regard people with partiality*'", 22: 34-35 – "*When*

These negative reactions of the scribes and the Pharisees to Jesus and his mission are mainly retained by Matthew from his two sources Mark and Q, without changing the tone, except in two places. Matthew's statement in 15:12, that the Pharisees were offended by Jesus' teaching, is unique to Matthew, and Matthew heightens the tone in 22:35 from Q (Luke 10:25) by making it explicit that the lawyer who tested Jesus was a member of the Pharisees.

However, amongst the unsympathetic responses of the Matthean Jesus to the scribes and the Pharisees, only a very few of them are retained by Matthew from his source Mark and Q without changing the tone, while he considerably heightens a good number of them. Furthermore, a large number of them are unique to Matthew. They can be seen as follows:[279] He describes the scribes and the Pharisees as a brood of vipers (3:7; *12:34*; 23:33); as hypocrites (15:7; *22:18*; *23:13, 15, 23, 25, 27-29*; cf. *6:2, 5, 16*; 23:3); as blind men (*15:14*; *23:16, 17, 19, 24, 26*); as children of Gehenna (*23:15*). Besides, the Matthean Jesus accuses them - of lacking righteousness (*5:20*); of placing their own tradition before the will of God (**15:2-3**; **23:15-26**); of failing to practice what they preach (**23:3, 27-29**); of placing intolerable burdens on others (*23:4*); of soliciting admiration (23:5-7); and even of committing murder (**23:29-36**; cf. *22:6*). Jesus also accuses them, as a result of their leadership roles, of leading the people astray (**15:14**); of preventing the people from entering the kingdom of heaven (*23:13*); of making the people twice as much children of Gehenna as they are (*23:15*). Jesus singles out the scribes (**9:4**) and the Pharisees (*12:34*; cf. **22:18**) as being evil. Jesus also labels them as the appropriate leaders of "this evil generation" because they themselves are inherently evil and are in league with Satan (**12:38-42**; **16:1-4**).[280]

In fact, while one is obliged to acknowledge on the basis of the two-document hypothesis, that Matthew draws a good deal of his anti-scribal and anti-Pharisaic materials from his major sources, namely Mark and Q, it is generally accepted, as also clearly indicated above, that Matthew has considerably intensified and developed what he found in his sources.[281] Such negative portrayals of scribes and

the Pharisees heard that he had silenced the Sadducees, they gathered together, 35 and one of them, a lawyer, asked him a question to test him."

279 Here, those underlined are taken by Matthew without changing the tone. Those put in **bold** are what he heightens the tone from his source. Those *italicized* are Matthew's unparalleled version. They are mentioned in this way here for easy identification. Since the references are too many, the texts will not be mentioned here.

280 Cf., Sim, *The Gospel of Matthew and Christian Judaism*, 119-120.

281 Sim, *The Gospel of Matthew and Christian Judaism*, 119. See also the following - Anthony J. Saldarini, "The Gospel of Matthew and Jewish-Christian Conflict," in David L. Balch, ed., *Social History of the Matthean Community. Cross-disciplinary Approaches* (Minneapolis: Augsburg, 1991), 39; Saldarini, "Delegitimation of Leaders in Matthew 23," 659-680.

Pharisees by Matthew, therefore, are understood as Matthew's description of his contemporary opponents.[282]

Besides these incidents of mutual attack between the scribes and the Pharisees on one hand and the Matthean Jesus on the other, the conflict between Matthew's community and formative Judaism is also indicated by the competition between the two groups, particularly in the response of Matthew's group to the development within formative Judaism, which can be inferred from Matthew's gospel. Overman gives a comprehensive argument in this regard,[283] and states that in the context of its competition with formative Judaism Matthew's community struggled to establish, order, and define the belief and life of the community.[284] To put it briefly, the response of Matthew's community to the developments within formative Judaism, as envisaged in Matthew's gospel, can be highlighted as follows – 1) Matthew's community developed its own gathering place, an *ekklēsia*, in response to the gathering place of formative Judaism, *autōn synagōgē*, their synagogue; 2) The disciples in Matthew's gospel resemble in significant ways the portrait of the scribes and the Pharisees in the gospel, who were leaders of formative Judaism; and the disciples were given authority analogous to that of the Pharisees, that is "to bind and to loose;" 3) Matthew claims that it is not the Jewish leadership, but his community that fulfills the law and the will of God who is in heaven.[285] In addition to these, W. D. Davies and Dale C. Allison, Jr. also note that while the Matthean community criticized Pharisaism, its parent body, at whose hands it suffered, it also emulated it. Therefore, like the Pharisees - it had prophets, wise men and scribes (10:41; 13:52); its members were to be "righteous" (5:20); and it was to engage in proselytism (23:15; 28:16-20).[286]

Matthew's gospel also indicates that because of the antagonism between the two groups, Matthew's community suffered different kinds of afflictions or persecutions[287] from formative Judaism, which can be briefly highlighted as follows.

---

282 See the following for example - Overman, *Matthew's Gospel and Formative Judaism*, 142; Sim, *The Gospel of Matthew and Christian Judaism*, 120-121.

283 For a comprehensive discussion, see Overman, *Matthew's Gospel and Formative Judaism*, 35-149.

284 Overman, *Matthew's Gospel and Formative Judaism*, 72.

285 See Overman, *Matthew's Gospel and Formative Judaism*, 152-155.

286 Davies and Allison, Jr., *Matthew*, Vol. III, 697. Cf. Gabriele Boccaccini, *Middle Judaism: Jewish Thought, 300 B.C.E. to 200 B.C.E.* (Minneapolis: Fortress, 1991), 7-25, who contends that prior to the second Jewish revolt in 135 C.E., Christianity and Rabbinism were two of the many forms of Judaism of their time. Therefore, the blood tie between the two is not to be conceived as parent (Rabbinism) and child (Christianity). Rather they are to be viewed as fraternal twins born of the same womb.

287 It seems that the term "persecution" is used by Matthew to characterize all the negative experiences / problems suffered by his community from the Jewish side. This is indicated in

1.4.3.2. *Persecutions Suffered by Matthew's Community in the Hands of Formative Judaism*

The main afflictions suffered by Matthew's community indicated in the gospel can be briefly stated as verbal attack (5:11-12), floggings in synagogues, deliverance to the Sanhedrin or local courts, persecution and expulsion (5:10-12, 44; 10:17, 23; 13:21; 23:34) and killings (22:6; 23:34).[288] Though scholars are not unanimous in their interpretation of these texts, it seems that all these problems can be seen as problems faced by Matthew's community from formative Judaism. Brief explanations of these different persecutions may be given as follows.

a. Verbal Attack: Matt 5:11-12 indicates that members of Matthew's community were "reviled" and "all kinds of evil" were uttered against them. According to Douglas R. A. Hare, all persecutions referred to in Matthew's gospel apply to the missionaries of Matthew's church, and those outside the missionary sphere were never involved.[289] However, such a generalization is not accepted by some scholars. It is suggested that such verbal abuses were not official acts, but were experienced by some of the Matthean community members in their day-to-day contact with people from the majority group, that is formative Judaism. The phrase "on my (Jesus') account" indicates that the reason behind such verbal denigration was their faith in Jesus, and it also suggests that those revilers also tried to defame Jesus as well.[290] Douglas Hare further maintains that the persecutors were not only the Pharisees, although their role becomes increasingly important in the later period. The Jewish community as a whole was indicted by Matthew for the rejection and ill-treatment of the Christian missionaries, who were basically Jewish Christians.[291] The reason behind the persecutions, according to Hare, was the perpetual obduracy of Israel.[292] This view holds true to some extent as it is also supported by Matthew 27:25. Matthew indicts here that the Jewish nation as a whole was responsible for the death of Jesus and this indictment is unique to Matthew. However, Matthew's strong polemics against the scribes and the Pharisees, as seen especially in Matthew chapter 23, which are very much heightened from their parallels in Mark and Luke, indicate that the Pharisees

---

Matt 5:10-12, 44; 10:23; 13:21; 23:34. See Stegemann and Stegemann, *The Jesus Movement*, 237, and 440, n. 279.

288 Stegemann and Stegemann, *The Jesus Movement*, 236-237. For a detailed study of Jewish persecution of Christians in Matthew's gospel, see Douglas Hare, *The Theme of Jewish Persecution of Christians in the Gospel according to St. Matthew.* Society for New Testament Series Monograph Series 6 (Cambridge: Cambridge University, 1967), 80-129.

289 Hare, *The Theme of Jewish Persecution,* 125, 169.

290 Sim, *The Gospel of Matthew and Christian Judaism*, 154-156. See also Stegemann and Stegemann, *The Jesus Movement*, 236-237.

291 Hare, *The Theme of Jewish Persecution,* 169.

292 *Ibid.,* 170.

and the scribes were primarily responsible for the persecutions of the Matthean community members.

b. Floggings in Synagogues, Deliverance to the Sanhedrin or Local Courts, Persecution and Expulsion (5:10-12, 44; 10:17, 23; 13:21; 23:34): All these kinds of afflictions were understood to have connections with the missionary activity of Matthew's community.[293] Sim suggests that Matthew's community had given up mission to Gentiles after the fallout between Peter and Paul in Antioch (Gal 2: 11ff.), but they faithfully carried on the mission to the Jews which was entrusted to Peter (as Paul indicated in Gal 2:7). In the course of such mission work it was inevitable to come into contact with the leaders of formative Judaism. In the situation where there was a bitter conflict between formative Judaism and Matthew's community, those missionaries were met with severe opposition, and all kinds of persecutions were inflicted upon them.[294] Sim also suggests that persecution in terms of physical injury to members of Matthew's community could happen from a few members of the opposing party even outside the missionary activity as well.[295]

c. Killings (Matt 22:6; 23:34): According to Stegemann and Stegemann, the assertion of the killing of the one sent by God, particularly in Matt 23:34, 37, is a generalization and an exaggeration of the rejection of the prophets,[296] and to infer from them anything about the historical experience of the Matthean community is extremely problematic.[297] Sim also agrees that it is difficult to establish the historical accuracy of the references made in these texts. However, Sim maintains at the same time, that such references are evidence for the intensification of the persecutions faced by the Matthean missionaries in the hands of formative Judaism in the period following the Jewish War. Because of such intensified persecution Matthew blames the leaders of Judaism, particularly the scribes and Pharisees, for all the violence which the messengers of God suffered in the past.[298]

What has become obvious at any rate is that Matthew's community suffered severe opposition, including persecutions of different kinds, in the hands of formative Judaism. Such a conflict situation underlies the writing of Matthew's gospel.[299] There has been an ongoing debate, however, whether Matthew's community was still part of the Jewish community by the time the first gospel was written or whether it had been separated from the parent body that is the Jewish community. While many scholars maintain that by the time Matthew's gospel was written the Matthean community was still part of the synagogue network

---

293 Stegemann and Stegemann, *The Jesus Movement*, 237.

294 Sim, *The Gospel of Matthew and Christian Judaism*, 157-162.

295 *Ibid.*, 156-157.

296 Cf., I Thes 2:15.

297 Stegemann and Stegemann, *The Jesus Movement*, 237.

298 Sim, *The Gospel of Matthew and Christian Judaism*, 157-162.

299 Sim, *The Gospel of Matthew and Christian Judaism*, 2.

and Judaism, many others maintain that, even though the Matthean community was still engaged in debate with the Jewish community, it had already separated itself from the Jewish community.[300] Although there is no scholarly consensus on the issue, it seems that the Matthean community was recently separated from the Jewish community when the first gospel was written, and it was still in a very close contact with it.[301]

1.4.4. Matthew's Community and the Gentiles

It has often been understood in general that Matthew's gospel, in spite of its overwhelming Jewish nature, is also characterised by a positive presentation of the Gentiles. Several passages of the gospel have been interpreted to support this understanding. The gospel texts that have been usually taken for this thought are – the description of Jesus as the son of Abraham, the father of all nations (1:1); the inclusion of four Gentile women in the genealogy such as Tamar, Rahab, Ruth and Bathsheba/the wife of Uriah (1:3, 5, 6); the story of the Magi worshipping the infant Jesus (2:1-12); two of the formula quotations (4:15-16; 12:18-21); the healing of the centurion's son (8:5-13); Jesus' visit to and work of miracles in the Gentile regions of Gadara (8:28-34), Tyre and Sidon (15:21-39); the healing of the daughter of a Canaanite woman (15:22-28); Parables of the kingdom (21:28-22:14); the Gentile centurion's confession (27:54); and Jesus' command to evangelize all nations (28:19).[302]

However, some scholars see Matthew's gospel as strongly anti-Gentile. As examples of this view, we will briefly highlight the arguments of S. G. F. Brandon and David C. Sim. S. G. F. Brandon, repudiating B. H. Streeter's suggestion that Matthew's gospel represents a compromise between James' ideas and Paul's ideas under the mediation of Peter,[303] argues that the apparent liberalism of the gospel may be easily exaggerated and misinterpreted, although there is no doubt about its Judaistic side. Brandon points out that Judaistic interest is displayed throughout the gospel, and the strongest piece of evidence of liberalism, that is the commission of the Apostles by the Risen Lord to evangelize all nations (28:19),

300 For an analysis of these two positions and their proponents and supporters, see Ewherido, *Matthew's Gospel and Judaism*, 20-27.

301 This is suggested by some of the Matthean passages, such as for example, Matthew's redaction of Mark's reference to synagogues and scribes by qualifying them as *their* synagogues and *their* scribes (see for example, Matt 10:17; cf. Mark 13:9; Matt 9:35; cf., Mark 6:2; Matt 12:9; cf. Mark 3:1; Matt 13:54; cf., Mark 6:2; Matt 7:29; cf. Mark 1:22), indicating that Matthew was distancing his community from the Jewish leadership. For this and for further analysis, see Ewherido, *Matthew's Gospel and Judaism*, 24-25, and the corresponding endnotes in 41-42.

302 See the following for example - F. J. Matera, *Passion Narratives and Gospel Theologies: Interpreting the Synoptics through their Passion Stories* (New York: Paulist Press, 1986), 137-139; R.T. France, *Matthew: Evangelist and Teacher* (Grand Rapids: Zondervan, 1989), 232-235; Kingsbury, *Matthew as Story*, 151.

303 Streeter, *The Four Gospels*, 512-516.

is also qualified by the words: "teaching them to observe all things whatsoever I commanded you" (28:20). Moreover, Brandon finds the uncompromising nature of Jewish interest in various sayings of Christ, such as, "I was sent only to the lost sheep of the house of Israel" (15:24); "Go nowhere among the Gentiles, and enter no town of the Samaritans" (10:5); "When you are praying, do not heap up empty phrases as the Gentiles do; for they think that they will be heard because of their many words" 6:7 (cf. 18:17); and "Do not give what is holy to dogs; and do not throw your pearls before swine, or they will trample them under foot and turn and maul you" (7:6) which is probably said in reference to the Gentiles. Because of all such sayings, Brandon contends that the gospel of Matthew "can scarcely be regarded as designed to conciliate Gentile Christians."[304] Brandon brings out his arguments for the anti-Gentile nature of Matthew's gospel mainly to refute Streeter's proposal of Antioch as the location of this gospel and to suggest Alexandria instead. According to him, the first Jewish war against Rome (66-73 C.E.) resulted in the downfall of the mother church of Jerusalem, and this downfall resulted in the rehabilitation of Paul in the Gentile churches. However, the Alexandrian church, a Jewish church, was strengthened by the passing of the mother church of Jerusalem. Matthew's gospel was produced by this reinvigorated church, and one of the main concerns behind its composition was to respond to the rehabilitation of Paul by the Gentile churches, "and the challenge which this fact implied to the essentially nationalistic factor in Jewish Christianity."[305] For Brandon, the anti-Gentile attitude and anti-Pauline attitude of the first gospel go together. While mentioning all these, our main interest here is to highlight Brandon's stand for the anti-Gentile attitude of the first gospel.

More recently, David C. Sim offers fresh arguments and further elaboration on the anti-Gentile attitude of the first gospel. He strongly questions the interpretations of those texts mentioned above that show the first evangelist as completely pro-Gentile. According to him, a fresh examination of these texts shows that they are not so much pro-Gentile as they are often thought to be. Rather, the narratives of the gospel contain both positive and negative attitudes toward

304 Brandon, *The Fall of Jerusalem and the Christian Church*, 219.

305 *Ibid.*, 226. Brandon, here, mentions two other major problems facing the Alexandrian Christians, which, according to him, were also the main influencing factors for the writing and shaping of Matthews gospel. (1) The overthrow of the Jewish nation and the destruction of their sacred city, Jerusalem, with its Temple was a grievous blow to the national faith and pride of the Jewish Christians. As a result, it became imperative for those who retained their faith in Christ even under the impact of such calamity, to readjust their ideas and their outlook. They also were required to find some explanation for the overthrow of their nation by the heathen, which would square with their faith in Jesus as the Messiah and their conviction of the essentiality of Judaism. (2) "The failure of their own people to accept the person and mission of Jesus raised more acutely than ever the question of the admittance into the church of those Gentiles who were willing to accept Jesus as their Lord." Therefore, Brandon maintains that it was in that mental atmosphere of the Jewish Christians and in response to such needs, that Matthew's gospel was produced.

the Gentiles.[306] Moreover, a closer examination of the anti-Gentile statements in Matthew, which have often been either down played or ignored, such as 5:46-47; 6:31-32; 6:7-8; 18:15-17, offers the true picture of Matthew's attitude towards the Gentiles.[307] It could be inferred from these texts that "Matthew and his readers viewed the Gentile world as a foreign place with foreign practices, and that they had minimal contact with the local Gentile society."[308] This means that Matthew's community was following a policy to avoid or shun its Gentile neighbours. The reason behind such a negative attitude towards the Gentiles, according to Sim, is that in addition to the suspicion of and contempt for the irreligious "pagan" world, which the community had from its Jewish heritage, the community had experienced persecution and oppression at the hands of certain Gentiles.[309] So, according to Sim, there are two main texts in Matthew that point to this situation. First, the mission discourse in Matt 10:17-22 indicates that because of their mission (to the Jews) Matthew's community suffered persecution from both the Jews and the Gentiles. Sim maintains that Matt 10:18 clearly refers to official Gentile persecution, and Matthew's addition of kai. toi/j e;qnesin (*and to the Gentiles/nations*) "is intended to make the further point that these Gentile officials conduct their persecution on behalf of the whole Gentile world." This point is reinforced in v. 22 where Matthew says (following Mark) that these missionaries will be hated by all because of Jesus' name.[310] Second, according to Sim, the Gentile persecution of the Matthean community is also clearly indicated in the apocalyptic discourse in Matt 24: 4-14. In this discourse the events listed in vv. 4-10 had already taken place, those events in vv. 11-12 were currently taking place, and the events in vv. 13-14 were still expected. Especially, v. 9 refers to tribulation, martyrdom and hatred by all nations for the sake of Jesus' name. Matthew's redaction of Mark (13:9) in this verse is seen in the references to tribulation and death, and in his expansion of Mark's "hated by all" to "hated by all the nations." These redactional alterations point to violent persecution under the perpetration of the Gentiles. Since this material refers to the past events, it indicates that Matthew's community had suffered severe persecution in the hands of the Gentiles. It was because of all such situations that Matthew's community had a negative attitude toward the Gentiles.[311] The events, which Matthew here refers to, were obviously the Gentile persecutions of the Jews in Antioch during and after the Jewish rebellion against Rome (66-73 C.E.), because these were the only known historical events, which match all the criteria, found in these texts.

306 Sim, *The Gospel of Matthew and Christian Judaism*, 218 [218-226].

307 *Ibid.*, 231 [226-231].

308 *Ibid.*, 231.

309 *Ibid.*, 231-232.

310 *Ibid.*, 232.

311 *Ibid.*, 232-233.

During these times, the community of Matthew was living among other Jews, sharing the same fear and trepidation with other Jews in Antioch.[312]

Thus, both Brandon and Sim see Matthew as strongly anti-Gentile, although they present different ideas on the reasons behind this anti-Gentile attitude. For Brandon, it was mainly a response of the re-invigorated Jewish church in Alexandria to the rehabilitation of Paul by the Gentile churches, as well as to respond to the challenge, which that rehabilitation implied to the essentially nationalistic factor in Jewish Christianity. However, for Sim, the anti-Gentile attitude of Matthew was mainly because the Matthean community in Antioch was sharing the same fear and trepidation with other Jews in Antioch during and after the Jewish rebellion against Rome (66-73 C.E.). Sim's argument seems to have more weight than Brandon's, which meets with certain problems, as discussed above.[313]

While Brandon and Sim offer important insights on the negative view of Matthew's gospel toward the Gentiles, it seems that they overstate this aspect and understate the positive view of the gospel toward the Gentiles. This is clearly highlighted by Donald Senior and it is not necessary to be repeated here.[314] However, a highly probable situation is that, as Sim suggests, Matthew's community lived in a close proximity with Gentiles and they had suffered, were suffering, and were in fear of suffering further persecutions from their Gentile neighbours. This is especially indicated by Matt 10:16-22 and 24:4-14. The official Gentile persecution is mentioned in 10:18, and it is taken over by Matthew from Mark. However, Matthew adds "*and the Gentiles/nations*" in 10:18, thus intensifying the connection of this persecution to the Gentiles (Cf. Mark 13:9 and Luke 21:12).[315] And, in the apocalyptic discourse (24:4-14), Matthew changes the Markan version "hated by all" (Mark 13:13) into "hated by all nations" μισούμενοι ὑπὸ πάντων τῶν ἐθνῶν (Matt 24:9). This addition seems to be a clear indication of the Gentile persecution suffered by the Matthean community. This could refer especially to what the Jewish members of the community suffered along with other Jews in

312 Sim, *The Gospel of Matthew and Christian Judaism*, 233-236. For the persecutions, which the Jews in Antioch (including Matthew's Jewish Christian community) suffered in the hands of their Gentile neighbours, see Josephus, *The War of the Jews* VII. III. 3, in *Josephus. Complete Works*, 591.

313 As we already discussed above, there are problems with Brandon's suggestion. First is, whether the city, which experienced a plundering of the Jews during the first Jewish war, would have accommodated again a big Jewish community by the time Matthew's gospel was written to facilitate the composition of Matthew's gospel. Second is, there is almost a total lack of knowledge about the origins of the Christian community in this city. See the discussion in "the Geographical location of Matthew's gospel," above.

314 See Senior, "Between Two Worlds...," 1-23.

315 As already indicated above, David C. Sim is of the opinion that the addition of καὶ τοῖς ἔθνεσιν in 10:18 indicates that these Gentile officials represent the Gentile world in their persecution. Sim, *The Gospel of Matthew and Christian Judaism*, 232.

Antioch during and after the Jewish War (66-67 C.E.).[316] However, in the context of the tense situation that was prevailing in Antioch between the Jews and the Gentiles,[317] there was a possibility that even the Gentile Christians could have suffered persecution from their Gentile fellows because of their association with the Jews.

The point that has become clear, at any rate, is that the Matthean community suffered persecution at the hands of the Gentiles. A possible implication of this situation is that because of such experience, the Matthean community could have had a negative attitude toward the Gentiles, and especially the Jewish members of the community could have maintained to some extent a negative attitude toward the Gentiles, which they had from their Jewish heritage.[318] Such an attitude could also worsen their relationship with their Gentile neighbours and this would in turn affect their mission to the Gentiles as well. Matthew would therefore have had to address this situation.

1.4.5. The Ethnic Composition of Matthew's Community

There are different opinions on the ethnic composition of the Matthean community, especially on the nature of the Gentile participation in this community. Some examples may be highlighted as representatives of different views.

Andrew J. Overman and Anthony J. Saldarini are of the view that Matthew's community was composed solely of Jewish Christians. According to Overman the people of Matthew's community were Jews, who, like many of their contemporaries and competitors, "understood themselves as the 'true Israel' and set themselves over against those they believed to be the false covenant people and false leaders who would lead the people astray."[319] Saldarini maintains, "the Matthean group and its spokesperson, the author of the Gospel of Matthew, are Jews who believe in Jesus as the Messiah and Son of God." Though this group praises Gentiles for their faith or for their partial recognition of Jews, which may imply that they are potential members of this group, none of them became members, and even the narrative does not indicate that they will become so.[320]

David C. Sim insists, on the other hand, that there were a few Gentile converts in Matthew's community, but those Gentile members were

316 For this and for further discussion, see Sim, *The Gospel of Matthew and Christian Judaism*, 232-236.

317 A series of bloody and very destructive anti-Jewish riot broke out in Antioch in 40 C.E., and a more destructive one took place during the war in 66-70 C.E. See Rodney Stark, "Antioch as the Social Situation for Matthew's Gospel," in David L, Balch, ed., *Social History of the Matthean Community. Cross-Disciplinary Approaches* (Minneapolis: Augsburg Fortress, 1991), 206.

318 Sim, *The Gospel of Matthew and Christian Judaism*, 231-232.

319 Overman, *Matthew's Gospel and Formative Judaism*, 5.

320 Saldarini, *Matthew's Christian-Jewish Community*, 1, 74, 82.

fully proselytized into Judaism before they were inducted by baptism into this Christian Jewish community.[321]

Keener S. Craig is of the view, slightly differing from Sim that claiming the Jews as Matthew's primary audience does not imply exclusion of Gentile converts among this audience. What it suggests rather is "that those Gentile converts recognized that in converting to Christianity they were adopting a Jewish faith and with it some elements of the Jewish culture that had brought it to them."[322]

There are some scholars who are of the opinion that there were also Gentiles in the Matthean community who were not converted to Judaism. According to Graham Stanton, "the evangelist Matthew was a learned Jew who wrote for Jews who had accepted some Gentiles into their Christian communities." Stanton states that the original recipients of Matthew's gospel, including the evangelist himself, "saw themselves as a 'new people', minority Christian communities over against both Judaism and the Gentile world at large."[323] Schnackenburg also states that Matthew's audience includes both Jewish Christians and Gentile Christians.[324] Raymond Brown maintains that the most plausible interpretation of the interplay of Jewish and Gentile interest in Matthew is that it "was addressed to a once strongly Jewish Christian church that had become increasingly Gentile in composition."[325] John P. Meier follows the same line of thought.[326] According to Magnus Zetterholm the Matthean community was composed of Jewish Christians and Gentile Christians, and those Gentile Christians remained in the community at the level of god-fearers.[327]

The views of scholars are quite varied that one cannot simply follow any of them without further explanation. Therefore, an attempt will be made in this sub-section to give a more detailed explanation about this community to suggest the ethnic composition of the Matthean community, especially the nature of the relationship between the Jewish and Gentile members. Since there is no direct reference in the first gospel itself about its audience, information will be drawn mainly from the accounts of the Book of Acts and Paul's letter to the Galatians on

321 Sim, *The Gospel of Matthew and Christian Judaism*, 256. Sim also admits at the same time (in pp. 49-50) that there were also some Gentiles at the level of God-fearer, but it seems that he does not include them among the proper members of the Matthean community.

322 Keener, *A Commentary on the Gospel of Matthew*, 49-50.

323 Stanton, *A Gospel for a New People*, 280, 378. See also Graham N. Stanton, "The Communities of Matthew," *Interpretation* XLVI/4 (Oct 1992), 379-391.

324 Rudollf Schnackenburg, *The Gospel of Matthew.* Translated by Robert R. Barr (Grand Rapids, Michigan: William B. Eerdmans Publishing Company, 2002), 5.

325 Brown, *An Introduction to the New Testament*, 213.

326 Brown, and Meier, *Antioch and Rome*, 50-51.

327 Zetterholm does not clearly specify the situation of the Matthean community. However, this can be inferred from his reconstruction of the history of the church at Antioch, which he understands as underlying the gospel of Matthew. See for example, Zetterholm, *The Formation of Christianity in Antioch*, 196-201.

the church at Antioch, which is identified here as the church behind Matthew's gospel, and from the detailed reconstructions of the history of this church by scholars like John P. Meier,[328] David C. Sim,[329] and Magnus Zetterholm.[330] The views of these three scholars will be taken as more or less representing the different major ideas on the nature of the Antiochene church. Insights from these sources will be combined with some possible internal and external supports. It is acknowledged here that the reliability of the Lukan accounts in Acts has been questioned on various points.[331] At the same time, however, the basic information on the church at Antioch drawn here from Acts will be taken as reliable, and the account of Paul in Galatians 2:1-11 will be taken here as trustworthy. And, this study assumes that the Matthean community comprised the whole membership of the Antiochene church and not only a specific portion of it.

As agreed by all the scholars mentioned above, the Church in Antioch began with the preaching of those who were scattered due to the persecution of the church, which resulted in the martyrdom of Stephen, as Acts 11:19-20[332] says:

> [19]Now those who were scattered because of the persecution that took place over Stephen traveled as far as Phoenicia, Cyprus, and Antioch, and they spoke the word to no one except Jews. [20] But, among them were some men of Cyprus and Cyrene who, on coming to Antioch, spoke to the Hellenists also, proclaiming the Lord Jesus (NRSV).

According to this account, the gospel of Jesus Christ was preached among both the Jews and the Greeks. The term "Hellenists" here seems to be understood to mean the Gentiles (Greeks) because the Jews are mentioned separately.[333] Since the place is outside Palestine, the Jews here may be understood as Hellenistic Jews, that is, the Greek-speaking Jews. Luke continues to say in the following verses (11:21-26) the way in which the church in Antioch grew within a short span of time:

---

328 Brown, and Meier, *Antioch and Rome*, 15-72.

329 Sim, *The Gospel of Matthew and Christian Judaism*, 63-107.

330 Zetterholm, *The Formation of Christianity in Antioch*.

331 For example, of the questions on the reliability of Acts, see DeSilva's brief discussion on the discrepancy between Lukan presentation of Paul in Acts and Paul's own account in Gal 1-2, and a possible solution on this, in DeSilva, *An Introduction to the New Testament*, 369-379.

332 See for example: Sim, *The Gospel of Matthew and Christian Judaism*, 72-73, 106; Brown and Meier, *Antioch and Rome*, 32-33; Zetterholm, *The Formation of Christianity in Antioch*, 89.

333 According to C. K. Barret, Luke uses the word "Hellenists" in Acts 6:1; 9:29 and 11:20 with different meanings. At 6:1 the word refers to the Greek speaking Jewish Christians, at 9:29 it refers to the Greek-Speaking Jews but who were not Christians, and at 11:20 it refers to Greek speaking Gentiles. For this and for further discussion, see C. K. Barret, *A Critical and Exegetical Commentary on the Acts of Apostles*, Vol. I, ICC (Edinburgh: T&T Clark, 1994), 309, 470, 550-551.

> 21 The hand of the Lord was with them, and a great number became believers and turned to the Lord. 22 News of this came to the ears of the church in Jerusalem, and they sent Barnabas to Antioch.23 When he came and saw the grace of God, he rejoiced, and he exhorted them all to remain faithful to the Lord with steadfast devotion; 24 for he was a good man, full of the Holy Spirit and of faith. And a great many people were brought to the Lord. 25 Then Barnabas went to Tarsus to look for Saul, 26 and when he had found him, he brought him to Antioch. So it was that for an entire year they met with the church and taught a great many people, and it was in Antioch that the disciples were first called "Christians."

There is a question on the accuracy of Luke's account in these verses, especially on the relationship between Barnabas and the Jerusalem church, as well as on how the meeting between Barnabas and Paul took place.[334] Whatever be the situation, what interests us here is that a good number of people came to believe in Jesus. Here, it would be safe to assume that those new believers in Jesus Christ would have come from both Jewish and Gentile backgrounds,[335] and, Gentile members were not required to undergo circumcision.[336] This is also indicated by Acts 15:1-2 which reads:

> 1 Then certain individuals came down from Judea and were teaching the brothers, "Unless you are circumcised according to the custom of Moses, you cannot be saved." 2 And after Paul and Barnabas had no small dissension and debate with them, Paul and Barnabas and some of the others were appointed to go up to Jerusalem to discuss this question with the apostles and the elders.

The picture that has come out now is that the gospel preached in Antioch was a Law-free gospel. Therefore, the Gentiles who adhered to this preaching did not have to follow the Jewish Law, especially circumcision. This is plain as indicated in the above quoted passage that circumcision was demanded only when some people came from Judea. On the other hand, it does not mean that even the Jews who came to follow this good news had to give up the Jewish Law. Rather, it means that it was a gospel that embraced each individual as he/she was. Jews continued to be Jews while Gentiles continued to be Gentiles.

Nevertheless, things changed when some people from Judea, obviously Jesus-believing Jews, came down to Antioch. They demanded that the Jesus-believing Gentiles must circumcise in order to get the salvation promised by Jesus Christ. These people had a heated argument with Paul and Barnabas. It seems

334 For a discussion on this question, see Sim, *The Gospel of Matthew and Christian Judaism*, 75.

335 The demand of circumcision in Acts 15:1 suggests that they were the Gentile members from whom circumcision was demanded; and Paul's letter to Galatians 2:11-14 indicates that Jews were also there.

336 Brown, and Meier, *Antioch and Rome*, 33.

that both sides did not persuade each other. Therefore, this controversy resulted in the Jerusalem Council (Acts 15:3-30). According to Luke's account here, even in the Jerusalem council Gentiles were not demanded to circumcise. Paul's letter to Galatians 2:1-10 also affirms this. According to Acts 15:19-20, however, they were required to follow Jewish food laws, and to abstain from sexual fornication. That means that while circumcision was not imposed upon the Gentile believers, some Jewish laws were imposed upon them.[337] The party of Paul also went back to Antioch and gave their report to the congregation and they read out the letter sent by representatives of the church in Jerusalem. The congregation was rejoicing at the exhortation expressed in the letter (Acts 15:30-31). This indicates that nothing was changed with regard to the situation of the relationship between the Jewish and Gentile Christians in Antioch. They continued to live as before, that is, having free fellowship between the members regardless of whether they were Jews or Gentiles.[338] Even Paul's letter to Galatians, though it does not give explicit details, could be understood as affirming this conclusion (Gal 2:11-14). Here, Paul mentions that Peter was eating with the Gentiles (2:11) and he indicates that Barnabas and the other Jews were also eating with the Gentiles (2:13).

Luke did not mention any further development in the Antiochene church. But Paul's letter to Galatians reveals that the problem was far from over. In Gal 2:11-14 Paul says:

> [11]But when Cephas came to **Antioch**, I opposed him to his face, because he stood self-condemned; [12] for until certain people came from James, he used to eat with the Gentiles. However, after they came, he drew back and kept himself separate for fear of the circumcision faction. [13]And, the other Jews joined him in this hypocrisy, so that even Barnabas was led astray by their hypocrisy. [14] But, when I saw that they were not acting consistently with the truth of the gospel, I said to Cephas before them all, "If you, though a Jew, live like a Gentile and not like a Jew, how can you compel the Gentiles to live like Jews?"

Based on this witness, it seems that James sent emissaries to Antioch sometime after the Jerusalem council.[339] It is not sure what message these messengers brought from James, and what was the result of their mission. David C. Sim suggests that James sent emissaries to demand circumcision from the Gentile Christians, thus abrogating the agreement reached in the Jerusalem council.[340] However,

337 Brown, and Meier, *Antioch and Rome*, 38.

338 Zetterholm, *The Formation of Christianity in Antioch*, 160.

339 Paul's account here is taken in this study as a situation after the Apostolic Council (Acts 15). For a discussion on this, see James D. G. Dunn, *Jesus, Paul and the Law. Studies in Mark and Galatians* (London: SPCK, 1990), 151-159.

340 Sim, *The Gospel of Matthew and Christian Judaism*, 95, 106-107. Sim is here basically following the view of Esler. See also Philip F. Esler, *The First Christians in Their Social Worlds. Social Scientific Approaches to New Testament Interpretation* (London and New York: 1994), 52-69.

According to Zetterholm, James did not abrogate the decree of the Jerusalem council. Although he could be understood as implicitly demanding circumcision, he did not explicitly demand it. The main problem underlying the incident in Antioch was the differing interpretation of covenantal theology between James and Paul. Paul maintains that in order to be saved Gentiles should be included in the covenant, but without excluding the Jews. What Paul means is that while the Torah remains valid and the covenant remains the same for the Jews, it should be reinterpreted through Christ in a new way, to include the Gentiles in the covenant. For James, however, the covenant does not need to be reinterpreted for the sake of the Gentiles. An established and halakhic-defined way of social intercourse must be maintained, "Gentiles could become god-fearers and as such they will be embraced by the final salvation."[341] Therefore, he was not happy with the interpretation of the decree and how it was carried out by the church at Antioch. He had a concern that if there is such a close intercourse between Jewish Christians and Gentile Christians, it would result in the confusion of the boundaries between Jews and Gentiles. Therefore, he sent emissaries with the message that there must not be unrestricted table-fellowship or covenantal fellowship between Gentile Christians and Jewish Christians. Both of them should form separate commensality groups. Zetterholm further observes, however, that in practice, this demand would soon function as an implicit demand on the Jesus-believing Gentiles formally to become Jews. Zetterholm also explicitly mentions that, James "further suggested a covenantal fellowship that, according to him, and presumably most Jews, would require that the Gentiles converted to Judaism."[342]

It is not possible to know about the demand of James with certainty, which his emissaries brought to Antioch. However, it seems, as Zetterholm suggests, that the main subject was abolition of free table fellowship between Jewish Christians and Gentile Christians. This is indicated by Paul's letter to Galatians 2:11-14, which is the main source of information on this incident in Antioch. At the same time, however, it seems that the question of circumcision was in the background of the question on table-fellowship. This is indicated by Paul's statement in Gal 2:12. Here, Paul deliberately mentions "the people from James" as "the circumcision faction," because of whom Peter withdrew from having table-fellowship with the Gentile Christians. Therefore, we could posit the situation in this way. The message that the emissaries of James brought to Antioch was primarily that the Jesus-believing Gentiles and Jesus-believing Jews should not have an unrestricted table-fellowship. But, behind this principal message there are underlying implications. (1) Free table fellowship was restricted because Jesus-believing Gentiles were not part of the covenant. (2) They were not part of the covenant because they were not circumcised. (3) If they wanted to be part of the

341 Zetterholm, *The Formation of Christianity in Antioch*, 156-157. Here, Zetterholm is basically following the view of Dunn. See also James Dunn, *Jesus, Paul and the Law*, 151-158, 161.

342 Zetterholm, *The Formation of Christianity in Antioch*, 166, 161-162.

covenant, and then have covenantal fellowship with the Jesus-believing Jews, they needed to become Jews, and therefore become circumcised. This was in total contrast to Paul's understanding.

So, according to Paul's account in Gal 2:11-14, when men from James came with such a message, Peter, who was already having an unrestricted fellowship with the Gentile Christians, withdrew from them. Then, Barnabas and the other Jewish Christians also followed him. Paul rebuked Peter severely for this. However, it seems, as Zetterholm suggests, that James (through his emissaries) convinced Peter, Barnabas and the other Jews to follow his model of relating to Gentiles, because it seems quite natural to them from the Jewish point of view. Because of this conviction, together with the authority of James as the brother of Jesus, "*Paul suffered an ideological defeat*," in Antioch.[343]

Paul does not mention in his letter any further developments after this incident. According to Luke's account, Paul and Barnabas remained in Antioch for some time after returning from Jerusalem council, teaching and proclaiming the word of God. However, when they were about to set out to visit the churches which they established before, a controversy arose between them over John Mark. Barnabas wanted to take him along with them, but Paul did not want to take him because he had deserted them in Pamphylia and did not accompany them in their work. Their disagreement became so sharp that they parted company. Barnabas took John Mark, while Paul took Silas (Acts 15:35-40; cf. 13:13).

David C. Sim is of the opinion that the main reason behind the separation of Paul and Barnabas here is not the question over John Mark, but because Barnabas changed his attitude toward the Gentile Christians, as Paul mentions in Gal 2:11-14.[344] This is quite possible based on Paul's account here. In addition, the disagreement between Paul and Barnabas which became so sharp (Acts 15:39), also seems to be in tune with the controversy which Paul reports in Gal 2:11-14, more than the controversy over John Mark. Whatever be the reason behind their controversy, it seems that Paul left Antioch not long after the Jerusalem council,[345] but soon after the people from James came to Antioch.[346] Acts reported that after this departure Paul returned to Antioch once again (Acts 18:22). However, Paul himself never mentions about this in his letters. Therefore, he probably never visited Antioch again.[347]

What exactly happened to the Gentile Christians in Antioch after this incident is not known. On the part of the Jewish Christians, Paul's statement shows that

343 Zetterholm, *The Formation of Christianity in Antioch*, 162.

344 Sim, *The Gospel of Matthew and Christian Judaism*, 100-101.

345 It is not certain how long exactly Paul remained in Antioch after coming back to it from the Jerusalem council. According Acts 15:35-41 they remained in Antioch…, and after some days … they left…. We could posit that "after some days"' here refers to "not long after."

346 Sim, *The Gospel of Matthew and Christian Judaism*, 100-101.

347 *Ibid.*

they followed the instruction of James and stopped having table-fellowship with the Gentile Christians (Gal 2:13). There is no more Biblical evidence about the church in Antioch after this incident. However, it is quite legitimate to posit, as it is usually asserted, that as Paul, the principal advocate of the law-free Christianity, was defeated by James's party and left the place, the church in Antioch became a Jewish-oriented church, probably under the leadership of Peter as the church tradition claims.[348] It is also natural to think that the Jewish Christians would have had no problem with this development at all.[349] However, there are differing opinions on what might have happened to the Gentile Christians there. We will briefly highlight the views of J. P. Meier, David C. Sim and Magnus Zetterholm, who have done detailed reconstructions of the church in Antioch, and it will be concluded with the view adopted in this study.

According to J. P. Meier, some Gentile Christians may have undergone circumcision after the departure of Paul. But, most probably both the Gentile and the Jewish Christians followed the instruction from James and held meals (probably Eucharist as well) separately. As long as this instruction was observed both James and Peter would not have demanded circumcision. So, some sort of fellowship, however tenuous and uneasy, was maintained in the Antiochene church between the Jewish members and the Gentile members. Peter played a moderating role in such a situation of tension and division, and kept the church in Antioch from disintegration and complete schism. His figure, even in his physical absence, was a rallying point in the late 40s and early 50s for Antiochene Christians who felt an antagonism toward the liberalism of Paul or the conservatism of James. The prominence given to him in the gospel of Matthew could be a reflection of the important role he played in holding these two groups together.[350]

Meier maintains that Peter's task of keeping peace between the two groups was not easy at all because of their conflicting viewpoints. On the left-wing, the pro-Paul Gentile Christians were preserving their desire for an unhindered universal mission with baptism as the initiation rite instead of circumcision, and Jesus as the ethical touchstone of Christian conduct rather than the Mosaic Law. The views of this group might be outlined in the universalistic traditions in Matthew, especially in 28:16-20. Peter might also have been sympathetic to this group to some extent, and this group viewed Peter's modification of table practice just because of pressure from James' party. At the same time, there were among the Jewish Christians "right-wing extremists" who opposed any circumcision-free mission, who made it difficult to practice the universalistic programme. This group might have been the creators or bearers of such mission statements as those found in 10:5-6 and 15:24. However, this Jewish extremist group did not gain

348 For the church tradition on Peter's connection with Antioch, see Downey, *A History of Antioch*, 583-586.

349 Zetterholm, *The Formation of Christianity in Antioch*, 196.

350 Brown, and Meier, *Antioch and Rome*, 40-41.

the upper hand in Antioch, and ultimately they probably broke away entirely and became Ebionites and other marginal Jewish Christian heretics.[351]

Meier further posits that sometime after the departure of Paul, either Peter or even the Jamesian group, made possible a closer fellowship between the Gentile Christians and the Jewish Christians as a gesture of moderation. To make this possible, abstinence from three 'kosher' laws and fornication[352] were imposed on the Gentile Christians which is enshrined in Acts 15:20, 29 and 21:25. These prohibitions come from Leviticus 17-18 in the same order as they appear in Acts, such as – prohibition of eating food offered to idols, drinking blood from animals, eating meat from strangled animal, and maintaining incestuous unions (*porneia*), and these are obligations which the Pentateuch considers as binding on resident aliens. "The very fact that the Gentile Christians would receive and obey these prohibitions indicates that a total split into two hostile churches had not occurred."[353] Apart from this factor, the Hellenist Jewish Christians in Antioch also seem to have helped in keeping the two groups together. They were the ones who started the work of converting the Gentiles at Antioch with law-free gospel. At least some of them may have remained in Antioch after Paul (and Barnabas) left Antioch for mission and stood firm in their theological stance. Although they would be technically part of the Jewish-Christian group, they would have been in agreement with the Gentile-Christian group due to the ascendancy of James' party, which Peter could not resist, and Paul could not defeat. In this way, they could have played important role in keeping the Jewish Christian group and the Gentile Christian group together.[354]

Meier asserts that through the observance of the four prohibitions by the Gentile members, both the Jewish Christians and the Gentile Christians of the Antiochene church were able to enjoy once again the full fellowship they had had in the earlier days of this church. They could meet together for meals, for Eucharist, and for other religious assemblies. This resumed fellowship resulted in a process, albeit slow, of mutual assimilation. "Symbiosis gradually became Osmosis." Persecutions from the synagogue and civil authorities produced a stronger bond between the two groups. Perhaps the extreme right wing went its own way at this time.[355]

So, according to Meier, the group left in the Antiochene church in the 80s when Matthew's gospel was written were the Gentile Christians (in ever increasing number), together with the liberal Jewish Christians who preserved the ideals of Paul and the Hellenists, as well as the more conservative Jewish Christians who

351 Brown, and Meier, *Antioch and Rome*, 41-42.

352 Meier uses 'kosher laws' for all the four prohibitions. However, prohibition of fornication does not seem to be part of kosher laws.

353 Brown, and Meier, *Antioch and Rome*, 42-43.

354 *Ibid.*, 44.

355 *Ibid.*, 50.

did not wish to break the bond of Christian fellowship and take the path leading to Ebionitism. "Despite all the changes after A.D. 70 or rather because of them," Meier asserts, "the church at Antioch still needed some way of synthesizing the various tendencies and groups which created tension within the community. This was the theological and pastoral problem Matthew had to face when he came to write his gospel."[356]

David C. Sim has quite a different view from that of Meier. According to him, after he was defeated on ideological grounds, Paul left Antioch and the Antiochene church became a law-observant community under the local leadership of Peter. The church was modelled on the traditions and practice of the Hebrews in Jerusalem, and it became a Christian Jewish community. Gentiles were welcomed to join the community, but they were required, unlike before, to convert to Judaism before they were accepted into the community.[357] With regard to the former Gentile members of the church, they were left to choose one of the three possible options – to become proselytes and join the church in full membership, or be content with the status of God-fearers and attach themselves to the Christian Jewish community of Antioch or to another local Jewish group, or to leave the Antiochene church altogether. Most probably, some of them became proselytes, while some others accepted God-fearer status, and most of them left the Christian movement altogether, or moved to other places where they could join Pauline Christianity without first becoming Jews.[358]

Sim further posits that under the mediating role of Peter the Antiochene church stood firmly in the tradition of the original Jerusalem church, and Paul, the self-designated apostle to the Gentiles (according to them), was severely denigrated. Paul, on the other hand, left Antioch soon after and travelled to Asia Minor and Greece conducting his mission to the Gentiles, independently of the churches in Jerusalem and Antioch. Though Acts states that he visited Antioch once again ((Acts 18:22-23), Paul himself never confirms this and therefore it is quite probable that he never returned to Antioch. The conflict between these two

356 Brown, and Meier, *Antioch and Rome*, 50-51. Brown here mentions the situation of the more conservative Jewish Christians as follows:

> These more conservative Jewish Christians found themselves in a unique plight. They had formerly had the upper hand; now they were definitely in the minority. They were too Christian to go back to the synagogue and too much in the mainstream of Christianity to follow the extreme right-wing out of the church. They had shown themselves willing to compromise by agreeing to the 'Apostolic Decree,' but they were determined to hold on to their particular traditions. No doubt, they viewed with some misgivings the large number of pagans now streaming into the church. Cut off from Jerusalem, cut off from the synagogue, how could they maintain monotheism, morality, and all the other aspects of their Jewish heritage which, in their view, made Christianity the true fulfilment of God's promise to Israel, and not another pagan religion?

357 Sim, *The Gospel of Matthew and Christian Judaism*, 107.

358 *Ibid.*, 103-104.

communities, that is, between the law-observant Christian Jewish community and law-free Pauline Christians, continued for decades and even centuries after the time of Paul and James, and the community of Matthew was an active participant in this dispute.[359]

According to Magnus Zetterholm, James demanded, using his authority as the brother of Jesus, that the Jewish Christians and the Gentile Christians must form separate commensality groups for each of them. For James Gentile Christians were not part of the covenant, but they could become god-fearers in order to be embraced in the final salvation. Therefore, he made this demand because he was afraid that too close a social intercourse would result in the confusion of the boundaries between Jews and Gentiles.[360] Then, after the incident in Antioch, and especially after Paul left, the Jesus-believing Gentiles were reduced to the status of God-fearers. They did not have access to the covenant of the God of Israel, and they did not have any separate religious identity. They were separated socially and theologically from both Jews and Gentiles. The only unifying feature they had was their belief in Christ. Moreover, their status within the polity of Antioch also became somewhat unclear. While the Jesus-believing Jewish community, as part of the Jewish community, still had a relation with the authorities of Antioch, the Jesus-believing Gentiles had lost their status because they did not fulfil their religious duties as Gentile inhabitants in a Greek *polis* anymore. The only way for them to relate to the authorities was to pass as Jews through their relation to the Jesus-believing Jewish community. However, this situation also became further complicated after the fall of the Temple. Since they did not have their own identity, the only way to resolve the tension in their relation to the civic authorities was to appear as Jews by paying the *fiscus Judaicus.* However, their association with the Jews also put them in a dangerous situation. In the context of the hostility of the Gentile population against the Jewish community, they could face persecution along with the Jews. In addition, they could also be accused of collaborating with the Jews and they could be beaten or killed as a result. Things could have become even worse under Domitian's enforcement of *fiscus Judaicus.* Because of all such problems, Zetterholm posits that, the Jesus-believing Gentiles, with "*a desire to create a situation within which one may – ideally and/or materially – live in comfort,*" probably under the leadership of Ignatius, and probably during the reign of Domitian, started to separate themselves from the Jesus-believing Jews, and to create a separate collegium.[361] Therefore, according to Zetterholm, "The parting of the ways in Antioch was primarily a separation – not between 'Judaism' and 'Christianity' – *but between Jewish and Gentile adherents to the Jesus movement.*"[362]

359 Sim, *The Gospel of Matthew and Christian Judaism*, 100-101, 165.

360 Zetterholm, *The Formation of Christianity in Antioch*, 161, 166.

361 *Ibid.*, 196, 198, 201-202.

362 *Ibid.*, 202.

Thus, Zetterholm does not specifically give the situation of the Antiochene community during the time in which Matthew's gospel was written. However, we could infer from his overall reconstruction that by the time Matthew's gospel was written the Matthean community was composed of both the Jewish and Gentile members. The Jewish members were in majority and hence the church was a Jewish-oriented church. The Gentile Christians were members of this church only at the level of God-fearers, and therefore they were never fully satisfied with their status.

As it is already mentioned at the beginning of this discussion, there is no explicit indication of the composition of Matthew's community. However, the overwhelming Jewish nature of the gospel and the prominence of Gentiles in the gospel from beginning to end, suggest that both Jews and Gentiles were members of this community, and that the Jews were in the majority. At the same time, as it is acknowledged in some of the recent studies, it seems that the Gentile members were notably increasing in the Matthean community.[363] The universal mission commanded by the Matthean Jesus to his disciples at the end of the gospel (28:19), which cancels the former exclusive mission to Israel (10:5-6),[364] may be an important indication of this situation. Moreover, the idea of the increasing Gentile membership in the Antiochene church is also supported by the fact that not long after Matthew's gospel was written, that is by the time of Ignatius, the church at Antioch became an overwhelmingly Gentile-oriented church.[365] If the Gentile members were increasing in the Matthean church, and if it became a Gentile-oriented church not long after Matthew's gospel was written,[366] we could fairly assume that the Gentile members could enter the Matthean community without circumcision, at least at the time Matthew's gospel was written.[367] However, it

363 See for example, Carl R. Holladay, *A Critical Introduction to the New Testament* (Nashville: Abingdon Press, 2005), 137; DeSilva, *An Introduction to the New Testament*, 238; Luz, *Studies in Matthew,* 11, 34.

364 Luz, *Studies in Matthew*, 26. According to Donald Senior Jesus focussed on the mission to Israel during his earthly ministry and his command after his resurrection from the dead was a mission to all the nations, inclusive of both Jews and Gentiles. See Senior, "Between Two Worlds…," 19.

365 See M. Hengel and C. K. Barrett, *Conflicts and Challenges in Early Christianity*, edited by D. A. Hagner (Harrisburg, PA: Trinity Press, 1999), 37. Here Hengel says that Ignatius "in his polemics shows himself to be the first author of a purely Gentile Christianity." See also Zetterholm, *The Formation of Christianity in Antioch*, 203.

366 If the gospel of Matthew was written between 75-93 C.E., as it is assumed in this study, and if the Antiochene church which underlies this gospel became a Gentile-oriented church in the time of Ignatius who died around 107 C.E. (see C. Trevett, *A Study of Ignatius of Antioch in Syria and Asia*, 3-9), there is no doubt that the Antiochene church became a Gentile-oriented church not long after the first gospel was written.

367 Luz is of the view that sometime after the destruction of the Jerusalem Temple in 70 C.E., Matthew's Jewish Christian community left the synagogue because they could no longer pray the Eighteen Benedictions because of the curse on the *minim*. They were integrated into a

is difficult to make out the actual relation between the Jewish members and the Gentile members of the Matthean church from the gospel itself. The only possibility is probably to make an assumption by speculating on the development in the Antiochene church between Paul's departure and the writing of Matthew's gospel, and relate it to Matthew's gospel.

As it is generally agreed, the demand of James for the Jewish and Gentile members of the Antiochene church to have Eucharist separately might have created serious tension in the church initially. Because of this, some of the Gentile Christians might have left the church and some of them might have undergone circumcision, as Meier and Sim suggest.[368] However, most of the Gentile members must have been in a dilemma, without knowing which way to take. They must have found it difficult to leave the church because of their faith in Jesus Christ. At the same time, they must also have found it difficult to undergo circumcision or be proselytised because it was totally contrary to Paul's teaching. In that situation, their only option, at least for the time being, was to go along with the demand of James and remain in the church, having separate Eucharist with the Jewish Christians.[369] We could fairly assume that the Gentile members were never satisfied with that condition, and there must have been certain tension in the Antiochene church without doubt.[370] Such a situation would not have been, satisfying at all even for Peter and some of the Jewish Christians. Therefore, most probably Peter would have tried to find a way to ease the situation. The table fellowship might not have been resumed quickly because of the fear of James. However, it is highly probable that Peter would have tried his best to persuade the Gentile members to accept the situation only as the maintenance on the part of the Jewish members of their Jewish identity in the sight of the rest of the Jewish community.[371] Such an effort of mediation could have helped to some extent

Gentile Christian church, which "had adopted their identifying rituals of baptism (and not circumcision) and the Lord's Supper (which was probably observed outside the framework of the annual Passover in Matthew's community)." Then they opened up to the mission to the Gentiles and gradually gave up circumcision and other requirements of the law, and were being absorbed by the Gentile Christian church. See Luz, *Studies in Matthew*, 9-11, 34-35.

368 See Brown and Meier, *Antioch and Rome*, 40; and Sim, *The Gospel of Matthew and Christian Judaism*, 103-104. While both of them suggest here that some of the Gentiles became proselytes, Sim also suggests that most of the Gentile Christians left the Antiochene church.

369 This follows to some extent the suggestion of Zetterholm, who posits that after Paul left, the Jesus-believing Gentiles were reduced to the status of God-fearers, without having either access to the covenant of the God of Israel, or any separate religious identity, thus they were separated socially and theologically both from Jews and Gentiles. Zetterholm, *The Formation of Christianity in Antioch*, 196.

370 According to Zetterholm the Gentile members were never satisfied and finally they formed their own collegium probably under Ignatius during the reign of Domitian. Zetterholm, *The Formation of Christianity in Antioch*, 201-202.

371 Dunn points out that there was an increasing pressure upon the Christian Jews to maintain their Jewish identity due to deterioration in Palestine and increasingly polemical response from

at least for some time. However, it is unlikely that the tension was ever totally quenched. Therefore, we could assume that sometime after Paul left, Peter and the other Jews made further concessions, so that they could have table fellowship together again, but maintaining the abiding validity of the Jewish law, of course, as interpreted by Jesus. To put it briefly, the Gentile members were required to observe the Jewish food laws stricter than before, but not circumcision.[372] Probably at this stage, some of the extreme Jewish Christians, unable to adjust to such mutual contact with the Gentiles, left the community and formed a separate Jewish Christian group, which came to be known as Ebionites.[373] On the other hand, this new situation encouraged more and more Gentile members to join the Antiochene church. Probably the Jewish members of the community saw the increasing Gentile membership in the community as a threat to their dominance and the Jewish-orientation of the church. Accordingly, they might have reacted by showing an attitude of superiority over the Gentile Christians. The stories of the healing of the centurion's son (Matt 8:5-13) and the healing of the daughter of the Canaanite woman (Matt 15:21-28) can be seen as Matthew's reaction to such an attitude.[374] And, Matt 18:6-7 may also be a warning to the Jewish Christians not

---

the Jews upon those that seem a threat to Judaism. That was the development behind James' demand upon Peter in Antioch. Dunn, *Jesus, Paul and the Law*, 135-136.

372 Meier maintains that Peter, and probably other Jewish Christians, established the joint table fellowship again sometime after Paul left, on the condition that the Gentile Christians observed the four Jewish laws. Brown, and Meier, *Antioch and Rome*, 42-43. The problem with this view of Meier's, however, is that these four Jewish laws were, according to Acts 15:1-30, already demanded by the Jerusalem council, and the Gentile Christians in Antioch already accepted the demand as soon as it was communicated to them after the council. Dunn further clarifies this situation. According to him, the Gentiles in Antioch already observed the basic food laws prescribed by the Torah. What the men from James demanded was "a much more scrupulous observance of the rulings on what the dietary laws involved, especially with regard to ritual purity and tithing." Dunn, *Jesus, Paul and the Law*, 154.

373 This is not far from Meier's view that the extreme right wing of the Jewish Christians probably left the church when the Jewish Christians and the Gentile Christians were experiencing mutual assimilation through the renewed joint table fellowship and when the bond between them was strengthened by persecutions form the synagogue and from the civil authorities.

374 The story of the healing of the centurion's child is taken from Q. Both Matthew and Luke emphasize the faith of the centurion's faith in comparing to the faith of the Jews. However, the importance of the Gentiles in the kingdom of God is further accentuated by Matthew by adding in 8:11-12 (Jesus says to his followers) "*I tell you, many will come from east and west and will eat with Abraham and Isaac and Jacob in the kingdom of heaven, while the heirs of the kingdom will be thrown into the outer darkness, where there will be weeping and gnashing of teeth.*" The story of the healing of the daughter of the Canaanite woman is taken from Mark. However, Matthew made significant changes to accentuate the differentiation between the Jews and the Gentiles (probably to reflect the attitude of the Jewish Christians), and the faith of this woman representing the Gentiles. He changes the woman's identity as "a Canaanite woman" in place of Mark's "a Greek, a Syrophoenician by birth." Matthew adds in Jesus' response to the request of the woman, "I was sent only to the lost sheep of the house of Israel." Matthew also changes Jesus' response to the woman. Matthew has "O woman, great is our faith!" in place of Mark's

to place a stumbling block to such new Gentile members.[375] At the same time, the increasing Gentile members also could have tended to play down the Jewishness of their Jewish Christian friends, and pressurised them to minimize their Jewish practices, seeing them as a hindrance to equality within their community. Matthew's emphasis on the abiding validity of the Law can be understood as a correcting reminder of such an attitude of the Gentile Christians.[376] Therefore, although there was no serious tension between the Jewish Christians and the Gentile Christians within the community, it seems that at least some degree of tension was created by the changing situation, and both sides needed a proper exhortation to cope with that changing situation properly, especially concerning their mutual relationship. Therefore, Matthew had to address this situation.[377]

1.4.6. The Socio-Economic Status of Matthew's Community

The intent of this section is to highlight the socio-economic status of Matthew's community, which is understood to be one of the factors that influenced the content of Matthew's gospel. For this purpose, an inference will be drawn from Matthew's gospel on the socio-economic condition of the Matthean community, and the social stratification system of the first century Mediterranean societies will be employed for determining and understanding their status in the society. First of all, the social stratification in the first century Mediterranean world will be highlighted because this whole region exhibited structurally similar economic and social living conditions under the rule of the Roman emperors.[378] Based on this insight we will have a closer look at the social stratification in Palestine to give us a clearer picture of the social stratification within the Jewish society. This is important for understanding the social status of Matthew's community, which, although located outside Palestine, was mainly a Jewish community. An insight into this will be applied to the Matthean community to understand their socio-economic standing in the society. In this analysis, the work of Ekkehard

"For this saying you may go your way." See also David Cortes-Fuentes, "Not like the Gentiles: The Characterization of Gentiles in the Gospel according to St. Matthew," *Journal of Hispanic / Latin Theology* 9/1 (2001), 15-18.

375 Foster, *Community, Law and Mission in Matthew's Gospel*, 252.

376 DeSilva, *An Introduction to the New Testament*, 237-238.

377 *Ibid.*, 237. Matthew's possible intention to this situation, that is to bring unity between the Jewish Christians and Gentile Christians, can be seen in his calling for a mission to Gentiles while at the same time recognizing Israel's special place (28:16-20; 10:5-6; 15:21-28); his insistence on a righteousness exceeding that of the Pharisees (5:20); and his silence on the explosive issue of circumcision although his community, especially the Jewish members, apparently practiced it. See Davies and Allison, Jr., *Matthew*, Vol. III, 703.

378 Stegemann and Stegemann, *The Jesus Movement*, 2-3. The Mediterranean world of the first century here includes the area around the Mediterranean Sea such as – Italy, the coast of Greece and Asia Minor, Syria, Israel (Palestine), and Bithynia.

W. Stegemann and Wolfgang Stegemann will be followed in general,[379] because, although one may not fully agree with their detailed stratification system,[380] their work represents, to a large extent, one of the more recent, detailed and refined works from the previous researches on the same subject. Moreover, they are the ones who give specifically a detailed treatment of the social stratification of the first century Mediterannean. Therefore, this work provides useful information for the basic understanding of the socio-economic status of the Matthean community. Of course, the work of Stegemann and Stegemann will be supplemented as far as possible with other relevant and available information.

1.4.6.1. *Social Description of the First Century Mediterranean*

The society of the first century Mediterranean world under the rule of the Roman emperors could be subsumed as agrarian, which characterized most of ancient societies.[381] The major characteristic of agrarian society was that farming comprised the main source of production while on the other hand a small social group controlled the distribution of a society's goods.[382] Various criteria have been proposed for the determination of the social position of a person in the ancient societies. In the midst of the complexity of factors Stegemann and Stegemann assume that the three "basic elements" that determine a society's system of

379 Stegemann and Stegemann, *The Jesus Movement*, 129-136.

380 For example, while Stegemann and Stegemann have only upper and lower strata and no middle stratum in their analysis, Joachim Jeremias, in his analysis of the economic status of the people of Jerusalem during the time of Jesus, divides them into the rich, the middle class, and the poor. See Jeremias, *Jerusalem in the Time of Jesus*, 87-119. Those who formed the middle class in the analysis of Jeremias (such as the retail traders who had shops in one of the bazaars, the small industrialists or craftsmen, who owned their own premises and did not hire themselves out for wages, and probably the priests also) can be basically grouped, in the analysis of Stegemann and Stegemann, among the first group of the urban lower stratum, who were relatively poor or relatively prosperous (*penēs/penētes*) [while the second group of the lower stratum comprised the absolutely poor (*ptōchos/ptōchoi*)]. See Jeremias, *Jerusalem in the Time of Jesus*, 100, 104; and Stegemann and Stegemann, *The Jesus Movement*, 71.

381 The name "Agrarian society" was given by Lenski to refer to the new society, which evolved through the second great social revolution of antiquity, which was made possible by a series of inventions and discoveries enhancing major advances in production, transportation and communication. According to Lenski, Agrarian societies first became established between 5000 B.C.E. to 6000 B.C.E. years ago in the Middle East, then from there they spread into the whole of Mediterranean world. By the end of the fifteenth century C.E., they became firmly established in the whole of Europe, North Africa, the Middle East, and south East Asia. See Gerhard E. Lenski, *Power and Privilege: A Theory of Social Stratification* (New York: McGraw Hill, 1966), 189-190. See also Stegemann and Stegemann, *The Jesus Movement,* 10.

382 For this and for further discussion on the nature of "agrarian society" see Stegemann and Stegemann, *The Jesus Movement,* 7-52. See also Richard A. Horsley, *Sociology and the Jesus Movement,* 2nd Edition (New York: Continuum, 1994), 67-101; Lenski, *Power and Privilege*, 193-200; and Helmut Koester, *History, Culture, and Religion of the Hellenistic Age* (Philadelphia: Fortress Press, 1983 [1982], 62-65.

distribution are *power, privilege, and prestige.* They hold the view that these are the most important variables in determining the social position of a person in the social system. Among these three factors, *power* is the primary variable, which determines the division of a society's surplus [the excess of production over need]. Then, *privilege*, which is understood as the possession or control of a part of the surplus from a society's produce, depends on power. Finally, *prestige* is, above all, a function of power and privilege. Consequently, Stegemann and Stegemann maintain that a decisive factor in a stratification analysis of ancient Mediterranean societies is power. Here, there are two types of power: Power through position (office or role) and power through property (influence). In the Roman Empire decisive for one's stratum membership was the exercise of a leading public function. At the same time, however, the role played by property as the foundation of social power could not be underestimated.[383]

The three variables mentioned above were employed for developing the social position of a person in the first century Mediterranean societies whereby *power* played the first and foremost role, followed by *privilege* and *prestige.* Accordingly, the societies of the first century Mediterranean were divided into two strata, the upper and lower strata or elite and non-elite (the masses). This division follows a *dichotomous model*, which has been maintained in principle, for the description of the social stratification of ancient societies.[384] To put it briefly, according to the *dichotomous model* social inequality within a society is understood through the assumption of upper and lower strata or elite and non-elite (the masses). There is no middle stratum.[385] The main criterion for this grouping is division of power. That is, power was concentrated in the small upper stratum on one hand while on the other hand the large lower stratum was powerless. Social privileges, personal possessions and legal advantages were also basically determined by this constellation. Those who were without prominent office and thus lacked a direct sharing of power (including single women and freed slaves) did not have any influence except only through a considerable fortune. This means that those people who possessed neither prominent office nor wealth did not belong to the

383 Stegemann and Stegemann, *The Jesus Movement,* 60-62.

384 *Ibid.,* 67.

385 Stegemann and Stegemann note that there is a controversy on the terminologies used for differentiating a populace. Different terms such as stratum, status group, class, position, and caste have been used. But, the problem is that none of these terms is clearly defined either sociologically or in everyday speech. They then use the term *stratum,* and according to them, "*a stratum comprises all the people of a society who find themselves in a similar social position on the basis of their share of power, privilege, and prestige.*" See Stegemann and Stegemann, *The Jesus Movement,* 58. Also Horsley, using the term "class," maintains that the ancient agrarian societies were basically divided into two structures, the rulers and the ruled, the aristocratic class and the peasant class, and there was no middle class between the rulers and the ruled. Horsley, *Sociology and the Jesus Movement,* 68-70.

elite of their society.[386] Important to note here again is that while the society is divided into two basic strata based on power, privilege, and prestige, both the strata, namely the upper stratum and the lower stratum, are made up of different groups.[387]

a. The Upper Stratum: There were three main categories in the upper stratum.

(i) The Roman Ordines: The first category of the upper stratum included the members of the Roman *ordines* or "estates" such as – "imperial aristocracy" that is emperor and imperial house (*domus Caesaris*), senatorial nobility (*ordo senatorius*),[388] and equestrians (*ordo equester*).[389] Members of these groups exercised *power* as authority in leading political offices. These offices also presuppose wealth in varying amounts, and their occupants enjoyed, through the possession of wealth, further *privileges* including privilege before judiciary. The members of these groups also enjoyed the highest *prestige* in different degrees. The wives and other family members of these groups also enjoyed a reduced share of the privilege and social prestige of their husbands and fathers. They also, in principle, exercised

386 Stegemann and Stegemann, *The Jesus Movement,* 67.

387 Gerhard E. Lenski, in his general analysis of the later Agrarian societies in general, divided the society into the privileged class and the common people. Under the privileged class, he includes the ruler, the governing class, the retainer class, and the merchant class. He divides the common people in the peasant class, the artisans, the unclean and degraded classes, and the expendables. See Lenski, *Power and Privilege,* 189-296. The division made by Stegemann and Stegemann in their analysis of the first century Mediterranean societies, is more or less the same, as we will continue to see.

388 The number of senators was set at 600 (six hundred) by Augustus. The minimum wealth of the senators amounted to one million sesterces, or 250,000 denarii, (1 denarii was the day's wage of a labourer) and most of them exceeded this amount. They were big landowners in Italy and the provinces, and majority of their income came probably from their agricultural possessions and from their administration of public offices in the provinces. The criteria for becoming member of the senatorial *ordo* are high birth, outstanding traits and wealth. See the following: Stegemann and Stegemann, *The Jesus Movement,* 71, 73; Ramsay MacMullen, *Roman Social Relations. 50 B.C. to A.D. 284* (New Haven and London: Yale University Press, 1974), 89; Everett Ferguson, *Backgrounds of Early Christianity* (Grand Rapids, Michigan: William B. Eerdmans Publishing Company, 1989 [1987], 42-43.

389 The Equestrian order had about 20,000 members and the minimum wealth for an individual member was 400,000 sesterces or 100,000 denarii. Many of them had very much higher amount than that, and they drew their largest income from their real estate. Among their numbers were wholesalers, bankers, and holders of leases for taxes and customs duties. The equestrian order was not homogeneous as the senatorial birth aristocracy was. While they were supposed to demonstrate in general, high birth, outstanding traits and wealth, among its members were also sons of freed slaves, aspirants from the military, and members of the provincial upper stratum. While, among the equestrians those who had an exalted post and a residence in Rome were more esteemed, the majority of the members probably belonged to the provincial or local upper stratum. See Stegemann and Stegemann, *The Jesus Movement,* 73. See also MacMullen, *Roman Social Relations,* 89; and Ferguson, *Backgrounds of Early Christianity,* 43-44.

influence, but not the authority of the office. In the same way the *decurions* (city councillors),[390] and members of ruling houses and the leading priestly and lay families in vassal states and provinces were members of their local or provincial upper stratum, and enjoyed their share of power, privilege, and prestige.[391]

(ii) The Wealthy People: The second category of the upper stratum was made up of wealthy people without prominent political offices, regardless of their sex or legal status. This means that it did not matter whether they were single men or women, whether born free or made free. Such wealthy people could exercise power in the form of influence on leading political figures and they could even command their own, sometimes large, staffs. Because of their income, they also could lead a lifestyle, which was beyond the reach of the general populace. They also could expect, in general, privileged treatment before the judiciary even if it was not necessarily based on law. Their social prestige was indeed less than that of the members of the *ordines*. However, as certain compensation to that, honorary social offices were bestowed on them, such as being a functionary of the imperial cult – *Augustules* - or patron or patroness of social organizations. These offices were mainly bestowed on wealthy freed slaves without political office. In this group were included the veterans of the Roman army who retired with the rank of a *primipilus* and received a settlement of 600,000 sesterces, or one and a half times the minimum equestrian wealth, and the freed slaves who became rich. Independent women, who did not have to work but lived from their property or wealth, also were comparable to them.[392]

(iii) The Retainers: In the third category were the retainers of the upper stratum. Included in this category were the free individuals, freed slaves, and slaves

390 The numbers of decurions (city councillors) in the Roman Empire was in all about 150,000 to 200,000. Their numbers in different towns were different, mainly from thirty to five hundred. These were provincial aristocracy with considerable property. Like the senators and equestrians, the decurions were also supposed to demonstrate honourable origin, wealth, and traits of character. The sons of freed slaves and certain veterans could also join them. The presupposed minimum income for the provincial aristocracy varied between 20,000 and 100,000 sesterces. Accordingly, their wealth also varied considerably and in several cases, they could be called rich in the context of their local situations. See Stegemann and Stegemann, *The Jesus Movement,* 74. See also Ferguson, *Backgrounds of Early Christianity*, 44. According to Ramsay MacMullen the qualification in *comum* in Italy was 25,000 denarii, that is one-tenth of a Roman senator's minimum. MacMullen, *Roman Social Relations*, 90.

391 Stegemann and Stegemann, *The Jesus Movement,* 68-69. The vassal kings or princes and their families, as well as the upper stratum families in Rome's vassal states and provinces could not appeal to their own noble heritage and never became members of a Roman *ordo*, but only received certain honorary privileges and Roman citizenship. However, on the basis of their power, property, privileges, and their prestige which they enjoyed at least in Rome, they were counted among the elite. In the same way, also the families of high priests and laity, who traditionally belonged to the upper-stratum groups in the land of Israel and who also enjoyed the esteem of the people, were included among the elite because of their property and power. See Stegemann and Stegemann, *The Jesus Movement,* 74.

392 *Ibid.*, 69, 75-76.

who fulfilled duties for their masters of the upper stratum groups in prominent political positions or performed important administrative task in the private sphere. Again, the share of power, privilege and prestige of members of this group would be different because of the difference in their masters.[393]

The upper stratum, including the families, shared between 1 and 5 percent of the total population of the Roman Empire.[394]

b. The Lower Stratum: Regarded in its totality the lower stratum was extremely heterogeneous, and therefore, differentiation of these groups is quite difficult. In the midst of this difficulty of differentiation Stegemann and Stegemann use *relative property (income) or privilege* and *relative status or prestige* as their central criteria. Based on these criteria (and in the view of the upper stratum) those who belonged to the lower stratum were, in principle, people who had to earn a living for themselves and their families through their own work. These people were dependent on their own work to provide their subsistence, not only because of their non-involvement in high political offices and hence their enormous lack of power, but also because of their minimum, or total lack of property. They were broadly divided into two groups: (a) relatively poor or relatively prosperous (*penēs/penētes*) and (b) the absolutely poor (*ptōchos/ptōchoi*).[395]

(i) The Relatively Poor or Relatively Prosperous (penētes): Those relatively poor or relatively prosperous (*penētes*) were, because of their income or property, in a position to provide for themselves and their families appropriate dwelling, sufficient food and clothing which were needed for adequate subsistence.[396]

(ii) The Absolutely Poor (ptōchos/ptōchoi): The absolutely poor lived at or under the level of minimum existence. They lacked all or some of the goods needed for subsistence such as food, clothing and dwelling.[397]

Most of the people in the lower stratum lived in the country. Included among them were small farmers and their families, small leaseholders, free wage earners, and day labourers, who constantly lived on the verge of minimum existence. Lower stratum in the city includes families of small artisans and their free wage earners, small traders, doctors (except for the "personal physicians" of the upper stratum), teachers, musicians, administrators of houses and fortunes,

---

393 Stegemann and Stegemann, *The Jesus Movement,* 69-70. Within the retainers of the upper stratum were included especially the important members of the *familia Caesaris,* and among them were the imperial freed slaves (*Augusti liberti*), who held politically privileged position, and also helpers of the Roman magistracy (*apparitores*), who probably were mostly freed slaves. Those people performed public and legal activities. They also worked in archives, and in the library. They even worked with the census or in other public projects. Apart from the remarkable power (conveyed by the emperor) those retainers had also the opportunity to acquire substantial wealth. Stegemann and Stegemann, *The Jesus Movement,* 76.

394 *Ibid.,* 77.

395 *Ibid.,* 70-71, 79.

396 *Ibid.,* 71.

397 *Ibid.*

harbour workers, urban day labourers, and other occasional workers, who were also constantly on the verge of minimum existence.[398] Other members of the lower stratum, who mainly comprised the absolutely poor, were - beggars, widows, orphans, chronically ill or disabled like the blind, the lame, and lepers. These people did not have enough to eat. They did not have lodgings or hope. They were hungry and thirsty and had only rags for clothes. They were dependent on the help of others, for example, through begging, for their livelihood. Many of them lived under bridges, under stairs or in the cellars of apartment houses. Some of them, especially in the city of Rome, could not afford to get proper burial even at death and their corpses were thrown out in the streets and were collected by public slaves.[399]

The basic social structure that has been discussed above was found throughout the Mediterranean world of the first century. However, there was a difference in the detailed social composition within that structure in different provinces of the Roman Empire because of differences in socio-religious set up. We will have a closer look at the specific social stratification in Palestine because it offers the best clue for understanding the social standing of the Matthean community.

1.4.6.2. *Social Stratification in the First Century Palestine*

As in all other areas of the first century Mediterranean, society in the first century Palestine also could be grouped broadly into small minority members of the upper stratum, including the ruling elite, their retainers in the administration, and the military on one hand, and the great majority of the lower stratum or non-elite, on the other. The small members of the upper stratum were the ones who skimmed off the surplus, while the great majority of the lower stratum was the ruled masses and producers of the wealth.[400] At the upper stratum were (a) the provincial aristocracy including the Herodian ruling house,[401] the priestly and lay aristocracy, and members of the Sanhedrin; (b) retainers of the upper stratum such as members of the Sanhedrin, administrative and military functionaries, priests, scribes, local judges, tax collectors, foreign traders, wholesalers.[402]

The lower stratum was made up of all those who did not have a share in the power and privilege of the ruling stratum and those who were not among those

398 Stegemann and Stegemann, *The Jesus Movement,* 71.

399 *Ibid.,* 92.

400 *Ibid.,* 99.

401 The Herod's ruling family ruled in the land of Israel, under the Roman emperor, in one way or the other until the death of Agrippa II in the time of Domitian. See Stegemann and Stegemann, *The Jesus Movement,* 130. Domitian was the emperor of Rome between 14, Sept. 81 till 18, Sept. 96. See Brian W. Jones, "Domitian (Emperor)," *ABD*, Vol. 2 (New York: Doubleday, 1992), 221-222. The exact date of the death of Agrippa II is uncertain. He seems to have died around A.D. 93 during the reign of Domitian. See, Braund, "Agrippa (Person)," 100.

402 Stegemann and Stegemann, *The Jesus Movement,* 135.

in its service. Again, they were divided into two groups. (a) Relatively prosperous members who comprised a smaller number of the lower stratum, such as - prosperous craftsmen, traders, peasant farmers, tenants, and service workers.[403] (b) poor or destitute people who could hardly eke out a subsistence living for their families, and which comprised probably a great majority, such as: in the cities – small traders, artisans, businessmen; and in the country - small farmers, tenants, day labourers and wage earners, fishermen, indebted servants and slaves. Those at the bottom of the lower stratum - that is, below the level of minimum existence, included – beggars, prostitutes, shepherds, widows, orphans, and bandits.[404]

The picture becomes clearer when this social stratification is applied to the religious groups of the first century in the land of Palestine: The Sadducees, some of the Pharisees, and some of the Essenes belonged to the elite (upper stratum) groups. The "Teacher of Righteousness," a prominent figure among the Essenes,[405] was a member of the upper stratum. At the same time, some of the Essenes, some of the Pharisees, leaders of social bandits, and one follower of Jesus namely, Matthew the tax collector, belonged to the retainer group of the upper stratum. John the Baptist was included in this group. In the relatively prosperous non-elite (lower stratum) groups, belonged some members of the Essenes, some members of the social bandits, some of the followers of John the Baptist and some of the followers of Jesus. Jesus himself belonged to this group. In the "minimum existence" group belonged some members of the social bandits, some of the followers of John the Baptist, some of the followers of Jesus, sign prophets and miracle workers.[406]

This picture mainly shows the situation before 70 C.E. After this, the composition of the members changed to some extent but the social stratification system remained the same. From this picture, we will be able to have a clearer view of the social profile of the Matthean community.

1.4.6.3. *The Socio-Economic Status of the Matthean Community*

Viewed from the social stratification system of its time, Matthew's gospel indicates that some of its community members were from the retainer group and a few from the upper stratum. The presence of members from the upper stratum is suggested in 27:57, where Joseph, a rich man (but not a respected member of the council as in Mark 15:43), is a disciple of Jesus. Matthew's presentation of the rich positively in the parable on the kingdom of Heaven (20:1ff.), although he maintains a negative attitude toward the rich (19:23, 24), also suggests the same

403 Cf., Jeremias classified these groups as "the middle class" in the context of Jerusalem. See Jeremias, *Jerusalem in the Time of Jesus*, 100.

404 Stegemann and Stegemann, *The Jesus Movement,* 129-135.

405 For the "Teacher of Righteousness", see J. Murphy-O'Connor, "Teacher of Righteousness," *ABD*, Vol. 6 (New York: Doubleday, 1992), 340-341.

406 Stegemann and Stegemann, *The Jesus Movement,* 157-160, 183-186.

phenomenon. The addition of "in spirit" in the first beatitude (5: 3) can also be an indicator of this situation.[407] The membership of the retainer group is indicated in the inclusion of the tax collectors (Matt 9:10-11; 11: 19; 21:31-32); and the centurion (Matt 8:5, 8, 13; 27:54) among the followers of Jesus. However, these are the lower ranks of the retainer group. The pre-dominant members of the Matthean community seem to have been from the urban lower stratum. Notably included among them were slaves and (former) prostitutes (e.g., Matt 21:31, 32, and several occurrences of slaves).[408] Based on the above analysis, Matthew's community is located in an urban setting,[409] and it seems that economically this community is relatively wealthier than the Lucan community and the Markan community.[410] However, it is important to remember that while the rich and the well to do members from the upper stratum and the retainer groups were there in the Matthean community, the majority of the members who came from the urban lower stratum group were not at all rich. This difference in economic status was another potential threat to create disunity and hatred among the members, which the first evangelist had to address.[411]

---

407 Kingsbury, *Matthew as Story*, 152. See also Stegemann and Stegemann, *The Jesus Movement*, 228; R. H. Smith also clearly notes the inclusion of affluent people among Matthew's community. However, his observation that Matthew's "audience seems to have consisted of 'affluent Christian Jews who probably belonged to upper class society,'" seems to miss the real situation. See R. H. Smith, "Were the Early Christians Middle-Class? A Sociological Analysis of the New Testament," *CurTheolMiss* 7 (1980): 266. Recently his view is adopted by Aaron M. Gale. See Gale, *Redefining Ancient Borders*, 73-76, 165-166.

408 Stegemann and Stegemann, *The Jesus Movement,* 228-230.

409 For the suggestion of the urban setting of Matthew's gospel, see the following: Smith, "Were the Early Christians Middle-Class?...," 266; Stegemann and Stegemann, *The Jesus Movement,* 227-228. See also point no. 3 of the section "Important Factors for determining the Geographical Location of Matthew's Gospel" above.

410 This is indicated in various ways in Matthew's gospel when compared with Mark and Luke. For examples – while Luke has only "the poor" in the first beatitude (Luke 6:20) Matthew has "the poor in spirit" (Matt 5:3). While the Markan Jesus commands the disciples to take with them "no copper coin" in their missionary journey (Mark 6:8) Matthean Jesus commands them to take neither "gold, nor silver, nor copper coin" (Matt 10:9). While, the Lucan Jesus tells a parable about "minas" (Luke 19:11-27) the Matthean Jesus tells the parable about "talents" (Matt 25:14-30). The widow's mite, found in Mark (12:41-44) and Luke (21:1-4) does not appear in Matthew. Also, the woes against the rich (which perhaps stood in Q), and the parable of the rich man and poor Lazarus, both found in Luke (6:24-26; 16:19-31) are not found in Matthew. And Joseph of Arimathea, who is a respected member of the council in Mark (15:43) also becomes a rich disciple of Jesus in Matthew (27:57). See the following - Kingsbury, *Matthew as Story*, 152; Davies and Allison, Jr., *Matthew*, Vol. III, 703.

411 Davies and Allison, Jr., *Matthew*, Vol. III, 703-704. According to Horsley, in the Jewish society of the first century Palestine, the fundamental conflict was basically between the rulers and the ruled. Peasants were forced to pay double or triple demands from the rulers, Romans, Herodians and Priests. They were driven to indebtedness and forced to borrow from those who controlled larger stores of grain, oil, or money at a high rate of interests, which further worsens their situations. Some lost their land, some gave their sons or daughters, family

1.4.7. Preliminary Conclusion

Our discussion in the present sub-section may be briefly concluded as follows.

In the aftermath of the Jewish war against Rome (66-73 C.E.), particularly after the destruction of Jerusalem and the Temple, there emerged a coalition force to rebuild the Jewish faith that was shattered by the war. This renewal movement, the so-called formative Judaism, adopted Pharisaic teaching as its basis, and the scribes and Pharisees were taking up the leadership roles. The leaders of formative Judaism exerted their influence upon all the Jews, both inside and outside Palestine. They emphasized the overcoming of factionalism within Jewish society and they did not tolerate any other groups that did not conform to their teaching. Because of its proximity to Palestine and because it had a large Jewish population in it, the city of Antioch, where Matthew's community was located, obviously became one of the early prime targets of the leaders of formative Judaism to exert their influence. When these leaders came to Antioch, they came into serious conflict with Matthew's community,[412] which, although it had some Gentiles among its members, was mainly a Jewish-oriented Christian community. The leaders of formative Judaism were particularly antagonistic towards the Jewish members of the Matthean community, mainly because of their differing interpretation of the Law, and their bestowal of Messiahship upon Jesus. Their hostility was also aggravated by the unsupportive attitude of the Jewish Christians during the Jewish War against Rome. Even due to the presence of the Gentiles within the Matthean community, the Jews questioned the faithfulness of the Jewish Christians towards the worship of Israel's one God. In these conflicts, formative Judaism got the upper hand. In consequence, Matthew's community suffered various kinds of persecutions from formative Judaism.[413] This historical situation seems to have been the primary factor that prompted the writing of Matthew's gospel and influenced its material arrangement and composition. At the same time, there were other important socio-historical experiences of the Matthean community, which the first evangelist obviously had to address. The more noticeable ones among such experiences could be briefly stated as follows – (1) Members of the Matthean community were experiencing persecutions in the hands of the Gentiles,

---

inheritance, etc. Horsley, *Sociology and the Jesus Movement*, 88-90. This situation indicates that there was a potential disunity and hatred between the rich and the poor even in the Matthean community.

412 The conflict between Matthew's community and the leaders of formative Judaism is most clearly indicated in the negative reaction of the scribes and the Pharisees, who were the leaders of formative Judaism, to the mission of Jesus, and in Jesus' response to those events by denouncing the scribes and Pharisees in the harshest of tones, in Matthew's gospel. For a detailed discussion on this, see the "The Antagonism between Matthew's Community and Formative Judaism," above.

413 See the discussion on "*Persecutions Suffered by Matthew's Community in the Hands of Formative Judaism*," above.

and they were expecting further persecutions to some extent.[414] (2) At the same time, while the community was failing in its mission to the Jews, more and more Gentiles were joining the community. This created some tension between the two communities. The Jewish members were apprehensive of their dominance within the community and the Jewish-orientation of their church. The Gentile members were, on the other hand, about to play down the importance of the Jewish practices in their Christianity.[415] (3) In addition to all this, there was economic inequality among the members of the Matthean community, which was a potential threat to create disunity and hatred among the members.[416]

Now, to conclude our survey of the socio-historical context of Matthew's gospel, we will briefly analyse the two sociological theories, which are usually proposed for the designation of the Matthean community, such as sectarianism and deviance, to see which one is more appropriate for the designation of the Matthean community.

1.5. Matthew's Community: A Sectarian or Deviant Community?

The Matthean community has often been termed as a "sectarian community" in modern sociological studies on this community.[417] However, this designation has been questioned by some scholars, claiming that the Matthean community (as well as the early church in general) does not fit into the sociologists' detailed explanation of "sect." And the term "deviant community" is suggested as a more appropriate designation.[418] An attempt will be made here to highlight the basic definitions and characteristics of these two theories that will help us to see which one is more appropriate for the designation of the Matthean community.

---

414 See the discussion on "Matthew's community and the Gentiles," above.

415 See the discussion on "The Ethnic composition of the Matthean Community," above.

416 Besides, those socio-historical features that have been highlighted above, it has been suggested that the hardships imposed by the Roman imperial regime on its subjects also seem to have influenced Matthew's gospel to some extent· For this suggestion see especially Warren Carter, *Matthew and Empire. Initial Exploration* (Harrisburg: Trinity Press International, 2001). See also, John Riches and David C. Sim, eds., *The Gospel of Matthew in Roman Imperial Context* (London/New York: T&T Clark International, 2005). However, this is not taken up here because the suggestion is at an initial level and not yet strongly established, and also because it does not seem to have any connection with the Matthean beatitudes.

417 A classic example would be Overman, *Matthew's Gospel and Formative Judaism*. David C. Sim also follows Overman overwhelmingly in terming Matthew's community as a sectarian community. See Sim, *The Gospel of Matthew and Christian Judaism*. See also Ewherido, *Matthew's Gospel and Judaism*, 200-217.

418 For example, of the questioning of terming the early church as "sect," and suggesting "'deviant community" instead, see J. T. Sanders, *Schismatics, Sectarians, Dissidents, Deviants: the First One Hundred Years of Jewish-Christian Relations* (Valley Forge, Pa.: Trinity Press International, 1993), 114-145. For the same question and suggestion specifically in relation to Matthew's gospel, see Stegemann and Stegemann, *The Jesus Movement*, 242ff.

1.5.1. Theory of Sectarian Movement

The use of the term "sect" for designating the early Christians is based mainly on the church-sect dichotomy, which goes back to scholars like Max Weber and Ernst Troeltsch, etc. Although Weber is the one who introduced the term "sect" in modern sociological studies, he does not develop an ideal type of sect with logically connecting attributes.[419] Therefore, discussions on this subject usually begin with Ernst Troeltsch's model of church-sect dichotomy.[420]

Basically viewing from the Christian situation in Germany and other European countries of the high Middle Ages, Troeltsch gives four basic points of difference between church and sect, such as - (1) The church is an overwhelmingly conservative organization, somewhat affirming the secular order, dominating the masses, and hence, in principle, is universal, that is, it desires to encompass the whole life of humanity. Sects, on the other hand, are relatively small groups, aspiring towards personal inward perfection. Their members have close fellowship with each other, and they have renounced the idea of dominating the world. They also behave apathetically toward the state and society. (2) While the churches encompass all strata, especially incorporating the "ruling strata," the sects, on the other hand, relate to the lower strata or to the strata that take a position against the state and society. (3) Members of the churches are initiated by birth whereas members of the sects are initiated through conscious conversion. (4) The church is a large institution, hierarchically organized, whereas a sect is a small group, chiefly organized autonomously.[421]

---

419 This is pointed out by David J. Chalcraft. Since Weber's work is enormous to be covered, it would be appropriate to mention here some of the observations on Weber's thought by Chalcraft, who is specialized in the study of Weber. According to Chalcraft the development of the concept of sect was progressing throughout Weber's thinking, and even in particular texts it develops over the course of his entire oeuvre and therefore it needs to be traced. Moreover, Weber does not develop an ideal type of a sect with a number of logically connecting attributes in the course of all his writings. He rather prefers a polar-type construction, and highlights one particular feature, which is essential for differentiating a sect-like religious movement from a church-like religious movement and for assessing the cultural significance of either, that is "*a religious community founded on voluntary membership achieved through qualification.*" Chalcraft further mentions that non-religious, artistic or other worldview /professional associations were also later included. Then, according to Weber, "all genuine sects" are sociologically speaking, those associations which accept only religiously qualified persons in their midst. Weber includes all the monks in the world in his concluding list. For this and for further insight into Weber's thought on "sect," see David J. Chalcraft, "The Development of Weber's Sociology of Sects: Encouraging a new Fascination," in *Sectarianism in Early Judaism. Sociological Advances*, edited by David J. Chalcraft (London, Oakville: Equinox, 2007), 26-51.

420 Lester L. Grabbe, "When is a Sect a Sect – or not? Groups and Movements in the Second Temple Period," in *Sectarianism in Early Judaism. Sociological Advances*, edited by David J. Chalcraft (London, Oakville: Equinox, 2007), 124.

421 Troeltsch, *The Social Teaching of the Christian Churches*, 331ff.

Although various attempts have been made after Troeltsch to explain the meaning of "sect," the explanation which is mostly quoted even now, is the one given by Bryan Wilson. According to Wilson the basic limitation of Troeltschean categories is the direct contrast of "the sect" with "the church." Wilson acknowledges that in the European Middle Ages, the sect was no doubt a protest against the church, its teaching, and its priests.[422] However, in today's secularized society, Wilson maintains, that sects "do not normally arise in schisms from established churches, nor do they usually arise in specific protest against the church." Instead, they arise in general "among those who are outside the churches, or at least arise without so much direct relevance to church involvement."[423] Therefore, the sect is a challenge to society at large and not to conventional religious beliefs.[424] Then, Wilson gives a brief definition of sect as "a self-consciously and deliberately separated religious minority which espouses a faith divergent from that of other religious bodies." According to him, the term "sect" encompasses minority movements, which are sometimes referred to as "cults" or "new religious movements."[425]

Although he contrasts Troeltsch's model of church - sect dichotomy, Wilson maintains that the basic characteristics of sects, as enunciated by Troeltsch and as subsequent sociologists have refined them, are still relevant in general. Then on that basis, he mentions eight characteristics of sects, which may be briefly summarized as follows:

> Sects are characterized by - (1) Commitment to only one body of religious teaching, and only one membership. (2) A claim to have a monopoly of the complete religious truth, which others do not enjoy. (3) Lay people with a body of professional functionaries and organizers, who are generally anti-sacerdotal. (4) Rejection of the religious division of labour, and special religious virtuosity to anyone, except, in some cases, to their own founders and leaders; and promotion of equal religious obligation for all members. (5) Voluntary membership, but with fulfillment of some mark of merit in order to be accepted as a member. (6) An exercise of sanctions against inadequate or wayward, to the point of expelling such individuals from the sect. (7) A demand of total religious allegiance, which is to be evident in its influence on all areas of the member's life. (8) A protest not against other religious bodies, but against the secular society, and, in some measure, possibly also against the state.[426]

According to Wilson non-sectarian persons accept the world as it is, with its mainstream culture and values, leaders and institutions, and sectarian groups by

422 Wilson, *Religion in Sociological Perspective*, 92.

423 *Ibid.*, 90.

424 Bryan Wilson, *The Social Dimension of Sectarianism. Sects and New Religious Movements in Contemporary Society* (Oxford: Clarendon Press, 1990), 46-47.

425 Wilson, *The Social Dimension of Sectarianism*, 47.

426 *Religion in Sociological Perspective*, 91-92.

contrast reject the world as evil. He then classifies sectarian groups according to the variety of their responses to the world, such as:

> *Conversionist* sects seek to change the individuals' hearts and are concerned with the recruitment of new members.
> *Revolutionist* sects wait for a supernatural intervention that will change the world.
> *Introversionist* sects tend to withdraw from society and to found isolated communities.
> *Manipulationist* sects claim to possess special or esoteric knowledge that enable them to influence the world.
> *Thaumaturgical* sects believe in oracles and miracles dispensed by super-natural agencies.
> *Reformist* sects try to provide a moral and ethical example for the rest of the society.
> *Utopian* sects are committed to the reconstruction of the world based on some divinely given principles, and to establish a new, evil-free social organization.[427]

Wilson puts together these seven types of sects into three larger categories on the basis of their focus, such as (1) *Objectivists*, - revolutionists, introversionists, reformists, and utopians; (2) *Subjectivists*, - conversionists; (3) *Relationists*, - manipulationists and thaumaturgists.[428]

Although there are several other attempts to define the term "sect," Wilson's definition and the models he proposes seem to be the most comprehensive, and most of the sectarian movements in modern times can be placed under at least one of them.[429] At the same time, these seven types are not rigid and they are not very separate from one another. A group can respond to the world at one time in more than one way, although one response would usually be dominant while the others would be subordinate.[430]

Out of the seven sectarian models proposed by Wilson, the Matthean community may fit into the first and the sixth, such as Conversionist sects and Reformist sects because their mission was to convert people into their faith

427 Bryan Wilson, *Magic and the Millennium: A Sociological Study of Religious Movements of Protest among Tribal and Third World Peoples* (London: Heinemann, 1973), 18-30.

428 *Ibid.*, 27.

429 Lester L. Grabbe says "Wilson's model of seven ideal types provides the valuable insight that we do not need to come up with new terminology." Grabbe, "When is a Sect a Sect – or not?...,"129. Pierluigi Piovanelli also comments, "Among the contemporary elaborations on religious sectarianism, Bryan R. Wilson's typology seems to be the most sensitive and operationally useful." Pierluigi Piovanelli, "Was there Sectarian Behaviour before the Flourishing of Jewish Sects? A Long-Term Approach to the History and Sociology of Second Temple Sectarianism," in *Sectarianism in Early Judaism. Sociological Advances*, edited by David J. Chalcraft (London, Oakville: Equinox, 2007), 157.

430 Saldarini, "The Gospel of Matthew and Jewish-Christian Conflict," 58.

of Jesus Christ, and they were emphasizing the moral and ethical quality of righteousness.[431] And Wilson's brief definition of sect as "a self-consciously and deliberately separated religious minority which espouses a faith divergent from that of other religious bodies," also seems applicable to the Matthean community if the term "sect" is to be understood only in terms of this definition. In the same way, out of the eight characteristics, which Wilson mentions, the first seven characteristics can be applied to the Matthean community. However, the eighth characteristic, which defines a "sect" as a protest movement against the secular society and the state, but not against other religious bodies, is not applicable to the Matthean community. In connection to this, Wilson's understanding of "sects" as protest groups arising from those outside the churches also does not correspond to the identity of the Matthean community. Therefore, while most of the characteristics of "sects" as mentioned by Wilson are more or less applicable to the Matthean community, and this community could fit into at least one or two of Wilson's seven models of sects, his basic understanding of sects as arising outside the church as a protest movement against the society and the state, but not against the church, makes it inappropriate to apply this term to the Matthean community.

Troeltsch's explanation of church-sect dichotomy is also not applicable to the Matthean community because, as far as we could understand, Matthew's community did not behave apathetically toward the state and society, and they did not relate only to the lower strata but also to the upper strata, and they did not take a position against the state and society.[432]

In addition to Troeltsch's and Wilson's explanations of the term "sect," even the explanations given by others[433] do not properly correspond to the identity of the Matthean community.

431 According to Saldarini the Matthean community had probably been a reformist movement. Saldarini, "The Gospel of Matthew and Jewish-Christian Conflict," 59.

432 See the section - "the Socio-Economic Status of the Matthean Community" above.

433 For example, of other definitions, the following may be mentioned in brief: (1) Benton Johnson: Churches accept their social environment whereas sects reject the social environment in which they exist. See Benton Johnson, "On Church and Sect," *American Sociological Review* 28/4 (August 1963): 539-549; (2) Baumgarten: "*A voluntary association of protest, which utilizes boundary marking mechanisms – the social means of differentiating between insiders and outsiders – to distinguish between its own members and those otherwise normally regarded as belonging to the same national or religious entity.*" See Albert I. Baumgarten, *The Flourishing of Jewish Sects in the Maccabean Era: An Interpretation* (Leiden: E.J. Brill, 1997), 7. (3) Philip R. Davies: "A social group that has socially segregated itself from its wider social matrix." See Philip R. Davies, "Sect Formation in Early Judaism," in *Sectarianism in Early Judaism. Sociological Advances*, edited by David J. Chalcraft (London, Oakville: Equinox, 2007), 135. (4) Saldarini: A sect is "a religiously based group which is either actively involved against society or withdrawn in reaction to it. Such groups are often political forces. In its classical Christian definition sect is contrasted with the dominant religious force, church." See Anthony J. Saldarini, *Pharisees, Scribes and Sadducees in Palestinian Society. A Sociological Approach* (Wilmington, Delaware:

Moreover, the term "sect" is an obscure term to some extent. It seems that there is no or there could not be a single universally applicable explanation or definition.[434] The term is apparently applied by different sociologists to describe the nature of different deviant religious movements which they are dealing with or are familiar with. Such different deviant religious groups usually have different characteristics, as rightly pointed out by Wilson in his seven models, hence different definitions. Wilson's seven models also would not be exhaustive,[435] and various groups, which can be placed within one model, will have different characteristics in detail. This means that there cannot be a single universally applicable explanation of "sect"[436] other than to apply Wilson's brief definition as "a religious minority movement," without further explanation, or to understand it simply to mean "a deviant religious movement" which Wilson also uses from time to time to refer to the so-called "sects."[437] However, as we have seen above, Wilson is also not content with these short renderings, but he gives emphasis on the nature of "sect" as a protest movement against the society. That is not, however, the nature of the Matthean community. Moreover, in spite of Wilson's effort to correct Troeltsch's definition, it seems that as of now, the use of the term "sect" is usually accompanied by an understanding of it with negative connotations as a split from the church.[438] Consequently, the term "sect" is not suitable for the understanding of the Matthean community, especially in its relation with the majority Jewish community after 70 C.E. Therefore, the term "deviant," which

---

Michael Glazier, 1988), 313. (5) Rodney Stark: Sect movements "occur by schism within a conventional religious body when persons desiring a more otherworldly version of the faith break away to 'restore' the religion to a higher level of tension with its environment." See Rodney Stark, "The Class Basis of Early Christianity: Inferences from a Sociological Model," *Sociological Analysis* 47/3 (1986): 216-225, http://www.jstor.org (accessed 30-Oct 2006); Stark's fresh definition with Bainbridge: "A *sect movement* is a deviant religious organization with traditional beliefs and practices." See Rodney Stark and William Sims Bainbridge, *A Theory of Religion* (New Brunswick, New Jersey: Rutgers University Press, 1996 [1987]), 124.

434 On the problem of defining the term "sect," Davies says, "we are unlikely to reach agreement on how to use the term." Davies, "Sect Formation in Early Judaism," 134.

435 Pierluigi Piovanelli, citing Wilson's models, mentions eight, instead of seven, adding *Spiritualistic* sects, which emphasize communication with the dead (e.g., Kardecism and Umbanda cult in Brazil). See Piovanelli, "Was there Sectarian Behaviour before the Flourishing of Jewish Sects?...," 158.

436 For a brief analysis on how the meaning of the term "sect" has been changing, see Kåre Sigvald Fuglseth, *Johannine Sectarianism in Perspective: A Sociological, Historical, and Comparative Analysis of Temple and Social Relationships in the Gospel of John, Philo and Qumran* (Supplements to Novum Testamentum. Leiden / Boston: Brill, 2005), 45-65.

437 See for example, Wilson, *Magic and the Millennium*, 19, 21, 26.

438 Grabbe rightly says, "Once 'sect' is shorn of its negative attitude and seen to indicate a 'minority religious movement,' without necessarily implying a split from a 'church,' it can serve the useful function of designating most and perhaps all the movements we know of in Second Temple Judaism." Grabbe, "When is a Sect a Sect – or not?...,"129. This implies that as of now the term "sect" is usually understood as having a negative connotation.

has been suggested by some scholars, seems more appropriate for the designation of the Matthean community,[439] which will be briefly looked into now.

1.5.2. Deviance Theory

The sociological theory of deviance is derived from Emil Durkheim's analysis of society in his *Division of Labour in Society.*[440] However, the person responsible for the major advance in the modern understanding of deviance theory is H. S. Becker with his work - *Outsiders: Studies in the Sociology of Deviance.*[441] According to H. S. Becker deviance is created by society itself. He maintains, "*social groups create deviance by making the rules whose infringement constitutes deviance*, and by applying those rules to particular people and labeling them as outsiders." Becker also maintains, "from this point of view, deviance is *not* a quality of the act the person commits, but rather a consequence of the application by others of rules and sanctions to an 'offender'." Therefore, "the deviant is one to whom that label has successfully been applied; deviant behavior is behavior that people so label."[442] Therefore, based on Becker's analysis, there is no static definition of the contents and aspects of deviant behavior for characterizing certain persons as outsiders or deviants. The majority society explains deviant behavior in each case.[443] Becker also holds that the person labeled as outsider, not accepting the rule by which he is being judged, and not regarding those who judge him as either competent or legitimately entitled to do so, may transfer back the labeling of outsider to them.[444] Thus, according to Becker's analysis, deviant community starts when, because of a deviant act, some people are labeled as outsiders by the public and isolated from the conventional society.[445] Consequently, the deviants, who share a common fate, in order to neutralize their exclusion, organize themselves into their own deviant groups and a deviant subculture gradually arises.[446] Becker further says that rules are usually made by groups who are more powerful for those who are less powerful; for example, elders make rules for young people, men for women, and the White people for the Negroes, the middle class for the lower class, etc. Thus, power differentials, either legal or extralegal, essentially constitute differences in ability to make rules and apply to other people. And, those groups who have power and weapons because of their social position are best able to enforce their rules. Differences in such power are all related to distinctions of age, sex, ethnicity and

439 Stegemann and Stegemann, *The Jesus Movement,* 242ff.

440 Originally published in 1893 as *De la division du travail social,* English translation in 1933, 1984. This is mentioned in Sanders, *Schismatics*, 129.

441 (New York: Free Press, 1963). This is mentioned in Sanders, *Schismatics*, 130.

442 Becker, *Outsiders*, 8-9.

443 Stegemann and Stegemann, *The Jesus Movement*, 244.

444 Becker, *Outsiders*, 2,

445 *Ibid.*, 1.

446 *Ibid.*, 38.

class, etc. "The rules created and maintained by such labeling," says Becker, "are not universally agreed to. Instead, they are the object of conflict and disagreement, part of the political process of the society."[447] Becker also maintains that the reason for branding others as deviants by certain persons or institutions lies mainly in the process of interaction between people wherein some of them, in order to serve their own interests, set up certain rules that declare others as deviants. On the other hand, those who are declared as deviants transgress those rules in pursuit of their own interests.[448] Such rules are formed by people based on values. That means that they shape values into rules when they perceive that some area of their existence is in difficulty and thus requires action. And, "the rule, framed to be consistent with the value, states with relative precision which actions are approved and which [are] forbidden, the situations to which the rule is applicable, and the sanctions attached to breaking it."[449]

Writing three years after Becker, Erikson offers another perspective of viewing deviance, not in opposition to, but as a supplement to what Becker has mentioned. According to Erikson, not the rules, but the specific crisis situations that necessitate the setting up of certain rules against deviants, are of crucial importance. He maintains that the majority society imposes its norms on deviants in crisis situations in order to draw or preserve boundaries. Such intensification of its boundaries or exclusion of others as deviants gives to a society a renewed assurance of its identity.[450]

In line with Eriksson, Ben-Yehuda also notes that deviance is most intimately connected with the identity of a society in that "it shows where a society draws its boundaries and indicates fundamental structures and values in its social and symbolic system."[451] He maintains, along with Erich Goode, that although the terms "deviance" and "deviant" are pejorative and condemnatory to most people, to the sociologists the use of the terms does not imply any condemnation, but are simply descriptive, referring "to behavior that, or persons who, are widely condemned – that, and nothing more."[452]

Saldarini maintains, "while deviant positions as such appear outside a society, they are still socially and historically a part of the whole."[453] In other words, "one cannot be deviant unless one is a member of the community."[454]

---

447 Becker, *Outsiders*, 17-18.

448 *Ibid.*, 163.

449 *Ibid.*, 131.

450 Erikson, *Wayward Puritans*, 13.

451 Ben-Yehuda, *Deviance and Moral Boundaries*, 19-20, as quoted in Stegemann and Stegemann, *The Jesus Movement*, 245.

452 Erich Goode and Nachman Ben-Yehuda, *Moral Panics. The Social Construction of Deviance* (Oxford UK & Cambridge USA: Blackwell, 1994), 70-71.

453 Saldarini, "The Gospel of Matthew and Jewish-Christian Conflict," 47.

454 *Ibid.*, 48.

Deviance theories outlined above seem to be very appropriate for explaining the experience of the Matthean community, although not every aspect of the explanations may necessarily apply.

1.5.3. Matthew's Community

A Deviant Jewish Community: The Jewish society faced a serious crisis after the destruction of the Temple in 70 C.E., and Judaism was badly in need of renewal. Important steps in the process of this renewal movement were redefinition of Judaism and establishment of boundaries. In this context, Pharisaic groups took control of the renewal movement and their convictions became the core of an ongoing process of integration. In this situation, the Christ-confessing Jews faced exclusion because of their deviant conception of the central symbols and values of Judaism.[455] Here, one could see that various explanations of deviance by Becker are in operation. First, the scribes and the Pharisees representing the Jewish society made the rules, and the Matthean community transgressed it and they were labeled as deviant by the Jewish society. The Torah as interpreted by the Pharisees comprised the rules for the Jews. However, for the Matthean community Jesus Christ and his interpretation of the law comprised the rule of the community.[456] Second, the Matthean community transferred the label back to the Pharisees and the Scribes. This is seen especially in the accusation of the Pharisees and scribes by the Matthean Jesus as hypocrites repeatedly in Matt 23, and in his demand of righteousness that surpass the righteousness of the Pharisees in Matt 5:20.[457] Third, in order to neutralize their exclusion, the Matthean community organized their own group, gradually developing a deviant subculture. This is indicated especially by the opening of the community's boundaries to non-Jews as shown in the Gentile interest, which is found in the first gospel from beginning to end.[458] The formation of *ekklesia* for Matthew's community as a gathering place distinct from the synagogue also could be another indication. Fourth, the scribes and the Pharisees formed the rules in their own interest because they were more powerful. The Matthean community wanted to carry on their own interest and then violated those rules. This is indicated in the various persecutions mentioned in Matthew's gospel, which were obviously suffered by Matthew's community at the hands of the Jewish leaders.[459] Erikson's emphasis on the importance of the crisis situation in which the rules are formed, also properly applies here because the enforcement of the Pharisaic teaching at this time was the upshot of the crisis situation in which the Jews were caught up in the aftermath of the destruction

455 Stegemann and Stegemann, *The Jesus Movement*, 245.

456 Saldarini, "The Gospel of Matthew and Jewish-Christian Conflict," 50.

457 Stegemann and Stegemann, *The Jesus Movement*, 246.

458 Saldarini, "The Gospel of Matthew and Jewish-Christian Conflict," 51.

459 Various persecutions are found in Matt 5:10-12, 44; 10:17, 23; 13:21; 22:6; and 23:34.

of Jerusalem and the Temple.[460] All these suggest that the Matthean community could be conveniently termed as a Jewish deviant community. This would not give a negative picture to the Matthean community from sociological point of view, as Erich Goode and Ben-Yehuda have clearly mentioned that the term does not carry any condemnation other than referring to the person or the behavior condemned.[461] And, this designation also affirms that they were part of the Jewish community, as Saldarini has explicitly pointed out.[462]

Saldarini has thoroughly dealt with how the Matthean community fits into a deviant Jewish community, giving various textual evidences.[463] According to him deviance associations have been conventionally classified into four types, such as *conformative* – those who seek acceptance by society; *alienative* – those who seek societal change; *expressive* – those who focus on the needs of their own members; and *instrumental* – those who seek to have an impact on society. And, by the time the first gospel was written Matthew's community seems "to be an *alienative-expressive* group offering its adherents a new Christian-Jewish world as an alternative to the conventional Jewish world (i. e., various types of traditional Jewish society with a range of norms and viewpoints)."[464]

Our discussion above shows that the sociological term "sect" does not properly fit for designating the Matthean community, and the more appropriate term is "deviance" or "deviant." Therefore, the Matthean community would be understood in this study as a "deviant Jewish community."

1.6. Preliminary Summary

Our investigation into the socio-historical setting of Matthew's gospel could be summarized as follows.

Matthew's gospel (the final redaction) was written around 75-93 C.E. It was written by a Hellenistic Jewish author, who was probably a former Jewish rabbi who became a Christian, extensively making use of Mark's gospel and the sayings source Q, and also a special tradition that was available to him, both in written and oral. The sayings source was probably collected by Matthew the apostle and written in Aramaic, and later translated into Greek and then took the form of Q. Most probably, the first evangelist used one of the two redacted forms of Q, which is now called Q^{mt}. The primary audience or target audience of the first evangelist was made up of Christ-believing Jews as the majority members, which were mixed with some Jewish-oriented Gentile Christians as minority members. Based on all the available internal and external evidences, Antioch of Syria is the most probable location where this final redaction took place.

460 See the section – "The Emergence of Formative Judaism" above.

461 Goode and Ben-Yehuda, *Moral Panics*, 70-71.

462 Saldarini, "The Gospel of Matthew and Jewish-Christian Conflict," 48.

463 *Ibid.*," 38-61.

464 Saldarini, "The Gospel of Matthew and Jewish-Christian Conflict," 56-57.

There were various socio-historical factors that affected the writing of Matthew's gospel and determined its contents.

The primary factor was the antagonism between the Matthean community and formative Judaism. In the aftermath of the Jewish war against Rome (66-73 C.E.), especially because of the destruction of Jerusalem and the Temple, which constituted the social, cultural and religious centre of the Jews, the Jewish society was in a chaotic and fluid state, and a new religio-cultural synthesis was required for the survival of Judaism. In this situation, the challenge to reclaim the faith of the Jews from the devastation of the war was taken up by a coalition of forces under the leadership of the scribes and the Pharisees. This renewal movement was called formative Judaism. The teachings of the Pharisees became the basis of the movement, and Jamnia was the centre of the movement. The influence of the Pharisaic rabbis in Jamnia was not confined within Palestine. All the Jews in the Roman Empire were dependent upon them for spiritual, temporal, and legal matters. This coalition movement strongly emphasized the overcoming of the previous separation of Judaism into different groups. As a result, the Jewish groups, which were not representing the majority consensus, including the followers of Jesus Christ, were not tolerated.

At this time Matthew's community (especially the Jewish members) were (most probably) part of the Jewish community in Antioch. They were not different from other Jews except in their belief in Jesus as the Messiah, and in their interpretation of the Law according to Jesus' interpretation. However, because of these very differences, the leaders of formative Judaism were very much hostile to them and there was a serious antagonism between the two groups. The hostility of the leaders of formative Judaism towards the Matthean community was further aggravated by the unsupportive behaviour of the Jewish Christians during the war, and the suspicion, because of their mixture with the Gentile (Christians), that they were no longer faithful to the belief in Israel's one God. Therefore, the leaders of formative Judaism looked upon Matthew's community as a deviant Jewish community. Formative Judaism got the upper hand in their conflict and as a result, Matthew's community suffered various kinds of persecutions in their hands. Matthew's community was confronted with various questions in this situation, such as – where does the community stand in relation to formative Judaism? How does the community understand and interpret the law? How does all this relate to their belief in Jesus of Nazareth? How do they order their lives and articulate their position? In what way are they different from the rest of the Jewish community? The need to clarify all these questions primarily prompted the writing of Matthew's gospel.

At the same time, there were also some other important concerns in relation to Matthew's community which the first evangelist had to address along with the primary concerns mentioned above.

In addition to the persecution from the Gentiles which the Matthean community endured along with other Jews during the Jewish war against Rome (66-73 C.E.), they were also suffering persecutions from the Gentiles (together with the Jews), probably because of their mission among the Jews,[465] and they were still in fear of further persecution from them. Because of such experiences, the Matthean community could have had a negative attitude toward the Gentiles. Such an attitude could also have worsened their relationship with their Gentile neighbours, which would in turn have affected their mission to the Gentiles as well.

Meanwhile, the mission of the Matthean community to the Jews was not successful and the Jewish membership of the community could no longer increase. On the other hand, more and more Gentiles were entering into the community. This situation created some sort of tension within the community. It seems that the Gentile members were showing signs of negligence to the importance of Jewish practices, because of which the Jewish members were apprehensive about the continuing Jewish-orientation of their community, as well as their leadership.

At the same time, there were some rich people among the members of the Matthean community while most of them were poor. This economic inequality was also a potential threat to the community to create disunity and hatred among the members, particularly between the rich and the poor.

In the midst of these varied problems and experiences undergone by the Matthean community, the gospel of Matthew was written. It is assumed in this study that the socio-historical situations experienced by Matthew's community played a decisive role in the selection, redaction and omission of the materials available to the writer (final redactor) of the first gospel. This means that while Matthew wrote/compiled his gospel from various gospel traditions available to him, he must have tried his best to make it meaningful and relevant to his target audience. For this purpose he must have retained those materials which served his purpose without alteration, he edited or redacted some of the materials to suit his purpose, and he omitted some of the materials which he felt were not useful for his purpose. Having said this, however, it is maintained in this study that while Matthew did all such literary exercises to make his message meaningful to his primary readers, he did not do anything to alter the fundamental meaning of the gospel traditions, but was faithful to their core meaning and implication. It is believed also in this study that while keeping his eye on his social setting, the first evangelist, who envisaged the gospel being preached to all nations (Matt 28:16-20), also would have definitely envisaged a broader readership including all Christians beyond his own time and place. With such a vision, and while it was obvious that many of the eye witnesses to Jesus were still alive, the author of

465 This is indicated in Matt 10:17-22.

the first gospel would have tried to be as accurate as possible in writing the story of Jesus.[466]

Finally, it is maintained in this study that an understanding of this socio-historical situation behind Matthew's gospel is of paramount importance for a proper understanding and interpretation of this gospel, which also will lead to a proper understanding of the story and teaching of Jesus the Christ. Accordingly, this insight into the socio-historical setting of Matthew's gospel will inform the final interpretation of the selected text for this study, that is the Matthean Beatitudes (Matt 5:3-12), supplementing insights from an exegetical study of the passage with the help of historical critical method, to which we now turn.

466 W. D. Davies and Dale C. Allison, Jr., seem right in pointing out that "a major and perhaps the primary impulse behind the first Gospel was 'the human desire to remember Jesus and preserve that memory accurately for the generations to follow.'" Davies and Allison, Jr., *Matthew*, Vol. III, 704.

Chapter 2

Exegesis of Matthew 5:3-12 (The Beatitudes)

2.1. Literary Analysis of Matthew's Gospel: An Overview

To begin the exegetical study of the Matthean Beatitudes (Matt 5:3-12), the literary characteristics of Matthew will be briefly analysed in order to establish the literary unity of the gospel and then to indicate the place where the selected passage is located within this unified gospel. The structure of the gospel will be analyzed first and then other literary characteristics of this gospel will be highlighted.

2.1.1. The Structure of Matthew's Gospel

Various suggestions have been put forth by Matthean scholars for the structure of Matthew's gospel, and among the various suggestions there are four most dominant theories out of which three are based on literary evidence and one is based on geographical framework. The theories based on literary evidence are the Pentateuchal theory, the chiastic arrangement, and the three-fold division.[1]

---

1 Excluded in this consideration are the topical outlines suggested by various commentators. For the list of scholars who made such topical outlines, see J. D. Kingsbury, *Matthew: Structure, Christology, Kingdom* (Philadelphia: Fortress, 1975), 2, and n. 6.
Besides the four dominant theories mentioned here, there is a lectionary hypothesis proposed by Michael Goulder in *Midrash and Lection in Matthew* (London: SPCK, 1974). However, Goulder's suggestion is criticised on several grounds, for example, (1) there is lack of knowledge about ancient Jewish liturgies, (2) Goulder's theory that Matthew is a Midrash on Mark is difficult to accept, and (3) Goulder's claim that Matthew knew and used Pauline corpus (including Ephesians) is doubtful. See the following: Davies and Allison, Jr., *Matthew*, Vol. I, 60-61. Carson, Moo and Morris, *An Introduction to the New Testament*, 61. And, especially for a detailed discussion of Goulder's suggestion, see L. Morris, "The Gospels and the Jewish Lectionaries," in *Gospel Perspectives: Studies of History and Tradition to the New Testament*, edited by R.T. France, David Wenham, and Craig Blomberg (Sheffield: JSOT, 1980-1986), 129-156.

These three hypotheses and the one based on geographical framework will be highlighted here, and following that a suggestion will be made on the theory which this study accepts as the most identifiable structure of Matthew's gospel.

2.1.1.1. *The Pentateuchal Theory*

B. W. Bacon first proposed a five–fold structure for Matthew's gospel and suggested that the first gospel was modelled by the first evangelist after the five books of the Pentateuch to produce a new Pentateuch and to present Jesus as the new Moses. According to Bacon, Matthew, a converted rabbi and a Christian legalist, systematically structures the commandments of Jesus based on the Pentateuch in order to meet the heresy of lawlessness that threatens his church. Bacon based his five-fold division on a more or less fixed statement καὶ ἐγένετο ὅτε ἐτέλεσεν ὁ 'Ιησοῦς.... "and when Jesus had finished...." which occurs five times in the gospel (7:28; 11:1; 13:53; 19:1; 26:1)[2] demarcating each section.[3] A good number of scholars are in agreement with Bacon's proposed outline,[4] although many of them

2 The formula is varied slightly from time to time: καὶ ἐγένετο ὅτε ἐτέλεσεν ὁ 'Ιησοῦς τοὺς λόγους τούτους (7: 28); καὶ ἐγένετο ὅτε ἐτέλεσεν ὁ 'Ιησοῦς διατάσσων τοῖς δώδεκα μαθηταῖς αὐτοῦ (11:1); καὶ ἐγένετο ὅτε ἐτέλεσεν ὁ 'Ιησοῦς τὰς παραβολὰς ταύτας (13:53); καὶ ἐγένετο ὅτε ἐτέλεσεν ὁ 'Ιησοῦς τοὺς λόγους τούτους (19:1); καὶ ἐγένετο ὅτε ἐτέλεσεν ὁ 'Ιησοῦς πάντας τοὺς λόγους τούτους (26:1).
All the scriptural quotations in Greek in this research will be taken from UBS Greek Text, 4th Revised Edition, and all the quotations in English will be taken from New Revised Standard Version (NRSV), otherwise it will be mentioned.

3 Each of the five books has a discourse preceded by a narrative, thus:
Preamble/Prologue -Birth narrative (1-2)
Book I: (a) Narrative material (3:1-4:25)
(b) Discourse - The Sermon on the Mount (5:1-7:27)
Formula: 7:28-29 - *and when Jesus had finished....*
Book II: (a) Narrative material (8:1-9:35)
(b) Discourse - on mission and martyrdom (9:36-10:42)
Formula: 11:1 - *and when Jesus had finished....*
Book III: (a) Narrative and debate material (11:2-12:50)
(b) Discourse – Teaching on the kingdom of heaven (13:1-52)
Formula: 13:53 - *and when Jesus had finished....*
Book IV: (a) Narrative and debate material (13:54-17:21)
(b) Discourse - on church administration (17:22-18:35)
Formula: 19:1 - *and when Jesus had finished....*
Book V: (a) Narrative and debate material (19:2-22:46)
(b) Discourse – on eschatology: farewell address (23:1-25:46)
Formula: 26:1-2 - *and when Jesus had finished....*
Epilogue: 26:3-28:20 - From the last supper to the resurrection.
See, B. W. Bacon, "The 'Five Books' of Matthew against the Jews," *Expositor* 15 (1918), 56-66, as quoted in Davies and Allison, Jr., *Matthew*, Vol. I, 59. See also B.W. Bacon, *Studies in Matthew* (New York: Henry Hold and Company, 1930), 145-335.

4 Kingsbury lists a huge number of scholars who, in general, are in agreement with Bacon. See Kingsbury, *Matthew: Structure, Christology, Kingdom*, 3, n. 13.

draw other inferences on the nature and purpose from Bacon's outline.[5] At the same time, Bacon's Pentateuchal theory has been criticized from various points.[6] Yet, in spite of various criticism levelled against Bacon's Pentateuchal theory, the five-fold division which he suggested has become the most frequently proposed structure for Matthew's gospel till now, albeit with slight variations in the actual demarcations of each section.[7]

2.1.1.2. *The Chiastic Arrangement*

The alternation between narrative and discourse in Matthew's gospel can be arranged in a chiastic pattern. C. H. Lohr is one of the leaders proposing a chiastic pattern for the structure of Matthew's gospel. Thus, Lohr's analysis shows that having chapter 13 as the centre ensures that discourses and narratives (without separate prologue and epilogue) in the two halves of the gospel parallel to each other.[8] The chiastic approach is also adopted by some other scholars but with slight

---

5 For examples of such scholars, Kingsbury mentions G. D. Kilpatrick, K. Stendahl, P. Benoit, P. Bonnard, David Hill, and W. Marxsen. See Kingsbury, *Matthew: Structure, Christology, Kingdom*, 3-4.

6 The main criticisms levelled against Bacon's theory are – his proposed connection between the five books of the Pentateuch and the five fold divisions of Matthew's gospel are too tenuous, and the ties between each discourse and the respective corresponding narrative are not always strong. Moreover the relegation of the entire passion and resurrection narrative to the status of epilogue is questionable. It is also argued that only with difficulty chapter 23 can be considered a part of the eschatological discourse that follows, and a considerable amount of Jesus' teaching in chapter 11 remains outside the five-fold structure. It is also argued that while Bacon divides each book of Matthew into a narrative section and a discourse section (taking discourse sections as legal materials), such a division between narrative and legal material is not found in Genesis, Leviticus, and Numbers. Only Exodus and Deuteronomy fit into such a division. Therefore, it seems that Matthew did not make the structure of his gospel in rigid parallel to the books of the Pentateuch. See these criticisms in the following: Carson, Moo and Morris, *An Introduction to the New Testament*, 62; Hagner, *Matthew 1-13*, li-liii; Davies, *The Setting of the Sermon on the Mount*, 19; and Kingsbury, *Matthew: Structure, Christology, Kingdom*, 4-7.

7 For examples of such five-fold divisions, see the following: Christopher, R. Smith, "Literary Evidence of fivefold Structure in the Gospel of Matthew," *NTStud* 43 (O 1997), 549; Carson, Moo and Morris, *An Introduction to the New Testament*, 63-65; DeSilva, *An Introduction to the New Testament*, 239-240; Brown, *An Introduction to the New Testament*, 174-203.

8 The arrangement goes as follows:

1-4	Birth and beginnings	Narrative
5-7	Blessings, entering the kingdom	Discourse
8-9	Authority and Invitation	Narrative
10	Mission discourse	Discourse
11-12	Rejection by this generation	Narrative
13	Parables of the kingdom	Discourse
14-17	Acknowledgment by disciples	Narrative
18	Community discourse	Discourse
19-22	Authority and invitation	Narrative
23-25	Woes, coming of the kingdom	Discourse
26-28	Death and rebirth	Narrative

variations from each other.[9] The chiastic arrangement is criticized on the ground that some of the corresponding elements seem arbitrary and are not compelling. There is also ambiguity in the evidence that can be gleaned from Matthew's text. As a result, the proponents of this structure have not gained a consensus.[10]

2.1.1.3. *The Tripartite Division*

Following the lead of Stonehouse, Lohmeyer, and Edgar Krentz, Jack Dean Kingsbury suggests a three-fold division for the structure of Matthew's gospel with the statement 'απὸ τότε ἤρξατο ὁ 'Ιησοῦς... "from that time on Jesus began..." which appears twice (Matt 4:17 and 16:21), as marking the boundary of each section.[11] This suggestion is also criticised on several grounds. It is questioned whether the statement 'απὸ τότε (*apo tote*) has a redactional importance so as to determine the entire structure of the gospel. It is also pointed out that the same statement is used by Matthew at 26:16 without any break in the flow of the narrative. It is also maintained that the breaking up of the important Peter passage in Matt 16 with this outline is unacceptable. Above all, the Christological development is not clear as Kingsbury alleges. It is argued that the person of Jesus which Kingsbury assigns to section 1 as its main theme (1:1-4:16), is still the focal point even in section 2 and 3 (e.g., 16:13-16; 22:41-46); and it is hardly possible to restrict the proclamation of Jesus to section 2 (4:17- 16:20), for two

---

See C. H. Lohr, "Oral Techniques in the Gospel of Matthew," *CathBibQuart* 23 (1961), 427. Ulrich Luz calls this "the *center model.*" Luz, *Matthew 1-7*, 36.

9 Scholars often quoted as adopting chiastic pattern are Fenton, Green, Gaechter, and Combrink. See in the following - Davies and Allison, Jr., *Matthew*, Vol. I, 60; and Hagner, *Matthew 1-13*, 60. See also P. F. Ellis, *Matthew: His Mind and His Message* (Collegeville: The Liturgical Press, 1974), 12. For more recent supporter of the chiastic structure, see Gary W. Derickson, "Matthew's Chiastic Structure and Its Dispensational Implications," *BiblSac* 163 (October-December 2006), 423-437.

Almost in line with this suggestion, Ulrich Luz is of the opinion that the first evangelist probably arranged the discourses in certain pattern according to length. The longest are the first, the sermon on the mount (chaps. 5-7) and the last, the apocalyptic discourse (chaps. 24-25); the shortest are the second, the mission discourse (chap. 10) and the fourth, the community discourse (chap. 18); and the middle discourse, which is the parable discourse is the medium-sized. See Luz, *Matthew 1-7*, 38.

10 See Hagner, *Matthew 1-13*, lii.

11 The three sections are therefore:

1. 1:1 - 4:16. The Person of Jesus the Messiah.
2. 4:17 - 16:20. The Proclamation of Jesus the Messiah.
3. 16:21 - 28:20. The Suffering, Death and Resurrection of Jesus Messiah. See, Kingsbury, *Matthew: Structure, Christology, Kingdom*, 7-25. See also the following: Ned B. Stonehouse, *The Witness of Matthew and Mark to Christ* (Grand Rapids: Eerdmans, 1944), 119-131; Ernst Lohmeyer, *Das Evangelium des Matthäus*, edited by W. Schmauck (Göttingen: Vandenhoeck & Ruprecht, 1956); Edgar Krentz, "The Extent of Matthew's Prologue: Toward the Structure of the First Gospel," *JournBibLit* 83 (1964), 410-411; Ulrich Luz calls this "the *Markan Model.*" Luz, *Matthew 1-7*, 36.

of the discourses (chaps. 18-24-25) and other important exchanges (21-23) are reserved for the third section.[12]

2.1.1.4. *A Structure based on Geographical Framework*

Besides the three theories proposed on the basis of literary evidence as mentioned above, some scholars suggest a structure based on a geographical framework, which is basically related to Mark's gospel.[13]

The suggestion of the structure based on geographical framework is criticized on the grounds that it does not reflect the literary markers in Matthew's gospel and therefore it tells very little of the purposes of the unique characters of Matthew's gospel. It is also claimed that with minor alterations this kind of analysis can be applied to all the gospels.[14]

Now, keeping in mind the four suggestions highlighted above for the structure of Matthew's gospel, we will try to make a suggestion on the structure, which is accepted in this study as the most identifiable for Matthew's gospel.

2.1.1.5. *Preliminary Conclusion on the Structure of Matthew's Gospel*

Since there is no consensus among scholars on the structure of Matthew's gospel, and at the same time, each of the proposals is not without criticism, it has often been asked whether the first evangelist had a particular structure as his master plan in mind. Some scholars hold that Matthew did not have a master plan, and an outline should not be imposed on this gospel.[15] In this context Dale C. Allison, Jr. seems right to some extent in suggesting that Matthew could "simply follow a rough chronological sequence – birth, baptism, ministry in Galilee, journey to Jerusalem, passion, resurrection – a sequence into which the five long and meticulously crafted sections of teaching material have been regularly inserted."[16]

---

12 Carson, Moo and Morris, *An Introduction to the New Testament*, 62.

13 According to this suggestion the basic structure of Matthew can be arranged as follows:

1. 1:1- 4:11 - Introduction (par. Mark 1: 1-13)
   1:1-2:23 - The prologue
   3:1-4:11 - Jesus' preparation for ministry
2. 4:12-13: 58 - Jesus' ministry in Galilee (par. Mark 1:14-6:13)
3. 14:1-16:12 - Extension of Jesus' ministry to other locales in the North (par. Mark 6:14-8:26)
4. 16:13–20:34 - Jesus begins to move toward Jerusalem (par. Mark 8:27–10:52)
5. 21:1-25:46 – The confrontation in Jerusalem (par. Mark 11:1-13:37)
6. 26:1-28:20 – Passion and Resurrection (par. Mark 14:1-16:8).

See for example A. H. McNeile, *The Gospel according to St. Matthew* (London: Macmillan, 1961), xii. See also Carson, Moo and Morris, *An Introduction to the New Testament*, 61.

14 See Carson, Moo and Morris, *An Introduction to the New Testament*, 61.

15 See for example, Gundry, *Matthew*, 10. See also Donald Senior, *What are They Saying about Matthew?* Revised and Expanded Edition (New York: Paulist Press, 1996), 35.

16 Allison Jr., "A New Approach to the Sermon on the Mount," 424.

At the same time, however, the argument, that "the five discourses are so clearly marked, from a literary point of view, that it is well-nigh impossible to believe that Matthew did not plan them,"[17] seems to be true.

Therefore, it is believed in this study that in presenting the life and teachings of Jesus, Matthew follows a rough chronological sequence, and he consciously chose to insert the teaching materials into five places in this sequence. The strongest support for this view is the literary evidence where each of the five discourses is closed remarkably with a similar statement, "now when Jesus had finished …," which obviously paves the way for the resumption of the narrative.[18] With these five discourses, which are all closed with a typical statement, Matthew creates a five-fold division for the basic structure of this gospel (as Bacon suggests) with the genealogy as introduction and the passion narrative as conclusion. This five-fold structure is further supported by the fact that each narrative that precedes a discourse can be seen as introducing a theme on which the following discourse expounds.[19] This means that each discourse and the preceding narrative can be seen as a unit, although the degree of the relationship between the discourses and their corresponding narratives may in fact be different in different sections.[20] The five-fold structure may be presented as follows:

Introduction: Genealogy (1:1-17)	
First Narrative (1:18-4:25)	First Discourse (5:1-7:29)
Second Narrative (8:1-9:38)	Second Discourse (10:1-42)
Third Narrative (11:1-13:9)	Third Discourse (13:10-53)

17 Carson, Moo and Morris, *An Introduction to the New Testament*, 62-63. Ulrich Luz also rightly points out that "Matthew puts together materials which are formally or materially similar." He further notes that although this principle of arrangement is not new as it is already found even both in Q and Mark, it is nevertheless new in Matthew for the fact that in several cases Matthew "brackets a block solidly in the thread of the narrative to enable it to receive a clear function in its place," for example, "the collection of miracle narratives in chs. 8-9 between the Sermon on the Mount and the discourse at the sending out of the disciples," as well as the collection of parables in 21:28-22:14 which has a clear function in the preparation of the great accounting with Israel. Luz, *Matthew 1-7*, 38.

18 Guthrie, *New Testament Introduction,* 40. See also Davies and Allison, Jr., *Matthew*, Vol. I, 412.

19 For a discussion on these, see the following: Talbert, *Reading the Sermon on the Mount*, 17-18; Smith, "Literary Evidence of fivefold Structure in the Gospel of Matthew," 545-549; and Gene R. Smillie, "'Even the Dogs': Gentiles in the Gospel of Matthew," *JournEvangTheolSoc* 45/1 (March 2002):96. Here, Smillie notes that several references to Gentiles are found in Matthew's gospel, which is evidently Jewish, wherein the conventional negative stereotypes of the Gentiles are juxtaposed with unconventional positive portraits of the same people. While, the negative stereotypes are often found in the discourses, the positive portraits are found in the narrative materials. Then, Smillie suggests that "the key to these ἔθνη puzzles … may possibly be found in understanding the relationship of the discourses to the narratives."

20 See Luz, *Matthew 1-7*, 35, who notes that the relationships between the narrative sections and the corresponding discourses are varied and at times are minimal ones.

Fourth Narrative (13:54-17:27) Fourth Discourse (18:1-35)
Fifth Narrative (19:1-23:39) Fifth Discourse (24:1-25:46)
Conclusion: Passion Narrative (26:1-28:20).[21]

The significance of this five-fold structure is, however, uncertain. It could be that Matthew just follows a widely used principle of organization in antiquity.[22] However, the socio-historical setting of Matthew's gospel suggests otherwise. It has been mentioned in the previous chapter that the main influencing factor behind the writing of Matthew's gospel was the antagonism between Matthew's community and formative Judaism where the first group suffered various persecutions at the hands of the latter. In such a context the Jewish author of the first gospel who wrote for a community, which was composed basically of Jewish/ Jewish oriented Christians, would have definitely tried his best to make the gospel attractive, meaningful and relevant for his target audience. Then the arrangement of the gospel into five blocks, after the number of the books in the Pentateuch would have been one of his strategies. Here, we uphold Bacon's Pentateuchal theory in principle, although not without some reservations. Every aspect of the Pentateuch and the five-fold divisions of Matthew's gospel may not or cannot be parallel,[23] because Matthew was not creating the gospel out of nothing, but from the traditions that were available to him, and he obviously was careful to be faithful to his traditions in presenting the life and work of Jesus.[24] However, viewed from the socio-historical setting of the first gospel, the choice of number five by the author for the arrangement of the discourse materials alongside the narratives, while he seemingly had freedom to choose other numbers as well, is difficult to

21 For this structure, see Smith, "Literary Evidence of fivefold Structure in the Gospel of Matthew," 549.

22 Talbert, *Reading the Sermon on the Mount*, 16-17. Here, Talbert maintains that the arrangement of the first gospel around five big discourse sections, does not prove in itself that a new Pentateuch is intended with the first gospel. Then he mentions how number five has been commonly used in antiquity for organizing structures of literature as follows:
The number five was widely used as a principle of organization in antiquity. Ancient Jewish materials use it: for example, the Pentateuch; the five books of Psalms (1-41; 42-72; 73-89; 90-106; 107-150); the five megilloth (Esther, Ruth, Song of Songs, Lamentations, Ecclesiastes); the five division of Proverbs (1-9; 10-24; 25-29; 30; 31); 1 Enoch (1-36; 37-71; 72-82; 83-90; 91-108); Jason of Cyrene's five books (mentioned by 2 Macc 2:23). Greco-Roman traditions uses it: for example, Diogenes Laertius says that Aristophanes of Byzantium, the renowned grammarian, literary critic, and lexicographer at Alexandria, was the first scholar to organize the *Corpus Platonicum*, doing so by arranging the Platonic dialogues into five trilogies (*Lives* 3.61-62); Xenophon's novel, *An Ephesian Tale*, is also organized in five books. Early Christian authors also used the number five as an organizing principle: for example, Papias' *Expositions of the Dominical Oracles* consisted of five books; Irenaeus's *Against Heresis* is in five books; Tertullian's *Against Marcion* is also in five books.

23 W. D. Davies' assessment is correct in this matter. See Davies, *The Setting of the Sermon on the Mount*, 19-20.

24 Davies and Allison, Jr., *Matthew*, Vol. III, 704.

explain meaningfully in any other way. Therefore, it is quite compelling to view in such a way that Matthew was trying his best to arrange the materials available to him, particularly the teaching materials, into five blocks, in parallel to the five books of the Pentateuch. Although other proposed structures also can indeed be deduced from the gospel, none of them enjoys, as compared to the five-fold structure, a strong support from the literary evidence and from the socio-historical setting of the first gospel.[25] Therefore, this five-fold arrangement of the teachings of Jesus by Matthew could well be defined as one of his strategies to portray these teachings as reminiscent to the teachings of Moses in the Pentateuch. This observation is also well supported by Matthew's presentation of Jesus in parallel to Moses in many ways.[26]

The primary significance of the identification of the five-fold structure with undeniable boundary markers is that it goes well with the suggested socio-historical setting of the first gospel in the previous chapter, and at the same time it strongly indicates the cohesive unity of this gospel,[27] showing that it is properly and meaningfully arranged by the author to be a united whole. Here, we can invite the support of other proposed structures as well for, although they do not

---

25 Luz, (in *Studies in Matthew,* 22) observes:

The impact of Matthew's Gospel owes a great deal to his inspired idea of assembling in five thematic discourses the sections of Jesus' preaching which were relevant for the present. Explicit references in Matt 5:1 and 8:1 to the Sinai narrative indicate that Matthew himself was inspired by the Pentateuch. Even though we cannot establish any clear correspondence between the individual books of the Pentateuch and individual passages of Matthew's Gospel, we can say that his basic literary model, i.e., the story of God's activity interspersed with discourses that address the current readers directly, corresponds to that of the Pentateuch.

Luz, however, further observes (in p. 31) that there is a (second) distinctive feature of Matthew in the five discourses:

Like the biblical Moses in the book of the Covenant, in Deuteronomy and the later in *Jubilees*, *Jesus* now speaks from the mountain directly into the present. The instruction he gives is valid for the present. It is not the Torah, but the εὐαγγέλιον τῆς βασιλείας (gospel of the kingdom) which incorporates the Torah. With the five discourses, the "proclamation of the kingdom" corresponds to the fivefold Torah. Jesus' discourses unfold a new proclamation of the valid will of God, given by one who is greater than Moses, that is, the Immanuel himself.

26 For example, as Moses received the Law from God on the mountain, Jesus gives his teaching on discipleship (the Sermon on the Mount) from the mountain (chaps. 5-7). The teaching of Jesus is contrasted with that of Moses throughout the Sermon on the Mount (Matt 5:22, 28, 32, 34, 39, 44). At the same time Matthew presents Jesus as coming to give the Law and the Prophets (the OT) their real meanings (Matt 5:17). Like Moses, Jesus miraculously escaped death as a child (Matt 2: 16-18). Like Moses Jesus is brought out of Egypt by divine guidance (Matt 2: 13-15). Because of all these, Matthew could be viewed as presenting Jesus as "the new Moses." See Newman, Jr., "Some Translational Notes on the Beatitudes," 107. For a detailed study of the parallelism of Jesus and Moses in the first gospel, see Dale C. Allison, Jr., *The New Moses, a Matthean Typology* (Minneapolis / Augsburg: Fortress, 1993). Cf. Luz says that he does not assume, unlike Dale C. Allison Jr., a unified Moses Christology in or behind the gospel of Matthew. Luz, *Studies in Matthew,* 32.

27 Davies and Allison, Jr., *Matthew*, Vol. I, 72.

enjoy a strong support from the socio-historical setting of the gospel as much as is enjoyed by the five-fold structure, all of them also point to the unity of the gospel and not otherwise. Then the selected passage for the present study is an important component within this united gospel. This area will be dealt with further later. Meanwhile, the unity of the gospel is indicated not only by the structures, but also by several other literary characteristics, which we will be looking at now.

2.1.2. Other Important Literary Characteristics of Matthew's Gospel

Apart from the basic literary structures (above), literary analysis of Matthew's gospel reveals that the first gospel is characterized by several identifiable literary characteristics, which in turn indicate the intrinsic unity of this gospel because they more or less characterize the gospel in its entirety. Such major literary characteristics may be briefly highlighted as follows.[28]

2.1.2.1. *Triadic Arrangement*

A very significant literary characteristic in Matthew's gospel is the arrangement of the materials in triads. A careful analysis shows that where Matthew composes on his own (as in chaps. 1-12 and the major discourses), he chiefly composes in triads (although not always so, as Talbert has pointed out[29]), and where Matthew closely follows Mark (as he does in 14:1 on, and in 13:1-23 and 24:1-36), the triad disappears.[30]

2.1.2.2. *Favourite Words and Expressions*

Matthew's gospel has several words and phrases, which can be taken as unique to this gospel. J. C. Hawkins listed ninety-five words and phrases which, according to him, are characteristic of Matthew. By "characteristic" he refers to those vocabularies, which occur at least four times in Matthew and which, are either not found in Mark or Luke, or which occur twice as often as in Mark and Luke put together. For example – ἀνατολη, ἀναχωρεω, ἀνομια, ἀποδιδωμι, ἀργυρια (pl), ἀρτι, ἀστηρ, βασιλεια των οὐρανων, βρυγμος των ὀδοντων, γαμος, etc.[31] W. D. Davies and Dale C. Allison Jr. also list other "hundred and forty three" words and phrases which they regard, although they do not satisfy Hawkins' criterion for

28 Davies and Allison, Jr., have analysed the literary characteristic of Matthew in detail. This sub-section will heavily depend upon their analysis. See Davies and Allison, Jr., *Matthew*, Vol. I, 72-96.

29 Talbert, *Reading the Sermon on the Mount*, 16. Here Talbert points out that Gaechter, *Das Matthäus Evangelium,* shows the use of five and sevens also in the material where the Evangelist is on his own.

30 For a detail discussion on this, see Davies and Allison, Jr., *Matthew*, Vol. I, 62-72, 86-87. See also Allison, Jr., "A New Approach to the Sermon on the Mount," 405-414.

31 See a complete list in Davies and Allison, Jr., *Matthew*, Vol. I, 75-76. Davies and Allison, Jr., however, note here, "not all of the words in Hawkins' list are of great importance."

"characteristic," to be very often editorial, for example – ἀγρος, ἀδελφος, ἀλλος, ἀπερχομαι, ἁρπαζω, ἀφιημι, βαλλω, βαπτιστης, βασιλευς, γεεννα, etc.[32] These favourite words are found throughout the gospel.

2.1.2.3. *Semitisms*

Matthew's gospel is full of Semitisms, that is, it is full of words and constructions, which need to be explained through the influence of Hebrew or Aramaic. These Semitisms derive from four different sources, such as - the author's tradition (Mark, Q and M), the author's imitation of the LXX, the author's translation of the Hebrew Old Testament, and the author's own Semitic mind-set. This Semitism is not unique to Matthew, for Mark and Luke also are characterised by Semitisms. However, certain words and expressions, apart from the formula quotations, strongly indicate the author's knowledge of more than the Greek language. Consequently, the Semitisms in Matthew "presumably reflect the evangelist's own style of thought."[33]

2.1.2.4. *The Penchant for Numbers (such as Triads, Two, Seven, and Fourteen)*

Literary analysis of Matthew's gospel shows that the evangelist had a strong inclination to arrange his thoughts around numerals. Apart from the triads (mentioned above) other numbers such as two, seven and fourteen are found in the first gospel.[34] At least three times Matthew has multiplied a Markan figure by two.[35] Also number seven occurs several times in Matthew's gospel. Most or all of them, however, are drawn from his sources Mark, Q and M. W. D. Davies and Dale C. Allison Jr. maintain that Matthew does not lend any significance to this number "seven."[36] However, this researcher believes that not only the Matthean redaction, but also the existing sources which he accepts as they are, have significance for the author. With regard to his retention of number seven from his tradition, they would at least support Matthew's penchant for numbers, which is indicated by his use of other numbers, as well as the significance of those numbers. To be more precise, Matthew's penchant for numbers is understood to

32 See a complete list in Davies and Allison, Jr., *Matthew*, Vol. I, 77-79. Cf. Luz, *Matthew 1-7*, 52-72.

33 For this and for the representative (but not exhaustive) list of Semitisms in Matthew, see Davies and Allison, Jr., *Matthew*, Vol. I, 80-85.

34 Ulrich Luz maintains that number *three* seems most important in Matthew's number schemes although *two*, *four* and *seven also* play certain role. Luz, *Matthew 1-7*, 38.

35 One demoniac in Mark 5:2 becomes two demoniacs in Matt 8: 28; an ass in Mark 11:1-10 becomes an ass and her foal in Matt 21:1-11; a blind man in Mark 10: 46-52 becomes two blind men in Matt 9:27-30; and also some false witness in Mark 14:57 becomes two false witnesses in Matt 26:57-58. For these and for other occasions where Matthew retain number "two" from his sources, namely Mark, Q and M, see Davies and Allison, Jr., *Matthew*, Vol. I, 87.

36 Davies and Allison, Jr., *Matthew*, Vol. I, 87.

be an indicator of his Jewishness, and especially of his place in a rabbinic world.[37] This would hold significance especially if we are reminded that the primary influencing factor behind the writing of Matthew's gospel was to respond to the teaching of the Pharisaic rabbis who were leaders of formative Judaism with whom the Matthean community was in serious conflict. Here, number seven would certainly contribute alongside other numbers. The number fourteen found in Matt 1:2-17 also indicates the Jewishness of the author. Various suggestions have been put forward as the key to understanding this number (fourteen). Although it is difficult to understand what Matthew exactly would mean with this number, most (or all) of the suggestions relate to the Jewish background of the author.[38]

2.1.2.5. *Thematic Thinking*

Matthew's gospel betrays a careful thematic arrangement by the author because every single saying is found in its proper thematic place. The difficulty to discern such a thematic unity in both Mark and Luke indicates that the first evangelist has often rearranged the materials in his traditions in order to bring the sayings on the same theme together. Obviously because of this, the subject matter of the major Matthean discourses can be easily summarized, such as – chaps. 5-7: law, cult, social attitudes and obligations; chap. 10: missionary instructions; chap. 13: parables on the kingdom of God; chap 18: community regulations; chaps. 24-25: eschatological teaching.[39]

---

37 Davies and Allison, Jr., *Matthew*, Vol. I, 85-86. Here, Davies and Allison, Jr. also mentions rabbinic writings such as *m.'Abot* 1 which contains triads; *m.'Abot* 5 which name numbers ten, seven, and four again and again; and *m. Kelim* 24 which contains seventeen triads.

38 Some of the suggestions are - 1) if the three fourteens are taken as multiples of seven (i.e., six sevens), then with the coming of Christ the seventh seven will begin to appear, that is the period of perfection and fulfilment. 2) The number fourteen could be seen as alluding to Daniel's reference to seventy weeks of years (Dan 9:24), for the same number, 490, is reached by reckoning a generation at thirty-five years. This will mean that after three periods of seventy weeks of years, God sends his Messiah into the world. 3) The numerical value of the Hebrew letters spelling David is fourteen (דוד = 4, 6, 4). Therefore, keeping this in mind Matthew may have structured the genealogy because David is very important to his purpose. 4) The waxing and waning of the moon (twenty-eight-day cycles) may have bearing on the use of fourteens in the genealogy, thus relating the alternating of - i.e., the Davidic kingdom, the Babylonian exile, the appearance of Christ - high and low points in the dividing points of the genealogy. 5) The forty-two months of evil in Rev 13:5 before the intervention of God may have influenced the use of these fourteens (3x14= 42). For these suggestions and comments on them, see Hagner, *Matthew 1-13*, 6-7.

39 Davies and Allison, Jr., *Matthew*, Vol. I, 87-88. According to Ulrich Luz Matthew also hints at his themes by central verses, which are, for example, 5:17, 20, 48; 6:1; 7:12, 21; 10:16, 26 or 18:10, 14. There are also or central texts in a figurative sense, such as for example, 5:17-20; 12:35-40; 22: 34-40 or 28:16-20. Such texts or verses open up larger contexts and they are distinguished by their positions. Luz, *Matthew 1-7*, 39.

2.1.2.6. *Repetition*

Matthew's gospel is prolific with repetitions of different types,[40] such as repetition of formulas in close succession,[41] repetition of formulas throughout the gospel,[42] twofold repetition of similar phrases or constructions in close proximity,[43] twofold or threefold repetition of similar or identical words or phrases not in close proximity[44] (excluding doublets), doublets due to overlapping of sources,[45] doublets due to Matthean redaction,[46] and similar stories.[47] Besides these there are miscellaneous repetitions, such as for example, ἔνοχος ἔσται – repeated three times in 5:22; μὴ μεριμνᾶτεή́σητε – repeated three times in 6:25-34;

40 For a comprehensive list of repetitions, see Davies and Allison, Jr., *Matthew*, Vol. I, 88-92.

41 For example – Abraham begat Isaac ... and so on (thirty nine times in a row - 1:2-16); blessed are the poor in spirit for... and so on (nine times in a row - 5:3-11); the kingdom of heaven is like + dative (three times in 13:44-47); woe to you (seven times in 23:13-36), etc.

42 For example, "all this took place to fulfill what had been spoken by the Lord through the prophet" (1:22; 2:15, 17, 23; 4:14; 8: 17; 13:35; 21:4; 27:9); "and it happened when Jesus had finished ...." (7:28; 11:1; 13:53; 19:1; 26:1), etc.

43 Instances are, παραγίνεται Ἰωάννης (3:1) and παραγίνεται ὁ Ἰησοῦς (3:13); "In that hour" (11:25) and "In that hour" (12:1)); "Watch then, because you do not know in what day..." (24:42) and "Watch then, because you do not know the day" (25:13). See further examples in – 2:22-23 and 4:14; 4:18 and 4:20; 5:13 and 5:14; 5:18 and 5:20; 5:29 and 5:30; 5:39 and 5:41; 5:40 and 5:42; 8:1 and 8:5; 9:26 and 9:31; 15:21 and 15:29; 17:22 and 17:24.

44 Example, "and behold a voice from the heavens saying, this is my beloved son, in whom I am well pleased" (in 3:17 and 17:5); "brood of vipers" (in 3:7 and 23:33); "Have mercy upon us, Son of David" (in 9:27; 15:22 and 20:29, 31). See further examples in – 4:10 and 16:23; 4:17 and 16:21; 5:17 and 10:34; 5:32 and 19:9; 7:12 and 22:40; 7:21 and 12:50; 8:2 and 9:18; 8:12 and 13:38; 9:4 and 12:25; 9:20 and 14:36; 9:36 and 14:14; 10:6 and 15:24; 12:39 and 16:4; 13:43 and 17:2; 14:21 and 15:38; 14:33 and 27:54; 16:12 and 17:13; 16:16 and 26:63; 17:6 and 27:54; 21:36 and 224.

45 Examples could be, eschatological persecution on account of Jesus (10:19-20; 24:9, 13 cf. Mark 13:11; Luke 12:11-12); "he who has to him shall be given" (13:12; 25:29, cf. Mark 4:25; Luke 19:26). See further examples in – Matt 10:32; 16:27 cf. Mark 8:38; Luke 12:8-9; Matt 10:38-39; 16:24-25 cf. Mark 8:34-35; Luke 14:27; 17:33; Matt 10:40; 18:5 cf. Mark 9:37; Luke 10:16; Matt 11:15; 13:9 cf. Mark 4:9, 23; Luke 14:35; Matt 12:38-42; 16:1-4 cf. Mark 8:11-12; Luke 11:16, 29-30; Matt 17:20; 21:21 cf. Mark 11:23; Luke 17:6.

46 For example, "Repent, for the kingdom of heaven is at hand" (3:2; 4:17); "the first will be last" (19:30; 20:16). See further examples in – 3:10 and 7:19; 5:29-30 and 18:8-9; 5:32 and 19:9; 7: 16 and 7:20; 9:1 and 12:7; 10:6 and 15:24; 10:15 and 11:24; 10:17-22 and 24:9-14; 16:19 and 18:18.

47 For example, Jesus and the sea (8:23-27; 14:22-33 from Mark); two blind men healed (9:27-31; 20:29-34); a dumb demoniac healed (9:32-34; 12:22-34); the feeding narratives (14:14-41; 15:32-38 from Mark).
Ulrich Luz observes that doublets in Matthew serve various purposes, for example, they create a compositional frame around certain sections; they set off important sections; they sometimes help in treating the same materials under different aspects; and they serve special intentions, for example, in demonstration of the continuity of the proclamation among John, Jesus and the disciples. Luz, *Matthew 1-7*, 39-40.

γρηγορεῖτεῆσαι – repeated three times in 26:38-41 (from Mark).[48] Matthew also has a habit of repeating key words to hint at his themes, for examples, "Αγγελος κυρίου (4 times in 1:18-2:23 as pointing to God's guidance); δικαιοσύνη (5 times in chaps 5-7); ἀποστέλλωἀπόστολος (4 times in 10:2-42); κρίσις (7 times in 11:20-12:45); Φαρισαῖος (4 times in 12:1-45); "Οχλος (16 times in chs 14f.); ἀδελφός μικρός ανδ ἀφίημι (4 times, 3 times and 4 times respectively in ch. 18); ἀκολουθέω (9 times in chs. 8f. and 6 times in chs 19f.).[49]

2.1.2.7. *Inclusio*[50]

Although the repetition of key words or phrases does not necessarily always make for a significant enclosure in Matthew's gospel, several undoubted examples of *inclusio* are found. Some of the examples are the following:[51]

(1) 1:23 – "God with us" ----------- 28:20 – "I am with you always."
(2) 4:23 - Jesus went throughout Galilee, teaching in their synagogues and proclaiming the good news of the kingdom and curing every disease and every sickness among the people.

9:35 - Jesus went about all the cities and villages, teaching in their synagogues, and proclaiming the good news of the kingdom, and curing every disease and every sickness.

(3) 5:1-2 - the crowds, the mountain, Jesus teaching. -------- 7:28-8:1 – the crowds, the mountain, Jesus teaching.
(4) 5:3b – for theirs is the kingdom of heaven. -------- 5:10b – for theirs is the kingdom of heaven.
(5) 5:17 – the law and the prophets --------- 7:12 – the law and the prophets.
(6) 5:20 – περισσεύσῃ --------------- 5:47-48 – περισσόν.
(7) 7:16 – "you will know them by their fruits" ----- 7:20 – "you will know them by their fruits."
(8) 15:12 – "they do not wash their hands when they eat" ---- 15:20 – "to eat with unwashed hands does not defile a man."

48 For other examples, see 5:34-36; 7:7-11; 10:26-31.

49 For this see Luz, *Matthew 1-7*, 39.

50 *Inclusio*, as defined by Brown, "is a stylistic technique for marking off or 'packaging' a unit: a detail mentioned at the beginning of a section is alluded to or repeated at the end." See Raymond E. Brown, *The Birth of the Messiah: A Commentary on the Infancy Narratives in the Gospels of Matthew and Luke* (New York: Doubleday, 1999 [1977]), 50.

51 Davies and Allison, Jr., *Matthew*, Vol. I, 92-93. See also Luz, *Matthew 1-7*, 40.

W. D. Davies and Dale C. Allison Jr. observe that "the Matthean *inclusio* does more than set off discrete units: it also gives expression to the major themes of those units."[52]

2.1.2.8. *Chiasmus*

Although the chiastic arrangement does not seem to be so compelling for the basic structure of Matthew's gospel, the attempts, which have been made to make out such a structure, suggest that the possibility cannot be totally ruled out. Moreover, it seems that at least at some points the first evangelist may have consciously arranged his material in chiastic sequences. Some of the possible chiastic arrangements, according to Davies and Allison, Jr., include 1:1, 18; 8: 14-15, 23-27, 28-34; 10:1-42; and 28:16-22.[53] Ulrich Luz also finds the Sermon on the Mount with the Lord's Prayer as its centre as an example of Matthew's chiastic composition. He further identifies examples of smaller text sections with chiastic structure in 9:1b-8; 13:13-18 and 18:10-14.[54]

2.1.2.9. *Headings and Conclusions*

The author of the first gospel has a habit of placing introductory or summarizing sentences at the beginning of sections. To see for instance, 1:1, 18; 4:23- 5:2; 5:13-16, 17-20; 6:1, 25; 10:16, 26; 11:20; 23:2; 24:3. This technique is reminiscent of the rabbinic *kĕlāl*,[55] and therefore, it is another clear indicator of the Jewishness of the author. Matthew also has a habit of concluding sections sometimes with summarizing statements, as in 5:48; 6:34; 7:12; and 18:35.[56]

2.1.2.10. *Foreshadowing*

The anticipation of the fate of Jesus and the outcome of his mission is found in the first four chapters of the first gospel in three different ways. This means that the beginning foreshadows the end. First, is the foreshadowing of the passion narrative in chapter 2, such as in the troubling of Jerusalem as a result of Jesus' birth (2:3), the conspiracy of the chief priests with Herod (2:4-5), and the threatening of Jesus' life (2;13). Second, is the anticipation of the Gentile mission, which Jesus commanded only in 28:19. This anticipation is found in the calling of Jesus as

52 Davies and Allison, Jr., *Matthew*, Vol. I, 93. Luz maintains that "an impressive inclusion which spans the whole Gospel is the resumption of Immanuel, 'God with us' (1:24f.), at the end in 28:20." He also holds that "inclusions in large contexts become evident only to continuous reading" thus indicating that "Matthew wishes that his book be read and meditated upon as a whole again and again." Ulrich Luz, *Matthew 1-7*, 40.

53 Davies and Allison, Jr., *Matthew*, Vol. I, 93.

54 Luz, *Matthew 1-7*, 40. Here Luz observes that a pre-Matthean example of chiastic arrangement is found in 23: 16-21.

55 Davies and Allison, Jr., *Matthew*, Vol. I, 93.

56 Davies and Allison, Jr., *Matthew*, Vol. I, 93.

the son of Abraham (1:1), in the visit of the Gentile magi to infant Jesus (2:1), in the saying of the Baptist about God raising up new children to Abraham (3:9), and in the appearance of Jesus in the "Galilee of the Gentiles" (4:15). Third is the foreshadowing of Jesus' fate in the arrest of John (4:12), which indicates, "the true prophet will be 'handed over'."[57]

2.1.2.11. *Parallelism*

The sayings of Jesus in Matthew often show a higher degree of parallelism when compared with those in Mark and Luke. This seems to be a characteristic of the first evangelist, and it probably is due to the influence of Semitic poetry. Then, this phenomenon is also another clear indicator of the Jewishness of the author and the intended audience of the first gospel. Typical examples of parallelisms may be found in 5:39-40 (par. Luke 6: 29); 6:22-23 (par. Luke 11:34-36); 18:8-9 (par. Mark 9:43-47).[58]

2.1.2.12. *Redactional Expansions of and Additions to the Sayings Tradition*

The author of the first gospel is understood to have reordered many events found in Mark, distributed Q material wherever he willed, and more notably expanded on occasions dominical sayings and also created a few of his own.[59] These were done by the evangelist to make the texts more adaptable to his own *Sitz im Leben*, to achieve certain literary ends, to explain events to his readers, and to make theological points. Consequently, he is labelled a "conservative redactor" and considered a "creative writer." Since it is often difficult to decide whether a verse should be ascribed to M or to pure redaction, it is not possible to determine the extent of the first evangelist's creativity with exactitude. However, the author's pure redaction seems to be found at least in 3:15; 5:10, 13, 14, 16, 20, 32; 6:14-15; 7:12, 15; 9:13; 10:8; 10:41; 11:29; 12:7; 18:10, 14; 19:9; 21:41c, 43; 23:32-34; 24:12, 20, 26.[60]

---

57 Davies and Allison, Jr., *Matthew*, Vol. I, 93-94. According to Ulrich Luz, the history of Herod and the Gentile Magi in Matt 2:1-12 preludes the whole tragic faith of Israel; Matt 4:8 contains a signal to 28: 15-20; Matt 2:23 and 4:12-16 together signal to the Gentile mission; Matt 3:15 signals to 5:17 and the Sermon on the Mount. Luz maintains that the signal technique of Matthew shows that the first gospel was meant to be read as a whole, and as a narrative. Luz, *Matthew 1-7*, 41.

58 For other examples, compare Matt 6:19-21 with Luke 12:33-34; Matt 7:24-27 with Luke 6: 47-49; and Matt 10:24-25 with Luke 6:40. Davies and Allison, Jr., *Matthew*, Vol. I, 94.

59 This understanding does not contradict the view that the author of the first gospel tried to be faithful to the traditions he had before him. The idea adopted here is that if the author created any events in the gospel of his own, they would not contradict the traditions available to him. They would only act as further clarification of the message (s) presented by the author through his traditions.

60 For these and for the statements in the verses mentioned, see Davies and Allison, Jr., *Matthew*, Vol. I, 95-96.

2.1.2.13. *Authorial Comments*

Matthew has inserted explicit authorial commentary into his work more regularly than his antecedents Mark and Q. Such authorial comments in the first gospel include the title in 1:1, the formula quotations and their introductions, as well as a number of parenthetical asides or illustrative notes, for example, in 1:23b; 7:29; 9:6; 12:8; 13:34; 22:33; 24:15; 27:8, 15-16, 33, 46; 28:15.[61]

Most of these literary characteristics are found throughout Matthew's gospel, albeit with differences in their degree of regularity. This clearly indicates that the gospel is the handiwork of one man. Above all, literary tools such as foreshadowing, repetition, and *inclusio* reveal the impressive unity of the gospel.[62] Moreover, these literary characteristics also firmly point to the Jewishness of the author. Especially, those literary devices such as chiasmus, *inclusio*, penchant for numbers, frequent repetition, and numerous Semitisms and Septuagintisms, signify that the author of the first gospel had a mind steeped in the Old Testament and Jewish tradition.[63]

Having established the integral unity of Matthew's gospel through analysis of its literary characteristics (above), we can now look into the place of the Matthean Beatitudes (Matt 5:3-12), within this unified gospel.

2.2. The Place and Significance of the Matthean Beatitudes (Matt 5:3-10) within the overall Structure of Matthew's Gospel

The Matthean Beatitudes (Matt 5:3-12) has substantial importance in the overall plan of Matthew's gospel. A brief analysis of this area will be taken up in this section because it has significant bearings on the importance of this research work.

The Matthean Beatitudes is an integral part of the Sermon on the Mount, which is the first of the five major discourses in Matthew's gospel. Therefore, it is imperative for our present purpose first to consider the place and significance of the Sermon on the Mount within Matthew's gospel. This will lead us to examine the place and significance of the Matthean Beatitudes within the Sermon on the Mount. The outcome of the two assessments will indicate the place and

61 Davies and Allison, Jr., *Matthew*, Vol. I, 96.

62 Ulrich Luz maintains that Matthew is to be read from beginning to end, to be viewed as a whole, because "in many a place it has a depth dimension which discloses itself only when the Gospel is viewed as a whole." In fact, it is the wish of the first Evangelist, according to Luz, that "his book be read and meditated upon as a whole again and a gain." Luz, *Matthew 1-7*, 40-41.

63 Davies and Allison, Jr., *Matthew*, Vol. I, 96. Aaron M. Gale maintains that apart from other literary characteristics, the Jewish literary techniques of *binyan av* and *kal vehomer* were incorporated in Matthew's gospel, which indicates the Jewish background of both the authors and the audience, and also that the authors were learned scribes and the audience were educated as well. Gale, *Redefining Ancient Borders*, 4-5, 121-142, 166-167. Gale obviously ascribes the authorship of the first gospel to more than one person.

significance of the Matthean Beatitudes within Matthew's gospel. This subject matter has been briefly highlighted in the section "Elaboration of the Problem" in chapter 1, and therefore this section will be, to some extent, a recapitulation and furtherance of what has been said there.

2.2.1. The Place and Significance of the Sermon on the Mount Within the Overall Structure of Matthew's Gospel

One of the primary emphases of Matthew in writing his gospel is undoubtedly to show the importance of Jesus' teachings. A comparison of the synoptic gospels clearly affirms this. While the teaching materials occupy about 50 percent of Mark's gospel and about 66 percent of Luke's gospel they occupy about 75 per cent of Matthew's gospel.[64] Moreover, the teaching materials are meticulously arranged in five major blocks of discourses. In other words, all the five major discourses in Matthew's gospel are presented in the form of teachings with Jesus as the subject, rather than in the form of simple sermons. Furthermore, it is interesting to note that all the teachings in these discourses are primarily directed to the disciples. This strongly suggests that Matthew has "discipleship" as the centre in which the teachings of Jesus revolve or are bound together.[65] Consequently, it can be surmised that Matthew's arrangement of the teaching materials into five major blocks of discourses is not only to emphasize Jesus' teachings in general, but also to accentuate Jesus' teachings on discipleship in particular. Here, the importance of the Sermon on the Mount within Matthew's gospel can be noted. Most of Jesus' major teachings on discipleship are contained in the Sermon on the Mount,[66] and this sermon is placed as the first of the five major discourses. This indicates that Matthew wants to project the Sermon on the Mount as the first of Jesus' teachings,

64 Newman, Jr., "Some Translational Notes on the Beatitudes," 108. See also Toussaint, *Behold the King. A Study of Matthew*, 22.

65 As Wilkins notes, each of the major discourses in Matthew's gospel is primarily directed to the disciples (5:1; 10:1, 5; 13:10, 36; 18:1; 23:1; 24:1–3), and Matthew often transforms the teaching segments into explicit discipleship-teaching pericopae by including the term "disciple/s" (8:21, 23; 9:37; 10:42; 12:49; 13:10; 15:23; 16:5; 17:6; 17:10; 18:1; 19:10; 21:20; 24:3; 26:8, 40, 45). See Wilkins, "Discipleship," 182. See also Smith, "Literary Evidence of fivefold Structure in the Gospel of Matthew," 543-544.

66 In connection to this, the structure of the Sermon on the Mount proposed by James A. Brook is enlightening. He identifies the actual beginning of the sermon at 5:3, taking 5:1-2 as the setting and 7:28-29 as the conclusion of the sermon. Then he divided the SOM into six major parts with "disciples" as the main subject in each parts, such as:

5:3-12 - the blessedness of the disciples
5:13-16 - the character of the disciples
5:17-48 - the new law for disciples
6:1-18 - the practice of piety by disciples
6:19-34 - the avoidance of materialism by disciples
7:1-27 - Warnings to disciples. See, James A. Brooks, "The Unity and Structure of the Sermon on the Mount," *CriswellTheolRev* 6 (Fall 1992), 28.

and that is obviously to emphasize his teachings on discipleship.[67] In support to this view, it has been maintained that the teaching materials in the Sermon on the Mount are not necessarily taken from the first teachings of Jesus or Jesus' teaching on one occasion, but were gleaned and systematically arranged by Matthew to suit his special purpose (that is to draw attention to the nature of discipleship) from the teachings of Jesus during his earthly ministry at different times under different circumstances.[68] This is affirmed especially by the presence of the parallel materials in different places of Luke's gospel.[69] Thus, at least two important conclusions can be drawn from here. First, Jesus' teachings on discipleship comprise one of the main emphases of Matthews's gospel. Second, among all the five major discourses Matthew bestows primacy of importance upon the Sermon on the Mount by way of accumulating in it Jesus' major teachings on discipleship and placing it at the first place, thus depicting it as the first of Jesus' teachings.[70]

Keeping this conclusion in mind, we will now examine the place and significance of the Matthean Beatitudes within the Sermon on the Mount.

2.2.2. The Place and Significance of the Matthean Beatitudes Within the Sermon on the Mount

Matthew introduces the Sermon on the Mount with nine beatitudes. The selection of the Beatitudes for the introduction of the Sermon on the Mount, which can be regarded as the most important discourse among the five Matthean major discourses, suggests that a very high importance is attached to the Beatitudes by

---

67 See the following - Schweizer, *The Good News According to Matthew*, 82-83; Newman, Jr., "Some Translational Notes on the Beatitudes," 107-109. Hagner, *Matthew 1-13*, 83-84. Kingsbury also, studying from the perspective of literary criticism, notes that the Sermon on the Mount is the example par excellence of Jesus' teaching, and its theme is "Greater Righteousness," and the primary addressees are disciples. See Kingsbury, "The Place, Structure, and Meaning of the Sermon on the Mount within Matthew," 136-137.

68 James A. Brooks rightly observes that such topical arrangement in one place by Matthew of Jesus' teachings at different occasions does not question the authenticity of any of the teachings attributed to Jesus. See Brooks, "The Unity and Structure of the Sermon on the Mount," 23.

69 Hagner, *Matthew 1-13*, 82-83. Hagner here highlights the parallel materials of the Sermon on the Mount in Luke's gospel as follows – Luke's "Sermon on the Plain" (Luke 6:17-49) contains parallels to Matt 5:1-12, 38-48, and 7:1-5, 12, 16-21, 27. Other parallels are found throughout Luke, thus –Matt 5:13 in Luke 14:34–35; Matt 5:14 in Luke 11:33; Matt 5:18 in Luke 16:17; Matt 5:25–26 in Luke 12:57–59; Matt 5:31–32 in Luke 16:18; Matt 6:9–13 in Luke 11:2–4; Matt 6:19–21 in Luke 12:33–34; Matt 6:21–23 in Luke 11:34–36; Matt 6:24 in Luke 16:13; Matt 6:25–34 in Luke 12:22–32; Matt 7:7–11 in Luke 11:9–13; Matt 7:13–14 in Luke 13:23–24; and Matt 7:22–23 in Luke 13:25–27. See also Newman, Jr., "Some Translational Notes on the Beatitudes," 107.

70 Cf., however, Stanton insists that all the five discourses are equally important and the Sermon on the Mount is only the first one. Graham N. Stanton, "The Origin and Purpose of Matthew's Sermon on the Mount," in *Tradition and Interpretation in the New Testament. Essays in Honor of E. Earle Ellis*, edited by Gerald F. Hawthorne with Otto Betz (Grand Rapids, Michigan: William B. Eerdmans Publishing Company, 1987), 189.

the author of the first gospel. This suggestion is supported by the contents of the Beatitudes, which obviously represent the core of the Matthean Jesus' teaching on the nature of discipleship, which on the other hand, is the main concern of the whole of the Sermon on the Mount. Hans Dieter Betz maintains that the introduction of the Sermon on the Mount with the Beatitudes is intentional, and the first beatitude stands out distinctively, with the other beatitudes unfolding and developing the first beatitude. All the beatitudes together constitute, according to Betz, the self-consciousness of the Matthean community whose self-expression is found in the sayings "You are the salt of the earth" (Matt 5:13) and "You are the light of the world" (Matt 5:14-16). Betz further maintains that it is not only that "the first macarism is unfolded and variously developed in the following macarisms (Mt 5:4-12)," but also "the rest of the Sermon is nothing else than the concretization and elucidation of the first macarism." Betz continues that on the basis of the first beatitude, the interpretation of the Torah is carried out in 5:17-48 and 7:12, the life of practical piety is constituted a new in 6:1-18, and the conquest of everyday anxiety is undertaken in 6:19-7:12.[71] Austin Farrer had already proposed, even before Betz, that the Sermon on the Mount, apart from the (eight) beatitudes (Matt 5:3-10), "was an orderly exposition or application of the Beatitudes," and the order is "ascending from the last to the first."[72] Farrer maintains that Matthew chapters 5-7 (the Sermon on the Mount) is modelled on Exodus chapters 20-24, and the Beatitudes occupy a place corresponding to that of the Decalogue in Exodus 20-24 thus, finding an orderly exposition or application in the rest of the Sermon, just as the Decalogue of chapter 22 finds its exposition in the Covenant Laws given in the rest of the section.[73] Following Farrer, but with little amendments, his student Michael Goulder also has suggested that the (eight) Matthean beatitudes (Mt 5: 3-10) are Matthew's creation in rabbinic style to form the summary of (that is the *kĕlāl*), or heading for, the Sermon on the Mount, and their meaning is explained by the relevant passages of the Sermon in reverse order, that is beginning from the last and ending with the first.[74] More recently, Kingsbury also notes that the Sermon on the Mount divides itself into five parts,[75] having "greater righteousness" as its theme, and this theme is specified in the introduction. This introduction (5:3-16) focuses on "the types of persons disciples are who practice the greater righteousness," and "in the second, third, and fourth parts he explicates what it is to practice this righteousness."[76]

71 Betz, *Essays on the Sermon on the Mount*, 25, 35.

72 Farrer, *St. Matthew and St. Mark*, 162, 176.

73 *Ibid.*, 160-161. See also Bruner, *The Christ Book*, 157. More recently, Benedict Green subscribes to this view. See Green, *Matthew, Poet of the Beatitudes*, 256.

74 Goulder, *Midrash and Lection in Matthew*, 250-252.

75 Excluding the narrative frame of the Sermon where Jesus is described as ascending the mountain to teach (Matt 5:1-2) and descending after finishing (Matt 7:28-8:1).

76 Kingsbury, "The Place, Structure, and Meaning...," 136-138.

Although one may not accept the view of these scholars on the Sermon on the Mount in toto,[77] their emphasis on the importance of the Beatitudes within the overall framework of the Sermon, however, cannot be ignored.[78] Dale C. Allison Jr., who proposes a triadic arrangement for the structure of the Sermon on the Mount, is of the view that the Beatitudes function as building up, encouraging, and consoling the Christian reader before they hear the hard imperatives of Jesus found in the sermon itself.[79] This view highlights the importance of the Beatitudes from another angle. Not only that, but it also supports the importance of the Beatitudes within the overall framework of the Sermon on the Mount as outlined above, because based on this understanding the Beatitudes can be viewed as expressions of the identity and destiny of those who follow the imperatives given by Jesus which are found in the Sermon that follows. The importance of the Beatitudes is further highlighted by the fact that the two catch words in these beatitudes, namely righteousness and kingdom (+ of Heaven/God), which together form "the righteousness of the kingdom of heaven," permeate the whole of the Sermon on the Mount, befitting to be called its themes.[80] Therefore, based on all this evidence, it seems right to term the Beatitudes, in the words of Casimir A. Delimat, "an eloquent summary of the meaningful Sermon on the Mount."[81]

The logic now is that among Matthew's five great discourses the Sermon on the Mount is the most important one, dealing particularly with the nature of discipleship, which is one of the main emphases of this gospel. It was especially designed by the author for that purpose. Then the Beatitudes constitute a

77 For example, Betz hypothesizes that the Sermon on the Mount is a pre-Matthean composition - taken and fitted by Matthew to a totally different setting in the composition of his gospel, and therefore the theology and *Sitz im Leben* of the Sermon on the Mount is also different from the rest of the gospel of Matthew. See Betz, *Essays on the Sermon on the Mount*, 18-19. But this hypothesis is difficult to accept, because literary analysis of the gospel (see above) clearly shows that the Sermon on the Mount is not isolated from the rest of the gospel. In fact, several scholars criticize Betz's view. Just for example, Graham N. Stanton, criticizing Betz for this view, points out certain examples that indicate the integrity of the sermon on the mount into the total context of Matthew's gospel, particularly the themes common to the Sermon on the Mount and the rest of Matthew's gospel, such as Christology, discipleship, ecclesiology, dual audience of Jesus' discourses, opposition to scribes and Pharisees etc. Therefore, Stanton insists that the Sermon on the Mount and the rest of Matthew's gospel have the same origin and the same purpose. See Stanton, "The Origin and Purpose of Matthew's Sermon on the Mount," 187-190. For another example of Betz's critique on this, see Allison, Jr., "A New Approach to the Sermon on the Mount," 405-414. Here Allison-Jr. points out that the Sermon on the Mount (Matt 5-7) is built largely of triads, which is the same structure with which Matthew builds all other discourses, as well as some of the narratives.

78 For a list of other suggestions on the structure of the Sermon on the Mount, see Allison, Jr., "The Structure of the Sermon on the Mount," 425.

79 Allison, Jr., "The Structure of the Sermon on the Mount," 437-440.

80 Luz, *Matthew 1-7*, 213-214.

81 Delimat, *Ascent: Spiritual Progress According to the Beatitudes*, 7.

programmatic summary of the Sermon on the Mount,[82] carrying in it the essence of the teachings on discipleship by the Matthean Jesus. Adam G. Cooper seems right in saying that in the Beatitudes, Matthew presents in pithy form, the primary themes of his entire gospel, such as kingdom, righteousness, mercy, suffering and heavenly reward.[83] Matthew attaches all these themes to the major theme of "discipleship." Thus, viewing from Matthew's emphasis on discipleship, the Beatitudes also hold substantial importance within Matthew's gospel as a whole.

We will now proceed to the detailed exegesis of the Matthean Beatitudes. We will begin with an investigation into the general background of the Matthean Beatitudes. This will be followed by an analysis of its literary features and an investigation of other aspects of the Matthean Beatitudes, which are important for an in-depth study of this passage. Then the exegetical comments will follow.

2. 3. The General Background of the Matthean Beatitudes

2.3.1. Beatitudes in the Greek Literature

According to Hans Dieter Betz the earliest instance of a beatitude is found in Homeric Hymn to Demeter (480-483),[84] which is dated around 700–600 B.C.E.[85] But, the word used here is ὄλβιος, which serves as a synonym for μακάριος.[86] The first appearance of the word μακάριος is in the work of Pindar around 522 or 518 B.C.E.[87] It is a subsidiary form of μὰκαρ, which referred at first predominantly to the gods, denoting the transcendent happiness of life beyond care, labour and death. Then the word came to be used of men to denote the state of godlike blessedness hereafter in the isles of the blessed. The word μακάριος also, in keeping with its relation to the word μάκαρ, was first used to describe the happy state of the gods who are above earthly suffering and labours. Then, it came to be used, like μάκαρ, to refer to the dead who have attained to the supra-terrestrial life of the gods. However, from the time of Aristotle it became a very common and much weaker everyday term, referring to the status of the wealthy people who, by virtue

82 Cf. Hermann Lichtenberger, "Makarisms in Mathew 5:3ff. in their Jewish Context," in *The Sermon on the Mount and Its Jewish Setting*, edited by Hans-Jürgen BECKER and Serge RUZER. Cahiers de la Revue Biblique, 60 (Paris: J. GABALDA et Cie Éditeurs: 2005), 55, who acknowledges that the position of the Beatitudes in the Sermon on the Mount is programmatic.

83 Adam G. Cooper, "'They Shall See God': The Gospel for all saint's Day, Matthew 5:1-11," *LuthTheolJourn* 38/2 (Ag 2004), 64.

84 Betz, *Essays on the Sermon on the Mount*, 26, citing from N. J. Richardson, *The Homeric Hymn to Demeter* (Oxford: Clarendon Press, 1974), 134. See also Hans Dieter Betz, *The Sermon on the Mount* (Minneapolis: Fortress Press, 1995), 97.

85 Richardson, *The Homeric Hymn to Demeter*, 10-11.

86 Betz, *The Sermon on the Mount*, 93.

87 Hauck, "μακάριος, μακαρίζω, μακαρισμός: The Greek Usage and The Stylistic Form of the Beatitude," *TDNT*, Vol. IV (Grand Rapids, Michigan: William B. Eerdmans Publishing Company, 1967), 362. See also Davies and Allison, Jr., *Matthew*, Vol. I, 431.

of their riches, are above the normal cares and worries of the common people. Thus, it is often used as synonymous with εὐδαίμων which denotes a wealthy person, one who has a good daemon. However, Aristotle himself never used the two terms synonymously. He differentiated between the two terms, applying μακάριος only to gods and εὐδαίμων to men.[88] In fact, the beatitudes took various forms on the Greek soil, and μακάριος ὅς(τις) is one of the most common forms in which it frequently occurred. Another very common form of the beatitudes is ὄλβιος ὅς(τις).[89] It is a poetic word extolling human happiness, and it inseparably connects happiness with possession.[90] Another favoured form is τρισμακάριος,[91] which is a strengthening form for μάκαρ, and it means "three times blessed."[92] εὐδαίμων, another synonym, looks to the origin of happiness and it simply means "rich." Although it has become a leading philosophical term for inner happiness, it seems that it has not come into common use.[93] Another related term is εὐτυχής which refers to "the one who is provided or favoured with a happy destiny."[94] The beatitudes, which are common in both poetry and prose throughout the centuries in Greek literature, reflect the sorrows and afflictions, the aspirations and ideals, of the Greeks. They are influenced by practical Greek philosophy. As the Greek mind, which is orientated to earth, first draws happiness from earthly goods and values,[95] the objects evoking the beatitude in Greek literature include praiseworthy children, virtue, piety, wisdom, and fame.[96]

2.3.2. Beatitudes in the Old Testament and Judaism

Beatitudes or blessings are also found in the Old Testament and Judaism where the key words are אַשְׁרֵי *ašrê* or בָּרוּךְ *bārûk*. The word אַשְׁרֵי is never applied to God in the Old Testament[97] and is less sacred and solemn than בָּרוּךְ. In the LXX only אַשְׁרֵי is translated as μακάριος and בָּרוּךְ is usually translated as εὐλογητός There is therefore a minimal significance of the בָּרוּךְ formulas for understanding

88 Hauck, "μακάριος, μακαρίζω, μακαρισμός: The Greek Usage…," 362. See also Davies and Allison, Jr., *Matthew*, Vol. I, 431.

89 Hauck, "μακάριος, μακαρίζω, μακαρισμός: The Stylistic Form of the Beatitude," *TDNT,* Vol. IV (Grand Rapids, Michigan: William B. Eerdmans Publishing Company, 1967), 363.

90 *Ibid.,*" 362.

91 *Ibid.,*" 363.

92 Henry George Liddell and Robert Scott, (comps), *A Greek-English Lexicon*, Vol. II, Revised Edition (Oxford: Clarendon Press, 1996 [1883]), 1823.

93 Hauck, "μακάριος, μακαρίζω, μακαρισμός: The Greek Usage…," 362.

94 *Ibid.*

95 *Ibid.*, 363.

96 *Ibid.*, 363-364. See also Davies and Allison, Jr., *Matthew*, Vol. I, 431.

97 One instance of its use to refer to God outside the OT may be in Philo, *De Sacrificiis Abelis et Cain* 101. See *The Works of Philo. Complete and Unabridged.* New Updated Edition. Translated by C. D.Yonge (Peabody, Massachusetts: Hedrickson, 1993), 107.

the background of the Beatitudes in Matthew (5:3-12) and Luke (6:20-22).[98] Thus, in sharp contrast to the Hellenistic usage, the word μακάριος is never applied to God in the Old Testament (LXX), but it always refers to a person. It also never refers to a thing or state.[99] Blessedness is understood in terms of fullness of life in the Old Testament and Judaism, and God is the giver of all blessedness. Blessedness first relates to earthly blessings, for example, wife (Sir 25;8; 26:1), children (Gen 30:13; 4Macc. 16:9; 18:9; Sir 25:7), beauty (Cant 6:9 [8]), earthly well-being, riches, honour, wisdom (Job 29:10, 11, cf. Isa 32:20). Wisdom is often the theme of the Old Testament beatitudes (e.g., Prov 3:13; Sir 14:20; 25:9; 37:24; 2 Chron 9:7; etc.), and wisdom and piety are understood as the presupposition of all blessedness in the Old Testament and Judaism (e.g., Prov 8:32, 34; 14:21; 20:7; 29:18; Sir 31 (34):8, 9; etc.).[100] The characteristic beatitudes of the Old Testament and Judaism mainly refer "to the one who trusts in God, who hopes and waits for him, who fears and loves Him" (e.g., Prov 16:20; 28:24; Sir 34:15 [31:17]; Isa 30:18; Tob 13:15).[101] The Old Testament beatitudes are part of the practical wisdom of the Old Testament, and they are controlled by prevailing desires and ideals.[102]

As such, probably in accordance with Egyptian influence, the μακάριος formula of the Old Testament appears first in wisdom literature or in literature influenced by wisdom.[103] Those μακάριος sentences praise the wise man and hold him up as a model. For example:

μακάριος δὲ ἄνθρωπος ὃν ἤλεγξεν ὁ κύριος νουθέτημα δὲ παντοκράτορος μὴ ἀπαναίνου "Behold! Blessed is the man whom God reproves" (Job 5:17).

> μακάριος ἀνήρ ὃς οὐκ ἐπορεύθη ἐν βουλῇ ἀσεβῶν καὶ ἐν ὁδῷ ἁμαρτωλῶν οὐκ ἔστη καὶ ἐπὶ καθέδραν λοιμῶν οὐκ ἐκάθισεν ἀλλ' ἢ ἐν τῷ νόμῳ κυρίου τὸ θέλημα αὐτοῦ καὶ ἐν τῷ νόμῳ αὐτοῦ μελετήσει ἡμέρας καὶ νυκτός "Blessed is the man who walks not in the counsel of the wicked, or stands in the way of sinners, nor sits in the seat of scoffers; but his delight is in the law of the Lord, and on his law he meditates day and night" (Ps 1:1-2).

> μακάριος ὁ συνοικῶν γυναικὶ συνετῇ καὶ ὃς ἐν γλώσσῃ οὐκ ὠλίσθησεν καὶ ὃς οὐκ ἐδούλευσεν ἀναξίῳ ἑαυτοῦ "Blessed is he who lives with an

98 Davies and Allison, Jr., *Matthew*, Vol. I, 431-432.

99 Bertram, " [μακαριος] in the LXX and Judaism," *TDNT*, Vol. IV (Grand Rapids, Michigan: Wm. B. Erdmann's Publishing Company, 1967), 365. The only exception in the whole of the Bible where it is applied to God may be 1Timothy 1:11, and 6:15.

100 Bertram, " [μακαριος] in the LXX and Judaism," 365.

101 Bertram, " [μακαριος] in the LXX and Judaism,"366. See the same for various scriptural references.

102 Bertram, " [μακαριος] in the LXX and Judaism," 365.

103 J. Dupont, " 'Béatitudes' égyptiennes," *Biblica* 47 (1966), 185-222, as quoted in Davies and Allison, Jr., *Matthew*, Vol. I, 432. See also Lichtenberger, "Makarisms in Mathew 5:3ff. in their Jewish Context," 43.

intelligent wife, and he who has not made a slip with his tongue, and he who has not served a man inferior to himself" (Ecclus 25:8).[104]

To put it in brief, wisdom beatitudes mainly "declared a person to have *worldly well-being* because he lived in conformity with the established ways of the world."[105] The basis of the declaration of the blessing is not the expectation of a different world-order to come, but a prudent estimation of ordinary human affairs. What is declared is not heavenly rewards but earthly blessings, such as for example, a good wife (e.g., Sir 26:1), children (e.g., Ps 127, 4-5), beauty (e.g., Song of Songs 6:9), and earthly prosperity in general (e.g., Isa 32:20). In short, the promised blessing is well-being and long life in this world, that is, an enjoyment of this life to its fullest and for a long, long time. With the belief that divine wisdom was imparted with the Law of Moses, the study and observance of the Mosaic Law had been frequently stressed by the Jewish sages as the indispensable path to wisdom's blessings (e.g., Ps 119:1).[106]

Then, resulting from an interpretation of wisdom-speech forms and apocalyptic thought-processes, the so-called "apocalyptic beatitudes" began to appear in late Judaism, especially in the apocalyptic writings.[107] For example:

μακάριος ὁ ἐμμένων καὶ συνάξει εἰς ἡμέρας χιλίας τριακοσίας τριάκοντα πέντε "Blessed is the man who has patience and perseveres

104 Davies and Allison, Jr., *Matthew*, Vol. I, 432. The translations of Davies and Allison, Jr. are taken here. See also the following: Gen 30:13; Ps 2:12; 32:1-2; 34:8; 41:1; 84:12; 119:1; 127:5; Prov 3:13; Wisd 3:13-14; Ecclus 14:1-2, 20; 26:1; 28:19; 31:8; 34:15; 48:11; 50:28; Tob 13:14.

105 R. J. Dillon, "The Text of the Sermon on the Mount," (Notes issued in his course on the Sermon on the Mount at Forbham University in 1980), 39.

106 Dillon, "The Text of the Sermon on the Mount," 39-40.

107 Dillon, "The Text of the Sermon on the Mount," 41. The term "apocalyptic" or "apocalyptic writings" is explained here as follows:

The word (apocalyptic) refers to a literature and a mentality which grew out of the condition of Palestinian Jewry as a subjugated, colonial people during the years between the Babylonian exile (ended 522 B.C.) and the first century of the Christian era. After the Babylonian conquest of Palestine, which brought mass deportations of Israelites and devastation of the land, no nation of Israel existed as such, and the territory of the "promised land" was ruled by a succession of foreign powers: Persia, Greece, Egypt, Syria, finally Rome (63 B.C. onward). Especially during the most repressive of these alien regimes, that of the Syrian Seleucid kings (200-142 B.C.), "Apocalyptic" came into its own as a literary expression of the captive people's hopes. Their hopes became increasingly focused upon a *different future age*, to be brought about by their God in a way known only to himself. Speculations about that completely new age, and the way of its establishment, were the fascination of a class of *visionaries*, whose visions carried them momentarily *beyond the closed gates of the heavens* to learn the secret plans of God for that dazzling future. The transmission of these visions in written form, usually under the name of some magical hero of a brighter past (like Daniel, Henoch, Esra, Baruch), created the genus of late-Jewish book known as "*apocalypse*" (= a literature of "un-veiling," or "dis-closure," = the Greek work *apo-kalypsis*). Heavenly secrets brought "*out of hiding*" by the visionary – such is the nature of the writings and the basis of the word, "apocalyptic."

until the one thousand three hundred and thirty-five days" (Dan 12:12).[108]

μακάριοι οἱ γενόμενοι ἐν ταῖς ἡμέραις ἐκείναις ἰδεῖν τὰ ἀγαθὰ Ισραηλ ἐν συναγωγῇ φυλῶν ἃ ποιήσει ὁ θεός
"Blessed be they that shall be in those days, in that they shall see the good fortune of Israel which God shall bring to pass in the gathering together of the tribes" (Ps. Sol. 17:44).[109]

In contrast to the wisdom beatitude, which has moral exhortation as its general object, the apocalyptic beatitude is usually addressed to people in desparate circumstances promising them a future consolation. It has assurance and the proffering of hope as its goal. It focuses on the future in which natural values and the present situation will be reversed. It envisages that the eschatological intervention of God will alter the dismal status quo of the addressees. Therefore, fulfilment will be found only in the future new world, but not in this world.[110] To put it briefly, the apocalyptic beatitudes pronounced blessings of salvation in the future judgment of the world and participation in God's new world for those who persevered in their religion, under severe toils, in the present world.[111]

In anticipation of what are found in Matthew and Luke, different beatitudes are sometimes brought together in Jewish literature, thus forming a pair or series of blessings.[112] However, while such pairs or series of beatitudes are found in eschatological or apocalyptic texts, only the pairs are found in wisdom literature, and neither are found in Greek literature.[113]

The eschatological woe, the counterpart of the eschatological blessings, forms another notable development in the history of makarism in the Bible/Judaism. For example:

Woe unto you sinners who are dead! When you are dead in the wealth of your sins,

those who are like you will say of you, "Happy are you sinners!" (1 En. 103:5).[114]

---

108 This translation is taken from NAB.

109 Davies and Allison, Jr., *Matthew*, Vol. I, 432. The translation of Davies and Allison, Jr. is taken here. For other examples, see the following: Ps 72:17; Isa 30:18; 31:9 LXX; Ecclus 48:11; 1 En 81:4; Ps. Sol 18:6; 2 Bar 10:6-7; 2 En 42:6-14; 52:1-14.

110 Davies and Allison, Jr., *Matthew*, Vol. I, 432. See also Guelich, *The Sermon on the Mount: A Foundation for Understanding*, 65.

111 Dillon, "The Text of the Sermon on the Mount," 41.

112 Davies and Allison, Jr., *Matthew*, Vol. I, 433. See the following for example: Ecclus 14:1-2; 25:8-10; Ps 32:1-2; 84:4-5; 119:1-2; Tob 13:14-15; and 2 En 52:1-4.

113 Davies and Allison, Jr., *Matthew*, Vol. I, 433.

114 Davies and Allison, Jr., *Matthew*, Vol. I, 433. See also 1 En 99:10-15; 2 Bar 10:6-7; 2 En 52:1-14.

Beatitudes in the second person are rare in the Old Testament, but are found in the later Jewish literature (e.g., *Eth. En* 58:2 – "Blessings on you elect and righteous, for glorious will be your lot!").[115]

The formal beatitude is not common in Philo, and it seems that Hellenistic influences are discernible. The word group of beatitude has a transcendental sense in Philo and it is often used of God. According to him, blessedness is the proper nature of the divine, and man can attain to it "in bearing the troubles of earthly existence … and in philosophical Endeavour."[116]

The Old Testament sense of beatitude is maintained in Rabbinic Judaism. For example, Rabban Johannan ben Zakkai (c. 80 C.E.) cried to two of his disciples, "Hail to you, and hail to the mothers that bare you! Hail to mine eyes, that they have seen this!" and it seems that the theological and legal ideals of the Rabbis controlled the content of the beatitudes in Rabbinic Judaism.[117]

There are five beatitudes found in the Qumran texts. They are dated between 50 B.C.E. to 50 C.E. They are wisdom beatitudes, comparable to Wisdom texts like Sirach 14:20-27. The main subject of these beatitudes is wisdom and they do not have a reward clause. Therefore, concerning content they are quite different from the beatitudes found in the gospels, which are mainly apocalyptic in nature.

The wisdom beatitudes focused on the formulas of blessings and curse enjoined in the obedience and disobedience of the Mosaic Law in Deuteronomy 27:15-28:68. This might have been the main influencing factor even behind the development of the eschatological woe as a counterpart to eschatological blessing in the late Judaism, as well as the alternation of the blessings and the woes in Luke 6:24-26. However, there is a formal distinction between the "blessing and curse" formula and the "beatitude and woe" formula, at least initially. The basic difference is in the difference of the vocabulary both in Hebrew and in Greek. In the "blessing and curse" formula, the Hebrew words used are ברוך (*bārûk*) and אׂרור (*'ārûr*) which are rendered by Greek εὐλογημένος and κατάρατος (LXX) respectively. On the other hand, the Hebrew vocabularies used in the "beatitude and woe" formula are אַשְׁרֵי (*'ashrê*) and הוֹי/אוֹי (*hôi/'ôi*) which are rendered by Greek μακάριος and οὐαί respectively. While the Hebrew word *bārûk* pronounced strict blessing, the word *'ashrê* declared people happy in terms of fortunate. So also the word "*hôi/'ôi*" is merely constative as against the strict curses *'ārûr*. Thus, the difference of vocabulary in these two formulas reflects the difference in intention in the speaking of them. In blessings and curses, there is a belief on the part of the speaker that his word had the prophetic power of bringing about the good or ill fortune, which it pronounced. The beatitudes and reproaches, on the other hand, are celebration and denouncement of fortunes, good or ill. The blessing and curse were mainly definitive. However, exhortation is attached in the beatitude and woe, which could move the listener to chart his course toward good fortune. In spite of these differences, however, late-Jewish texts tend to mingle blessings and beatitudes (e.g., Tobit 14:14-16; 2 Enoch 52). Therefore, strict separation cannot be insisted in the intentions of Jesus and the evangelists. See Dillon, "The Text of the Sermon on the Mount," 39, 40.

115 As mentioned in Schweizer, *The Good News According to Matthew*, 80.

116 Bertram, " [μακαριος] in the LXX and Judaism," 366. See the same place for a list of references of the beatitude word group in Philo's writings.

117 Bertram, " [μακαριος] in the LXX and Judaism," 367.

They, however, have some similarities in form with the Matthean beatitudes, in that they are presented in third person and the last one is somewhat longer than the previous ones.[118]

2.3.3. Beatitudes in the New Testament

The Matthean Beatitudes (5:3-12) and the Lukan Beatitudes (6:20-23) are not the only beatitudes found in the New Testament, for in fact, beatitudes are found also in other places of the New Testament. In this sub-section we will briefly highlight the beatitudes in the New Testament just for information without going into a detailed study of them. This is expected to help us to have a clearer picture of the Matthean Beatitudes (5:3-12) within the framework of the New Testament.

In the New Testament the word μακάριος occurs fifty times: thirteen in Matt (5:3, 4, 5, 6, 7, 8, 9, 10, 11; 11:6; 13:6; 16:17; 24:46), fifteen in Luke (1:45, 48; 6:20, 21(2), 22; 7:23; 11:27, 28; 12:37, 38, 43; 14:14, 15, 23, 29), two in Jn (13:17; 20:29), two in Acts (but neither of them are a beatitude – 20:35; 26:2), seven in the Pauline corpus (only three - Rom 4:7, 8; 14:22, are beatitudes. Others are Rom 4: 9; Gal 4:15; I Tim 6:15; Tit 2:13); two in Jas (1:12; 1:25); two in 1Pet (3:14; 4:14); seven in Rev (1:3; 14:13; 16:15; 19:9; 20:6; 22:7, 14). Thus, there are 44 beatitudes in the New Testament altogether.[119] While the related noun μακαρισμός appears three times, in Rom 4:6, 9, and Gal 4:15, the verb μακαρίζω appears twice in Luke 1:48, and Jas 5:11. As in the Greek world and the Old Testament, even the μακάριος in the New Testament usually does not refer to things but to persons. Only occasionally, it refers to things, such as for example, ὀφθαλμοὶ "eyes" and ὦτα "ears" in Matt 13:16, and κοιλία "womb" and μαστοὶ "breasts" in Luke 11:27. These usages are influenced by the Jewish modes of thought, which in some sense, regards members of the body as bearing independent life.[120] The New Testament makarisms exhibit diverse form and function, and display all of the features heretofore noted in Jewish literature (excluding Philo). Hence, there are beatitudes belonging to the sapiential/wisdom tradition (Rom 14:22) and to the eschatological tradition (Rev 19:9; 20:6; 22:7, 14). There are also isolated beatitudes (Jn 13:17; 20:29; Rom 14:22; Jas 1:12), as well as beatitudes in series (Matt 5: 3-12; Luke 6: 20-22; 11:27-28; 14:14-15; cf. Rev 20:7, 14). Eschatological woes are also found in the New Testament (Mark 13:17; Luke 6:24-26; Rev 8:13; 9:12; 11:14; 12:12; 18:10, 16, 19).[121]

At the same time, the formula of the beatitudes in the New Testament exhibits a sign of independence from its surrounding world that is the Greek world. While the formula μακάριος ὅς (τις) based on the Heb. אַשְׁרֵי הָאִישׁ אֲשֶׁר

118 See Viviano, *Matthew and His World*, 64-68.

119 Davies and Allison, Jr., *Matthew*, Vol. I, 434. See also Robert Guelich, *The Sermon on the Mount: A Foundation for Understanding* (Dallas: Word Publishing, 1982), 63.

120 Hauck, "[μακάριος] The Word Group in the New Testament," 367.

121 Davies and Allison, Jr., *Matthew*, Vol. I, 434.

are often found both in the Greek world and in the LXX they are seldom found in the New Testament, but only in Matt 11:6 and its parallel in Luke 14:15. As in many cases of the LXX, the New Testament prefers the form of a predicative μακάριος first, then the person with article, and finally followed by the reason for a blessedness or a description of it in a subsidiary clause; for example: Matt 5:3ff.; Luke 1:45; Rev 1:3; 14:13 etc.[122] Moreover, there is a clear distinction of the beatitudes in the New Testament from those of the Greek beatitudes in that all secular goods and values which form the basis of the beatitudes in the Greek world, "are now completely subsidiary to the one supreme good, the kingdom of God, whether it be that the righteous man may hope for this, is certain of it, has a title to it, or already has a part in it."[123] In the New Testament the μακάριος word group "refers overwhelmingly to the distinctive religious joy which accrues to man from his share in the salvation of the kingdom of God."[124]

In this connection it may be good to mention that there are also beatitudes in early Christian literature outside the New Testament, but they take over the Gospel tradition, for example, *Gospel of Thomas*, 45, 68-69; Acts of Paul 5-6.[125]

The above survey shows that most of the beatitudes in the New Testament are individual or isolated beatitudes, and even among the beatitudes in series, the Matthean Beatitudes (5:3-12) and the Lukan Beatitudes (6:20-23) are the most prominent ones, and they stand out distinctively with distinctive teachings.

2.3.4. A Brief Summary on the General Background of the Matthean Beatitudes

What has become obvious from the above analysis is that while the Matthean Beatitudes, with their parallels in Luke, have clear distinction from those of the beatitudes in the Greek world, they are typical of the Old Testament beatitudes in many ways. While the form of the Matthean and Lukan Beatitudes, such as μακάριος + subject + ὅτι is attested (Gen 30:13; Tob 13:16; Matt 16:17),[126] parallels of other characteristics, both of Matthew and Luke, are also found in the OT, such as the eschatological content, the grouping of beatitudes (and woes), as well as the third person and second person forms.[127] Therefore, according to Davies and Allison, the only exceptional formal characteristic of the synoptic beatitudes, probably, is their brevity, that is that those blessed are described with

122 Hauck, "[μακάριος] The Word Group in the New Testament," 367.

123 *Ibid.*, 368.

124 *Ibid.*, 366, 367.

125 See Lichtenberger, "Makarisms in Mathew 5: 3ff. in their Jewish Context," 48-49.

126 Cf., however, while other NT beatitudes use the ὅτι clause, it is uncommon outside the NT, and the consistent use of it by Matthew is a distinctive one. Hagner, *Matthew 1-13*, 88-89.

127 Davies and Allison, Jr., *Matthew*, Vol. I, 434. Second person form is rarer, and they are found in Deut 33:29; Ps 128: 2; Eccl 10:17; Isa 32: 20; I En. 58:2; Matt 16:17; Luke 14:14; Jn 13:17.

utmost succinctness. If there is anything beyond this, setting apart the Beatitudes of the Sermon on the Mount/Plain, it would not be their form, but their content on the one hand, and their context in the proclamation of Jesus, as well as the theology and context of the Evangelist, on the other.[128]

An implication, then, is that the beatitudes in the Old Testament and Judaism form the general background for the Matthean and Lukan Beatitudes.[129] In addition, of the two categories of beatitudes found in the Old Testament and Judaism, namely wisdom and apocalyptic, the Apocalyptic beatitudes form their background. This is obvious especially because of the promises in each of the beatitudes, in which eschatological blessing is promised to the people felicitated in each statement.[130] Moreover, the parallel beatitudes in Matthew (5:3-4, 6) and Luke (6:20-21) in particular, which are supposed to go back to Jesus himself, present the promises in anti-thetical manner: "poor now, but rulers of the future; mourners now, but then consoled; hungry now but fully satisfied then," as

---

128 Davies and Allison, Jr., *Matthew*, Vol. I, 434. Davies and Allison Jr. here exclude the context of the evangelist, and it is added by this researcher, because he believes that the context of the evangelists is instrumental in the final shaping of the content of the Beatitudes.

129 According to Hans Dieter Betz, there were four kinds of beatitude in the ancient literature both of the Hellenistic and of the Jews, such as the religious beatitude (e.g. Ps 1:1), the secular beatitude (which praises one on account of wealth, strength, beauty, etc.), the beatitude of the wise man (in which one is praised for wisdom and virtue), and the satirical beatitude (e.g., *Eth. En.* 103:5-6, which says: "Blessed are the sinners; they saw all their days. And now they have died in prosperity and wealth..."). Betz maintains that the Matthean beatitudes belong to the type of religious beatitude, the earliest instance of which is found in the *Homeric Hymn to Demeter* (480-83) which is formulated in the third person and addressed to those who have been initiated into the Eleusinian mysteries. Betz further maintains that in the field of Jewish literature basically the apocalyptic literatures contain the religious beatitude (e.g., *Slav. En.* 42:6ff.; 52:1 ff.; *4 Ezra* 8:46-54), and there is a notable parallel between the ancient Greek mysteries and Jewish apocalyptic within the phenomenology of religion. The beatitude of the wise man, an anti-beatitude, formulated in opposition to the conventional beatitude, is frequently encountered in Cynic and Stoic traditions. But they are also found in great numbers in OT-Jewish Wisdom literature, in apocalyptic, and in early Christian literature. According to Betz, the first line of the first Matthean beatitudes is an anti-beatitude, which opposes the conventional beatitude, which says, "Blessed are the rich." The second line is a Semitism and it derives from the Jewish "piety of the poor." By the combination, it goes however far beyond the elements of which it was built and constitutes a new form of religious beatitude, and is elevated to the status of a fundamental theological definition. Now, "it contains everything one must know to pass through his life into paradise." See, Betz, *Essays on the Sermon on the Mount*, 25-35. Although such parallels might be discerned between the Matthean (or Synoptic) beatitudes and the beatitudes in the Hellenistic literature, the analysis above shows that the beatitudes in OT (and Judaism) form the general background of the Matthean beatitudes. See Guelich, "The Matthean Beatitudes...," 416; and also Guelich, *The Sermon on the Mount: A Foundation for Understanding*, 63.

130 Cf. Dillon, "The Text of the Sermon on the Mount," 42.

Trilling puts it.[131] Even the balancing of the beatitudes with the woes in Luke 6:24-26 portents a reversal of all values in the future kingdom of God.[132] All these characteristics clearly show that both the Matthean and Lukan beatitudes belong to the category of apocalyptic beatitudes.[133]

At the same time, however, it is important to note that while the Matthean Beatitudes can be subsumed basically under the category of apocalyptic beatitudes, ethical aspects are also infused through its pre-Matthean developments, that is, in the addition of the third, fifth, sixth and seventh beatitudes.[134]

We may conclude that the Matthean Beatitudes has its background in the beatitudes of the Old Testament/Judaism, and particularly in the apocalyptic beatitudes of the late-Judaism. Ethical elements are added into the original beatitudes through the pre-Matthean development, and the first evengaelist carried them forward as they are suitable for his context. The author also made some redactional addition, especially in the first, fourth and eighth beatitudes, mainly making clarifications as required in his community's context. However, the apocalyptic nature is not lost, as it is clearly indicated especially in the promises of each of the beatitudes. Therefore, the Matthean Beatitudes can be subsumed in the category of apocalyptic beatitude.

2.4. Literary Features of the Matthean Beatitudes

In the analysis of the literary features of the Matthean Beatitudes, its common characteristics will be highlighted first and this will be followed by analysis of its structure.[135]

131 Dillon, "The Text of the Sermon on the Mount," 42, quoting Wolfgang TRILLING, *Christusver-kündigung in den synoptischen Evangelien. Beispiele gattungsgemässer Auslegung* (München: Köesel-Verlag, 1969), 77.

132 *Ibid.*

133 See also Lichtenberger, "Makarisms in Mathew 5:3ff. in their Jewish Context," 50.

134 For some scholars, the Matthean redaction, such as the addition of "in spirit" in the first beatitude, and "and thirst for righteousness" in the fourth beatitude, as well as the composition and addition of the eight beatitude, carries ethical flavour. See for example, Dillon, "The Text of the Sermon on the Mount," 45-47. It is believed in this study, however, that Matthean redactions are basically done to make clarifications as needed by the context of his community, without ethicizing them. This assumption will be further clarified in the exegetical comments below.

135 In the present study, the text of the Matthean Beatitudes in view is the UBS Greek NT, 4th Revised Edition, which is the same with Nestle Aland Greek NT, 26th Edition. For the translation New Revised Standard Version will be mainly followed, otherwise it will be indicated. Discussions on textual problems will be taken up in the exegesis proper of each of the beatitudes.

2.4.1. The Common Characteristics of the Matthean Beatitudes

First of all, the word μακάριοι, "blessed" is placed at the beginning of nine successive sentences, thus clearly demarcating the Beatitudes from the verses preceding it and following it.

Second, each of the first eight beatitudes has the μακάριοι "blessed" at the beginning, followed by designation of those called "blessed", and then a ὅτι clause which describes the reason or ground of the predication of blessedness.[136] There is, however, a marked change in the ninth and last beatitude (vv. 11–12). The third person plural is changed to the second person plural ("blessed are you"), and the lengthy ὅταν ("whenever") clause is added. The ὅτι ("for") clause is also delayed by the placing of the verbs at the beginning of v. 12 ("rejoice and be exceedingly glad").

Third, the eighth beatitude has the same ending with the first, that is ὅτι αὐτῶν ἐστιν ἡ βασιλεία τῶν οὐρανῶν "for theirs is the kingdom of heaven." Therefore, it could be seen as forming an *inclusio*.[137]

Fourth, the word δικαιοσύνη "righteousness" punctuates the fourth and the eighth beatitudes respectively, thus dividing the first eight beatitudes which are similar in form (third person plural) into two stanzas of equal length.[138]

There are also other slight differences in the parallelism between the beatitudes. The first and sixth beatitudes add defining datives such as τῷ πνεύματι, "in spirit" (v. 3), and τῇ καρδίᾳ, "in heart" (v. 8). Even the fourth and the eighth beatitudes have more expanded subjects such as οἱ πεινῶντες καὶ διψῶντες τὴν δικαιοσύνην "those who hunger and thirst for righteousness" (vv. 6), and οἱ δεδιωγμένοι ἕνεκεν δικαιοσύνης, "those who are persecuted for righteousness' sake" (v. 10). The second, fourth, and fifth beatitudes (vv. 4, 6, and 7) have the strict parallelism of the simple future passive in the ὅτι clause such as αὐτοὶ

136 According to Daniel Patte, the ὅτι clause, the second part of each beatitude is framed by Matthew to convince his readers whom he does not expect to be convinced by the first part in itself. Daniel Patte, *The Gospel According to Matthew. A Structural Commentary on Matthew's Faith* (Philadelphia: Fortress Press, 1987), 66. However, this does not seem to be Matthew's creation because Luke also has the same construction (Luke 6:20-21). It seems therefore that Matthew has taken what he has in his source.

137 According to Daniel Patte the application of the rhetorical device of "*inclusio*" "shows that it is taken for granted that participation in the kingdom is the ultimate blessing," and all other blessings pronounced in the beatitudes are part and parcel of the participation in the kingdom. Patte, *The Gospel According to Matthew*, 66. Ulrich Luz notes that the apodoses of the first and eight beatitudes are the longest ones, and with the frame of their composition, this length shows the unending importance of the kingdom of heaven in the Sermon on the Mount. Luz maintains that Matthew is here taking up again the central catch word of Jesus' proclamation given in 4:17, 23, with a desire to uphold the meaning of the "gospel of the kingdom of heaven" in terms of context. Luz, *Matthew 1-7*, 224.

138 Cf. R. A. Guelich, while noting the grouping of the first eight beatitudes into two groups, maintains that this division reflects in no way a propensity for any special number or grouping. Guelich, "The Matthean Beatitudes...," 432.

παρακληθήσονται "they will be comforted," αὐτοὶ χορτασθήσονται "they will be filled," and αὐτοὶ ἐλεηθήσονται "they will receive mercy," (cf. also the seventh beatitude, v. 9, which has the simple future passive without strict parallelism). One more parallel of note is found in the ἕνεκεν δικαιοσύνης, "for righteousness' sake," of the eighth beatitude (v. 10) and the ἕνεκεν ἐμοῦ, "for my sake," of the ninth beatitude (v. 11).[139]

There are important observations, which can be made out of the literary characteristics of the Matthean Beatitudes mentioned above. While the ninth beatitude cannot be excluded from the whole group of the Beatitudes here, the first eight beatitudes nevertheless form a closer unit. This is indicated, first, by the *inclusio* found in the first and the eighth beatitudes ("for theirs is the kingdom of heaven"), and second, by the punctuation of the fourth and the eighth beatitudes by the word "righteousness" which is an important term in Matthew's gospel, especially in the Sermon on the Mount, thus dividing the first eight beatitudes into two equal parts. Because of these two factors, compounded by the difference in form and structure of the ninth beatitude, some commentators conclude that the original collection comprises the first eight beatitudes, and the ninth beatitude is an addition from another source or is the creation of the author.[140] Davies and Allison, Jr., who acknowledge that Matthew inherited eight beatitudes from his tradition, however, maintain that the eight beatitudes inherited by Matthew are the first seven and the ninth, and the eighth beatitude is added by the author to make the total number of beatitudes to nine, that is a multiple of 3. They observe that if 5:3b and 5:11a were to be combined the result would be very close to 5:10.[141]

It is upheld in this study that there are nine beatitudes and not eight or ten beatitudes.[142] And, the difference in form and structure of the ninth beatitude from the other eight beatitudes indeed seems to suggest that Matthew inherited the first eight beatitudes from his main source, and added the ninth from another source or he created it. The possibility of this cannot be totally ruled out. If this is the case, one could explain that the author of the first gospel found the first eight beatitudes having an *inclusio* "for theirs is the kingdom of heaven" in the first and eighth beatitudes. He also found the word "righteousness" punctuating the eight beatitudes in the fourth and eighth, dividing them into equal parts. He found all

139 Hagner, *Matthew 1-13*, 89.

140 See the following for example - Hagner, *Matthew 1-13*, 89. Gundry, *Matthew: A Commentary on His Handbook*, 73. Here, Hagner can be seen as viewing that the ninth beatitude is Matthew's addition. However, according to Gundry the ninth beatitude is not part of or continuation of the first eight beatitudes. He views it as the beginning of the next section and he sees it as taken and altered by the author from another tradition to serve his emphasis on persecution.

141 Davies and Allison, Jr., *Matthew*, Vol. I, 430-341. See also Guelich, "The Matthean Beatitudes…," 432.

142 Betz finds two beatitudes in Matt 5:11-12, and thus has ten beatitudes altogether. See Betz, *The Sermon on the Mount*, 109. See also Betz, *Essays on the Sermon on the Mount*, 23.

these characteristics very much suited to his purpose and took them as they are. Then, in order to make them more connected to his purpose, he added the ninth beatitude thus making the total number of the beatitudes to a multiple of 3. He further put the ninth beatitude in second person plural, thus indicating that the beatitudes are addressed to his primary audience.

However, the view of Davies and Allison, Jr., that Matthew added the eighth beatitude, is more convincing to this researcher. The explanation of this view may not have much difference from the above explanation. However, it places more emphasis on the role of the author. Matthew's purpose in composing and adding one more to the eight beatitudes which he inherited from his tradition would be, as suggested by Davies and Allison Jr., to make the number in agreement with the rest of the Sermon on the Mount. That is, the materials in the Sermon on the Mount (Matt 5-7) are built largely around triads, and a triadic arrangement is found almost everywhere in the first gospel.[143] If this is the sole purpose of the author, however, it seems that he can make an addition with the combination of any of the beatitudes and place it at any position. Therefore, his selection of the eighth position to place his additional beatitude and his selection of the materials, which contain "kingdom of heaven" and "righteousness," seems significant. This suggests that not only the complete number (9) seems to be in view, but the content of the additional beatitude, as well as the position. That means that if the eighth beatitude is added by the author, the position and the content tell that the special importance of "the kingdom of heaven" and "righteousness," which the author wanted to emphasize, is clinched here. This is because, the statement "for theirs is the kingdom of heaven," in the eighth beatitude serves as an *inclusio* with that of the first beatitude, thus accentuating on the phrase "kingdom of heaven." In the same way, the word "righteousness" in the eighth beatitude signifies the emphasis given to this term by the author because, with this arrangement, this word can be seen as a concluding formula of the first four beatitudes, and of the second four beatitudes respectively. With this analysis we could well agree with the observation of Ulrich Luz, that righteousness and kingdom of heaven, which permeate the whole of the Sermon on the Mount, are the two catchwords of the Matthean Beatitudes forming "the righteousness of the kingdom of heaven," befitting to be called its theme.[144] Then, the ninth beatitude could be understood as retained by the author as a direct address to his primary audience, indicating that all the beatitudes apply to them. This is quite possible because of the fact that Luke (6:22-23) also has a parallel of the ninth Matthean beatitude.

This analysis of the literary features of the Matthean Beatitudes is also important for the determination of its structure, to which we now turn.

143 Davies and Allison, Jr., *Matthew*, Vol. I, 86-87, 431.

144 Luz, *Matthew 1-7*, 103.

2.4.2. The Structure of the Matthean Beatitudes

A very common suggestion for the structure of the Matthean Beatitudes made by a good number of scholars, based on its literary features, is a division into two sets of four.[145] The first set consists of 5:3-6 and the second set consist of 5:7-10. The important literary features mainly taken as a support for such a division into two sets of four are – 1) the letter π characterizes the identities or designations of those called blessed in the first set (or the first four beatitudes), such as "the poor (πτωχοί)," "those who mourn (πενθοῦντες)," "the meek (πραεῖς)," and "those who hunger (πεινῶντες) and thirst," thus functioning as a unifying instrument. 2) The first four beatitudes are also held together by the same subject matter, that is, the persecuted (passive) condition of the disciples. 3) The second set, such as – "Blessed are the merciful," "Blessed are the pure in heart," "Blessed are the peacemakers," and "Blessed are those who are persecuted for righteousness' sake" uniformly treat the ethical (active) qualities leading to persecution and therefore they can be taken as a unit.[146] 4) The word δικαιοσύνη "righteousness" punctuates the fourth and the eighth beatitudes respectively, thus dividing the first eight beatitudes into two stanzas of equal length, both containing 36 words each.[147] 5) The ὅτι clause of the eighth beatitude, that is "for theirs is the kingdom of heaven," has a verbatim agreement with that of the first beatitude and therefore it forms an *inclusio*.[148]

Davies and Allison Jr. argue that although the division of the Matthean Beatitudes into two sets of equal length seems quite attractive because of the suggested supporting literary features, there are some problems with this division. First, the phrase, καὶ διψῶντες "*and thirst*" disrupts the π pattern in 5: 6. Second, if the first set (5:3-6) is based on a unifying letter (that is π), then an inevitable question is – why is there no unifying letter in the second set (5:7-10)? Third, the ninth beatitude (5:11-12) is totally excluded in this division.[149]

The first two criticisms may be explained in the following way. First, the addition of "καὶ διψῶντες" in 5:6 does not replace οἱ πεινῶντες, and the meaning of οἱ πεινῶντες καὶ διψῶντες in this verse is more or less the same with οἱ πεινῶντες alone.[150] Therefore, the addition of "καὶ διψῶντες" does not

145 See the following for example - Schweizer, *The Good News According to Matthew*, 82; Gundry, *Matthew: A Commentary on His Handbook*, 73; Lambrecht, *The Sermon on the Mount*, 61.

146 See Davies and Allison, Jr., *Matthew*, Vol. I, 429, who summarize the arguments of the scholars who suggest this structure, but without supporting it.

147 Schweizer, *The Good News According to Matthew*, 82. Guelich, while noting the grouping of the beatitudes in two groups, maintains that this division reflects in no way a propensity for any special number or grouping. Guelich, "The Matthean Beatitudes...," 432.

148 For example, see Hagner, *Matthew 1-13*, 89. See also Guelich, *The Sermon on the Mount: A Foundation for Understanding*, 93.

149 Davies and Allison, Jr., *Matthew*, Vol. I, 430.

150 See "exegetical comment" on this verse below.

disrupt the implication of the π pattern in 5:6. Second, the first four beatitudes are undoubtedly alliterated with the letter π, and this alliteration seems to have taken place in Q^{mt}, before Matthew.[151] And, this does not necessarily mean that the second set of four beatitudes (vv. 5-8) also must have a unifying letter. The only notable redaction of Matthew in the first four beatitudes seems to be the addition of τῷ πνεύματι in the first beatitude and καὶ διψῶντες τὴν δικαιοσύνην in the fourth beatitude. Therefore, Matthew does not play a role in the alliteration of the first four beatitudes with the letter π. However, it seems that he deliberately concludes the first four beatitudes with τὴν δικαιοσύνην in the fourth beatitude. This is strongly suggested by his conclusion of the second set of four beatitudes (vv. 7-10) with the same phrase in the eighth beatitude, which obviously is his addition.[152]

In spite of such explanations, the exclusion of the ninth beatitude is unacceptable, because the most distinguishing feature of this pericopae, that is the beginning of each of the beatitudes with the word μακάριοι "blessed," clearly indicates that it is part of the Beatitudes' pericope.[153]

Another notable suggestion for the structure of the Matthean Beatitudes is a chiastic arrangement. This arrangement is given by N. J. McEleney, who also thinks that the first eight beatitudes (5:3-10) divide themselves into two units, such as 5:3-6 and 5:7-10 respectively and the two units are arranged in a chiastic pattern.[154]

---

151 Dillon points out that the π alliteration is responsible for at least two noteworthy changes in the content of this basic series of beatitudes: first, the substitution of the word *peinontes* ("mourning") for *klaiontes* ("weeping") in Matt 5: 4, as against Luke 6:21b; and second, the wholly new beatitude of the *praeis* ("meek") in Matt 5:5, unmatched in Luke. Dillon, further suggests that the π alliteration could have resulted from a kind of literary artifice which does not appear elsewhere in Matthew's composition, or more probably to serve the mnemonic needs of the spoken tradition. Dillon, "The Text of the Sermon on the Mount," 48.

152 See "the Redaction of the Matthean Beatitudes" below.

153 Davies and Allison, Jr., *Matthew*, Vol. I, 430. Davies and Allison, Jr. here notes that the ninth beatitude (5:11-12) is admittedly different in form from the preceding beatitudes, in that it is much longer, it contains imperatives, and it is directly addressed to the reader (that is that the second person is used). However, they maintain that there is a good precedent for making the last member of a series much longer than the preceding members and for the abrupt switch from the third to second person. They claim that both of such things are found in Jewish prayer texts, in the Bible, and even in English literature. They take examples, such as Isa 63:10-14; Ecclus 47:12-22; 48:1-11; Matt 1:2-16; 23: 3-36; Luke 1: 68-79; 6:37-38.

154 Such as: Matt 5:3 - inclusory formula: "because theirs is the kingdom of heaven"'
5:4 - divine passive: "because they shall be comforted"
5:5 - future active with object: "because they shall inherit the earth"
5:6 - divine passive: "because they shall be satisfied"
5:7 - divine passive: "because they shall receive mercy"
5:8 - future middle with object: "because they shall see God"
5:9 - divine passive: "because they shall be called sons of God"
5:10 - inclusory formula: "because theirs is the kingdom of heaven"

In fact, a chiastic structure can be undeniably deduced from the first eight beatitudes as McEleney highlighted. As the chiastic arrangement is found also in other places of this gospel,[155] McEleney's proposal seems possible to some extent. However, a closer look at the Matthean Beatitudes reveals that there are problems even with this proposal. First, the key word "righteousness" occurs in vv. 6 and 10 and therefore it does not fall into the chiastic pattern. Second, as in the case of the previous suggestion, this proposal also left the ninth beatitude (5:11-12) aside.[156] Therefore, the chiastic pattern does not seem to be the intended structure of Matthew for the Beatitudes.

Alexander A. Di Lella proposes that numerical concern plays a role in the structure of the Matthean Beatitudes. He identifies eight beatitudes, and divides them into two strophes with 36 words each. Then he notes that each strophe has beatitudes with six words, with eight words, with ten words, and with twelve words, all even numbers. But, the μακάριοι clause of each strophe, as well as the ὅτι clause of each strophe has three, five or seven words, all uneven numbers. He suggests that the addition of τῷ πνεύματι in v. 3, the article τὴν of τὴν γῆν in v. 5, καὶ διψῶντες in v. 6, and the omission of the article τὴν before δικαιοσύνην in v. 10a (against τὴν δικαιοσύνην in v. 6a), all have to do with the numerical concern of the author.[157] In fact, such numerical arrangement can be detected in the first eight beatitudes, and the author might have such a numerical concern for the sake of better symmetry. Apart from that, such numerical concern does not seem to have any particular significance for the theology of the author, nor any relevance to the socio-historical context of the author.[158] Yet, a major problem with the suggestion of this structure is that it also leaves the ninth beatitude aside. Moreover, the suggested redactions in verses 3, 5, 6, and 10 seem to have better reasons than the numerical concern, which is suggested by Di Lella, such as theological and contextual reasons.[159]

Frederick Dale Bruner suggests a division into three groups on thematic grounds, such as, A) The Inaugural Need (or Poor) Beatitudes of Grace and Faith, 5:3-6. B) The Central Help (or Full) Beatitudes of Service and Love, 5:7-9. C)

See McEleney, "The Beatitudes of the Sermon on the Mount/Plain," 1-13. The proposal for chiastic arrangement is also upheld by H. Benedict Green. See Green, *Matthew, Poet of the Beatitudes*, 37-39.

155 See "Literary analysis of Matthew's gospel" above.

156 Davies and Allison, Jr., *Matthew*, Vol. I, 430.

157 Alexander A. Di Lella, "The Structure and Composition of the Matthean Beatitudes," in *To Touch the Text. Biblical and Related Studies in Honor of Joseph A. Fitzmyer, S.J.*, edited by Maurya P. Horgan and Paul J. Kobelski (New York: Crossroads, 1989), 238-241.

158 The author of this article, Di Lella himself, also seems to admit this by stating that there is nothing earthshaking in this proposal. See Di Lella, "The Structure and composition of the Matthean Beatitudes," 242.

159 The significance of these additional words are spelled out in the "Redaction of the Matthean Beatitudes" and in the exegetical comments of the specific verses below.

The Concluding Hurt (or Persecution) Beatitudes of Joy and Hope, 5:10-12.[160] The problem with this suggestion is that the Matthean redaction of the Beatitudes does not seem to have any significance in relation to this structure, and therefore this structure does not seem to be the one intended by the author.

Davies and Allison, Jr. suggest that the author of the first gospel inherited eight beatitudes from his tradition. Then he created additional beatitude in order to correspond to the triads with which he arranged the materials in the Sermon on the Mount, thus making three triads of the Beatitudes (3+3+3). Therefore, the complete number nine to fulfil a triadic formula was the main concern of Matthew for the structure of the Beatitudes.[161]

Davies and Allison, Jr. seem right in saying that "every attractive analysis need not be correct."[162] Especially the omission of the ninth beatitude is incompatible because, as already indicated above, the μακάριοι formula at the beginning clearly indicates that it is an integral part of the Matthean Beatitudes. Consequently, it seems quite possible that the triadic arrangement (3+3+3) was what Matthew had in mind as the basic structure for the arrangement of his nine beatitudes. This is supported by Matthew's penchant for numbers and especially the triads, for his arrangement of materials in his gospel. At the same time, however, there seems to be a stronger suggestion than a simple triadic arrangement, that is, 4+4+1, for the structure of the Matthean Beatitudes.

It is believed in this study that the author of the first gospel deliberately arranged the first eight beatitudes into two sets of four. This "two sets of four" arrangement is clearly supported especially by – (1) the punctuation of each set with the word "righteousness" at the fourth and eighth beatitudes respectively, apparently by Matthew's own hand; and (2) the enclosure, at the same time, of the first eighth beatitudes with the same ὅτι clause "for theirs is the kingdom of heaven," which is found in the first beatitude and deliberately added by Matthew in the eighth beatitude. With this arrangement, the ninth beatitude is not excluded from the group of the Matthean Beatitudes, but only is placed outside the eight beatitude as a conclusion to all. It is presented in second person plural form, while the first eight beatitudes are presented in third person plural form, to indicate that the author of the first gospel deliberately presented the ninth beatitude as a conclusion to these two sets of four. The direct address to the disciples/the intended audience with second person plural form indicates that the first eight beatitudes which are presented in third person plural form as universally applicable are also applicable to, or rather primarily meant for, them.

160 Bruner, *Matthew 1-12*, 155.

161 Davies and Allison, Jr., *Matthew*, Vol. I, 430-431, 459. Davies and Allison, Jr. here assert that Matthew did not have any other concern in his addition of the eighth beatitude, but only numerical arrangement, that is, to make the beatitudes into nine in line with his triadic arrangement of the Sermon on the Mount.

162 Davies and Allison, Jr., *Matthew*, Vol. I, 430.

Furthermore, the subject of the eighth beatitude, that is persecution, bridges the final beatitude with the preceding eight beatitudes (which, on the other hand, are bound together with an *inclusio* in the first and the eighth beatitudes).[163] Therefore, it seems that Matthew consciously arranged the Beatitudes in 4+4+1 format. This assumption is reasonable for the fact that number 2 (4=2+2) is also one of the favourite numbers of the first Evangelist.[164] Moreover, this suggestion is strongly supported by the notable redactions of the Beatitudes by the author of the first gospel. One of the most remarkable redactions of the author is the addition of the eighth beatitude.[165] For this additional beatitude, Matthew deliberately chooses his favourite terms like "righteousness" and "kingdom of heaven," which are the two catchwords in the Sermon on the Mount. Therefore, Matthew deliberately forms an *inclusio* with the term "kingdom of heaven" which is already there in the first beatitude. The enclosure of the first eight beatitudes (vv. 3-10) by the phrase ὅτι αὐτῶν ἐστιν ἡ βασιλεία τῶν οὐρανῶν "for theirs is the kingdom of heaven," in the first and eighth beatitudes, indicates that all the promises in the first eight beatitudes are enclosed in the promise, "for theirs is the kingdom of heaven," and the enclosed apodoses "unfold what 'kingdom of heaven' means."[166] Another important redaction of Matthew is the addition of καὶ διψῶντες τὴν δικαιοσύνην, in the fourth beatitude. With the addition of καὶ διψῶντες Matthew has πεινῶντες καὶ διψῶντες in place of Luke's (or Q's) only πεινῶντες. Matthew's addition of καὶ διψῶντες seems to have been influenced by the OT frequent parallelism of the two words "πεινῶντες" and "διψῶντες" (e.g., 107:5-9; Isa 49:19; 65:13), and the meaning of these two expressions seems to be more or less the same.[167] However, with the addition of the term τὴν δικαιοσύνην in the fourth beatitude, the first eight beatitudes are divided into two equal stanzas both of which are concluded with the term δικαιοσύνην. Thus, with the addition of the eighth beatitude, and the redaction of the fourth beatitude, the importance of the terms "kingdom of heaven" and "righteousness"

163 Cf. Guelich, *The Sermon on the Mount: A Foundation for Understanding*, 93.

164 In fact, Talbert is of the view that the pre-occupation of Davies and Allison, Jr. with triads as the structure of the Sermon on the Mount and then of the Beatitudes seems forced, and he asks, "why see 3x3 Beatitudes instead of 4+4+1?" Then Talbert points out that number 2 is used widely as well in Matthew's gospel, for example, two images – 5:13-16; two groups of antithesis – 5:21-48; 6:19-7:12 sub divides into two units; the two ways – 7:13-14; two houses – 7:24-27. Talbert, *Reading the Sermon on the Mount*, 23. See also Betz, *Essays on the Sermon on the Mount*, 23, who maintains that "In patristic exegesis, the number eight (according to other reckonings, the number seven) is discussed at great length, for it, too, must be explained in terms of number symbolism. The number eight (or seven) symbolizes perfection as well."

165 See "The Form, Sources and *Sitz im Leben* of the Matthean Beatitudes" below.

166 Luz, *Matthew 1-7*, 235. See also Dillon, "The Text of the Sermon on the Mount," 48.

167 See "Redaction of the Matthean beatitudes" and an exegetical comment on v. 6 below.

within the Beatitudes has been deliberately accentuated by the author.[168] This corresponds well with the importance of these two terms in the First gospel as a whole, and especially in the Sermon on the Mount.[169] Moreover, it also seems that Matthew deliberately included the term "persecution" for his additional beatitude (Matt 5:10) in order to connect it with the following ninth beatitude which has the theme of persecution.

Thus, the structures of the Matthean Beatitudes may be given as follows:[170]

Strophe I

3 Blessed are the poor in spirit, for theirs is the kingdom of heaven.
4 Blessed are those who mourn, for they will be comforted.
5 Blessed are the meek, for they will inherit the earth.
6 Blessed are those who hunger and thirst for righteousness, for they will be filled.

Strophe II

7 Blessed are the merciful, for they will receive mercy.
8 Blessed are the pure in heart, for they will see God.
9 Blessed are the peacemakers, for they will be called children of God.
10 Blessed are those who are persecuted for righteousness' sake, for theirs is the kingdom of heaven.

Concluding Beatitude

11 Blessed are you when they revile you and persecute you and utter all kinds of evil against you falsely on my account.
12 Rejoice and be glad, for your reward is great in heaven, for in the same way they persecuted the prophets who were before you.

---

168 So, Luz also observes thus: "the redactional beatitude of the persecuted in v. 10 does not go beyond v. 3 and v. 11f. It reinforces once more the two main aspects of the whole series, δικαιοσύνη and kingdom of heaven." Luz, *Matthew 1-7*, 241.

169 See "Redaction of the Matthean Beatitudes" below.

170 While 4+4+1 structure is adopted here, it is also recognized that Matthew would have been aware of the fact that his addition of the eighth beatitude also satisfies the triadic formula (3+3+3), with which he largely arranged the SOM and his gospel as a whole. However, while the triadic structure seems to have significance in indicating the Jewish background of the author and his intended audience, the 4+4+1 structure seems to have higher degree of significance for Matthew's theology especially giving emphasis on righteousness and kingdom of heaven. Therefore, viewing from Matthew's redactional contribution in the fourth and eighth beatitudes, the 4+4+1 seems to be the structure the author had in mind.

2.5. The Matthean Beatitudes and the Lukan Beatitudes: A Comparison and Contrast

The Matthean Beatitudes (Matt 5:3-12) has a parallel in Luke 6:20b-23. However, there are obvious differences between these two parallel Beatitudes. The aim of this section is only to highlight the differences between the two versions, and the significance of these differences will be given in detail in the exegetical comments below as and when necessary.[171]

2.5.1. The Major Differences

(1) Matthew has nine beatitudes while Luke has four beatitudes.

(2) All the four Lukan beatitudes have parallel in Matthean beatitudes, of course, with certain differences in wordings and in length, such as –

Luke 20b – *"Blessed are you who are poor, for yours is the kingdom of God."*
par.
Matt 5:3 – "*Blessed are the poor in spirit, for theirs is the kingdom of heaven.*"

Luke 6:21a – "*Blessed are you who are hungry now, for you will be filled.*"
par.
Matt 5:6 – "*Blessed are those who hunger and thirst for righteousness, for they will be filled.*"

Luke 6:21b – "*Blessed are you who weep now, for you will laugh.*"
par.
Matt 5:4 – "*Blessed are those who mourn, for they will be comforted.*"

Luke 22:22-23 –*Blessed are you when people hate you, and when they exclude you, revile you, and defame you on account of the Son of Man.*
23 *Rejoice in that day and leap for joy, for surely your reward is great in heaven; for that is what their ancestors did to the prophets.*
par.
Matt 5:11-12 - *Blessed are you when people revile you and persecute you and utter all kinds of evil against you falsely on my account.*
12 *Rejoice and be glad, for your reward is great in heaven, for in the same way they persecuted the prophets who were before you.*

Most of the major differences in these parallel beatitudes are ascribed to the Matthean redaction, such as the addition of "in spirit" and the use of "kingdom of heaven" in the first beatitude; the addition of "and thirst for righteousness" in the fourth beatitude.[172]

171 See also the "Redaction of the Matthean Beatitudes" below.

172 For a detailed analysis, see "the Redaction of the Matthean Beatitudes" and the exegetical comments of the specific verses below.

Five of the Matthean beatitudes (Matt 5:5, 7, 8, 9, and 10) do not have parallels in Luke. While the absence of the third, fifth, sixth and seventh Matthean beatitudes in Luke is ascribed to the difference of traditions used by the two evangelists, the eighth Matthean beatitude is understood to be a Matthean addition.[173]

(3) Matthew has third person plural in the ὅτι clause of the first eight beatitudes and the second person plural in the ninth beatitude, while Luke has second person plural in all the four beatitudes. In this case, there is no consensus among scholars on which form is the original. It is, however, quite possible that Matthew's third person form is the original and Luke's second person form is the author's redaction.[174]

(4) Besides the differences mentioned above, Luke furthermore has four corresponding woes (Luke 6:24-26) directly following the beatitudes and serving as their counterparts[175] while Matthew has no such corresponding woes. It is uncertain whether Matthew did not see the woes in his tradition, or he saw them and omitted them or he inserted them in a different place.[176] Even in this case, it is quite possible that the two evangelists used two different traditions and Matthew did not find the "woes" in his tradition.[177]

2.5.2. The Minor Differences

Besides the basic differences mentioned above there are also minor differences between the Beatitudes in Matthew and Luke, particularly in the vocabularies they use. The significant ones are:

(1) Matthew 5:4 has οἱ πενθοῦντες, ὅτι αὐτοὶ παρακληθήσονται. "those who mourn, for they will be comforted." The parallel beatitude in Luke 6:21b

173 For a detailed explanations, see "the Redaction of the Matthean Beatitudes" and the exegetical comments of the specific verses below.

174 For further explanations, see "the Redaction of the Matthean Beatitudes" and the exegetical comments of the specific verses below.

175 Dodd rightly observes that the four Lukan woes "balance the beatitudes so closely that we cannot doubt that the evangelist intended beatitudes and woes to form a single whole." Dodd, "The Beatitudes: A form Critical Study," 3.

176 Of course, Matthew has a list of woes in chapter 23. But these woes do not seem to correspond to the beatitudes. Their closer parallels seem to be found in Luke 11:42-52. At the same time, however, it could also be that Matthew found the woes corresponding to the Beatitudes in his tradition, but used them for heightening the woes in chap 23, and applies them to the scribes and Pharisees, just as he deliberately omitted the subject οἱ ἄνθρωποι of Q/Luke (6:22) to leave unspecified "they" (Matt 5:11) to refer to the leaders of formative Judaism. Cf. Cooper, "'They Shall See God':..," 66, who sees the woes in Luke 6:24-26 and the seven woes in Matt 23:13ff. as forming a parallel frame.

177 See also "the Form, Source and *Sitz im Leben* of the Matthean Beatitudes" and the "Redaction of the Matthean Beatitudes" below.

has οἱ κλαίοντες νῦν, ὅτι γελάσετε "those who weep now, for you will laugh." It is uncertain which evangelist preserves the original form.[178]

(2) Matthew 5:11 has ὅταν ὀνειδίσωσιν ὑμᾶς καὶ διώξωσιν καὶ εἴπωσιν πᾶν πονηρὸν καθ' ὑμῶν [ψευδόμενοι] ἕνεκεν ἐμοῦ "when they revile you and persecute you and utter all kinds of evil against you falsely on my account." The parallel beatitude in Luke 6:22 has ὅταν μισήσωσιν ὑμᾶς οἱ ἄνθρωποι καὶ ὅταν ἀφορίσωσιν ὑμᾶς καὶ ὀνειδίσωσιν καὶ ἐκβάλωσιν τὸ ὄνομα ὑμῶν ὡς πονηρὸν ἕνεκα τοῦ υἱοῦ τοῦ ἀνθρώπου "when people hate you, and when they exclude you, revile you, and defame you on account of the Son of Man." Here, Matthew seems to be responsible for the omission and change of the wordings.[179]

There are also slight differences in the wordings of Matt 5:12 and its parallel Luke 6:22. Matthew does not have "in that day" which is found in Luke. Here, Matthew seems to be responsible for omitting what is found in the Q. Matthew has "rejoice and be [exceedingly] glad" in place of Luke's "leap for Joy." Luke seems to be responsible for this difference in wordings. For other minor differences like the plural "in the heavens" in Matthew and the singular "in the heaven" in Luke, it is not certain which one is original.[180]

2.6. The Forms, Sources, and Sitz im Leben of the Matthean Beatitudes

2.6.1. The View of Earlier Form Critics

According to the earlier form critics, the earliest memories of Jesus (his sayings and stories about him) were circulated by word of mouth and in the process of circulation, they were shaped into forms according to principles of oral communication such as miracle stories, parables, etc. In the course of the repeated retelling, they took on additional details and emphases, and new stories were created to meet the ongoing needs of the believing community.[181]

Viewing from the background of this understanding, Bultmann is of the opinion that the Beatitudes (of Matthew and Luke) belong to prophetic and apocalyptic sayings, and precisely under a sub category of "preaching of salvation." With regard to the number of Beatitudes in Matthew and Luke, Bultmann believes that the number in Luke is the more original. He divides the Beatitudes into two groups, such as Luke 6:20f. par. Matt 5:3-9, and Luke 6:22f. par. Matt 5:10-12, and he thinks that in the case of the first group Luke is probably more original in

178 For a detailed discussion, see the "Redaction of the Matthean Beatitudes" and the exegetical comment on v. 4 below.

179 For further discussion, see the "Redaction of the Matthean Beatitudes" and the exegetical comment on v. 11 below.

180 For a detailed discussion see the "Redaction of the Matthean Beatitudes" and the exegetical comment on v. 12 below.

181 See William Baird, "New Testament Criticism," *ABD*, Vol. I (New York: Doubleday, 1997 [1992]), 732.

general. He, however, opines that the third person in Matthew is more original and Luke changed it to second person in order to introduce a comparison with vv. 22f., in which the second person was in the traditional form. With regard to the second group, that is Luke 6:22f. par. Matt 5:10-12, Bultmann believes that Matt 5:10 is a Matthean formulation with an intention to bring the number of the beatitudes in vv. 3-9 up to seven (here Bultmann excludes Matt 5:5, terming it as a secondary in Matthew). He views Matt 5:11f. (par. Luke 6:22) as a new element of the tradition undoubtedly different from the older element (that is Luke 6:20f. par. Matt 5:3-9) in form and content. He contends that this portion arose *ex eventu* and for that reason it was created by the church.[182]

For Dibelius the Beatitudes (of Matthew and Luke) belong to the group of "prophetic appeals." He takes the form that is found in Luke as original and according to him, they belong to those very earliest traditions which could be recovered.[183]

Thus, according to Bultmann and Dibelius the original form of the Beatitudes is found in Luke, and their social setting (*Sitz im Leben*) was the church's preaching of salvation or church's prophetic appeals.

2.6.2. The Present Understanding

On the basis of the "Markan Priority" which is subscribed to by the majority of New Testament scholars at present,[184] four of the nine Matthean Beatitudes, such as Matt 5:3-4, 6 and 11-12 could be ascribed to the Q source mainly because their parallels are found in Luke (Luke 6:20-22).[185] However, there are difference in the wordings of these parallel Beatitudes in Matthew and Luke.[186] Ever since the introduction of redaction criticism, Matthean scholars usually took Luke as representing Q[187] and often ascribe the differences between the Matthean Beatitudes and the Lukan Beatitudes, such as the difference in wordings as well

182 Rudolf Bultmann, *History of the Synoptic Tradition* (Peabody, Massachusetts: Hendrickson Publishers, 1963), 108-110.

183 Martin Dibelius, *The Message of Jesus Christ*, translated by Frederick C. Grant (New York: Charles Scribner's Sons, 1939), xx.

184 Either in terms of two document hypothesis (proposed by Holtzmann in 1863) which suggests that Mark wrote first and both Matthew and Luke used Mark and another source called Q, or four document hypothesis (proposed by Streeter in 1924) which further suggests that besides Mark and Q, both Matthew and Luke used another source peculiar to each of them. See Baird, "New Testament Criticism," 733-734.

185 Davies and Allison, Jr., *Matthew*, Vol. I, 434.

186 See the comparison between the Matthean and Lukan Beatitudes above.

187 According to Stanton, Scholars accept in general that Luke, though not necessarily original wording, has preserved the original order of Q tradition, and therefore it has become customary for recent writers to refer to Q passages with the chapters and verses in Luke's gospel. G. N. Stanton, "Q," *DJG*, edited by Joel B. Green, Scott McKnight and I. Howard Marshall (Downers Grove, Illinois: InterVarsity Press, 1992), 644. See also Lichtenberger, "Makarisms in Mathew 5:3ff. in their Jewish Context," 41.

as the difference in number, to Matthew's hand.[188] However, it does not seem to be as simple as that. In this context, Hagner's argument seems quite reasonable. According to him, ascribing primacy to one (Luke) and terming the other (Matthew) as secondary would amount to accusing one or the other of omitting indispensible material (for Luke, several beatitudes, and for Matthew, the woes).[189] At the same time, however, there is a possibility for Matthew to omit the woes even if he found them in his tradition, because he was very much conscious about his audience (perhaps more than Luke) and he realizes that they (the woes of Luke 6:24-26) would be very disruptive and inappropriate in a sermon which was directed, above all, to disciples. That is, therefore, a reason good enough for him to omit them. Not only that, but also "in Matthew the beatitudes are antithetically correlated with the warnings in 7:13-26, and the woes would not fit into this scheme"[190] On the other side, if Luke had the other beatitudes in his tradition at all, it is very unlikely that he would omit them, as Hagner suggests. Therefore, apart from the differences in wordings, these two major differences between Matthew and Luke, namely Matthew's lack of the woes, which are found in Luke 6:23-26, and Luke's lack of Matthew's 5:5, 7-9 (excluding 5:10, which betrays Matthew's redaction) does not seem to be the result of redaction from the two evangelists. A highly probable situation, rather, is that Matthew and Luke used two different versions of Q, which scholars usually refer to as Q^{mt} and Q^{lk}.[191] This is quite possible because it has been suggested that different traditions both written and oral lie behind the Q material.[192] Moreover, typical Matthean vocabulary or interests are not represented in four of the remaining five beatitudes in Matthew, such as Matt 5:5, 7, 8, and 9 (excluding Matt 5:10), and therefore they cannot be simply attributed to Matthew's hands. In fact, they are usually assigned to Q^{mt}.[193] Such an attribution of these beatitudes to Q is also supported by the fact that a comparison of Matt 5:7, 8, and 9 with Luke 6 (not with Matthew 5:5) shows that

188 See for example, Gundry, *Matthew: A Commentary on His Handbook*, 65-75. See also Lichtenberger, "Makarisms in Mathew 5:3ff. in their Jewish Context," 41.

189 Hagner, 89-90. Hagner here holds that "this material, as it is found in both of the Gospels, exhibits content and form that the early Church very likely would have committed to memory."

190 Davies and Allison, Jr., *Matthew*, Vol. I, 435-436, n. 11.

191 See Strecker, *The Sermon on the Mount*, 12. See also Luz, *Studies in Matthew*, 39-53. Here, (in p. 44-45) Luz lists the following texts which according to him, are probably in Matthew's copy but not in Luke's copy - Matt 5:5, 7-9; Matt 5:19(?); Matt 5:41; Matt 6:34; Matt 7:6(?); 10:5-6(?); Matt 10: 16b; Matt 10:23(?); Matt 10:41(?); 18:15b-17, 18; Matt 23:15(?). These question marks are given by Luz to indicate very uncertain passages.

192 See W. F. Albright and C. S. Mann, *Matthew*. The Anchor Bible, Vol. 26 (New York: Doubleday, 1971), xliv-liii. Cf. however, Tuckett, "Q (Gospel Source)," 567-571, for the idea that Q was a single source existed in written form at some stage and was available in Greek to Matthew and Luke.

193 Davies and Allison, Jr., *Matthew*, Vol. I, 434. See also Luz, *Studies in Matthew*, 44.

there is a linking up of these beatitudes, through their catchwords and themes, with the passages that are to be assigned to Q's Sermon on the Mount/Plain. The comparison may be seen as follows:[194]

Matt 5	**Luke 6**
The *merciful* will obtain mercy (v. 7)	Be *merciful*, even as your Father is *merciful* (v. 36)
The pure in *heart* will see God (v. 8)	The good man out of the treasure of his *heart* brings forth the good (v. 45)
The peacemakers will be called *sons of God* (v. 9)	Those who love their enemies and do good to them will be *sons of the Most High* (v. 35; cf. Matt 5:45)

With regard to the "meek" of the third Matthean beatitude (Matt 5:5), Guelich's observation is highly probable. He asserts that this beatitude betrays a characteristic Matthean term, and it does not show any trace of being a part of the original beatitude. At the same time, however, there is no evidence of its omission from the original beatitudes, while differing evidence for its location is there, which thus rules out its being later interpolation.[195] Therefore, this also seems to be a pre-Matthean addition to the Q tradition simultaneously with 5:7-9.[196]

According to W. D. Davies and Dale C. Allison, Jr. (more or less in agreement with R. A. Guelich[197]), the formation of the Beatitudes in Matthew and Luke took four stages. In the first stage, Jesus uttered three paradoxical beatitudes, which have eschatological reversal as their theme, such as blessed are the poor, blessed are those who mourn, and blessed are those who hunger. It is highly probable that Jesus formulated these three beatitudes based on Isa 61:1-3.[198] In the second stage, these

194 For this comparison, see Davies and Allison, Jr., *Matthew*, Vol. 1, 435. Davies and Allison Jr., here, note the difference of the Greek words used for the similar meaning (mercy/merciful) in Matt 5:7 and Luke 6:36, that while Matthew has ἐλεήμονες and ἐλεηθήσονται, Luke has οἰκτίρμονες and οἰκτίρμων. They maintain that Q^{mt} probably had οἱ οἰκτίρμονες in Matt 5:7, and Matthew's use of ἐλε-root is probably due of Matthew.

195 Some manuscripts place this beatitude in the second position. See "Redaction of the Matthean Beatitudes" in the next sub-section.

196 Guelich, "The Matthean Beatitudes…," 423-426.

197 *Ibid.*, 415-434. See also Guelich, *The Sermon on the Mount: A Foundation for Understanding*, 63-118. Ulrich Luz is also of the opinion that the first three beatitudes might go back to Jesus in their Lukan form of text, but probably without the Lukan νῦν in Luke 6:21. Luz, *Matthew 1-7*, 227.

198 Davies and Allison, Jr., *Matthew*, Vol. I, 438.

three dominical beatitudes were, after they were translated into Greek,[199] joined to what is now Luke 6:27-28, and to at least part of what is now Luke 6: 39-49. This resulted in the creation of the early form of the Sermon on the Mount/Plain. A fourth beatitude, that is on persecution (Matt 5:11-12 par. Luke 6:22-23), was added or composed, probably to make the transition from the beatitudes to the section on the love of enemies. This beatitude links up verbally with the previous beatitudes, as well as with the pericopae that follow it. In the third stage, Q took two different forms, Q^{lk} and Q^{mt}.[200] In Q^{lk} four woes corresponding to the four beatitudes were composed. In Q^{mt}, "Blessed are the meek…" was added to explain the potentially misleading "Blessed are the poor…" (which was not yet qualified by "in spirit"), and in order to establish a correlation between beatitudes and what follows, three more beatitudes were composed. This resulted in eight beatitudes. In the fourth stage, Matthew and Luke edited the different versions of Q available to them. That is that, Matthew used Q^{mt} for his final edition while Luke used Q^{lk}. Matthew composed and added another beatitude (Matt 5:10), to make the number of the Beatitudes to nine.[201]

It is not possible to know with certainty whether the four-stage development of the Matthean Beatitudes, proposed above, is true or not. However, it seems that there is no proposal, which is more convincing yet. This research will assume, based on the above arguments and suggestions, that Matthew inherited eight beatitudes[202] (which probably underwent three stages toward the final production of Q^{mt}), and (probably in the fourth stage of the history of the Matthean Beatitudes) he redacted the tradition which he inherited in Q^{mt} to produce their present form. This researcher would like to add here (against Davies and Allison, Jr.), that while Matthew added 5:10 to make the number of the beatitudes to nine, the selection of its content by the first evangelist is influenced by his context.[203] It follows then, that the (pre-redacted) three beatitudes, namely, the *poor* beatitude (Matt 5:3 par. Luke 6:20b), the *mourning* beatitude (Matt 5:4 par. Luke 6:21b), and *the*

199 Cf., Green, *Matthew, Poet of the Beatitudes*, 41, who contends that the Matthean beatitudes were written in Greek.

200 Q (the abbreviation for German *Quelle*, which means "source") is the name given by scholars to the hypothetical source that would account for the gospel material, common to both Matthew and Luke, but not found in Mark. It is generally accepted as a written document, and it is also often called "the Sayings Source." Luz's observation seems quite reasonable, that according to him Q material underwent a process of expansion from a smaller collection, Qmt represents a version of Q, which is altered and enlarged only minimally, while Qlk represent a very much enlarged version. See Luz, *Matthew 1-7*, 46. See also Tuckett, "Q (Gospel Source)," 567.

201 Davies and Allison, Jr., *Matthew*, Vol. I, 435-436. Cf. Luz, *Matthew 1-7*, 228-229. See also analysis of "the Structure of the Matthean Beatitudes," above.

202 Cf., Hagner, *Matthew 1-13*, 90, who suggests that Matthew drew the nine Beatitudes from the Q tradition which is different from the one used by Luke and adapted to his gospel with minor redactions.

203 For this argument, see the exegetical comment below.

hungry (and thirsty) beatitude (Matt 5:6 par. Luke 6:21a), have their *Sitz im Leben* in the preaching/teaching/ministry of Jesus.[204] The other four beatitudes (Matt 5:5, 7-9) have their Sitz *im Leben* in the Q community.[205] The last beatitude (Matt 11-12) could have its Sitz *im Leben* in Jesus' ministry (or probably in the Q community).[206] Matt 5:10 has its *Sitz im Leben* in the experience of the Matthean community.[207]

The four Lukan woes corresponding to his four beatitudes will be left to an open question here. They could be a Lukan origin,[208] or they could have been added in Q^{lk}, as Davies and Allison, Jr. suggested. They could also have been part of the Q tradition before it was split into Q^{mt} and Q^{lk}, and they probably went back to Jesus also. It is also possible that the first evangelist omitted them because of his consciousness of his primary audience, which included some affluent members.[209]

2.7. Redaction of the Matthean Beatitudes

According to Guelich the Matthean redaction of the Beatitudes took place in the first, third, fourth and eight beatitudes mainly to link them up with Isa 61:1-3. Guelich thus observes that Matthew adds τῷ πνεύματι "in spirit" to the πτωχοὶ "poor" in the first beatitude to align the "poor beatitude" with the "poor" (*'ănāwîm*) of Isa 61:1. Then Matthew reverses the order of the second and third beatitudes because the (present) second beatitude is closer to the order

204 Guelich, *The Sermon on the Mount: A Foundation for Understanding*, 71-72. Cf., Hagner, *Matthew 1-13*, 90, who maintains that it is too restrictive to ascribe only the three beatitudes as going back to Jesus and it presumes that we know more than we can know.

205 Ulrich Luz, following Paul Hoffmann, identifies the historical site of the Q source at the end of the mission to Israel when the Q community turns away from Israel because of its failure in its mission to Israel. He maintains that the "tridents of Q and Matthew's communities are in historical continuity" and therefore "Matthew and Q are probably temporally close." This is supported by, or "corresponds to the fact that Matthew's version Q-Matt. is relatively close to the basic material of the source and is Jewish Christian in character, as are both Q itself and Matthew's Gospel." Luz, *Studies in Matthew*, 52-53.

206 It is quite uncertain whether the last beatitude was composed by Jesus and was collected and added by the Q community among the three dominical beatitudes, or it was composed by the Q community on the basis of Jesus' teaching and added to the three dominical beatitudes. It is believed in this study, however, that it was spoken by Jesus and was in circulation separately from the other three beatitudes. It was then collected and added to the other three beatitudes by the editor for the Q community. An explanation to this view will be given in the exegetical comment below.

207 It is presumed in this study that the five beatitudes, which are ascribed to have their *Sitz im Leben* in the Q community and the Matthean community, were formulated on the basis of Jesus' authentic teachings found in other places of the (synoptic) gospels. This will be substantiated in the exegetical comments below.

208 Lichtenberger, "Makarisms in Mathew 5:3ff. in their Jewish Context," 41.

209 For the idea of the possibility that Matthew omitted the woes, see Nolland, *The Gospel of Matthew*, 280. See also Schweizer, *The Good News According to Matthew*, 85.

and vocabulary of Isa 61:2.[210] He expands the fourth beatitude by adding καὶ διψῶντες τὴν δικαιοσύνην "and thirsty for righteousness," and added the eighth beatitude focusing on "righteousness" to correspond to Isa 61:3 (10-11).[211]

While Matthew's redaction seems obvious in the places suggested by Guelich, his suggestion of the reversal of the second and the third beatitude by Matthew is not apparent.[212] Also his suggestion that Matthew attempted to link the Beatitudes with Isa 61:1-3, is questioned by Davies and Allison, Jr. who maintain that Matthew has done nothing to underline the parallel between Matt 5 and Isa 61. They hold that Matt 5:3, 4, and 5, where the most obvious allusions in the Matthean Beatitudes to Isa 61 are found, go back to Jesus, and Matt 5:10 where the redactional contributions of Matthew are most evident apparently do not have any links with Isa 61.[213] Therefore, while there is in fact exegetically significant association between the Matthean Beatitudes and Isa 61, the connection between the two goes back to Jesus, and not to Matthew.[214]

Alexander Di Lella gives an interesting support from a different angle for the reversal of the second and third beatitude. He suggests a numerical arrangement of the Beatitudes, and he finds that by reversing the second and third beatitudes, a chiastic pattern is deduced. That is that the first two beatitudes together have 20 words and the last two (seventh and eighth) beatitudes together have 20 words; the third and fourth together have 16 words and corresponding to this the fifth and sixth together have 16 words.[215] Although Di Lella's proposal

210 Guelich is not the first one to propose such an order. He is reiterating the proposals of others scholars before him, for example, Austin Farrer, *St. Matthew and St. Mark*, 162-163.

211 Guelich, "The Matthean Beatitudes," 426-432.

212 See for example, Dupont maintains that the alternative reading is influenced by Luke, and since Luke moved things around to associate hunger with poverty, the present Matthean order is original. Dupont, *Les Béatitudes*, Vol. 3, 271-272, as quoted in Davies and Allison, Jr., *Matthew*, Vol. I, 436.

213 Davies and Allison, Jr., *Matthew*, Vol. I, 434, 438. See also the works cited by Davies and Allison here.

214 *Ibid.*, 438.

215 Di Lella, "The Structure and Composition of the Matthean Beatitudes," 241-242. Di Lella here further argues that if the second and third beatitudes are reversed, then the order of the nouns in the first two beatitudes namely τῶν οὐρανῶν and τὴν γῆν would follow the order found at the beginning and end of the first creation account in Gen 1:1 and 2:4a. He further says that the connection between the Beatitudes and the creation account is also seen in the author's presentation of eight beatitudes, instead of seven which is one of the most sacred numbers of the Bible. This number eight, according to him, corresponds to the eight works of creation in Genesis 1. The implication of this numerical correlation between the Beatitudes and the eight works of creation, according to Di Lella, is that there are eight conditions met by members of the new order of creation, which is the kingdom of heaven inaugurated by Jesus. Di Lella's proposal of the symmetrical arrangement of the Beatitudes, especially of the reverse order of the second and third beatitudes, is also supported by F. Manns. See Manns, "Blessed are the Meek for They shall inherit the Earth," 40. There is, however, a major problem with Di Lella's proposal for the co-relation between the beatitudes and Genesis 1, that is that according

of numerical symmetry, especially in relation to the reversal of the second and third beatitude, is quite possible, it does not seem to have any significance to the theology or context of the author, except for aesthetic purpose.[216] Again, Di Lella rightly mentions that if the present order of the second and the third beatitudes is reversed, the noun τῶν οὐρανῶν in the first beatitude will be followed by τὴν γῆν in the second beatitude.[217] However, this is exactly the intended reason for the alternative reading pointed out by the textual committee of the UBS Greek text. The editorial committee of the present UBS Greek text of the New Testament are of the opinion that the reversal of (the present) verses 4 and 5 is the result of an intention to put πραεῖς, "the meek" (v. 5a), immediately after οἱ πτωχοὶ τῷ πνεύματι "the poor in spirit" (v. 3a), and thereby to juxtapose the reference to τῶν οὐρανῶν, "heaven" (v. 3b), and τὴν γῆν, "earth" (v. 5b).[218]

Based on these observations, it is unlikely therefore, that Matthew reversed the original order of the second and third beatitudes, but took them over as he found in his tradition.

According to Donald Hagner, Matthew derived the Beatitudes as they appear in the Gospel from oral tradition and the essential structure of the Beatitudes might go back to Jesus himself. It is also possible that the evangelist drew the ninth beatitude from different tradition and added it to the eight shaping it in his own way. Or, more probably Jesus spoke the beatitudes originally using the second person plural form as Luke has it, and it was altered by the first evangelist, or someone before him, to the third person plural so as to objectify these teachings and thus make clear their universal significance.[219]

This view does not give enough credit to insights from redaction criticism which is given due importance in the present research work.

It is difficult to ascertain the exact extent of Matthean redaction in the passage under study. However, on the basis of a comparison of the Matthean Beatitudes with the parallel Beatitudes in Luke (6:20-23), as well as because of the fact that Luke is usually regarded as preserving the original form of the Q tradition where the two have parallel Q passages, Matthew's redaction seems quite apparent in certain places such as:

(1) The addition of τῷ πνεύματι "in spirit" to the πτωχοὶ "poor" of the first beatitude (v. 3, cf. Luke 6:20b), seems to be a Matthean addition. Although the in-

to him the eight beatitudes relates to the eight works of creation in Gen 1. However, according to this study, there are nine beatitudes, and not eight.

216 Besides, if the alternative reading as proposed by Di Lella is the original one, then the question is, who was responsible for the reversal of the second and the third beatitudes in the present order, and why? Neither Di Lella nor Manns give the possible reason(s) for the arrangement of the second and third beatitudes in their present order.

217 Di Lella, "The Structure and Composition of the Matthean Beatitudes," 242.

218 Bruce M. Metzger, *A Textual Commentary on the Greek New Testament* (New York: United Bible Societies, 1994 [1971]), 10. See also Hagner, *Matthew 1-13*, 88.

219 Hagner, *Matthew 1-13*, 90.

depth meaning of both πτωχοὶ and πτωχοὶ τῷ πνεύματι are more or less the same (see the exegetical comment below), only the πτωχοὶ could be misunderstood as appreciative of poverty itself. Therefore, it seems that the first evangelist added τῷ πνεύματι as a corrective to such possible misunderstanding.[220] It is highly possible that Matthew sees that the meaning conveyed with this addition is obvious in Isa 61:1, which is the most apparent Old Testament basis of this beatitude.[221] At the same time, it is obvious that his community, which comprised both rich and poor, influenced him to give such a corrective addition to avoid the possible misunderstanding of the term πτωχοὶ by his community members.[222]

(2) The use of βασιλεία τῶν οὐρανῶν "kingdom of heaven" in vv. 3 and 10 is obviously Matthew's replacement of βασιλεία του Θεοῦ "kingdom of God" found in Luke 6:20. This is clearly indicated by Matthew's use of "kingdom of heaven" in most of the places throughout his gospel in place of "kingdom of God" found in the parallel passages in Mark and Luke. The orthodox Jews considered too sacred to speak the name "God" and they usually used the term "Heaven" to refer to God. Therefore, most probably Matthew uses the term "kingdom of heaven" instead of "kingdom of God" because it was a more familiar term to his community, which was a Jewish/Jewish-oriented community.[223]

(3) The addition of διψῶντες τὴν δικαιοσύνην "thirsty for righteousness" in v. 6 (cf. Luke 21) also seems to be the result of Matthew's redaction. The addition of the phrase "and thirsty" is probably influenced by the Old Testament frequent parallelism of the two words "hungry" and "thirsty" (e.g., 107:5-9; Isa 49:19; 65:13).[224] And, the addition of "for righteousness"' is also obviously a Matthean redaction because the Lukan parallel does not have it, and at the same time "righteousness" is one of Matthew's favourite terms. It appears seven times in Matthew (3:15; 5: 6, 10, 20; 6:1, 33; 21:32), all from the lips of Jesus, while it occurs only once in Luke (1:75) and not a single time in Mark.[225]

(4) Matthew also uses the terms of persecution such as διώξωσιν "they persecute (you)" and εἴπωσιν πᾶν πονηρὸν καθ' ὑμῶν "they utter all kinds of evil against you" in v. 11, in place of the terms used by Luke in the parallel passage (Luke 6:22) such as ἀφορίσωσιν ὑμᾶς "they exclude you" and ἐκβάλωσιν

220 Schweizer, *The Good News According to Matthew*, 88.

221 Guelich, *The Sermon on the Mount: A Foundation for Understanding*, 74-75.

222 W. D. Davies and Dale C. Allison, Jr., have four reasons for the possible redaction of this passage. Such as: (1) Another Q passage, Matt 11:5 par. Luke 7:22 has "poor" without qualification; (2) "the qualification disrupts what would otherwise be perfect parallelism in Q: μακάριοι οἱ πτωχοι, μακάριοι οἱ πεινῶντες, μακάριοι οἱ κλαίοντες; (3) The first woe in Luke 6:24 "has 'the rich' without qualification, which probably implies an unqualified 'the poor' in at least Q^{lk}"; (4) Matthew has a habit of adding qualifying phrases (as in 5:6a, 32; 6:13b; 13:12b; and 19:9). See, Davies and Allison, Jr., *Matthew*, Vol. I, 442.

223 See Dillon, "The Text of the Sermon on the Mount," 58.

224 Cf. Harrington, *The Gospel of Matthew*, 79.

225 See also Schweizer, *The Good News According to Matthew*, 91.

τὸ ὄνομα ὑμῶν "they cast out your name." These usages seem to be part of Matthean redaction under the influence of his community's concrete experience of persecution. Out of the other two forms of persecution found in Luke 6:22 such as ὀνειδίσωσιν ὑμᾶς "they revile you," and μισήσωσιν ὑμᾶς "they hate you," Matthew (in 5:11) retains the first one and omits the second one. Probably Matthew omits μισήσωσιν ὑμᾶς "they hate you," because he already has three forms of persecutions which corresponds to the triadic formula with which he arranges the Sermon on the Mount,[226] and probably also because he opines that the vacancy created by his omission of μισήσωσιν ὑμᾶς "they hate you" is already implied in the other terms of persecution which he uses.

In the same verse, Matthew also omits the subject οἱ ἄνθρωποι found in the Lukan parallel, and he has ἕνεκεν ἐμου "on account of me" in place of the Lukan parallel ἕνεκα τοῦ υἱοῦ τοῦ ἀνθρώπου "on account of the Son of Man." It seems that Matthew deliberately omits the subject οἱ ἄνθρωποι of Q/Luke to leave unspecified "they" to refer to the leaders of formative Judaism/Jewish leaders.[227] It also seems that Matthew replaced Luke's ἕνεκα τοῦ υἱοῦ τοῦ ἀνθρώπου with ἕνεκεν ἐμου in order to make for conformity with 10:18, 39; and 16:25 (cf., in place of the "Son of Man" in Mark 8:31 [par. Luke 9:22] Matthew uses a simple pronoun "he" for Jesus in Matt 16:21).[228]

There are also some differences between Matt 5:12 and the parallel beatitude in Luke 6:23. However, there is no certain evidence of Matthew's redaction in these cases.[229]

(5) The eighth beatitude also, as suggested by Davies and Allison, Jr. seems to be a redactional addition of the first evangelist, to make a triadic structure for the Beatitudes in line with his triadic arrangement of materials largely in the Sermon on the Mount.[230] At the same time, the author's choice of the terms, such as "righteousness" and "kingdom of heaven" in this beatitude again corresponds to the obvious reasons behind his choice of the same terms in his redactions of other beatitudes (5:3, 6) as mentioned above.[231] It is also quite possible that Matthew, after the introduction of the new beatitudes (5:7-9) alien to the original beatitudes, deliberately added the eighth beatitude to preserve the theme of the

---

226 Davies and Allison, Jr., *Matthew*, Vol. I, 461. Cf. Guelich, *The Sermon on the Mount: A Foundation for Understanding*, 94, who maintains that Matthew's omission of μισέω and his use of διώκω may have happened in the pre-Matthean tradition because διώκω is pre-Matthean in 10:23 (M) and 23:34, par Luke 11:49 (Q).

227 Davies and Allison, Jr., *Matthew*, Vol. I, 462.

228 *Ibid.*, 462. See also Luz, *Matthew 1-7*, 229, 242.

229 For further discussion see "Exegetical Comments" below.

230 See "Other Important Literary Characteristics of Matthew's gospel" and "the Structure of the Matthean Beatitudes" above.

231 More will be said on this in the exegetical comment below.

"Q" source-text, which is a consolation to the despised disciples.[232] His selection of the term "persecution" also reflects the actual experience of his community.

(6) It is uncertain whether Matthew's redaction plays any role in the use of the third person plural in the first eight beatitudes and the second person plural in the ninth and the last beatitude while Luke has second person plural in all his beatitudes.[233] However, it is highly probable that Matthew just reproduced what he got in his tradition. David Daube clearly highlights that the conclusion of a series of equal length with third person form, with a lengthened second person form was a practice in the Old Testament and Judaism (e.g., Isa 63:7ff.; Sir 47:12ff.; 48:1ff.). Therefore, the Matthean form of the Beatitudes, that is a series of third person concluded with second person, seems to be the form from the outset of their collection in Q.[234] It will follow from this view, that based on the practice of ancient literature, the original collector of the Beatitudes for the Q community arranged the first three (dominical) beatitudes in third person, and he connected the fourth (Matt 5:11-12) one in second person. Then, following the same pattern all the other four beatitudes (Matt 5:5, 7-9) added in Q were also composed in third person form. Matthew took over this and when he composed and inserted another beatitude (Matt 5:10) he composed it in third person, so that the original form of arrangement was not disturbed even when the Beatitudes took their final form. This also indicates, on the other hand, that Luke is responsible for the second person form of the first three beatitudes. In support of this view, Daube rightly proposes that based on the principle of *lectio difficilior*,

232 Dillon, "The Text of the Sermon on the Mount," 48-49.

233 This uncertainty is indicated by the fact that scholars have Different views on this. Some of them may be mentioned, as examples - Schnackenburg asserts that the original form is not actually known. Schnackenburg, *The Gospel of Matthew*, 47. Ulrich Luz also notes the difficulty of this question. At the same time he maintains that the third person belongs to the genre of macarism, that probably Jesus addressed the suffering ones in the second person, and later they have been adapted to the third person which is the usual form for macarism, but that took place presumably before Matthew. Luz, *Matthew 1-7*, 227. According to Lichtenberger, the Matthean arrangement of the beatitudes, 8+1, in contrast to Luke's, 3+1, "has to be regarded as an enlargement attributable to scribal exegesis;" so also is the use of the third person because it was used both in the OT and in rabbinic literature. Lichtenberger, "Makarisms in Mathew 5:3ff. in their Jewish Context," 41. John Nolland, however, observes that the lack of a corresponding second person indication in the first half of the beatitude makes the Lukan construction of the beatitudes awkward, and this suggests that Luke's could possibly be secondary. Nolland, *Luke 1-9:20*, 280. Schweizer, on the other hand, assumes that as the second person is found in the Jewish literature contemporary to Jesus (*Eth. En* 58:2), as well as elsewhere in place of Matthew (13:16; 16:17), the second person was the form Jesus used. Schweizer, *The Good News According to Matthew*, 80.

234 David Daube, "The Last Beatitude," in *New Testament Judaism. Collected Works of David Daube*, Vol. 2, edited by Calum Carmichael. Studies in Comparative Legal History (Berkeley: The Robbins Collection, 2000), 321-324. Daube also here asserts that there are many instances in the NT, which indicate that the pattern Matthew uses was also used in the period of the NT, for example, Luke 1: 68ff.

"Matthew's transition from the minor key of the third person to the major of the direct address looks more original than Luke's smoother version."[235] Therefore, Matthew was not responsible for the switch over from third person to second person in the last beatitude. However, it would be correct to assume that he took over this as he found the arrangement pleasant and effective for addressing his community, in that it shows the first eight beatitudes as universally significant and the last beatitude as an application of those universally significant beatitudes to the immediate audience.

(7) Other major differences of the Matthean Beatitudes from the Beatitudes in Luke, such as four ethical beatitudes (Matt 5:5, 7-9) which are found in Matthew but not in Luke, and Matthew's lack of the corresponding woes found in Luke, could be attributed to the difference of traditions behind the two gospels.[236]

Thus, it is maintained in the above discussion that the Matthean redaction within the Beatitudes is obvious in the first beatitude where he adds "τῷ πνεύματι" "in spirit" to the πτωχοὶ "poor" in the first beatitude; in his use of βασιλεία τῶν οὐρανῶν "kingdom of heaven" in the first and eighth beatitudes instead of βασιλεία του Θεοῦ "kingdom of God" as found in Luke 6:20; in the addition of καὶ διψῶντες τὴν δικαιοσύνην "and thirsty for righteousness" in the fourth beatitude; in his use of the word διώξωσιν "they persecute (you)" and εἴπωσιν πᾶν πονηρὸν καθ' ὑμῶν "they utter all kinds of evil against you" in the ninth beatitude instead of ἀφορίσωσιν ὑμᾶς "they exclude you" and ἐκβάλωσιν τὸ ὄνομα ὑμῶν "they cast out your name" which are found in the parallel passage in Luke (6:22); and in his addition of the eighth beatitude.[237]

It is believed in this study that all the Matthean redactions of the beatitudes have been influenced by his socio-historical context, and at the same time, those beatitudes, which he took over from his tradition without redaction have correspondence with his socio-historical context. In other words, he took them over without redaction because they were suitable for addressing his community without further redaction. An exegesis that follows will clarify this assumption. We will now look at the literary context in which Matthew presents his Beatitudes.

---

235 Daube, "The Last Beatitude," 324.

236 See "the Form, Source and *Sitz im Leben* of the Matthean Beatitudes" above. Cf. Lichtenberger, "Makarisms in Mathew 5:3ff. in their Jewish Context," 41; who maintains that "the woes in Luke could be of Lucan origin."

237 Cf. Luz maintains that "linguistically only the addition of τὴν δικαιοσύνην (v.6), all of v. 10, and βασιλεία τῶν οὐρανῶν can be demonstrated as redactional. Such, a demonstration is not possible for the addition of τῶ πνεύματι in v. 3, which often is considered redactional. Thus, more speaks in favor of assigning the remaining additions and changes to a text recension prior to the redaction." Luz, *Matthew 1-7*, 226-227.

2.8. The Literary Context of the Matthean Beatitudes

Much has been said in the preceding section about the wider context of the selected passage in terms of the significance of the Beatitudes within Matthew's gospel. Our concern here will be a brief highlight of the literary context, that is, the literary device with which Jesus is introduced by the author of the first gospel before Jesus started his ministry and teaching. This is important because Matthew's introduction of Jesus before the commencement of his ministry has a significant bearing upon the Matthean community, which, according to the first evangelist, was composed of the Jewish Christians and the Jewish-oriented Gentile Christians, or we may say in brief as a "Jewish-oriented church."[238]

Matthew properly introduces Jesus before Jesus started his ministry and teaching, by means of his genealogy, the story of his birth and infancy, his baptism and temptation. Matthew does not simply tell about all these accounts as a simple story, but he arranges all of them meticulously with explanations to show clearly that Jesus is the Messiah. Therefore, when Jesus begins his ministry and his teaching in Matthew's gospel his identity has already been revealed clearly through these accounts.

First, Matthew begins the gospel with the genealogy and infancy narrative as a preparation for the first main narrative.[239] At the very beginning, Matthew replaces Mark's statement, "the beginning of the good news of Jesus Christ, the Son of God," with "an account of the genealogy of Jesus the Messiah, the son of David, the son of Abraham." Here Matthew reflects Old Testament phraseology (Gen 2:4; 5:1 LXX). This reflection of the Old Testament phraseology and the description of Jesus as the son of David son of Abraham make the genealogy portray Jesus as the goal and fulfilment of the Old Testament.[240] Matthew's substitution of Mark's

---

238 As we already indicated elsewhere in this thesis, the Jesus movement or the Jesus community as envisaged by Matthew was mainly a movement/community of the Jews who believed in Jesus as the Messiah. They still followed the Jewish way of life and their main difference from the other Jews was their interpretation of Jesus as the Messiah. Of course, there were also some Gentile members among them. Such a mixed community was suggested by both the Jewish and Gentile interest found in Matthew. According to the analysis of some scholars, some of those Gentile members were proselytized to Judaism. They underwent circumcision and they followed all the Jewish way of life. Some other Gentile members followed the Jewish way of life without undergoing circumcision. This subject matter is discussed in different places of this thesis, such as in – the "Intended Audience of Matthew's Gospel," "Important Factors for Determining the Geographical Location of Matthew's Gospel," "the Social Setting of Matthew's Gospel" (especially in - *The Ethnic Composition of Matthew's Community*, and *The Socio-economic Status of the Matthean Community*,) and "Matthew's Community: A Deviant Jewish Community," in the first chapter. For a detailed discussion on this, see "Intended Audience of Matthew's Gospel," and "*The Ethnic Composition of Matthew's Community*."

239 Hagner, *Matthew 1-13*, 2.

240 Robert H. Gundry, *Matthew: A Commentary on His Handbook for a Mixed Church Under Persecution* (Grand Rapids, Michigan: William B. Eerdmans Publishing Company, 1982), 13.

"Son of God" with "Son of David, Son of Abraham" seems to have dual function. First, "Son of David" would represent Jesus as the king of Israel, the rightful heir to the Davidic promises, and second, "son of Abraham" would imply that the blessing of all the nations of the earth, which was promised to the patriarch (Gen 12:1-3; 18:18; 22:15-18; cf. Matt 18:18-20), has been fulfilled in Jesus, the seed of Abraham.[241] Then Matthew presents the genealogy (1:2-17) in a different way from its counterpart in Luke (3:23-38). In Luke the genealogy goes back from Jesus to Adam and finally to God. But, in Matthew it goes in a reverse order to conform to I Chronicles 1-3, which makes the genealogy build up to climax in Jesus. Furthermore, in contrast with Luke and I Chronicles 1-3, Matthew omits all names prior to Abraham, thus leading to the identification of Jesus as "the King of the Jews."[242] And while Luke has 56 generations between Jesus and Abraham (including both Jesus and Abraham) Matthew has 41 generations (including Jesus and Abraham). Moreover, Matthew also has different names from those of Luke especially in the genealogies of monarchical and post-monarchical periods.[243] The most plausible reason for this difference is the theological purposes of the two evangelists, for Matthew to show that Jesus is the Davidic Messiah, and for Luke to show that Jesus is the son of God.[244] The genealogy is arranged into three groups of fourteen,[245] and it is held together by an *inclusio* (v. 1- Christ ... David ... Abraham; v. 17 – Abraham ... David ... Christ). Although, it is difficult to give an exact explanation to the grouping of the genealogy into fourteen, it probably is derived by the author from the consonantal value of David's name in Hebrew, that is *gematria,* דוד = 4+6+4= 14.[246] It is therefore highly possible that Matthew, a Jewish author, who wrote primarily for a Jewish/Jewish oriented Christian audience, wanted to indicate to his intended readers that Jesus, about whom he is writing, has special significance in the history of Israel.[247] Particularly, Matthew shows with this genealogy that the history of Israel, which has now

---

241 Davies and Allison, Jr., *Matthew*, Vol. I, 159-160. See also Gundry, *Matthew: A Commentary on His Literary and Theological Art*, 13.

242 Gundry, *Matthew: A Commentary on His Literary and Theological Art*, 15.

243 See the tables of comparison between the genealogies in Matthew and Luke, in Brown, *The Birth of Jesus the Messiah*, 76-81.

244 Brown, *The Birth of Jesus the Messiah*, 85, 94.

245 It is mentioned in Matt 1:17, "so all the generations from Abraham to David are fourteen generations; and from David to the deportation to Babylon, fourteen generations; and from the deportation to Babylon to the Messiah, fourteen generations." It seems that the author here count the name of Jechoniah twice, as the last of the second group and the first of the last group. If the name of Jechonaiah is counted only in the second group, then the last group has only thirteen generations.

246 Brown, *The Birth of the Messiah*, 80. See also Davies and Allison, Jr., *Matthew*, Vol. I, 87. For other suggested explanations, see Hagner, *Matthew 1-13*, 6-7.

247 This is also suggested by Matthew's presentation of the genealogy in a different way from that of Luke (as just mentioned above).

fulfilled three fourteen generations, is reaching its goal that is the coming of the Messiah in the person of Jesus.[248] The *inclusio* found at v. 1 and v. 17 also seems to indicate this. To say in other words, the genealogy acts as "an artistically devised theological statement" providing "the vehicle for the initial presentation of Jesus as the fulfilment of the promises to Abraham and David."[249]

Then, after introducing the genealogy of Jesus in such a careful and meaningful way, Matthew gives an account of how the birth of Jesus took place. In the first part (1:18-25) the emphasis is laid on the fact that the birth of Jesus took place in fulfilment of the Old Testament promise (especially 1:22-23).[250] The second part of the infancy narrative (2:1-12) also emphasizes on the fulfilment of the Old Testament promise, particularly the fact that the Messiah should be born in Bethlehem (2:5-6). In the third part of the infancy narrative (2:13-23) Matthew still emphasizes on the fulfilment of Old Testament prophecy (2:15, 17-18, 23). Along with that, and may be more to Matthew's emphasis, there is a parallelism between (the story of) Moses and (the story of) Jesus, that is so to say, "Moses-Christ typology." In the story, Herod tried to kill Jesus (2:13). Jesus was saved by fleeing to Egypt (2:14-15). Herod killed all the male infants (2:16), but Jesus was saved. After the death of Herod, Jesus came back from Egypt to the land of Israel (2:19-21). In the Exodus story Pharaoh killed all male Hebrew infants, but the infant Moses was delivered (Exod 1:22). However, Moses fled later from Egypt because Pharaoh threatened his life (Exod 2:15). When Pharaoh died he was directed to return to Egypt (Exod 4:19-20). All this parallelism shows that Matthew, when narrating the story of Jesus in this passage, obviously has the story of Moses in mind: "Herod is the antitype of Pharaoh; Jesus is the antitype of Moses."[251] This can be seen as the first instance where Matthew's intention to present Jesus as the new Moses is indicated.[252] At the same time, the flight of Jesus (and his family) to Egypt and their return to the land of Israel after the death of Herod also parallels the sojourn of the Israelites in Egypt during the time of Joseph and their exodus from Egypt in the time of Moses, as affirmed by the citation of Hosea 11:1 in Matt 2:15. This typology implies for Matthew that "all Israel's history finds its recapitulation in the life of Jesus."[253]

---

248 Hagner, *Matthew 1-13*, 7.

249 *Ibid.*, 12. For a more detailed discussion on Matthew's purpose with the genealogy, see Brown, *The Birth of the Messiah*, 66-95.

250 Hagner, *Matthew 1-13*, 16.

251 *Ibid.*, 34.

252 Talbert here notes that the parallelism between Jesus and Moses go beyond Matthew 5-7, especially in the miracles of Jesus. Talbert, *Reading the Sermon on the Mount*, 14-15. For a detailed study of Moses-Christ typology, see Allison, Jr., *The New Moses.*

253 Hagner, *Matthew 1-13*, 34. Brown observes that five formula quotations of the Matthean infancy narrative were added by Matthew in the pre-Matthean birth narratives to underline certain themes, such as: (1) The addition of Isa 7:14 underlines the themes of the "who" (*Quis*) and the "how" (*Quomodo*) which are dominant in the two sections of chap. 1, the genealogy

After clearly highlighting the identity of Jesus through the genealogy and birth narratives - that he is the Messiah, who was born according to, and in the fulfilment of, the Old Testament promise, and that he is the new Moses, - Matthew narrates the baptism of Jesus as a preparation for his (Jesus') ministry (3:1-4:11). It is obvious that Matthew took this from Mark (1:2-11 par. Luke 3:1-22). However, unlike Mark and Luke, Matthew presents Jesus' baptism as the fulfilment of righteousness. John, in fulfilment of the Old Testament prophecy, appears in the wilderness of Judea, preparing the way for the ministry of Jesus/ the Lord (3:1-6). John gives baptism with water as a mark of repentance, and a multitude come to him. However, he is only the forerunner of Jesus who is coming after him, to give baptism with Holy Spirit and fire (3:11).[254] Thus, the magnitude of Jesus' ministry is highlighted before it really begins. Then Jesus receives baptism at the hands of John (3:13-17). John knows that Jesus does not need to take baptism from him, but Jesus insists that he should take it in order that he (and John) would fulfil all righteousness (3:15). So, the baptism of Jesus here is clearly depicted in such a way that it is a preparation for, or the beginning

---

and the annunciation, respectively; 2) The addition of Micah 5:1 (2) underlines the theme of the "where" (*Ubi*) which is dominant in the first half of chap 2; (3) The addition of Hos 11:1 and Jer 31:15; as well as that of "He will be called a Nazorean" turn the readers attention to the "whence" of Jesus' destiny, evoking three stages in the salvation history, namely the exodus (analogy between Jesus and Moses Hosea 11:1), the exile (parallelism between the history of Jesus and the history of Israel Jer 31:15), and the ministry of Jesus ("He will be called a Nazorean). See Brown, *The Birth of the Messiah*, 118 (96-119 for a detailed discussion).

254 Baptism comes from the Greek verb βαπτιζείν which means "dip frequently or intensively, plunge, immerse." It is formed from βαπτειν which means "dip." The verb appears four times in the LXX (2Kings 4:14 – Naaman in the Jordan; Judith 12:7 – purification; Sir 34:30 [Eng 34:25] – purification after touching a corpse; Isa 21:4-figuratively of lawlessness). The noun βαπτισμα is used only in Christian literature where it refers to the baptism of John or Christian baptism. Even if the word βαπτιζείν is not necessarily used, Baptism is always associated with water except when it is used metaphorically. However, the term implies not only the external act of baptism, but also denotes the inner meaning and force of the act, and therefore it may be appropriately employed for both spirit baptism and water baptism. The practice of baptism is not a distinctive Christian rite, but is widespread, especially in early times and its functions include initiation, removal of guilt, cleansing, and the granting of a new start. However, the context of John's baptism and Christian baptism is informed by the OT, Judaism and practices of the Qumran community, where it is frequently connected with the symbolism of purification – from sin, from destruction, from profane sphere before entering a holy area, from something under a taboo, etc. For example, Lev 16:4, 24 (the high priest before and after the rites of atonement); Lev 15:19-27 (on menstruating woman); 1QS 3:4-9; 6:14-23 (cleansing from sin); Sib.Or 4:165 (a baptism of repentance). John's baptism also seems more probably a purificatory, rather than initiation. See the following – Lars Hartman, "Baptism," *ABD*, Vol. 1 (New York: Doubleday, 1992), 583; and D. S. Dockery, "Baptism," *DJG*, edited by Joel B. Green, Scot McKnight, I. Howard Marshall (Downers Grove, Illinois/Leicester, England: Inter Varsity Press, 1998 [1992]), 55-56; and, Jacob Neusner and William Scott Green, (eds.), *Dictionary of Judaism in the Biblical Period 450 B.C.E to 600 C.E.* (Peabody, Massachusetsts: Hendrickson Publishers, 1999), 76.

of, his ministry, but not for repentance. This is affirmed by the Holy Spirit descending upon Jesus (3:16) and a voice from heaven declaring that he is the beloved Son of God (3:17).[255] It is difficult to understand the exact meaning of the statement, "fulfilment of all righteousness through baptism" here. However, it is quite possible that it means the fulfilment of God's will, in the sense of God's saving activity. Then, the implication would be that through the baptism and the accompanying anointing by the Spirit "John and Jesus together ('for us') inaugurate the fulfilment of God's saving purposes."[256] In other words, John, through his obedience to give baptism to Jesus, will accomplish the transition to the Promised One, and he will bring his preparatory mission to its climax. On the other hand, Jesus, through his reception of baptism in obedience to the will of the Father, "proves to be the occasion of the formal beginning of his ministry."[257] Therefore, through the story of Jesus' baptism Matthew scores another crucial point that Jesus is the Son of God, who begins his ministry through divine inauguration and Holy Spirit anointing.[258] Correctly pointing out Matthew's strong emphasis of "righteousness" in the Sermon on the Mount (5:6, 10, 20; 6:1, 33), Talbert rightly observes that "given the linguistic and thematic links between preceding narratives and subsequent discourses in Matthew," the depiction of the Matthean Jesus as fulfilling all "righteousness" before he teaches his disciples about righteousness cannot be a coincidence.[259] He further points out, giving various examples from Greco-Roman paganism, ancient Judaism, and early Christian writings outside the New Testament, that there was a strong emphasis in Mediterranean antiquity on the ideal of unity of life and teaching. Therefore, Talbert maintains, "When Matthew's auditors heard that Jesus fulfilled all righteousness before he spoke to his disciples about seeking a righteousness that surpassed other models, they would have inferred the legitimacy of Jesus' teachings and would have accorded the authority due a true teacher."[260]

With such preparations Jesus is about to start his ministry. However, before he takes a practical step, his faithfulness to his sonship of God is tested (4:1-11), and he overcomes all the temptations. The temptation account of Jesus is closely parallel to the experience of the Israelites, the sons of Yahweh, in the wilderness

255 Hagner, *Matthew 1-13*, 59.

256 *Ibid.*, 56.

257 *Ibid.*

258 *Ibid.*

259 Talbert, *Reading the Sermon on the Mount*, 18. Davies and Allison, Jr. also note the significance of this passage in this way - "In his own deeds Jesus 'fulfilled all righteousness.' This means: what believers are called to perform, Jesus has fulfilled. Thus, there is implicit in the First Gospel an *imitatio Christi*. In seeking to fulfil the gospel's demand for righteousness, the believer has an example in his Lord." Davies and Allison, Jr., *Matthew*, Vol. I, 345.

260 Talbert, *Reading the Sermon on the Mount*, 18-20. As to the meaning of "righteousness"' here, Gundry seems right in saying that it "implies a quantitative concept of righteousness that fits 5:20." Gundry, *Matthew: A Commentary on His Literary and Theological Art*, 50.

after they were delivered from Egypt (Exod chs. 14-16). In fact, it seems that Matthew has two sources, Mark and Q for the temptation narrative. While Mark goes as far as to note the presence of wild animals (1:13b) so as to compare between Jesus and Adam, Matthew omits the reference to the wild animals thus presenting the experience of Jesus with that of the Israelites in the wilderness, but with a major difference, that whereas Israel failed the test, Jesus succeeds.[261] This is another important indicator of what has been indicated once in the infancy narrative (2:15), that Jesus is an embodiment of Israel and the fulfiller of all her hopes.[262]

Now, Matthew's introduction of Jesus before the starting of his ministry is complete. Unmistakably for the readers, particularly the Matthean community, which was composed of Jewish Christians and Jewish-oriented Gentile Christians, Jesus, is the Messiah, who was born according to and in the fulfilment of the Old Testament promise. He is the new Moses, the Son of God who begins his ministry through divine inauguration and the Holy Spirit's anointing, who overcomes all the temptations of Satan, and who is an embodiment of Israel and the fulfiller of all her hopes.[263]

Then, Jesus begins his ministry (4:12-25). Again, Matthew introduces the beginning of Jesus' ministry with the affirmation that Jesus chooses his dwelling place according to the Old Testament prophecy (4:12-16; cf., Isa 9:1-2), thus clearly indicating that Jesus is the Messiah, the promise of the Old Testament.[264] Jesus begins his public ministry from that time on with the proclamation, "Repent, for the kingdom of Heaven has come near (4:17)." Here, the main theme of the whole gospel, that is the "kingdom of heaven," is introduced at the very outset of Jesus' ministry. Then Matthew tells about the calling of the first four disciples (4:18-22), which probably takes place after Jesus begins to proclaim about the kingdom of heaven (as the preceding verse suggests) but before he starts his actual ministry (as suggested by no reporting of such as yet). Only the calling of four disciples is reported here. The calling of another disciple, Matthew, is reported in 9:9, and there is no other report of the calling of disciples. Twelve disciples are introduced at 10:2 and the calling of seven of them is never reported. Therefore, the calling of the four here is understood to represent in a sense the calling of the others, and Matthew's point with this passage "is to account for Jesus' disciples prior to the teaching discourse of chaps. 5-7, which is primarily addressed to them

---

261 Gundry, *Matthew: A Commentary on His Literary and Theological Art*, 53.

262 Hagner, *Matthew 1-13*, 62.

263 Cf. Wayne S. Baxter, "The Narrative Setting of the Sermon on the Mount," *TriJourn* 25/1 (2004): 32; and Bruner, *Matthew 1-12*, 152.

264 It seems that Matthew redacted Mark (1:14, 21) based on his interest, and connected it with a quotation from Isaiah 9:1-2. For a detailed comment, see Davies and Allison, Jr., *Matthew*, Vol. I, 375-392.

(cf. 5:1)."[265] That is to say, Matthew places the calling of the four disciples here as a mark of his emphasis on the importance and nature of discipleship which he is going to accentuate in discourse material soon after in chaps 5-7, following a brief description of the ministry of Jesus in 4:23-25. Thus, the calling of the disciples here is a preparation for this important discourse.[266]

Then Matthew, preparing to set a stage for the first discourse, highlights the initial ministry of Jesus in a nutshell (4:23-25). Jesus was going through the whole of Galilee doing a ministry of preaching and healing (4:23). His fame, obviously because of his healing ministry in particular,[267] was spread even into the whole of the surrounding Syrian territory, and people with all kinds of sicknesses were brought to him, and he healed them (4:24). With such a wonderful ministry, Jesus has exerted a very great influence upon the people and large crowds from Galilee, Decapolis, Jerusalem, and Judea were following him (4:25). Now, the stage is set for a very important teaching on the nature of discipleship (chaps 5-7). It has been established beyond doubt that the one who is going to give this important teaching is the Messiah, whom God promises to His people in the Old Testament through the prophets, and he is a new leader like Moses for God's people. He is also an embodiment of Israel and the fulfiller of all her hopes. On top of that, he is the Son of God, anointed with the Holy Spirit by God, whose faithfulness to God has been tested and absolutely proved. Not only that, but he has already proved his divine sonship by his miraculous healing of all kinds of sickness.[268] With this entire introduction, Matthew's audience would have understood undoubtedly that Jesus, who teaches about the Beatitudes (as well as the Sermon of the Mount as a whole) to his disciples, is an authority figure, who is representing God.[269]

265 Hagner, *Matthew 1-13*, 76.

266 Hagner, *Matthew 1-13*, 78. Hagner here rightly points out that the calling of the disciples here also serves a historical purpose that it shows the way in which Jesus gathered disciples, and also a pastoral purpose, that it shows to his readers that "the calling of these disciples serves as a model of the nature of true discipleship generally," that is that "the call of God through Jesus is sovereign and absolute in its authority; the response of those who are called is to be both immediate and absolute, involving a complete break with old loyalties."

267 This is indicated by what follows in 4:24b – "and they brought to him all the sick, those who were afflicted with various diseases and pains, demoniacs, epileptics, and paralytics, and he cured them."

268 Talbert, taking Matthew 1:1-5:2 as the introduction to the Sermon on the Mount, notes the significance of this introduction as follows:

By reading Matthew 1:1–5:2 consecutively the auditors have a sense of who is speaking in the Sermon. He is son of Abraham, son of David (1:1-17), one conceived by the Spirit (1:18, 20), Saviour (1:21), Immanuel (1:23), King of the Jews (2:2), Messiah (2:4), fulfiller of all righteousness (3:15), God's beloved Son (3:17), God's victorious Son (4:1-11), a preacher of repentance (4:17), a gatherer of disciples (4:18-22, 23-25), a healer (4:23-24), and a teacher of disciples (5:1-2). See Talbert, *Reading the Sermon on the Mount*, 14.

269 Talbert, *Reading the Sermon on the Mount*, 20. Talbert here rightly points out that the conclusion of Matthew's Gospel also strongly affirms the identity of Jesus, which Matthew establishes

Then, Matthew sets Jesus on a mountain (5:1-2) to begin his first teaching. We will now have a closer look at the significance of this setting for Matthew.

2.9. The Literary Setting of the Matthean Beatitudes (5:1-2)

Matthew tells in 5:1-2 that Jesus went up the mountain as he saw the crowd before he started his teaching. He sat down there and his disciples came to him, and then he began to speak and taught them.

The literary setting of the Beatitudes in Matthew has three significant differences from the parallel passage in Luke (6:17-20) – (1) In Matthew, Jesus taught his disciples from the mountain, while in Luke he taught from a level place, (2) In Matthew, Jesus sits down while teaching, but in Luke he stood, (3) In Matthew, Jesus "opened his mouth"[270] and began to teach, but in Luke he looked up at (the great crowds) of his disciples.

It is highly probable that Matthew 5:1-2 is a redaction by the author, making use of Mark 3:13 and Q's introduction to the sermon on the plain.[271] It could be perceived that the main purpose of the author with this (obvious redactional) introduction is to make it meaningful to his Jewish-Christian audience. This can be explained in three ways:

(1) First of all, the setting of the Matthean Beatitudes (Sermon on the Mount) on a mountain seems to have special significance for Matthew, because the image of a mountain is prominent in Matthew's gospel. The prominence of "mountain" in Matthew's gospel is apparent when compared with other gospels. Mountain occurs 10 times in Matthew, while it occurs 5 times in Mark, and 4 times each in Luke and John. Moreover, Matthew also adds "mountain" to some of Markan materials (see Mark 1:40-45 par. Matt 8:1-4; Mark 7:31-37 par. Matt 15:29-31). These situations suggest that Matthew's interest in "mountain" is not purely a topographical matter.[272] The special importance of mountain in Matthew is self evident in the gospel itself. It is a place where special events occur, such as the temptation of Jesus on the mountain (4:8), the transfiguration on the mountain (17:1), and the mountain of the resurrection appearance and the great commission (28:16).[273] Mountain is also a place of prayer (14:23),

---

through his introduction of him in the beginning. It is clearly stated in 28:18-20 that he is the one to whom God has given all authority in earth and in heaven. The one who teaches his disciples with authority in the Sermon on the Mount is the same Jesus who gives his command with authority to his disciples at the end.

270 In Greek "he opened his mouth" is ἀνοίξας τὸ στόμα αὐτοῦ. Although, it is translated in different ways in different English versions, the Greek language seems to allow the present translation.

271 Davies and Allison, Jr., *Matthew*, Vol. I, 420-421.

272 Keener, *A Commentary on the Gospel of Matthew*, 164.

273 Harrington, *The Gospel of Matthew*, 78. Harrington here mentions that it is useless to try to determine the exact site.

of healings (15:29), of revelation (17:1; 28:16), and of teaching (24:3).[274] The Olivet discourse also took place in a somewhat similar setting to the present text: Jesus sits down on Mount Olives, his disciples come to him (but κατ ' ἰδιαν, "privately"), and Jesus teaches them (24:3). The importance Matthew gives to mountains, especially in narratives that have to do with revelation, suggests that ὄρος, "the mountain," in the present text (5:1-2) functions as a literary device. That is that, through this device Matthew tries to show the fulfilment of Judaism in Christianity. Obviously what Matthew kept in mind was Moses' going up Mount Sinai to receive the law (Exod 19–20; 34. see also Matt 23:2).[275] And by locating Jesus' teaching on the mountain (while Luke 6:17 has it on the plain) Matthew tries to indicate that the teaching of Jesus is a new revelation which supersedes and fulfils the Law given to Moses on Mount Sinai, thus, depicting Jesus as the "New Moses,"[276] but very much superior to (the Old) Moses. This view is supported by Jesus' statement in Matt 5:17 that he came to fulfil the law and the prophets; and his contrasting at the same time of Moses' teaching with his teaching in several places of the sermon on the mount (5:22, 28, 32, 34, 39, 44). Moses typology in the infancy narratives (chap 2) also supports the same view.[277] In addition, Matthew's emphasis on the importance of mountain in his gospel in general, and in the Beatitudes (the Sermon on the Mount) in particular, must have been influenced by the importance of mountain in the Old Testament. This is because the Old Testament accounts must have special significance to Matthew's intended audience, the Jewish-Christian community. The importance of mountain is depicted in various ways in the Old Testament. For example, numerous theophanies took place on a mountain (Gen 22:14; Exod 3:1; 4:27; 18:5; Deut 4:11; 5:4; 9:15; 1Kgs 19:11-14). Mountains are depicted, although not all in a positive manner, as a symbol of power, but to reveal the power of God above it (e.g., Ps 97:5; Jer 51:25; Dan 2: 45; Zech 4:7), Mountains are depicted as having been created at the beginning of creation (Prov 8:25; Job 15:7); and as enduring forever (Gen 49:26; Ps 125:1; Hab 3:6). Besides, mountains also played an important role in salvation-history, as attested by the names Moriah (Gen 22:2), Horeb (Exod 3:1ff.), Sinai (Exod 19:11ff.), Zion (Ps 14:7, etc.). All these

---

274 Luz, *Matthew 1-7*, 224.

275 Hagner, *Matthew 1-13*, 85-86. See also Schnackenburg, *The Gospel of Matthew*, 46.

276 According to Hagner, "Jesus, somewhat like a new Moses, goes up to the mount to mediate the true interpretation of the Torah." Hagner, *Matthew 1-13*, 86.

277 Newman, Jr., "Some Translational Notes on the Beatitudes," 107. C.f., however, Luz, maintains that Matthew does not want to place Jesus antithetically to Moses, nor he understands the law of the second Moses as the invalidation of the Mosaic Law. Luz, *Matthew 1-7*, 224. Strecker also, in line with Luz's view, maintains that this mountain motif does not depict Jesus as the "new Moses" and the mountain motif itself is not set up as parallel to mount Sinai, the place of old covenant and the law of Moses. The teaching of Jesus on the mountain rather means that divine epiphany occurs in his speech. See, Strecker, *The Sermon on the Mount*, 25.

depictions of mountains in the Old Testament must have played some role in the setting of the Beatitudes (Sermon on the Mount) on a mountain by Matthew.[278]

(2) Second, Matthew's picture of Jesus as sitting down, while his disciples were coming to him (5:1b), also seems to have importance for Matthew's Jewish-christian community. Teaching from a seated position was customary for the rabbis in Judaism. Thus, according to Matthew, Jesus sat down (καθίσαντος αὐτου/[279]) like a rabbinic master before he began to teach (cf. 13:2; 24:3).[280]

(3) Third, Matthew introduces Jesus with an elaborate construction "he opened his mouth and taught them, saying..." (5:2). This is also significant in the context of the Matthean community, which was made up of Jewish/Jewish-oriented Christians. The phrase ἀνοίξας τὸ στόμα αὐτοῦ, "he opened his mouth," is a Semitic idiom used at the beginning of a public address (e.g., Job 3:1; 33:2; Dan 10:16; Acts 8:35; 10:34) and it points here to the weighty significance of what Jesus is about to say.[281] Gundry contends that here it echoes Matt 4:4 "every word that comes from the mouth of the Lord," and since Jesus is "God with us" (1:23) "when he opens his mouth, his disciples hear nothing less than the Word of God."[282]

Thus, Matthew's presentation of Jesus as teaching from a mountain, in a standing position, and beginning with the phrase "he opened his mouth" are understood as Matthew's literary work to make the teaching of Jesus more meaningful to his community. However, there is a question on who are the actual audience of the Beatitudes (the Sermon on the Mount).

In fact, there is an ambiguity about the actual audience of the Beatitudes (or the Sermon on the Mount as a whole) as presented by Matthew.[283] The setting of the Sermon (5:1-2) could be viewed as suggesting Jesus' disciples (a small

---

278 Davies and Allison, Jr., *Matthew*, Vol. I, 422-423.

279 According to Gundry this genitive absolute typifies Matthew's style. Gundry, *Matthew: A Commentary on His Handbook*, 66.

280 Hagner, *Matthew 1-13*, 86. Gundry observes that the "sitting" here contrasts the "standing" in Luke (6:17), and by sitting in the normal position of teachers Jesus replaces the scribes and Pharisees (23:2; cf. 13:1-2; 24:3; 26:55; Luke 4:20; 5:3). Gundry, *Matthew: A Commentary on His Literary and Theological Art*, 66.

281 Hagner, *Matthew 1-13*, 86. See also Harrington, *The Gospel of Matthew*, 78, quoting D. A. Black, "The Translation of Matthew 5:2," *BibTrans* 38 (1987), 241-43.

282 Gundry, *Matthew: A Commentary on His Handbook*, 67. Gundry further says here that, 'εδίδασκεν is an inceptive imperfect, meaning "he began to teach," and the Sermon falls under the rubric of teaching only in Matthew (Luke has only ἔλεγεν "he was saying," which means that Jesus simply says instead of teaching). According to Strecker the phrase "he opened his mouth" shows that this speech is raised above the secular world, and it indicates that Jesus' ethical teaching in the Sermon on the Mount is an eschatological demand. Strecker, *The Sermon on the Mount*. 26.

283 The "audience" here will be treated as the audience of the Sermon on the Mount as a whole because there is no separate audience of "the Beatitudes" other than that of the Sermon on the Mount.

group?) as the audience of this teaching.[284] The ending of the Sermon (7:28-29), on the other hand, suggests that the crowds were also listening to this teaching. Therefore, some scholars suggest that the audience of this teaching include the disciples and the crowds.[285] Some other scholars however take the term "disciples" here to include both the crowds[286] and those whom Jesus had specially called.[287] We could well assume on the basis of the text that the audience of Jesus' Sermon on the Mount includes both his newly called disciples (5:1-2) and the crowd (in part or in whole) who were following him (7:28). This crowd can also be understood as disciples in some sense because Matthew sometimes speaks of Jesus' disciples other than the twelve (8:19, 21); and his knowledge of the wider circle of disciples is indicated in various places (10:24, 25, 42; 27:57). Moreover, the crowd that follows Jesus in Matt 4:23-25 can best be understood as part of the wider circle of Jesus' disciples.[288] Consequently, David Hill could be right in suggesting that the word "disciples" in Matt 5:1 may denote all those who wish to hear the instruction of Jesus.[289] The introductory phrase, "he opened his mouth," which is a Semitic idiom used at the beginning of a public address,[290] also suggests that Jesus intended his teaching to be heard by a larger group of people. According to Stanton, the Sermon is clearly addressed to the newly called disciples, but the crowds also heard it. This dual audience is deliberate because while Jesus' teachings in the five discourses of Matthew are directed to the disciples, parts of them are appropriate (or rather meant) for the wider audience. This is indicated even in chs. 13 and 23, which have a dual audience.[291] Luz maintains that the two centric circles of hearers, disciples and the multitude indicate that the Sermon on the Mount contains ethics for both the disciples and the listening people.[292] Finally, the instruction given by the risen Jesus to his disciples to teach all those whom they have made "disciples of Jesus" from all the nations to keep all that he has commanded (28:18-20), affirms the appropriateness for a larger audience

284 Albright and Mann indeed maintain that the Sermon on the Mount is addressed to the inner circle, the disciples. Albright and Mann, *Matthew*, 45.

285 See for example Kingsbury, "The Place, Structure, and Meaning…," 134 [131-143]. See also Fitch, *The Beatitudes of Jesus*, 6.

286 According to Schnackenburg the "crowds" here "are the persons who have thronged together from all corners of the land (4:25) and who represent the people of Israel about to hear the message and teaching of Jesus." Schnackenburg, *The Gospel of Matthew*, 46.

287 See for example, Gundry, *Matthew: A Commentary on His Handbook*, 66; Schweizer, *The Good News According to Matthew*, 79; Patte, *The Gospel According to Matthew*, 60; and Newman, Jr., "Some Translational Notes on the Beatitudes," 109.

288 Talbert, *Reading the Sermon on the Mount*, 13.

289 David Hill, *The Gospel of Matthew.* New Century Bible (Grand Rapids/London: Eerdmans, Marshall Morgan & Scott, 1972), 108.

290 Hagner, *Matthew 1-13*, 86.

291 Stanton, "The Origin and Purpose of Matthew's Sermon on the Mount," 188.

292 Luz, *Matthew 1-7*, 224.

of some parts of Jesus' teaching to his disciples.[293] The Sermon on the Mount (including the Beatitudes) is one of such teachings of Jesus and that is why the crowd also listened to it. The going up of Jesus to the mountain to teach this lesson also indicates that he was looking for a convenient place to address such a larger crowd who were already following him.[294] Luz seems right in suggesting that the command of Jesus in 28:20 to his disciples to teach to all nations all that he has commanded them is probably a recalling of the Sermon on the Mount.[295] According to Strecker, the addressing of both the disciples and the crowd by Jesus indicates that the demands of Jesus exclude no one, for, in the Sermon on the Mount Jesus addresses all those who belong to him and those who do not belong to him.[296]

The literary setting thus shows that the first Matthean discourse is depicted by the first evangelist as an authoritative teaching of Jesus to both his selected disciples and to the crowds. It would be correct to understand that the disciples are the primary addressees, but at the same time, it is also meant for the crowds to hear. And, Matthew presents it to his Jewish-Christian audience in a way that would be more convincing to them, by locating it on a mountain, being taught by Jesus in a sitting position as a Jewish rabbi, and beginning the teaching with a Semitic idiom "he opened his mouth."

The stage, which Matthew carefully sets for the first and the most remarkable of the five discourses which he is going to present (i.e., the Sermon on the Mount: chaps. 5-7) is the same stage for "the Beatitudes" which is a programmatic introduction to this extraordinary discourse.

With all this information, we will now go to the exegetical comment of the Matthean Beatitudes (Matt 5:3-12), beginning with the highlight of its semantic fields.

2.10. The Semantic Fields of the Matthean Beatitudes

There are four main terms and one phrase which are dominant in this passage such as μακάριος, πτωχος διωκώ δικαιοσύνη and βασιλεία τῶν οὐρανῶν.

The term μακάριος "blessed" occurs 9 times in the plural form μακάριοι, beginning all the nine beatitudes, and it is also related to three other words which occur once each such as αἱρετε "rejoice," ἀγαλλιᾶσθε "be glad," and μισθὸς "reward."

The term πτωχός "poor" occurs only once in the passage (that is in the plural form πτωχοί). But, it is the principal term underlying other expressions

293 Stanton, "The Origin and Purpose of Matthew's Sermon on the Mount," 188.

294 Strecker, *The Sermon on the Mount*, 25.

295 Luz, *Matthew 1-7*, 214.

296 Strecker, *The Sermon on the Mount*, 26.

which occur once each, such as οἱ πενθοῦντες "those who mourn," οἱ πραεῖς, "the meek," οἱ πεινῶντες "the hungry" (οἱ) διψῶντες "the thirsty."[297]

The term διωκω "to persecute" (here) occurs two times; once in perfect passive participle οἱ δεδιωγμένοι and another time in aorist active subjunctive διώξωσιν. There are two phrases related to it which occur once each, such as ὀνειδίσωσιν "they revile" (aorist subjunctive, indefinite clause), εἴπωσιν πᾶν πονηρὸν "they utter all kinds of evil" (aorist subjunctive, indefinite clause).[298]

The term δικαιοσύνη "righteousness" occurs two times at regular intervals, in the fourth (in accusative form δικαιοσύνην) and in the eighth beatitudes (in genitive form δικαιοσύνης) dividing the first eight beatitudes into two equal groups,[299] thus appearing as the concluding term for each group. It is especially related also to such terms and phrase οἱ ἐλεήμονες_"the merciful," οἱ καθαροὶ τῇ καρδίᾳ "the pure in heart," and οἱ εἰρηνοποιοί "the peacemakers," which occur once each.

The phrase βασιλεία τῶν οὐρανῶν "kingdom of heaven" occurs at the first and the eight beatitudes, forming an *inclusio*, and thus acting as the concept that underlies all the major terms mentioned above.

The dominance of these four main terms and one phrase, such as μακάριος πτωχός διώκω δικαιοσύνη ανδ βασιλεία τῶν οὐρανῶν indicates that they are the main emphases of the author in this pericope.

2.11. Exegetical Comment

V. 3. μακάριοι οἱ πτωχοὶ τῷ πνεύματι, ὅτι αὐτῶν ἐστιν ἡ βασιλεία τῶν οὐρανῶν "***Blessed are the poor in spirit, for theirs is the kingdom of heaven.***" The first beatitude is ascribed to Jesus' own saying, which was preserved in Q. It has its Old Testament basis in Isa 61:1, where the servant of the Lord says that the Lord sends him to bring good news to the poor/oppressed.[300] The parallel beatitude in Luke 6:20 is understood to contain the original Q form and the Matthean version betrays a redacted form.

μακάριοι οἱ πτωχοὶ τῷ πνεύματι, "***blessed are the poor in spirit.***" According to Friberg Lexicon, the word μακάριος (plural - μακάριοι) is used in different ways, such as: (1) It is used of persons, characterised by transcendent happiness or religious joy, thus meaning "blessed," "happy," (e.g., Matt 5:3);

297 Bultmann also maintains, in his comments on the second beatitude, that as the word παρακληθήσονται of the second beatitude stands in synonymous parallelism to the promises of the other beatitudes, so also πενθοῦντες of the second beatitude stands in synonymous parallelism to πτωχοί (τῷ πνεύματι), πραεῖς, and πεινῶντες καὶ διψῶντες (τὴν δικαιοσύνην) of the first, third and fourth beatitudes respectively. See Bultmann, "πένθος, πενθέω," *TDNT,* Vol. VI (Grand Rapids, Michigan: William B. Eerdmans Publishing Company, 1968), 43.

298 ὀνειδίσωσιν and εἴπωσιν are also aorist active subjunctive third person plural, used in indefinite clause with ὅταν.

299 Schweizer, *The Good News According to Matthew*, 82.

300 Hagner, *Matthew 1-13*, 91-92.

or without religious connotation, thus referring to "fortunate" or "lucky" (e.g., Luke 23:29). (2) It is also used of "parts of the body viewed as happy because of favourable circumstances" (e.g., Matt 13:6; Luke 11:27); and (3) also "of things closely related to God, as hope" (e.g., Tit 2:13).[301] The Hebrew word mostly translated as μακάριος in the LXX is אַשְׁרֵי *'ašrê* (adj.). According to BDB *Lexicon* the noun אֶשֶׁר or אֹשֶׁר means happiness, blessedness,[302] and this indicates that the adjective אַשְׁרֵי means "happy" or "blessed." According to Cazelles, in the Wisdom vocabulary of the Old Testament, probably under the influence of the Egyptian culture, "the divine blessing demands deeds of faithfulness to God and his law in order to give happiness to the faithful," and "this is precisely the meaning of *'ashre*."[303] Cazelles further mentions that while the word *'ashre* does not occur in the Qumran literature, its traditional usage is preserved in the Rabbinic literature, and the last stage in the development of the pronounced blessing is encountered in Sirach, which uses the word six times. In Sir 37:24, the blessings and happiness are put in parallelism, "and this prepares the way for the Sermon on the Mount, where the Gk. *makários*, 'blessed,' is connected with fulfilment of the law."[304]

However, the meaning of the Greek word μακάριος (with its Hebrew equivalent אַשְׁרֵי) brought out here reflects its meaning from wisdom perspective, and therefore there is a problem in directly applying this meaning to the Matthean beatitudes, which are basically apocalyptic beatitudes rather than wisdom beatitudes.

According to Guelich, the translation of the Greek word μακάριος is integral to the function of the beatitude. In the context of a cultic setting, the more accurate translation would be "blessed." However, against the background of Wisdom the more appropriate translation would be "happy" or "fortunate." In a less sacramental setting, it would convey the meaning of "congratulation to." Then, Guelich maintains that the translation of μακάριος in the present passage (Matt 5:3-12), would depend upon "whether Matthew 'ethicized' the Beatitudes to become 'entrance requirements' for the Kingdom or whether they are eschatological promises announced to the unsuspecting or undeserving." Then he concludes, "by using *blessed* in the translation, we have maintained the familiar-even if ambiguous-term."[305] Since Guelich interprets the Matthean beatitudes as eschatological blessings (thus apocalyptic beatitudes), we may understand him to

---

301 See "Freiberg Lexicon." C. D. Rom. Bible Works, LLC, 2001.

302 Francis Brown, S. R. Driver and Charles A. Bridges, eds., *Hebrew and English Lexicon of the Old Testament* (Oxford: Clarendon Press, 1959 [1907]), 80.

303 Cazelles, "אַשְׁרֵי *'ashrê*," *TDOT*, Vol. I (Grand Rapids, Michigan: William B. Eerdmans Publishing company, 1974), 448. *'ashre* here, is Cazelles' transliteration.

304 Cazelles, "אַשְׁרֵי *'ashrê*," 448.

305 Guelich, *The Sermon on the Mount: A Foundation for Understanding*, 66-67. See also Thomson, "The Background and Function of the Beatitudes…," 10.

mean that the term *blessed*, although ambiguous, is acceptable for translating the word μακάριος in that context.[306]

From its Old Testament basis, especially of its Hebrew equivalent אַשְׁרֵי *ašrê*, it would be correct to render the word μακάριος as blessed, happy or fortunate.[307] However, as the Matthean beatitudes are mainly apocalyptic beatitudes, any of the renderings in Matthew would refer to the blessed situation and the concomitant deep inner joy of the faithful followers of Jesus Christ who put their faith and hope only in him even under all difficult situations, for whom Jesus announced participation in the eschatological kingdom of God / Heaven.[308] As the NRSV translation is followed in this study, the rendering of "blessed" will be adopted here.

Etymologically πτωχός is related to πτώσσειν which means "to bow down timidly," and as an adjective it means "destitute," "mendicant." While πένης, another Greek word translated as "poor" refers to one who has to earn his living because of lack of property, πτωχός refers to "the complete destitution which forces the poor to seek the help of others by begging."[309]

There are three Hebrew words translated in the LXX as πτωχός such as עָנִי *ʿāni*, דַּל *dal*, and אֶבְיוֹן *abeiwn*. The word πτωχός is used 37 times for עָנִי, it is used 22 times for דַּל and 11 times for אֶבְיוֹן.[310]

From the stem ענה, the word עָנִי denotes the situation of answering and readiness to answer. Then in the more developed form, it denotes the position of inferiority before the one who demands an answer. In concrete sense עָנִי is the hearer, the dependant, and therefore the word primarily expresses a relation rather than a state of social distress. When the word is used for an economic position, it is for the first instance combined with דַּל *dal* (e.g., Ps 82:3) or אֶבְיוֹן *abeiwn* (e.g., Deut 24:14; Ezra 16:49; 18:12; 22:29). Only in a more developed usage the word עָנִי is used to denote a state of lowliness or distress. In this case, it refers to a man in a state of reduced competence and lesser worth, and predominantly signifies poverty. The antonym of עָנִי is "violent" (רָשָׁע, פָּרִיץ, עוֹשֵׁק). The term עָנִי denotes one who is "wrongfully impoverished or dispossessed" and it is not used to refer to deserved poverty. The term also takes on religious significance referring to "humble" and even "pious" which is translated in Ps 18:27/17:28LXX, as

306 Guelich, "The Matthean Beatitudes: 'Entrance-Requirements' or Eschatological Blessings?," 415-434 [433].

307 Guelich highlights the difficulty of expressing the meaning of μακάριος in English, and mentions the following as examples: "Blessed" – KJV, RSV, ASV; "how blest" – JB, PHILLIPS; "happy" – TEV; "fortunate" – LB. Guelich, *The Sermon on the Mount: A Foundation for Understanding*, 66.

308 Cf. Hagner, *Matthew 1-13*, 91.

309 Hauck, "πτωχος in the Greek World," *TDNT,* Vol. VI (Grand Rapids, Michigan: Wm. B. Eerdmans Publishing Company, 1968), 886.

310 Bammel, "The Poor in the Old Testament," *TDNT,* Vol. VI (Grand Rapids, Michigan: Wm. B. Eerdmans Publishing Company, 1968), 888.

ταπεινός.[311] Thus, a comprehensive meaning of the word עָנִי may be understood as a person, wrongfully impoverished or dispossessed, thus forced into a position of inferiority, and who became humble and pious before God, looking to Him as his/her only help. This must throw light on the meaning of the "poor" in the first Matthean beatitude, because the word for "poor" used in its Old Testament basis Isa 61:1 is עָנִי.

The word דַּל *dal* is rendered as πτωχός for 22 times in the LXX. The word דַּל has different shades of meaning in the Old Testament. It is used to refer to physical weakness in Gen 41:19; and 2Sam 13:4. It is also used to denote social status, such as "lowly," "poor," "wretched," and "insignificant" in Lev 19:15; 1Sam 2:8, etc. The term also denotes the lower orders in 2Kings 24:14; 25:12; cf. Jer 40:7; 52:15f.; 39:10; and it also is used to substitute the sense "humble" in Isa 25:4; 26:6; and especially Zeph 3:12.[312] Thus, the word דַּל also can be understood as referring to a lowly, poor, wretched person, who humbles himself/herself before God as his/her only helper.

Πτωχός is used 11 times in the LXX for אֶבְיוֹן *abeiwn*, for which the Greek word more frequently used is πένης. The root of אֶבְיוֹן ס אבה which means "to will," as well as "to be willing." From this root the word אֶבְיוֹן originally denotes "the one who seeks alms," that is "the beggar." Then the word came to be used in more general term for "the poor man," and where the word is used in non-figurative sense it often refers to the very poor, "those with no roof over their heads" etc. (e.g., 1Sam 2:8, etc.). אֶבְיוֹן also often has a religious nuance like the word עָנִי, especially when it is used in a double form עָנִי וְאֶבְיוֹן. This is the regular expression in the Psalms for the attitude of the one who prays to God (see Ps 35:10; 37:14; 40:17; 70:5; 74:21; 86:1; 109:16, 22).[313] The word אֶבְיוֹן also thus refers to economically poor person, who prays to God with the feeling of helplessness, and it is not far from the meaning of עָנִי and דַּל.

Besides these three words there are other Hebrew words sometimes translated in the LXX as πτωχός such as רָשׁ and מִסְכֵּן. רָשׁ is participle of the רוש, which means "to be poor, needy, famished," in an exclusively social and economic sense. It is a favourite word in the Wisdom literature. It is commonly translated as πτωχός in Proverbs (11 times), usually as an antithesis to "rich."[314] The word מִסְכֵּן means the "dependent" and then the "socially inferior." The LXX translates it once as πτωχός in Sir 30:14. πτωχός is also once used for the uncertain word חֵלְכָה in Ps 9:35 while the same word is translated as πένης in Ps 9:29.[315]

Thus, the main Hebrew words which are often translated as πτωχός and which are sometimes synonymously used are עָנִי דַּל and אֶבְיוֹן. However, in several

311 Bammel, "The Poor in the Old Testament," 888.

312 *Ibid.*

313 *Ibid.*, 888-889.

314 *Ibid.*, 889.

315 *Ibid.*

passages they are also differentiated in translations like the Greek words πένης and πτωχός, especially when two words are used in parallel or linked by ו, (Amos 8:6; Isa 26:6; 41:17; etc.), and sometimes their antitheses are also differentiated (Isa 11:4 (?); 14:30; 32:7; etc.).[316] However, even in such cases they refer more or less to the same or similar situation, and still can be understood as synonymous.

Viewing from its Old Testament basis Isa 61:1-2, the meaning of the word πτωχός in Matt 5:3 may be derived primarily from the word עני (Isa 61:1). Then, the meaning of πτωχός in Matt 5:3 could be understood as referring to the poor, famished, wretched, and lowly people, both economically and socially, who are wrongfully impoverished and dispossessed, and forced into a position of inferiority by forces like social, political, religious, etc., and who look to God with a humble and pious heart, praying to Him as their only helper.[317] This meaning is supported by the two synonyms of עני, such as דַּל and אֶבְיוֹן,[318] as well as other Hebrew words such as רֹשׁ and מִסְכֵּן. which are often translated as "poor" in the OT.

Most scholars take τῷ πνεύματι "in spirit" as a Matthean addition to his source which has only "the poor" (as Luke 6:20 has),[319] and it refers to human spirit, rather than divine spirit.[320] There are two main lines of thought, however,

316 Bammel, "The Poor in the Old Testament," 889.

317 According to Davies and Allison, Jr., in the LXX, the word πτωχός and its Hebrew equivalents primarily refer to economic poverty. However, in the OT, especially in the Psalms, they already refer to those who are in special need of God's help. Then in time, the word came to be a self-designation for the meek, humiliated, and oppressed people of God, and this is the sense in which the word πτωχός is used in the Beatitudes. However, the religious meaning of πτωχός does not exclude the economic meaning. The two rather go together. For many of Jesus' followers, probably for the majority of them, their religious state of poverty was matched by economic poverty. Therefore, they were poor both in spirit and in fact. See Davies and Allison, Jr., *Matthew*, Vol. I, 443. According to Ulrich Luz, the LXX translation of עני and דַּל as πτωχός emphasizes the social aspect of the beatitude and it corresponds to its meaning in Jesus' usage. See Luz, *Matthew 1-7*, 232. Guelich rightly points out, "*The poor* in Judaism referred to those in desperate need (socio-economic element) whose helplessness drove them to a dependent relationship with God (religious element) for the supplying of their needs and vindication." Guelich, *The Sermon on the Mount: A Foundation for Understanding*, 69.

318 Cf., Davies and Allison, Jr., *Matthew*, Vol. I, 443.

319 Guelich, *The Sermon on the Mount: A Foundation for Understanding*, 74.

320 One of the few exceptions would be Robert H. Smith, who takes "the poor in spirit" as referring to "the poor in the Holy Spirit" as apposed to those who are rich in the Holy Spirit, the charismatically endowed Christian leaders who are disturbing the community. According to Smith, the poor in the Holy Spirit (5:3) are those who are hunger and thirst for righteousness (5:6), and they are the same people who are persecuted for righteousness' sake (5:10). On the other hand, those who are rich in the Holy Spirit, are those "powerful prophetic personalities" (7:15) who call Jesus "lord" and have acted in his name (7:22). Jesus rejects these people because they are poor in deeds of righteousness. They are the "workers of lawlessness" (ἀνομία 7:23). They are the false prophets referred to in Matt 24:11, 24. See, Robert H. Smith, "'Blessed are the Poor in (Holy) Spirit'? (Matthew 5:3)," *Word & World* 18

on the interpretation of Matthew's addition of τῷ πνεύματι "in spirit." According to some scholars, Matthew, by adding the phrase τῷ πνεύματι "in spirit," spiritualized or ethicized the poor in Luke 6:20 (or Q). For example, Newman maintains that Luke's emphasis on God's special concern for the poor and the needy are not emphasized by Matthew (elsewhere) to any noticeable extent. Therefore, the "poor in spirit" in Matthew refers to those who feel and recognize their spiritual need, their need of God. Newman further contends that Matthew added "in spirit" because he understood it to be implicit in the original words of Jesus.[321] According to Luz the qualification of πτωχός by τῷ πνεύματι in the Matthean text apparently changes its meaning. The dative τῷ πνεύματι could be either dative of means or dative of reference, and it could refer either to divine spirit or human spirit. In this text, however, it should be taken as dative of reference referring to human spirit. The meaning of "the poor in spirit," would then be "those who stands before God as beggars in regard to their inner life… in the feeling of their inability to help themselves." Therefore, πτωχός in the first beatitude refers to an attitude rather than circumstance, and the first beatitude thus means "blessed are the lowly in spirit, i.e., the humble." Luz concludes that not only the language is changed (by Matthew) but also the content is shifted, that "social poverty moves to the background; inner need moves to the foreground. It reaches over into the ethical attitude of humility. Thus, one has to speak of a tendency to internalize and ethicize the first beatitude."[322] Strecker maintains that the encouragement of the first beatitude is for the people of low self-esteem, who are humble, and it confronts the high self-esteemed Pharisees and scribes as mentioned in 6:2 and 23:1ff.[323]

A good number of scholars, on the other hand, are of the view that Matthew's addition of τῷ πνεύματι does not spiritualize or ethicize the "poor" in Luke. For example, Joseph Pathrapankal traces the meaning of both πτωχός and πνεύμα in the Greek language and the Hebrew (OT) background, and he maintains that this is not a spiritualization of the "poor" in Luke. Pathrapankal interprets οἱ πτωχοὶ τῷ πνεύματι, as referring to those who have "no power, no prestige, no influence to defend themselves against the insults and assaults of the world around," as well as "those who were economically poor" – thus "the poor, the humble and faithful people who have no help on earth and who in perfect and humble trust have wholly committed themselves to God."[324] According to Hagner, "the poor in

(Fall 1998), 392-394. Smith's analysis gives an impression that the spiritually rich people were the persecutors of the spiritually poor people. However, this is very unlikely because, according to Smith, the spiritually rich people are the insiders.

321 Newman, Jr., "Some Translational Notes on the Beatitudes," 112-113.

322 Luz, *Matthew 1-7*, 232-233.

323 Strecker, *the Sermon on the Mount*, 32.

324 Joseph Pathrapankal, *The Christian Programme: A Theological and Pastoral Study of The Sermon on the Mount* (Bangalore: Dharmaram, 1999), 115 [110-115].

spirit" refers to the frame of mind of those who are literally poor, and the addition of "in spirit," does not "spiritualize" the Lukan form, which has only "poor" and which is probably the original.[325] Hagner further quotes Broer, who notes that the two phrases "poor" and "poor in spirit" are synonymous in the Judaism of Jesus' time and they convey the notion that the poor are almost always poor in spirit and the poor in spirit are also almost always the poor.[326] According to Schweizer, the term "poor" had become a kind of honorific title for the righteous in the Judaism of Jesus' time (first century C.E.), and Matthew's addition of "in spirit," points out the danger of thinking poverty as an honour, which is not a virtue or something to be boasted.[327] Davies and Allison also maintain that the addition of "in spirit" does not pervert the meaning of the unqualified "poor" as found in Luke. The addition only shifts the emphasis from the economic to the religious sphere, and the religious sphere is also not altogether lacking in the pre-Matthean tradition. Rather, in spite of the third evangelist's several simple contrast between the rich and the poor (see, Luke 12:13-21; 14:7-14; and 16:19-31), the religious meaning also should be read into Luke, because in Luke the rich have little sense of need for God (Luke 12:16-21; 16:19-31), while the poor depend upon Him (see Luke 1:46-53; 14:25-33). Therefore, the words "rich" and "poor" in Luke cannot be purely economic, in as much as "Luke does not hold forth salvation for the poor simply because they are poor."[328]

While Matthew's addition of the phrase "in spirit" to the "poor" of the first beatitude has been interpreted in different ways, it is believed in this research that

325 Hagner, *Matthew 1-13*, 91. Cf. Schnackenburg, *The Gospel of Matthew*, 46, who maintains that Matthew stresses the moral attitude demanded of the poor, hungry and weeping, thus is highlighting the unity of Divine grace, moral requirements, and promises.

326 Hagner, *Matthew 1-13*, 91, quoting I Broer, *Die Seligpreisungen der Bergpredigt* (BBB 61. Bonn: Peter Hanstein, 1986), 71. Hagner observes that this reflects also the situation in the post-exilic Israel, where "poverty and piety often went together," and "the poor were driven to complete reliance upon God, and the righteous poor were thought especially to be the objects of God's special concern (cf. Ps 9:18; 33[34]:18; 40:17; Isa 57:15; Jas 2:5)." Hagner further says that Ps. 61:1, which talks about eschatological hope, having particularly the poor in view, and alluded to in Matt 11:4 (cf. Luke 4:19-19), is the basis of this beatitude. Hagner, *Matthew 1-13*, 91-92. Cf., however, Harrington, *The Gospel of Matthew*, 78, who notes that the word *ptōchos* denotes a "beggar" and the qualification "in spirit" defines the poor as the ones who recognized God's kingdom as a gift that cannot be forced.

327 Schweizer, *The Good News According to Matthew*, 81, 83, 88. See also Albright and Mann, *Matthew*, 46, who maintains that the "poor in spirit" is produced by the original editor from Qumran saying (1QM XIV 7) because of the feeling that the tradition as it is found in Luke, which has, only "poor" would be misunderstood. Cf., J. C. Fenton, *Saint Matthew.* The Pelican New Testament Commentaries (Harmonsworth: Penguin Books, 1963), 80, who takes "in spirit" to mean "willingly," "voluntarily" so that "the poor in spirit" are "those who have renounced their possessions in order to follow Jesus." For a similar interpretation, see also G. E. P. Cox, *The Gospel According to Saint Matthew* (London: SCM Press Ltd, 1952), 45.

328 Davies and Allison, Jr., *Matthew*, Vol. I, 444. See also Guelich, *The Sermon on the Mount: A Foundation for Understanding*, 67, 75.

the socio-historical context of the Matthean community has an important bearing for understanding the meaning of the first beatitude. It has been highlighted in the first chapter that the Matthean community was suffering, along with other Jews, socio-political and economic hardships at the hands of the Romans in the aftermath of the first Jewish Revolt against Rome (66-73 A.D.), and religious persecutions at the hands of both the Jews and the Gentiles. Although a few of the members were well-to-do, most of them were economically poor. Therefore, they were in such a severe plight and they looked only to God/Jesus for their help.[329] To console them in such situations Matthew drew the first beatitude from Jesus' apocalyptic beatitudes, which Jesus most probably spoke based on Isa 61:1-2. However, he had to clarify that Jesus did not promise the blessing of the kingdom of God to the downtrodden because of their poverty as such, but because they put their complete trust in God in the midst of their difficult situations. Such a clarification was necessary because there was a tendency in some circles of the Jews to elevate poverty as such as the basis of God's blessing. Such tendency in turn could cause the few well-to-do members of the Matthean community to misunderstand the meaning of the "poor" and exclude themselves from the promise of the blessing. However, Matthew did not compromise the apocalyptic nature of the beatitudes with this clarification. Therefore, the "poor in spirit" of the first beatitude can be understood as primarily referring to the frame of mind of the poor and the downtrodden people of God, who put their trust only in God for which they are promised the blessing to inherit the kingdom of Heaven/God. At the same time, this addition also clarifies, especially in the context of the Matthean community, that all those who have the same frame of mind are not excluded from the blessing promised in the first beatitude.[330]

---

329 Here, we see certain parallels with the situation of the "poor" in Isaiah 61:1, although the meaning cannot be exactly the same between the two. In Isaiah 61:1, the "poor" "poignantly describes the dispirited Jewish community around the ruins of Jerusalem before Ezra returned." See John D. W. Watts, *Isaiah 34-66*, WBC, Vol. 25 (Dallas, Texas: Word Books Publisher, 1987), 302. Obviously those people were also, like the Matthean community, in a very severe plight and they looked only to God for their help.

330 Here, viewing from Matthew's socio-historical context, we maintain the view of Davies and Allison, Jr. that the addition of "in spirit" does not pervert the meaning of the unqualified "poor" as found in Luke, but only shifts the emphasis from the economic to the religious sphere, while the religious sphere is also not altogether lacking in the pre-Matthean tradition. See Davies and Allison, Jr., *Matthew*, Vol. I, 444. We also uphold Guelich's rendering, that the *poor in spirit* in Matthew are "those who find themselves waiting, empty-handed, upon God alone for their hope and deliverance while beset with abuse and rejection by their own social and religious context." See Guelich, *The Sermon on the Mount: A Foundation for Understanding*, 75. For a contrary view, see Luz, *Matthew 1-7*, 233-234, who maintains that in the first beatitude "social poverty moves to the back ground; inner need moves to the foreground. It reaches into the ethical attitude of humility," and "the expression 'poor in spirit' does not indicate whether the humble are poor or rich," for "in principle the rich are just blessed as the poor, for there is no distinction of persons before God."

ὅτι αὐτῶν ἐστιν ἡ βασιλεία τῶν οὐρανῶν, ***"for theirs is the kingdom of heaven."*** According to Daniel Patte, αὐτῶν is in an emphatic position here, referring to the "poor in spirit."[331] Gundry ascribes the use of the third person to Matthew's redaction, assimilating Jesus styles to the word of God in the Old Testament, in order to make it to a didactic manner as well as to conform to Old Testament Beatitudes.[332] Guelich maintains, on the other hand, that although some have taken Luke's form to be the earlier, some factors weigh in favour of Matthew's form. Since both forms occur in Greek and Jewish literature without connoting any significant difference in *Sitz im Leben*, these differences have been proven more apparent than real. Therefore, the question is primarily of style rather than content. As "either form could have been used without detracting from the force of the Beatitudes for their audience," ultimately the question of person is academic.[333] According to David Daube, the conclusion of a series of equal length with third person form, with a lengthened second person form was a practice in the Old Testament and Judaism (e.g., Isa 63:7ff.; Sir 47:12ff.; 48:1ff.). Therefore, the Matthean form of the Beatitudes, that is a series of third person concluded with second person, seems to be the form from the outset of their collection in Q.[334] It seems, therefore, that Matthew took over them as he found in his tradition, for the format suits well his purpose. Therefore, even when he inserted an additional beatitude at the eighth position, he used the third person form to retain the same format.[335] Then, for Matthew, the repetition of αὐτῶν in the second clause of each of the beatitudes except in the ninth could have an antithetical effect, referring to "these" people rather than "those." In this case, "these" people would refer to Christians (represented by the Matthean community) and "those" people would refer to the Jewish leaders, as the two groups emerge in Matt 5:17-7:12.[336]

Concerning the use of "kingdom of heaven" by Matthew in place of Luke's "kingdom of God," the term "heaven" is a Jewish substitution for "God," and "kingdom" refers to the reign or sovereignty of God,[337] thus "kingdom of heaven" is an equivalent to the "kingdom of God" found in other gospels and other parts of the New Testament.[338] An obvious reason for Matthew's replacement of the term

331 Patte, *The Gospel According to Matthew*, 66.

332 Gundry, *Matthew: A Commentary on His Handbook*, 68.

333 Guelich, *The Sermon on the Mount: A Foundation for Understanding*, 76.

334 Daube, "The Last Beatitude," 321-324.

335 For further discussion, see the "Redaction of the Matthean Beatitudes" above.

336 For this and for the possible arguments, see Davies and Allison, Jr., *Matthew*, Vol. I, 445-446, 447.

337 Harrington, *The Gospel of Matthew*, 79.

338 Patte, *The Gospel According to Matthew*, 66. However, Guelich notes that Matthew uses the term "the kingdom" (e.g., Matt 4:23; 6: 33) as well as the more common "kingdom of God" (e.g., Matt 12:28) with the same meaning as "kingdom of heaven;" and he also uses "kingdom of heaven" and "kingdom of God" interchangeably in 19:23, 24. Matthew's use of these different terms, according to Guelich, is more indicative of his inconsistency of style

"kingdom of God" with "kingdom of heaven" in 5:3 as well as in other places must be a concern for his primary audience. As we have noted in the previous chapter, Matthew's community was made up of Jewish Christians and Jewish-oriented Gentile Christians, and the term "kingdom of heaven" was more familiar to them than the term "kingdom of God." Therefore, it seems that Matthew chooses the term "kingdom of heaven," which is a familiar term to his target audience. The phrase "kingdom of heaven" (= kingdom of God) here, however, does not refer to "some 'pie-in-the-sky' wonderland that all good folks are 'going to'," but the "*ultimate salvation of the human race wrought by God,*" or "*God's creation restored to God's rule,*" that is "the eschatological restoration of the entire universe to its Creator's rule."[339]

The present tense ἐστιν is used here and in the eighth beatitude. Gundry asserts that the present tense here is to be taken futuristically because of the future tenses that come in the second half and also because of the phrase "in heaven" in v. 12, which almost demands a futuristic understanding (the ninth beatitude is also future in orientation).[340] According to Daniel Patte, however, it may be rather correct to understand that the present tense is used here because the kingdom is already present in the presence of Jesus, while the future aspect of the eschatology is also indicated in the use of the future tenses in all the beatitudes other than the first, the eighth and ninth.[341] Schweizer also points out that "with the exception of the Ethiopic Enoch 58:2,[342] Jesus' Beatitudes are totally new in taking a future blessing and declaring it as right now present." According to him, the salvation promised in the Beatitudes is not only future, but present as well. Speaking with

---

rather than of his theology. Guelich further observes that while most have explained Matthean "kingdom of heaven" as a circumvention of the divine name with a metonym, Matthew does not show any tendency for avoiding the divine name otherwise. Therefore, "heaven" (οὐρανός) has a much broader function in Matthew's gospel than simply as a metonym for God. In continuity with the OT concept of "heaven", it stands for the realm of God where God is enthroned and is ruling over the entire world. Therefore, "heaven" symbolizes God in his sovereign activity. When the biblical understanding of βασιλεία, as referring primarily to a dynamic rule or reign in contrast to a static concept of a realm, is added, then "*Kingdom of Heaven* is a double reference to the sovereign rule or reign of God whose heavenly designation has great import for Matthew." See Guelich, *The Sermon on the Mount: A Foundation for Understanding*, 77. Guelich has rightly pointed out that Matthew uses the term "kingdom of heaven" synonymously with "kingdom" and "kingdom of God." However, it is an undeniable fact that Matthew changes "kingdom of God" of Mark and Luke with "kingdom of heaven," in several places including the present place.

339 Dillon, "The Text of the Sermon on the Mount," 58. Cf. Gundry, *Matthew: A Commentary on His Handbook*, 68, who holds that Matthew's version of "kingdom of heaven" in place of Luke's "kingdom of God" harks back to Daniel 4.

340 Gundry, *Matthew: A Commentary on His Handbook*, 68.

341 Patte, *The Gospel According to Matthew*, 66. See also Hagner, *Matthew 1-13*, 92.

342 Since, this is a translation from the Greek between 4th and 6th century C.E., [See, Rochus Zuurmond, "Ethiopic Versions," *ABD*, Vol. 6 (New York: Doubleday, 1991), 808-809], it could not have anything to do with Matthew's gospel.

the authority of God, Jesus promises joys on the Beatitudes everyday to everyone who can hear his word in an inward application.[343] Davies and Allison, Jr. are of the view that this should be understood as a futuristic or proleptic present expressing vividness and confidence. At the same time, they express the possibility that the present tense also could hint at the presence of the kingdom at present in some sense, and therefore a blessing is enjoyed even now. In either case, they say, however, "there would have been no verb in the Semitic original."[344] Nevertheless, they cling more to the futuristic aspect and they maintain that the phrase "for theirs is the kingdom of heaven" here does not mean that the poor now possess the kingdom, or, the kingdom consists of the poor. It must be rather understood as the proclamation of the outcome of the last judgment. Therefore, what is meant here is that the kingdom of heaven will be given to the poor. "The world will be turned upside down; 'those who are on top here are at the bottom there, and those who are at the bottom here are on the top there'."[345] This seems to be what the apocalyptic nature of this beatitude, in fact, conveys. At the same time, however, the present aspect is also not totally negated by the first evangelist. Guelich seems right in saying that "the choice of ἔστιν rather than ἔσται may correlate with the specific promise – *the Kingdom of Heaven / God*." Guelich notes that whereas the other beatitudes combine the present (declarations) and the future (promises), the Kingdom in Jesus' ministry involved both the present ("already") and the future ("not yet"). "Jesus came to announce and effect the Kingdom, God's redemptive reign, now." Therefore, "the Beatitude announces that God is entering now into a new relationship of blessing, one anticipated in the Old Testament promise, with those turning to him in desperation." Consequently, "the *Kingdom of Heaven* is present as God's sovereign rule from heaven in his Son, Jesus Messiah." This is evident in Jesus' ministry of healing of the sick, in his sharing of the table with sinners, in his defeating of Satan and the forces of evil, in his preaching/teaching where he announces that the Kingdom has come, etc. Meanwhile, "the *Kingdom of Heaven* is also future as the ultimate consummation through the appearance of the Son of Man to effect vindication and judgment." The "present" and the "future" "are not two separate realities but rather are continuous aspects of God's sovereign rule in history."[346] In the words of Kingsbury, it means, "from the unprecedented activity of God in the person of Jesus in the present there will issue in the future the consummated Kingdom of Heaven."[347]

343 Schweizer, *The Good News According to Matthew*, 81, 97.

344 Davies and Allison, Jr., *Matthew*, Vol. I, 446.

345 *Ibid.*, 445.

346 Guelich, *The Sermon on the Mount: A Foundation for Understanding*, 76-78.

347 Kingsbury, *Matthew: Structure, Christology, Kingdom*, 146. Cf. David L. Turner, "Whom does God Approve? The Context, Structure, Purpose and Exegesis of Matthew's Beatitudes [Mt 5: 3-12]," *CriswellTheolRev* 6 (Fall 1992): 37-38. Turner here emphasizes the significance of the present tense in the first and the eighth beatitudes as follows:

Now, we may draw a conclusion on the first Matthean beatitude based on our analysis above. Initially Jesus announced the first beatitude to his followers based on Isa 61:1. The meaning of the first beatitude in Jesus' ministry was that God's promise of salvation for the poor through the prophet Isaiah (Isa 61:1) has come to its fulfilment in the ministry of Jesus.[348] The Kingdom of God/Heaven, that is God's sovereign rule, is now present in Jesus the Messiah, the Son of God.[349] The poor and the downtrodden people, those who look to God with humble and pious heart, praying to Him as their only helper, are now the recipient of the blessing of this kingdom.

In its original setting in the OT and Judaism, the "poor" refers to the famished, wretched, and lowly people, both economically and socially, who are wrongfully impoverished and dispossessed, and forced into a position of inferiority by forces like social, political, religious, etc. Those people were driven by their helplessness to a dependent relationship with God for the supplying of their needs and vindication.[350] This is indicated, especially by the Hebrew word עָנִי used for "poor" in Isa 61:1, which is the basis of the first domonical beatitude. This is further supported by the other Hebrew synonyms such as דַּל and אֶבְיוֹן, which are also often translated as "poor" in the OT. When Jesus announced this blessing to the poor applying Isa 61:1 to his own situation, his listeners, those who were attracted by hi ministry, were mainly the social and religious outcasts of the Jewish religious society. Therefore, although their situation was not exactly the same with them, Jesus' followers stood in continuity with the poor of the OT (especially with Isa 61:1), because they too stood empty handed, without a power base and pretense before God. They were the ones who fully depended upon God's mercy (Luke 18:9-14).[351]

When Matthew adapted this beatitude to the situation of his community, he and his community would have been, indeed, reminded of God's promise through the prophet Isaiah. However, they would surely have understood it as Jesus' message to their own situation, or rather as Jesus' announcement of the fulfilment of God's promise through the prophet Isaiah to their own situation. Therefore, in

---

The whole thrust of the beatitudes is upon the present blessedness of the disciples, and this blessedness is rather hollow if their actual experience of this blessings is postponed until millennial times. Therefore it is better to take the present tense as a simple statement of the disciples' present experience of the kingdom. Granted, their present experience of the kingdom is partial, but it is genuine. Granted, the disciples' hope is primarily in the future eschaton, but they have already experienced its saving power. God has already begun His eschatological work of blessing those who acknowledge their spiritual bankruptcy and hunger for spiritual fullness. In the eschaton they will be filled full.

348 Guelich, *The Sermon on the Mount: A Foundation for Understanding*, 97.

349 *Ibid.*, 78.

350 *Ibid.*, 69.

351 *Ibid.*, 71.

the context of the Matthean community, the "poor in spirit" of the first Matthean beatitude would primarily refer to the Matthean community, who suffered severe socio-political and economic hardships (along with other Jews) in the hands of the Romans and their representatives, and further religious persecutions in the hands of both the Jews and the Gentiles. They are, therefore, the recipients of the blessing of the kingdom of God/Heaven announced by Jesus. The kingdom of God/Heaven already belongs to them because they put their complete trust in God in the midst of their sufferings. They can begin to experience the blessings of the kingdom from now itself in their relationship with Jesus, although partially, because Jesus had already inaugurated that future kingdom. They will experience the blessings of that kingdom in full at the eschaton. That means that there is an apocalyptic reversal of fate awaiting them in the eschatological kingdom. Those who are materially in a better situation within the community are are not excluded because, they shared the same persecutions and hardships with all other members. The community as a whole are powerless before their persecutors, and all of them are one in spirit and poor in spirit. [352] Yet, Matthew might have an apprehension that those few well-to-do members of his community may feel excluded if he use Luke's term "blessed are the poor" because of their material well-being in spite of all their sufferings along with all other members. Therefore, he replaces it with "poor in spirit" which has more or less the same meaning, but which is easier to understand for those well-to-do members among his community.

V. 4. μακάριοι οἱ πενθοῦντες, ὅτι αὐτοὶ παρακληθήσονταὶ ***"Blessed are those who mourn, for they will be comforted."***[353] The second beatitude is ascribed to

352 This understanding seems to reflect the meaning of the first beatitude as Jesus spoke it (as found in Luke 6:20), as well as its OT background in Isa 61:1ff. Dillon, "The Text of the Sermon on the Mount," 50, rightly observes that what the prophet Isaiah principally addressed was the *state of mind and spirit*, that is *the oppressed spirit* of the Jewish exiles after they return from captivity, although material poverty and physical distress were certainly part of their condition. The two Hebrew words עָנִי and דַּל which are most frequently translated as πτωχός in the LXX also "referred more to the *weak and vulnerable position in society* which less fortunte people held" rather than "poor" in the sense of "having little of this world's goods." "The Hebrew words thus expressed a *social inferiority* which made weaker people prey to those who were more powerful, brought them continual misfortunes and humiliations, and made it extremely difficult for them to obtain justice from the society in which they ranked so low." Even " 'the poor' of the first beatitude, as Jesus spoke it, are the powerless of the present order, whose condition in this world gives them nowhere to turn except to their Creator. They stand before God without resources or achievements of their own to rely on, hence they can hope for salvation *by him alone*, i.e., *by grace alone.* According to Jesus' proclamation, this is not simply the way some people stand before God, this is the way all must stand before him in order to experience his reality, his salvation."

353 Several MSS, particularly Western and Syriac readings (such as D 33 it$^{a, aur, e, d, ff^1, g^1, h, k, l}$ vg syr^{c} cop^{boms} Origen Eusebian Canons Chrysostom$^{1/2}$ Theodoret^{vit}; Hilary Ambrose Jerome Augustine), reverse the present order of the second (5:4) and third beatitude (5:5). However, the present order is attested in several major MSS including Codex Sinaiticus (א) and Codex

the dominical saying, which was preserved in Q. It has its basis in Isaiah 61:2, which talks about the comfort for all those who mourn. Its parallel is found in Luke 6:21b. Probably Matthew's version represents the original Q form, which would suggest that the Lukan version represents authorial redacted form.

μακάριοι οἱ πενθοῦντές ***"blessed are those who mourn"***. The parallel passage in Luke 6: 21b has μακάριοι οἱ κλαίοντες νῦν, ὅτι γελάσετε, "*blessed are you who weep now.*" It is uncertain whether Matthew drew this from the same source as Luke and redacted it,[354] or whether he drew it from a tradition different from that of Luke and preserves what he found in is tradition.[355] According to W. D. Davies and Dale C. Allison, Jr., οἱ κλαίοντες in Luke is probably redactional and οἱ πενθοῦντες in Matthew is probably from the Q source, because πενθοῦντες has a parallel in the third Lukan woe: "woe to you that laugh now, for you shall mourn and weep" (Luke 6:25). On the other hand, there is a possibility that the first evangelist redacted it, if he tries to connect the first, third and fourth beatitudes with Isa 61:1-3, as Guelich suggests, because Isa 61:2 speaks of comfort for those who mourn[356] (but, note that Davies and Allison, Jr. reject Guelich's suggestion[357]). It could also be that neither of them has preserved the original wording of Q.[358] According to Ulrich Luz, the replacement of κλαίοντες "weeping" with πενθοῦντες "mourning" already took place before Matthew.[359] In any case this second beatitude apparently alludes to Isa 61:2 (in the LXX), in which the one anointed by the Spirit says that he has come παρακαλέσαι πάντας τοὺς πενθοῦντας, "to comfort all those who mourn."[360] Because of its apparent connection with Isa 61:2, and in view of the fact that this beatitude goes back to

---

Vaticunus (B) (and other MSS such as - C W Δ Θ $f f^{3}$ 28 157 180 205 565 579 597 700 892 1006 1010 1071 1241 1243 1292 1342 1424 1505 *Byz* [E Σ] *Lect* $\text{it}^{\text{b, f, q}}$ $\text{syr}^{\text{s, p. h. pal}}$ $\text{cop}^{\text{sa, meg, bo}}$ arm eth geo slav Macarius/Symeon Chrusostom[1/2]; tertullian Chromatius). The present order has a stronger manuscript support and therefore the editors of the present UBS Greek text adjudge the present text as quite reliable and in their grading system, they give "B" mark that is next to the highest mark "A." See *The Greek New Testament*, 4th Revised Edition (D-Stuttgart: United Bible Societies, 1998), 11.

354 As Gundry suggests in Robert H. Gundry, *Matthew: A Commentary on His Handbook for a Mixed Church Under Persecution* (Grand Rapids, Michigan: William B. Eerdmans Publishing Company, 1982), 68.

355 As Hagner suggests in Hagner, *Matthew 1-1 3*, 89.

356 Guelich, "The Matthean Beatitudes," 426-432. See also Guelich, *The Sermon on the Mount: A Foundation for Understanding*, 80.

357 Davies and Allison, Jr., *Matthew*, Vol. I, 434-438.

358 *Ibid.*, 447.

359 Luz, *Matthew 1-7*, 235. Here, Luz maintains, however, that the meaning in Matthew is probably the same with that of Luke's. πενθέω comes from Isa 61:2f.; and the subject there is mourning in this world quite generally; and it particularly refers to the mourning for Jerusalem. Therefore, both in Luke and Matthew, "with 'mourning' is encompassed mourning of this eon which in the coming eon will be replaced by comfort."

360 Hagner, *Matthew 1-13*, 92.

Jesus' speech (as maintained in the redaction of the passage above), it is highly possible that Jesus uses an Aramaic word in the second beatitude, which was equivalent to the Hebrew word אֲבֵלִים of Isa 61:2 translated in the LXX as πενθοῦ ντας.[361] Then, Jesus' word was translated into Greek as πενθοῦντες, and preserved in Q, and Matthew took it over, as he found it very appropriate for his context.

The term πενθοῦντες comes from the verb πενθέω/πενθεῖν. In the Greek usage the verb usually means, "to mourn," "to grieve" (intrans.), and also "to bewail" (with accusative object). The noun πένθος can mean both "sorrow," "grief," and also a painful event or fact. Originally πενθεῖν or πένθος denotes sorrow of heart. However, such expression is at least associated in most instances with outward expression by tears or laments. πένθος can also have the sense of public mourning. The words πενθεῖν or πένθος are used especially for mourning for the dead although they are used for other sufferings as well.[362] The two words πένθος and πενθεῖν are frequently used in the LXX, mostly for the derivatives from the stem אבל. Both the noun אֵבֶל and the verb אָבַל denote sorrow expressed in tears, lamentations and rites, especially mourning for the dead, which includes individual sorrow of heart (e.g., Gen 37:34; Dan 10:2).[363] The use of the word (אֲבֵלִים – pl) in Isa 61:2 also may be understood as primarily referring to the mourning for the dead, and in addition to that the mourning for the loss of possessions and land rights.[364] According to Bultmann, even in the NT πενθεῖν and πένθος denote the sorrow expressed in lamentation and tears. It is however, neither open lamentation nor quiet sorrow of the heart, but it means a passionate grief that leads to corresponding action. πενθεῖν/πένθος in some instances, such as Matt 9:15; Rev 18:7f., and probably 1Cor 5:2, seems to indicate the specific sense of mourning for the dead.[365]

Thus, the second beatitude can be understood as a promise of divine comfort for those who mourn because of deep sorrow in their heart, the cause of which may be of various natures, regardless of the ways in which they express their sorrow. However, scholars' opinions are varied on the question of the people who are referred to by πενθοῦντες in the second Matthean beatitude, and of the reason(s) behind their sorrow and mourning.

According to Albright and Mann "those who mourn" refers to "those who lament the sin which mars God's choice of Israel" (cf. Isa 61:2), thus referring "to those who mourn man's disobedience to God."[366] Bultmann maintains that the blessing of the second beatitude takes up the prophetic promises and it is to

361 This is suggested by fact that the first three beatitudes ascribed to Jesus are apparently composed on the basis of Isaiah 61. See Davies and Allison, Jr., *Matthew*, Vol. I, 438.

362 Bultmann, "πένθος, πενθέω," 40-41.

363 *Ibid.*, 41-42.

364 See Watts, *Isaiah 34-66*, 303.

365 Bultmann, "πένθος, πενθέω," 42.

366 Albright and Mann, *Matthew*, 46.

be taken eschatologically. According to him οἱ πενθοῦντες here refers to those who suffer under the present aeon, which is an aeon of suffering, and those who see this suffering aeon as it is, but are not led astray by its charms. At the same time, it is also evident that all those who mourn are not called blessed. And, παρακληθήσονται here denotes eschatological consolation in the "kingdom of heaven" for those who mourn because of their suffering in this present aeon. Also, πενθοῦντες here is not to be narrowly understood as penitent sorrow for sin, but it cannot be excluded either.[367] While he accepts that πενθοῦντες here encompasses mourning of this aeon, Ulrich Luz asserts that he does not see "any examples from contemporary literature in which πενθέω without further additional definition carries the meaning of mourning over imperfection or sin."[368] Hagner is of the view that the focus even in this second beatitude is the eschatological expectation of the downtrodden and the poor, those who suffer. What is proclaimed here is, then, that the time of their salvation/comfort has found its beginning as the kingdom has arrived in the person of Jesus. Therefore, they have to rejoice now, even in their troubled circumstances.[369] Balz suggests that while this could be its meaning from its Old Testament basis, in the context of Matthew's gospel it rather seems to refer to the mourning/suffering of the poor and the downtrodden because of the seeming slowness of God's justice.[370] According to W. D. Davies and Dale C. Allison, Jr., this verse reflects its Old Testament source in Isa 61:2. In Isaiah, the people of God mourn because of the oppression they suffered in the hands of their heathen captors. They mourn because the righteous people of God suffer while their wicked captors prosper, and God has not yet acted to reverse the situation. Matt 5: 4 reflects a similar situation. The righteous people of God mourn because they are still persecuted and they are still waiting to see the kingdom of God in its fullness (5:10-12); they have not yet seen the twelve sitting on the twelve thrones judging the twelve tribes of Israel (19:28); they have not yet seen the Son of Man coming in his glory (24:29-31); and God's will is not done on earth as it is in heaven (6:10). In sum, the wicked are holding the upper hand against the righteous (2:1-23; 5:10-12; 7:15-22; 13:53-58; 21:12-13; 26:1; 27:66). The righteous are mourning because of all these circumstances as they are waiting for the eschatological reversal.[371] Guelich also maintains that the

367 Bultmann, "πένθος, πενθέω," 43.

368 Luz, *Matthew 1-7*, 235.

369 Hagner, *Matthew 1-13*, 92.

370 The LXX frequently uses the verb πενθέω to refer to grief in the face of death or God's punishment. However, the verb here refers to "the grief of those who suffer under this world and place their hope in God alone." H. Balz, "πενθέω *pentheō*," *EDNT*, Vol. 3, edited by Horst Balz and Gerhard Schneider (Grand Rapids, Michigan: William B. Eerdmans Publishing Company, 1993 [1982-83]), 69.

371 Davies and Allison, Jr., *Matthew*, Vol. 1, 448. Here, Davies and Allison, Jr. note that the seeming contradiction between Matt 5:4 and 9:15 (where Jesus says that the wedding guests cannot mourn as long as the bridegroom is with them), "is only one aspect of the tension created

meaning of "those who mourn" here would at least partially be conditioned by Isaiah's context because Isa 1-2 played an influential role in shaping this beatitude. "The bereavement of the mourners in Zion," he says, "stems from their national loss resulting from their sin and God's judgment." Therefore, "*those who mourn* here has the more comprehensive sense of Isa 61:2-3, an inclusive grief that refers to the disenfranchised, contrite, and bereaved," but not only one's expression of sorrow for one's sin or grief surrounding death. In fact, "it is an expression of the intense sense of loss, helplessness, and despair."[372]

In fact, in Isa 61:2 πενθοῦντες refers to the mourning of Israel for the loss of lives of their relatives and friends at the hands of their enemies, as well as the loss of their possessions and land rights to their heathen captors.[373] When Jesus taught this beatitude to his followers, he would have said it on the basis of Isa 61:2, but the implication of the "mourning" would have not been exactly the same because the contexts were different. While his listeners would have been reminded of the words of the prophet Isaiah, they would surely have applied it to their own context. So, that they would have listened to Jesus as proclaiming a message of comfort to their mourning due to the various hardships they were undergoing, some of which may be similar to the hardships undergone by the people addressed by Isaiah, while some of their sufferings would have been certainly different. Given the fact that most of Jesus' followers were poor and downtrodden people, afflicted with the concomitant problems such as illness and death, the mourning in this beatitude, in its original context of Jesus' teaching, could largely refer to grief because of bereavement, affliction with acute illness and lack of proper treatment, heavy burdens because of heavy debts amidst their acute poverty, and other hardships caused by the imperial powers, etc.[374]

When Matthew took over this beatitude, and especially the term πενθοῦντες, he would have remembered in his mind its implication in Isa 61:2, as well as its implication in Jesus' context. So also, his intended audience, the Jewish Christians, would have been reminded, especially of Isa 61:2 when they read/listened to it. However, both Matthew and his intended readers would certainly have applied

---

by the fact that the kingdom of God is both present and coming in the gospel tradition." Therefore, "while in 5:4 the weight comes down on the future coming of the kingdom, in 9:15 the presence of the kingdom is being proclaimed."

372 Guelich, *The Sermon on the Mount: A Foundation for Understanding*, 80-81.

373 Watts, *Isaiah 34-66*, 303.

374 Warren Carter, reading from a socio-political and religious perspective, maintains that on the basis Isa 61:1-3 what the people of God mourn or lament is the destructive impact of imperial powers such as Babylon (and Rome) which oppress God's people. Carter, *Matthew and the Margins*, 132. Asserting that the second beatitude refers to the mourning of real deaths, W. R. Domeris, also says, "to the people of Jesus' time, with a life expectation of only 25 years, death was a constant companion. Not the quiet death of a hospital ward, the privilege of the well-to-do, but the brutal and violent death of the poor." William R. Domeris, "Exegesis and Proclamation. 'Blessed are You …' (Mt 5:1-12)," *JournTheolSAfric* 73 (D 1990), 69.

it to their own mourning caused by the various hardships they were undergoing. Matthew's community had various reasons to mourn. First, (particularly for the Jewish members of the Matthean community) the impact of the War affected them like other Jews, especially in their social and economic life. The destruction of Jerusalem (and probably also of the Temple) was painful to them in as much as it was painful to other Jews. Like other Jews, they must have lost some of their relatives and friends in the War. They must have lost their possessions. They were stricken with poverty in the aftermath of the War, and they were burdened with heavy taxes in the midst of their poverty, which exacerbated their poverty and resulted in illness and death.[375] Second, apart from their suffering alongside other Jews they were also suffering various kinds of persecutions, including killing, from both the Jews and the Gentiles. Third, as it was the case in many other cities, it is obvious that in the unhygienic situation of the first century Antioch, and the repeated natural calamities, which struck it,[376] death was a regular experience of the people of Antioch, and apparently, the community members of Matthew would not have been excluded from such experience. Consequently, death was one of the most common experiences of the Matthean community.[377] Therefore, viewing from the context of the Matthean community, πενθοῦντες of the second Matthean beatitude encompasses *mourning* because of all kinds of sufferings, but particularly sufferings because of and at the hands of their adversaries. This is the meaning even in Isa 61:2, which forms the basis of the second Matthean beatitude.

ὅτι αὐτοι παρακληθήσονται, ***"for they will be comforted."*** The parallel passage in Luke has ὅτι γελάσετε, "for you will laugh." Since, it appears that Luke redacted the first part of his third beatitude, that is that he replaced the word "mourn" with "weep" (as it is contended above),[378] the word "laugh" also seems to be used by Luke to correlate with the word "weep" and probably under

375 According to Rukundwa and Van Aarde, who view from post-colonial perspective, "people mourned and longed for justice and righteousness, because they had been denied justice and they lived under the pressure of debts, taxes and landlessness," and in short, they lived constantly under the shadow of death. Rukundwa & Van Aarde, "Revisiting Justice…," 934.

376 For a vivid highlight of the unhygienic situation of the ancient Greco-Roman city, and for a list of natural and social disaster that frequently struck Antioch in the first century, See Stark, "Antioch as the Social Situation for Matthew's Gospel," 189-208.

377 Viewing from post-colonial perspective Rukundwa and Van Aarde maintain, "Matthean audience were not strangers to mourning. They too fell victim to daily injustice and violence perpetrated by brutal colonial powers. Those who were not killed by the sword were killed by famine and disease due to a lack of health care." Rukundwa & Van Aarde, "Revisiting Justice…," 934.

378 See also Neil J. McEleney, "The Beatitudes of the Sermon on the Mount/Plain," CathBibQuart 43 (1981): 9 [1-13]. Here, McEleney mentions that κλαίω is a characteristically Lukan.

the influence of Eccl 3:4 where weeping and laughing are paired as opposites.[379] Therefore, it seems that Matthew retains the original Q form.

The verb παρακληθήσονται here is a divine passive and it assumes God as the acting subject.[380] The "divine passive" means that the Jews, so as not to pronounce the name of God, often used the passive voice to speak of God. Therefore, a Jew who reads- "they shall be comforted" - would understand at once that God is the one who will comfort.[381] According to Guelich, the passive form and the future tense (παρακληθήσονται) here express the divine comfort integral to the promise for Israel's future (e.g., Isa 49:13; 51:12; 66:13; Jer 31:13).[382]

The verb παρακαλεῖν originally goes back to the sense of "to call someone to oneself." However, in ordinary Greek usage, the word is used in great variations, such as "to call to," "to beseech," "to exhort," and "to comfort." The word is rarely used in the sense of "to comfort" and even where it is used in this sense, it mostly refers to the consolation that is at the level of exhortation or encouragement to those who sorrow.[383] However, the use of the word in the LXX changed its significance. In the LXX the word παρακαλεῖν is used for translating about 15 Hebrew words, and it is also used in many verses with no Hebrew equivalent, thus indicating either a free rendering or an introduction of a new sense because of the deficient understanding of the basic Hebrew. When the LXX translated different Hebrew words with παρακαλεῖν, however, it concentrated on divine and human comfort, referring to comfort in bereavement (e.g., Gen 24:67; 37:35; 38:12, etc.), words of comfort in any human grief (e.g., Judith 6:20; Job 2:11, etc.), encouragement (e.g., Deut 3:28) or friendly exhortation (e.g., Esther 5: 1e, 2b). When the word is used in those parts of the LXX, which are not translations of the Hebrew Bible, the sense of divine and human comfort is almost completely absent. The case is the same with the extra-canonical writings and Hellenistic Judaism outside the Greek translation of the Old Testament. The most common Hebrew equivalent for παρακαλεῖν in the LXX is נחם, which has an outstanding sense of "to comfort," in many verses where it stands for the Greek translation of παρακαλεῖν. And, the LXX especially used παρακαλεῖν "to promise and to testify to the comfort of God which is to be given to his people when under divine judgment, or to the individual in time of temptation."[384] Therefore, according to Schmitz, this is the sense in which it is used in the second Matthean beatitude. It

379 See John Nolland, *Luke 1-9:20*, WBC, Vol. 35A (Dallas, Texas: Word Books, Publishers, 1989), 284. See also McEleney, "The Beatitudes of the Sermon on the Mount/Plain." Here, McEleney mentions that γελάω is correlative to κλαίω.

380 Gundry, *Matthew: A Commentary on His Handbook*, 69.

381 Newman, Jr., "Some Translational Notes on the Beatitudes," 115.

382 Guelich, *The Sermon on the Mount: A Foundation for Understanding*, 81.

383 Schmitz, "παρακαλεω, παρακαλησις, 'Gommon Greek Usage' and 'in Greek Judaism,'" *TDNT*, Vol. V (Grand Rapids, Michigan: William B. Eerdmans Publishing Company, 1967), 773-776.

384 *Ibid.*, 776-779.

refers here to the eschatological comforting act of God, which "already reaches into the present time to the degree that the πενθοῦντες who stand under the promise are already μακάριοι," in as much as the rich in Luke 6:24, conversely, "have already received their consolation in their riches, so that they cannot look for the consolation of God in the world to come."[385] According to Guelich, "the comfort promised in this Beatitude is the ultimate consolation and encouragement that God alone can effect for those whose mourning expresses their sense of total loss and helplessness." Guelich further says that the promise in this beatitude is not simply a repetition of Isa 61:2-3. "The fulfilment motif in Jesus' ministry sets the promise of the Beatitude in another dimension. The mourner is pronounced *blessed* by Jesus, in whom God is already at work fulfilling Isaiah 61 and through whom the consummation will be accomplished."[386]

Based on the above analysis, we may put it briefly now, that the second beatitude is a promise of ultimate comfort from God to His faithful believers, from their *mourning* due to all kinds of sufferings. The promise is a reality now itself ("blessed are ..."), and its consummation will come in the eschatological kingdom of God/Heaven ("for they will be comforted").

In the context of the Matthean community, the second beatitude would function as a promise of ultimate comfort from God, because of and through Jesus Christ, from their *mourning* due to all kinds of sufferings, which include their sufferings - under the oppressive Romans administration, under the persecution from both the Jews and the Gentiles, and because of all the poverty-related illnesses and death, as well as because of natural calamities, etc. That means that they will experience God's comfort in its fullness, in the eschatological kingdom of God as against all their mourning at present. That is the basic message carried by the apocalyptic nature of this beatitude. At the same time, however, it would function as a comfort at present as well, although partially, because "the comfort from God" is one of the attributes of the "kingdom of heaven," which is already a present reality in and through the ministry of Jesus, although it will come into its fullness at the end of the age.[387]

V. 5. μακάριοι οἱ πραεῖς, ὅτι αὐτοὶ κληρονομήσουσιν τὴν γῆν. ***"Blessed are the meek, for they will inherit the earth."*** The third beatitude is ascribed to Q^{mt}. Apparently it has been formulated on the basis of Jesus' own life and teaching as found in Matt 11:29; 18:4; 21:5, and its formulation seems to have

385 Schmitz, "παρακαλεω and παρακαλησις in the NT," *TDNT*, Vol. V (Grand Rapids, Michigan: William B. Eerdmans Publishing Company, 1967), 798.

386 Guelich, *The Sermon on the Mount: A Foundation for Understanding*, 81.

387 As noted above, Guelich rightly observes, "The mourner is pronounced *blessed* by Jesus, in whom God is already at work fulfilling Isaiah 61 and through whom the consummation will be accomplished." Guelich, *The Sermon on the Mount: A Foundation for Understanding*, 81.

been influenced by Ps 37:11.[388] Luke does not have a parallel beatitude. Matthew probably took over from Q^{mt} as it is. There is no trace of redaction.[389]

μακάριοι οἱ πραεῖς, ***"blessed are the meek."*** πραεῖς is the adjective, nominative, plural form of πραΰς, which, in the Greek usage denotes "gentle" and "pleasant." When it is used of things, it refers to "mild," "soothing," and "allaying." When it is used of animals, it means tamed, or calmed after having been irritated. When it is used of persons, it denotes "mild," "friendly," "gentle," and "pleasant" as opposite to "rough," "hard," and "violent or angry." The adverb πράως is often used to refer to the quiet and friendly composure which does not become embittered or angry at unpleasant people or fate. It is not a passive submission, but an active attitude and deliberate acceptance.[390] The noun form πραΰτης is used of "mild and gentle friendliness" in opposite to "roughness," "bad temper," "sudden anger" and "brusqueness."[391]

While the Hebrew synonyms עָנִי , עָנָו , דַּל , אֶבְיוֹן , and רָשׁ are variously translated with the Greek words πένης, πτωχός, ταπεινός, and πραΰς in the LXX, πραΰς is the most common rendering of עָנָו. The root of both עָנִי and עָנָו is ענה which means "to find oneself in a stunted, humble, lowly position."[392] עָנָו first means "the one who is in subjection," then it takes on the predominant sense of "one who feels that he is a servant in relation to God and who subjects himself to Him quietly and without resistance," and the Greek term πραΰς which the translators of the LXX chose as the best rendering of עָנָו "often has the sense of the calm acceptance of fate or human injustice."[393] In the Pentateuch (LXX) the adjective πραΰς is used only at Num 12:3 with reference to Moses. It is understood to be a more recent addition probably on the basis of the later ideal of piety or the Hellenistic concept of the ideal ruler (cf. Sir 45:4).[394] No pre-exilic prophecy refers to the gentle and patient believer.[395] Even if that were the case, the meaning of the word in relation to Moses would be the same. It could simply mean that Moses was not self-assertive.[396] However, it seems that the idea becomes more important from the context of the exile. Thus, the king of salvation is depicted as the king of peace in Zech 9:9f. According to Hauck and Schulz, in the context of the exile, "the quiet, patient, hopeful, expectant bearing" of their severe destiny

388 Schweizer, *The Good News According to Matthew*, 83.

389 Guelich, *The Sermon on the Mount: A Foundation for Understanding*, 81. See also "The Forms, Sources, and *Sitz im Leben* of the Matthean Beatitudes."

390 F. Hauck/S. Schulz, "πραΰς, πραΰτης," *TDNT*, Vol. VI (Grand Rapids, Michigan: William B. Eerdmans Publishing Company, 1968), 645.

391 Hauck/Schulz, "πραΰς, πραΰτης," 646.

392 *Ibid.*, 647.

393 *Ibid.*

394 *Ibid.*

395 *Ibid.*

396 Philip J. Budd, *Numbers*, WBC, Vol. 5 (Waco, Texas: Word Books Publishers, 1984), 136.

by the Israelites, "without resistance or complaint, without vehement anger, is a sign of piety which stands out sharply from an earlier even disposition in times of national prosperity."[397] So, in the Old Testament, "meekness" (πραΰτης - the noun form of πραΰς) "is based on the eschatological hope (Ps 76:9) that God will judge (147:6; 149:4) and give the land to the lowly, that is those who wait (37:9)." This eschatological hope is connected in Ps 37:9-11 with the promises of the land, which were originally given to Abraham and his descendants and with it the Psalmist refers to his own age.[398]

In the New Testament Paul uses the noun πραΰτης once in Gal 5:23. It is translated as "gentleness" in most of the English versions. The adjective genitive singular πραέως is used in 1Pet 3:4. It is translated as "gentle" in most of the English versions. Besides these two, it is only Matthew in the whole of the New Testament, who uses either the adjective or noun. Besides the adjective nominative plural πραεῖς in the third beatitude, he uses the adjective singular πραΰς twice in reference to Jesus in 11:29 and 21:5. In these two occurrences, most of the English versions translate the word as "gentle," "humble" and "meek." The word "lowly" is used only once for its occurrence in 21:5 by NKJV.

The third beatitude is attributed to Q^{mt} and it is basically a quotation of the LXX of Ps 36[37]:11 - οἱ δὲ πραεῖς κληρονομήσουσιν γῆν, "the meek shall inherit the land (NRSV)."[399] The Hebrew word translated as πραεῖς here is עֲנָוִים, *'ănāwîm*. On the basis of the underlying Hebrew word common to them, many scholars take πραεῖς here and πτωχοί of 5:3 as more or less synonymous. For example, Donald Hagner, noting the occurrence of the same word in Isa 61:1 and its translation in the LXX as πτωχοὶ "poor," contends that the thought of the third beatitude is approximately the same thought of the first beatitude. He suggests that πραεῖς here does not refer to those who are submissive, mild, and unassertive but to those who are humbled because of oppression by the ungodly. Such, people have no choice but only to depend upon God. Hagner further mentions that the Qumran community took Ps 37 as prophesying their struggles with their enemies and saw themselves as the ones about to experience the proof which would come with messianic fulfilment (4QpPs 37).[400] Schweizer also points out that the words for both "poor" and "meek" here are almost identical in Aramaic, and he suggests that the better translation may be "powerless."[401] Davies and Allison, Jr. also, supporting Schweizer's suggestion, contend that "the πραεῖς are not so much actively seeking to avoid hubris (an attitude) as they are, as a matter of fact, powerless in the eyes of the world (a condition)."[402] Guelich

397 Hauck/Schulz, "πραΰς, πραΰτης," 648.

398 Hauck/Schulz, "πραΰς, πραΰτης," 648.

399 Luz, *Matthew 1-7*, 236. For other possible parallels, see Ps 25:13; En 5:9; Did 3:7.

400 Hagner, *Matthew 1-13*, 92. See also Harrington, *The Gospel of Matthew*, 79.

401 Schweizer, *The Good News According to Matthew*, 83, 89-90.

402 Davies and Allison, Jr., *Matthew*, Vol. I, 449.

suggests that two different but synonymous terms such as *'nyym/'nwm* (of Isa 61:1) and *'nwm* (of Ps 37 [36LXX]:11) probably underlie the *poor* of Matt 5:3 and the *meek* of Matt 5:5 respectively, or more probably an identical term *'nwm* (5:5) underlies them. He maintains that even if the two terms, *'nyym* and *'nwm*, underlie them, the only possible difference between the two terms would be one of emphasis. While *'nwm* = πραεῖς focuses on one's dependent relationship to God, *'nyym*=πτωχοί focuses more on one's socio-economic status. Even then, these two terms were used interchangeably in Qumran, thus indicating that they were not exclusive. Moreover, there is no evidence that the *poor* in Luke 6:20, regardless of its underlying Hebrew term, was ever intended in an exclusively socio-economic manner. "Therefore, *the meek*, like *the poor*, refers to those who stand empty-handed before God in total dependence upon him. The term in no way connotes weakness or softness, an attitude rather than a condition."[403]

Some other scholars, however, see ethical connotation in πραεῖς of the third beatitude. For example, Schnackenburg, points out that while this is not a specific appeal for non-violence "it does carry the connotation of peaceful behaviour."[404] Gundry sees Jesus as an example of meekness in Matthew corresponding to Moses (Num 12:3).[405] Ulrich Luz also points out that for the people living in proximity of Semitic languages, the word πραΰς means "humble." He further notes that Matthew's knowledge of the sense is also demonstrated in 11:29 and 21:5 where the element of non-violence and kindness is included. He also observes that also in Jewish parenesis, the nuances of humility and kindness can hardly be separated from each other such that πραΰτης is humility demonstrated in kindness.[406] According to Benedict Green, humility in the third beatitude "is to be seen as in general a humility towards people, which can be qualified as gentle, non-assertive and non-violent."[407]

It is assumed in this study that there is, in fact, a close relationship between πραεῖς and πτωχοὶ, especially in terms of the underlying Hebrew word, that is עֲנָוִים. At the same time, however, they are used in their respective places with difference in emphasis, but without negating or excluding each other. To be more precise, while πτωχοί of the first beatitude mainly expresses the humble frame of mind of the powerless and the downtrodden people before God, πραεῖς of the third beatitude emphasizes an ethical attitude of humility, that is, peaceful behaviour of God's people before fellow human beings, while an endurance of their oppressed situation with humble mind is not excluded. This is also indicated by the attitude of Jesus found in Matt 11:29 and 21:5, which apparently form the basis on which the third beatitude has been formulated. The fact that the

403 Guelich, *The Sermon on the Mount: A Foundation for Understanding*, 82-83.

404 Schnackenburg, *The Gospel of Matthew*, 48.

405 Gundry, *Matthew: A Commentary on His Handbook*, 69.

406 Luz, *Matthew 1-7*, 236.

407 Green, *Matthew, Poet of the Beatitudes*, 188.

third beatitude is a pre-Matthean addition also supports this view because the other three ethical beatitudes infused into the three dominical beatitudes are also ethical in nature. It may be further substantiated in the following ways: First of all, the Hebrew word עֲנָוִים is translated in different ways in different places in the Old Testament, suggesting that the same Hebrew word which can have different meanings (or different emphasis among various synonyms) in different contexts is rendered in different ways in the Greek language on the basis of its implication or emphasis in different contexts.[408] Therefore, the translation of עֲנָוִים as πτωχοὶ in Isa 61:1 (the basis of the first beatitude) and as πραεῖς in Ps 37:11 (the basis of the third beatitude) also must have been done with a different connotation or emphasis behind them. Consequently, it is appropriate to assume that the word πραεῖς of Matt 5:5 could have a different connotation/emphasis from that of πτωχοὶ of Matt 5:3 in Matthew's context.[409] Second, it is only Matthew, among all the gospel writers, who uses the adjective πραεῖς both in its plural and singular forms. The only other appearance of adjective in the whole of the New Testament is 1Peter 3:4, and the noun form πραΰτης appears once in Gal 5:23. The word πτωχοὶ, on the other hand, appears twice in Luke (6:20 and 7:22), and once in 2Cor. 6:10. This suggests that the word πραεῖς must have special significance in Matthew's context. At this juncture the socio-historical context of Matthew seems to hold significance in suggesting that the word πραεῖς emphasizes an active attitude of "meekness" "humbleness," which includes a passive submission (with one's conscious choice) to endure difficult situations with humility. This may further be elaborated based on the socio-historical context of the Matthean community. In the previous chapter, we have identified various situations in which Matthew's community was caught up in different difficult situations. First, they were in strong opposition from formative Judaism, because of which they suffered even persecutions. In this context, the third beatitude would be an important exhortation to them, as followers of Jesus Christ, to endure such situations with meekness. Besides, they were called to carry on their mission to the Jews in spite of all the hard oppositions they met from them. In this context, meekness would be a very important strategy for their mission. Second, we propose in the previous chapter that there was an unequal partnership between the Jewish members and the Gentile members of the Matthean community.[410] To be more precise, the Gentile

408 It is translated as - πτωχοὶ in Isa 61:1; πραεῖς in Ps 37:11; πτωχός in Ps 9:19; πτωχοὶ in Ps 69[68-LXX]:33; and Isa 29:19; πτωχῶν in Amos 2:7; as πενήτων in Ps 10:17; as πένητες in Ps 22[21-LXX]:27; as πραεῖς in Ps 25[24-LXX]:9 (two times); 34[33-LXX]:3; 147[146-LXX]:6; 149:4; and as ταπεινοὺς in Isa 32:7.

409 Betz maintains that "it would be a mistaken conclusion to take the MT of Ps 37:11 using the term ענוים and interpret the Greek equivalent on the basis of the Hebrew instead of the Greek. The opposite is the case: as in many other instances the LXX translators have chosen the Greek concept of *πραΰς* ("meek") to make the Jewish *'ănāwîm* piety intelligible for Greek-speaking readers." Betz, *The Sermon on the Mount*, 126.

410 See "The Ethnic Composition of Matthew's Community" in the previous chapter.

members were not able to have full table fellowship with the Jewish members. In this situation, we could fairly assume that there would have been a certain amount of tension between the Jewish members and the Gentile members, which could lead to open hostility at any time. Especially the Gentile members were likely to have a certain amount of hostility to the situation they were put into. Although they could adjust to that situation in normal situations, there would have been a possibility of enraging them if they were pressed further. In this circumstance, the third beatitude would be a befitting exhortation, to emulate Jesus' meekness for the unity of the church. In addition, such exhortation would be easier for the Gentile members to accept, as Matthew at the same time gives a clear hint to the failure of the mission to the Jews and more emphasis on the prospect of mission to the Gentiles. As such, Schweizer seems right in maintaining that it is an exhortation to the community to "serve one another according to the rule of love, without regard to any consequences of reward or punishment."[411] Third, we also see that the Matthean community was not in good terms with their Gentile neighbours. They have been persecuted and were in fear of further persecution along with other Jews. Even if they were not persecuted, their relation with their Gentile neighbours was not at all cordial. Therefore, as it is human nature, it would be very easy for the members of the Matthean community to show an unfriendly attitude towards their Gentile neighbours as much as it was shown to them, and to retaliate in the same manner whatever they experienced from them. In such situations the call to be meek, befitting to be followers of Jesus Christ, would be very important. This view is further supported by the greater emphasis given to the Gentile mission. That means that, as the Gentiles were becoming more and more of their prime target in their mission it would be very important to show meekness, gentleness, friendliness toward them, regardless of whatever experience they had from them. Therefore, the socio-historical context in which Matthew's gospel was written, suggests that while the third beatitude could refer to the oppressed situation of the Matthean community, the emphasis is more on an exhortation to exhibit a meek, humble, friendly, and gentle life, especially to endure difficult situations they were going through with humility (with one's conscious choice). While Matthew might have such socio-historical implications in his mind when he took over this beatitude, it is above all the situation which Jesus himself had undergone, and it is his own nature as well (see Matt 11:29 and 21:5). Therefore, Matthew must remember its validity for all the followers of Jesus Christ, particularly for those who undergo difficult situations because of Jesus Christ. It is true that the Qumran community took Ps 37 as prophesying their struggles with their enemies, and saw themselves as the congregation of the poor who would accept the appointed time of affliction and wait for messianic

411 Schweizer, *The Good News According to Matthew*, 90.

deliverance (4QpPs 37).[412] However, it would be correct to assume that even the Qumran community interpreted the Psalm on the basis of their situation and theology, and therefore it cannot be the same with the interpretation of Matthew.

ὅτι αὐτοὶ κληρονομήσουσιν τὴν γῆν, "***for they will inherit the earth.***" In the Greek usage the verb κληρονομέω / κληρονομεῖν means "to be heir," "to inherit something," "to be the heir of someone" including non-material things.[413] But in the LXX the verb is used to translate the Hebrew verb יָרַשׁ *yāraš* and so it comes to mean "to possess" or "to acquire."[414] The implication of "to inherit," "to possess," or "to acquire" may be more or less the same in this beatitude.

There is a question as to what τὴν γῆν here refers. Ps 37:11 does not have the article τὴν before γῆν. However, the counterpart of Matthew's τὴν γῆν is found in the Targum on Ps 37:11, and in Isa 61:7. Then, is Matthew's τὴν γῆν to be understood as 'the earth?' Or does it mean "the Land" referring to the land of Israel as a promise in this beatitude (Matt 5:5)? Or, is it to be understood in a more general term as "all land?" or is it to be understood simply as referring to a symbol of inheriting the spiritual kingdom of heaven?[415]

According to Hagner, τὴν γῆν "the earth" originally referred to the land promised to the Israelites beginning with the Abrahamic covenant (cf. Gen 13:15). But in the present context of messianic fulfilment it connotes the regenerated earth (Matt 19:28; cf. Rom 4:13, where κόσμος, "world," replaces γῆ), which is promised by the eschatological passages in the prophets (e.g., Isa chaps. 65-66). Thus, the "kingdom of heaven" of the first beatitude and the "regenerated earth" of the third beatitude can be understood as something similar, and this makes the parallelism between the first and the third beatitudes more vivid in that both the "poor" and the "meek" have the same Hebrew root.[416] Guelich observes that the promise of the third beatitude stands as a parallel to the promise of the first beatitude, that is, the kingdom of heaven. According to him, "the inheritance of the land was part of Israel's prerogative as the people of God (Deut 4:1; 16:20)," and "it came to be an expression of God's intervention on their behalf in the future as seen, for example, in Isa 61:7." Therefore, the only difference between Matt 5:3 and 5:5 is the temporal perspective of the promise.[417] According to Davies and Allison, Jr. the nationalistic hopes are undone throughout Matthew (cf. 8:11 and 19:28). Therefore, a simple equation of τὴν γῆν with the Land of

412 See the following: Davies and Allison, Jr., *Matthew*, Vol. I, 449; Hagner, *Matthew 1-13*, 92, and Harrington, *The Gospel of Matthew*, 79.

413 Foerster, "The Greek Usage of the Word Group κληρονόμος," *TDNT*, Vol. III ((Grand Rapids, Michigan: William B. Eerdmans Publishing Company, 1965), 768.

414 Davies and Allison, Jr., *Matthew*, Vol. I, 450.

415 *Ibid.*

416 Hagner, *Matthew 1-13*, 92-93,

417 Guelich, *The Sermon on the Mount*, 82-83.

Israel is unlikely. Besides, the unqualified γῆ appears in Matthew to refer to the earth in various places, but not Palestine (as in 5:13, 18, 35; 6:10, 19; 9:6; 10:34; 11:25; 12:42; 16:19; 18:18-19; 23:9; 24: 30, 35; 28:18). Moreover, the kingdom is necessarily spiritualized and divorced from geography, as it is already present in some sense (Matt 4:17). Because of all these, "to inherit the land" in Matt 5:5 has been spiritualized and it means, "'the one who humbles himself will be exalted (in the kingdom of God)'."[418] F. Manns also points out, "to inherit the land was understood in the sense of entering the messianic Kingdom" in Isa 60:21, and to inherit the land means to inherit eternal life in Zech 13:1; Isa 11:1, and 16:21.[419] Seeing the "poor" beatitude and the "meek" beatitude as parallel, Mann further says, that τὴν γῆν in this beatitude has a generic meaning as it often has, and therefore, to inherit the land means to inherit the kingdom.[420]

Based on the scholars' analyses mentioned above, τὴν γῆν of the third Matthean beatitude can be understood as meaning the future regenerated earth, the eschatological kingdom of God. And, the third Matthean beatitude is a promise of inheritance of the eschatological kingdom of God for the meek and the humble, probably meaning, in the words of Davies and Allison, Jr. that they will be exalted in the eschatological kingdom of God.[421] The apocalyptic nature of this beatitude affirms this understanding, that the meek and the humble people of God, who get the lower places in this world, will get their situation reversed into exaltation, in the eschatological kingdom of God. As many scholars agreed upon, the promise of the third beatitude is, thus, similar to the promise of the first beatitude.[422] Of course, the meek shall experience their exaltation in full in the eternal kingdom of heaven/God at the end of the age. However, as the kingdom of heaven/God has already been inaugurated by Jesus Christ, the exaltation of the meek can be viewed as already beginning to take place even now.

V. 6. μακάριοι οἱ πεινῶντες καὶ διψῶντες τὴν δικαιοσύνην, ὅτι αὐτοὶ χορτασθήσονται. "***Blessed are those who hunger and thirst for righteousness, for they will be filled.***" The fourth beatitude is ascribed to the original dominical beatitude, which was preserved in Q. The parallel beatitude in Luke (6: 21) is understood to represent the original Q form, indicating that the Matthean version

418 Davies and Allison, Jr., *Matthew*, Vol. I, 450-451.

419 Manns, "Blessed are the Meek for They Shall Inherit the Earth," 38, 46.

420 Manns, "Blessed are the Meek for They Shall Inherit the Earth," 50-51. To support this beatitude as a promise to eternal life, Manns here also quotes the interpretation of the church Fathers such as: Did 3,7 (quotes Psalm 37.11); Origen, *Contra Celsum* 7,29; Irenaeus of Lyon, *Adversus haereses* 5,32,2; 33; 36,3.

421 Davies and Allison, Jr., *Matthew*, Vol. I, 450-451.

422 See for example, Hagner, *Matthew 1-13*, 92-93; Guelich, *The Sermon on the Mount*, 82-83; Davies and Allison, Jr., *Matthew*, Vol. I, 450-451; Dillon, "The Text of the Sermon on the Mount," 58.

represents an authorial redacted form. Its formulation was probably influenced by Ps 37 and 107.[423]

οἱ πεινῶντες καὶ διψῶντες τὴν δικαιοσύνην, ***"those who hunger and thirst for righteousness."*** The parallel beatitude in Luke (6:21a) has οἱ πεινῶ ντες νῦν "those who hunger now." Therefore, καὶ διψῶντες τὴν δικαιοσύνην is usually taken as a Matthean addition. The addition of καὶ διψῶντες seems to have been influenced by the Old Testament frequent parallelism of "hunger" and "thirst" (e.g., Ps 107:5-9; Isa 29:19; 32:6; 49:10; 65:13),[424] and the addition of τὴν δικαιοσύνην seems to have been influenced by Psalm 106:3 (LXX, 105:3).

Literally, πεινῶντες means "be hungry" "hunger." Figuratively it means "strongly desire" something, "long for" "want very much." And διψῶντες literally means "thirst" "be thirsty" "suffer from thirst." Figuratively it means "long earnestly for" "have strong desire for."[425] Therefore, in the sense of the figurative usage, both οἱ πεινῶντες and οἱ πεινῶντες καὶ διψῶντες have more or less the same meaning. They refer to those who earnestly long for, or have a strong desire for some thing. Thus, the addition of καὶ διψῶντες does not change the meaning, but only conveys the style of the first evangelist.[426]

In the Old Testament the word πεινᾶν is regularly used for the Hebrew word רָעֵב rāᶜēḇ, which is mostly translated as "famine" and also often as "hungry/ hunger." Therefore, in the Old Testament, the word πεινᾶν first denotes the effect of famine (Gen 41:55; 2 Kings 7:12). It is also used to refer to exhaustion caused by military campaign (Judg 8:4ff.; 2 Sam 17:29; cf. Isa 5:27), or a desert journey (Deut 25:18; Ps 107: 4-9). In this second sense it is often the rendering of the Hebrew עָיֵף *ᶜāyēp̄*. However, it mostly denotes "persistent hunger" רָעֵב in consequence of national or social distress.[427] καὶ διψῶντες is Matthew's redactional addition without changing the meaning from the single πεινῶντες, but only under the influence of the frequent parallelism of the two words in the Old Testament (e.g., Ps 107:5-9; Isa 29:19; 32:6; 49:10; 65:13).[428]

---

423 For the suggestion on the influence of Ps 37 and 107, see Schweizer, *The Good News According to Matthew*, 83; and Harrington, *The Gospel of Matthew*, 79.

424 See Davies and Allison, Jr., *Matthew*, Vol. I, 451; See also Harrington, *The Gospel of Matthew*, 79.

425 See Freiberg Lexicon," C.D. Rom.

426 This also probably has to do with Matthew's love of parallelism. See "Other Important Literary Characteristics of Matthew's Gospel" above.

427 Goppelt, "πεινάω (λιμός)," *TDNT*, Vol. VI (Grand Rapids, Michigan: William B. Eerdmans Publishing Company, 1968), 15.

428 See also Harrington, *The Gospel of Matthew*, 79. Gundry observes that by adding καὶ διψῶ ντες Matthew "conforms Jesus' words to Isa 49:10 'they shall not hunger or thirst'." Gundry, *Matthew: A Commentary on His Handbook*, 70. See also Schweizer, *The Good News According to Matthew*, 84, who attributes it to an assimilation to OT language found in such places as: Ps 107:9; Isa 49:10; 65:13; Amos 8:11. Fenton, however, says that fasting is a form of prayer and therefore "hunger and thirsty for righteousness" here means praying for righteousness,

Thus, in the context of the fourth beatitude in Matthew, πεινῶντες καὶ διψῶντες can be understood as referring to "a strong desire for righteousness." However, there is an ongoing debate on whether this should be understood as a passive longing or an active desire. For example, Goppelt and Hagner are of the view that it should be understood as a passive longing. According to Goppelt, the original meaning of πεινῶντες in the Matthean and Lukan beatitudes could be found by deducting Matthew's explanation addition καὶ διψῶντες and turning to the original history of the term and the total witness of the Synoptic gospels. According to him, "the hungry are men who both outwardly and inwardly are painfully deficient in the things essential to life as God meant it to be, and who, since they cannot help themselves, turn to God on the basis of His promise."[429] Goppelt further contends that both Matthew and Luke give a particular reference to the original comprehensive sense of the beatitude, and Matthew construes hunger as a hungering and thirsting after righteousness because of the controversy with Judaism, which insists on its own righteousness. Therefore, the hunger in Matthew is not a concern or striving for uprightness, but is the desire, fed by painful lack, that God's will should be done (Matt 6:10, 33). The promised quenching of the hunger for righteousness will be had in Jesus because the kingdom of God comes in him.[430] Hagner suggests that "the hungry and thirsty" of the fourth beatitude refers to the downtrodden and oppressed, who are hungry and thirsty especially for the justice associated with the coming of God's eschatological rule.[431] On the other hand, some other scholars, for example, Davies and Allison, Jr., Newman, Jr., and Ulrich Luz, understand it as an active desire. Davies and Allison, Jr. are of the view that the meaning of "hunger and thirst" here is not passive longing, but active seeking. They maintain, "Righteousness is to be earnestly and habitually sought, as though it were meat and drink."[432] According to Newman, to "hunger and thirst" for something, in biblical language, means to seek with all of one's heart, that is, to desire it above all else.[433] Luz also maintains that on the basis of the Jewish and Hellenistic parallels "'hunger and thirst' may mean both 'to long for' and 'to make an effort for'," which in turn suggests that this beatitude

that is, for "the obedience of the world to the will of God, the coming of his kingdom." Fenton, *Saint Matthew*, 81. According to Guelich, with the addition of "*and thirst*" "Matthew underscores the element of need by combining the ultimate human needs for food and drink." He further notes that this combination is reminiscent of God's provision of food and drink during the exodus (See Ps 107:6; Isa 48:21; Neh 9:15, cf. Exod 17:6 and Deut 8:15), which is also typologically applied to the eschatological promise. Therefore, Guelich maintains that, *hungry and thirsty* of Matt 5:6 had its history in the OT expectation. See Guelich, *The Sermon on the Mount: A Foundation for Understanding*, 83.

429 Goppelt, "πεινάω (λιμός)," 17-18.

430 *Ibid.*, 18.

431 Hagner, *Matthew 1-13*, 93.

432 Davies and Allison, Jr., *Matthew*, Vol. I, 450-451.

433 Newman, Jr., "Some Translational Notes on the Beatitudes," 116.

should be interpreted ethically, which even the early church almost exclusively advocated.[434] Scholars' interpretations of πεινῶντες καὶ διψῶντες of the fourth beatitude as either passive or active are also related to their interpretation of the word τὴν δικαιοσύνην "for righteousness" in the fourth beatitude, which apparently is a Matthean addition,[435] with which Matthew clarifies the object of hunger (and thirst) which is not specified in Q.[436]

In fact, δικαιοσύνη is an important term for Matthew. The noun δικαιοσύνη occurs seven times in Matthew[437] and it is a key concept in this gospel, and it appears only on the lips of Jesus.[438] It is especially a prominent theme in the Sermon on the Mount (5:10, 20; 6:1, 33), in which it is presented especially as the goal of discipleship (5:20; 6:1, 33), that is, to accomplish the will of God in its fullness. It is also closely connected to the coming of the kingdom (cf. 5:6, 10; 6:33),[439] and its addition in the fourth beatitude brings the Beatitudes into a closer connection with the rest of the Sermon on the Mount.[440]

However, just as the phrase πεινῶντες καὶ διψῶντες in Matt 5: 6 has been interpreted in different ways, even the meaning of its object δικαιοσύνη (here and in other places of Matthew's gospel) has been a matter of debate. Davies and Allison, Jr. list four options, which have been suggested by various scholars, such as –

> (1) It is justification, the gift of God, given to those who ask for it.... (2) It is the eschatological vindication of the elect: those who hunger and thirst after righteousness are seeking the overthrow of the ungodly, the salvation of the saints, and, the establishment of divine justice in general. (3) "It is the fulfilment by man of God's will *and* the fulfilment by God of His own

---

434 Luz, *Matthew 1-7*, 238.

435 See, "Redaction of the Matthean Beatitudes" above.

436 Davies and Allison, Jr., *Matthew*, Vol. I, 451-452. Davies and Allison, Jr., following Goppelt, maintains here, that with the addition of righteousness in this beatitude, Matthew is not spiritualizing a physical need, in as much as the "hungry" in Luke=Q also does not mean only physical hunger, but "the hungry are men who both outwardly and inwardly are painfully deficient in the things essential to life as God meant it to be, and who, since they cannot help themselves, turn to God on the basis of His promise." See also Goppelt, "πεινάω (λιμός)," 18.

437 See, Matt 3:15; 5: 6, 10, 20; 6:1, 33; 21:32.

438 While the noun δικαιοσύνη occurs seven times in Matthew it occurs once in Luke and it does not at all occur in Mark. The adjective δίκαιος occurs 18 times in Matthew while it occurs ten times in Luke and two times in Mark. Only the verb δικαιόω occurs more times in Luke than in Matthew. It occurs twice in Matthew and five times in Luke. Mark does not have it.

439 Hagner, *Matthew 1-13*, 56.

440 Davies and Allison, Jr., *Matthew*, Vol. I, 451.

purposes of grace and mercy." (4) It is the right conduct, which God requires, as in 6:33. The thought of gift is not involved ....[441]

In the Greek secular usage, the word δικαιοσύνη "righteousness," particularly in the legal view of the term, refers "to the thought of the judge allotting to each what is his due."[442] According to Kertelge, its concrete meaning is taken in the New Testament with a variety of usages such as righteousness, legality, honesty, correct condition, equality, and it competes with the Old Testament and Jewish meaning, that is "gift of salvation." Both of them influence the meaning of δικαιοσύνη in several places of the New Testament, but the meaning is determined in most passages by the Old Testament and Jewish history of the concept.[443] In the New Testament other than Pauline writings, according to Shrenk,[444] the term "occasionally means the just judgment of God exercised by Christ at His return."[445] In most places, however, it is used "for the right conduct of man which follows the will of God and is pleasing to Him, for rectitude of life before God, for uprightness before His judgment."[446]

Davies and Allison, Jr. contend that the usage of the word "righteousness" in other places of the Sermon on the Mount, such as 5:10, 20; 6:1, 33, must probably be a deciding factor to construe its meaning in 5:6. In all these four usages, the word "righteousness" refers to "the right conduct required by God," and therefore this must probably be its meaning in 5:6 also.[447] Various scholars hold a similar view.[448]

---

441 Davies and Allison, Jr., *Matthew*, Vol. I, 452. See also Guelich, *The Sermon on the Mount: A Foundation for Understanding*, 84.

442 Shrenk, "δικαιοσύνη," *TDNT,* Vol. II (Grand Rapids, Michigan: Wm. B. Eerdmans Publishing Company, 1964), 193.

443 Kertelge, "δικαιοσύνη, ης, ἡ *dikaiosynē* righteousness, justice," *EDNT,* Vol. 1, edited by Horst Balz and Gerhard Schneider (Grand Rapids, Michigan: William B. Eerdmans Publishing Company, 1990 [1978-80]), 326.

444 In the Pauline writings, the concept of righteousness occupies a central place and it has an especially prominent place in the letter to the Romans. The term occurs 57 times in Pauline literature and out of that it occurs 33 times in Romans alone. Righteousness for Paul basically refers to God's covenant faithfulness, that is that God shows his faithfulness to his covenant with human beings in various ways in various stages of human history, and it was culminated in the death and resurrection of Jesus. So, God is righteous and He also declares righteous those who believe in Jesus (who is the final expression of God's faithfulness). James D. G. Dunn, *The Theology of Paul the Apostle* (Grand Rapids: William B. Eerdmans Publishing Company, 1998), 337.

445 E.g., Acts 17:31; Rev 19: 11, cf. Mark 16:13-15; 2 Pet 1:1; Heb 11: 13.

446 Shrenk, "δικαιοσύνη," 198.

447 Davies and Allison, Jr., *Matthew*, Vol. I, 452-453.

448 See for example, in a full study on the subject of *Righteousness in Matthew*, Przybylski concludes that in all the seven occurrences the demand of God upon human beings, i.e., proper conduct before God is involved. See B. Przybylski, *Righteousness in Matthew and His World of Thought.* SNTSMS 41 (Cambridge: Cambridge University, 1980), as quoted in Hagner, *Matthew 1-13*,

On the other hand, Hagner asserts that though ethical conduct is incontestably in view in some instances (5:20; 6:1; and perhaps 5:10; 6:33), this is not necessarily so in every case. Matthew could use the word in different senses in different occasions and the meaning of the word should be determined from its immediate context.[449] In this verse, therefore, the context of the passage suggests that δικαιοσύνη means "justice" rather than "personal righteousness," that the poor, the grieving, and the downtrodden who have experienced injustice are longing for God to act for their justice. But, the sense of δικαιοσύνη as personal righteousness is not excluded altogether here, for "the justice of God's eschatological rule presupposes the δικαιοσύνη of those who enjoy its blessings (cf. 2 Pet 3:13)."[450] Harrington suggests that this beatitude also seems to reflect the language of Ps 107 (LXX: 106), which talks about God delivering the hungry and thirsty. This is also supported, according to him, by the fact that "in an apocalyptic context righteousness refers to the vindication of the just at the last judgment."[451]

It is believed in this study that the socio-historical situation of the Matthean community should play an important role for understanding the meaning of οἱ πεινῶντες καὶ διψῶντες τὴν δικαιοσύνην in the fourth beatitude. As we have seen in the previous chapter, the Matthean community experienced so much injustice done to them. First, they were sharing with other Jews injustice in terms of social, political and economic, in the hands of the Romans in the aftermath of the Jewish war (66-73 C.E.). On top of this, they were suffering religious persecutions in the hands of the Jewish leaders and their Gentile neighbours. Obviously one of the reasons for their persecution was the consequence of unjust legal treatment meted out to them. Moreover, most of the members of the Matthean community were economically poor and they had no power to claim justice. Even the few well-to-do among them suffered the same injustice, which all other community members were suffering. Under such situations, it is apparent that they were deeply longing to experience justice in their life, in terms of social,

---

56. Newman believes that in all the occurrences in Matthew's gospel the word "righteousness" refers to "what God requires of His people," and this is indicated by the appearance of the word only on the lips of Jesus. Newman, Jr., "Some Translational Notes on the Beatitudes," 117. Luz also holds that in line with the interpretation of the early church δικαιοσύνη can be understood as referring to human behaviour in all Matthean passages. Luz, *Matthew 1-7*, 237. According to Strecker, in all its occurrences in Matthew's gospel, with the exception of 6:33, the word "designates the righteousness of people, a human attitude that is supposed to be realized through active deeds." Strecker, *the Sermon on the Mount*, 37. Shrenk also maintains that "righteousness" in the fourth beatitude refers to a right state before God, which is "the supreme goal for πεινῶντες καὶ διψῶντες." Shrenk, "δικαιοσύνη," 198. See also Schnackenburg, *The Gospel of Matthew*, 48.

449 Hagner, *Matthew 1-13*, 56.

450 *Ibid.*, 93. See also Gundry, *Matthew: A Commentary on His Handbook*, 70.

451 Harrington, *The Gospel of Matthew*, 79.

political, economic, and legal as well. At the same time, the Matthean community presumably felt that they could not expect any human being to restore justice due to them. Therefore, it is obvious that they were earnestly longing for God to act to give them justice.[452] Then, the longing of the Matthean community is in two fronts, 1) to experience justice in their life; and 2) for God's justice (just judgment) to act for them, to give them justice. Consequently, the word δικαιοσύνη also could have two connotations – 1) justice done by human beings, that is the fulfilment of God's will, which has positive effect upon other human beings;[453] and 2) justice done by God, that is the just judgment of God that restores justice to the downtrodden, and of course, overthrows those who act with injustice, which is basically to be exercised by Christ at his return, that is, at the *eschaton*. In both cases, πεινῶντες καὶ διψῶντες refers to the passive longing for justice which the oppressed people are lacking. The apodosis, that is ὅτι αὐτοὶ χορτασθήσονται "for they will be filled," also supports the understanding of πεινῶντες καὶ διψῶντες as referring to a passive longing. This clause indicates that those who are "hungry and thirsty" suffer from the lacking of something with which they need to be filled. They cannot do anything to quench their hunger and thirst, and therefore, they expect only God to satisfy their hunger and thirst. Therefore, we could understand δικαιοσύνη of the fourth beatitude as basically referring to "God's justice (just judgment)" for which the oppressed people are longing with the expectation of experiencing its realization to come to them. Here, justice is related to judgement, especially the just judgment of God (which restores justice to the poor and the downtrodden), and it is also related to the Greek secular usage of the term, especially in the legal context.[454] However, the aspect of δικαιοσύνη as meaning an active longing to fulfil God's will is not totally negated, because, as Hargner rightly has pointed out, "the justice of God's eschatological rule presupposes the δικαιοσύνη of those who enjoy its blessings (cf. 2 Pet 3:13)."[455] Moreover, it is appropriate to assume that those who are longing to experience justice in their life would try to act with justice. Now, we could assume with confidence that Matthew drew the fourth beatitude from the

452 Hagner, *Matthew 1-13*, 93.

453 From this perspective, πεινῶντες καὶ διψῶντες τὴν δικαιοσύνην of the fourth beatitude can be understood as, in the words of Goppelt, "the desire, fed by painful lack, that God's will should be done (Matt 6: 10, 33)." Goppelt, "πεινάω (λιμός)," 18.

454 Shrenk, "δικαιοσύνη," 193.

455 Hagner, *Matthew 1-13*, 93. See also Gundry, *Matthew: A Commentary on His Handbook*, 70. Mary Ann Hinsdale, following John Meyer and John Reumann, suggests that perhaps the best answer to the question of the meaning of δικαιοσύνη in Matt 5:6 and 5:10 may be to see both beatitudes as reflecting the dual character of *dikaiosúne*, such as an active longing to fulfil God's will and a passive longing for God's justice. See Mary Ann Hinsdale, "Blessed Are the Persecuted … Hungering and Thirsting for Justice: Blessings for Those Breaking Boundaries," in *New Perspectives on Beatitudes*, edited by Francis A. Eigo (Villanova: The Villanova University Press, 1995), 165 [161-189].

beatitude of Jesus to console and encourage his community, which experienced injustice and were earnestly longing to experience justice. Without the qualifying word δικαιοσύνη, the fourth beatitude can be (mis)understood as referring to or emphasizing physical hunger. Therefore, in line with the actual experience of his community, that is their acute longing for justice, Matthew added a clarifying word δικαιοσύνη, to address the concrete situation of his community.

ὅτι αὐτοὶ χορτασθήσονται, ***"for they will be filled."*** The intransitive verb χορτασθήσονται (future passive third person plural) "they will be filled," comes from χορταζω, which literally means "feed," "satisfy," "fill (up)." In the passive, it means "eat one's fill," "be satisfied." Figuratively the passive means "be satisfied." In the fourth beatitude, it is used in the figurative sense "be satisfied."[456] And the passive χορτασθήσονται here is the divine passive, because God is the one who will satisfy their hunger and thirst.[457] Therefore, the fourth beatitude is a consolation to the Matthean community that God will satisfy their hunger, meaning that He will fill them with what they are lacking and eagerly longing for, that is "justice." God, with his just judgment, will restore justice to them. Here, the apocalyptic nature of this beatitude becomes obvious. The beatitude implies that the oppressed people of God will experience a total reversal of their situation, getting restoration of justice due to them, while their oppressors, on the other hand, will also receive a reversal of their situation, getting punishment for all the injustice they had done to the poor and the downtrodden people of God. The future tense, of course, indicates its eschatological aspect, meaning that the full restoration of justice to the poor and the downtrodden by God will take place in the eschatological kingdom of God.[458] However, as the kingdom of heaven/God has been inaugurated by Jesus Christ,[459] those who are "hungry and thirsty for righteousness" could experience justice in Jesus even now. This implies that wherever the Lordship of Jesus Christ is proclaimed, justice must be experienced by the people, especially the poor and downtrodden people.

V. 7. μακάριοι οἱ ἐλεήμονες, ὅτι αὐτοὶ ἐλεηθήσονται. ***"Blessed are the merciful, for they will receive mercy."*** The fifth beatitude does not have a parallel in Luke. It is ascribed to Q^{mt}.[460] Its formulation was probably influenced by Prov 14:21b; and 17:5c (LXX). Most probably, its formation in the Q^{mt} took place in the context of Q community which was very similar to the context of Matthew's community, or which had a historical continuity with Matthew's community, not long before Matthew's gospel was written.[461] Therefore, Matthew took it over because it suits

456 See "Freiberg Lexicon." C.D. Rom.

457 Hagner, *Matthew 1-13*, 93.

458 Davies and Allison, Jr., *Matthew*, Vol. I, 453. See also Gundry, *Matthew*, 70.

459 See the discussion on "the kingdom of God" in the first beatitude above.

460 See "the Form, Source and *Sitz im Leben* of the Matthean Beatitudes" above.

461 *Ibid.*

the situation of his community at the time the gospel was written. The ascription of the source to Q^{mt} does not question its authenticity as Jesus' teaching, for its formulation in Q^{mt} is not a creation out of nothing. It is apparent that it has been formulated to suit the need of the situation, based on Jesus' teaching found elsewhere. This would be the case not only with this fifth beatitude, but with all those beatitudes which are not found in Luke, and which are ascribed to Q^{mt}. With regard to the fifth beatitude, even though there is no parallel beatitude in Luke, a similar teaching on showing mercy is found in Luke 6:27-38. Although the Greek word used by Luke here is οἰκτίρμονες, it is more or less synonymous with ἐλεήμονες. Moreover, some scholars believe that Matthew's fifth beatitude could possibly have οἰκτίρμονες in Q^{mt} in its original form and it was changed to ἐλεήμονες by Matthew because of his fondness of ἐλε-root.[462] The teaching on showing mercy is also found in the parable of the Good Samaritan (Luke 10: 25-37). And in Matthew the teaching on mercy to fellow human beings is found in 18:21-35 (cf. 9:9-13; 12:1-8; 23:23), and a parallel sentiment is found in 6:12-15; 7:1-5.[463] Therefore, even if this beatitude was not spoken by Jesus in its present form, there is no doubt that it was composed later on the basis of Jesus' authentic teaching.[464]

This beatitude probably has its background in Prov 14:21b which reads (in the LXX) ἐλεῶν δὲ πτωχοὺς μακαριστός, "blessed is the one who have mercy on the poor" (cf. Prov 17: 5c of the LXX text also has ὁ δὲ ἐπισπλαγχνιζόμενος ἐλεηθήσεται, "the one who has compassion will be shown mercy").[465]

μακάριοι οἱ ἐλεήμονες, ***"blessed are the merciful."*** 'ελεήμονες is the plural form of the adjective ἐλεήμων which means, "merciful," "compassionate," "sympathetic."[466] It comes from the verb ἐλεέω/ἐλεεῖν which means "to have pity on," "to show mercy upon."[467] The noun ἔλεος means "mercy," "compassion," and it is used both of attitudes of man and God. It is used to refer to an attitude and emotion roused by the affliction of another, and especially of gracious action demonstrating God's compassion.[468] In the LXX, although the verb ἐλεεῖν is often used for רִחַם (in Piel form) it is mostly used for חָנַן.[469] In Prov 14:21b, which possibly influenced the composition of the fifth Matthean beatitude, the word

462 See for example, Davies and Allison, Jr., *Matthew*, Vol. I, 454. See also Guelich, *The Sermon on the Mount: A Foundation for Understanding*, 88-89.

463 Davies and Allison, Jr., *Matthew*, Vol. I, 454. See also Thomson, "The Background and Function of the Beatitudes…," 114.

464 Cf. Schweizer, *The Good News According to Matthew*, 92.

465 Cf. Hagner, *Matthew 1-13*, 93.

466 "Freiberg Lexicon." C.D. Rom.

467 Liddel and Scott, (comps), *A Greek-English Lexicon*, 531.

468 "Freiberg Lexicon." C.D. Rom.

469 Bultmann, "ἔλεος, ἐλεέω, ἐλεήμων, ἐλεημοσύνη, ἀνέλεος, ἀνελεήμων," *TDNT*, Vol. II (Grand Rapids, Michigan: William B. Eerdmans Publishing Company, 1964), 479.

חנן is used. And the noun ἔλεος is usually used for the Hebrew word חֶסֶד and less frequently for רַחֲמִים.[470]

According to BDB Lexicon, the verb חָנַן, in the Qal form, means "shew favour," "be gracious." When used of man, it refers to – a) showing favour by giving something, b) showing favour in dealing with the poor, needy and orphans, c) showing favour by considering and sparing. When used of God, it usually refers to the bestowal of redemption from enemies, evils and sins. In Piel it means – "make gracious, favourable."[471] The verb רָחַם in demonstrative form means "love." In Piel form, it means, "have compassion." It is usually used of God's compassion to His people. When used of man, it usually refers to the compassion of the conquerors.[472] The noun חֶסֶד, means "goodness," "kindness." When used of man, it refers to – 1) "kindness" of men towards men, in doing favours and benefits, 2) "kindness" (especially as extended to the lowly, needy and miserable), "mercy," 3) (rarely) "affection" (of Israel to God), "love to God," "piety," 4) lovely appearance. When used of God it refers to His "kindness," "loving-kindness," in condescending to the needs of his creatures. Specifically it is used of God's loving-kindness – a) in redemption from enemies and troubles, b) in preservation of life from death, c) in quickening of spiritual life, d) in redemption from sin, and e) in keeping the covenant with Abraham, with Moses and Israel, with David and his dynasty, and with the wife of Zion.[473] The noun רַחֲמִים means "compassion," referring usually of God, but also sometimes of man.[474] According to Bultmann חֶסֶד in the Old Testament denotes an attitude of man or God which arises out of mutual relationship. Primarily it is not a disposition but a helpful act, and it corresponds to a relationship of trust, and faithfulness as the appropriate attitude. On the other side, it also denotes help or kindness as the grace of a superior. The element of obligation may yield before that of favour in human relationship. But in regard to God, חֶסֶד particularly denotes grace, which rests on the בְּרִית "covenant" by which God has freely bound himself to his people. On the part of men, they are obliged to keep their obligations to their fellow men, to be called חֲסִידִים the "righteous," and thus can appeal to God's חֶסֶד. In religious usage, God's חֶסֶד always means God's faithfulness and merciful help. On the other hand, רַחֲמִים originally denotes emotion, or the seat of feeling which is felt physically. It refers to the original oneness within a family, such as parents and children or brothers and sisters. It often amounts to "pity" or "sympathy" as it is especially evoked when the other is in trouble. However, the better rendering is "love." In

470 Bultmann, "ἔλεος, ἐλεέω, ἐλεήμων, ἐλεημοσύνη, ἀνέλεος, ἀνελεήμων," 479.

471 Brown, Driver and Bridges, eds., *Hebrew and English Lexicon of the Old Testament*, 335.

472 *Ibid.*, 933.

473 *Ibid.*, 338.

474 *Ibid.*, 933.

the later Judaism, however, חֶסֶד and רַחֲמִים are used interchangeably just as ἔλεος and οἰκτιρμοί are used synonymously.[475]

Thus, all the three Hebrew words, such as חָנַן, רִחַם and חֶסֶד which are mainly used for the Greek ἐλεεῖν, ἔλεος, taken together can be understood as referring to "showing favour, compassion and kindness," and in short "showing mercy."

According to Bultmann, the verb ἐλεεῖν (as well as the noun ἔλεος) in the New Testament often refers to the divinely required attitude of man to man.[476] According to Davies and Allison, Jr., the word ἐλεήμων, which appears only twice in the New Testament, in Matt 5:7 and Heb 2:17 means "merciful."[477]

Guelich has rightly pointed out that to put it briefly, the concept of mercy (ἔλεος, ἐλέω, ἐλεήμων), both in the Old Testament and New Testament points to two directions: First, the pardon granted to one in the wrong (e.g., Exod 34:6-7; Isa 55:7; Matt 18:32-34). Second, the kindness rendered to one in need (e.g., Ps 86:15-16; Isa 30:18; Ezek 39:25; Mark 10:47). "This latter usage becomes an 'act of mercy' or 'alms'"[478]

Guelich, maintaining the fifth beatitude as introduced into the pre-Matthean tradition, asserts that the meaning of "merciful" in Matt 5:7 can best be understood on the basis of its relation to the Sermon section on Judging (Luke 6:36-42, cf. Matt 5:48; 7:1-5). He contends, "In the pre-Matthean Sermon tradition, *merciful* refers to the act of judging rather than to the acts of kindness." It refers to the showing of mercy to others who are in the wrong, just as one has already experienced mercy from God (e.g., Matt 6:12; 18:21-35 cf. Luke 6:36). Therefore, the fifth beatitude "declares such a demonstration of mercy to others in the wrong as *blessed.*"[479] Guelich's suggestion may be correct in the pre-Matthean setting. However, it does not seem to be necessarily so in the Matthean setting. What Matthew actually means by οἱ ἐλεήμονες in the fifth beatitude, or, what this term refers to in the Matthean setting, may be deduced from Matthew's overall emphasis on the importance of mercy in his gospel, which must have a connection with his context or the context of his community.

First, in Matt 9:13; 12:7; and 23:23, we see mercy as a fundamental demand, which the Pharisees failed to accomplish. If we look at the contexts in which Matthew presents these sayings, especially of Matt 9:13, it refers to the context where Jesus eats with the tax collectors, who are looked upon as "sinners" but who are on the other hand spiritually hungry people; and in Matt 12:17 it refers to the situation where the physically hungry disciples of Jesus plucked heads of grains on the Sabbath and ate. Jesus' response to the criticisms of the Pharisees indicates that

---

475 Bultmann, "ἔλεος, ἐλεέω, ἐλεήμων, ἐλεημοσύνη, ἀνέλεος, ἀνελεήμων," 479-481.

476 Bultmann, "ἔλεος, ἐλεέω, ἐλεήμων, ἐλεημοσύνη, ἀνέλεος, ἀνελεήμων," 482.

477 Davies and Allison, Jr., *Matthew*, Vol. I, 454.

478 Guelich, *The Sermon on the Mount: A Foundation for Understanding*, 88.

479 *Ibid.*, 88-89.

the Pharisees were lacking compassion and mercy for the spiritual hunger of the tax collectors, and for the physical hunger of the disciples. That means that they lack sympathy for those who are spiritually hungry and physically hungry. It is because of the same reason that they are criticized in Matt 23:23. These passages indicate that "mercy" in Matthew include compassion for those who are spiritually hungry (the so-called "sinners") and physically hungry. Second, in Jesus' teachings - on love for enemies in Matt 5:43-48; on forgiveness of fellow human beings in Matt 18:21-35; and on helping those who are in difficult situations of different kinds in Matt 25:31-46, we see that "mercy" in Matthew covers "love and compassion" for the poor, the prisoners, the sick, the debtors, and the enemies. This shows that all are included under the purview of "mercy." Third, we see in various places (Matt 9:27-31; 15:21-18; 17:14-18; 20:29-34) that people asked Jesus to have mercy upon them, that is basically to help them in their difficulties, such as in their blindness, and from demon possession. Then Jesus showed mercy upon them by helping them in their difficulties.

If we take all these together, the implication is that in Matthew "mercy" or "showing mercy" includes both the kindness rendered to one in need, as well as the pardon granted to one in the wrong. It means showing loving compassion and sympathy accompanied by relevant actions, to people in difficult situations of every kind.[480] And, the inclusion of enemies in the object of mercy indicates that nobody should be excluded from the purview of mercy. Mercy should be shown to everyone who needs it.[481] Then, those who show compassion with the required action to anyone in need are called οἱ ἐλεήμονες in Matt 5:7. And, doing such things is a demand from God. According to F. Staudinger, the Hebrew word חֶסֶד which is used in the Old Testament for ἐλεέω/ἔλεος, has the Old Testament original meaning "kindness," a conduct which God demanded from person to person.[482] Newman, Jr. rightly maintains that the fifth beatitude does not mean that believers in Christ should be merciful to others so as to get the same from them. What it means is that whoever is merciful to others will receive mercy from God.[483]

ὅτι αὐτοὶ ἐλεηθήσονται, ***"for they will receive mercy."*** The verb ἐλεηθήσονται "they will receive mercy" is a divine passive, indicating that those

480 The relevant action would include to help them in their spiritual hunger, or to feed them when they are physically hungry and needing help. It may be to help them when they are sick, by visiting them and comforting them, or by giving them financial help for their treatment and other needs. It may be to help the poor providing them with financial and material help. It may be to visit the prisoners and help them for their spiritual and physical well-being. It may be to forgive their debts, or may be to forgive them when they commit mistakes, etc.

481 See also Davies and Allison, Jr., *Matthew*, Vol. I, 454-455.

482 F. Staudinger, "ἐλεέω *eleeō*," *EDNT*, Vol. 1, edited by Horst Balz and Gerhard Schneider (Grand Rapids, Michigan: William B. Eerdmans Publishing Company, 1990 [1978-80]), 430 [429-431]. See also Davies and Allison, Jr., *Matthew*, Vol. I, 455.

483 Newman, Jr., "Some Translational Notes on the Beatitudes," 118.

who are merciful will receive mercy from God. As the verb is future, the time for obtaining mercy by the merciful may be at the last judgment.[484] However, it must have present implication as well, given the fact that the kingdom, which is the binding factor of all the beatitudes, has both present and future implications in Matthew.[485] It could briefly be stated that whoever has mercy on people will obtain mercy from heaven (God)[486] in its fullness in the future kingdom of God. Not only that, but they will also partially experience it at present. Davies and Allison, Jr. point out that if mercy is known in the future, it is also known in the past. This is seen in Matt 18:21-35 (cf. Luke 6:36) where it is indicated that disciples can show mercy because God has first shown mercy to them.[487] If then, mercy is shown in the past and will be shown in the future by God, He will also show it at present. Guelich rightly maintains, "In this beatitude God's mercy to be experienced at the final judgment belongs already to the merciful and furnishes the basis for their behaviour towards others." And, in the final judgment one will simply receive in full what he/she "has already freely experienced through Jesus Messiah, namely, the pardoning acceptance of God."[488] At the same time, this beatitude also implicitly refers to the judgment upon the wicked oppressors, that those who have *not* shown mercy will not receive mercy (cf. Jas 2:13)[489] in the last judgment. At the same time, however, this also must have a present implication as well.

Then, what would be the implication of this beatitude in the context of Matthew? First, it could relate to the relationship between Matthew's community and the leaders of formative Judaism, and particularly it could be a call to covenant loyalty for the members of the community as against the disloyal scribes and Pharisees. As noted above, the Hebrew word חֶסֶד, which is an equivalent of ἔλεος, carries a covenant relationship whereby the people of God are required to fulfil their obligations of חֶסֶד to their fellow humans. Against this understanding, the scribes and the Pharisees, the main opponents of Matthew's community, are accused of failing to fulfil their covenant obligation of חֶסֶד to their fellow humans in Matt 9:13; 12:7; and 23:23. This means that they are not faithful to God. This is clearly seen especially in their persecutions of the followers of Jesus Christ (the Matthean Community). Consequently this implies that while their Pharisaic opponents are not faithful to God, the followers of Jesus (= the Matthean community) are faithful to Him by showing mercy and acts of loving-kindness.[490] Therefore, they

484 Harrington, *The Gospel of Matthew*, 79.

485 See the comment on v. 3 above.

486 Albright and Mann, *Matthew*, 47.

487 Davies and Allison, Jr., *Matthew*, Vol. I, 455.

488 Guelich, *The Sermon on the Mount: A Foundation for Understanding*, 89-90.

489 Hagner, *Matthew 1-13*, 93-94. See also Betz, *The Sermon on the Mount*, 134.

490 Davies and Allison, Jr., *Matthew*, Vol. I, 455. Schweizer also observes that in Matthew, the message of Jesus has mercy as its focal point while the Pharisees have already forgotten it,

will receive God's mercy in full at the eschaton. While this beatitude must be referring to the present situation of the Matthean community, it must also be understood as a call to them to faithfully carry out their obligation of loyalty to God, by continually showing mercy. Davies and Allison, Jr. rightly point out that "throughout Matthew (including 5:7) 'mercy' and its cognates imply that merciful action is the concrete expression of loyalty to God, and that what God demands is not so much activity directed Godward ('I desire ... not sacrifice') but loving-kindness benefiting other people ('I desire mercy')."[491] Second, as the Matthean community comprised some affluent members while the majority of them were poor, the fifth beatitude would also be a call to the better off people to have a concern for the poorer people, especially when they were undergoing specific problems. It was also highly probable that the poor people would have borrowed money from the rich people in times of problems, as that was the usual practice in the agrarian society of the first century. It was natural to think that the poor people would have often failed to repay their debt unless they had a bumper harvest. In such situations, the fifth beatitude is a call to the creditors to show mercy to the debtors. Third, the Matthean community did not live alone in a secluded area. They lived in a city/town context having been in regular contact with the wider society, both Jews and Gentiles. Therefore, they were living their daily lives, they were doing their businesses, and they were carrying on their various activities with and in the midst of other people. In such situations, they must have come across various situations, which called for expressions of "mercy" in concrete manners, not necessarily to their fellow believers in Jesus Christ. The third beatitude can be seen as a call in such situations, to show mercy to everyone who is in need of it, without making any exception or discrimination. This would include even their persecutors. This befits their identity as the faithful people of God, and faithful followers of His Messiah. Fourth, in the context whereby the community was called to continue its mission among all the people, including both Jews and Gentiles, such a behaviour would be a very important way of convincing people to join them in their faith in Jesus Christ. That means that showing mercy is a very important approach for the success of their mission. Indeed, if they do not show mercy where it is called for, they are unlikely to convince people with their message.

Because of all these situations, mercy plays a very important role in Matthew's gospel. Gundry also notes that the ethic of mercy is prominent in Matthew's gospel even where the term mercy does not necessarily occur.[492] Davies and Allison, Jr. rightly observe that while the demand for mercy was inherent in

as indicated by a unique Matthean passage 23:23. Schweizer, *The Good News According to Matthew*, 92.

491 Davies and Allison, Jr., *Matthew*, Vol. I, 455.

492 Gundry, *Matthew: A Commentary on His Handbook*, 71. Here, Gundry mentions the places in Matthew's gospel where mercy is implicitly prominent such as:

the Old Testament and Jewish tradition, the Matthean Jesus gives it a "renewed emphasis and vividness by placing it at the centre of his proclamation (9:13; 12:7; 23:23; 25:31-46) and by making it plain that mercy should be shown to all ..., not only to those on the fringes of society but even enemies (5:43-8; cf. Lk 10: 29-37)."[493] Such, an understanding of renewed emphasis is affirmed by the inclusion of "mercy" in the Beatitudes, which is a programmatic introduction to the Sermon on the Mount, the most outstanding discourse on discipleship in Matthew's gospel. While the main thrust of the fifth beatitude is ethical exhortation, the aspect of the eschatological judgement emphasized in its apodosis indicates its apocalyptic orientation.

V. 8. μακάριοι οἱ καθαροὶ τῇ καρδίᾳ, ὅτι αὐτοὶ τὸν θεὸν ὄψονται. ***"Blessed are the pure in heart, for they will see God."*** The sixth beatitude is ascribed to Q^{mt}.[494] This beatitude corresponds to the thought of Ps 24[LXX:23]:3–4, which links (in the LXX) καθαρὸς τῇ καρδίᾳ, "the pure in heart" with those who will go up to the Lord's mountain and stand in his holy place (cf. for "pure heart," - Ps 51:10; 73:1).[495] Its formulation in the Q community must have been based on Jesus' teaching such as found in Luke 6:43-45 par. Matt 7:16-20; 12:33-35, etc.[496]

μακάριοι οἱ καθαροὶ τῇ καρδίᾳ, ***"blessed are the pure in heart."*** In Greek literature the word καρδία is used primarily and literally referring to "the heart" in physiological sense, as the central organ of the body of man and beast. However, it is also used figuratively "as the seat of moral and intellectual life," referring to – (1) "the seat of emotions and passions" which include anger, courage or fear, joy or sadness, and love; (2) "the seat of power and thought," (3) "the seat of the will and resolves." Besides these, it is also used figuratively with regard to nature, referring to the "inward part," the "core" of a plant, or a "kernel" of a tree.[497]

In the LXX καρδία is used in the true equivalent of the Hebrew לֵב or לֵבָב. Apart from their translations with καρδία these Hebrew words are also translated,

---

Joseph shows mercy in not wanting to put Mary to open shame (1:19); a husband is to show mercy to his wife by not divorcing here (5:31-32 with comments); the parable of the debtors describes forgiveness as an act of mercy (18:23-35); paying a full day's wage to laborers who have worked only one hour is also such an act (20:1-16); Jesus' attention to "the little ones" (chap. 18), to the children, the blind, and the lame in the Temple (21:14-16), and to publicans and prostitutes (21:28-32) exhibits mercy; and acts of mercy distinguish the sheep from the goats at the last judgment (25:31-46).

493 Davies and Allison, Jr., *Matthew*, Vol. I, 454-455.

494 See "The Forms, Sources, and *Sitz Im Leben* of the Matthean Beatitudes" above.

495 Hagner, *Matthew 1-13*, 94. See also Davies and Allison, Jr., *Matthew*, Vol. I, 456.

496 Cf. Davies and Allison, Jr., *Matthew*, Vol. I, 434-435.

497 Behm, "καρδια among the Greeks," *TDNT*, Vol. III (Grand Rapids, Michigan: William B. Eerdmans Publishing Company, 1965), 608-609.

but more rarely, as διάνοια and ψυχή, and very rarely as φρένες, νοῦς and στῆ θος.[498] In the literal sense, לֵב means "heart" in men and animals (Hos 13:8). It is used in the sense of the seat of vitality which vitalizes by nourishment (e.g., Gen 18:5), as well as physical brokenness (Isa 1:5). Figuratively it means "innermost part of man" (e.g., 1 Sam 16:7 par. Jer 31:33), that is, "the seat of mental or spiritual powers and capacity." This is expressed in various ways, such as – (1) it stands firm in bravery and courage (e.g., Ezek 22:14; Dan 11:25, etc.); (2) it is the seat of rational functions (e.g., Deut 29:3; Prov 19:8, etc.); (3) from the heart comes planning and volition (e.g., Jer 23:20; Isa 10:7, etc.); and (4) religious and moral conduct is rooted in the heart (e.g., 1 Sam 12: 20, 24; Jer 32:40; Prov 7:3, etc.).[499] The use of καρδία in the LXX reflects the wealth of nuances in the underlying Hebrew words לֵב or לֵבָב. First, it is the principal organ of man's personal life, the focus of his being and activity as a spiritual personality (cf. Prov 4:23, etc.). It is also, therefore, the source and seat of man's moral and religious life (cf. Deut 6:5, etc.). Although it is often interchangeable with ψυχή, διάνοια, πνεῦμα, νοῦς, etc., in contrasts to these synonyms καρδία "relates to the unity and totality of the inner life represented and expressed in the variety of intellectual and spiritual functions."[500] Even Hellenistic Judaism, when it follows the Old Testament lines of thought, uses καρδία in the same sense as the LXX. Rabbinic Judaism also, in its use of לֵב or לֵבָב, follows the Old Testament.[501]

The New Testament's use of καρδία reflects the Old Testament background as distinct from the Greek usage, and "even more strongly than the LXX it concentrates on the heart as the main organ of psychic and spiritual life, the place in man at which God bears witness to Himself."[502] Only Luke 21: 34; Acts 14:7; and James 5:5, in the New Testament, use καρδία as the central organ of the body and the seat of physical vitality. On the other hand, it is attested in many ways in the New Testament that "the heart is the centre of the inner life of man and the source or seat of all the forces and functions of soul and spirit," such as - (a) the dwelling place or centre of feelings, emotions, desires, passions, and joy (Acts 2:26; Jn 16:22; etc.); (b) the seat of understanding, the source of thought and reflection (Mark 7:21 and par.; Matt 12:34 and par.; Jn 12:40b; etc.); (c) the seat of will, the source of resolves (Luke 21:14; Acts 11:23; 2 Cor 9:7; etc.), and thus, (d) "supremely the one centre in man to which God turns, in which the religious life is rooted, which determines moral conduct" (Luke 16:15; 1 Thes 2:4; Rev

498 Behm, "[καρδία] in the LXX, and Hellenistic and Rabbinic Judaism," *TDNT*, Vol. III (Grand Rapids, Michigan: William B. Eerdmans Publishing Company, 1965), 609.

499 Baumgaertel, "לֵב, לֵבָב in the OT," *TDNT*, Vol. III (Grand Rapids, Michigan: William B. Eerdmans Publishing Company, 1965), 606-607.

500 Behm, "[καρδια] in the LXX, and Hellenistic and Rabbinic Judaism," 609-610.

501 *Ibid.*, 610-611.

502 Behm, "καρδια in the New Testament," *TDNT*, Vol. III (Grand Rapids, Michigan: William B. Eerdmans Publishing Company, 1965), 611.

2:23; etc.). Besides the above usages, Matt 12:40, in reference to nature, uses the word to refer to the inward part, the bosom, of the earth (cf. Jon 2:4; Ezek 27:4, 25ff.; 28:2; 4 Ezra 13:3, etc.).[503]

Thus, the basic meaning of the word καρδία –"heart" (= לֵב or לֵבָב) in biblical tradition, refers to – "the real or true self" that is "the psyche at its deepest level," the seat of emotions (Deut 28:47; Prov 27:11; Isa 35:4; Acts 14:17, etc.), volition (Prov 6:18; Jer 3:17; 23:20; Dan 1:8, etc.), the intellect (Gen 27: 41; Judg 5:16; Mark 2:6; etc.); as well as the internal sphere where the divinity is encountered (Ps 27:8; Eph 3:17, etc.).[504]

From the above discussion, one could infer the theological meaning of the word καρδία –"heart," which runs through the OT, the NT, as well as the Rabbinic Judaism and Hellenistic Judaism, that it is the center of a human being's moral and spiritual/religious life, the place in the human being at which God bears witness to Himself. So, the word καρδία in Matt 5:8 also must be understood in this manner.

The word καθαροὶ is used in various ways in the Greek literature. It means literally - clear of dust, clean, pure, spotless, unsoiled, open, and free. In a moral sense, it is used for "clear from shame or pollution," especially "clear of guilt or defilement." In relation to water, it is used for - clear of "admixture," "clear," "pure." In relation to birth, it is used to refer to "pure," "genuine," such as "citizens of pure blood." It is also used as "without blemish" to refer to the sound portion of the army. With regard to accounts, it relates to "clear," "exact," that is "exactly balanced."[505] According to Thayer's Greek Lexicon, its usage in Matt 5: 8 is ethical, and it means "free from corrupt desire, from sin and guilt."[506] In Freiberg Lexicon its usage in Matt 5:8 comes under moral and spiritual usage, and it means "pure," "good in God's eyes," "without sin."[507] Then, "pure in heart" may be understood as referring to "pure and good in God's eyes, free from corrupt desire, from sin and guilt, from the heart."

Scholars interpret καθαροὶ τῇ καρδίᾳ "pure in heart," of Matt 5:8 in different ways. According to Hagner, it refers to the state of the inner core of a person, and takes for granted doing right actions with integrity of mind.[508] According to Schnackenburg, καθαροὶ τῇ καρδίᾳ especially includes "truthful speech, keeping one's word, dealing honestly with one's neighbour (Ps 15:2-5), and conduct oriented to God's trustworthiness, goodness, and fidelity (Ps 26;

503 Behm, "καρδια in the New Testament," 611-612.

504 Davies and Allison, Jr., *Matthew*, Vol. I, 456.

505 For these and other nuances, see Liddel and Scott, (comps.), *A Greek-English Lexicon*, Vol. 1, 850-851.

506 Joseph Henry Thayer, *Greek-English Lexicon of the New Testament* (New York: Harper & Brothers, 1887), 312.

507 "Freiberg Lexicon." C.D. Rom.

508 Hagner, *Matthew 1-13*, 94.

Mic 6:8)."[509] According to Ulrich Luz, the meaning of καθαροὶ τῇ καρδίᾳ could be briefly stated as "undivided obedience toward God without sin."[510] Schweizer maintains that what Matthew has in mind is a simple heart set on God, and it is similar to faith (cf. 14: 31). According to him, in Judaism, purity of heart is seen in general as obedience to God rather than ritual sacrifice (e.g., 1 Sam 15:22; Isa 1:10-17; Jer 7:3-7). Therefore, since it is contrasted to the outward purity brought about by cultic means (23:26) the sixth beatitude calls all the cultic practices of the Jews and of the Gentiles into question, and it has essentially to do with one's conduct toward a neighbour.[511] While Schweizer correctly states that this beatitude is contrasted to the outward purity brought about by cultic means, his view that this beatitude questions all the cultic practices of the Jews and Gentiles, seems to be an over-interpretation.[512] Hagner seems right in saying that this beatitude anticipates the internalizing of Jesus' commandments that follow in the Sermon.[513] Also, Davies and Allison hold that "the pure (or clean) in heart" presupposes external, ceremonial purity as its counterpart (cf. 23:25-26), and this is given full body in several pericope of the Sermon on the Mount, such as – Purity of heart from adulterous thought is demanded in 5:27-30. A piety, which is concerned with the private encounter with God, but not with outward show, is portrayed in 6:1-18. It is declared in 6:21 that one's heart is to be in heaven where one's treasure is. The strict correlation between observable behaviour and the true internal self is propounded in 7:16-20. "So, purity of heart must involve integrity, a correspondence between outward action and inward thought (cf. 15:8), a lack of duplicity, singleness of intention ... and the desire to please God above all else. More succinctly: purity of heart is to will one thing, God's will, with all of one's being."[514] Guelich, identifying the background of this beatitude in Ps 24 (23):4, 6, maintains that this Psalm has a cultic setting, and "clean hands" and "pure heart" in this Psalm "describe the whole person standing in total honesty and integrity before God." And, "this meaning of the *pure in heart* corresponds to the section of the Sermon tradition involving behaviour consistent with one's character (Luke 6:43-45, par. Matt 7:16-20)." Therefore, Guelich asserts, "the *pure in heart* viewed against the background of Ps 24(23):4 and the Sermon tradition of Luke 6:43-44 cannot be narrowly defined in terms of thoughts and intentions. Rather, the

509 Schnackenburg, *The Gospel of Matthew*, 48.

510 Luz, *Matthew 1-7*, 239.

511 Schweizer, *The Good News According to Matthew*, 92-93.

512 Davies and Allison, Jr., *Matthew*, Vol. I, 456. See also Luz, *Matthew 1-7*, 239.

513 Hagner, *Matthew 1-13*, 94.

514 Davies and Allison, Jr., *Matthew*, Vol. I, 456. See also Hamm *The Beatitudes in Context*, 99-100; and Thomson, "The Background and Function of the Beatitudes...," 114.

designation refers to the complete integrity and sincerity of one's existence before God."[515]

ὅτι αὐτοὶ τὸν θεὸν ὄψονται, ***"for they will see God."*** It is generally accepted that the promise of the sixth beatitude is eschatological in tone.[516] Those who have a pure heart are promised that they will see God in the eschaton. However, Matthew does not mention the exact meaning of "seeing God" here. It has been interpreted in various ways.[517] We may have an inclusive interpretation by taking together an interpretation of Guelich and Allison, Jr. According to Guelich, "seeing God" here refers to standing "before God, in his very presence, accepted by him at the last judgment."[518] Allison, Jr. is of the view that "seeing God" in Matt 5:8b assumes an embodied deity, and in the context of the first evangelist, it refers to a literal view of God. To support his view, he finds an assumption on the anthropomorphic God in some of the Old Testament passages, such as for example, Gen 1:26-27; 3:8; 32:30; Exod 33:23; Deut 34:10; Isa 6:1; Dan 7:9-13. His strongest support, however, is Matt 18:10, which tells about the angels continually seeing the face of God/the Father.[519] On the basis of such assumptions, he maintains that, Matt 5:8 means "the beatific vision, which the angels enjoy even now, will be bestowed upon the saints in the world to come, just as in other ways the redeemed will become like the angels in heaven (22:30).[520] At the same time, after surveying various interpretations from the past upto the present, Allison, Jr. concludes that the changes in the context of the readers always result in the changing of the reading, and the various interpretations need not be mutually exclusive. Rather, all the diverse interpretations can be held together in the interpretation of "seeing God" as "experiencing the vision of God."[521]

Taking the interpretations of Guelich and Allison, Jr. together, the meaning of "seeing God" in the sixth beatitude may be understood as, standing before God, being accepted by Him at the last judgment, and having an opportunity to view His beauty and to worship him face to face eternally. As Allison, Jr. rightly says,

---

515 Guelich, *The Sermon on the Mount: A Foundation for Understanding*, 90. See also Betz, *The Sermon on the Mount*, 135, who maintains that rather than merely quoting Psalm 24, the sixth beatitude "confirms ideas that were commonly accepted in Judaism at the time. Beginning in the Old Testament, but even more so at the time of early Christianity, purity of heart was the great virtue sought by the truly religious."

516 See for example, Harrington, *The Gospel of Matthew*, 79, quoting M. Barré, "Blessed are the Pure of Heart," *BibToday* 22 (1984), 236-242.

517 For a comprehensive history of interpretations of the meaning of "seeing God" in Matt 5:8b, see Dale C. Allison, Jr., *Studies in Matthew. Interpretation Past and Present* (Grand Rapids, Michigan: Baker Academic, 2005), 43-63.

518 Guelich, *The Sermon on the Mount: A Foundation for Understanding*, 91.

519 Allison, Jr., *Studies in Matthew*, 45-48.

520 *Ibid.*, 48.

521 *Ibid.*, 45-62.

this understanding would include all other interpretations.[522] The implication of this beatitude, therefore, is that those whose hearts are pure before God, and which is, of course, accompanied by their bebaviour, will be blessed with an opportunity to have the beatific vision of God in the eschatological kingdom of God, and to worship Him face to face forever.[523] As in the fifth beatitude, the future aspect of the promised blessing from God indicates the apocalyptic aspect of this beatitude, although the ethical exhortation to pursue purity of heart is the main emphasis. This means that those who strive after purity of heart here and now will experience the beatific vision of God in the eschatological kingdom. To say in other words, in order to experience the beatific vision of God in the age to come, one has to pursue purity of heart here and now.

What then is the significance of purity of heart in the context of Matthew? Primarily, what Strecker says leads us to one possible direction. According to Strecker the "pure in heart" refers to "one who fulfils the demand of righteousness," and it is directed against the attitude of the Pharisees.[524] This seems quite possible.

---

522 For examples of other interpretations, see the following - According to Davies and Allison, Jr., the promise of the future was associated in Judaism with the knowledge or vision of God (e.g., Isa 52:6; 60:16; Jer 24:7; 31:31-34; Heb 12:14; 1 Jn 3:2). It is a privilege, which the angels enjoy even now (Matt 18:10). In line with this Matt 3:8 also has to do with the promise of the eschatological future, and "to see God" here means "to know him." Davies and Allison, Jr, further notes that there are two biblical traditions about "seeing God." One tradition seems to put "seeing God" out of the realm of possibility (e.g., Exod 3:6; 19:21; 33:20, 23; Jn 1:18; 1 Tim 6:15, etc.). The other tradition seems to make "seeing God" a blessed goal (e.g., Ps 11:7; 17:15; Job 19:26, etc.). So, Davies and Allison, Jr. maintain that "perhaps the ancients harmonized things in this way; the former texts have in mind physical sight, the latter inner or spiritual insight; or perhaps they thought one to pertain to this world, the other to the world to come." Davies and Allison, Jr., *Matthew*, Vol. I, 456-457. According to Hagner, "to see God" is the highest possible eschatological reward, which includes all other blessings. This is promised to those who are righteous in the eschatological age (as against the strong Old Testament declaration that no one can see God's face and live, e.g., Exod 33:20). Hagner, who sees all the other Matthean beatitudes as having special reference to the poor, points out that this beatitude does not have any specific relationship to the poor and is quite different from others. Therefore, it could mean that inner purity is required even of the downtrodden and oppressed, for those to whom the good news of the kingdom comes, and it is not something that can be presupposed. Hagner, *Matthew 1-13*, 94. Gundry suggests that Matthew may be trying to make his readers understand that they will see God in the future in the face of Jesus (whom he identified as "God with us") when he returns in glory. Gundry, *Matthew: A Commentary on His Handbook*, 71. According to Schweizer, the vision of God "comprehends everything that men call salvation, life, glory." Schweizer, *The Good News According to Matthew*, 93.

523 Guelich points out that "Ps 24:3-6, in its cultic setting of worship, expresses the hope of "seeing God" found in similar contexts (Ps 17:15; 63:2; Jn 19:26, cf. Isa 38:11). The cultic setting of being accepted into the presence of God becomes the basis for the eschatological hope of "seeing God" found in apocalyptic and rabbinic Judaism (Str-B 1:206-315) and in the New Testament (Heb 12:14; 1 Jn 3:2; Rev 22:4)." Guelich, *The Sermon on the Mount: A Foundation for Understanding*, 91. See also Luz, *Matthew 1-7*, 239.

524 Strecker, *the Sermon on the Mount*, 39-40.

It is our contention in the previous chapter, that the chief opponents of Matthew's community were the scribes and Pharisees who were the leaders of formative Judaism. And, the accusation of these people by the author of the first gospel is seen in various places in the materials which he took from Mark, from Q and in his peculiar material as well.[525] Based on all these accusations, it seems quite possible that the sixth beatitude is directed against the scribes and the Pharisees. The understanding of Schweizer that this beatitude is contrasted to the outward purity brought about by cultic means,[526] and the view of Davies and Allison, Jr., that external, ceremonial purity, is presupposed as its counterpart by "the pure (or clean) in heart," also point to the same direction.[527] This is seen in the fact that Matthew especially connects the Pharisees (and the scribes) with external, ceremonial purity or purity brought about by cultic means (e.g., 23:15, 25, 27).

While, this beatitude is directed mainly against the attitude of the scribes and the Pharisees, that does not seem to be the only focus of Matthew. It seems that Matthew also focuses on an exhortation to his community, having the scribes and the Pharisees at the background, though. This is clearly indicated in Matt 5:20, where the Matthean Jesus explicitly says to his disciples, "unless your righteousness exceeds that of the scribes and Pharisees, you will never enter the kingdom of heaven." And, he also says in 23:2ff., that the scribes and the Pharisees don't practice what they teach (v. 2-3). Therefore, keeping in mind that the scribes and the Pharisees are impure in their hearts, and there is no correspondence between their speech and their actions, Matthew emphasizes to his community members the importance of purity in heart corresponded with outward actions. This is further affirmed by the Matthean Jesus' emphasis upon the unity of thought and action in Matt 5:21ff. On the basis of our analysis above, purity in heart here could or should be understood as doing right actions with integrity of mind;[528]

525 See for example, in 5:20 the Matthean Jesus says to his disciples – "unless your righteousness exceeds that of the scribes and Pharisees, you will never enter the kingdom of heaven." The scribes think evil in their hearts (9:4). The scribes and Pharisees are termed as "evil and adulterous generation" (12:38; 16:4). The scribes and Pharisees broke the commandments of God (15:3). The Pharisees are blind guides of the blind (15:12-14). The Pharisees are pictured as unfaithful tenants (21:33-46). And, especially Matt chap 23 is full of condemnation of the scribes and Pharisees – they don't practice what they teach (v. 2-3); they stop people from entering the kingdom of God and they themselves do not go in (v. 13); they make their convert twice as much a child of hell as themselves (v. 15); They tithe mint, dill, and cummin, but they have neglected the weightier matters of the law: justice and mercy and faith (v. 23); they clean the outside of the cup and of the plate, but inside they are full of greed and self-indulgence (v. 25). They are like whitewashed tombs, which on the outside look beautiful, but are full of the bones of the dead and of all kinds of filth inside (v. 27); they are descendants of those who murdered the prophets, and who fill up the measure of their ancestors. They are snakes, brood of vipers! (vv. 29-33).

526 Schweizer, *The Good News According to Matthew*, 92-93.

527 Davies and Allison, Jr., *Matthew*, Vol. I, 456.

528 Hagner, *Matthew 1-13*, 94.

which includes "truthful speech, keeping one's word, dealing honestly with one's neighbour (Ps 15:2-5)."[529] It relates to the strict correlation between observable behaviour and the true internal self (propounded in Matt 7:16-20), and therefore it involves "integrity, a correspondence between outward action and inward thought (cf. 15:8), a lack of duplicity, singleness of intention … and the desire to please God above all else."[530] This beatitude also probably reflects that there was a situation within the Matthean community, which necessitates an emphasis on such teaching. Then, this will be another way of calling the community members to shun the way of the Pharisees, who appeared to be pure outside, but were impure in the heart. While the primary purpose of Matthew with this beatitude would be to encourage his community members to pursue a purity of heart, it would also imply a warning to them that even if they are members of the Matthean community, those who are impure in their hearts like the Pharisees, will not see God. Those, whose way is the same with that of the Pharisees, will have the same lot with the Pharisees, who are not entering the kingdom of heaven (23:13). Besides that, it is also an assurance to them that the Matthean community members, who were trying to keep their heart pure before God in spite of all the difficulties and hardships they were undergoing, will finally see God with joy and happiness at the eschaton while their opponents the Scribes and the Pharisees will not have that opportunity.

V. 9. μακάριοι οἱ εἰρηνοποιοί, ὅτι αὐτοὶ υἱοὶ θεοῦ κληθήσονται."***Blessed are the peacemakers, for they will be called children of God.***" The seventh beatitude is attributed to Q^{mt}, and on verbal and thematic grounds, it is linked up with Matt 5:38-48 par. Luke 6:27-30, 32-36 (on turning the other cheek and loving enemies),[531] and also probably with Mark 9:50c.[532] This means that its formulation in the Q community was based on those gospel traditions. Although, wisdom and rabbinical parenesis has "to make peace" as their central theme of admonition, and they contain statements which articulate Israel's sonship with God as future hope, "the admonition to make peace is never coupled with the

529 Schnackenburg, *The Gospel of Matthew*, 48.

530 Davies and Allison, Jr., *Matthew*, Vol. I, 456. See also Guelich, *The Sermon on the Mount: A Foundation for Understanding*, 90.

531 Davies and Allison, Jr., *Matthew*, Vol. I, 457. See also Thomson, "The Background and Function of the Beatitudes…," 114. Betz points out that although it does not use the term "peacemaking", the antitheses of the Sermon on the Mount (Matt 5:21-48) present six cases of peacemaking. Moreover, the issues of forgiveness (Matt 6:12, 14-15) and judging (7:1-5) are also related to peacemaking. Betz, *The Sermon on the Mount*, 138.

532 Gundry is of the view that the seventh beatitude is especially in accord with Jesus' teaching in Mark 9:50c, which says, "have salt in yourselves, and be at peace with one another," and since Matthew uses this teaching here he omitted it when he took over the material in Mark 9:42-50 (in Matt 18:6-9). Gundry, *Matthew: A Commentary on His Literary and Theological Art*, 72.

eschatological promise of being children of God."[533] Therefore, the first part of the seventh beatitude probably has its basis in Ps 34:15b (14b), which says ζήτησον εἰρήνην καὶ δίωξον αὐτήν "seek peace, and pursue it,"[534] and Israel's future hope of sonship with God found in some of the Jewish writings[535] might have been joined with it in Q[mt].[536]

μακάριοι οἱ εἰρηνοποιοί, ***"blessed are the peacemakers."*** The word εἰρηνοποιοί is a New Testament's hapax legomenon. It does not occur even in the LXX. However, the verbal equivalent of "peacemakers" occurs in Prov 10:10 LXX (ὁ δὲ ἐλέγχων μετὰ παρρησίας εἰρηνοποιεῖ "*He who boldly rebukes makes peace*") and Col 1:20 (καὶ δι' αὐτοῦ ἀποκαταλλάξαι τὰ πάντα εἰς αὐτόν, εἰρηνοποιήσας διὰ τοῦ αἵματος τοῦ σταυροῦ αὐτοῦ, [δι' αὐτοῦ] εἴτε τὰ ἐπὶ τῆς γῆς εἴτε τὰ ἐν τοῖς οὐρανοῖς, "*and through him God was pleased to reconcile to himself all things, whether on earth or in heaven, by making peace through the blood of his cross*"). Therefore, Davies and Allison, Jr. assert that Matthew's εἰρηνοποιοί comes from the LXX.[537] They further state that besides the fact that the word εἰρηνοποιοί is a hapax legomenon, the theme of "peace" is not prominent in the first gospel. These two facts, therefore, indicate that the origin of the seventh beatitude is pre-Matthean.[538]

The action that the word εἰρηνοποιοί might refer to in this beatitude is interpreted in different ways. However, based on the views of the majority of the scholars, and some related Jewish and NT texts, οἱ εἰρηνοποιοί can be understood as primarily referring to those who make peace between human beings. At the same time, however, those who make peace between human beings and God cannot be excluded.[539] It is quite uncertain, however, whether there could be any

533 Luz, *Matthew 1-7*, 241.

534 Gundry, *Matthew: A Commentary on His Handbook*, 72.

535 E.g., Jubilees 1:24f.; T.Judah 24:3; Ps. Sol. 17:27 (future!); cf. Wisd. 5:5. For these references, see Luz, *Matthew 1-7*, 241.

536 Davies and Allison, Jr., *Matthew*, Vol. I, 459.

537 Davies and Allison, Jr., *Matthew*, Vol. I, 457.

538 *Ibid.*

539 See the following interpretations as examples - Guelich maintains that "we should take the adjective in its more literal, active sense of one who makes peace, who brings reconciliation between opposing parties rather than one who patiently endures in a passive posture of nonresistance for the sake of peace." He further says that "in light of Luke 6:27-35, par. Matt, the peacemakers are those who demonstrate love and concern for their enemies," and therefore, *peacemaking* "is much more than a passive suffering to maintain peace or even 'bridge-building' or reconciling alienated parties. It is the demonstration of God's love through Christ in all its profundity." Guelich, *The Sermon on the Mount: A Foundation for Understanding*, 91-92. See also Dupont, *Les Beatitudes*, 3: 635-640, quoted by Guelich here. Denis Hamm notes that the Hebrew word for peace, *Shalom* (and its usual Greek counterpart in the LXX, *eirēnē*) means not simply absence of war but "the fullness of life, abundance, right relationship all round," and, "the most immediate background of the ninth beatitude is the rabbinical *asah shalom*, which refers to the establishment of peace and concord between human beings." Hamm, *The*

reference beyond these two spheres.[540] Concerning making peace between human beings, the Old Testament bases (esp. Ps 34: 15b [14b], and Prov. 10:10) and the related texts in the NT such as Matt 5:38-48 par. Luke 6:27-30, 32-36; and Mark 9:50c., seem to refer primarily to taking positive action, instead of simply being a pacifist or peaceful, to make peace between oneself and others. However, as Guelich asserts, the adjective εἰρηνοποιοί in its literal and active sense, also points to peacemaking between opposing parties. This seems to be the point also of the extrabiblical texts which are related to the seventh beatitude (such as *m. Pe'a* 1:1; *Mek.* on Exod 20:25, etc.).[541]

Beatitudes in Context, 102. According to Cox, however, it refers to the work of reconciliation between human being and another human being, and more fundamentally between human being and God. Cox, *The Gospel According to Saint Matthew*, 47. Schnackenburg, on the other hand, asserting that the word "peaceable" would be too weak for a translation of the word εἰρηνοποιοί, maintains that the word denotes, "an active concern for peace, as God wills it and as Jesus embodies it (Matt 21:4-5)," and seeking "to propagate among humans the peace proclaimed by God (Lk 2:14), in conformity with the Reign of God throughout the world, even among the Gentiles (Isa 2:4; Mic 4:3)." Schnackenburg, *The Gospel of Matthew*, 49. See also Doohan, *Matthew. Spirituality for the 80's and 90's*, 129. Newman is also of the view that while the "peacemakers" here could refer both to those who make peace between human being and God, as well as between human being and another human being. He says that both the extra-biblical Jewish literature and the biblical writings themselves give support to the idea that the peace spoken of is, that which is established among human beings. Newman further mentions here for example that the phrase εἰρήνην ποιεῖν ("to make peace") is used in the same sense in Eph 2:15 and Jas 3:18; and Heb 12:14 exhorts the believers to be at peace with all human beings. Newman, Jr., "Some Translational Notes on the Beatitudes," 118. Ulrich Luz also asserts that "the admonition to make peace has a central place in wisdom and in rabbinical parenesis," and "in each case, concrete steps in interhuman relationship are meant." Luz, *Matthew 1-7*, 241. According to Davies and Allison, Jr., the correct translation of εἰρηνοποιός is "peacemakers" and not pacifist or "peaceful," for what is envisioned is a positive action, reconciliation. That is, the "peacemakers" seek to bring about peace. They further note that other biblical texts (quoted above) and extra biblical texts (such as *m.Pe'a* 1:1; *Mek.* on Exod 20:25, etc.), which are related to the seventh beatitude in theme and vocabulary, consistently have a social dimension, thus indicating that religious peace (peace with God) is probably not the subject. They, however, maintain, "because there is no qualification for 'peacemakers', it would be wrong to delimit precisely the sphere to which 'peacemakers' bring peace." They are also of the view that the seventh beatitude was perhaps formulated during the Jewish war or shortly after and thereby, it reflects the conviction that revolution against Rome was the wrong course to take. Davies and Allison, Jr., *Matthew*, Vol. I, 457-458.

540 Davies and Allison Jr. mention that Origen (in *Philocal* 6:1) includes among the "peacemakers" those who reconcile contradictory Biblical texts. But, they (Davies and Allison, Jr.) comment that it "is only a curiosity which evokes a smile." Davies and Allison, Jr., *Matthew*, Vol. I, 458.

541 Gundry notes that especially in Prov 10:10 LXX (cf. Nas 3:18), peacemaking means one's own peace with others. But making peace between others is obtained in *m.Pe'a* 1:1 and other rabbinic literature cited by Str-B. 215-18. Gundry, *Matthew: A Commentary on His Literary and Theological Art*, 72.

ὅτι αὐτοὶ υἱοὶ θεοῦ κληθήσονται, ***"for they will be called children of God."*** υἱοὶ θεοῦ literally "sons of God" appears only here in Matthew. Its equivalent "sons of your father in heaven" occurs in 5:45 (cf. Luke 6:35). Gundry, however, rightly points out that the promise to call the peacemakers "sons of God" here suits Matthew's interest in the sonship of the disciples to God the Father, especially in the Sermon on the Mount.[542] Although the phrase υἱοὶ Θεοῦ literally means "sons of God," Hagner renders it as "children of God" which includes both men and women.[543] This seems to be a better rendering than the literal translation "sons of God" because neither Jesus nor Matthew is likely to exclude women. It rather seems that they just use the normal usage of the time without any idea of exclusion.[544] In the first century Judaism, women might have never been viewed to take part in peace making. That is indicated by this verse. That seems to be one of the reasons why an inclusive language is not used by the first evangelist. It does not seem that women are deliberately excluded. Therefore, whether the literal meaning is retained in the translation, thus "sons of God," or it is translated with the inclusive language, thus "children of God," this beatitude seems to emphasize the importance of peace making for the followers of Jesus Christ, for both women and men. Therefore, the translation "children of God" is preferred in this study.

The verb κληθήσονται is a divine passive, and it is future. This indicates that the expectation here is "to be called" sons/children of God by God in the future, that is in the eschaton.[545] However, just as the kingdom of heaven has both present and future dimensions, meaning that, it is already experienced here but to be consummated in the future, the promise of this beatitude also must have a present dimension as well. That means that the peacemakers (i.e., believers in Jesus Christ) are already called children of God even here on earth, although the full significance will be experienced in the future kingdom of God. Indeed, in harmony with Johannine and Pauline tradition (see, Jn 1:12; Rom 8:14-15; Gal 3:26-27; 4:5; Eph 1:5), there is a notion in Matthew that believers in Jesus are

542 Gundry, *Matthew: A Commentary on His Literary and Theological Art*, 72. Here, Gundry mentions the following verses – Matt 5: 16, 45, 48; 6:1, 4, 6, 8, 9, 14, 15, 18, 26, 32; 7:11; and also 10:20, 29; 13:43; 18:14; 23:9, all unique in this respect except for 5:45, 48; 6:9, 14; 7:11.

543 Hagner, *Matthew 1-13*, 94. See also Schnackenburg, *The Gospel of Matthew*, 49.

544 Cf. however, Harrington observes, "a gender neutral translation might obscure the allusion to joining the angels in God's kingdom" in Gen 6:1-4. Harrington, *The Gospel of Matthew*, 80. Carson also is of the view that the literal meaning should be preferred to the inclusive translation. Carson, *The Sermon on the Mount*, 26-27. Dennis Hamm connects "sons of God" of the seventh beatitude with the presentation of Jesus as God's Son in Matt 2:15; 3:17, and 4:3, 6. He asserts that "Son of God" in these episodes connotes Jesus' obedience to the Father. Therefore, those who participate in the peace-making initiative of God the Father in Jesus, both male and female, are called to share in the sonship of Jesus Christ. Hamm, *The Beatitudes in Context*, 103-106.

545 Davies and Allison, Jr., *Matthew*, Vol. I, 458-459.

already children or sons of God (Matt 5:45; 6:9).[546] This also supports the idea that the future promise in Matt 5:9, "to be called children of God" also has a present dimension. According to Davies and Allison, Jr., there are two dimensions symbolized by the notion of the expected eschatological sonship, such as – (a) a degree of intimacy with God which has never been experienced so far, and (b) a likeness to God (cf. 5:48).[547] According to Newman, Jr., the term υἱοὶ θεοῦ "sons of God" usually refers in the biblical and extra-biblical literature to the one who "bears the likeness of God in terms of the particular quality under discussion," and hence in the present context it will mean that the peace-makers will bear the likeness of God in peace-making.[548] Guelich also states that κληθήσονται here "denotes the divine act by which one becomes a son of God," and it is more than a label (as Matt 5:45 par. Luke 6:35 notes), but an actual becoming of a son of God. He further notes that the *son of God* in Matt 5:9 and 5:45, "is an expression of the future intimate relationship with God as Father, as well as of the similarity of character between Father and Son." Therefore, these two verses indicate, "by exhibiting conduct corresponding to that of the Father ..., they show themselves indeed to be *sons of God*," and "the ultimate status of sonship declared at the consummation expresses the complete acceptance by God."[549]

Thus, the meaning of the seventh beatitude may be briefly given as: by peace making, believers in Jesus Christ bear the likeness of God. Therefore, they already show themselves as children of God. However, they will experience the full significance of their sonship / childrenhood of God in the eschaton by being fully accepted by God, and enjoying a degree of intimacy with God, which has never been experienced so far. At the same time, however, this would also imply that those who are not peacemakers are not entitled to the name "children of God."[550] The apocalyptic aspect of this beatitude is apparent here.

Now, what would be the implication of this beatitude in the context of Matthew? According to Hanger this beatitude is based on Jesus' teaching that the status of υἱοὶ θεοῦ, "children of God" belongs not to the violent but to those who live peaceably (cf. Rom 9:26). And, in the context of Matthew's gospel, it could be the evangelist's exhortation to the oppressed and the downtrodden to shun the way of the zealots who were hoping to bring the kingdom of God through violence.[551] In its original setting, whether it was in Jesus' own time, or, during the first Jewish War or soon after it, it could well mean an exhortation to the followers of Jesus to shun the Zealots' way. However, the poor and the downtrodden could not have necessarily been the sole object of the exhortation (against the view of

546 Davies and Allison, Jr., *Matthew*, Vol. I, 458-459.

547 *Ibid.*, 459.

548 Newman, Jr., "Some Translational Notes on the Beatitudes," 119.

549 Guelich, *The Sermon on the Mount: A Foundation for Understanding*, 92.

550 Betz, *The Sermon on the Mount*, 141.

551 Hagner, *Matthew 1-13*, 94.

Hagner). Even if the members of Jesus' followers were composed, probably and basically of the poor, no one among Jesus' followers would have been excluded. And, in the context of Matthew's community which is identified as located in Antioch, and especially at the time of the writing of this gospel, the question of Zealot's way may have not been so prominent among the members of the community. Therefore, this beatitude seems to have another focus in the context of Matthew.

In the previous chapter, we have maintained that in their conflict with the leaders of formative Judaism, especially the scribes and the Pharisees, members of the Matthean community were suffering persecutions from those people. Therefore, one of the implications of the seventh beatitude would be that the scribes and the Pharisees are not at all εἰρηνοποιοί "peacemakers." The corollary would then be that they will not be called "sons/children of God,"[552] and therefore they are not to be imitated at all for the Matthean community. More importantly, this beatitude would be an exhortation to the members of the Matthean community not to retaliate against those who persecute them. Instead, they must try to make peace between themselves and those who persecute them. This is strongly supported by Matt 5:44-45 in which the Matthean Jesus exhorts his disciples to love their enemies and pray for those who persecute them, so that they will be able to become sons of their Father in heaven.[553] In addition to that, this beatitude could also be a call for unity among the community of Matthew. As we have indicated in the previous chapter, the community of the first evangelist was made up both of Jews and Gentiles who could not have free table fellowship, or to say in other words, who could not have fellowship on equal terms. The Gentile members had to adjust themselves to an inferior position. In such a situation, there were chances of misunderstandings even on slight pretexts. Through this beatitude, the first evangelist is exhorting his community members to avoid such misunderstandings, and when a situation arose for such quarrel, they are exhorted to try to make peace between them and their opponents, or between other opposing groups or members. Moreover, we have highlighted in the previous chapter that the Jews in Antioch suffered persecutions at the hands of the Gentiles, and they were in fear of further persecutions. Even if such persecutions did not happen, the relation between the Jews and the Gentiles in Antioch was not good at all. The community of Matthew also would certainly have shared

552 Gundry claims that the "peacemakers" here "stand against the men who hate the disciples in the final beatitude of the final tradition (Luke 6:22)." See, Gundry, *Matthew: A Commentary on His Handbook*, 72.

553 Ulrich Luz maintains that this beatitude, together with the following ones, points to the commandments of love of enemies in Matt 5:44-48, as "there also the promise is made that they shall be children of God (5:45);" and "there also, the subject is, as in vv. 10-12, enemies and persecutors." Luz further says, "Matthew is thinking not only of a peaceful living together of members of the community, but thinks beyond the limits of the community." Luz, *Matthew 1-7*, 241.

the experience of the Jews. In such situations, the seventh beatitude could be a call to be peacemakers between Jews and Gentiles in Antioch. This possibility is also well supported by the emphasis on mission among the Gentiles. In view of the experiences they had undergone from the Gentiles, it would have been very difficult from the Jewish perspective to emphasize mission to the Gentiles. However, based on Jesus' teaching, the Matthean community members could view the situation from a different perspective.

V. 10. μακάριοι οἱ δεδιωγμένοι ἕνεκεν δικαιοσύνης, ὅτι αὐτῶν ἐστιν ἡ βασιλεία τῶν οὐρανῶν. "***Blessed are those who are persecuted for righteousness' sake, for theirs is the kingdom of heaven.***" Although we could not know for sure, it is accepted in this study that the eighth beatitude is a Matthean addition.[554] Davies and Allison, Jr. explicitly assert that Matthew added this beatitude solely to make the number of the beatitudes into nine from the eight, which he got in his tradition, and Matthew did this to correspond to his triadic arrangement of the materials in the Sermon on the Mount. According to them, the content of this beatitude does not play any important role for the explanation of its addition by Matthew. It was added only for the numerical concern, that is, to make the eight beatitudes into nine, to agree with the triadic arrangement of other materials in the Sermon on the Mount.[555]

Davies and Allison, Jr. seem right in saying that Matthew added the eighth beatitude to make the number of the beatitudes to nine. However, that does not seem to be the only concern of Matthew. There are some pertinent questions which are not answered by Davies and Allison, Jr., such as why did Matthew select the eighth position for adding this beatitude, and why did he choose such prominent terms like persecution, righteousness, and kingdom of heaven, connecting all of them? It is believed in this research, as already indicated in the structure of the Matthean Beatitudes above that Matthew deliberately selected the eighth position for inserting an additional beatitude, and he purposely selected the content of this beatitude. To put it briefly, the first evangelist wanted to accentuate the importance of these three terms, such as righteousness, persecution, and kingdom of heaven, by selecting them for his additional beatitude and by deliberately placing them at the eighth position of his beatitudes.[556]

It is also appropriate to clarify here that in the view of this researcher Matthew did not create this beatitude out of nothing. Rather he renders in the

554 See "the Redaction of the Matthean Beatitudes" above.

555 Davies and Allison, Jr., *Matthew*, Vol. I, 459. Here, Davies and Allison, Jr. argue that the addition of this beatitude does not have anything to do with emphasis on the beatitude of persecution because this is satisfied by 5:11-12. It also does not have anything to do with giving "righteousness" a home in the beatitudes because it has already been named in 5:6. To connect persecution and righteousness was not also his purpose because if that was his concern he could easily do it by adding "and righteousness" at the end of 5:11.

556 See also "the Structure of the Matthean Beatitudes" above.

form of this beatitude what he found in Jesus' teaching. The teaching of Jesus with such a notion can be found at least in Matt 10:26-33 (par. Luke 12:1-12). Moreover, although "a suffering person or a person in hardship would never be called *makarios*" in the Old Testament,[557] it was widely emphasized in Judaism of Jesus' time that the persecuted are among God's favourites. Such idea was contained in Ps 22; 34:19-20; and Wisd. 2:10-20.[558] Moreover, given the fact that the Hebrew/Aramaic equivalent of διώκω that is רָדַף refers to both persecute and pursue,[559] the eighth beatitude also can be understood as alluding to Deut 16:20.[560] Giving an interesting analysis in this aspect, C. R. Day maintains that the eighth beatitude talks about the fact that "being *persecuted for righteousness' sake* is the result of *pursuing righteousness.*" Then, he gives a paraphrase of Matt 5:10 as follows – "*Blessed are those whose pursuit of what God requires causes them to become persecuted, for they receive the kingdom of Heaven.*"[561] The passages mentioned above could have formed the basis of the formulation of the eighth beatitude by Matthew, or the teaching of Jesus behind it, or both of them. Moreover, the idea of blessedness for the suffering righteous is also found in 1Peter 3:14 which reads, "But, even if you do suffer for doing what is right, you are blessed. Do not fear what they fear, and do not be intimidated." While this could be taken from Matthew, it could also be the Petrine adaptation of Jesus' saying, which underlies the eighth beatitude of Matthew.[562] If the second were the case, it would be a strong supporter of the contention that the eighth beatitude of Matthew is the first evangelist's adaptation from Jesus' authentic sayings.[563] Therefore, the eighth beatitude of Matthew seems to have been formulated by the first evangelist on the basis of Jesus' authentic teaching and some of the Old Testament passages such

557 Lichtenberger, "Makarisms in Mathew 5:3ff. in their Jewish Context," 44, quoting W. Zimmerli, "Die Seligpreisungen der Bergpredigt und das AT," in E. Bammel, et al (eds.), *Donum Gentilicium, FS D. Daube* (Oxford: Clarendon Press, 1978), 8-26, esp. 16.

558 Schweizer, *The Good News According to Matthew*, 95-96.

559 See Brown, Driver and Bridges, eds., *Hebrew and English Lexicon of the Old Testament*, 922.

560 Which says: "Justice, and only justice, you shall pursue, so that you may live and occupy the land that the LORD your God is giving you."

561 C. R. Day, "Those who are persecuted because of Righteousness, are those who pursue Righteousness: An Examination of the Origin and Meaning of the Eighth Beatitude," *ActaPatByz* 16 (2005), 164 [157-165]. Although Day's analysis of the possible allusion of the eighth beatitude to Deut 16:20 is taken here, his understanding (following Goulder) that Matt 5:11-12 forms part of Jesus' explanation to the eighth beatitude (see p. 162), is not subscribed to in this study.

562 J. Ramsey Michaels, *I Peter*, WBC, Vol. 49 (Dallas, Texas: Word Books Publishers, 1988), 185. See also Davies and Allison, Jr., *Matthew*, Vol. I, 460. Davies and Allison, Jr. also mention here other possible implications of the parallel between Matt 5:10 and IPet 3:14. They also mention that a similar saying in Polycarp, *Ep.* 2:3, "Blessed are the poor and those who are persecuted for righteousness' sake, because theirs is the kingdom of God" undoubtedly betrays a direct dependence upon Matthew.

563 Guelich, *The Sermon on the Mount: A Foundation for Understanding*, 93.

as Deut 16:20; Ps 22; 34:19-20; and Wisd 2:10-20, under the influence of his community's experience.

μακάριοι οἱ δεδιωγμένοι ἕνεκεν δικαιοσύνης, ***"blessed are those who are persecuted for righteousness' sake."*** The perfect passive participle δεδιωγμένοι comes from διώκω which has two basic meanings such as "to impel" and "to persecute." The LXX uses it in the sense of religious persecution accusing the persecutors as offenders. Though it is used in the sense of "impelling" in the New Testament, the more common use is in the sense of religious persecution with the guilt being laid on the persecutors. That is the sense even in this place.[564]

Luz maintains that the use of the perfect participle here "lifts the actual event of persecution as described in vv. 11f., into a more universal sphere." According to him, Matthew, looking back to a persecution which happened earlier, understands persecution almost as a general sign of being a Christian."[565] On the other hand, Guelich maintains, "the rather unexpected perfect participle, δεδιωγμένοι, makes the subject quite concrete, focussing on the community's actual experience rather than on a more general, indefinite possibility."[566] According to Gundry, "δεδιωγμένοι is typical of Matthew's diction" and it "does not necessarily refer to killing, but means hounding ... and here it corresponds to ἀφορίσωσιν 'exclude' in the final beatitude of the tradition (Luke 6:22)."[567] According to Davies and Allison, Jr., the verb διώκω may refer either to physical violence or to verbal abuse or it may also refer to both. The perfect tense, which is used here, entails that persecution is a fact of the past as well as of the present.[568] Although, scholars have different views, it may be correct to take διώκω, especially in this verse, as referring to different kinds of negative experience (persecutions) suffered by members of the Matthean Community at the hands of the Jewish leaders and their Gentile neighbors.[569] The perfect would indicate, as Davies and Allison, Jr., assert (see above), that it is something that has happened, and is still in operation.[570] While, it would be correct to assume that it primarily indicates what has happened and are still happening to the primary audience, that is the Matthean community, it would not exclude all the persecutions suffered by the faithful followers of Jesus Christ (i.e. "because of righteousness").

---

564 Oepke, "διωκω," *TDNT,* Vol. II (Grand Rapids, Michigan: William B. Eerdmans Publishing Company, 1964), 229-230.

565 Luz, *Matthew 1-7*, 241-242.

566 Guelich, *The Sermon on the Mount: A Foundation for Understanding*, 93.

567 Gundry, *Matthew: A Commentary on His Handbook*, 72.

568 Davies and Allison, Jr., *Matthew*, Vol. I, 459.

569 In fact, Matthew uses the term "persecution" to characterize all the negative experiences / problems suffered by his community from the Jewish side. This is indicated in Matt 5:10-12, 44; 10:23; 13:21; 23:34. See Stegemann and Stegemann, *The Jesus Movement*, 237, and 440, n. 279.

570 See also Betz, *The Sermon on the Mount*, 146.

Hare suggests that ἕνεκεν here simply identifies the persecuted, meaning that "blessed are the persecuted righteous."[571] However, Davies and Allison, Jr. argue that the word ἕνεκεν here most naturally implies that "righteousness" is the occasion or cause of persecution.[572] δικαιοσύνη "righteousness" here means "doing the will of God" or "doing what God requires of his people."[573] It is not used here in terms of "justification" or "vindication."[574]

Thus, the phrase οἱ δεδιωγμένοι ἕνεκεν δικαιοσύνης "who are persecuted on account of righteousness" here refers to the persecution which the believers in Jesus Christ had undergone because of their loyalty to God, that is their faith in Jesus Christ.[575] This is clarified by the phrase ἕνεκεν ἐμοῦ, "on account of me" in v. 11, which is the counterpart of ἕνεκεν δικαιοσύνης, "on account of righteousness" in this verse. This also further indicates that to be in the way of righteousness one has to identify himself/herself with Jesus and the kingdom (cf. 21:32).[576] Strecker is of the view that the absence of a definite article before δικαιοσύνη here is intentional and it means that Christians are persecuted not because of their faith in Christ, but because of their ethical behaviour.[577] However, on the part of Christians as focused on in this beatitude, it seems that their faith in Christ and their ethical behaviour cannot be clearly demarcated. It rather seems that because of their faith in Jesus Christ they acted according to his teaching, as Luz rightly says, "the confession of Christ manifests itself in deeds" of righteousness, which is affirmed even in other places like Matt 7:21-23; 25:31-46.[578] Therefore, it seems right to assume that the persecutions suffered by Christians seem to be because of both their faith in Christ and their ethical behaviour, which were like two sides of the same coin. Guelich rightly notes that persecution for righteousness' sake in the Matthean context "comes to those who live according to the will of God," and in Matthew, such conduct is based on and grows "out of the new relationship offered by God to humankind in the gospel of Jesus' ministry. Such, conduct led inevitably to conflict with the standards of that day, Jewish and Greek, for the disciple just as certainly as it did for Jesus' own

571 Hare, *The Theme of Jewish Persecution*, 131.

572 Davies and Allison, Jr., *Matthew*, Vol. I, 459. Gundry also maintains, "Since for Matthew a Christian is righteous by definition (otherwise he is a hypocrite), we have no reason to distinguish between righteousness as the occasion of persecution and righteousness as the cause of persecution." Gundry, *Matthew: A Commentary on His Literary and Theological Art*, 73.

573 For this meaning of δικαιοσύνη see Newman, Jr., "Some Translational Notes on the Beatitudes," 117. See also Davies and Allison, Jr., Matthew, Vol. I, 459-460; and Luz, Matthew 1-7, 242.

574 Davies and Allison, Jr., *Matthew*, Vol. I, 460.

575 Guelich, *The Sermon on the Mount: A Foundation for Understanding*, 93.

576 See the following: Hagner, *Matthew 1-13*, 94; and Luz, *Matthew 1-7*, 242. See also comment on 5:6 above.

577 Strecker, *The Sermon on the Mount*, 45.

578 Luz, *Matthew 1-7*, 242.

ministry (5:11-12)."[579] Daniel Patte also rightly says that the ultimate goal of the disciples is to act for righteousness' sake (5:10), or, better, "for Jesus' sake" (5:11), and ultimately for God's sake, because when they act in this way … people may "give glory to the Father who is in heaven" (5:16).[580]

ὅτι αὐτῶν ἐστιν ἡ βασιλεία τῶν οὐρανῶν, ***"for theirs is the kingdom of heaven."*** The same ὅτι clause, *"for theirs is the kingdom of heaven,"* is found in the first beatitude. Therefore, this ὅτι clause forms an *inclusio* between the first and the eighth beatitudes.[581] This *inclusio* performs important functions. First, it marks the beginning and end of the first eight beatitudes, which are similar in forms. The ninth and the last beatitude, which follows these eight beatitudes is quite different in form. Second, this *inclusio* also implies that the promises in the beatitudes (second to seventh) are different ways of saying the same promise of the first and the eighth beatitudes, that is, "for theirs is the kingdom of heaven."[582] Thus, by forming an *inclusio* with the first beatitude, the eighth beatitude is bound to the beatitudes, which precede it. At the same time, with its subject matter, that is "persecution," it also points or is attached to the last beatitude, 5:11-12, which follows it because the theme of this last beatitude is also "persecution."[583] The attachment of the eighth beatitude to the beatitudes preceding it and to the one following it clearly indicates that the nine beatitudes are inseparable.

Now, what is the significance of this beatitude for Matthew? Eduard Schweizer points out that the inclusion of the persecuted among God's favourite was widely stressed in Judaism of Jesus time, and the statement, such as found in Matthew, was familiar in various forms.[584] The persecution of the righteous is prominent especially in Wisdom chaps. 1-5, an apocryphal book of the Old Testament. However, there is no blessing of the persecuted in the Old

---

579 Guelich, *The Sermon on the Mount: A Foundation for Understanding*, 93.

580 Patte, *The Gospel According to Matthew*, 67.

581 According to Guelich, not only the ὅτι clause, but both the protasis and the apodosis form an *inclusio*. He maintains that *those having been persecuted for righteousness' sake* of the eighth beatitude pick up the synonymous *poor in spirit ('nwm)* of 5:3, therefore the content of the eight beatitude parallels to that of the first, and forms a deliberate *inclusio*. Guelich, *The Sermon on the Mount: A Foundation for Understanding*, 93.

582 Davies and Allison, Jr., *Matthew*, Vol. I, 460. In other words, we may say that all the promises in the beatitudes from 2 to 7 are attributes of the kingdom of heaven. Betz puts in this way - "For the SM, the meaning of the *inclusio* is clear: the sequence of virtues in vss 3a-9a, combined with the eschatological promises in vss 4b-9b, is held together by the theme of the kingdom of the heavens, in which righteousness reigns and will ultimately prevail." Betz, *The Sermon on the Mount*, 146. For a detailed discussion on the meaning of "for theirs is the kingdom of Heaven," see the exegetical comment on the first beatitude above.

583 Davies and Allison, Jr., *Matthew*, Vol. I, 460.

584 Schweizer quotes Ps 22; 34:19-20; Wis 2:10-20 as containing this idea, and 1Pet 3:14; 4:13-14 as showing its familiarity in various forms. See Schweizer, *The Good News According to Matthew*, 95-96.

Testament.[585] Therefore, it is quite uncertain how far Matthew might have drawn the idea for this beatitude from the Old Testament.[586] On the other hand, it seems quite clear that Matthew reflects upon the practical experience of his community in this beatitude. Schnackenburg has rightly pointed out that persecution for righteousness' sake was the actual experience of the Matthean community.[587] Moreover, the theme of persecution has special importance in Matthew, probably because of the concrete experience of the community behind the first gospel who experienced persecution, both from the Jews and from the Gentiles.[588] Therefore, it is quite apparent that in the context of the persecutions they were undergoing, especially in the hands of the leaders of formative Judaism, and probably also from the Gentiles, they needed to be exhorted on the basis of Jesus' teaching, especially on how to regard and endure persecution. This is what the first evangelist does with this beatitude.[589] It is composed by the first evangelist in the form of apocalyptic beatitude for the exhortation of his community members to remain faithful under the circumstances of persecution. An eschatological reversal is promised to them, that all their sufferings will turn into glory and exaltation in the eschatological kingdom of God.

VV. 11-12. 11μακάριοί ἐστε ὅταν ὀνειδίσωσιν ὑμᾶς καὶ διώξωσιν καὶ εἴπωσιν πᾶν πονηρὸν καθ' ὑμῶν [ψευδόμενοι] ἕνεκεν ἐμοῦ. ***"Blessed are you when they revile you and persecute you and utter all kinds of evil against you falsely on my account."***

12χαίρετε καὶ ἀγαλλιᾶσθε, ὅτι ὁ μισθὸς ὑμῶν πολὺς ἐν τοῖς οὐρανοῖς· οὕτως γὰρ ἐδίωξαν τοὺς προφήτας τοὺς πρὸ ὑμῶν. ***"Rejoice and be exceedingly glad, for your reward is great in heaven, for in the same way they persecuted the prophets who were before you."*** The ninth beatitude belongs to Q. It has its Old Testament bases in Isa 51:7 (v. 11) and 61:10-11 (v. 12). Probably it was spoken by Jesus (on the basis of these OT passages). Then it was circulating in isolation from the other three dominical beatitudes; and was collected and added to them before the other beatitudes (Matt 5:5, 7-9) were added, or it was composed in

585 Davies and Allison, Jr., *Matthew*, Vol. I, 459. See also Lichtenberger, "Makarisms in Mathew 5:3ff. in their Jewish Context," 44, quoting Zimmerli, "Die Seligpreisungen der Bergpredigt und das AT," 8-26, esp. 16.

586 Gundry notes that "righteousness" here means the disciples' right conduct, and has twofold allusion to Ps 15:1[-2], "O LORD, … who shall dwell on your holy hill? He who … does righteousness," and Isa 51:7a, "Listen to me, you who know righteousness, a people in whose heart is my law." Gundry, *Matthew: A Commentary on His Literary and Theological Art*, 72.

587 Schnackenburg, *The Gospel of Matthew*, 49.

588 Sim, *The Gospel of Matthew and Christian Judaism*, 5-8. See also Stanton, "The Origin and Purpose of Matthew's Sermon on the Mount," 189. According to Hagner, The theme of persecution in the last three verses of the Matthean Beatitudes (5:10-12) as well as the similar motif of 5:44 and 10:23 are unique to Matthew. Hagner, *Matthew 1-13*, 95.

589 Cf. Hagner, *Matthew 1-13*, 95.

the Q community on the basis of Jesus' teaching found elsewhere in the gospel tradition (such as Matt 10:26-33 par. Luke 12:1-12 which also form the basis of the eighth beatitude) and was added to the first three dominical beatitudes to make a smooth transition from the Beatitudes to the section on the love of enemies in the following pericopae.

The form of the ninth beatitude is different from the other beatitudes. It is much longer than the preceding eight beatitudes, and the ὅτι clause is also delayed. Moreover, a notable difference of the ninth beatitude is the use of second person pronoun, as against third person pronoun, in all the preceding beatitudes. Such difference in form and especially its use of second person pronoun can be viewed as suggesting the possibility of its original independence from the collection of the preceding eight beatitudes. However, since there is a parallel beatitude in Luke (6:22-23) with similar structure, this beatitude and the other three beatitudes common to Matthew and Luke (Matt 5:3, 4, 6 par. Luke 6:20-21) had most probably been brought together in the pre-Matthean and Lukan tradition.[590] As it is contended above, it seems that the original collector of the Beatitudes for the Q community brought them together, and following a common literary practice in ancient literature, he arranged them in the form of third person, concluded with an extended second person form.[591] It is obvious, therefore, that the final beatitude was part of the tradition which Matthew received, which he reproduced in second person form as he received it. There could be two probable reasons behind Matthew's retention of the present form of the Beatitudes, that is the formulation of a series in third person form and concluded with a second person form, such as: (1) It could be that he wished to smooth the transition from the Beatitudes to the following pericope (5:13-16 – which has second person), or (2) he thought that to switch from the third to the second person makes it climactic.[592] It is believed in this study that Matthew retains the form that he found in his source as it is, because of the emphasis it carries.[593] This emphasis has significance at least in two ways. First, it indicates the importance of the theme of persecution

590 Guelich, *The Sermon on the Mount: A Foundation for Understanding*, 94. Guelich, here, points out that this view is supported by the fact that each of the final beatitudes of Matthew and Luke has lexical similarity with their respective subsequent material on loving one's enemies. To be more precise, "hatred" (μισέω) of Luke 6:22-23 has its counterpart in 6:27; and "persecution" (διώκω) of Matt 5:11-12 has its counterpart in 5:44. Guelich maintains here, "consequently, this rather complex Beatitude had once formed a transition between the other three Beatitudes and the following section addressed in the second person plural (5:44, par. Luke 6:27) in the Sermon tradition." See also Schnackenburg, *The Gospel of Matthew*, 49.

591 See "the Redaction of the Matthean Beatitudes" above.

592 Davies and Allison, Jr., *Matthew*, Vol. I, 461. Davies and Allison, Jr. mention these two probable reasons if Matthew was responsible for the third person form of 5:3-10. They are taken in this study as the reasons behind Matthew's retention of the form which he found in his tradition.

593 Although, it is not explicitly mentioned, this is also implied in Daube, "The Last Beatitude," 321-325.

in Matthew. The theme of persecution is already presented in the eighth beatitude in the form of third person, like the first seven beatitudes. Now it is elaborated in the ninth beatitude emphatically with direct address to the audience. All these indicate that the theme of persecution occupies a very important place in the Matthean Beatitudes as well as in Matthew's gospel as a whole. The most probable reason for such emphasis is to relate it to the persecution experienced by the Matthean community. Second, this climactic presentation of the final beatitude in second person indicates that all the previous beatitudes, which are presented in third person as universally applicable, are also primarily meant for the immediate audience. This is supported especially by a close link between the eighth and ninth beatitudes with the same subject matter, that is, persecution, and the inclusion of the first eight beatitudes with the promise of "kingdom of heaven" in the first and eighth beatitudes.

The ninth Matthean beatitude (5:11-12) parallels the fourth Lukan beatitude (6:22-23). Matt 5:11 parallels Luke 6:22, and Matt 5:12 parallels Luke 6:23. However, Matthew has certain different wordings from its parallel in Luke. If, as it is usually held, Luke has preserved the Q form, and so even in this beatitude, then it means that Matthew redacted the same material which he shared with Luke for this last beatitude. However, all the differences in this beatitude may not necessarily be attributed to Matthean redaction. This aspect will be further clarified in the exegesis of the two verses, which follows from here.

11μακάριοί ἐστε ὅταν ὀνειδίσωσιν ὑμᾶς καὶ διώξωσιν καὶ εἴπωσιν πᾶν πονηρὸν καθ' ὑμῶν [ψευδόμενοι] ἕνεκεν ἐμοῦ, ***"blessed are you when they revile you and persecute you and utter all kinds of evil against you falsely on my account."*** The parallel beatitude in Luke (6:22) reads: μακάριοί ἐστε ὅταν μισήσωσιν ὑμᾶς οἱ ἄνθρωποι καὶ ὅταν ἀφορίσωσιν ὑμᾶς καὶ ὀνειδίσωσιν καὶ ἐκβάλωσιν τὸ ὄνομα ὑμῶν ὡς πονηρὸν ἕνεκα τοῦ υἱοῦ τοῦ ἀνθρώπου· "Blessed are you when people hate you, and when they exclude you, revile you, and defame you on account of the Son of Man."

Here, out of the four forms of persecution found in the Lukan version, Matthean version retains only ὀνειδίσωσιν ὑμᾶς "they revile you." In the place of Luke's ἀφορίσωσιν ὑμᾶς "they exclude you," Matthew has διώξωσιν "they persecute (you);" and in the place of Luke's ἐκβάλωσιν τὸ ὄνομα ὑμῶν "they cast out your name," he has εἴπωσιν πᾶν πονηρὸν καθ' ὑμῶν [ψευδόμενοι] "they utter all kinds of evil against you [falsely]." Matthew omits Luke's μισήσωσιν ὑμᾶς "when they hate you." He also drops the subject οἱ ἄνθρωποι "men," and he has ἕνεκεν ἐμοῦ "on my account" in place of Luke's ἕνεκα τοῦ υἱοῦ τοῦ ἀνθρώπου "on account of the Son of Man."

Luz observes that Matthew's replacement of the words like ἀφορίζω and ἐκβάλλω τὸ ὄνομα with a much more generalized term such as διώκω and λεγω indicates his tendency to generalize.[594] But, according to Davies and Allison, Jr., Matthew wants to keep ὀνειδίζω "revile" (also found in Isa 51:7 LXX); he wants to use his favourite word διώκω (also found in Matt 5: 9, 12), and wants to retain a reference to speech (εἴπωσιν πᾶν πονηρὸν "utter all kinds of evil"). Since all these result in three verbs, corresponding to his preferred number that is "three," Matthew omits μισέω "hate" and ἀφορίζω "exclude."[595] Davies and Allison, Jr. seem right in this in view of Matthew's penchant for triadic arrangement especially in the Sermon on the Mount. However, there could be further clarification on why Matthew favoured the word διώκω and why he wanted to keep εἴπωσιν πᾶν πονηρὸν, so as to replace with them Lukan words ἐκβάλωσιν τὸ ὄνομα ὑμῶν and to omit μισέω and ἀφορίζω. The apparent answer to this is that Matthew loves these two expressions because they indicate the actual experience of his community. In the previous chapter, we have already mentioned about the persecutions suffered by Matthew's community at the hands of both Jews and Gentiles. It is also obvious that apart from physical abuse, they would have suffered verbal abuse as well. This is indicated by the denouncement of Jesus by the scribes and Pharisees, especially such as – accusing him of blaspheming (9:3); attacking him for eating with sinners (9:11); charging him of demon possession (9:34; 12:24); and attacking him for breaking the law (12:2; cf. 15:1-2). Since these two words together with ὀνειδίζω made up three, which is the perfect number for his arrangement of the Sermon on the Mount, Matthew omitted Q's μισέω and ἀφορίζω. It is highly probable that in the opinion of the first evangelist the vacancy created by his omission of these words are made up by the words he uses because when the disciples are reviled, persecuted, and all kinds of evil are uttered against them, it is obvious that they are also hated and excluded by their persecutors. It is especially obvious that the opponents of Matthew's community were saying all sorts of evil things against it as a group or against individual members, without proper foundation, or in other words, falsely. Pathrapankal notes that the church of the Catacombs (c.a. 300 C.E.), in fact, experienced the meaning of Jesus' words expressed in this beatitude. He says, "false accusations that the prayer gatherings of the Christians were scenes of obscene revelry, that they were cannibals, that they were trying to upset the stability of the Roman empire and that they were upsetting the peaceful atmosphere of the families, were all levelled against them."[596] Highly probably, such was a common experience of Matthew's community members, as this beatitude indicates. Such evil talks could

594 Luz, *Matthew 1-7*, 242.

595 Davies and Allison, Jr., *Matthew*, Vol. I, 461.

596 Pathrapankal, *The Christian Programme*, 124-125. See also Barclay, *The Plain Man Looks at the Beatitudes*, 97-120, where the author elaborates about the accusations levelled against the early church as the context of the ninth beatitude.

have taken place in any situation, including denouncement in the synagogue, accusation in court, etc.[597]

μακάριοί ἐστε ὅταν ὀνειδίσωσιν ὑμᾶς καὶ διώξωσιν, ***"blessed are you when people revile you and persecute you."*** The verb ὀνειδίζω means, here, "unjustifiably bringing reproach on someone" or "to speak disparagingly of a person in a manner which is not justified." It is synonymous with upbraid, denounce, revile, disparage, or insult.[598] According to Guelich, it refers to verbal abuse directed at one personally.[599]

The verb διώκω may be understood, as in the preceding verse, as encompassing all the negative experiences suffered by the followers of Jesus Christ at the hands of their persecutors.[600] Its use here, along with other two forms of persecution (ὀνειδίσωσιν and εἴπωσιν πᾶν πονηρὸν καθ' ὑμῶν), seems to refer to the fact that the other two are especially common among the primary audience. And in order to include all other forms of persecution which also can happen to them, the author uses this general term διώκω.[601]

καὶ εἴπωσιν πᾶν πονηρὸν καθ' ὑμῶν [ψευδόμενοι] ἕνεκεν ἐμοῦ, ***"and when they utter all kinds of evil against you falsely on my account."*** The authenticity of the word ψευδόμενοι ("lying") here is doubted.[602] Whether it is authentic or not, however, it is obvious that the persecutors do not speak the truth.[603] The Lukan parallel has ἐκβάλωσιν τὸ ὄνομα ὑμῶν ὡς πονηρὸν "cast out your name as evil" (Luke 6:22). In spite of their difference both the Matthean version and

597 Davies and Allison, Jr., *Matthew*, Vol. I, 462-463.

598 See, "Freiberg Lexicon," C.D. Rom; "Louw-Nida Lexicon," C. D. Rom; and UBS Greek Dictionary, C.D. ROM, in Bible Works, LLC, 2001.

599 Guelich, *The Sermon on the Mount: A Foundation for Understanding*, 94.

600 For the meaning of διώκω see the explanation given for the preceding verse above.

601 According to Schweizer, this passage (5:11) reflects a period when the community suffered only verbal abuse as yet, but not physical abuse which came later. Schweizer, *The Good News According to Matthew*, 96. The use of the verb 'διώκω', however, seems to include physical abuse as well.

602 The word ψευδόμενοι, "lying," is attested by MSS such as ℵ B C W Δ Θ *f* *f*^{3} 28 33 157 180 205 565 579 597 700 892 1006 1010 1071 1241 1243 1292 1342 1424 1505 *Byz* [E Σ] *Lect* it$^{a?, aur, f, ff, l, q}$ vg syr$^{c, p, h, pal}$ cop$^{sa, meg, bo}$ arm eth geo slav Origen$^{1/2}$ Basil Apostolic Constitutions Gregory-Nyssa Didymus Epiphanius Chrysostom Cyril Hesychius Theodoret; Chromatius$^{1/2}$ Jerome Rufinus Augustine$^{6/11}$. But it is omitted in MSS such as D it$^{b, c, d, g, h, k}$ syr^{s} Origen$^{1/2}$; Tertullian Hilary Lucifer Ambrosiaster Ambrose Chromatius$^{1/2}$ Augustine$^{5/11}$ Speculum. See *The Greek New Testament*, 12. While,the omission of the word in some MSS could be attributed to an intention to harmonize with Luke 6:22, its inclusion in more MSS also could be attributed to the result of the scribal addition for clarifying the text. Since, these two analyses are equally possible, it is very difficult to choose between the two readings. As a result the editorial committee of the present UBS Greek text is also quite indecisive about it and therefore places the word ψευδόμενοι, "lying," in square brackets, and they give the "C" mark. See the following - *The Greek New Testament*, 12; Metzger, *A Textual Commentary on the Greek New Testament*, 10-11; and Hagner, *Matthew 1-13*, 88.

603 Hagner, *Matthew 1-13*, 95. See also Schweizer, *The Good News According to Matthew*, 85.

the Lukan parallel are supposed to have come from the same source that is Q. It is believed by Davies and Allison, Jr. that behind the Q version there is a Semitic expression – "to cause an ill name to go out" - which Luke reproduces. This is suggested by the fact that the Lukan expression "cast out your name as evil" (ἐκβάλωσιν τὸ ὄνομα ὑμῶν ὡς πονηρὸν) is very awkward in Greek. Then for the sake of clarity the awkward Q's translation of the Semitic idiom was rewritten by Matthew, and he changed "on account of the Son of Man" to "on account of me" in order to make for conformity with 10:18, 39; and 16:25 (cf. in place of "the Son of Man" in Mark 8:31 [par. Luke 9:22] Matthew uses a simple pronoun "he" for Jesus in Matt 16:21).[604] This suggestion is further supported by the fact that Luke never adds the title Son of Man.[605] So, the Lukan version betrays what Luke got from the tradition.

Although, the authenticity of the word ψευδόμενοι is doubted, its inclusion here is essentially significant at least in two ways. First, it accentuates that the evils spoken of the followers of Jesus' Christ, or of the members of the Matthean community are far from true. Second, it implies that the mere fact of persecution or being spoken of evil does not carry blessedness, but only when it is falsely done for the sake of Jesus Christ. Chrysostom had rightly written on this: "Lest thou shouldest think that the mere fact of being spoken evil of makes men blessed, He hath set two limitations; when it is for His sake, and when the things that are said are false: for without these, he who is evil spoken of, so far from being blessed, is miserable."[606] Luz also fittingly observes that the word ψευδόμενοι here throws light on Matthean ethical interest, meaning that "a promise applies not to any persecution but to persecution which happens for the sake of Christ, i.e., for the sake of righteousness," for, confession of Christ manifests itself in deeds of righteousness.[607] The connection between "for the sake of righteousness" and "for the sake of Christ" is made plain in 5:10 and 5:11. Even if they are not the same in other places, "for the sake of righteousness" and "for the sake of Christ" are the same in these two beatitudes, for those who are persecuted because of righteousness are the followers of Jesus Christ who pursue righteousness because of their faith in Christ, as Luz righly observes.[608]

The use of the indefinite clause (ὅταν + subjunctive) indicates something that has been experienced and is still going on, and very much likely to come in the future. This is in consonant with the use of the perfect tense δεδιωγμένοι in the preceding verse referring to all forms of persecutions.

The subject οἱ ἄνθρωποι "men" which Luke has, but which Matthew omits, may have a word-play with "Son of Man" in Q. In its place Matthew simply leaves

604 Davies and Allison, Jr., *Matthew*, Vol. I, 462.

605 Guelich, *The Sermon on the Mount: A Foundation for Understanding*, 95.

606 Chrysostom, *Hom. on Mt.* 15:7, as quoted in Davies and Allison, Jr., *Matthew*, Vol. I, 462.

607 Luz, *Matthew 1-7*, 242.

608 *Ibid.*

an unspecified "they" and with this he seems to refer to the Jewish leaders, as it is clearly indicated even in the whole of the Sermon on the Mount.[609]

[12]χαίρετε καὶ ἀγαλλιᾶσθε, ὅτι ὁ μισθὸς ὑμῶν πολὺς ἐν τοῖς οὐρανοῖς· οὕτως γὰρ ἐδίωξαν τοὺς προφήτας τοὺς πρὸ ὑμῶν, ***"rejoice and be glad, for your reward is great in heaven, for in the same way they persecuted the prophets who were before you."*** This verse consists of three parts and it contains the only two imperatives in the Beatitudes, such as χαίρετε "rejoice" and ἀγαλλιᾶσθε "be glad." The thought of this verse is that the ill-treatment, which the disciples are suffering, is the same with what the prophets of old had suffered. This indicates that like those prophets, the disciples are also the servants of God, and they have a great reward awaiting them in heaven. With the knowledge of this, they can rejoice and be glad even now.[610] The sentence construction also implies that the reward, which is awaiting them, is the same reward that is meant for those prophets before them. We may put in this way: the prophets were persecuted because of their faithfulness to God and they have great reward in heaven. In their faithfulness to God the prophets raised their voice against the sin of the people to lead them back to God,[611]and they addressed social issues like injustice, oppression, corruption, etc.,[612] and as a result they suffered persecutions. However, a great reward for their faithfulness to God and the resultant sufferings is waiting for them in heaven. The followers of Jesus Christ are persecuted like the prophets before them because of their faithfulness to Jesus Christ. By implication, in their faithfulness to Jesus Christ, the followers of Jesus Christ stood firm in Jesus' teachings, and the same great reward, which was awaiting the prophets, is awaiting them in heaven.[613]

609 Davies and Allison, Jr., *Matthew*, Vol. I, 461. For the parallel saying of Matt 5:11 in Gospel of Thomas 68, Clement of Alexandria, *Strom.* 4:6; and IPeter 4:14, see Davies and Allison, Jr., *Matthew*, Vol. 1, 463.

610 Davies and Allison, Jr., *Matthew*, Vol. I, 463. See also Betz, *The Sermon on the Mount*, 152.

611 For example, Isa 1:1-20.

612 A classic example of the prophetic voice against oppression is found in Exodus where Moses raised his voice against the oppression of the Israelites by the Egyptians. Many of the later prophets also raised their voice for justice and against injustice, oppression, corruption, etc. See for example, Isa chaps. 1:17-31; 5:1ff.; 10:1-4; 16:1-5; 59:1ff.; Jer 5:20-29; 21:11-14; 22:1-5; Amos 5:4ff.; Mic 3:8ff.; 6:1-8; 7:1ff. We may include the ministry of John the Baptist. See especially Matt chap. 3; 14:3-4; Luke 3:10-14. For a discussion on the prophets' concern of social issues, see James Limburg, *The Prophets and the Powerless* (Lima, Ohio: Academic Renewal Press, 2001), 25-99; and R.B.Y. Scott, *The Relevance of the Prophets*, Revised edition (London: the Macmillan Company, 1968 [1944]), 171-192.

613 We know that like the prophets of OT times, the main concern of Jesus is to lead the people back to God. This is indicated by Jesus' proclamation, "Repent, for the kingdom of heaven has come near," at the beginning of his ministry (Matt 4:17 [par. Mark 1:15]). At the same time, however, it is seen in various places that Jesus upheld the prophets' concern for social issues. First of all, it is clearly seen where Jesus says in Matt 5:17 (cf. Matt 22:40), that he comes to fulfil the law and the prophets. Moreover, Jesus' concern for justice is seen in Matt 12:18-20; 23:23 (par. Luke11:42); Luke 18:3-8. And his concern for the oppressed is seen where he healed the people with all kinds of sicknesses and he taught his disciples to do the same (e.g.,

With the knowledge of this, they can rejoice and be glad now, even under the circumstances of their sufferings. Thus, Betz is right in saying that "one must read the argument [of 5:12] in reverse, so to speak. The historical verdict rendered in v. 12c leads to the dogmatic judgment in v. 12b, and both together constitute the basis for the macarism in v. 12a."[614]

χαίρετε καὶ ἀγαλλιᾶσθε, ***"rejoice and be glad."*** These opening words serve as a parenthetic expansion of μακάριοι in v. 11, and heighten the paradox of suffering and blessedness.[615] The parallel beatitude in Luke 6:23a has χάρητε ἐν ἐκείνῃ τῇ ἡμέρᾳ καὶ σκιρτήσατε *"Rejoice in that day and leap for joy."* There are three differences between the two versions here. While Matthew has present imperative, Luke has aorist imperative. Luke has ἐν ἐκείνῃ τῇ ἡμέρᾳ which Matthew does not have; and Matthew has ἀγαλλιᾶσθε in place of Luke's σκιρτήσατε. Luke's use of aorist tense may be explained by the accompanying ἐν ἐκείνῃ τῇ ἡμέρα "in that day," which Matthew does not have, because present tense seems less appropriate than aorist tense for such a specified time.[616] The expression seems to refer to any day in which a disciple of Christ is or may be persecuted. It is a continuation of the previous verse (Luke 6:22) and if the two verses are taken together the structural construction suggests that ἐν ἐκείνῃ τῇ ἡμέρα of Luke 6:23 refers back to ὅταν +... (two times) of Luke 6:22.[617]

It is uncertain why Matthew does not have ἐν ἐκείνῃ τῇ ἡμέρα "in that day" (which has an eschatological tone[618]) which Luke has. It is quite possible that the Lukan version (including the aorist) is traditional as Luke is usually regarded as preserving the Q form more than Matthew does.[619] If that is the case, we could assume that when Jesus taught this beatitude, persecution was not much experienced by his disciples/followers as yet, but their situation indicated that it was a possibility at any time, and it is (going to be) part and parcel of the eschatological experience for the followers of Jesus Christ (see Luke 21:12).[620]

4:24; 8:16; 10:7-8); in his attitudes toward the socially downcast people, such as the sinners like tax collectors and harlots (e.g., 9:10-13 [par. Mark 2:5-17]; Luke 5:29-32]; 21:31-32); in his concern for the poor (5:3 [par. Luke 6:20]; 11:4-5 [par. Luke 7:22]; 19:21 [par. Mark 10:21]), etc.

614 Betz, *Essays on the Sermon on the Mount*, 25.

615 Hagner, *Matthew 1-13*, 95.

616 Gundry, *Matthew: A Commentary on His Literary and Theological Art*, 74.

617 According to Guelich the aorist imperative of Luke "most likely refers to the judgment day in the setting of the synagogue ban ... when one is to celebrate the occasion with 'jumping for joy'" Guelich, *The Sermon on the Mount: A Foundation for Understanding*, 95.

618 Davies and Allison, Jr., *Matthew*, Vol. I, 463.

619 Davies and Allison, Jr. suggest that Luke's "in that day" is probably traditional and Matthew omitted it for reasons not known to us or he did not find it in Q[mt]. Davies and Allison, Jr., *Matthew*, Vol. I, 463.

620 It is assumed here that Luke preserves the tradition as found in Q, which reflects the original saying of Jesus.

Therefore, "in that day" would mean that whenever a persecution, which they could expect at any time, came to a reality, in that day, they must rejoice and be glad rather than being sorry. Then, when Matthew wrote his gospel, persecution was an ongoing experience by his community. Therefore, when he incorporated the ninth beatitude, he omitted "in that day" because it was no more relevant or necessary. Rather he wanted to exhort members of his community to rejoice and be glad always in spite of the persecutions they had suffered, they were suffering, and they were expecting to suffer in the future. Accordingly, he also uses present imperative in place of Luke's or Q's aorist imperative.

With regard to Matthew's use of ἀγαλλιάομαι, while Luke has σκιρτάω, John Nolland is of the opinion that Matthew conformed the text to the established pairing of χαίρειύ "to rejoice," and ἀγαλλίασθαι "to exult."[621] But, according to Davies and Allison, Jr., in this case, Matthew probably preserves the Q version of ἀγαλλιάομαι and Luke probably changed it to the classical σκιρτάω (leap for joy).[622] Dupont also argues that 1Pet 1:6–8; 4:13 which used ἀγαλλιᾶσθϵ echo an early form of the beatitude, and the use of σκιρτάν "to leap for joy," by Luke is in line with his taste for more precise psychological terminology.[623] The possibility of Matthew's preservation of the Q version in this is also suggested by the use of the same verb (ἀγαλλιάομαι) in Isa 61:10 LXX.[624] This idea is drawn from the supposition that as the Matthean Beatitudes (5:1-12) seem to depend heavily upon Isa 61, the words like δικαιοσυύη of Matt 5:10 and ἀγαλλιάομαι of Matt 5:12 could be influenced by or taken from Isa 61 verses 11 and 10 respectively.

ὅτι ὁ μισθὸς ὑμῶν πολὺς ἐν τοῖς οὐρανοῖς, "***for your reward is great in heaven***." The delayed ὅτι clause here gives the reason why the disciples should always rejoice and exult. It is because their reward is great in heaven.[625] Guelich seems right in saying that "the promise appears to come as an assurance rather than an expected 'reward'".[626]

The Lukan parallel (6:23b) has ἰδοὺ γὰρ "for behold" (RSV[627]) in place of Matthew's ὅτι "for/because," and it has singular ἐν τῷ οὐρανω in place of Matthew's plural ἐν τοῖς οὐρανοῖς. While the expression ἰδοὺ γὰρ appears 5 times

621 Nolland, *Luke 1-9:20*, 286. Here Nolland mentions Tob 13:13; Rev 19:7; cf. 1 Pet 4:13 as the texts where the pairing of the two words appear.

622 Davies and Allison, Jr., *Matthew*, Vol. I, 463-464.

623 Dupont, *Les Beatitudes*, Vol. I, 245-246, as quoted in Nolland, *Luke 1-9:20*, 286.

624 So, Gundry opines that Matthew's use of ἀγαλλιάομαι is probably influenced by Isa 61:10 LXX. Gundry, *Matthew: A Commentary on His Literary and Theological Art*, 74. See also Davies and Allison, Jr., *Matthew*, Vol. I, 464.

625 Hagner, *Matthew 1-13*, 95. Cf., however, Albright and Mann, *Matthew*, 47, who maintain that "the reward idea is not so much a precise calculation of reward for past conduct. Rather it is a contrast between coming pain and persecution, and future blessedness.

626 Guelich, *The Sermon on the Mount: A Foundation for Understanding*, 95.

627 ἰδοὺ γὰρ is rendered in different ways. NRSV rendered it as "for surely." RSV translation is quoted here as it seems to refer to the literal meaning.

in Luke (1:44, 48; 2:10; 6:23; 17:21), it does not appear at all in Matthew and Mark. Therefore, in this case, the difference may be ascribed to Luke.[628] However, with regard to the use of singular ἐν τῷ οὐρανῷ "in heaven" by Luke and plural ἐν τοῖς οὐρανοῖς "in heavens" by Matthew, it is very difficult to decide from word statistics. Davies and Allison, Jr. suggest that this also may be ascribed to Luke. In support of their suggestion they mention that the singular "heaven" appear fifty three times in Luke/Acts and the plural "heavens" only six times.[629] However, it is found in this study that while the plural "heavens" is found six times, the singular "heaven" is found fifty five times in Luke/Acts (twenty one times in Luke's gospel alone). At the same time, the plural "heavens" is also found fifty four times in Matthew, and the singular "heaven" is found twenty eight times. Therefore, while Luke could be viewed as responsible for the use of singular "heaven," Matthew can be equally viewed as responsible for the plural "heavens." In any case, the meaning of Luke's singular "heaven" would be a reverential circumlocution meaning "with God," and Matthew's plural "heavens" would mean "in the kingdom of heaven."[630] There does not seem, however, any significant difference between the two terms, because the implication in both cases is that the followers of Jesus Christ who faithfully endure persecutions will receive great reward from God in the eschatological Kingdom of God. Thus, ἐν τοῖς οὐρανοῖς, "in heaven" also indicates the futuristic nature of the reward. However, the thought of this future reward gives confidence about the joyful future, which is in full contradiction with the present painful circumstances, to produce joy in the present, or at least to make the suffering of the present bearable.[631]

ὁ μισθὸς ὑμῶν "your reward" belongs to Q as both Matthew and Luke have it. However, Matthew gives much more importance to the idea of μισθός than any other Gospel. It occurs ten times in Matthew (5:12, 46; 6:1,2,5, 16; 10:41[2], 42; 20:8), two times in Mark (5:12; 9:41), three times in Luke (6:23, 35; 10:7), and once in John (4:36). The importance of the concept of reward in Matthew is found even where the word is not used (as for example in 25:31-46; 6:4). The actual content of the reward, however, is left vague despite its importance.[632] According to Strecker, the word μισθός is a technical term for the heavenly reward beyond this world in Matthew's gospel.[633] According to Davies and Allison, Jr., the significance of "reward" lies in the fact that it signals that what matters most is being approved by God.[634] Although the actual content of the

628 Davies and Allison, Jr., *Matthew*, Vol. I, 464.

629 *Ibid.*

630 Davies and Allison, Jr., *Matthew*, Vol. I, 464. See also M. Pamment, "Matthew and the Kingdom of Heaven," *NTStud* 27 (1981): 211-232, quoted by Davies and Allison, Jr. here.

631 Hagner, *Matthew 1-13*, 95. See also Davies and Allison, Jr., *Matthew*, Vol. I, 463.

632 Hagner, *Matthew 1-13*, 95.

633 Strecker, *The Sermon on the Mount*, 46.

634 Davies and Allison, Jr., *Matthew*, Vol. I, 464.

reward is not mentioned, viewing from the perspective of the apocalyptic nature of the beatitude, we could assume that the eschatological reversal of situation is an integral part of it. This would mean that because of their sufferings, the persecuted Christians would enter the eschatological kingdom as victors rather than as victims anymore. The idea of rewarding the persecuted is also found even in the Jewish literature, contemporary or a little earlier to Matthew's time (such as 1 En 108:10; 4 Ezra 7:88-101). The difference, however, is that while the reason behind the persecution in this literature is "perfectly keeping the Law of the Lawgiver" (4 Ezra 7:89), Christians suffered because of their faith in Jesus.[635]

οὕτως γὰρ ἐδίωξαν τοὺς προφήτας τοὺς πρὸ ὑμῶν, ***"for in the same way they persecuted the prophets who were before you."*** The Lukan parallel (Luke 6:23c) has κατὰ τὰ αὐτὰ γὰρ ἐποίουν τοῖς προφήταις οἱ πατέρες αὐτῶν "*for that is what their ancestors did to the prophets.*" It is quite uncertain whether the expression, κατὰ τὰ αὐτα is Lukan or not. Davies and Allison, Jr. note that the expression occurs only three times in the New Testament and all of them are in Luke (6:23, 26; 17:30). They, however, suggest that it could be a pre-Lukan tradition and not of Luke.[636] This would mean that it belongs to Q or Q^{lk}. On the other hand, οὕτως and ἐδίωξαν seem to be Matthean. This is indicated by the words statistics. The word οὕτως occurs 32 times in Matthew, ten times in Mark and twenty one times in Luke. The word διώκω occurs six times in Matthew, it does not occur in Mark, and it occurs three times in Luke.[637] Therefore, they could be replacements of the κατὰ τὰ αὐτα if this expression belongs to Q, or if it belongs to Q^{lk} then they are replacements of Q form which is not known to us. Especially, with regard to the word διώκω this is the third time Matthew inserted it in three successive verses. According to Gundry, "these insertions show how much Matthew emphasizes persecution as the present fate of the righteous."[638]

οἱ πατέρες αὐτῶν "their fathers" on the other hand seems to be Lukan. This is suggested by Luke's stylistic tendency to avoid impersonal subjects, as well as by the word statistics. The plural of πατήρ with the meaning of "forefathers" or "ancestors" is used six times in Luke and nineteen times in Acts whereas it is used only twice in Matthew and is never used in Mark.[639] Moreover, Matthew's reference to "the fathers" in connection with the persecution of the prophets in 23:29-30, 32, also suggests that if Matthew found the term in the ninth beatitude, he is unlikely to have omitted it. Therefore, the unexpressed subjects in 5:11-12

---

635 Harrington, *The Gospel of Matthew*, 80.

636 Davies and Allison, Jr., *Matthew*, Vol. I, 464.

637 *Ibid.*

638 Gundry, *Matthew: A Commentary on His Literary and Theological Art*, 74.

639 Davies and Allison, Jr., *Matthew*, Vol. I, 464-465. See also Guelich, *The Sermon on the Mount: A Foundation for Understanding*, 96, quoting Dupont, *Les Beatitudes*, I, 248.

seem to reflect the Q form.[640] At any rate, it seems that the implication of the unexpressed subjects in Matthew can be drawn from Matt 23:31 and 34. In Matt 23:31, the "scribes and Pharisees" are accused of being the sons of those who murdered the prophets. They are also accused of killing prophets in 23:34. Because of this, it is quite possible that Matthew has in mind "the scribes and Pharisees" as the unexpressed subjects even in Matt 5:11-12.[641] In fact, it is our contention in our socio-historical study in the previous chapter that in most of the occurrences of persecutions in Matthew, including 5:11-12, the subjects are the leaders of formative Judaism, who are mainly the scribes and Pharisees.

προφήτας τοὺς πρὸ ὑμῶν, ***"the prophets who were before you."*** It is not possible to say with certainty whether Matthew's πρὸ+ὑμῶν (which Luke does not have) is a reproduction of Q.[642] Davies and Allison, Jr. rightly note that in any case, with the mention of those who killed the prophets, Matt 5:12 is put in a well-established tradition. The notion that the true prophets are put to death by the disobedient people of Israel is already found in the Old Testament itself, and the link between prophet and martyrdom becomes almost fixed in inter-testamental sources. Then, the New Testament picks up where the Jewish sources leave off. For example, 1 Thes 2:14-16 connects the motif of the prophets' martyrdom not only with the rejection of Jesus, but also with the persecution of Jesus' followers (in this case Paul and his co-workers). Matt 5:12 carries a similar motif. Here, the persecution of Jesus' disciples[643] is likened to the persecution of the prophets of old. Such, a reference to the persecution of God's special messengers, the prophets, illumines the reason for the persecution of Christians in these two texts.[644] As prophets suffered because of their faithfulness to God, Christians also suffered

640 Guelich maintains that "there is no particular reason for Matthew to have dropped the subject from his source." Guelich, *The Sermon on the Mount: A Foundation for Understanding*, 96.

641 Davies and Allison, Jr., *Matthew*, Vol. I, 464.

642 *Ibid.*,465. cf. Luz, *Matthew 1-7*, 242, which maintains that it is a reproduction of Q.

643 Schweizer seems right in saying that the disciples, whose fate is compared with the fate of the prophets here, include not only the twelve, but every disciple of Jesus to whom verses 13-16 apply, is a prophet of God. Schweizer, *The Good News According to Matthew*, 97. Schweizer here further says that the wish for all God's people to become prophets, was expressed in Numbers 11:29; then God's reward in the eschaton was predicted in Joel 3:1-2; Jer 31:34; and Isa 54:13 (=Jn 6:45). And, it is now fulfilled.

644 Davies and Allison, Jr., *Matthew*, Vol. I, 465. See the following references mentioned here by Davies and Allison, Jr. - the OT references, such as: Neh 9:26; I Kings 18:4, 13; 19:10, 14; 2 Chron 24:20-21; 36:15-21; Jer 2:30; 26:20-24; The Jewish sources during the intertestamental period such as: Jub 1:12; 4QpHos[a] 2:3-6; Josephus, *Ant.* 10:38; Asc. Isa. 2:16; 5:1-14; par. Jer. 9:21-32; Tg. on Isa 21.8; and the NT references such as: Matt 13:57; 21:35-36; 22:6; 23: 29-32, 34-37; Mark 6:4; 12:2-5; Luke 4:24; 11:47-51; 13:33-34; Jn 4:44; Acts 7:51-52; Rom 11:3; Heb 11:32-38; James 5:10-11; Rev 11: 3-7; 16:6; 18:24. and 1 Thess 2:14-16 which is specially noteworthy for connecting the motif of the prophets' martyrdom not only with the rejection of Jesus, but also with the persecution of Jesus' followers (in this case Paul and his co-workers).

because of their faithfulness to the same God. They are following the footsteps of the faithful prophets.[645] Hagner seems right in observing that "the prophets before you," here should be taken as referring to all God's earlier spokespersons (cf. 2 Chron 36:16; Mt 23:35) and not only the literary or canonical prophets.[646]

The significance of the final sentence of the ninth beatitude in Matthew is especially informed by the socio-historical context of the Matthean community. In the context of the persecutions, which they were suffering especially from the leaders of formative Judaism, and from the Gentiles, this is a reminder to them that suffering is not a new thing for God's people. Rather, they are standing in an honoured tradition when they suffer persecution.[647] In the light of this it could well be that Matthew deliberately added πρὸ+ὑμῶν so as to equate the persecutions suffered by his community members to the sufferings of the true prophets of God.

2.12. Summary of the Exegetical Insights

A brief summary of the exegetical insights on the Matthean Beatitudes may be given as follows:

1) The Matthean Beatitudes (Matt 5:3-12 par. Luke 6:20-26) probably underwent four stages of development. In the first stage, Jesus uttered three beatitudes (Matt 5:3, 4, 6) based on Isa 61:1-3. In the second stage, these three dominical beatitudes were, after they were translated into Greek, joined to what is now Luke 6:27-28 (par. Matt 5: 44-48) by the Q community, and to at least part of what is now Luke 6:39-49. This resulted in the creation of the early form of the Sermon on the Mount/Plain. A fourth beatitude, that is on persecution (Matt 5:11-12 par. Luke 6:22-23), was added by the Q community, perhaps to make the transition from the Beatitudes to the section on the love of enemies (Luke 6: 27-36 par. Matt 5:44-48). It could have been composed by the Q community on the basis of Jesus' teaching or more probably it could have been spoken by Jesus and was in circulation separately from the first three beatitudes, and was collected and added by the Q community. In either way, the purpose was to make a smooth transition from the Beatitudes to the next pericope on love of enemies (Luke 6:27ff. par. Matt 5:43-48). In the third stage, Q took two different forms, Q^{lk} and Q^{mt}. In Q^{lk} four woes (Luke 6:24-26) corresponding to the four beatitudes were composed. In Q^{mt}, "Blessed are the meek…" (Matt 5:5) was added to explain the potentially misleading "Blessed are the poor…" (not yet qualified by "in spirit"),

645 According to Gundry, Matthew "changes the treatment of the prophets by the fathers (so Luke) to 'the prophets who were before you' in order to imply that Jesus' disciples are now prophets (cf. Gal 1:17)." Gundry, *Matthew: A Commentary on His Literary and Theological Art*, 74. According Guelich, in this beatitude, the fate of the prophets becomes a paradigm for the disciple. Guelich, *The Sermon on the Mount: A Foundation for Understanding*, 96.

646 Hagner, *Matthew 1-13*, 96.

647 *Ibid.*

and in order to establish a correlation between Beatitudes and what follows, three more beatitudes (Matt 5:7-9) were composed. This resulted in eight beatitudes. In the fourth stage, Matthew and Luke edited the different versions of Q available to them. That is that, Matthew used Q^{mt} for his final edition while Luke used Q^{lk}. Matthew added another beatitude (Matt 5:10), which he composed to make the number of the Beatitudes to nine.[648] However, for this additional beatitude he deliberately chose the eighth position and he purposely selected important terms like "righteousness," "kingdom of heaven," and "persecution," in order to accentuate their importance in the context of his community.[649]

All the Matthean beatitudes are mainly apocalyptic in nature. The beatitudes spoken by Jesus (the first, second, fourth and probably the ninth) are purely apocalyptic in form. The four beatitudes which the Q community composed (the third, fifth, sixth and seventh) and which they added to the four dominical beatitudes carry ethical exhortation that was obviously required in the Q community. However, they were formulated in the form of apocalyptic beatitude. This is clearly indicated by the apodoses of all these four beatitudes in which eschatological blessings are promised. The additional beatitude (the eighth) composed by the first evangelist and the authorial redactions are done mainly under the influence of the Matthean community's concrete experience and therefore they were not done to spiritualize them. Therefore, the Matthean Beatitudes can be subsumed in the category of apocalyptic beatitude.

2) All nine Matthean beatitudes have their bases in the Old Testament, or they allude to the Old Testament. The three dominical beatitudes (Matt 5:3, 4, 6) have their bases in Isaiah 61:1-3. The ninth beatitude (Matt 5:11-12), which was either spoken by Jesus or composed by the Q community has its possible basis in Isa 51:7 (Matt 5:11) and Isa 61:10-11 (Matt 5:12). The third beatitude (Matt 5:5, composed in the Q community) has its basis in Ps 37:11. The fifth beatitude (Matt 5:7, composed in Q community) has its basis in Prov 14:21b; and 17:5c(LXX). The sixth beatitude (Matt 5:8, composed in Q community) has its basis in Ps 24[LXX: 23]:3-4. The seventh beatitude (Matt 5:9, composed in Q community) has its basis in Ps 34:15b (14b) and in some of the Jewish writings.[650] The eighth beatitude (Matt 5:10, a Matthean addition) has its basis in Psalms 22; 34:19-20; and Wis. 2:10-20.[651]

---

648 Up to this, the view of Davies and Allison, Jr., are basically followed in this summary. For a discussion on their view, see "the Form, Source, and *Sitz im Leben* of the Matthean Beatitudes" above.

649 Here, this researcher departs from Davies and Allison, Jr. For a discussion, see "the Form, Source and *Sitz im Leben* of the Matthean Beatitudes" above.

650 E.g., Jubilees 1:24f.; T. Judah 24:3; Pss. Sol. 17:27 (future!); cf. Wis. 5:5.

651 Cf. Green, *Matthew, Poet of the Beatitudes*, 266-267. Here, Green, who maintains that the Matthean Beatitudes are composed by Matthew in a poetric form on the basis of the Old Testament, mentions various texts of the LXX as the roots of the Matthean Beatitudes.

All the five beatitudes (other than the three demonical beatitudes) composed by the Q community (Matt 5:5, 7, 8, 9) and by Matthew (Matt 5:10), were based on Jesus' teachings (by his words and his own life), found elsewhere in the gospel traditions. The third beatitude (Matt 5:5) was composed on the basis of Jesus' own life and teaching as found in Matt 11:29; 18:4; 21:5. The fifth beatitude (Matt 5:7) was composed on the basis of Jesus' teachings as found in Luke 6:27-38; 10:25-37; Matt 18:21-35 (cf. 6:12-15; 7:1-5; 9:9-13; 12:1-8; 23:23). The sixth beatitude (Matt 5:8) was composed based on Jesus' teachings as found in Luke 6:43-45 (par. Matt 7:16-20; 12:33-35). The seventh beatitude (Matt 5:9) was composed based on Jesus' teachings as found in Matt 5:38-48 (par. Luke 6:27-30, 32-36; and probably Mark 9:50c). The eighth beatitude (Matt 5:10) was composed based on Jesus' teaching as found in Matt 10:26-33 (par. Luke 12:1-12). The same passages must have formed the basis of the ninth beatitude (Matt 5:11-12), if it was composed by the Q community.

When Matthew redacted the eight beatitudes, which he got from the tradition available to him, he was primarily influenced by the background and practical experience of his community. He did not do anything to spiritualize or to compromise the in-depth meaning of the traditions available to him, which were based on the authentic teachings of Jesus. 1) Matthew uses "kingdom of heaven" in places of Luke's/Q's "kingdom of God" throughout the beatitudes only because the term "kingdom of heaven" was more familiar to his Jewish/Jewish oriented community. The two terms have the same meaning. 2) He added "in spirit" to "the poor" of the first beatitude because he had an apprehension that few economically well-to-do members of his community might feel left out with only "the poor." In fact, the meaning of "the poor" (of Luke) and "the poor in spirit" (of Matthew) are more or less the same. They primarily refer to the frame of mind of the poor and the downtrodden people of God (the Matthean community), who put their trust only in God in the midst of all the persecutions and hardships they suffer, for which they are promised the blessing to inherit the kingdom of Heaven/God. Thus, all the members of the Matthean community are "poor in spirit" and are included in the blessing announced in the first beatitude. 3) The addition of "and thirsty" in the fourth beatitude (Matt 5:6) is influenced by the frequent parallelism of "hunger" and "thirst" in the Old Testament. The meaning of "hungry and thirsty" is more or less the same with "hungry" alone. Matthew followed the Old Testament phraseology because members of his community were more familiar and attuned to it. He also added "righteousness" as the object of "hunger and thirst," which was not specified in Q/Luke. The addition of "righteousness" here seems to have been influenced by two factors. First, it was added according to the actual experience of Matthew's community, who were weighed down with the experience of injustice in their lives, thus earnestly longing to experience – (a) justice in their lives and (b) also God's eschatological vindication. Second, it was influenced by the Old Testament phraseology (Psalm 106:3 [LXX, 105:3]), which was familiar to his community. 4) Matthew's redaction of the ninth beatitude (Matt 5:11-12) also was done under the influence of his community's concrete experience, as well as the author's literary style which was influenced by his community's and his own Jewish background. Out of the four forms of persecutions in Luke 6:22/Q Matthew replaces "they exclude you" and "they cast out your name" with "they persecute (you)" and "they utter all kinds of evil against you." He retained "they revile you" and he omits "they hate you." The three forms of persecutions in Matthew reflect the concrete experience of his community. Although, "they hate you" is also applicable to the experience of Matthew's community, he omits it because he already has the triads, which is important for his literary arrangement, and because other forms of persecutions already indicate that, they are hated too. He also omits the subject "men" to leave unspecified "they" to refer to the Jewish leaders who were the main opponents of his community as the persecutors. 5) In addition to the eight beatitudes, which he received from his tradition, Matthew composed and added one more to them. Thus, he has nine beatitudes altogether. Matthew did this in order to make triads of three beatitudes, because the triad is important to his literary arrangement. His choice of important terms like "righteousness," "kingdom of heaven," and "persecution" for his additional beatitude and his selection of the eighth position to accentuate their significance, however, was influenced by the concrete experience, as well as the Jewish background, of his community (including himself). Consequently, the primary influence behind the formulation of the additional beatitude was the concrete experience of his community.

We can thus say that most (or all) of Matthew's redactions of the Beatitudes are influenced and determined by the socio-historical experience of his community and of himself. This also implies that those beatitudes, which Matthew took over without redaction, are relevant to the context of his community without redaction. All these finally indicate that the socio-historical context of Matthew's gospel offers a primary ground for understanding the meaning and implication of the Matthean Beatitudes. In the light of this understanding, the implications of the Matthean Beatitudes may be briefly highlighted again as follows:

The first beatitude implies that the poor and the downtrodden people of God are the recipients of the eschatological kingdom of God/heaven announced by Jesus. This is because the poor and the downtrodden people of God usually/always put their complete trust in God alone to help them in all their difficulties. They will experience the blessings of the kingdom in full at the eschaton, which include above all, restoration of justice and equality. However, they can begin to experience them from now itself in their relationship with Jesus, although partially, because Jesus has already inaugurated that future kingdom.

The second beatitude implies that the faithful believers in Jesus Christ who experience mourning due to all kinds of sufferings and hardships will receive the comfort from God in the coming kingdom of God from their mourning. Of course, the promise is to be experienced in its fullness in the age to come (future). At the same time, however, as "the comfort from God" is one of the attributes of the "kingdom of heaven," it can be experienced even now although partially, because the kingdom of heaven, which will come into its fullness at the end of the age, is already present in Jesus and his ministry.

The third beatitude implies that the followers of Jesus Christ (the Matthean community) must emulate his meekness in different situations, such as - when facing adversaries, when they are in difficult situations, and whenever they are called to serve others with love. Exaltation in the kingdom of God is promised to such people, which is more or less the same with the promise of the first beatitude. In the context of Matthew's community, the third beatitude is an exhortation to exhibit meekness/humility, – 1) in the situation of persecutions they were suffering at the hands of both the Jews and the Gentiles, and where at the same time they were called to continue their mission to both the Jews and the Gentiles. 2) in the context of possible racial problems within their community where the Gentile members could not have free table-fellowship with the Jewish members. Of course, the meek shall experience their exaltation in full when the kingdom of heaven/God comes to its fullness at the end of the age. However, as Jesus Christ has already inaugurated the kingdom of heaven/God, the exaltation of the meek can be viewed as already beginning to take place even now, especially among the believers in Jesus Christ.

The fourth beatitude implies that the followers of Jesus Christ, who experience injustice in their lives and who are longing for justice, will receive justice from God in its fullness on the last day, in the eschatological kingdom of God. However, as the kingdom of heaven/God has been inaugurated by Jesus Christ, they could experience justice in Jesus even now. This also would imply that wherever the Lordship of Jesus Christ is proclaimed, justice must be experienced by the people, especially the poor and the downtrodden people. In the context of the Matthean community, the injustice they experienced is two fold. They were suffering injustice along with other Jews at the hands of the Romans in terms of social, political and economic, in the aftermath of the Jewish war (66-73 C.E.). At the same time, they were suffering religious persecutions at the hands of the Jewish leaders and their Gentile neighbours. Under such situations, they were deeply longing to experience justice in their lives, in terms of social, political, economic, and legal as well. They were longing for justice in two fronts - 1) to experience justice in their life; and 2) for God's justice (just judgment) to act for them, to give them justice. Consequently, the word δικαιοσύνη could have two connotations – 1) justice done by human beings, that is the fulfilment of God's will, which has positive effect upon other human beings; and 2) justice done by God, that is the just judgment of God that restores justice to the downtrodden and overthrows those who act with injustice, which is to be exercised by Christ at his return, that is, at the *eschaton*.

The fifth beatitude implies that the followers of Jesus Christ must show mercy to everyone who needs it including the sinners, the poor, and the sick, the prisoners, and even the enemies. Those who show mercy will surely receive mercy in its fullness from God in the age to come, and they will experience it partially even now itself. However, this does not mean that believers in Jesus Christ should show mercy with expectation of receiving mercy in return, but they should show it because they already received the pardoning acceptance of God. In the context of Matthew's community, this beatitude is a call – 1) to the members of the community to show mercy as a sign of their faithfulness to God, in contrast to the scribes and Pharisees who failed to do so; 2) to the rich members of the community to show mercy to the poor members; 3) to the members of the community to show mercy to everyone in need, including the poor and the sinners among their Jewish and Gentile neighbours, as well as their persecutors among them; 4) to the members of the community to remember that such an action is imperative for the success of their mission among the Jews and the Gentiles.

The sixth beatitude implies that the believers in Jesus Christ must have a pure heart before God, which is free from corrupt desire, from sin and guilt, both in thought and outward action. Those whose hearts are pure before God will be blessed with an opportunity to enter the eschatological kingdom of God, to view God's beauty and to worship Him face to face (eternally). In the context of the Matthean community, it is a call to shun the way of the scribes and the Pharisees, who practiced outward ceremonial purity but were impure inside, and at the same time, it is an encouragement to them to pursue a purity of heart corresponded with outward action. This could also indicate that such a tendency began to creep into the midst of the Matthean community, and it is also a warning to such members, that if they are impure in heart like the Pharisees, who are not entering the kingdom of God/heaven, they also will not enter the kingdom of God/heaven.

The seventh beatitude implies that the followers of Jesus Christ must take the initiative to make peace between themselves and others whenever problems arise, and they must take initiative to make peace between warring or opposing groups. By doing such thing, they already show themselves as children of God. However, they will experience the full significance of their sonship/childrenhood of God in the eschaton by being fully accepted by God, and enjoying a degree of intimacy with God, which has never been experienced so far. In the context of Matthew's community, it is an exhortation to them – 1) to take initiative to make peace between them and their persecutors, both the Jews and the Gentiles, instead of retaliating against them; 2) to take initiative to make peace within the community whenever problems arise, especially because of the unequal partnership between the Jewish and Gentile members, and because of unequal economic conditions. To take such an initiative to make peace is their obligation as the followers of

Jesus Christ, and at the same time, it is imperative for the success of their ministry among the Jews and the Gentiles.

The eighth beatitude implies that whoever suffers persecution both verbal and physical because of their faith in Jesus Christ/God, will receive the blessing of the kingdom of God/heaven with all the attributes, which are expressed in the other beatitudes (2-7). In the context of the Matthean community, it is an exhortation to the community members to remain faithful under the circumstances of persecutions at the hands of both the Jews and the Gentiles. At the same time, it is also an assurance that their faithfulness to Jesus Christ under such situations will not go unnoticed or unrewarded. They will surely receive the blessings of the kingdom of heaven/God, undoubtedly with all its attributes as expressed in other beatitudes.

The ninth beatitude is essentially an exhortation to the believers in Jesus Christ to endure all kinds of persecutions with a joyful heart because there are plenty of rewards for their sufferings awaiting them in the coming kingdom of God. In the context of the Matthean community, it is especially an exhortation to endure the persecutions they were undergoing, at the hands of both leaders of formative Judaism and the Gentiles, with the assurance that they will be richly rewarded in the coming kingdom of God. It is also a reminder to all the persecuted Christians, that suffering is not a new thing for God's people. Rather, they are standing in an honoured tradition when they suffer persecution.

The history of the developments of the Matthean Beatitudes indicates that the teachings of Jesus have been adapted to the ongoing needs of the Christ-believing communities, namely the Q community and the Matthean community. Even after such adaptation, however, they are firmly rooted in Jesus' authentic teachings, as well as in the Biblical/Old Testament traditions. Such a situation, and especially the adaptation of the Beatitudes by Matthew to his community's context without losing their authenticity as Jesus' teachings, as well as Biblical truths, shows that the Matthean Beatitudes are applicable even today to address the ongoing situation of the Christ-believing community. Taking a cue from this, we will try to see the implication of the Matthean Beatitudes for contemporary Christian discipleship in the next chapter. Before that, however, we will briefly discuss an ongoing debate on the primary functions of the Matthean beatitudes, and conclude it with the view adopted in this study, for one's view on this issue has an important bearing on one's understanding of the implication of the Matthean beatitudes for contemporary Christian discipleship.

2.13. The Primary Function of the Matthean Beatitudes

There has been an ongoing debate on what constitutes the basic function of the Matthean Beatitudes. The main arguments fall on the question of, whether they are basically ethical requirements for entering the kingdom or whether they are primarily eschatological blessings in character. Various positions which have been represented in this debate may be briefly highlighted as follows:

2.13.1. The Matthean Beatitudes are Entrance Requirements for the Kingdom

It has been argued by some scholars like Windisch, Dodd, Strecker and Dupont, that the beatitudes, which were once straightforward eschatological blessings (as in Luke 6:20-23), were ethicized by Matthew so that they become hortatory or paraenetic in nature, and thus they are entrance requirements for the kingdom of God.[652] The main argument for this view, as summarised by Davies and Allison, Jr., is that the "Lukan beatitudes, which fit rather well in the eschatological or apocalyptic tradition, have in Matthew been modified along wisdom lines; the 'poor in spirit' and 'the meek' have become ideal characters to be imitated."[653]

2.13.2. The Matthean Batitudes are Pronouncements of Eschatological Blessings

The interpretation of the Matthean Beatitudes as entrance requirements for the kingdom has been opposed by some scholars. For example, Guelich argues that - Matthew, no more than Luke, sets forth a list of ethical requirements for the Kingdom.[654] Guelich admits that the form of the Matthean Beatitudes, in fact, exhibits to some extent the characteristics of wisdom beatitudes, such as third person construction, and virtuous behaviour ("merciful" of 5:7; "pure in heart" of 5:8; and "peacemakers" of 5:9), which is approved by God. Moreover, the Matthean Beatitudes lack the prophetic-apocalyptic woes of Luke, and at the same time they tend to be structurally more elaborate than Luke's beatitudes (especially "poor in spirit" of 5:3; and "thirst after righteousness" of 5:6). However, Guelich argues that, while the Matthean Beatitudes, viewed purely from the perspective of form, "do appear to be at home with the majority of the beatitudes of practical wisdom found in the OT and Judaism," more important in the examination of the Matthean Beatitudes is a consideration of the question of source and the analysis of the content.[655] So, Guelich contends that regarding the source, the first three beatitudes (Matt 5:3,4,6 par. Luke) which are eschatological in nature, have

652 See the following: H. Windisch, *The Meaning of the Sermon on the Mount*, translated by S. M. Gilmour (Philadelphia: Westminster Press, 1951), 26-27, 87-88; Dodd, "The Beatitudes: A form Critical Study," 7-8; Strecker, *The Sermon on the Mount*, 30; and Dupont, *Les Béatitudes*, Vol. I, 254-258.

653 Davies and Allison, Jr., *Matthew*, Vol. I, 439. Note that Davies and Allison, Jr. here do not mention their own argument, but of those who view the Matthean Beatitudes as entrance requirements. For a more recent support and arguments for the beatitudes as entrance requirements, see Thomson, "The Background and Function of the Beatitudes...," 109-116.

654 Robert A. Guelich, "The Matthean Beatitudes: 'Entrance-Requirements' or Eschatological Blessings?," *JournBibLit*, 95/3 (1976), 433.

655 Guelich, "The Matthean Beatitudes...," 419.

their original *Sitz im Leben* in Jesus' ministry. The ninth beatitude (Matt 5:11-12 par. Luke 6:22-23) was an isolated logion, and added to combine the first three beatitudes with the material on love for one's enemies. These four beatitudes were expanded with the addition of other four beatitudes (Matt 5:5, 7-8). These eight Matthean beatitudes (Matt 5:3-9, 11-12) are all pre-Matthean in origin. Then Matthew redacted these eight beatitudes to align with Isa 1:1-3, which is basically eschatological pronouncement of the presence of the New Age.[656] The Matthean redactions are found in the qualification of "the poor" with "in spirit" in the first beatitude (5:3); the reversing of the order of the second (5:4) and the third (5:5) beatitudes; the expansion of the fourth with "and thirst for righteousness" (5:6); and the addition of the eighth beatitude (5:10).[657] With regard to content, the first three beatitudes (Matt 5:3, 4, 6 par. Luke) are eschatological in nature, and the other four beatitudes (Matt 5:5, 7-9) were introduced into this clearly eschatological context of the Q beatitudes. Therefore, these four beatitudes (Matt 5:5, 7-9) did not arise out of the wisdom or ethical teaching of the day, but from the content and context of Jesus' ministry as expressed in the Q sermon.[658] Therefore, according to Guelich, Matthew's main intention with the Beatitudes is to express the fulfilment of the OT promise of God's favourable time (*Heilszeit*) in the person and proclamation of Jesus. In the "hearing" of the proclamation of Jesus, one - experiences his desperate need (Matt 5:3); experiences and reflects God-like mercy (5:7, Luke 6:36-38 cf. Matt); experiences a new allegiance of his person (5:8, Luke 6:43-45 par. Matt); and, in experiencing the underserved and unexpected *šālôm,* one becomes himself an agent of the same (5:9, Luke 6:27-29 par. Matt). Therefore, "for Matthew, as for Q, the Beatitudes are the eschatological pronouncement of the presence of the New Age."[659]

2.13.3. The Matthean Beatitudes are Pronouncement of Blessing Upon the Faithful as They are Now

Slightly different from Guelich, but in a similar manner, Davies and Allison, Jr. argue that although imperatives are implicit in the Matthean Beatitudes, their main function is pronouncement of blessing upon believers for their present faithfulness. Davies and Allison, Jr. note that there is no denying the initial plausibility of the view that Matthew ethicized the beatitudes. In fact, according to them, after hearing the promise of salvation to the "peacemakers" and "the pure in heart," the reader cannot avoid the implicit imperative to be pure in heart, and to be a peacemaker. This is made more apparent by the correspondences between certain beatitudes and imperatives elsewhere in the Sermon on the Mount (e.g.,

656 Guelich, "The Matthean Beatitudes...," 432.

657 *Ibid.*, 426.

658 *Ibid.*, 432-433.

659 *Ibid.*, 433.

5:6 with 5:20; 5:7 and 5:9 with 4:43-48).[660] However, several reasons suggest that the Matthean Beatitudes do not function primarily as imperatives, Davies and Allison, Jr. assert. That is, the ethical thrust does not overshadow the elements of consolation and promise. The main arguments of Davies and Allison, Jr. may be summarised as follows: (1) On the basis of form, there is no explicit imperative except in 5:11-12. Moreover, the apodosis of each of the beatitudes has an eschatological content, which points to the apocalyptic tradition rather than the wisdom tradition for the place of the Matthean Beatitudes. (2) The qualities upheld in the beatitudes appear very infrequently in NT virtue lists. (3) Instead of having created links between the beatitudes and other material in his sermon, Matthew seems to have dissolved several that existed in Q^{mt}. This suggests that he did not attempt to offer paraenesis. (4) In 5:10-12 those who are persecuted are blessed, and persecution is hardly a virtue in itself to be attained on one's own. (5) The last two beatitudes (5:10-12) presuppose a promise of consolation to the readers' present suffering and consolation. So, no behaviourial change is envisaged. (6) The Matthean beatitudes which have no parallel in Luke (Matt 5:5, 7, 8, 9), which usually lead scholars to the assertion that Matthew's beatitudes are ethicized, are not redactional, but they originated in Q^{mt}. If a tendency to ethicize be detected in these beatitudes, it should be traced to Q^{mt} and not to the first evangelist. (7) If the setting for the beatitudes was originally initiation into the Christian cult, as Betz suggests,[661] then the Matthean Beatitudes would be reminder more than imperative. (8) On the basis of structure, the Matthean Beatitudes is sandwiched between 4:23-5:2, which puts the words of the Messiah within the context of grace, and 5:13-16, which calls the disciples to be salt and light and thus acts as the heading for the main imperatives that follow (5:17-7:12). This implies that the Matthean Beatitudes functions as grace before imperatives. Davies and Allison, Jr., then conclude that although imperatives are undeniably implicit in Matt 5:3-12, the primary function of the Matthean Beatitudes is to bless the faithful as they are now.[662]

2.13.4. The Matthean Beatitudes are Ethicized but the Element of Grace is not Eliminated

Ulrich Luz, on the other hand, maintains that Matthew, in fact, ethicized the beatitudes although the element of grace is not abolished. According to Luz, the Matthean beatitudes are adapted to the linguistic usage of wisdom and therefore the *Sitz im Leben* is parenesis.[663] And, "through the pre-Matthean additions and through the Matthean interpretations, a *shift in the meaning of the beatitudes in*

660 Davies and Allison, Jr., *Matthew*, Vol. I, 439.

661 For Betz's suggestion quoted by Davies and Allison, Jr., here, see Betz, *Essays on the Sermon on the Mount*, 27-30.

662 Davies and Allison, Jr., *Matthew*, Vol. I, 439-440.

663 Luz, *Matthew 1-7*, 229.

the direction of parenesis apparently has taken place."[664] At the same time, however, Luz maintains, "the ethical reworking of the Beatitudes in the Gospel of Matthew by no means entailed an elimination of grace."[665] Luz's points of argument may be briefly summarised as follows: (1) the message of grace had been preached for about fifty years or so before the writing of Matthew's gospel. By the time of the writing of Matthew's gospel the Matthean community was facing a problem of how to remain loyal to the faith given to it, a situation in which the message of grace, if repeated without ceasing, could become "cheap grace."[666] Compelled by this situation, Matthew ethicized the beatitudes precisely to help the community. (2) Matthew's ethical beatitudes are gifts of virtues within the expression of grace which occupies Matthew's priority within the whole narrative framework of his gospel. Jesus, who made the ethical demands, is Immanuel who helps and accompanies his community. (3) An element of the promise of grace is also found in the apodoses of the Matthean Beatitudes, and all of them are to be understood eschatologically. This does not mean that the promises are to be attained by one's effort alone. Rather, to Matthew, those Christians who make efforts to attain the promise will be helped by God to attain that promise. Therefore, the promises are a full and pure bestowal of grace for Matthew. (4) As the Torah functions in the Old Testament-Jewish understanding as an aid towards remaining in the covenant which God has made for his people, the gospel functions, for Matthew, to help Christians to remain faithful to Jesus. And, the commands of Jesus as well as the ethical beatitudes in the gospel are part of this gospel. Therefore, God's demanding will, such as found in the Matthean ethical beatitudes, is an element of grace for Matthew.[667]

2.13.5. The Stance Adopted in this Research: The Matthean Beatitudes are Primarily Pronouncement of Eschatological Blessing. But they also Carry Ethical Exhortation

Of the four views mentioned above, the view of Davies and Allison, Jr. fits best to the insights of the exegesis of the Matthean Beatitudes in the previous chapter, although with slight modification, especially viewing from the socio-historical context of the Matthean community. A brief explanation may be given as follows: (1) Out of the eight beatitudes inherited by Matthew from his tradition (Matt 5:1-9, 11-12), four of them, such as the first (5:3 – *the poor*), second (5:4 - *those who mourn*), fourth (5:6 – *those who are hungry*) and the last (5:11-12 -

664 Luz, *Matthew 1-7*, 232.

665 *Ibid.*, 245.

666 Luz, *Matthew 1-7*, 245, quoting from Bonhoeffer, *The Cost of Discipleship*, 13-27.

667 For these points, see Luz, *Matthew 1-7*, 245-246.

persecuted for Jesus' sake) are purely apocalyptic in nature before his redaction.[668] The Matthean redaction, such as the addition of "in spirit" in the "poor" of the first beatitude, as well as "and thirsty for righteousness" in the fourth beatitude, does not spiritualize or ethicize them. They are only clarifications made on the basis of the Matthean community's socio-historical context.[669] Therefore, they are primarily pronouncements of consolation to the Matthean community in their current situation. They are consolations in the context of various difficulties they were undergoing.[670] (2) The other four, such as the third (5:5 – *the meek*), fifth (5:7 – *the merciful*), sixth (5:8 – *the pure in heart*) and seventh (5:9 – *the peacemakers*) carry ethical element, yet their apodoses are apocalyptic in nature. Matthew took them over without altering them because they were relevant for addressing his community as they were. While the protases are expressions of the identities of the Matthean community in contrast to the leaders of Formative Judaism, they are also exhortations to continue to pursue ethical behaviours which are greatly required in their social context, befitting the follower of Jesus Christ with the assurance that such conducts carry a promise of eschatological blessings.[671] It would be correct to assume that they are exhortations to continue what they have been doing, as well as to pursue it more vigorously, but not an exhortation to start what they have never been doing (i.e. ethical requirements for entering into the eschatological kingdom). (3) The Matthean addition of the eighth beatitude (Matt 5:10) is also formulated in the nature of apocalyptic beatitudes, and its content clearly indicates that it is a pronouncement of eschatological blessing to the Matthean community in their existing situation of persecution.[672] Therefore, Davies and Allison, Jr. are right in observing that the primary function of the Matthean beatitudes is to bless the faithful (= followers of Jesus Christ/the Matthean community) as they are now, and, they constitute grace before imperatives that follows in the Sermon

668 In fact, also those who understand the Matthean Beatitudes as entrance requirements for the kingdom, such as Windisch, Dodd, Strecker and Dupont, see these four beatitudes as straightforward eschatological blessings before they were redacted by Matthew. See the above sub-section 2.13.1. "The Matthean Beatitudes: Entrance Requirements for the Kingdom."

669 See the exegetical comments of the mentioned verses above.

670 It has been established in the first chapter (especially in 1.3 and 1.4), that the Matthean community was undergoing various difficulties. They shared with other Jews unjust treatment from the Romans socio-politically and economically. At the same time, they also suffered persecutions at the hands, primarily of the Jewish leaders, and also of their Gentile neighbours.

671 Besides the difficulties faced by the Matthean community mentioned above, there was a potential disunity among the Matthean community, especially between the Jewish members and the Gentile members, as well as between the few well-to-do and the majority poor members of the community, which, together with other difficulties, called the Mathean community to exhibit an ethical conduct stipulated in the third, fifth, sixth and seventh beatitudes. See the sections 1.4.5 and 1.4.6 of the first chapter.

672 See the exegetical comment on 5:10 above.

on the Mount.[673] At the same time, however, they also carry an exhortation to continue their ethical conduct befitting the followers of Jesus Christ, for it is highly demanded in their social situation.

With this conclusion, we will try to see in the following chapter the implication of the Matthean Beatitudes for contemporary Christian discipleship.

673 Davies and Allison, Jr., *Matthew*, Vol. I, 439-440.

Chapter 3

Implication of the Matthean Beatitudes for Contemporary Christian Discipleship

3.1. Prelude

The intent of this chapter is to bring out the implication of the Matthean Beatitudes for contemporary Christian discipleship. At this point, it may be good to give first a brief explanation of the term discipleship in general and in Matthew.

As already mentioned in the introduction, the English term "discipleship" derives from the noun "disciple," which in general refers to "someone who believes in, and follows, the teachings of another." It is also used at the same time to refer to "one of the twelve close followers of Christ."[1] The noun "discipleship" as such would therefore mean "being a believer and follower of the teachings of another" in general or "being a follower of Jesus Christ" in particular. Then, the term is used in this study to mean, "being a follower of Jesus Christ." From this general definition, let us try to see the meaning of the term discipleship in the context of Matthew's gospel. For this purpose, it would be helpful to refer to the explanation given by Bornkamm.

According to Bornkamm, the whole Matthean understanding of discipleship is embraced by the concept of μαθητής "disciple." Bornkamm maintains that οἱ μαθηται is the specific ecclesiological concept of the evangelist, and therefore it also embraces his whole understanding of the church. According to him, μαθητής is characteristic of discipleship in Matthew in that it is defined in terms of being called by Jesus to follow him. It signifies an enduring relationship with Jesus, and it proves itself by obedience, humility, and readiness to suffer. Bornkam further notes that the corresponding verb μαθητεύειν originally comes from the relationship to the earthly Jesus, and is apparently used by Matthew (in 28:16ff.)

1 *Chambers 21st Century Dictionary.*

to make it clear that the same relationship is permanently binding also now, after the Resurrection.[2]

Bornkamm's analysis of the noun *mathētēs* in Matthew clearly shows that the noun undoubtedly refers not only to the twelve, but also to all the followers of Jesus Christ. And accordingly, discipleship in Matthew can be understood as referring to being called by Jesus to follow him, to have an enduring relationship with him. And, the call of discipleship demands or carries with it obedience, humility, and readiness to suffer for the sake of Jesus Christ, and the call embraces every member of the church.

Keeping this general understanding of discipleship in mind, the intent of this chapter is to suggest to the contemporary Christians, what the Matthean beatitudes implies to them in their lives and in the different circumstances they are undergoing, as followers of Jesus Christ. And, the particular focus will be contemporary Christians in India, although the suggestion would be applicable to the different Christian groups of the world who have experiences similar to those of Christians in India. Meanwhile, the situation of Christianity in India is also quite complex, and Christians in different parts of India have different experiences. Therefore, an attempt will be made to highlight particular situations where the relevance of particular beatitudes is obvious.

It has been concluded in the previous chapter that the Matthean Beatitudes are basically apocalyptic in nature and they are primarily pronouncements of eschatological blessings (especially the first, second, fourth, eighth and ninth beatitudes), and that they are a consolation to the Matthean community in the context of various difficulties they were undergoing. At the same time, they (especially the third, fifth, sixth and seventh beatitudes) also carry an exhortation to continue to pursue an ethical conduct which is highly demanded in their social situation, of course, with promises of concomitant eschatological blessings. In spite of the complexity of the situations experienced by the contemporary Christians in different parts of India, the main functions of the Matthean Beatitudes (particularly as envisaged in the context of the Matthean community) apply even to them. To be more precise, both the functions of consolation and ethical exhortation of the Matthean beatitudes are highly significant for the Christians in contemporary India. Now, we will first look into the implications of the beatitudes which primarily carry consolation (the first, second, fourth, eighth and ninth) and following this we will look into the implications of the beatitudes which carry ethical exhortations (the third, fifth, sixth and seventh).

2 Günther Bornkamm, "The Risen Christ and the Earthly Jesus. Matt 28:16-20," in *The Future of Our Religious Past: Essays in Honor of Rudolf Bultmann*, edited by J. M. Robinson, translated by Charles E. Carlston and Robert P. Scharlemann (New York: Harper & Row, 1971), 218.

3.2. The Matthean Beatitudes: Pronouncement of Consolation to the Downtrodden and Suffering Christians in India

It has been highlighted in the second chapter that the Matthean community experienced various difficulties, and under such experiences they did not have any one to turn to for their help, except God. The Matthean beatitudes, especially the first, second, fourth, eighth and ninth, reflect the experience of the Matthean community in such situations and they function primarily as consolation to them in their sufferings. At the same time, this consolation would also have undoubtedly encouraged them to stand firm in their faith in Jesus Christ. In the same way, the Matthean Beatitudes functions as a pronouncement of consolation for many Christians in India, who, in their life, experience various difficulties like the Matthean community. Although, the sufferings of the Indian Christians may not be exactly the same with the sufferings of the Matthean community, there are many parallels between the two. The implication of the first, second and fourth beatitudes are more obvious to the sufferings of the Dalit Christians, while the implication of the eighth and ninth beatitudes are more relevant to the situations of persecution suffered by Indian Christians in general.

3.2.1. The Implication of the First, Second, and Fourth Beatitudes for the Downtrodden Christians in India, especially the Dalit Christians

Dalits are the lowest in the social hierarchy of Indian society, particularly under the Hindu religious system, in which there are four major castes such as the Brahmins (the highest and the priestly class), the Kshatriyas (the second highest and the warrior class), the Vaisyas (the third and the trading class), and the Sudras (the lowest and the servants of the above three class).[3] There are different theories regarding the historical background of the Dalits. According to some writers the Dalits are those who come from the Sudra background.[4] According to some others, Dalits form the fifth group below the four main castes, and they do not have caste.[5] Mahatma Phule, one of the great leaders of the Dalit movement in the nineteenth century, used the term *sudra-atisudra* for Dalits. *Shudras are* "touchable backward castes" and *atisudras* are "untouchable backward castes." B. R. Ambedkar, the most well-known leader of the Dalit movement in the twentieth century, used the

---

3 Robert W. Brown, *Dalits and the Church: An Initial Investigation into the Place of the Dalit Community within the Church of North India and the Church of South India* (New Delhi: Centre for Dalit/Subaltern Studies, 2006), 8-9. See also S. Lourduswamy, *Equal Rights to All Dalits (with special reference to Dalit Christians)*, CDS Pamphlet 2 (New Delhi: Centre for Dalit Studies, 2001), 1-2.

4 See for example, Buta Singh, *The Dalits and Dalit Awakening in India* (New Delhi: Gyan Publishing House, 2004), 24.

5 See for example, Prem K. Shinde, ed., *Dalits and Human Rights*, Vol. 2 (Delhi: Isha Books, 2005), 1-2.

English term "untouchable" for "Dalit."[6] It, then, seems correct to understand that Dalits come from the Sudra background, but they are *atisudras* "the untouchables" who are different from the "touchable" Sudras. They do not have caste and are therefore outcastes.[7] These untouchable people called themselves "Dalits," a term derived from a Sanskrit root *dal*, which means burst, split, broken or torn asunder, downtrodden, scattered, crushed, destroyed."[8] From administrative parlance the expression "Scheduled Castes" has been used to designate the "Dalits" or the "Untouchables" since 1932 under the British rule of India.[9] The name "Harijans" was given to these people by Mahatma Gandhi. It means "God's Children/men of God," but the people themselves preferred to be called "Dalits" because, according to them, the word "Harijans" does not describe their condition adequately. To them, "the word 'Dalit' is an expression of hope to recover their self-identity."[10] Thus, Dalits are the downtrodden people of India, who are outside the social structure because of the hatred and contempt shown by others, and thus have been considered "outcastes" in the caste structure of the Indian society, who are usually looked upon as untouchables,[11] and who, because of that status, "have been made to bear extreme forms of disadvantage and oppression for centuries, a continuous assault on their humanity which virtually reduced them to a state of being 'no-people'."[12] At the close of the twentieth century the Dalits (Scheduled Castes) comprise about 17% of the Indian population which is approximately 1000 million (or 1 billion).[13] Within the Dalit population of about 170 million,

6 James Massey, *Down Trodden. The struggle of India's Dalits for Identity, Solidarity and Liberation* (Geneva: WCC Publications, 1997), 1.

7 K. C. Das, *Indian Dalits. Voices, Visions and Politics* (Delhi: Global Vision Publishing House, 2004), 58.

8 Massey, *Down Trodden*, 1, 2-3.

9 *Ibid.*, 20-21. According to Ghanshyam Shah the term "Dalits" includes the so-called Scheduled Castes (SCs), Scheduled Tribes (STs), and Other Backward Classes (OBCs) in administrative parlance. However, Shah himself uses the term "Dalits" mostly in connection with the Scheduled Castes. See, Ghanshyam Shah, "Dalits and the State," in *Essay on Dalits*, edited by Raj Kumar (New Delhi: Discovery Publishing House, 2003), 115 [114-136]. According to the manifesto of the Dalit Panther Movement of the Maharastra state in India, the Dalits are "members of scheduled castes and tribes, neo-Buddhists, the working people, the landless and poor peasants, women and all those who are being exploited politically, economically and in the name of religion." See Massey, *Down Trodden*, 1.

10 See Ram Rattan, "Gandhiji and Untouchability," in *Essay on Dalits*, edited by Raj Kumar (New Delhi: Discovery Publishing House, 2003), 63 [62-69]; and Massey, *Down Trodden*, 2-3, 20.

11 According to Lourduswamy untouchability has been practiced for almost three millennia in the Hindu society. See Lourduswamy, *Equal Rights to All Dalits*, 2.

12 Massey, *Down Trodden*, 1-2.

13 See Lourduswamy, *Equal Rights to All Dalits*, 10. Here, Lourduswamy mentions the population of Scheduled Castes as 170 millions and Scheduled Tribes as 80 millions in the year 2000. See also Brown, Dalits and the Church, 8-9, who mentions the population of the Dalits as comprising about 20 % of the Indian population.

approximately 10% of them, that is about 16 million, are Christians, which makes up about 66% of the total Christian population in India that is about 24 million.[14]

There are various theories on the historical roots of the Dalits that is how the untouchable class came into existence. Some people thought that historically Dalits are the descendants of the aborigines of India from time immemorial, or of the Dravidians, one of the native inhabitants of ancient India (who were mixed up with the aborigines), who were conquered by the Indo-Aryans and whom they made domestic and village slaves around 2nd millennium B.C.[15] Some others argue that the untouchables (Dalits) were non-Aryan, non-Dravidian aboriginals who were conquered and subjugated by the Dravidians. There is another theory which rejects racial theory. According to this theory, the untouchability came into existence as a result of a continuous feud between the Sudra kings and the Brahmins. Under this feud the Brahmins were subjected to many tyrannies and indignities, as a result of which the Brahmins refused performing the *upanayana* of the *Shoetrees*. Then the fourth varna below the rank of *Vaishyas* came to be formed. Consequently, the Brahmanical Hindu religion evolved purity-pollution concepts, and treated some sections of the Sudras, those who were competing with the Brahmins, as untouchables.[16]

Although, it may be difficult to trace the historical root of the Dalits/untouchables with certainty, we may agree with the conclusion of Massey that Dalits are the descendants of the earliest settlers of India.[17] And, it is an undeniable fact that the Dalits/untouchables form the lowest hierarchy in the caste society of India. According to the earliest literary sources available, such as the Rigveda (1500-1000 B.C.), the Upanishads (800-600 B.C), the Ramayana and the Mahabharata, the Dalits "were reduced by their oppressors to a non-human level, with no identity or dignity."[18] They are often assigned tasks too ritually polluting and therefore they do not merit inclusion within the traditional caste system. Consequently they are deemed polluting and therefore "untouchable." While

14 See Lourduswamy, *Equal Rights to All Dalits*, 10. According to Sathianathan Clarke, the Dalits constituted about 16 percent of the Indian population in 1991 census, that is 138 million of 846 million. Clarke maintains that the figure would, however, be substantially higher if the Dalits who embraced non-Hindu religion are taken into consideration, because the Indian government includes (at that time) only the Hindu Dalits under scheduled castes. According to Clarke, 50-70 percent of the Indian Christians come from the Dalit background. See Sathianathan Clarke, *Dalits and Christianity. Subaltern Religion and Liberation Theology in India* (New Delhi: Oxford University Press, 1999 [1998]), 64.

15 See Singh, *The Dalits and Dalit Awakening in India*, 15-18; and Massey, *Down Trodden*, 12.

16 For a brief discussion of these different theories, see Shah, "Dalits and the State," 119-121. For a more detailed discussion see the works cited by Shah in the same essay.

17 James Massey, *Roots of Dalit History, Christianity, Theology and Spirituality* (Delhi: ISPCK, 1996), 53 [1-53].

18 See Singh, *The Dalits and Dalit Awakening in India*, 18-25; and Massey, *Down Trodden*, 12-15.

the first four castes have freedom to choose and change their occupation, Dalits have usually been confined to the occupational structures into which they were born.[19] Inspite of the fact that "untouchability" was abolished in 1950 under Article 17 of the Indian constitution, its practice continues,[20] especially in rural India, and atrocities towards Dalits seem increasing rather than diminishing. Discrimination against the Dalits include prohibitions - to draw water from the public ponds/wells/taps/tanks; to visit the same temples with the dominant castes, to drink from the same cups in tea stalls with them, and to carry their dead through their villages, or to bury them in the latter's graveyards; to sit on par with them in public or private places; to conduct marriage procession in their locality, etc. Atrocities against the Dalits include confiscation of land that is legally theirs, beatings, torture, rape, attempt to murder, and actual murder by dominant castes.[21] Because of all such conditions they are the most deprived community of India. Many of the Dalits are deprived of enough food, health care, housing and clothing, education and employment.[22] They are met with injustice from all

19 Shinde, ed., *Dalits and Human Rights*, Vol. 1, 80-81. See also Godwin Shiri, *The Plight of Christian Dalits – A South Indian Case Study* (Bangalore: Asian Trading Corporation, 1997), 78-90. Here, Shiri mentions about the continuity of traditional occupations by Christian Dalits. This could reveal to some extend the condition of the Dalits in general, and probably the condition of the non-Christian Dalits could even be worse.

20 See Shinde, ed., *Dalits and Human Rights*, Vol. 1, 81; and Massey, *Down Trodden*, 21.

21 See Lourduswamy, *Equal Rights to All Dalits*, 8-9. See also Jayshree P. M, et al. eds., *Dalit Human Rights Violations. Atrocities against Dalits in India*, Vol. 1. Case Papers: Summary & Jury's Interim Observations and Recommendations (National Campaign on Dalit Human Rights, 2000), 9; and James Massey, *India. 50 Years of Independence: 1947-97. Status, Growth & Development 20. Dalits: Issues and Concerns* (Delhi: B.R. Publishing Corporation, 1998), 7. Here, Massey mentions the numbers of murders, grievous hurt, rape, arson and other offences committed against the Dalits during 1981-1986.

22 K. D. Gangrade gives a brief profile of Dalits as follows:
Dalits constitute 20 per cent of all households while they won only eight per cent of land. Their family budget tends to be 30 to 50 per cent lower than the rest of the middle-class in India. The scheduled castes and the scheduled tribes spend 70 to 75 per cent of their money on food items alone. They account for bulk of India's two million bondage labourers. They have the dubious distinction of having the largest number of the world's absolute poor. The female illiteracy rate in rural areas is as high as 91 per cent amongst the SCs in the rural areas and 93 per cent amongst the STs in tribal area. They have suffered the same experience of deprivation. Their representation in public services is very low: in Class I and II of central services 6.9 per cent and 10 per cent, respectively. See K. D. Gangrade, "Gandhi and Dalits," in *Essay on Dalits*, edited by Raj Kumar (New Delhi: Discovery Publishing House, 2003), 76-77 [75-80].
In her case study on Christian Dalits (see above), which also can be taken as representing to some extend the condition of Dalits in general, Shiri found that 95 percent of those in the study areas live in huts, while the rest 5 per cent live in cemented or tiled houses. Only 14 percent of them in average have electricity in their homes, while the actual situation varies greatly in different villages. Only in 49 percent of the households under study were literates found, while there was not a single literate in 51 percent of the households. The main causes of poor education among them are – poor economic condition, poor infrastructure in village schools,

corners.[23] Most of them live on the brink of destitution. A large number of them work as agricultural labourers with very small wages. According to the 1991 census, 77 percent of the Dalit work force was engaged in the Agricultural sector. Those who own land among them usually fall into the category of marginal land owners.[24] In addition to their poverty and oppressed social and economic situation, the condition of the Dalits was worsened by the abuse of their women. Dalit women are often induced into prostitution called Devadasi system in the name of religion. And, the upper-caste men and the landlords often raped Dalit women. They were also often raped by the police.[25] It can be said that they are the poorest of the poor within the Indian society.

Dalit Christians share all the oppressions faced by the Dalits in general. Their conversion into Christianity does not change their social, educational and economic status.[26] Furthermore, their suffering is doubled by discrimination they suffer from the government and also from the church.

---

and hostile environments for (Christian) Dalits in villages. Shiri, *The Plight of Christian Dalits*, 60-62, 116-117,129-132. For a discussion on Dalits' education, see also Shah, "Dalits and the State," 117-119.

23 This is not an exaggeration. A clear proof can be seen in the many cases documented by National Campaign on Dalit Human Rights. See Jayshree P. M, et al. eds., *Dalit Human Rights Violations*, Vol. I. At least 57 cases are recorded only in this volume.

24 Shah, "Dalits and the State," 116-117. Through a case study on Christian Dalits (around 1993-94), which also gives the picture of Dalits in general, Shiri found that 89 % of those in the area under study are engaged in agricultural occupations, mostly as agricultural coolies with a very low wages, between Rs. 5 to Rs. 20 a day. 69 % of them have an income between Rs. 1000 to Rs. 4000 per annum. About 62 % of them have land, but most of them are small ones, two acres or less, and only 29 % of them owned wet land. Many of them could not make use of their land properly because of lack of water. Shiri, *The Plight of Christian Dalits*, 34-35, 134-150.

25 See Jayshree P. M, et al. eds., *Dalit Human Rights Violations*, 176-202. See also Shiri, The Plight of Christian Dalits, 95-97; Shah, "Dalits and The State," 125-126; and Massey, *Down Trodden*, 27.

26 Lourduswamy, *Equal Rights to All Dalits*, 11. See also Brown, *Dalits and the Church*, 35. This situation is clearly indicated in the case study done by Godwin Shiri in the villages of the Bellary district of Karnataka and Kurnool district of Andra Pradesh. Shiri found in her study that – Christian Dalits, like all other Dalits, are barred from entering village tea shops (p. 62), many traditional village functionaries like barbers and washer-men, refuse to serve Christian Dalits (p. 66), Christian Dalits are not allowed to use wells situated in localities other than their own and they face several restrictions while using village tanks or canal embankments (p. 67-68), most of the Christian Dalits do not have free access to the village shops and many of them do not have free access even in ration shops (p. 70), Christian Dalits are not allowed to take processions, especially marriage procession, in many villages (p. 71), Christian Dalits cannot move around freely in the Dalit localities of their villages, especially in the areas where the upper castes are concentrated (p. 75), Christian Dalits are generally restricted from standing in or entering public places and platforms in villages, such as the Panchayat platform, the (upper castes') temples. They dare not sit even at the Bus stops/shelters (p. 75), non-Dalits do not want to have inter-dining with Dalit Christians and the later are not allowed to enter

Dalit Christians are deprived of those constitutional rights and privileges which are enjoyed by Dalits who are Hindu, Sikh or Buddhist. Under the constitution of India, certain disadvantaged groups are referred to as the "Scheduled Castes," and are given special rights to compensate for the disadvantages they have been suffering in the past. Dalit Christians are not included in the scheduled castes by the Indian Government. When a Dalit becomes a Christian, the privileged which he/she has enjoyed as a member of scheduled caste, is confiscated from him/her.[27]

In addition to the discrimination they suffer from the society and the government, the Dalit Christians suffer discrimination even within the church, both in the Catholic and protestant churches. In some of the Indian churches non-Dalit Christians usually occupy the central part of the church, and the Dalits occupy the corners. Even in the Holy Communion service the Dalits usually have an opportunity to take the communion only after the non-Dalit Christians have done so. In some churches, separate cups are given to the Dalits at the Eucharistic celebration, and separate communion rails and separate cemeteries were assigned to the Dalit Christians in some of the catholic and protestant churches.[28] This does not mean that discrimination on grounds of caste has been officially perpetuated by the Indian churches among its members, or that any attempt has never been made to abolish such discriminations. In fact, the Church in India, particularly for the past thirty years, has been actively involved in denouncing caste system and discrimination against the Dalits. It has also taken positive measures for their development.[29] Inspite of such efforts, however, the fact is that the situation still continues in various places, and it is manifested in various ways and forms. It is quite uncertain when the caste discrimination against Dalits will be totally eradicated from among the Indian Christians.

The situations of the Dalit Christians in India highlighted above indicate that they are really the poor, who are poor in all areas – social, economic, education, etc. They are the people who are subjugated, oppressed, tortured, and deprived of most of the privileges, which consequently make them really poor in

---

the house of non-Dalits (pp. 76-77). Besides those restrictions, many Christian Dalits are forced by their poor economic conditions to continue their traditional occupation of doing demeaning tasks like skinning, beating drums, cobbler work, and *Madigathana-Okkaluthana* (pp. 78-84). Apart from such restrictions and compulsions to do menial works, many Christian Dalits suffer severe harassments, physically, socially and economically, which include – verbal abuse, physical assaults, forced labor, land grabbing, forcible eviction, molestation and rape of women, etc. (pp. 90-109). See Shiri, *The Plight of Christian Dalits*, 62-109.

27 Massey, *Down Trodden*, 22-24. See also Lourduswamy, *Equal Rights to All Dalits*, 25-31.

28 See Lourduswamy, *Equal Rights to All Dalits*, 13-16.

29 For example, see excerpts of the statements, resolutions and actions plans made by the Catholic Bishops Conference of India (CBCI) for equality and brotherhood in the church, and the response of the Church of North India (CNI) in Lourduswamy, *Equal Rights to All Dalits*, 17-24.

their spirit. In addition to all these situations, when persecution of Christians by non-Christians happens in India, the Dalits Christians are obviously the most affected people not only because they contribute the largest number of Christians in India, but also because they do not get respect from all corners. Therefore, like the Matthean community, the Dalits Christians truly deserve to be called "the poor in their spirit," and like the Matthean community they have many reasons to mourn. In addition to all the disadvantages that befall them which we have mentioned above, they are the ones who are deprived of proper medical cares, proper sanitation, proper nutrition, etc., as a result of which they obviously experience illness and death more frequently than the people around them.[30] Like the Matthean community the Dalit Christians are the people who are really hungry and thirsty for righteousness, that is, because of so many injustices they experience in their lives, they are really longing to experience justice in their lives and they are longing for God's justice to vindicate them. Therefore, the first, second, and fourth Matthean beatitudes are especially very meaningful for the Dalit Christians in India, and these beatitudes are consolation to them that the kingdom of heaven/God belongs to them. They are going to experience the blessings of the kingdom of heaven/God, which above all includes restoration of justice and equality, in full at the eschaton. Meanwhile, they can begin to experience those blessings from now itself, although partially, because Jesus had already inaugurated that future kingdom. This would also imply that wherever the lordship of Jesus Christ is experienced, the Dalit Christians also will or must experience the blessings of the kingdom of heaven/God. This assurance is also an encouragement to them to stand firm in their faith in Jesus Christ even in the midst of their difficulties.

Not only for the Dalits, however, even for many other Christians in different parts of India, especially the tribal Christians and the Adivasi Christians, who experience situations similar to those experienced by the Dalit Christians these beatitudes are consolation in their difficult situations, and encouragement to faithfully stand firm in their faith.

3.2.2. The Implication of the Eighth and Ninth Beatitudes for the Persecuted Christians in India

Apart from the suffering of poverty and injustice in various forms by the Dalit Christians and other Christians in India, persecution from other religious followers, particularly the Hindu extremists, has been a common experience of

30 According to Buta Singh, Dalits "were used as bonded laborers; very young children were employed to rear animals, and perform several other functions whether their physique permitted them or not. Very often they were victims of deadly diseases on account of pressure of work." Singh, *The Dalits and Dalit Awakening in India*, 305.

Christians in various parts of India for sometime.[31] The level of violence against Christians has multiplied since the Hindu nationalist Bharatiya Janata Party (BJP) came to power in the central government in March 1998 and it continued even during the congress and its allies came to power in 2004. Again, it escalated since BJP came to power again in 2014. The acts of violence against Christians include arson of churches, forced re-conversion of Christians to Hinduism and threats of physical violence, distribution of threatening literature, burning of Bibles, raping of nuns, murder of Christian priests and destruction of Christian schools, colleges, and cemeteries, etc.[32] According to the data released to the press by the Church in India on Tuesday, 24th November 1998, the violence against Christians in 1998 alone is far more than the total incidents of crime against the Christian community from 1964 to 1997. There were 38 incidents of violence against Christians reported during 1964 to 1996. And 24 such incidents were reported in 1997. Then from 1998, Christians in India have suffered a wave of violence.[33] This can be clearly seen in a list of atrocities committed against Christians across India released by the Concerned Christians of India in 1998.[34] This list contains atrocities against Christians only during the period between 15 August 1997 to the end of 1998, and it would be correct to assume that the list is far from exhaustive.[35] And, such incidents happened even afterwards in several places at several times. Although a list of such incidents is not available to this researcher, some of the incidents could be mentioned as examples.

Graham Staines, an Australian Christian missionary, who had worked in India for more than 30 years, and his two sons Timothy (aged 9) and Philip (aged 7), were burnt to death while they were sleeping in their station wagon at Manoharpur village in Keonjhar district in Orissa in January 1999. Staines was running the Evangelical Missionary Society of Mayurbhanj, an Australian Missionary society.[36]

---

31 From 1964 to 1996, 38 incidents of violence against Christians had been reported. See "Anti-Christian Violence in India" (modified on 25 March, 2009), 2 of 6, http:/christianpersecution-india.blogspot.com, Retrieved from http://en.wikipedia.org/wiki/Anti-Christian_violence_in_India, (accessed 02.04.2009)

32 See "Anti-Christian Violence in India," 1 of 6.

33 See "Anti-Christian Violence in India," 2 of 6.

34 See, "A List of Atrocities Commited Against Christians Across India in the Golden Jubilee Year of Independence August 15, 1997 to August 15, 1998 and beyond" (updated on 02.12.1998), 1-5 of 5, http://www.angelfire. com/pe/indianchristians/persecution.html (accessed 23.02.2009).

35 In fact, it has been mentioned that 38 incidents of violence against Christians were reported during 1964 to 1996, 24 such incidents were reported in 1997, and, 90 incidents were reported in 1998 alone. See "Anti-Christian Violence in India," 2 of 6.

36 See "Anti-Christian Violence in India," 3 of 6. See also "Attacks on Christians in Orissa" (no date of posting), 1-4 of 4, http://www.dalitchristians.com/Html/attacksOrissa.htm (accessed 23.02.2009). This incident was much publicized in the Media.

In August 23, 2008, Lakshmanananda Saraswati, a Vishwa Hindu Parishad (VHP) leader, was attacked and killed, along with four others. Hindu extremists accused Christians as the killer. Christians denied the accusation.[37] However, the incident was followed by violence against Christians. After a few days the Maoist outfit (People's Liberation Guerrilla Army) claimed responsibility.[38] Even then, the Hindus continued to accuse Christians and the violence against Christians continued. In the course of the violence, since August 2008 till 4th, Feb., 2009, it has been reported that, "at least 60 Christians have been killed; 18,000, wounded; 181 churches razed or destroyed; 4,500 Christian homes burned; and more than 50,000 Christians, displaced. More than 30,000 of those displaced were staying in refugee camps or hiding in the jungle." Many Christian schools and colleges were also destroyed or damaged.[39] Two women, one of whom was a Christian nun, were gang-raped.[40] Following the violence against Christians in Orissa, and probably under its influence, Christians were attacked even in Karnataka state in the later part of 2008. A Hindu extremist group, Bajrang Dal, targeted Christian churches and prayer halls, and the ruling BJP government was also accused of involvement. The violence started from 14 September 2008 when about 20 churches were vandalized in Mangalore, Udupi, Chikkamagaluru, and in other districts of Karnataka.[41] In relation to these incidents minor violence was later reported from the border state of Kerala.[42] In fact, incidents of targeting Christians happen at

37 See Sandeep Mishra, "Orissa violence: Cracks in BJP-BJD alliance" (26 Aug 2008, 0409 hrs IST), 1-2 of 2, http://timesofindia. indiatimes.com/articleshow/ 3405376.cms (accessed 10.04.09). See also "More Violence, Roads blocked in Kandhamal" (29 Aug 2008, 1327 hrs IST, IANS), 2 of 2, http://timesofindia. indiatimes.com/article show/3421412.cms (accessed 10.04.09).

38 "Maoists claim killing Swami," *The Times of India, Bangalore* (August, 30, 2008), 11.

39 See Michelle A.Vu, "Orissa Gov't to Boot Christians from Refugee Camps" (05.02.2009), 1 of 2, http://www.christianpost.com/Intl/Persecution/2009/02/ (accessed 23.02.2009). According to the report in the "Persecution Update" on 8th April, 2009, in the course of this event "more than 75 Christians have been killed, 5000 Christian houses looted, damaged and burnt along with 250 churches and Christian institutions." See "Kandhamal carnage orchestrated, not 'spontaneous' reaction, says Journalist author" (08.04.2009), 2 of 6, in *Persecution Update India. Window to the Persecuted and Suffering Christian Faith of India* (accessed 09.04.2009), available at http://persecution.in. Here, the website reports about what is written in a new book, entitled "Kandhamal – a Blot on Indian Secularism" authored by Anto Akkara, a journalist, who visited Kandhamal half a dozen times to make an arduous investigation. See also "Anti-Christian Violence in India," 3 of 6.

40 See "Anti-Christian Violence in India," 3 of 6. See also "Orissa Nun Breaks Silence: Cops Failed Me," *Times of India, Bangalore* (25.10.2008), 1; and "Hindu Orphan Raped, Murdered in Orissa," *Sunday Times, Bangalore* (05.10.2008), 1.

41 See "14 churches, clergy attacked in 3 dists. Bajrang Dal Activists Suspected," *The Times of India, Bangalore* (15.09.2008), 1. See also "Undying Fury: 3 more churches targeted. Miscreants Strike in DK, Chikmagalur, Kolar Districts," *The Times of India, Bangalore* (18.09.2008), 1.

42 "Conversion fire spreads to Kerala" (16 Sep 2008, 0329 hrs IST, TNN), 1-2 of 2, http:// timesofindia. indiatimes.com/articleshow/348 7282.cms (accessed 10.04.2009).

regular intervals in different parts of India.[43] Since BJP came to power again in 2014, there has been an increase of violence against Christians in different parts of India. Just to show few incidents - Several churches were attacked in the capital Delhi since December 2014, including St. Sebastian's Church, which was burned. A church in Mangalore was attacked in February 2015. In March 2015, a 71-year-old nun was gang raped in West Bengal during an attack on a convent school in which the school's chapel was ransacked and sacred items stolen, a church building under construction was vandalised in Haryana. St. George church in Mumbai was also attacked by masked persons, and the cathedral of Jabalpur was attacked and more than a dozen people were injured. In April 2015, St. Mary's Church in Agra was vandalised and statues of Mother Mary and the Infant Jesus were damaged.[44]

To the Christians in India who suffer persecution because of their faith in Jesus Christ and because of their good deeds in Jesus' name, the eighth and ninth beatitudes are consolation in the midst of their sufferings and an encouragement to stand firm in their faith. They are reminded, like the Matthean community, that they are following the footsteps of the faithful prophets, and they are assured that the kingdom of God belongs to them, and their sufferings will not go unrewarded. In the same way, even to all those Christians in different parts of the world, notably those who suffer under the Islam fundamentalists (ISIS & ISIL, etc.) who experience persecutions of different kinds, these beatitudes speak to them just as they speak to the persecuted Christians in India and just as they spoke to the Matthean community.

3.3. The Matthean Beatitudes Carry Ethical Exhortation to Many Christians in India

Just as the Matthean beatitudes (especially the third, fifth, sixth and seventh) are also exhortation to the Matthean community to continue to pursue an ethical conduct which is highly demanded in their social situation, they are also exhortation to the Indian Christians to pursue ethical conducts befitting to be the followers of Jesus Christ. This exhortation would apply to all the Christians in India although the degree of its application may vary from place to place. We will try to highlight some of the places where the implications of these beatitudes are more obvious, as examples.

3.3.1. The Implication of the Third and the Seventh Beatitudes

We may first take together the third beatitude and the seventh beatitude which are calls to be meek and to be peacemakers. In our exegesis in the previous chapter,

43 See Soumittra S. Bose, "Church in Mahastra Vandalized," *The Times of India* (Bangalore), 19 April 2009.

44 Anti-Christian violence in India (5 of 10). From Wikipedia, the free encyclopedia. http: // en.wikipedia.org/wiki/Anti-Christian_violence_in_India (accessed 22.05.2015).

we conclude that to the Matthean community, the call to be meek in the third beatitude is a call to emulate Jesus' meekness especially in the context of - 1) persecutions they were suffering at the hands of both the Jews and the Gentiles, and where at the same time they were called to continue their mission to both the Jews and the Gentiles; 2) possible racial problems within their community where the Gentile members could not have free table-fellowship with the Jewish members. The call to be peacemakers in the seventh beatitude applies to the Matthean community. It especially applies as a call - 1) to take initiative to make peace between them and their persecutors, both the Jews and the Gentiles, instead of retaliating against them; 2) to take initiative to make peace within their community whenever problems arise, especially because of the unequal partnership between the Jewish and Gentile members. The situations in India would not be exactly the same. However, there are various situations in which the call to be meek and to be peacemaker in the third and seventh beatitudes respectively are quite obvious.

First of all, the call to be meek in the third beatitude implies to the Christians in India a call to exhibit humility or meekness in the context of various persecutions they suffer such as in the hands of Hindu fundamentalists (as mentioned above). This does not mean that they should not raise their voice against the unjust treatments they received or claim their rights. It would primarily mean that they should not retaliate with violence. They should rather try to solve the problem with an attitude of humility. This is also important in their continuing responsibility and endeavour to preach the good news about Jesus Christ to the millions in India who have not yet heard about or believe in him.

Second, it is also very important for promoting a good relationship between the Dalit Christians and non-Dalit Christians who look down upon the Dalit Christians and discriminate against them. Especially, for those Christians who discriminate against the Dalit Christians, the third beatitude is a reminder that they are not living a humble life taught by Jesus, and they are rather living its opposite. With such discriminations, there cannot be proper unity and good relationships within the Christian community. Therefore, for the promotion of unity and Christian brotherhood/sisterhood among all the sections of Christians in India, it is important to follow Jesus' teaching on humility as found in the third beatitude.

Third, even for the good relationship among different church denominations in India, the third beatitude has important implication. There are various church traditions and many denominations in India.[45] Sometimes the relationship between them is not so good. Denomination rivalry often happens in different places, and the so-called 'sheep stealing' often happens especially in places where

45 For example, the Roman Catholics, the Syrian Orthodox church, the Mar Thoma church, the Protestant, the Baptist, the Presbyterian, the Pentecostals, the Salvation Army, etc. to name only a few.

Christian mission takes place. When Christians of different denominations fight each other the image of our Lord Jesus Christ is tarnished, and it always have negative effects in Christian mission. Therefore, it is very important for all the different Christian denominations to try to promote unity and good relationship with other denominations. For this purpose, humility is very important, and it cannot happen without humility. If anyone (church) takes initiative and concrete step with humble mind, it will usually yield good result. This has a very important bearing, especially for the churches in Mizoram.

Mizoram is one of the states in North East India. The first Christian missionaries among the Mizos came in 1894.[46] Within 50 years from that time, almost all the Mizos became Christian. According to 1951 government census, 80.31 per cent of the total population of Mizoram was Christian.[47] It would be safe to assume that the percentage of Christians among the Mizos has not decreased since that time on.[48]

46 The first missionaries were J. H. Lorrain and F. W. Savidge, sent by Arthington Aborigines Mission. They entered Mizoram, the then known as Lushai Hills District, on 11th, January, 1894, and started mission work among the Mizos. See Chhangte Lal Hminga, *The Life and Witness of the Churches in Mizoram* (Serkawn: Baptist Church of Mizoram, 1987), 48. See also J. Meirion Lloyd, *History of the Church in Mizoram (Harvest in the Hills)*, Gospel Centenary Series, No. I (Aizawl: Synod Publication Board, 1991), 32. Of course, William Williams, one of the missionaries of the Welsh Calvinistic Methodist Foreign Mission, working in the Khasi hills, came to Mizoram before Lorrain and Savidge. He visited Aizawl in March 20, 1891. He stayed for 27 days and went back on 17th April, 1891. He was, in fact, the first Christian missionary to set foot in the soil of Mizoram, the then known as Lushai Hills District. He remained in Aizawl for 29 days, till 27th April. He distributed Bible pictures to the Mizos, and he seems to be the first to make an attempt to communicate about Christian God to the Mizos. However, the purpose of his visit was mainly to explore the prospect of mission work among the Mizos. He persuaded the Welsh Calvinistic Methodist's General Assembly of 1892 to adopt the Lushai Hills District as its mission field. However, William died in April, 1892, and because of this, together with the difficulty to find another suitable missionary, the Welsh Mission delayed the commencement of the project. In the meantime two missionaries from the Arthington Aborigines Mission, namely James Herbert Lorrain and F. W. Savidge entered into the Lushai Hills District on 11th, January, 1894, and started missionary work among the Mizos. Therefore, they were the first two missionaries who did actual mission work among the Mizos. See Lalsangkima Pachuau, *Ethnic Identity and Christianity: A Socio-Historical and Misiological Study of Christianity in Northeast India with Special Reference to Mizoram* (Frankfurt: Peter Lang, 2002), 71-73. See also Lloyd, *History of the Church in Mizoram*, 32; and Hminga, *The Life and Witness of the Churches in Mizoram*, 48.

47 The rest 19.69 per cent non-Christian population must have been composed mainly of non-Mizos, such as Chakmas, Reangs, businessmen and government officials from outside, as well as some Mizo sub-tribes in the border areas. See Hminga, *The Life and Witness of the Churches in Mizoram*, 205-206.

48 In fact, the percentages of Christians were 86.64 in 1961 census, 86.09 in 1971 census, 83.81 in 1981 census, 83.81 in 1991 census, and 86.97 in 2001. This increase in the Christian percentage might indicate that all the Mizos became Christians and also some non-Mizos became Christians through the work of mission and evangelism among them by Mizo

In the course of time from its inception, various denominations and sectarian groups came up among the Mizo Christians. The bigger groups are the Presbyterian Church of Mizoram (PCM), Baptist church of Mizoram (BCM), United Pentecostal Church (UPC [North East India]), Salvation Army, United Pentecostal Church (UPC [Mizoram]), Evangelical Church of Maraland (ECM), Lairam Isua Krista Baptist Kohhran (LIKBK [Jesus Christ Baptist Church Lairam]), Seventh Day Adventist (SDA), and Roman Catholic Church. Besides these churches, there are many smaller groups which have less than 10000 (ten thousand) members respectively.[49] It is very important to have humility in order to have cordial relationship among these Christian groups. This is true especially for the Presbyterian and the Baptist churches, the two biggest denominational groups among the Mizo Christians. These two churches had been having a very cordial relationship from the time of their founding missionaries. They maintained a proper boundary. The Presbyterians were in the North while the Baptists were in the South. They also maintained mutual acceptance. Whenever a person from one side had to live to the other side temporarily, he/she was automatically accepted as a regular member of the church where he/she went. When a church elder migrated from one side to the other side he was usually accepted to continue as a church elder in the new place. Moreover, there was an agreement that pastors of each side would administer church rituals for those who came from the other side when the need arose. For example, if a Baptist member who lived in the North wanted his child to be baptised, the Presbyterian pastor where he lived would administer baptism according to the Baptist's norm, by dipping into the water. In the same way, if a Presbyterian member who lived in the South wanted his child to take baptism, the Baptist pastor where he lived would give baptism according to the norm of the Presbyterian Church that is by dropping water upon the child.[50] However, such

---

Christians. These statistics are taken from Hminga, *The Life and Witness of the Churches in Mizoram*, 9; and Lalhmachhuana Zofa, comp., *Mizoram General Knowledge*, 3rd Edition (Aizawl: J. L.Publication, 2007), 9. The decrease in the Christian percentage in 1981 and 1991 could be contributed by the influx of Chakma migrants from Bangladesh in these two periods respectively.

49 *Baptist Church of Mizoram. Statistical Handbook 2008*, compiled and published by Pastoral Ministry Department, BCM Hqrs, Lunglei, 6. Here, 18 churches are mentioned, among whom eight churches have less than 10000 members in 2005-2006 such as Congregational church of India Maraland (3500), Evangelical Free Church of India (8733), Fundamental Baptist Church of Mizoram (3172), Isua Krista Kohhran (Bualpui Ng – 3500), Isua Krista Kohhran (Hqrs. Venghlui Aizawl, 9800), Lalchhungkua Unity (3352), Mizo Kohhran (4022), Rinna Kohhran (1450).

50 This matter had been told to this researcher verbally when he newly joined pastoral ministry under the Baptist church of Mizoram as a probationary pastor in 1997 by Rev. K. T. Chungnunga, one of the senior pastors of the Baptist church of Mizoram then. See also the following for information on the relation between the Baptist church of Mizoram and the Presbyterian church of Mizoram: Hminga, *The Life and Witness of the Churches in Mizoram*; Lloyd, *History of the Church in Mizoram.*

mutual relationship has been broken since 1984. The physical boundary was also crossed from each side. Each side accused the other side as responsible for breaking the relationship. The Presbyterian church of Mizoram accused the Baptist church of Mizoram as breaking the boundary, which resulted in the breaking of their relationship. The Baptist accused the Presbyterians as creating a situation, which forced the Baptist church to break the boundary.[51] Since, then mutual crossing of the boundary took place and many Baptist churches have come up in North Mizoram, while many Presbyterian churches have come up in South Mizoram. Efforts have been made to restore good relationship between the two churches. There are, of course, some positive developments. However, it seems that there is still a long way to go to restore or to re-establish normal relationship between the two churches. For this purpose, humility/meekness, as taught by Jesus in the third Matthean beatitude, would be one of the most important things from both sides. In the same way, it is very important for various denominations in different parts of India to adopt humility for a good relationship with other denominations, and also to solve whatever problem they have.

The implication of the call to be peacemakers in the seventh beatitude for the Christians in India could be seen in various situations. First of all, it would imply that Christians in India should take initiative to make peace between them and their persecutors by peaceful means. We have seen above the severe persecutions suffered by Christians in India. In this context it is not enough to be silent sufferers. But, it is important to take active steps to make peace with the persecutors by peaceful means, with an attitude of humility. Second, it is a call to the Indian Christians to take initiative for the cordial co-existence of different Christian communities. The call is especially important for those places where there are problems between Dalits and non-Dalit Christians. We see that the complaints are usually from the Dalit Christians, and therefore the non-Dalit Christians are more responsible to take initiative to make peace between them and the Dalits. Even in the context where there are problems between Christians of different denominational backgrounds, which is especially experienced by the Christians in Mizoram, it is a call to each denomination to be an initiator of the peace process. Third, the seventh beatitude is also a call to the churches or Christians in India to take initiative to make peace between opposing or rival groups in their context where they themselves are not necessarily involved in the rivalry. Many of us may remember the ethnic conflict in Manipur state in the 1990s, especially between the Kukis and Nagas. Hundreds of people died in that conflict and several houses and villages were burnt. A very sad thing is that the communities involved in this conflict were Christians. It seems that the conflict was a result of a long time

51 See for example, Synod Executive Committee, *Mizoram Presbyterian Kohhran leh Mizoram Baptist Kohhran Inkar Thu* (Aizawl: Mizoram Presbyterian Church Synod, 1994); and *Mizoram Baptist Kohhran leh Mizoram Presbyterian Kohhran Inkar Thu* (Serkawn: Communication Department, Baptist Chruch of Mizroam, 1997).

rivalry, and it may take a long time to get completely healed.[52] In this context the call to be peacemaker in the fifth beatitude is very important for both sides. Another important example is the situation in Nagaland, where two underground groups, most probably belonging to Christian community, often fight each other and kill each other. Nagaland is one of the states in the North Eastern region of India. According to the 1991 census 85% of the total population (12.16 lakhs) of Nagaland are Nagas who belong to seventeen tribes, out of which 95 of them are Christians. There was an insurgency among some of the Nagas called Naga National Council (NNC) fighting for independence from India since 1947, the year of India's independence. This led to an undeclared war between the rebels and the Indian Army. In the course of this insurgency several Naga leaders who advocated the path of peace were also killed by the insurgents. Although, peace accord was signed between the Indian government and the Naga Underground in 1975, some of the groups in the underground movement, called National Socialist Council of Nagaland (NSCN) did not accept the accord and continued the armed rebellion. Later NSCN was divided into two groups – one led by Isaac and Muva/ Muivah, and the other led by Khaplang. These two movements are still going on till today.[53] In the rival fighting between these two groups many people had died. Just for example, only during 2008 to March 2009, more than 40 people had been killed.[54] In this context it is very important for the Nagaland churches to take initiative to make peace between these two rival insurgent groups, which has a high implication for the peace of all the people in Nagaland. The seventh beatitude is a reminder to them that they should continue to make efforts to make peace between these two rival groups as well as between the rebels and the

52 Lee and Deepa Khosla, *Nagas in India*, 1-19 of 19.

53 For this brief general information about the Nagas, see M. M. Thomas, *The Nagas Towards A.D. 2000* (Madras: Centre for Research on New International Economic Order, 1992), v-vii.

54 See the following for example, Vibou Ganguly, "Three killed in Naga factional violence," (April 18th, 2008 April 18th, 2008 - 6:18 pm ICT by admin -), 1 of 1, http://www.thaindian.com/news-portal/health/three-killed-in-naga-factional-violence_10039441.html, (accessed 09.04.09); Vibou Ganguly, "Factional killings continue unabated in Nagaland," (May 6th, 2008 - 6:14 pm ICT by admin -), 1 of 1, http://www.thaindian.com/newsportal/india-news/factional-killings-continue-unabated-in-nagaland_10045699.html (accessed 09.04.09); "12 underground cadres killed in a factional clash in Nagaland," (May 16th, 2008 - 7:13 pm ICT by admin), 1 of 1, http://www.thaindian.com/newsportal/lifestyle/12-underground-cadres-killed-in-a-factional-clash-in-nagaland_10049476.html, (accessed 09. 04.09); "12 killed as separatist gangs fight in Nagaland," (June 4th, 2008- 2:07 pm ICT by IANS), 1-2 of 2, http://www.thaindian.com/newsportal/world-news/12-killed-as-separatist-gangs-fight-in-nagaland_10056362.html (accessed 09.04.09); "Seven Naga rebels killed in fresh factional fight," (June 27th, 2008 - 5:54 pm ICT by IANS), 1-2 of 2, http://www.thaindian.com/newsportal/world-news/ seven-naga-rebels-killed-in-fresh-factional-fight_10065192.html (accessed 09.04.2009); "NSCN (IM) admit role in killing of sub-divisional officer," (March 4th, 2009 - 10:17 pm ICT by ANI), 1-2 of 2, http://www.thaindian.com/newsportal/india-news/nscn-im-admit-role-in-killing-of-sub-divisional-officer-2_100162718. html (accessed 09.04.09).

Indian government.[55] And, even for the two rebel groups, who obviously belong to a Christian community, the seventh beatitude is a call to them to examine their discipleship to Jesus, and take steps to be peace-makers.

We have thus far highlighted the implication of the third and the seventh beatitude mainly for the Christians in India as a group or as churches. This does not mean that the implication of the two beatitudes for individual Christians is neglected or abandoned. Indeed, the call to be meek and to be peacemakers also applies to individual believers in Christ, in their respective contexts in as much as it applies to the Christians as a group or as a church.

3.3.2. The Implication of the Fifth Beatitude

We have concluded in the exegesis that the fifth beatitude calls the followers of Jesus Christ to show mercy to everyone who needs it including the sinners, the poor, and the sick, the prisoners, and even the enemies. To the Matthean community the fifth beatitude especially implies - 1) a call to show mercy as a sign of their faithfulness to God, unlike the scribes and the Pharisees who failed to show mercy and thus were not faithful to God. 2) a call to the rich members of the community to show mercy to the poor members, 3) a call to the members of the community to show mercy to everyone in need, including the poor and the sinners among their Jewish and Gentile neighbours, as well as among their persecutors. 4) It is also a reminder to them that showing mercy is very important for the success of their mission among the Jews and the Gentiles.

This beatitude has a very important implication for the Christians in India, especially because of the various challenging situations in India which call them to show mercy befitting to be the followers of Jesus Christ. First of all, it is generally understood by those who travel on trains and visit the cities, that the Indian cities are infested with poor people living on the streets, beggars on the roads of the cities and in the trains, innumerable slum dwellers, people who survive on rag-picking, etc. Although the Indian economy is growing at a fast pace in recent years, basically because of technological development and economic globalization, the beneficiaries are mainly the rich who become richer, while the suffering of the poor is unabated. One of the very clear examples, besides the situations indicated above, is the plight of the farmers, many of whom have

55 This does not mean that the church had never taken any step in this regard. In fact, the Nagaland Baptist Church Council (NBCC) appointed a peace mission in 1964 to bring together the Naga rebels and the Indian government to come together to a conference table for negotiating a peaceful resolution to the Naga political problem. The council took another initiative to form Nagaland Peace Council to continue peace talks between the rebels and the Indian government which consequently resulted in the signing of the historic "Shillong Accord" in 1975. See Thomas, *The Nagas towards A.D.2000*, vi. However, as the rivalry between the two rebel groups continues, and the political problem of Nagaland remains, the seventh beatitude is an exhortation to the Nagaland churches to continue their effort to make peace between the two rebel groups, and also between the rebels and the Indian government.

committed suicide because of debt burdens. It is claimed that during 1997 to July 2005 more than 25000 (twenty five thousand) farmers committed suicide, and in 2006 alone more than 1000 (thousand) farmers have committed suicide in Maharastra state alone.[56] In such a situation, the Christians in India are called to show mercy whenever there is an opportunity to do so and in whatever way possible. It should be remembered that giving small amounts to the beggar is also an important way of showing mercy in Jesus' name. Giving financial/material aid, however small amount it may be, to the people who are hungry without having money to buy food, who are sick without any means to get medical treatment, etc., are important ways of showing mercy. People from all walks of life, from all religions, including persecutors must be included in the purview of such mercy. Second, at the same time, there are many Christians too among those poor people who are in need of help. This is very clear at least from the situation of the Dalit Christians highlighted above. Therefore, the fifth beatitude is a call to the well-to-do among the Christians to show mercy to the poor members in whatever way they need help and in whichever way the better-off members can help them. It may be by giving a loan when they are badly in need, forgiving them when they cannot repay the loan due to unforeseen problems, helping them by giving money for medical treatment, giving financial/material help when they could not afford to buy food or necessary clothing, etc. Third, it is also very important for the Indian Christians to remember that showing mercy is a very important strategy for the success of their mission. Christians in India comprise only about 2.5% of the total Indian population. Therefore, there are lots of tasks to do to communicate the good news of Jesus Christ. Indeed, many churches and para-church organizations are engaged in mission. For example, the Baptist church of Mizoram is supporting about 714 missionaries in various states working among various people groups.[57] For the missionary sending bodies, and especially for the missionaries themselves who are working in the mission fields, it is very important to remember that showing mercy is a very important strategy for the success of their mission whatever may be their experience from the people. Christians have to show mercy in whatever way possible because they receive mercy from God even now and they will receive it in full at the end of the age.

3.3.3. The Implication of the Sixth Beatitude

In the conclusion of the exegesis in the previous chapter it has been maintained that the sixth beatitude implies a call to the believers in Jesus Christ to have a

---

56 See Heeter, *Rough Cut. Seeds of Suicide. India's desparate farmers*, 1-2 of 6. See also Gadkari, *Over 1000 farmers committed suicide in 2006* (Maharastra News, 29. 11. 2006), 1 of 1, available from www.newsKerala. com, accessed 11.12.2006.

57 "BCM Mission Workers (as on March 2015)" *Missionary Tlangau* (May 2015), 33. I omit here - recognized (17), school support (209), and missionary nupui/pasal (158), which appear in the report.

pure heart before God, which is free from corrupt desire, from sin and guilt, both in thought and outward action. We may say it briefly as purity inside/of heart corresponded with outward action. In the context of the Matthean community, while it is an encouragement to pursue a purity of heart corresponded with outward action, it also implies a call to shun the way of the scribes and the Pharisees, who practiced outward ceremonial purity but were impure inside. It is also a warning that those who have an impure heart like the Pharisees will not enter the kingdom of God/heaven (23:13), they also will not enter the kingdom of God/heaven (Matt 5:20).

The call to be pure in heart in the sixth beatitude has an important implication for the Christians in India. A very clear example can be taken from the Mizo Christians in Mizoram, one of the states of India in the North East. To put it in a more direct way, the sixth beatitude is a call to the Mizo Christians to have a pure heart, and it is also a warning to them that if they fail to have a pure heart they may not enter the kingdom of heaven.

As it has been highlighted above, most of or all the Mizos in Mizoram are Christian. However, many of the Mizo Christians live a life that clearly indicates that there is no purity in their hearts. Among them are secret prostitutes and their customers,[58] drug abusers and drug peddlers,[59] illegal producers of and

58 For example, *Zozam*, a weekly magazine, reported in June 2006, and April 2007, that there were many illegal/unauthorized prostitutes in Aizawl, the capital city of Mizoram state, at that time. Most of them were of the age group 20-30, followed by of the age group 10-20, and there were a few from the age group 30-40. These prostitutes were categorized into four groups, such as (1) Supper Class – those who have other occupations, and were engaged in the business secretly; (2) First Class – Those who do not have any other occupation, and were engaged in the business secretly, and maintaining high standard of living. These two classes mainly take Rs. 1000-2000 per session or per night. (3) Second Class – those who charge basically between Rs 300-500, and also indulge in intoxicants like alcoholic drinks and drugs. (4) Third class – those who indulge in all types of intoxicants. *Zozam* reported in April 2007, that many married men used to have sex with such secret prostitutes without any preventive measure and it resulted in the spreading of HIV/AIDS. See "Sex leh Aizawl Khawpui [Sex and the Aizawl City]," *Zozam* (May 30-5 June, 2006), 9; and "Sex avangin HIV/AIDS a Hluar [Sex Spreads HIV/AIDS]," *Zozam* (April 18-24, 2007), 11.

59 Drug abuse has been known among the Mizos since 1984, and from that time on till September 2004, 982 Mizo youths died because of drug abuse. At the same time, it is alleged that the Mizoram government neglects the Act concerning prohibition of drugs. See "Thalaite Suattu Ruihhlo Khapna Dan Ngaihthah [An Act for Prohibition of Drugs that Massacre Young People is Neglected]," *Zozam* (September 14-20, 2004), 5. Probably out of dissatisfaction with the actions taken by the government, the Young Mizo Association (YMA), in its 59th Annual General Conference held on 20-21, Oct., 2004, declared the year 2005, "the Year of Fighting Against Drugs." See, *Zozam* (September 14-20, 2004), 5. This has been continued in the following three years, till 2008. The main intention of the organization was to control the supply of drugs as far as possible. Especially in Aizawl, a special cell called Supply Reduction Service (SRS) was formed to carry out the task. There were occasional reports that these groups acted extreme on some occasions, and some drug peddlers were tortured and some died in their hands. See for example, "SRS an che rapthlak [SRS acted dreadfully]," *Zozam* (June 7-13,

dealers in local alcoholic drinks,[60] and of course the drunkards, etc. Such people obviously have self-awareness that their heart is not pure. Though they claim to be Christians, such people hardly participate in church activities. However, a more serious problem among the Mizo Christians is that even among church-goers and active participants in church activities and even among church elders and deacons, there are many who indulge in financial corruption. It seems that in the opinion of the general public in Mizoram most of the government officers and legislators, many of whom are active participants in church activities, including church elders and deacons, are suspected to be involved in financial corruption. Even revelations of such corruption and reports of alleged corruptions do not shock the people of Mizoram any more for they have taken it for granted.[61] It

2005), 7; "YMA Duty An Hrang Lua Em Ni? [Are YMA on Duty Too Violent?]," *Zozam* (May 3-9, 2005), 7. However, as a result of the service of these people, the number of drug related death has been greatly reduced, comparing to the previous years. It has been reported that while 137 people died because of drug abuse in 2003, and 143 died in 2004, only 42 persons died in 2005, 22 persons in 2006, 29 persons in 2007, and 6 persons in 2008 (till September). Unquestionably this is the result of the efforts of the YMA. See, "Mizoramah Drugs Vanga Thi Tlem Tial Tial [Drug-Related Death Decreases in Mizoram]," *Christian Outlook* (October, 2008), 2.

60 Just for example, in March, 2005, more than 300 such factories have been destroyed and more than 1800 litres of local alcoholic beverage made from those factories have been seized by the volunteers of YMA. See "Operation Totê in Rangvamual a Nuai [Operation Storm Shocked Rangvamual]," *Zozam* (March 29-4 April, 2005), 5. Destruction of such factories by the YMA and the Mizoram Excise department took place at regular intervals. Such raid is done because *Mizoram Liquour Total Prohibition Act* was passed in 1995 by the Mizoram state government and it has been in operation since February, 1997, albeit it's being viewed as quite unsuccessful as expected. See "Zu Zuar, Zu Sa leh in te chunga Synod Thuchhuak Rum [Tough Resolution of the Synod Concerning Liqour Sellers, Liqour Makers, and Liqour Drinkers]," *Christian Outlook* (October, 2008), 4-6.

61 See for example, Bureau Report in News Link on 22, August, 2008 says that "in what could be a shocking revelation in other places other than Mizoram but not in Mizoram," it has been revealed by one vernacular magazine on 22, August, 2006 that 15 out of 38 members of Mizoram state legislators availed Leave Traveling Concession, amounting to lakhs of rupees per person without going on actual travels. The report further says that "the magazine only highlighted these 15 legislators coming from all parties because they were the ones who could be proved that they were in Mizoram while the claim in their TA bills said they were traveling." See Bureau Report, "Legislators Fake TA Bills Revealed," 1 of 1. In May, 2008, the names of 19 MLA, who were involved in the scam, with the amount they took, were mentioned in *Zoram Today* weekly. See "MLA Dawt Bill Tunge La? [Who Availed the MLA Fake Bills?]," *Zoram Today* (26-31, 2008), 19-22. It has been alleged that government officers other than MLAs are also involved in such scam. Rochama once mentioned that, a government officer who is also a church elder said to him that even all the government officers, including many church elders among them, are drawing advance bill for traveling concession, but either without really going for the trip or spending only a portion of the bill for traveling. See Rochama, "Zin Loh Hlawh (Bonus for not Traveling)," 1. It is also alleged that the Tuirial Hydel Project came to a stand still without completion because of so much amount of compensation claimed by the relatives of some of the ministers, who, though living in distant places from the project, owned lands

may be under the influence, either directly or indirectly, of rampant financial corruptions in the government offices that many other Mizo Christians also get involved in financial corruption.[62] The sixth beatitude is a warning bell to such corrupt Mizo Christians. Their practice of corruption clearly indicates that their heart is not pure before God. Like the Scribes and the Pharisees, many of them look pure outside, actively participating in church activities, taking up even leadership posts, and contributing a good amount in the church account. Therefore, it seems that the lot of the scribes and the Pharisees is going to be their lot unless they clean up the impurity in their hearts.

In the same way, we could assume that there are many Christians in India who indulge in financial corruption. The fact that the practice of financial corruption is a common phenomenon everywhere in India, suggests this situation.[63] This

---

in the area lately for the purpose of compensation. See for example, "CM-in House-ah Dawt a Sawi Em Ni? [Did the CM Tell a Lie in the Session]," *Zozam* (April 2-8, 2008), 18-21. More recently it has been revealed in Vanglaini Daily News paper that a sum of Rs. 10 crore, which the government of Mizoram entrusted to Mizoram Health Care Society, was deposited in the Bajaj Allianz Insurance Company by the name of 17 persons, out of which 11 of them are the relatives of a minister in the previous ministry, and the rest are officials. See "Mirethei damlo enkawlna tur sum Bajaj Allianz-ah dah [Money meant for taking care of the sick among the poor people is deposited in Bajaj Allianz]," *Vanglaini* (2009.04.08[09?]), available from http://vanglaini.org/index.php? module =Pagesetter&func= viewpub &tid=3&pid=3123 (accessed 10.04.2009).

62 A very clear indication is the financial scam that shock Mizos in 2008. A fake banking system, popularly known as "Chiahpuam" was run by some people. The name indicates that something is dipped into the water and its volume is greatly increased. Taking this notion as a metaphor, this fake banking system was given the name. In this system a very high rate of interest was promised, like 20% per month. Under the bankers there were agents and collectors. Initial depositors were given the high interest. Agents were paid high benefits. More and more people were attracted and many people invested whatever they have. But, it has been found that the money deposited later was given to the earlier depositors, and many people are at the brink of losing their deposits. This problem is severely affecting the Mizo society, especially those who deposit their money. Since many people deposited all that they have it is not yet known how severe the effect is going to be. At the time, of writing this (24.11.2008) it is reported that the amount which the depositors cannot draw is more than 2500 million Rupees, and more than twenty people have been arrested so far. More than 2000 FIR have been submitted to the Police. This matter has been written so-much in the print media. Just for example, see the following, "Pawisa Tihpun Hluaina Hi? [The Bank that Gives Unusually High Interest]," *Zoram Today* (27 Oct.-1 Nov., 2008), 22; "Chiahpuamin Zoram Chiah Hneh [Chiahpuam, a Burning Issue in Mizoram]," *Zoram Today* (10-15, November, 2008), 16; "CS leh Press Mite'n Chiahpuam Sawiho [CS and Media Discussed about Chiahpuam]," *Vangalini*, 17.11.08, 1. See also "Sum Tang Zawng Zawng Rs. Nuai 20000 Chuang Niin Chhut [Unreturned Money Estimated to be More Than Rs 2000 Million]," (06. 11. 2008), 1 of 1, available from http://www. khampat.com (accessed 07. 11. 2008).

63 Rev. P. R. Hmuaka once told this researcher in March 2009, that a Catholic Father once asked him about the problem among the Mizo Christians. In his reply Hmuaka mentioned that financial corruption is one of the main problems among the Mizo Christians. Then, the Catholic father said that such thing happens everywhere in India. This conversation is one of

does not mean that every Christian in India indulges in this practice. Rather, it means that among the Christians everywhere in India there is a good portion or a good number who indulge in this practice. The sixth beatitude is a call to all such Christians to give up their corrupt practice. On top of that, even church offices are not free from financial and power corruption. Some of the leaders manipulate church money, and misuse their power for favouritism in appointments for jobs, for training, and for promotion inside the church.[64] The sixth beatitude is a warning bell even to such people. Unless they give up such impure practice, they will be surprised at the eschaton and they may be surprised even during their lifetime.

Finally, the Matthean beatitudes are an eschatological call to the Christians today, to remain faithful for Jesus Christ in the midst of all their sufferings because the blessings of the kingdom of heaven are waiting for them. They can already experience that blessing even now although partially, and they will experience it in full at the end of the age. They are also an eschatological call to live an ethical life as demanded by their situations, befitting the follower of Jesus Christ, and eschatological blessings are waiting for them for whatever they do in the name of Jesus Christ.

---

the clear indicators that financial corruption is there among the Christians almost everywhere in India.

64 This writer feels that he has a firsthand knowledge about this through his participation in some of the important church meetings and in the ministry of the church.

Conclusion

In conclusion, the major insights of the present research will be briefly recapitulated.

The basic assumption of this research is that the socio-historical experience of the Matthean community played an important role in affecting the writing and shaping the content of Matthew's gospel, including the Matthean Beatitudes. Accordingly, an investigation has been done on the socio-historical context of Matthew's gospel. Then insights gained from it have been employed for drawing conclusions from the exegetical study of the Matthean beatitudes. In the light of these exegetical insights, an attempt has been made to see the implication of the Matthean beatitudes for contemporary Christians in India in their discipleship to Jesus Christ. The main points of insights gained in the study can be briefly summarized as follows:

The gospel of Matthew was written around 75-93 C.E. by a Hellenistic Jewish author for a Christian community in Antioch of Syria, composed of Jewish Christians and Jewish-oriented Gentile Christians.

The most outstanding experience of the Matthean community was its antagonism towards formative Judaism, a movement for the renewal of Judaism shattered by the destruction of Jerusalem and the Temple in 70 C.E. in the course of the first Jewish war against Rome (66 C.E.-73 C.E.). In this conflict, formative Judaism got the upper hand and the Matthean community suffered various kinds of persecution at their hands. Apart from this major experience, the Matthean community had other significant experiences such as persecution from the Gentiles, unequal partnership between the Jewish members and the Gentiles members within the community, and difference in economic status among the members. In addition to these experiences, they also shared with other Jews the socio-political and economic hardships caused by the destruction of Jerusalem and the Temple. All those experiences of Matthew's community influenced Matthew in his selection, omission, redaction and composition of materials for his gospel. Therefore, even the Matthean Beatitudes (Matt 5:3-12), which is the selected passage for this research, can best be understood by viewing it from the perspective of those experiences undergone by the Matthean community.

When Matthew wrote the first gospel, he inherited eight beatitudes in the tradition available to him. Out of those eight beatitudes the first, the second, the fourth, and probably the last were spoken by Jesus, based on Isa 61, for consolation of the people of God who found themselves in a crisis. Therefore, they are apocalyptic in nature. The third, the fifth, the sixth and the seventh were composed by the Q community based on Jesus' teachings and were added to the dominical beatitudes. The protases of these four beatitudes carry ethical nuance. However, their apodoses indicate that they are also apocalyptic in nature. Then, the function of the eight beatitudes in the Q community was two fold: primarily it was a consolation to the followers of Jesus Christ caught in a difficult situation. At the same time, it was also an exhortation to pursue an ethical life in the midst of their sufferings that was obviously called for in their context. When Matthew took over these eight beatitudes, he redacted the first, the fourth, and the last ones on the basis of his community's experience, but without compromising their in-depth meaning. He took over the second, the third, the fifth, the sixth and the seventh beatitudes without alteration because they were suitable for addressing his community without modification. He composed one more (the eighth) apocalyptic beatitude, probably to fulfil a triadic formula (3+3+3) which is outstanding in his arrangement of the Sermon on the Mount. He, however, purposely selected its wordings carefully and deliberately placed it at the eighth position, both to emphasize the experience of his community. Thus, Matthew's redactions of the three beatitudes, his composition of additional beatitude, and his taking over of five beatitudes without modification, are done from the perspective of his community's experience. All the nine Matthean beatitudes are apocalyptic in nature. Matthew's redaction also punctuates this apocalyptic nature rather than ethicizing them. All the nine Matthean beatitudes have their bases in the Old Testament.

Matthew carefully arranged his gospel keeping his target audience in mind. He divided the whole gospel into five blocks of discourses preceded by narratives, with the infancy narratives as introduction and the passion narrative as conclusion. He deliberately placed the Sermon on the Mount, which contains most of Jesus' teachings on discipleship, at the first position, thus punctuating his emphasis on discipleship. The Matthean Beatitudes is a programmatic introduction to this Sermon, and it contains the essence of Christian discipleship in a nutshell. However, while the Sermon on the Mount is mainly occupied with imperatives, the Matthean Beatitudes function as grace before those imperatives. It is primarily a consolation and encouragement, before the hard imperatives that follow in the rest of the Sermon on the Mount.

Through historical and literary analysis, the following outstanding characteristics of the Matthean beatitudes can be identified: (1) three or four of the nine Matthean beatitudes were originally spoken by Jesus. (2) The Q community preserved these beatitudes and made use of them for addressing the need of their community. In addition, the Q community composed four other beatitudes, which carry ethical nuance and at the same time are apocalyptic in nature, most probably to address the need of the community in their specific context. These four beatitudes are firmly rooted in Jesus' authentic teachings found elsewhere in the gospel tradition. (3) Matthew inherited these eight beatitudes and adapted them to the ongoing needs of his community, but without compromising their authentic meaning in their original contexts. He also composed additional beatitude probably because of a concern for his literary style to make the number of the beatitudes to nine. However, he purposely selected its contents and deliberately placed it at the eighth position to reflect on the experience of his community. This additional beatitude is also firmly rooted in the teaching of Jesus found elsewhere in the gospel tradition. Moreover, all the beatitudes have their bases in the Old Testament.

All these features indicate that the Matthean beatitudes are still relevant for addressing the contemporary Christians who are faced with different situations in their discipleship to Jesus. With this conclusion, an attempt has been made to see the relevance of the Beatitudes for contemporary Christians in India. Different situations are highlighted as examples, such as the plight of the poor and downtrodden Dalit Christians, persecutions suffered by Christians in various parts of India, the relationship problem between different Christian denominations in India, the deadly ethnic conflict among Christians on ethnic grounds, the unending mutual killings among the Christian rebel groups in Nagaland, and the rampant corruption among the Mizo Christians in Mizoram.

Thus, an application of insights from socio-historical studies for understanding the meaning of the Matthean beatitudes and their implication for contemporary Christian discipleship has proven to be very fruitful in this study. And, we could assume with confidence that greater benefits may be gained by contemporary Christians if the same insights are applied for understanding the meaning of the Sermon on the Mount and its implication for contemporary Christian discipleship, because the Beatitudes functions basically as a programmatic introduction to this outstanding discourse of Matthew's gospel.

Bibliography

Entries from Encyclopaedias and Dictionaries

Baird, William. "New Testament Criticism." *ABD*. Vol. 1. New York: Doubleday, 1997 [1992], 730-736.

Balz, H. "πενθέω *pentheō*." *EDNT*. Vol. 3. Edited by Horst Balz and Gerhard Schneider. Grand Rapids, Michigan: William B. Eerdmans Publishing Company, 1993, 69.

Bammel. "The Poor in the Old Testament." *TDNT*. Vol. VI. Grand Rapids, Michigan: Wm. B. Eerdmans Publishing Company, 1968, 888-902.

Baumgaertel. "לֵב, לֵבָב in the OT." *TDNT*. Vol. III. Grand Rapids, Michigan: William B. Eerdmans Publishing Company, 1965, 606-607.

Behm. "καρδια." *TDNT*. Vol. III. Grand Rapids, Michigan: William B. Eerdmans Publishing Company, 1965, 608-613.

Bertram, " 'μακαριος' in the LXX and Judaism." *TDNT*. Vol. IV. Grand Rapids, Michigan: William B. Eerdmans Publishing Company, 1967, 364-366.

Braund, David C. "Agrippa (Person)." *ABD*. Vol. 1. New York: Doubleday, 1992, 98-100.

______________ . "Herod Antipas (Person)." *ABD*. Vol. 3. New York: Doubleday, 1992, 160.

Brown, Francis, S. R. Driver and Charles A. Briggs. *Hebrew and English Lexicon of the Old Testament*. Oxford: Clarendon Press, 1959 [1907].

Bultmann. "ἔλεος, ἐλεέω, ἐλεήμων, ἐλεημοσύνη, ἀνέλεος, ἀνελεήμων." *TDNT*. Vol. II. Grand Rapids, Michigan: William B. Eerdmans Publishing Company, 1964, 477-487.

______________ . "πένθος, πενθέω." *TDNT*. Vol. VI. Grand Rapids, Michigan: William B. Eerdmans Publishing Company, 1968, 40-43.

Cazelles. "אַשְׁרֵי *'ashrê*." *TDOT*. Vol. I. Grand Rapids, Michigan: William B. Eerdmans Publishing Company, 1974, 445-448.

Chambers 21st Century Dictionary.

Chilton, B. D. "Rabbis." *DNTB*. Edited by Craig A. Evans and Stanley E. Porter. Downers Grove, Illinois/Leicester, England: InterVarsity Press, 2000, 914-917.

Collins, Raymond F. "Beatitudes." *ABD*. Vol. 1. New York: Doubleday, 1997 [1992], 629-631.

Dockery, D. S. "Baptism." *DJG*. Edited by Joel B. Green, Scott McKnight and I. Howard Marshall. Downers Grove, Illinois/Leicester, England: InterVarsity Press, 1998 [1992], 55-58.

Evans, C. A. "Shammai, House of." *DNTB*. Edited by Craig. A. Evans and Stanley E. Porter. Downers Grove, Illinois/Leicester, England: InterVarsity Press, 2000, 1106-1107.

Foerster. "The Greek Usage of the Word Group κληρονόμος." *TDNT*. Vol. III. Grand Rapids, Michigan: William B. Eerdmans Publishing Company, 1965, 768-769.

Goppelt. "πεινάω (λιμός)." *TDNT*. Vol. VI. Grand Rapids, Michigan: William B. Eerdmans Publishing Company, 1968, 12-22.

Grintz, Yehoshua M. "The Significance of the [First] Temple." *Encyclopaedia Judaica*. Second Edition. Vol. 19. Detroit, et al.: Thomson Gale, 2007, 608.

Hartman, Lars. "Baptism." *ABD*. Vol. 1. New York: Doubleday, 1992, 583-594.

Hauck. "μακάριος, μακαρίζω, μακαρισμός: The Greek Usage and The Stylistic Form of the Beatitude." *TDNT*. Vol. IV. Grand Rapids, Michigan: William B. Eerdmans Publishing Company, 1967, 362-364.

_____. "[μακάριος] The Word Group in the New Testament," *TDNT*. Vol. IV. Grand Rapids, Michigan: William B. Eerdman's Publishing Company, 1967, 367-370.

Hauck. πτωχος in the Greek World." *TDNT*. Vol. VI. Grand Rapids, Michigan: Wm. B. Eerdmans Publishing Company, 1968, 886-887.

Hauck, F. / S. Schulz. "πραΰς, πραΰτης." *TDNT*. Vol. VI. Grand Rapids, Michigan: William B. Eerdmans Publishing Company, 1968, 645-651.

Holmes, M. W. "Ignatius of Antioch." *DLNTID*. Edited by Ralph P. Martin and Peter H. Davids. A Compendium of Contemporary Biblical Scholarship. Downers Grove, Illinois/Leicester, England: InterVarsity Press, 1997, 530-531.

Isaac, Benjamin and Aharon Oppenheimer. "Bar Kokhba Revolt." *ABD*. Vol. I. New York: Doubleday, 1992.

Johnson, T. S. "Roman Emperors." *DNTB*. Edited by Craig A. Evans and Stanley E. Porter. Downers Grove, Illinois / Leicester, England: InterVarsity Press, 2000, 968-974.

Jones, Brian W. "Domitian (Emperor)." *ABD*. Vol. 2. New York: Doubleday, 1992, 221-222.

______________. "Titus (Emperor)." *ABD*. Vol. 6. New York: Doubleday, 1992, 580-581.

Kertelge, "'δικαιοσύνη' *dikaiosynē* righteousness, justice." *EDNT.* Vol. 1. Edited by Horst Balz and Gerhard Schneider. Grand Rapids, Michigan: William B. Eerdmans Publishing Company, 1990 [1978-80], 325-334.

Lapin, Hayim. "Rabbi." *ABD*. Vol. 5. New York: Doubleday, 1992, 600-602.

Lewis, Jack. P. "Jamnia (Jabneh), Council of." *ABD*, Vol. 3. New York: Doubleday, 1992, 634-637.

Liddel, Henry George and Robert Scott, comps. *A Greek-English Lexicon*, Revised Edition. Oxford: Clarendon Press, 1996 [1883].

Mason, S. "Pharisees." *DNTB*. Edited by Craig A. Evans and Stanley E. Porter. Downers Grove, Illinois / Leicester, England: InterVarsity Press, 2000, 782-787.

McKnight, S. "Matthew, Gospel of." *DJG*. Edited by Joel B. Green, Scott McKnight and I. Howard Marshall. Downers Grove, Illinois: InterVarsity Press, 1992, 526-541.

Murphy-O'Connor, J. "Teacher of Righteousness." *ABD*. Vol. 6. New York: Doubleday, 1992, 340-341.

Neusner, Jacob and William Scott Green, eds. *Dictionary of Judaism in the Biblical Period, 450 B.C.E to 600 C.E.* Peabody, Massachusetts: Hendrickson Publishers, 1999.

Oepke. "διωκω." *TDNT.* Vol. II. Grand Rapids, Michigan: William B. Eerdmans Publishing Company, 1964, 229-230.

Oppenheimer. "Bar Kokhba Revolt." *ABD*. Vol. 1. New York: Doubleday, 1992, 597-601.

Rengstorf. "κλαίω, κλαυθμός." *TDNT*. Vol. III. Grand Rapids, Michigan: William B. Eerdmans Publishing Company, 1965, 722-726.

Safrai, Shmuel. "The Significance of the [Second] Temple for the People." *Encyclopaedia Judaica.* Second Edition. Vol. 19. Detroit, et al.: Thomson Gale, 2007, 624-625.

Sanders, James A. "Canon [Hebrew Bible]." *ABD*, Vol. 1. New York: Doubleday, 1992, 837-852.

Schmitz. "παρακαλεω, παρακαλησις, 'Gommon Greek Usage' and 'in Greek Judaism.'" *TDNT*. Vol. V. Grand Rapids, Michigan: William B. Eerdmans Publishing Company, 1967, 773-779.

______________. "παρακαλεω and παρακαλησις in the NT." *TDNT*. Vol. V. Grand Rapids, Michigan: William B. Eerdmans Publishing Company, 1967, 793-799.

Schoedel, William R. "Ignatius, Epistles of." *ABD*. Vol. 3. New York: Doubleday, 1992, 384-387.

Schweizer. "[πνεῦμα] in the New Testament." *TDNT*. Vol. VI. Grand Rapids, Michigan: William B. Eerdmans Publishing Company, 1968, 396-451.

Shrenk. "δικαιοσύνη." *TDNT.* Vol. II. Grand Rapids, Michigan: William B. Eerdmans Publishing Company, 1964, 192-210.

Stanton, G. N. "Q." *DJG*. Edited by Joel B. Green, Scott McKnight and I. Howard Marshall. Downers Grove, Illinois: InterVarsity Press, 1992.

Staudinger, F. "ἐλεέω *eleeō*." *EDNT*. Vol. 1. Edited by Horst Balz and Gerhard Schneider. Grand Rapids, Michigan: William B. Eerdmans Publishing Company, 1990 [1978-80], 429-431, 1992, 1090-1093.

Strange, James F. "Sepphoris." *ABD*. Vol. 5. New York: Doubleday, 1992, 1090-1093.

Sundberg, A. C. "Sadducees." *IDB*. Vol. IV. New York/Nashville: Abingdon Press, 1962, 160-163.

Tuckett, C. M. "Q (Gospel Source)." *ABD*. Vol. 5. New York: Doubleday, 1992, 567-572.

Twelftree, G. H. "Scribes." *DJG*. Edited by Joel B. Green, Scott McKnight, and I. Howard Marshall. Downers Grove, Illinois/Leicester, England: InterVarsity Press, 1998 [1992], 732-735.

Wilkins, M. J. "Discipleship." *DJG*. Edited by Joel B. Green, Scott McKnight and I. Howard Marshall. Downers Grove, Illinois: InterVarsity Press, 1992. 182-189.

Zuurmond, Rochus. "Ethiopic Versions." *ABD*. Vol. 6. New York: Doubleday, 1992, 808-810.

Books

Albright, W. F. and C. S. Mann. *Matthew.* The Anchor Bible. Vol. 26. New York: Doubleday, 1971.

Allison, Jr., Dale C. *Studies in Matthew: Interpretation Past and Present.* Grand Rapids, Michigan: Baker Academic, 2005.

______________ . *The New Moses, A Matthean Typology*. Minneapolis/Augsburg: Fortress, 1993.

Alon, Gedalyahu. *Jews, Judaism and the Classical World. Studies in Jewish History in the Times of the Second Temple and Talmud.* Translated from Hebrew by Israel Abrahams. Jerusalem: the Magnes Press, the Hebrew University, 1977.

Andrews, C. F. *The Sermon on the Mount.* London: George Allen & Unwin Ltd., 1949 [1942].

Applebaum, S. "The Economic Life in Palestine." In S. Safrai and M. Stern, eds. *The Jewish People in the First Century.* Vol. 2, 631-700. Philadelphia: Fortress Press, 1976.

Bacon, B. W. *Studies in Matthew*. New York: Henry Hold and Company, 1930.

Baptist Church of Mizoram: Statistical Handbook 2008. Compiled and Published by Pastoral Ministry Department, BCM Hqrs., Lunglei.

Barclay, William. *The Plain Man Looks at the Beatitudes.* London: Fontana Books, 1963.

Barret, C. K. *A Critical and Exegetical Commentary on the Acts of Apostles*. Vol. 1. ICC. Edinburgh: T&T Clark, 1994.

Bauer, David R. *The Structure of Matthew's Gospel: A Study in Literary Design.* Sheffield: Almond Press, 1988.

Bauer, David R. and Mark Allan Powell, eds. *Treasures New and Old: Recent Contributions to Matthean Studies.* SBL Symposium Series 1; Atlanta: Scholars, 1996.

Baumgarten, Albert I. *The Flourishing of Jewish Sects in the Maccabean Era: An Interpretation.* Leiden: E.J. Brill, 1997.

Becker, H. S. *Outsiders: Studies in the Sociology of Deviance.* New York: Free Press, 1963.

Ben-Yehuda, H. *Deviance and Moral Boundaries: Witchcraft, the Occult, Deviant Sciences and Scientists.* Chicago: University of Chicago Press, 1985.

Berger, Peter and Thomas Luckmann. *The Social Construction of Reality: A Treatise in the Sociology of Knowledge*. Garden City: Doubleday and Co., 1967.

Betz, Hans Dieter. *Essays on the Sermon on the Mount.* Philadelphia: Fortress, 1985.

________________ . *The Sermon on the Mount.* Minneapolis: Fortress Press, 1995.

Binder, D. D. *Into the Temple Courts: the Place of the Synagogue in the Second Temple Period.* Atlanta: Society of Biblical Literature, 1999.

Blomberg, Craig L. *Matthew.* The New American Commentary. Nashville: Broadman Press, 1992.

Boccaccini, Gabriele. *Middle Judaism: Jewish Thought, 300 B.C.E. to 200 B.C.E.* Minneapolis: Fortress, 1991.

Bonhoeffer, Dietrich. *The Cost of Discipleship*. Complete Edition. London: 1978 [1937, 1959].

Bornhäuser, Karl. *The Sermon on the Mount.* Translated by Rev. & Mrs. C. Sandegren. Madras: The Christian Literature Society for India, 1951 [1935].

Bornkamm, Günther. "The Risen Christ and the Earthly Jesus. Matt 28:16-20." In *The Future of Our Religious Past: Essays in Honor of Rudolf Bultmann.* Edited by J. M. Robinson. Translated by Charles E. Carlston and Robert P. Scharlemann, 203-229. New York: Harper & Row, 1971.

Brandon, S. G. F. *The Fall of Jerusalem and the Christian Church.* London: SPCK, 1981 [1951].

Broadus, John A. *Commentary on Matthew.* Grand Rapids, Michigan: Kregel Publications, 1990.

Broer, I. *Die Seligpreisungen der Bergpredigt.* BBB 61. Bonn: Peter Hanstein, 1986.

Brooks, Stephenson, H. *Matthew's Community: The Evidence of His Special Sayings Material.* Sheffield: Sheffield Academic, 1987.

Brown, Raymond E. *An Introduction to the New Testament.* Bangalore: Theological Publications in India, 2000 [1996].

______________. *The Birth of the Messiah: A Commentary on the Infancy Narratives in the Gospels of Matthew and Luke.* New York: Doubleday, 1999 [1977].

Brown, Raymond E. and John P. Meier. *Antioch and Rome. New Testament Cradles of Catholic Christianity.* New York/Ramsey: Paulist Press, 1983.

Brown, Robert W. *Dalits and the Church: An Initial Investigation into the Place of the Dalit Community within the Church of North India and the Church of South India*. New Delhi: Centre for Dalit/Subaltern Studies, 2006.

Bruner, F. D. *The Christ Book: A Historical Theological Commentary: Matthew 1-12*. Waco: Word Books, Publisher, 1987.

Budd, Philip J. *Numbers.* WBC. Vol. 5. Waco, Texas: Word Books Publishers, 1984.

Bultmann, Rudolf. *History of the Synoptic Tradition.* Peabody, Massachusetts: Hendrickson Publishers, 1963.

Burkett, Delbert. *An Introduction to the New Testament and the Origins of Christianity.* Cambridge: Cambridge University Press, 2002.

Carson, D. A., Douglas J. Moo and Leon Morris. *An Introduction to the New Testament.* Grand Rapids, Michigan: Zondervan, 1992.

______________. *The Sermon on the Mount: Evangelical Exposition of Matthew 5-7*. Grand Rapids, Michigan: Baker Book House, 1978.

Carter, Warren. *Matthew and the Margins: A Socio-political and Religious Reading.* Journal for the Study of the New Testament Supplement Series 204. Sheffield: Sheffield Academic Press Ltd., 2000.

______________. *Matthew and Empire: Initial Exploration.* Harrisburg: Trinity Press International, 2001.

______________. *What are They Saying about Matthew's Sermon on the Mount?* New York: Paulist Press, 1994.

Chalcraft David J. "The Development of Weber's Sociology of Sects: Encouraging a new Fascination." In *Sectarianism in Early Judaism. Sociological Advances.* Edited by David J. Chalcraft, 26-51. London, Oakville: Equinox, 2007.

Clarke, Sathianathan. *Dalits and Christianity: Subaltern Religion and Liberation Theology in India*. New Delhi: Oxford University Press, 1999 [1998].

Cox, G. E. P. *The Gospel according to Saint Matthew.* London: SCM Press Ltd, 1952.

Crosby, Michael H. *The Spirituality of the Beatitudes: Matthew's Challenge for First World Christians.* Maryknoll: Orbis, 1981.

Das, K. C. *Indian Dalits. Voices, Visions and Politics.* Delhi: Global Vision Publishing House, 2004.

Daube, David. "The Last Beatitude." In *New Testament Judaism. Collected Works of David Daube.* Vol. 2, 321-325. Edited by Calum Carmichael. Studies in Comparative Legal History. Berkeley: The Robbins Collection, 2000.

Davies, Philip R. "Sect Formation in Early Judaism." In *Sectarianism in Early Judaism. Sociological Advances.* Edited by David J. Chalcraft, 133-155. London, Oakville: Equinox, 2007.

Davies, W. D. *The Setting of the Sermon on the Mount.* Cambridge: Cambridge University, 1990 [1966].

Davies W. D. and Dale C. Allison, Jr. *A Critical and Exegetical Commentary on the Gospel According to St. Matthew.* 3 Volumes. ICC. Edinburgh: T&T Clark, 1988.

Delimat, Casimir A. *Ascent: Spiritual Progress according to the Beatitudes.* New York: St. Paul Publication, 1960.

DeSilva, David A. *An Introduction to the New Testament: Contexts, Methods and Ministry Formation.* Downers Grove, Illinois: InterVarsity Press / Leicester, England: Apollos, 2004.

Dibelius, Martin. *The Message of Jesus Christ.* Translated by Frederick C. Grant. New York: Charles Scribner's Sons, 1939.

Di Lella, Alexander A. "The Structure and Composition of the Matthean Beatitudes." In *To Touch the Text. Biblical and Related Studies in Honor of Joseph A. Fitzmyer, S.J.* Edited by Maurya P. Horgan and Paul J. Kobelski, 238-241. New York: Crossroads, 1989.

Dobschütz, Ernst von. "Matthew as Rabbi and Catechist." In *The Interpretation of Matthew.* Edited by Graham Stanton, 19-29. Philadelphia: Fortress Press; SPCK: London, 1983.

Dodd, C. H. "The Beatitudes: A form Critical Study." In *More New Testament Studies*, 1-10. Grand Rapids: Eerdmans, 1968.

Downey, G. *A History of Antioch in Syria from Seleucus to the Arab Conquest.* Princeton: Princeton University Press, 1961.

Dunn, James D. G. *Jews and Christians: The Parting of the Ways, A.D. 70-135.* Tübingen: J. C. B. Mohr (Paul Siebeck), 1992.

______________ . *Jesus, Paul and the Law. Studies in Mark and Galatians.* London: SPCK, 1990.

_______________ . *The Theology of Paul the Apostle.* Grand Rapids: William B. Eerdmans Publishing Company, 1998.

_______________ . *Unity and Diversity in the New Testament: An Inquiry into the Character of Earliest Christianity*. London: SCM Press, Ltd, 1977.

Dupont, J. *Les Béatitudes*. 3 Vols. Paris: J. Gabalda, 1958-73.

Eigo, F. A., ed. *New Perspective on the Beatitudes.* Villanova, Pennsylvania: The Villanova University Press, 1995.

Elliot, John H. *A Home for the Homeless: A Social-Scientific Criticism of I Peter, Its Situation and Strategy.* Minneapolis: Fortress, 1990.

Ellis, P. F. *Matthew: His Mind and His Message*. Collegeville: The Liturgical Press, 1974.

Erikson, K. T. *Wayward Puritans: A Study in the Sociology of Deviance.* New York: John Wiley and Sons, 1966.

Esler, P. F. The First Christians in Their Social Worlds. Social Scientific Approaches *to New Testament Interpretation.* London and New York: 1994.

Eusebius. *Ecclesiastical History to the Twentieth Year of the Reign of Constantine. Being the 324th of the Christian Era*. Translated by Cruse, C. F. 4th Revised ed. London: Samuel Bagster and Sons, 1847.

Ewherido, Anthony O. *Matthew's Gospel and Judaism in the Late First Century C.E.: The Evidence from Matthew's Chapter on Parables (Matthew 13:1-52.* New York, et al.: Peter Lang, 2006.

Farmer, William R. *The Synoptic Problem*. New York: Macmillan, 1976 [1964].

Farrer, Austin. *St. Matthew and St. Mark*. Westminster: Dacre, 1954.

Ferguson, Everett. *Backgrounds of Early Christianity.* 2nd Ed. Grand Rapids, Michigan: Wm. B. Eerdmans Publishing Company, 1993 [1987].

Filson, F. V. *The Gospel according to Saint Matthew.* BNTC. London: A & C Black, 1977.

Fitch, William. *The Beatitudes of Jesus.* Bombay: Gospel Literature Service, 1961.

Foster, Paul. *Community, Law and Mission in Matthew's Gospel.* Tübingen: Mohr Siebeck, 2004.

Fox, Emmet. *The Sermon on the Mount: A General Introduction to Scientific Christianity in the Form of a Spiritual Key to Matthew V, VI and VII.* New York: Grosset & Dunlap, 1938 [1934].

France, R. T. *Matthew: Evangelist and Teacher*. Grand Rapids: Zondervan, 1989.

Frend, W. H. C. *The Rise of Christianity*. London: Darton, Longman and Todd, 1984.

Fuglseth, Kåre Sigvald. *Johannine Sectarianism in Perspective: A Sociological, Historical, and Comparative Analysis of Temple and Social Relationships in the Gospel of John, Philo and Qumran.* Supplements to Novum Testamentum. Leiden. Boston: Brill, 2005.

Gager, J. G. *Kingdom and Community: The Social World of Early Christianity.* Eaglewood Cliffs, N.J.: Prentice Hall, 1975.

Gale, Aaron M. *Redefining Ancient Borders: The Jewish Scribal Framework of Matthew's Gospel.* New York/London: T&T Clark, 2005.

Galilea, Segundo. *The Beatitudes: To Evangelize as Jesus Did.* Maryknoll: Orbis, 1984.

Giner, Salvador. *Sociology.* London: Martin Robertson, 1972.

Gnanavaram, M. *Treasure in Heaven and Treasure in Earth: Attitude towards Poverty and Wealth in the New Testament Communities and in the Early Church.* Delhi: ISPCK, 2012 [2008].

Goode, Erich and Nachman Ben-Yehuda. *Moral Panics: The Social Construction of Deviance.* Oxford UK & Cambridge USA: Blackwell, 1994.

Goodman, Martin. *The Ruling Class of Judea: The Origins of the Jewish Revolt against Rome, A.D. 66-70.* Cambridge: Cambridge University Press, 1987.

Gore, Charles. *The Sermon on the Mount: A Practical Exposition.* London: Hasell, Watson & Viney, Ltd., 1947 [1896].

Goulder, Michael. *Midrash and Lection in Matthew.* London: SPCK, 1974.

Grabbe, Lester L. "When is a Sect a Sect – or not? Groups and Movements in the Second Temple Period." In *Sectarianism in Early Judaism: Sociological Advances.* Edited by David J. Chalcraft, 114-132. London, Oakville: Equinox, 2007.

Graetz, Heinrich. *History of the Jews.* Vol. II. Philadelphia: The Jewish Publication Society of America, 1893.

Graham, Billy. *The Secret of Happiness.* Garden City, New York: Doubleday & Company, Inc., 1955.

Green, H. Benedict. *Matthew, Poet of the Beatitudes.* Journal for the Study of the New Testament Series 203. Sheffield: Sheffield Academic Press, 2001.

Guelich, R. A. *The Sermon on the Mount: A Foundation for Understanding.* Dallas: Word Publishing, 1982.

Gundry, Robert H. *Matthew: A Commentary on His Handbook for a Mixed Church under Persecution.* Grand Rapids, Michigan: William B. Eerdmans Publishing Company, 1982.

______________ . *Matthew: A Commentary on His Literary and Theological Art.* Grand Rapids: William B. Eerdmans Publishing Company, 1982.

Guthrie, Donald. *New Testament Introduction.* Revised Edition. Downers Grove, Illinois: Intervarsity Press, 1990.

Hagner, Donald. *Matthew 1-13.* WBC. Vol. 33A. Dallas, Texas: Word Books, Publisher, 1993.

Hamm, Dennis. *The Beatitudes in Context.* Wilmington, Delaware: Michael Glazier, 1990.

Hanson, K. C., and Douglas E. Oakman. *Palestine in the Time of Jesus: Social Structures and Social Conflicts.* Minneapolis, MN: Fortress, 2002 [1998].

Hare, Douglas. *The Theme of Jewish Persecution of Christians in the Gospel according to St. Matthew.* Society for New Testament Series Monograph Series 6. Cambridge: Cambridge University, 1967.

Häring, Bernard. *The Beatitudes: Their Personal and Social Implications.* Middlegreen, Slough: St. Paul Publication, 1981 [1976].

Harrington, Daniel J. *The Gospel of Matthew.* Sagra Pagina. Collegeville, Minnesota: The Liturgical Press, 1991.

Hawthorne, Gerald F. with Otto Betz, eds. *Tradition and Interpretation in the New Testament: Essays in Honor of E. Earle Ellis.* Grand Rapids, Michigan: William B. Eerdmans Publishing Company, 1987.

Hendricks, Herman. *The Sermon on the Mount.* London: Geoffrey Chapman, 1984.

Hengel, M. and C. K. Barrett. *Conflicts and Challenges in Early Christianity.* Edited by D. A. Hagner. Harrisburg, PA: Trinity Press, 1999.

Hengel, M. *The Zealots: Investigations into the Jewish Freedom Movement in the Period from Herod I until 70 A.D.* translated by D. Smith. Edinburgh: T&T Clark, 1989 [1976a].

Hill, David. *The Gospel of Matthew.* New Century Bible. Grand Rapids/London: Eerdmans, Marshall Morgan & Scott, 1972.

Hinsdale, Mary Ann. "Blessed Are the Persecuted…Hungering and Thirsting for Justice: Blessings for Those Breaking Boundaries." In *New Perspectives on Beatitudes.* Edited by Francis A. Eigo, 161-189. Villanova: The Villanova University Press, 1995.

Hminga, Chhangte Lal. *The Life and Witness of the Churches in Mizoram.* Serkawn: Baptist Church of Mizoram, 1987.

Holladay, Carl R. *A Critical Introduction to the New Testament.* Nashville: Abingdon Press, 2005.

Holmberg, Bengt. *Sociology and the New Testament: An Appraisal.* Minneapolis: Fortress Press, 1990.

Horsley, Richard A., and John S. Hanson. *Bandits, Prophets, and Messiahs: Popular Movements in the Time of Jesus.* Harrisburg, Pensylvania: Trinity, 1999 [1985].

______________. *Sociology and the Jesus Movement.* 2nd edition. New York: Conti nuum, 1994.

Hunter, A. M. *Design for Life: The Sermon on the Mount.* London: SCM Press Ltd., 1978 [1953].

Jayshree, P. M., et al. eds. *Dalit Human Rights Violations. Atrocities against Dalits in India*. Vol. 1. Case Papers: Summary & Jury's Interim Observations and Recommendations. National Campaign on Dalit Human Rights, 2000.

Jeremias, Joachim. *Jerusalem in the Time of Jesus: An Investigation into Economic and Social Conditions during the New Testament Period.* Study edition. Translated by F. H. Cane and C. H. Cane. London: SCM, 1969 [1962].

_____________ . *The Sermon on the Mount.* Facet Books, Biblical Series. Philadelphia: Fortress, 1963.

_____________ . *Josephus. Complete Works*. Translated by William Whiston. Grand Rapids, Michigan: Kregel Publications, 1983 [1960].

Judge, E. A. *The Social Pattern of Christian Groups in the First Century*. London: Tyndale, 1960.

Kee, Howard C. *Miracle in the Early Christian World: A Study in Socio-Historical Method.* New Haven: Yale University, 1983.

Keener, Craig S. *A Commentary on the Gospel of Matthew.* Grand Rapids, Michigan /Cambridge, U.K.: William B. Eerdmans Publishing Company, 1999.

Kilpatrick. G. D. *The Origins of the Gospel According to St. Matthew.* Oxford: Clarendon Press, 1966 [1946].

Kimelman, Reuven. "*Birkat haminim* and the Lack of Evidence for an Anti-Christian Jewish Prayer in Late Antiquity." In *Jewish and Christian Self-Definition*. Vol. 2: *Aspects of Judaism in the Greco-Roman Period,* 226-244. E.P. Sanders et al. eds. Philadelphia: Fortress, 1981.

Kingsbury, Jack Dean. "Conclusion: Analysis of Conversion." In *The Social History of the Matthean Community. Cross-Disciplinary Approaches*. Edited by David L. Balch, 259-269. Minneapolis: Fortress Press, 1991.

Kingsbury, Jack Dean. *Matthew as Story.* Philadelphia: Fortress, 1986.

_____________ . *Matthew: Structure, Christology, Kingdom*. Philadelphia: Fortress, 1975.

Knibb, M. A., ed. *The Ethiopic Book of Enoch: A New Edition in the Light of Aramaic Dead Sea Fragments.* Oxford: Clarendon Press, 1978.

Koester, Helmut. *History, Culture, and Religion of the Hellenistic Age*. Philadelphia: Fortress Press, 1983 [1982].

Kumar, Raj, ed. *Essay on Dalits*. New Delhi: Discovery Publishing House, 2003.

Kummel, W. G. *Introduction to the New Testament*. Bloomsbury Street, London: SCM Press Ltd, 1977 [1973].

Lambrecht, Jan. *The Sermon on the Mount. Proclamation and Exhortation.* Wilmington, Delaware: Michael Glazier, 1985.

Lapide, Pinchas. *The Sermon on the Mount.* Maryknoll: Orbis, 1986.

Lenski, Gerhard E. *Power and Privilege: A Theory of Social Stratification.* New York: McGraw Hill, 1966.

Levine, Amy-Jill. *The Social and Ethnic Dimensions of Matthean Salvation History. "Go Nowhere Among the Gentiles…" (Matt. 10:5b).* Studies in the Bible and Early Christianity 14. Lewiston: the Edwin Mellon Press, 1988.

Levinskaya, I. *The Book of Acts in Its First Century Setting.* Volume 5: *The Book of Acts in Its Diaspora Setting.* Grand Rapids, MI: Eerdmans, 1996.

Lichtenberger, Hermann. "Makarisms in Mathew 5:3ff. in their Jewish Context." In *The Sermon on the Mount and Its Jewish Setting.* Edited by Hans-Jürgen BECKER and Serge RUZER. Cahiers de la Revue Biblique, 60. Paris: J. GABALDA et Cie Éditeurs, 2005.

Limburg, James. *The Prophets and the Powerless.* Lima, Ohio: Academic Renewal Press, 2001.

Lloyd, J. Meirion. *History of the Church in Mizoram (Harvest in the Hills).* Gospel Centenary Series, No. I. Aizawl: Synod Publication Board, 1991.

Lohmeyer, Ernst. *Das Evangelium des Matthäus.* Edited by Schmauck. W. Göttingen: Vandenhoeck & Ruprecht, 1956.

Lohse, Eduard. *The New Testament Environment.* Abingdon, Nashville: Parthenon Press, 1976.

Lourduswamy, S. *Equal Rights to All Dalits (with Special Reference to Dalit Christians).* CDS Pamphlet 2. New Delhi: Centre for Dalit Studies, 2001.

Luz, Ulrich. *Matthew 1-7: A Continental Commentary.* Translated by Wilhelm C. Linss. Minneapolis: Augsburg Fortress, 1989 [1985].

_____________ . *Studies in Matthew.* Translated by Rosemary Selle. Grand Rapids, Michigan Cambridge, U.K.: William B. Eerdmans Publishing Company, 2005.

MacMullen, Ramsay. *Roman Social Relations: 50 B.C. to A.D. 284.* New Haven and London: Yale University Press, 1974.

Malherbe, Abraham J. *Social Aspect of Early Christianity.* 2nd and Enlarged Edition. Philadelphia: Fortress, 1983 [1977].

Malina, B. J., and R. L. Rohrbaugh. *Social-Science Commentary on the Synoptic Gospels.* Minneapolis: Fortress, 1993.

_____________ . *The New Testament World: Insights from Cultural Anthropology.* Atlanta: John Knox, 1981.

Massaux, E. *The Influence of the Gospel of Saint Matthew on Christian Literature before Saint Irenaeus.* Edited by A. J. Bellinzoni. 3 Vols. New Gospel Studies 5. Vol. 1. Macon, GA: Mercer University Press, 1990.

Massey, James. *Down Trodden. The Struggle of India's Dalits for Identity, Solidarity and Liberation.* Geneva: WCC Publications, 1997.

_____________ . *India. 50 Years of Independence: 1947-97. Status, Growth & Development 20. Dalits: Issues and Concerns.* Delhi: B.R. Publishing Corporation, 1998.

_____________ . *Roots of Dalit History, Christianity, Theology and Spirituality.* Delhi: ISPCK, 1996.

Matera, F. J. *Passion Narratives and Gospel Theologies: Interpreting the Synoptics through their Passion Stories*. New York: Paulist Press, 1986.

Matthew, Sam P. *Temple Criticism in Mark's Gospel: The Economic Role of Jerusalem Temple During the First Century CE.* Delhi: ISPCK, 1999.

Maurus, J. *Live a Happier Life: 8 Steps to Success and Happiness*. Allahabad: Better Yourself Books, 1970.

McNeile, A. H. *The Gospel according to St. Matthew*. London: Macmillan, 1961.

Meeks, W. A. *The First Urban Christians: The Social World of the Apostle Paul.* New Haven and London: Yale University Press, 1983.

Meeks, W. A. and R. L. Wilken. *Jews and Christians in Antioch in the First Four Centuries of the Common Era.* Society of Biblical Literature sources for Biblical Study 13. Missoula, Mont.: Scholars, 1978.

Meier, John P. *The Vision of Matthew: Christ, Church, and Morality in the First Gospel.* New York: Paulist Press, 1978.

Metzger, Bruce M. *A Textual Commentary on the Greek New Testament.* New York: United Bible Societies, 1994 [1971].

Michaels, J. Ramsey. *I Peter*. WBC. Vol. 49. Dallas, Texas: Word Books, Publishers, 1988.

Moore, George Foot. *Judaism in the First Century of the Christian Era.* 3 Vols. 7th Ed. Cambridge: Harvard University Press, 1954.

Morris, Leon. *The Gospel According to Matthew*. Grand Rapids: William B. Eerdmans Publishing Company, 1992.

_____________ . "The Gospels and the Jewish Lectionaries." In *Gospel Perspectives: Studies of History and Tradition to the New Testament.* Edited by R.T. France, David Wenham, and Craig Blomberg, 1980-1986. Sheffield: JSOT. Nepper-Christensen, P. *Das Matthausevangelium: Ein Judenchristliches Evangelium?* Aarhus: Universitätsforlaget: 1958.

Neusner, Jacob. *Formative Judaism: Current Issues and Argument.* 2 Vols. South Florida Studies in the History of Judaism, 133, 145. Atlanta, GA: Scholars Press 1996/1997.

_____________ . *From Politics to Piety: The Emergence of Pharisaic Judaism.* Englewood Cliffs, New Jersey: Prentice Hall, 1978.

_____________ . *Judaism in the Beginning of Christianity*. Whitstable, Kent: Whitstable Litho Ltd, 1984.

_____________ . "The Formation of Rabbinic Judaism: Yavneh (Jamnia) from A.D. 70 to 100." In *ANRW* II, 3-42. Berlin /New York: Walter de Gruyter, 1979.

Nolland, John. *The Gospel of Matthew. A Commentary on the Greek Text.* Grand Rapids, Michigan/Cambridge, U.K.: William B. Eerdmans Publishing Company, 2005.

_____________ . *Luke 1-9:20.* WBC. Vol. $35_{A.}$ Dallas, Texas: Word Books, Publisher, 1989.

Norquist, Marylin. *Jesus' Pattern for a Happy Life: The Beatitudes.* Liquori, Missouri: Loquori Publications, 1981.

Oesterley, W. O. E. *A History of Israel.* Vol. II. Oxford: Clarendon Press, 1934 [1932].

Otzen, Benedikt. *Judaism in Antiquity: Political Development and Religious Currents from Alexander to Hadrian.* Translated by Frederick H. Cryer. Sheffield: JSOT Press, 1990.

Overman, J. Andrew. *Matthew's Gospel and Formative Judaism: The Social World of the Matthean Community.* Minneapolis: Fortress Press, 1990.

Pachuau, Lalsangkima. *Ethnic Identity and Christianity: A Socio-Historical and Missiological Study of Christianity in Northeast India with Special Reference to Mizoram.* Frankfurt: Peter Lang, 2002.

Pathrapankal, Joseph. *The Christian Programme: A Theological and Pastoral Study of the Sermon on the Mount.* Bangalore: Dharmaram, 1999.

Patte, Daniel. *The Gospel According to Matthew: A Structural Commentary on Matthew's Faith.* Philadelphia: Fortress Press, 1987.

Pentecost, J. Dwight. *The Sermon on the Mount: Contemporary Insight for a Christian Lifestyle.* Portland, Oregon: Multnomah Press, 1980.

Pirovanelli, Peirluigi. "Was there Sectarian Behaviour before the Flourishing of Jewish Sects? A Long-Term Approach to the History and Sociology of Second Temple Sectarianism." In *Sectarianism in Early Judaism. Sociological Advances.* Edited by David J. Chalcraft. London, Oakville: Equinox, 2007.

Pobee, John S. *Who are the Poor? The Beatitudes as a Call to Community.* Geneva: World Council of Churches, 1987.

Powell, Mark Allan. *What is Narrative Criticism?* London: SPCK, 1993.

Przybylski, B. *Righteousness in Matthew and His World of Thought.* Society for New Testament Studies Monograph Series 41. Cambridge: Cambridge University, 1980.

Rajak, T. "The Jewish Community and Its Boundaries." In *The Jews among Pagans and Christians.* Edited by J. Lieu, North and Rajak, 9-28. London: Routledge, 1992.

Rattan, Ram. "Gandhiji and Untouchability." In *Essay on Dalits.* Edited by Raj Kumar, 62-69. New Delhi: Discovery Publishing House, 2003.

Reicke, Bo. *The New Testament Era. The World of the Bible from 500 B.C. to A.D. 100.* Translated by David E. Green. Philadelphia: Fortress Press, 1979 [1964].

Repschinski, Boris. *The Controversy Stories in the Gospel of Matthew. Their Redaction, Form and Relevance for the Relationship between the Matthean Community and Formative Judaism.* Forschungen zur Religion und Literatur des Alten und Neuen Testaments 189. Göttingen: Vandenhoeck & Rupprecht, 2000.

Rhoads, David. "Social Criticism: Crossing Boundaries." In *Mark and Method: New Approaches in Biblical Studies.* Edited by Janice Capel Anderson and Stephen D. Moore, 135-161. Minneapolis: Fortress, 1992.

Richardson, N. J. *The Homeric Hymn to Demeter.* Oxford: Clarendon Press, 1974.

Riches, John and David C. Sim, eds. *The Gospel of Matthew in Roman Imperial Context.* London/New York: T&T Clark International, 2005.

Ripoll, F. *The Beatitudes: The Blueprint for Happiness.* 4th Edition. Bombay: St. Paul's, 1994 [1981].

Safrai, S., and M. Stern, eds. *The Jewish People in the First Century.* Vol. 1. Philadelphia: Fortress Press, 1974.

Saldarini, Anthony J. *Matthew's Christian-Jewish Community.* Chicago: University of Chicago, 1994.

______________ . *Pharisees, Scribes and Sadducees in Palestinian Society: A Sociological Approach.* Wilmington, Delaware: Michael Glazier, 1988.

Saldarini, Anthony J. "The Gospel of Matthew and Jewish-Christian Conflict." In Balch, David L, ed. *Social History of the Matthean Community. Cross-disciplinary Approaches,* 38-61. Minneapolis: Augsburg, 1991.

Sanders, E. P. *Judaism: Practice and Belief, 63 BCE - 66 CE.* London: SCM Press/ Philadelphia: Trinity Press International, 1992.

______________. *Schismatics, Sectarians, Dissidents and Deviants: The First One Hundred Years of Jewish-Christian Relations.* Valley Forge, Pa.: Trinity Press International, 1993.

Sandmel, Samuel. *The First Christian Century in Judaism and Christianity: Certainties and Uncertainties.* New York: Oxford University Press, 1969.

Schnackenburg, Rudolf. *The Gospel of Matthew.* Translated by Robert R. Barr. Grand Rapids, Michigan: William B. Eerdmans Publishing Company, 2002.

Schoedel, W. R. "Ignatius and the Reception of the Gospel of Matthew in Antioch." In *Social History of the Matthean Community: Cross-Disciplinary Approaches.* Edited by David L. Balch, 129-177. Minneapolis: Fortress Press, 1991.

Schoeps, Hans Joachim. *Jewish Christianity: Factional Disputes in the Early Church.* Philadelphia: Fortress, 1964.

Schürer, Emil. *The History of the Jewish People in the Age of Jesus Christ (175 B.C. - A.D. 135).* Revised and Enlarged. Edited by G. Vermes, F. Millar and M. Black. Edinburgh: T&T Clark, 1979 [1901/1909].

_____________ . *The History of the Jewish People in the Age of Jesus Christ (175 B.C. - A.D.135).* 3 Vols. A New English Version, Revised and Edited by Geza Vermes & Fergus Millar. Edinburgh: T&T Clark Ltd., 1973.

Schweizer, Eduard. *The Good News According to Matthew.* Translated by David E. Green. Atlanta: John Knox Press, 1975.

Scott, R. B. Y. *The Relevance of the Prophets.* Revised Edition. London: The Macmillan Company, 1968 [1944].

Scroggs, R. "The Earliest Christian Communities as Sectarian Movements," in Jacob Neusner, ed. *Christianity, Judaism and Other Greco-Roman cults: Studies for Morton smith at Sixty.* Vol. 2, 1-23. Studies in Late Judaism in Late Antiquity 12. Leiden, Neth: Brill, 1975.

Segal, Alan F. "Matthew's Jewish Voice." In *Social History of the Matthean Community.* Edited by David L. Balch, 3-37. Minneapolis: Fortress Press, 1991.

Senior, Donald. *What are they Saying About Matthew?* Revised and Expanded Edition. New York: Paulist Press, 1996.

Shah, Ghanshyam. "Dalits and the State." In *Essay on Dalits.* Edited by Raj Kumar, 114-136. New Delhi: Discovery Publishing House, 2003.

Shinde, Prem K. ed. *Dalits and Human Rights.* 3 Vols. Delhi: Isha Books, 2005.

Shiri, Godwin. *The Plight of Christian Dalits: A South Indian Case Study.* Bangalore: Asian Trading Corporation, 1997.

Sim, David C. *The Gospel of Matthew and Christian Judaism. The History and Social Setting of the Matthean Community.* Edinburgh: T&T Clark, 1998.

Singh, Buta. *The Dalits and Dalit Awakening in India.* New Delhi: Gyan Publishing House, 2004.

Stambaugh, John and David Balch. *The New Testament in Its Social Environment.* Philadelphia: Westminster, 1988.

_____________ . *The Social World of the First Christians.* London: SPCK, 1986.

Stanton, Graham N. *A Gospel for a New People: Studies in Matthew.* Louisville: Westminster Press, 1993 [1992].

Stark, Rodney. "Antioch as the Social Situation for Matthew's Gospel." In David L, Balch, ed. *Social History of the Matthean Community: Cross-disciplinary Approaches,* 189-210. Minneapolis: Augsburg Fortress, 1991.

Stark, Rodney and William Sims Bainbridge. *A Theory of Religion.* New Brunswick, New Jersey: Rutgers University Press, 1996 [1987].

Stegemann, W., B. J. Malina and G. Theissen, eds. *The Social Setting of Jesus and the Gospels*. Minneapolis, MN: Fortress, 2002.

Stegemann, Ekkehard W. and Wolfgang Stegemann. *The Jesus Movement: A Social History of Its First Century.* Translated by O. C. Dean, Jr. Minneapolis: Fortress Press, 1999 [1995].

Stendahl, Krister. *The School of St. Matthew and Its Use of the Old Testament.* Ramsey, New Jersey: Sigler Press, 1991 [Philadelphia: Fortress, 1968 [1954]].

Stonehouse, Ned B. *The Witness of Matthew and Mark to Christ.* Grand Rapids: Eerdmans, 1944.

Strecker, George. *Der Weg der Gerechtigkeit,* 3rd ed. Göttingen: Vandenhoeck & Ruprecht, 1971.

______________. *The Sermon on the Mount. An Exegetical Commentary.* Translated by O. C. Dean. Edinburgh: T&T Clark, 1988.

Streeter, Burton H. *The Four Gospels.* New York: Macmillan, 1925.

Swift, Helen Cecilia. *The Beatitudes: Pattern for Christian Living.* New York: Alba House, 1990.

Synod Executive Committee. *Mizoram Presbyterian Kohhran leh Mizoram Baptist Kohhran Inkar Thu.* Aizawl: Mizoram Presbyterian Church Synod, 1994.

Talbert, C. H. *Reading the Sermon on the Mount. Character Formation and Decision Making in Matthew 5-7.* Columbia: South Carolina Press, 2004.

Tcherikover, Victor A., and Alexander Fuks, eds. *Corpus Papyrorum Judaicarum.* 2 Vols. Cambridge / Massachusetts: Harvard University Press, 1957.

Thayer, Joseph Henry. *Greek-English Lexicon of the New Testament.* New York: Harper & Brothers, 1887.

The Greek New Testament. 4th Revised Edition. D-Stuttgart: United Bible Societies, 1998.

Theissen, Gerd. *Sociology of Early Palestinian Christianity.* Translated by John Bowden. Philadelphia: Fortress Press, 1978.

______________ . *The Social Setting of Pauline Christianity: Essays on Corinth.* Edinburgh: T&T Clark, 1982.

The Works of Philo: Complete and Unabridged. New Updated Edition. Translated by C. D. Yonge. Peabody, Massachusetts: Hedrickson, 1993.

Thomas, M. M. *The Nagas towards A.D. 2000.* Madras: Centre for Research on New International Economic Order, 1992.

Tisera, G. *Universalism According to the Gospel of Matthew.* European University Studies 23. Frankfurt: Peter Lang, 1993.

Toussaint, Stanley D. *Behold the King: A Study of Matthew.* Portland: Multnomah Press, 1980.

Traub, Stuart H. and Craig B. Little, eds. *Theory of Deviance.* Fourth edition. Itasca, Illinois: F. E. Peacock Publishers, Inc., 1994 [1975].

Trevett, C. *A Study of Ignatius of Antioch in Syria and Asia.* SBEC. Vol. 29. Lewiston: Edwin Mellen, 1992.

Trilling, Wolfgang. *Christusverkündigung in den synoptischen Evangelien. Beispiele gattungsgemässer Auslegung.* München: Köesel-Verlag, 1969.

Troeltsch, Ernst. *The Social Teaching of the Christian Churches.* Translated by Olive Wyon. Vol. 1. London: George Allen & Unwin Ltd.; New York: The Macmillan Company, 1956 [1931/1922].

Tugwell, Simon. *Reflections on the Beatitudes. Soundings in Christian Tradition.* London: Darton, Longman and Todd, 1980.

Vann, Gerald. *The Divine Pity: A Study in the Social Implications of the Beatitudes.* London and Glasgow: Fontana Books, 1956 [1945].

Viviano, Benedict T. *Matthew and His World: The Gospel of the Open Jewish Christians Studies in Biblical Theology.* Fribourg: Academic Press; Göttingen: Vandenhoeck & Ruprecht, 2007.

Wainwright, Elaine Mary. "The Gospel of Matthew." In Elisabeth Schüssler Fiorenza, ed. *Searching the Scriptures: A Feminist Commentary.* Vol. 2. New York: Crossroad, 1994.

Watts, John D. W. *Isaiah 34-66.* WBC. Vol. 25. Waco, Texas: Word Books, Publisher, 1987.

Weber, Max. *The Sociology of Religion.* Boston: Beacon Press, 1963.

Whiston, William, trans. *The New Complete Works of Josephus.* Revised and expanded edition. Commentary by Paul L. Maier. Grand Rapids, MI: Kregel Publications, 1999.

Wilkins, Michael J. *The Concept of Disciple in Matthew's Gospel: As Reflected in the Use of the Term Mathetes.* Supplements to Novum Testamentum 59; Leiden: E. J. Brill, 1988.

Wilson, Bryan. *Magic and the Millennium: A Sociological Study of Religious Movements of Protest among Tribal and Third World Peoples.* London: Heinemann, 1973.

____________. *Religion in Sociological Perspective.* Oxford/New York: Oxford University Press, 1982.

____________. *The Social Dimension of Sectarianism.* Oxford: Oxford University Press, 1990.

Windisch, H. *The Meaning of the Sermon on the Mount.* Translated by S. M. Gilmour. Philadelphia: Westminster press, 1951.

Zetterholm, Magnus. *The Formation of Christianity in Antioch: A Social-Scientific Approach to the Separation between Judaism and Christianity.* London and New York: Routledge, 2003.

Zimmerli, W. "Die Seligpreisungen der Bergpredigt und das AT." In E. Bammel, et al. (eds.), *Donum Gentilicium, FS D. Daube*, 8-26. Oxford: Clarendon Press, 1978.

Zofa, Lalhmachhuana, comp. *Mizoram General Knowledge*. 3rd Edition. Aizawl: J. L. Publication, 2007.

Periodicals

Allison, Jr., Dale C. "A New Approach to the Sermon on the Mount." *EphTheolLov* 64 (1988): 405-414.

_____________ . "The Structure of the Sermon on the Mount." *JournBibLit* 106/3 (Sept 1987): 423-445.

Ambrozic, Aloysius M. "Reflections on the First Beatitude." *Communio* 17 (1990): 95-104.

Bacon, B. W. "The 'Five Books' of Matthew against the Jews." *Expositor* 15 (1918): 56-66.

Barré, M. "Blessed are the Pure of Heart." *BibToday* 22 (1984): 236-242.

Baxter, Wayne S. "The Narrative Setting of the Sermon on the Mount." *Trinity J* 25/1 (2004): 27-37.

Black, D. A. "The Translation of Matthew 5:2." *BibTrans* 38 (1987): 241-243.

Brooke, George J. "The Wisdom of Matthew's Beatitudes (4QBeat and Mt. 5:3-12)." *ScriptBull* 19 (1989): 35-41.

Brooks, James A. "The Unity and Structure of the Sermon on the Mount." *CriswellTheolRev* 6 (Fall 1992): 15-28.

Cahill, Lisa Sowle. "The Ethical Implications of the Sermon on the Mount." *Interpretation* XLI/2 (Apr 1987): 144-156.

Carlston, Charles. "Betz on the Sermon on the Mount." *CathBibQuart* 50 (1988): 47-57.

Carter, Warren. "Matthew and the Gentiles: Individual Conversion and/or Systemic Transformation?" *JournStudNT* 26/3 (2004): 259-282.

Catchpole, David R. "Paul, James and the Apostolic Decree." *NTStud* 23 (1977): 428-444.

Charlesworth, James H. "The Qumran Beatitudes (4Q 525) and the New Testament (Mt 5: 3-11, Lk 6: 20-26)." *RevHistPhilRel* 80/1 (Jan - March 2000): 13-35.

Clark, K. W. "The Gentile Bias in Matthew." *JournBibLit* 66 (1947): 165-172.

Cooper, Adam G. "'They Shall See God': The Gospel for All Saint's Day, Matthew 5:1-11." *LuthTheolJourn* 38/2 (Ag 2004): 63-75.

Cortes-Fuentes, David. "Not like the Gentiles: The Characterization of Gentiles in the Gospel according to St. Matthew." *Journal of Hispanic / Latin Theology* 9/1 (2001): 15-18.

Day, C. R. "Those who are persecuted because of Righteousness, are those who pursue Righteousness: An Examination of the Origin and Meaning of the Eighth Beatitude." *ActaPatByz* 16 (2005): 157-165.

Derickson, Gary W. "Matthew's Chiastic Structure and Its Dispensational Implications." *BiblSac* 163 (October-December 2006): 423-437.

Domeris, William R. "Exegesis and Proclamation. 'Blessed are You …' (Mt 5:1-12)." *JournTheolSAfric* 73 (D 1990): 67-76.

Dupont, J. " 'Béatitudes' égyptiennes." *Biblica* 47 (1966): 185-222.

Elliot, J. H. "Social Scientific Criticism of the New Testament: More on Methods and Models." *Semeia* 35 (1986): 1-33.

Forest, Jim. "Pilgrims of the Cross: the Beatitude of Persecution." *Touchstone* (US) 14/9 (Nov. 2001): 26-31.

Gager, J.G. "Social Description and Sociological Explanation." *RelStudRev* 5 (1979b): 174-180.

Goodman, Martin. "The First Jewish Revolt: Social Conflict and the Problem of Debt." *JournJewStud* 33/1-2, (1982): 417-427.

Guellich, Robert A. "Interpreting the Sermon on the Mount." *Interpretation* XLI/2 (Apr. 1987): 117-130.

____________. "The Matthean Beatitudes: 'Entrance-Requirements' or Eschatological Blessings?" *JournBibLit* 95/3 (1976): 415-434.

Hays, Richard B. "The Gospel of Matthew: Reconfigured Torah." *HervTeolStud* 61/1&2 (2005): 165-190.

Hinnebusch, Paul. "The Messianic Meaning of the Beatitudes." *BibToday* (1972): 707-717.

Holmes, Michael W. "The Text of Matthew 5:11." *NTStud* 32/2 (Apr. 1986): 283-286.

Horsley, Richard A. "Ancient Jewish Banditry and the Revolt against Rome." *CathBibQuart* 43 (1981): 409-432.

Johnson, Benton. "On Church and Sect." *American Sociological Review* 28 (1963): 539-549.

Kennard, J. "The Place of Origin of Matthew's Gospel." *AngTheolRev* 31 (1949): 243-246.

Kingsbury, Jack Dean. "The Place, Structure, and Meaning of the Sermon on the Mount within Matthew." *Interpretation* XLI/1 (1987): 131-143.

Klark, K. W. "The Gentile Bias in Matthew." *JournBibLit* 66 (1947): 165-172.

Kraeling, C. H. "The Jewish Community at Antioch." *JournBibLit* 51 (1932): 130-160.

Krentz, Edgar. "The Extent of Matthew's Prologue: Toward the Structure of the First Gospel." *JournBibLit* 83 (1964): 409-414.

Lohr, C. H. "Oral Techniques in the Gospel of Matthew." *CathBibQuart* 23 (1961): 403-435.

Mandel, S. "Who paid the Temple Tax when the Jews were under Roman Rule?" *HarTheolRev* 77/2 (1984): 223-242.

Manns, F. "Blessed are the Meek for They shall inherit the Earth." *StudBibFranlibAnn* 50 (2000): 37-51.

McEleney, Neil J. "Beatitudes of the Sermon on the Mount/Plain." *CathBibQuart* 43 (1981): 1-13.

Meier, John P. "Matthew 5: 3-12." *Interpretation* 44 (1990): 281-285.

Neusner, Jacob. "Judaism after Moore: A Programmatic Statement." *JournJewStud* 331 (1980): 141-56.

Newman, Jr., Barclay M. "Some Translational Notes on the Beatitudes." *BibTrans* 26/1 (Jan 1975): 106-120.

Osborne, R. E. "The Provenance of Matthew's Gospel." *StudRel* 3 (1973): 222-235.

Pamment, M. "Matthew and the Kingdom of Heaven." *NTStud* 27 (1981): 211-232.

Powell, Mark Allan. "Matthew's Beatitudes: Reversal and Rewards of the Kingdom." *CathBibQuart* 58 (Jl 1996): 460-479.

Riches, John. "The Social World of Jesus." *Interpretation* 50 (1996): 383-393.

Riga, Peter J. "Reflections on the Beatitudes." *BibToday* (1968): 2731-2739.

Rohrbaugh, Richard L. "Methodological Considerations in the Debate over the Social Class Status of Early Christians." *Journal of American Academy of Religion* 52 (1983): 521-543.

Rukundwa, Lazare S. & Andries G. Van Aarde. "Revisiting Justice in the First Four Beatitudes in Matthew (5:3-6) and the Story of the Canaanite Woman (Mt 15:21-28): A Postcolonial Reading." *HervTeolStud* 61/3 (2005): 927-951.

Saldarini, A.J. "Delegitimation of Leaders in Matthew 23." *CathBibQuart* 54 (1992): 659-680.

Senior, Donald. "Between Two Worlds: Gentiles and Jewish Christians in Matthew's Gospel." *CathBibQuart* 61 (Jan. 1999): 1-23.

Shin, In-Cheol & Andries van Aarde. "Matthew's and Paul's Inclusive Tendencies: A Comparison." *HervTeolStud* 61/4 (2005): 1353-1372.

Sibinga, J. Smith. "Exploring the Composition of Matt 5-7: The Sermon on the Mount and Some of Its 'Structures.'" *Filologia NT.* 7 (Nov. 1994): 175-195.

____________. "Ignatius and Matthew." *NovTest* 8 (1966): 263-283.

Sim, David C. "The Gospel of Matthew and the Gentiles." *JournStudNT* 57 (Mr. 1995): 19-48.

____________. "The Social Setting of the Matthean Community: New Paths for an Old Journey." *HarvTheolRev* 57/1&2 (2001): 268-280.

Slater, Thomas B. "Social Methodology and the New Testament." *Bible Bhashyam* 19 (1993): 237-248.

Slingerland, H. D. "The Transjordanian Origin of Matthew's Gospel." *JournStudNT* 3 (1979): 18-28.

Smillie, Gene R. "'Even the Dogs': Gentiles in the Gospel of Matthew." *JournEvangTheolSoc* 45/1 (March 2002): 73-97.

Smith, Christopher, R. "Literary Evidence of Fivefold Structure in the Gospel of Matthew." *NTStud* 43 (Oct. 1997): 540-551.

Smith, Robert H. "'Blessed are the Poor in (Holy) Spirit'? (Matthew 5:3)." *Word & World* 18 (Fall 1998): 389-396.

______________ . "Were the Early Christians Middle-Class? A Sociological Analysis of the New Testament." *CurTheolMiss* 7 (1980): 260-276.

Stanton, Graham N. "The Communities of Matthew." *Interpretation,* XLVI/4 (Oct 1992): 379-391.

______________ . "The Gospel of Matthew and Judaism." *BullJohnRylLibMan* 66/2 (1984): 264-284.

Taylor, Justin. "The Jerusalem Decrees (Acts 15:20, 29 and 21: 25) and the Incident at Antioch (Gal 2:11-14)." *NTStud* 46 (2001): 372-380.

Thomson, James W. "The Background and Function of the Beatitudes in Matthew and Luke." *RestorQuart* 41/2 (1999): 109-116.

Trevett, C. "Approaching Matthew from the Second Century: The Under-Used Ignatian Correspondence." *JournStudNT* 20 (1984): 59-67.

Tuckett, C. M. "'The Beatitudes' A Source Critical Study…." *NovTest* 25 (1983): 193-216.

Turner, David L. "Whom does God Approve? The Context, Structure, Purpose, and Exegesis of Matthew's Beatitudes." *CriswellTheolRev* 6 (1992): 29-42.

Van Aarde, Andries G. "A Study of the New Testament Beatitude and the Beatitude Series in Matthew 5:3-10. A New Approach to 'Gattungforschung." *HervTeolStudSupp* 5 (1994): 151-179.

Viljoen, F. P. "The Matthean Community according to the Beginning of His Gospel." *ActaTheol* 26/2 (2006): 242-262.

Viviano, B.T. "Where was the Gospel according to St. Matthew Written?" *CathBibQuart* 41 (1979): 533-546.

Vledder, E.J., and A. G. Van Aarde. "The Social Location of the Matthean Community." *HarvTheolRev* 51/2 (1995): 388-408.

White, Leland. "Grid and Group in Matthew's Community: The Righteousness/Honor Code in the Sermon on the Mount." *Semeia* 35 (1986): 61-90.

Williams, Nathan E. "A Second Look at the First Beatitude." *ExpTimes* 98 (Apr 1987): 208-209.

Unpublished Thesis and Notes

Day, Charles R. "An Investigation of the Beatitudes of Matthew: Between the Oral Tradition and the Greek Text." D. Lit. Thesis, University of Pretoria, 2004.

Dillon, R. J. "The Text of the Sermon on the Mount." Notes issued in his course on the Sermon on the Mount at Forbham University in 1980.

Newspapers and Newsmagazines

"Chiahpuamin Zoram Chiah Hneh [Chiahpuam, a Burning Issue in Mizoram]." *Zoram Today* (November 10-15, 2008): 16.

"CM-in House-ah Dawt a Sawi Em Ni? [Did the CM Tell a Lie in the House]." *Zozam* (April 2-8, 2008): 18-21.

"Kohhran leh Politics [Church and Politics]." *Zozam* (July 4-10, 2006): 18.

"Mizoramah Drugs Vanga Thi Tlem Tial Tial [Drug-Related Death Decreases in Mizoram]." *Christian Outlook* (October, 2008): 2.

"MLA Dawt Bill Tunge La? [Who Availed the MLA Fake Bills?]." *Zoram Today* (May 26-31, 2008): 19-22.

"Operation Totê in Rangvamual a Nuai [Operation Storm Shocked Rangvamual]." *Zozam* (March 29 - April 4, 2005): 5.

"Pawisa Tihpun Hluaina Hi? [The Bank that Gives Unusually High Interest]." *Zoram Today* (October 27 - November 1, 2008): 22.

"Sex avangin HIV/AIDS a Hluar [Sex Spreads HIV/AIDS]." *Zozam* (April 18-24, 2007): 11.

"Sex leh Aizawl Khawpui [Sex and the Aizawl City]." *Zozam* (May 30 - June 5, 2006): 9.

"SRS an che rapthlak [SRS acted dreadfully]." *Zozam* (June 7-13, 2005): 7.

Sunday Times (Bangalore), 05 October 2008.

"Thalaite Suattu Ruihhlo Khapna Dan Ngaihthah [An Act for Prohibition of Drugs that Massacre the Youths is Neglected]." *Zozam* (September 14-20, 2004): 5.

The Times of India (Bangalore), 30 August 2008.

The Times of India (Bangalore), 15 September 2008.

The Times of India (Bangalore), 18 September 2008.

The Times of India (Bangalore), 25 October 2008.

The Times of India (Bangalore), 19 April 2009.

Vanglaini (Aizawl), 09 April 2009.

Vanglaini (Aizawl), 06 September 2006.

Vanglaini (Aizawl), 21 September 2006.

Vangalini (Aizawl), 17 November 2008.

"YMA Duty An Hrang Lua Em Ni? [Are the YMA on Duty Too Violent?]." *Zozam* (May 3-9, 2005): 7.

"Zu Zuar, Zu Sa leh in te chunga Synod Thuchhuak Rum [Tough Resolution of the Synod Concerning Liqour Sellers, Liqour Makers, and Liqour Drinkers]." *Christian Outlook* (October, 2008): 4-6.

Electronic Sources

Online Sources

"12 killed as separatist gangs fight in Nagaland" (June 4th, 2008- 2:07 pm ICT by IANS), 1-2 of 2. http://www.thaindian.com/ newsportal/world-news/12-killed-as-separatist-gangs-fight-in-nagaland_10056362.html (accessed 09.04.09).

"12 underground cadres killed in a factional clash in Nagaland" (May 16th, 2008 – 7:13 pm ICT by admin), 1 of 1. http://www.thaindian.com/newsportal /lifestyle/12-underground-cadres-killed-in-a-factional-clash-in-nagaland_ 10049476.html (accessed 09.04.09).

"2002 Gujarat violence" (January 2009),1-2 of 2. http://en.wikipedia.org/ wiki/2002-Gujarat_violence (accessed 10.04.2009).

"A List of Atrocities Committed Against Christians Across India in the Golden Jubilee Year of Independence August 15, 1997 to August 15, 1998 and Beyond" (updated on 02.12.1998), 1-5 of 5. http://www.angelfire. com/pe/ Indianchristians/ persecution.html (accessed 23.02.2009).

"Anti-Christian Violence in India" (modified on 25 March, 2009), 2 of 6. http:/ Chrianperecution-india.blogspot.com (accessed 02.04.2009). Retrieved from http://en.wikipedia.org/wiki/Anti-Christian_ violence_in_India.

"Attacks on Christians in Orissa" (no date of posting), 1-4 of 4. http://christian-persecutionindia. blogspot.com (accessed 23.02.2009).

A. Vu, Michelle. "Orissa Gov't to Boot Christians from Refugee Camps" (05.02.2009),1of2.http://www.christianpost.com/Intl/Persecution/2009/02/ (accessed 23.02.2009).

Bureau Report. "Legislators Fake TA Bills Revealed." *News Link* (22.08.2006), 1 of 1. Available from http:/www.zoram.com (accessed 11.12.2006).

"Conversion fire spreads to Kerala" (16 Sep 2008, 0329 hrs IST, TNN), 1-2 of 2. http://timesofindia.indiatimes.com/articleshow /3487282.cms (accessed 10.04.2009).

Ganguly, Vibou. "Factional killings continue unabated in Nagaland" (May 6th, 2008 -6:14 pm ICT by admin -), 1 of 1. http://www.thaindian. com/newsportal/india-news/factional-killings-continue-unabated-in-nagaland_10045699.html (accessed 09.04.09).

Ganguly, Vibou. "Three killed in Naga factional violence" (April 18th, 2008 April 18th, 2008 - 6:18 pm ICT by admin -), 1 of 1. http://www.thaindian.com/news -portal/health/three-killed-in-naga-factional-violence_10039441.html (accessed 09.04.09).

"Godhra train burning" (October, 2008), 1-2 of 2. http://en.wikipedia.org/wiki/Godhra-train_burning (accessed 10.04.2009).

Hare, Douglas R.A. "How Jewish is the Gospel of Matthew?" *CathBibQuart* 62/2, (Apr. 2000), 264-277. Available from http://search.atlaonline.com (accessed 30. Oct 2006).

Heeter, Chad. *Rough Cut. Seeds of Suicide. India's desparate farmers* (26. 07. 2005), 1-2 of 6. http://www.pbs.org/frontlineworld/rough (accessed 12.12.2006).

"Kandhamal carnage orchestrated, not 'spontaneous' reaction, says Journalist author" in *Persecution Update India. Window to the Persecuted and Suffering Christian Faith of India* (08.04.2009), 2 of 6. http://persecution.in (accessed 09.04.2009).

Lee, Shin-wha and Deepa Khosla. *Nagas in India* (updated 09/04/99), 1-19 of 19. http://www.bsos.umd.edu/cidcm/mar/indnaa.htm (accessed 12. 12. 2006).

Meyers, Eric M. "Early Judaism and Christianity in the Light of Archaeology." *Biblical Archaeologist* 51/2, (1988), 69-79. Available from http://search.atla-online.com (accessed 30. Oct. 2006).

Mishra, Sandeep. "Orissa violence: Cracks in BJP-BJD alliance" (26 Aug 2008, 0409 hrs IST), 1-2 of 2.http://timesofindia.indiatimes.com/articleshow/3405376.cms (accessed 10.04.09).

"More Violence, Roads blocked in Kandhamal" (29 Aug 2008, 1327 hrs IST, IANS), 2 of 2. http://timesofindia.indiatimes.com/articleshow/3421412.cms (accessed 10.04.09).

"MUP-in MLA hlawh nawr hniam tum" (Posted on 20 February 2009), 2 of 2. http://emizoram.com/news/?p=4387&cpage=1 (accessed 23.04. 2009).

"NSCN (IM) admit role in killing of sub-divisional officer" (March 4th, 2009 - 10:17 pm ICT by ANI), 1-2 of 2. http://www.thaindian.com/newsportal/india-news/nscn-im-admit-role-in-killing-of-sub-divisional-officer-100162718(accessed 09. 04.09).

"Over 1000 farmers committed suicide in 2006." *Maharastra News* (29. 11. 2006), 1 of 1. Available from www.newsKerala.com (accessed 11.12.2006).

"Seven Naga rebels killed in fresh factional fight" (June 27th, 2008 – 5:54 pm ICT by IANS), 1-2 of 2. http://www.thaindian.com/newsportal/world-news/seven-naga-rebels-killed-in-fresh-factional-fight_10065192.html (accessed 09.04. 2009).

Sherwin-White, A. N. "Why Were the Early Christians Persecuted? An Amendment." *Past and Present* 27 (1964), 23-27. Available from http://search.atlaonline. com (accessed 30. Oct. 2006).

Stark, Rodney. "The Class Basis of Early Christianity: Inferences from a Sociological Model." *Sociological Analysis* 47/3 (1986), 216-225. http://www.jstor.org (accessed 30-Oct 2006).

"Sum Tang Zawng Zawng Rs. Nuai 20000 Chuang Niin Chhut [Unreturned Money Estimated to be More Than Rs 2000 Million]" (06. 11. 2008), 1 of 1. http:// www.khampat.com (accessed 07. 11. 2008).

"Title page for ETD etd-09022005-094257" (2004-11-15), 1 of 1. http://upetd.up.ac.za/thesis/available/etd-09022005-094257/ (accessed 02.06.2006).

CD-ROM Sources

"Freiberg Lexicon." CD-Rom. Bible Works, LLC, 2001.

"Louw-Nida Lexicon." CD-Rom. Bible Works, LLC, 2001.

"UBS Greek Dictionary." CD-Rom. Bible Works, LLC, 2001.

Index

Q

R

S